Chevrolet S-10
GMC S-15
Olds Bravada
Automotive
Repair
Manual

by Robert Maddox
and John H Haynes
Member of the Guild of Motoring Writers

Models covered:
Chevrolet: S-10 pick-up (1982 thru 1993)
and S-10 Blazer (1983 thru 1994)
GMC: S-15 and Sonoma pick-ups (1982 thru 1993)
and S-15 Jimmy (1983 thru 1994)
Oldsmobile: Bravada (1991 thru 1994)

*Does not include Typhoon or Syclone models or
diesel engine information*

(4C18 - 24070
(831)

ABCDE
FGH

Haynes Publishing Group
Sparkford Nr Yeovil
Somerset BA22 7JJ England

Haynes North America, Inc
861 Lawrence Drive
Newbury Park
California 91320 USA

Acknowledgements

We are grateful for the help and cooperation of Tomco Industries, 1435 Woodson Road, St. Louis, Missouri 63132, for their assistance with technical information and illustrations. Wiring diagrams originated exclusively for Haynes North America, Inc. by Valley Forge Technical Information Services. Technical consultants who contributed to this project include Mike Stubblefield, Jeff Killingsworth and Larry Warren.

A book in the Haynes Automotive Repair Manual Series

Printed in the U.S.A.

ISBN 1 56392 116 2

Library of Congress Catalog Card Number 94-76569

Contents

Introductory pages

About this manual   0-5
Introduction to the Chevrolet S-10 and GMC S-15 Pick-ups   0-5
Vehicle identification numbers   0-6
Buying parts   0-8
Maintenance techniques, tools and working facilities   0-8
Booster battery (jump) starting   0-16
Jacking and towing   0-17
Automotive chemicals and lubricants   0-18
Conversion factors   0-19
Safety first!   0-20
Troubleshooting   0-21

Chapter 1
Tune-up and routine maintenance   1-1   **1**

Chapter 2   Part A
1.9L four-cylinder engine   2A-1   **2A**

Chapter 2   Part B
2.0L four-cylinder engine   2B-1   **2B**

Chapter 2   Part C
2.5L four-cylinder engine   2C-1   **2C**

Chapter 2   Part D
2.8L V6 engine   2D-1   **2D**

Chapter 2   Part E
4.3L V6 engine   2E-1   **2E**

Chapter 2   Part F
General engine overhaul procedures   2F-1   **2F**

Chapter 3
Cooling, heating and air conditioning systems   3-1   **3**

Chapter 4
Fuel and exhaust systems   4-1   **4**

Chapter 5
Engine electrical systems   5-1   **5**

Chapter 6
Emissions control systems   6-1   **6**

Chapter 7   Part A
Manual transmission   7A-1   **7A**

Chapter 7   Part B
Automatic transmission   7B-1   **7B**

Chapter 7   Part C
Transfer case   7C-1   **7C**

Chapter 8
Clutch and drivetrain   8-1   **8**

Chapter 9
Brakes   9-1   **9**

Chapter 10
Suspension and steering systems   10-1   **10**

Chapter 11
Body   11-1   **11**

Chapter 12
Chassis electrical system   12-1   **12**

Wiring diagrams   12-14

Index   IND-1   **IND**

Haynes mechanic, author and photographer with S-10 Blazer

About this manual

Its purpose

The purpose of this manual is to help you get the best value from your vehicle. It can do so in several ways. It can help you decide what work must be done, even if you choose to have it done by a dealer service department or a repair shop; it provides information and procedures for routine maintenance and servicing; and it offers diagnostic and repair procedures to follow when trouble occurs.

We hope you use the manual to tackle the work yourself. For many simpler jobs, doing it yourself may be quicker than arranging an appointment to get the vehicle into a shop and making the trips to leave it and pick it up. More importantly, a lot of money can be saved by avoiding the expense the shop must pass on to you to cover its labor and overhead costs. An added benefit is the sense of satisfaction and accomplishment that you feel after doing the job yourself.

Using the manual

The manual is divided into Chapters. Each Chapter is divided into numbered Sections, which are headed in bold type between horizontal lines. Each Section consists of consecutively numbered paragraphs.

At the beginning of each numbered Section you will be referred to any illustrations which apply to the procedures in that Section. The reference numbers used in illustration captions pinpoint the pertinent Section and the Step within that Section. That is, illustration 3.2 means the illustration refers to Section 3 and Step (or paragraph) 2 within that Section.

Procedures, once described in the text, are not normally repeated. When it's necessary to refer to another Chapter, the reference will be given as Chapter and Section number. Cross references given without use of the word "Chapter" apply to Sections and/or paragraphs in the same Chapter. For example, "see Section 8" means in the same Chapter.

References to the left or right side of the vehicle assume you are sitting in the driver's seat, facing forward.

Even though we have prepared this manual with extreme care, neither the publisher nor the author can accept responsibility for any errors in, or omissions from, the information given.

NOTE

A **Note** provides information necessary to properly complete a procedure or information which will make the procedure easier to understand.

CAUTION

A **Caution** provides a special procedure or special steps which must be taken while completing the procedure where the Caution is found. Not heeding a Caution can result in damage to the assembly being worked on.

WARNING

A **Warning** provides a special procedure or special steps which must be taken while completing the procedure where the Warning is found. Not heeding a Warning can result in personal injury.

Introduction to the Chevrolet S-10 and GMC S-15

These models are available in pick-up and 2- and 4-door sport utility body styles.

The inline four and V6 engines used in these vehicles are equipped with a carburetor or fuel injection, depending on model. The engine drives the rear wheels through either a four- or five-speed manual or three- or four-speed automatic transmission via a driveshaft and solid rear axle. A transfer case, driveshaft and front differential are used to drive the front independent driveaxles on 4WD models.

The steering box is mounted to the left of the engine and is connected to the steering arms through a series of rods. Power assist is optional on most models.

The brakes are disc at the front and drums at the rear, with power assist standard. Some later models are equipped with an anti-lock braking system.

Vehicle identification numbers

Modifications are a continuing and unpublicized process in vehicle manufacturing. Since spare parts manuals and lists are compiled on a numerical basis, the individual vehicle numbers are essential to correctly identify the component required.

Vehicle Identification Number (VIN)

This very important identification number is stamped on a plate attached to the left side of the dashboard, just inside the windshield on the driver's side of the vehicle (see illustration). The VIN also appears on the Vehicle Certificate of Title and Registration. It contains information such as where and when the vehicle was manufactured, the model year and the body style.

Service parts identification label

This label, used on most models, is located inside the glove box door. It lists the VIN, wheelbase, paint information and all production options or special equipment on the vehicle when it was shipped from the factory. Always refer to this label when ordering parts.

Certification label

The Certification label is normally affixed to the left door pillar. The label contains the name of the manufacturer, the month and year of production, the Gross Vehicle Weight Rating (GVWR) and the certification statement.

Engine identification number

The engine ID number on 1.9L and 2.5L four-cylinder engines is located on a machined surface on the lower left side of the engine block (see illustration). The engine ID number on 2.0L four-cylinder engines is stamped into a machined surface on the front of the engine block, just below the cylinder head. On 2.8L V6 engines, the number is either on a machined surface, facing up on the right-front of the engine block, just below the cylinder head or on the left front of the engine block, just above the water pump (see illustration). On 4.3L V6 engines, the number is either on the right front of the engine block just above the water pump, or on the left rear side of the engine block, where the transmission is joined to the engine.

The Vehicle Identification Number (VIN) is visible from outside the vehicle through the driver's side of the windshield

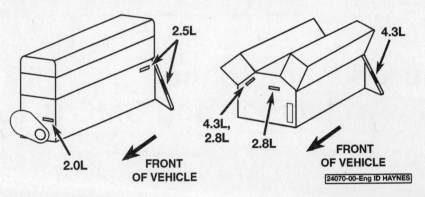

Engine location numbers - 2.0L and 2.5L four-cylinder engines

Engine location numbers - V6 engines

The location of the engine ID number on 1.9L engines; on 2.5L engines, the number is in the same general location, except it's stamped into the edge of the flange where the engine connects to the transmission

The Vehicle Emissions Control Information (VECI) label is always located in the engine compartment, usually on the fan shroud, as shown here

Transmission identification number

On manual transmissions, the number is stamped on a steel plate attached to the extension housing case bolt, on the left side. On automatic transmissions, the number is in one of the following locations:

a) *On the 180C three-speed transmission, it is on a steel tag attached to the left front of the transmission case.*

b) *On the 200C three-speed transmission, it is stamped on the right rear side of the transmission case, behind the vacuum modulator.*

c) *On 700R4 and 4L60 transmissions, the number is stamped on the right or left rear side of the transmission pan rail.*

Transfer case identification number

This number is on a tag attached to the rear half of the transfer case. The tag gives the model number, the low range reduction ratio and the assembly part number.

Axle/differential numbers

On rear axles, the number is stamped on the right front side of the axle tube, next to the differential. On 4WD models, the differential is identified by a number stamped on a metal tag attached to the differential cover by a cover bolt.

Vehicle Emissions Control Information (VECI) label

This label is located under the hood, on top of the fan shroud on most models **(see illustration)**. See Chapter 6 for more information on the VECI label.

Buying parts

Replacement parts are available from many sources, which generally fall into one of two categories - authorized dealer parts departments and independent retail auto parts stores. Our advice concerning these parts is as follows:

Retail auto parts stores: Good auto parts stores will stock frequently needed components which wear out relatively fast, such as clutch components, exhaust systems, brake parts, tune-up parts, etc. These stores often supply new or reconditioned parts on an exchange basis, which can save a considerable amount of money. Discount auto parts stores are often very good places to buy materials and parts needed for general vehicle maintenance such as oil, grease, filters, spark plugs, belts, touch-up paint, bulbs, etc. They also usually sell tools and general accessories, have convenient hours, charge lower prices and can often be found not far from home.

Authorized dealer parts department: This is the best source for parts which are unique to the vehicle and not generally available elsewhere (such as major engine parts, transmission parts, trim pieces, etc.).

Warranty information: If the vehicle is still covered under warranty, be sure that any replacement parts purchased - regardless of the source - do not invalidate the warranty!

To be sure of obtaining the correct parts, have engine and chassis numbers available and, if possible, take the old parts along for positive identification.

Maintenance techniques, tools and working facilities

Maintenance techniques

There are a number of techniques involved in maintenance and repair that will be referred to throughout this manual. Application of these techniques will enable the home mechanic to be more efficient, better organized and capable of performing the various tasks properly, which will ensure that the repair job is thorough and complete.

Fasteners

Fasteners are nuts, bolts, studs and screws used to hold two or more parts together. There are a few things to keep in mind when working with fasteners. Almost all of them use a locking device of some type, either a lockwasher, locknut, locking tab or thread adhesive. All threaded fasteners should be clean and straight, with undamaged threads and undamaged corners on the hex head where the wrench fits. Develop the habit of replacing all damaged nuts and bolts with new ones. Special locknuts with nylon or fiber inserts can only be used once. If they are removed, they lose their locking ability and must be replaced with new ones.

Rusted nuts and bolts should be treated with a penetrating fluid to ease removal and prevent breakage. Some mechanics use turpentine in a spout-type oil can, which works quite well. After applying the rust penetrant, let it work for a few minutes before trying to loosen the nut or bolt. Badly rusted fasteners may have to be chiseled or sawed off or removed with a special nut breaker, available at tool stores.

If a bolt or stud breaks off in an assembly, it can be drilled and removed with a special tool commonly available for this purpose. Most automotive machine shops can perform this task, as well as other repair procedures, such as the repair of threaded holes that have been stripped out.

Flat washers and lockwashers, when removed from an assembly, should always be replaced exactly as removed. Replace any damaged washers with new ones. Never use a lockwasher on any soft metal surface (such as aluminum), thin sheet metal or plastic.

Fastener sizes

For a number of reasons, automobile manufacturers are making wider and wider use of metric fasteners. Therefore, it is important to be able to tell the difference between standard (sometimes called U.S. or SAE) and metric hardware, since they cannot be interchanged.

All bolts, whether standard or metric, are sized according to diameter, thread pitch and length. For example, a standard 1/2 - 13 x 1 bolt is 1/2 inch in diameter, has 13 threads per inch and is 1 inch long. An M12 - 1.75 x 25 metric bolt is 12 mm in diameter, has a thread pitch of 1.75 mm (the distance between threads) and is 25 mm long. The two bolts are nearly identical, and easily confused, but they are not interchangeable.

In addition to the differences in diameter, thread pitch and length, metric and standard bolts can also be distinguished by examining the bolt heads. To begin with, the distance across the flats on a standard bolt head is measured in inches, while the same dimension on a metric bolt is sized in millimeters (the same is true for nuts). As a result, a standard wrench should not be used on a metric bolt and a metric wrench should not be used on a standard bolt. Also, most standard bolts have slashes radiating out from the center of the head to denote the grade or strength of the bolt, which is an indication of the amount of torque that can be applied to it. The greater the number of slashes, the greater the strength of the bolt. Grades 0 through 5 are commonly used on automobiles. Metric bolts have a property class (grade) number, rather than a slash, molded into their heads to indicate bolt strength. In this case, the higher the number, the stronger the bolt. Property class numbers 8.8, 9.8 and 10.9 are commonly used on automobiles.

Strength markings can also be used to distinguish standard hex nuts from metric hex nuts. Many standard nuts have dots stamped into one side, while metric nuts are marked with a number. The greater the number of dots, or the higher the number, the greater the strength of the nut.

Metric studs are also marked on their ends according to property class (grade). Larger studs are numbered (the same as metric bolts), while smaller studs carry a geometric code to denote grade.

It should be noted that many fasteners, especially Grades 0 through 2, have no distinguishing marks on them. When such is the case, the only way to determine whether it is standard or metric is to measure the thread pitch or compare it to a known fastener of the same size.

Standard fasteners are often referred to as SAE, as opposed to metric. However, it should be noted that SAE technically refers to a non-metric fine thread fastener only. Coarse thread non-metric fasteners are referred to as USS sizes.

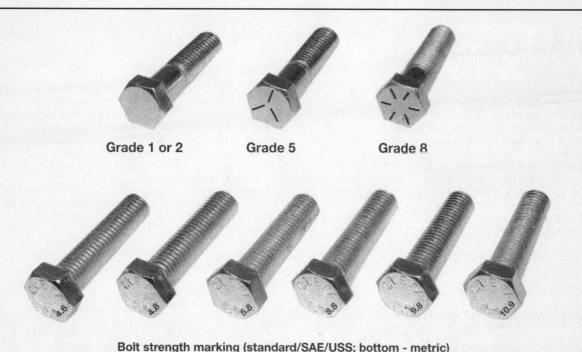

Grade 1 or 2   **Grade 5**   **Grade 8**

Bolt strength marking (standard/SAE/USS; bottom - metric)

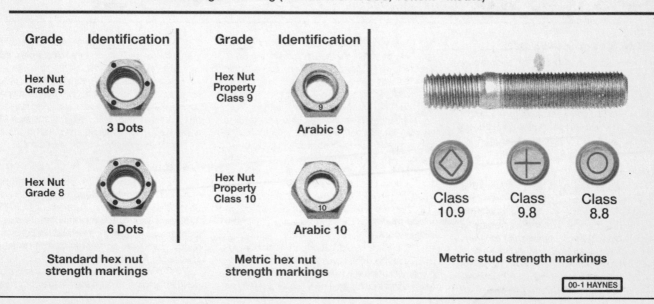

Grade	Identification
Hex Nut Grade 5	3 Dots
Hex Nut Grade 8	6 Dots

Standard hex nut strength markings

Grade	Identification
Hex Nut Property Class 9	Arabic 9
Hex Nut Property Class 10	Arabic 10

Metric hex nut strength markings

Class 10.9   Class 9.8   Class 8.8

Metric stud strength markings

Since fasteners of the same size (both standard and metric) may have different strength ratings, be sure to reinstall any bolts, studs or nuts removed from your vehicle in their original locations. Also, when replacing a fastener with a new one, make sure that the new one has a strength rating equal to or greater than the original.

Tightening sequences and procedures

Most threaded fasteners should be tightened to a specific torque value (torque is the twisting force applied to a threaded component such as a nut or bolt). Overtightening the fastener can weaken it and cause it to break, while undertightening can cause it to eventually come loose. Bolts, screws and studs, depending on the material they are made of and their thread diameters, have specific torque values, many of which are noted in the Specifications at the beginning of each Chapter. Be sure to follow the torque recommendations closely. For fasteners not assigned a specific torque, a general torque value chart is presented here as a guide. These torque values are for dry (unlubricated) fasteners threaded into steel or cast iron (not aluminum). As was previously mentioned, the size and grade of a fastener determine the amount of torque that can safely be applied to it. The figures listed here are approximate for Grade 2 and Grade 3 fasteners. Higher grades can tolerate higher torque values.

Fasteners laid out in a pattern, such as cylinder head bolts, oil pan bolts, differential cover bolts, etc., must be loosened or tightened in sequence to avoid warping the component. This sequence will normally be shown in the appropriate Chapter. If a specific pattern is not given, the following procedures can be used to prevent warping.

Metric thread sizes	Ft-lbs	Nm
M-6	6 to 9	9 to 12
M-8	14 to 21	19 to 28
M-10	28 to 40	38 to 54
M-12	50 to 71	68 to 96
M-14	80 to 140	109 to 154

Pipe thread sizes		
1/8	5 to 8	7 to 10
1/4	12 to 18	17 to 24
3/8	22 to 33	30 to 44
1/2	25 to 35	34 to 47

U.S. thread sizes		
1/4 - 20	6 to 9	9 to 12
5/16 - 18	12 to 18	17 to 24
5/16 - 24	14 to 20	19 to 27
3/8 - 16	22 to 32	30 to 43
3/8 - 24	27 to 38	37 to 51
7/16 - 14	40 to 55	55 to 74
7/16 - 20	40 to 60	55 to 81
1/2 - 13	55 to 80	75 to 108

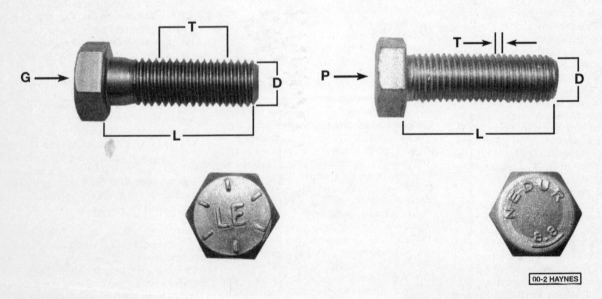

00-2 HAYNES

Standard (SAE and USS) bolt dimensions/grade marks

- G   Grade marks (bolt strength)
- L   Length (in inches)
- T   Thread pitch (number of threads per inch)
- D   Nominal diameter (in inches)

Metric bolt dimensions/grade marks

- P   Property class (bolt strength)
- L   Length (in millimeters)
- T   Thread pitch (distance between threads in millimeters)
- D   Diameter

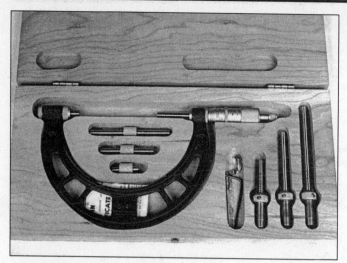

Micrometer set

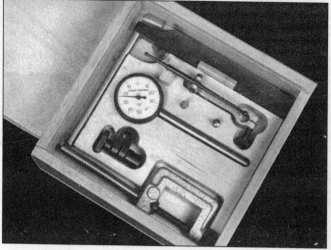

Dial indicator set

Initially, the bolts or nuts should be assembled finger-tight only. Next, they should be tightened one full turn each, in a criss-cross or diagonal pattern. After each one has been tightened one full turn, return to the first one and tighten them all one-half turn, following the same pattern. Finally, tighten each of them one-quarter turn at a time until each fastener has been tightened to the proper torque. To loosen and remove the fasteners, the procedure would be reversed.

Component disassembly

Component disassembly should be done with care and purpose to help ensure that the parts go back together properly. Always keep track of the sequence in which parts are removed. Make note of special characteristics or marks on parts that can be installed more than one way, such as a grooved thrust washer on a shaft. It is a good idea to lay the disassembled parts out on a clean surface in the order that they were removed. It may also be helpful to make sketches or take instant photos of components before removal.

When removing fasteners from a component, keep track of their locations. Sometimes threading a bolt back in a part, or putting the washers and nut back on a stud, can prevent mix-ups later. If nuts and bolts cannot be returned to their original locations, they should be kept in a compartmented box or a series of small boxes. A cupcake or muffin tin is ideal for this purpose, since each cavity can hold the bolts and nuts from a particular area (i.e. oil pan bolts, valve cover bolts, engine mount bolts, etc.). A pan of this type is especially helpful when working on assemblies with very small parts, such as the carburetor, alternator, valve train or interior dash and trim pieces. The cavities can be marked with paint or tape to identify the contents.

Whenever wiring looms, harnesses or connectors are separated, it is a good idea to identify the two halves with numbered pieces of masking tape so they can be easily reconnected.

Gasket sealing surfaces

Throughout any vehicle, gaskets are used to seal the mating surfaces between two parts and keep lubricants, fluids, vacuum or pressure contained in an assembly.

Many times these gaskets are coated with a liquid or paste-type gasket sealing compound before assembly. Age, heat and pressure can sometimes cause the two parts to stick together so tightly that they are very difficult to separate. Often, the assembly can be loosened by striking it with a soft-face hammer near the mating surfaces. A regular hammer can be used if a block of wood is placed between the hammer and the part. Do not hammer on cast parts or parts that could be easily damaged. With any particularly stubborn part, always recheck to make sure that every fastener has been removed.

Avoid using a screwdriver or bar to pry apart an assembly, as they can easily mar the gasket sealing surfaces of the parts, which must remain smooth. If prying is absolutely necessary, use an old broom handle, but keep in mind that extra clean up will be necessary if the wood splinters.

After the parts are separated, the old gasket must be carefully scraped off and the gasket surfaces cleaned. Stubborn gasket material can be soaked with rust penetrant or treated with a special chemical to soften it so it can be easily scraped off. A scraper can be fashioned from a piece of copper tubing by flattening and sharpening one end. Copper is recommended because it is usually softer than the surfaces to be scraped, which reduces the chance of gouging the part. Some gaskets can be removed with a wire brush, but regardless of the method used, the mating surfaces must be left clean and smooth. If for some reason the gasket surface is gouged, then a gasket sealer thick enough to fill scratches will have to be used during reassembly of the components. For most applications, a non-drying (or semi-drying) gasket sealer should be used.

Hose removal tips

Warning: *If the vehicle is equipped with air conditioning, do not disconnect any of the A/C hoses without first having the system depressurized by a dealer service department or a service station.*

Hose removal precautions closely parallel gasket removal precautions. Avoid scratching or gouging the surface that the hose mates against or the connection may leak. This is especially true for radiator hoses. Because of various chemical reactions, the rubber in hoses can bond itself to the metal spigot that the hose fits over. To remove a hose, first loosen the hose clamps that secure it to the spigot. Then, with slip-joint pliers, grab the hose at the clamp and rotate it around the spigot. Work it back and forth until it is completely free, then pull it off. Silicone or other lubricants will ease removal if they can be applied between the hose and the outside of the spigot. Apply the same lubricant to the inside of the hose and the outside of the spigot to simplify installation.

As a last resort (and if the hose is to be replaced with a new one anyway), the rubber can be slit with a knife and the hose peeled from the spigot. If this must be done, be careful that the metal connection is not damaged.

If a hose clamp is broken or damaged, do not reuse it. Wire-type clamps usually weaken with age, so it is a good idea to replace them with screw-type clamps whenever a hose is removed.

Tools

A selection of good tools is a basic requirement for anyone who plans to maintain and repair his or her own vehicle. For the owner who has few tools, the initial investment might seem high, but when compared to the spiraling costs of professional auto maintenance and repair, it is a wise one.

To help the owner decide which tools are needed to perform the tasks detailed in this manual, the following tool lists are offered: *Maintenance and minor repair,*

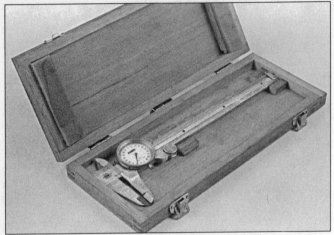

Dial caliper

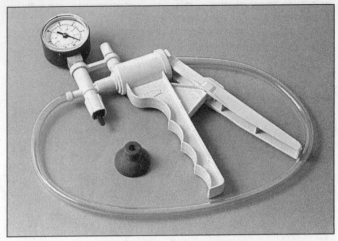

Hand-operated vacuum pump

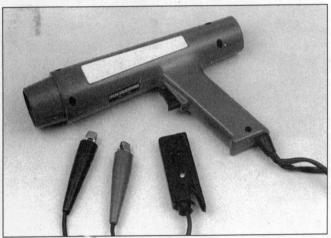

Timing light

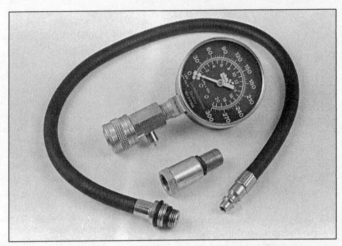

Compression gauge with spark plug hole adapter

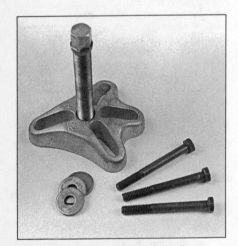

Damper/steering wheel puller

General purpose puller

Hydraulic lifter removal tool

Repair/overhaul and *Special*.

The newcomer to practical mechanics should start off with the *maintenance and minor repair* tool kit, which is adequate for the simpler jobs performed on a vehicle. Then, as confidence and experience grow, the owner can tackle more difficult tasks, buying additional tools as they are needed.

Eventually the basic kit will be expanded into the *repair and overhaul* tool set. Over a period of time, the experienced do-it-yourselfer will assemble a tool set complete enough for most repair and overhaul procedures and will add tools from the special category when it is felt that the expense is justified by the frequency of use.

Maintenance and minor repair tool kit

The tools in this list should be considered the minimum required for performance of routine maintenance, servicing and minor repair work. We recommend the purchase of combination wrenches (box-end and open-

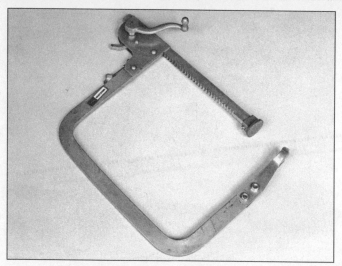

Valve spring compressor

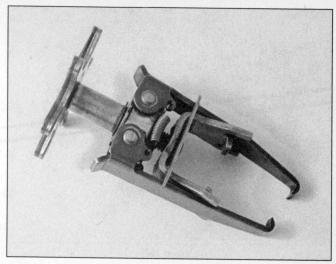

Valve spring compressor

Ridge reamer

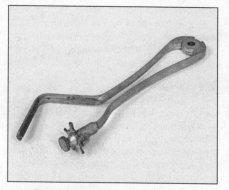

Piston ring groove cleaning tool

Ring removal/installation tool

Ring compressor

end combined in one wrench). While more expensive than open end wrenches, they offer the advantages of both types of wrench.

> *Combination wrench set (1/4-inch to 1 inch or 6 mm to 19 mm)*
> *Adjustable wrench, 8 inch*
> *Spark plug wrench with rubber insert*
> *Spark plug gap adjusting tool*
> *Feeler gauge set*
> *Brake bleeder wrench*
> *Standard screwdriver (5/16-inch x 6 inch)*
> *Phillips screwdriver (No. 2 x 6 inch)*
> *Combination pliers - 6 inch*
> *Hacksaw and assortment of blades*
> *Tire pressure gauge*
> *Grease gun*
> *Oil can*
> *Fine emery cloth*
> *Wire brush*
> *Battery post and cable cleaning tool*
> *Oil filter wrench*
> *Funnel (medium size)*
> *Safety goggles*
> *Jackstands (2)*
> *Drain pan*

Note: *If basic tune-ups are going to be part of routine maintenance, it will be necessary to purchase a good quality stroboscopic timing*

light and combination tachometer/dwell meter. Although they are included in the list of special tools, it is mentioned here because they are absolutely necessary for tuning most vehicles properly.

Repair and overhaul tool set

These tools are essential for anyone who plans to perform major repairs and are in addition to those in the maintenance and minor repair tool kit. Included is a comprehensive set of sockets which, though expensive, are invaluable because of their versatility, especially when various extensions and drives are available. We recommend the 1/2-inch drive over the 3/8-inch drive. Although the larger drive is bulky and more expensive, it has the capacity of accepting a very wide range of large sockets. Ideally, however, the mechanic should have a 3/8-inch drive set and a 1/2-inch drive set.

> *Socket set(s)*
> *Reversible ratchet*
> *Extension - 10 inch*
> *Universal joint*
> *Torque wrench (same size drive as sockets)*
> *Ball peen hammer - 8 ounce*
> *Soft-face hammer (plastic/rubber)*

> *Standard screwdriver (1/4-inch x 6 inch)*
> *Standard screwdriver (stubby - 5/16-inch)*
> *Phillips screwdriver (No. 3 x 8 inch)*
> *Phillips screwdriver (stubby - No. 2)*
> *Pliers - vise grip*
> *Pliers - lineman's*
> *Pliers - needle nose*
> *Pliers - snap-ring (internal and external)*
> *Cold chisel - 1/2-inch*

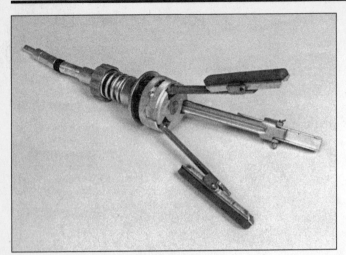

Cylinder hone

Brake hold-down spring tool

Scribe
Scraper (made from flattened copper tubing)
Centerpunch
Pin punches (1/16, 1/8, 3/16-inch)
Steel rule/straightedge - 12 inch
Allen wrench set (1/8 to 3/8-inch or 4 mm to 10 mm)
A selection of files

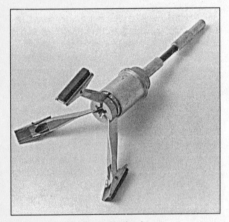

Brake cylinder hone

Wire brush (large)
Jackstands (second set)
Jack (scissor or hydraulic type)

Note: *Another tool which is often useful is an electric drill with a chuck capacity of 3/8-inch and a set of good quality drill bits.*

Special tools

The tools in this list include those which are not used regularly, are expensive to buy, or which need to be used in accordance with their manufacturer's instructions. Unless these tools will be used frequently, it is not very economical to purchase many of them. A consideration would be to split the cost and use between yourself and a friend or friends. In addition, most of these tools can be obtained from a tool rental shop on a temporary basis.

This list primarily contains only those tools and instruments widely available to the public, and not those special tools produced by the vehicle manufacturer for distribution to dealer service departments. Occasionally, references to the manufacturer's special tools are included in the text of this manual. Generally, an alternative method of doing the job without the special tool is offered. How-

ever, sometimes there is no alternative to their use. Where this is the case, and the tool cannot be purchased or borrowed, the work should be turned over to the dealer service department or an automotive repair shop.

Valve spring compressor
Piston ring groove cleaning tool
Piston ring compressor
Piston ring installation tool
Cylinder compression gauge
Cylinder ridge reamer
Cylinder surfacing hone
Cylinder bore gauge
Micrometers and/or dial calipers
Hydraulic lifter removal tool
Balljoint separator
Universal-type puller
Impact screwdriver
Dial indicator set
Stroboscopic timing light (inductive pick-up)
Hand operated vacuum/pressure pump
Tachometer/dwell meter
Universal electrical multimeter
Cable hoist
Brake spring removal and installation tools
Floor jack

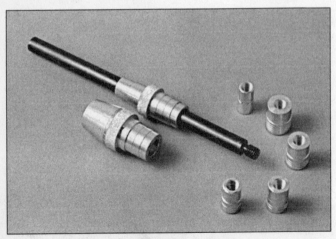

Clutch plate alignment tool

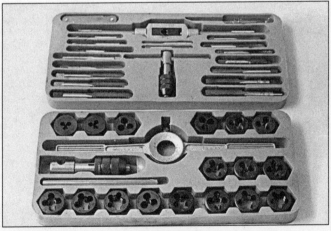

Tap and die set

Buying tools

For the do-it-yourselfer who is just starting to get involved in vehicle maintenance and repair, there are a number of options available when purchasing tools. If maintenance and minor repair is the extent of the work to be done, the purchase of individual tools is satisfactory. If, on the other hand, extensive work is planned, it would be a good idea to purchase a modest tool set from one of the large retail chain stores. A set can usually be bought at a substantial savings over the individual tool prices, and they often come with a tool box. As additional tools are needed, add-on sets, individual tools and a larger tool box can be purchased to expand the tool selection. Building a tool set gradually allows the cost of the tools to be spread over a longer period of time and gives the mechanic the freedom to choose only those tools that will actually be used.

Tool stores will often be the only source of some of the special tools that are needed, but regardless of where tools are bought, try to avoid cheap ones, especially when buying screwdrivers and sockets, because they won't last very long. The expense involved in replacing cheap tools will eventually be greater than the initial cost of quality tools.

Care and maintenance of tools

Good tools are expensive, so it makes sense to treat them with respect. Keep them clean and in usable condition and store them properly when not in use. Always wipe off any dirt, grease or metal chips before putting them away. Never leave tools lying around in the work area. Upon completion of a job, always check closely under the hood for tools that may have been left there so they won't get lost during a test drive.

Some tools, such as screwdrivers, pliers, wrenches and sockets, can be hung on a panel mounted on the garage or workshop wall, while others should be kept in a tool box or tray. Measuring instruments, gauges, meters, etc. must be carefully stored where they cannot be damaged by weather or impact from other tools.

When tools are used with care and stored properly, they will last a very long time. Even with the best of care, though, tools will wear out if used frequently. When a tool is damaged or worn out, replace it. Subsequent jobs will be safer and more enjoyable if you do.

How to repair damaged threads

Sometimes, the internal threads of a nut or bolt hole can become stripped, usually from overtightening. Stripping threads is an all-too-common occurrence, especially when working with aluminum parts, because aluminum is so soft that it easily strips out.

Usually, external or internal threads are only partially stripped. After they've been cleaned up with a tap or die, they'll still work. Sometimes, however, threads are badly damaged. When this happens, you've got three choices:

1) *Drill and tap the hole to the next suitable oversize and install a larger diameter bolt, screw or stud.*
2) *Drill and tap the hole to accept a threaded plug, then drill and tap the plug to the original screw size. You can also buy a plug already threaded to the original size. Then you simply drill a hole to the specified size, then run the threaded plug into the hole with a bolt and jam nut. Once the plug is fully seated, remove the jam nut and bolt.*
3) *The third method uses a patented thread repair kit like Heli-Coil or Slimsert. These easy-to-use kits are designed to repair damaged threads in straight-through holes and blind holes. Both are available as kits which can handle a variety of sizes and thread patterns. Drill the hole, then tap it with the special included tap. Install the Heli-Coil and the hole is back to its original diameter and thread pitch.*

Regardless of which method you use, be sure to proceed calmly and carefully. A little impatience or carelessness during one of these relatively simple procedures can ruin your whole day's work and cost you a bundle if you wreck an expensive part.

Working facilities

Not to be overlooked when discussing tools is the workshop. If anything more than routine maintenance is to be carried out, some sort of suitable work area is essential.

It is understood, and appreciated, that many home mechanics do not have a good workshop or garage available, and end up removing an engine or doing major repairs outside. It is recommended, however, that the overhaul or repair be completed under the cover of a roof.

A clean, flat workbench or table of comfortable working height is an absolute necessity. The workbench should be equipped with a vise that has a jaw opening of at least four inches.

As mentioned previously, some clean, dry storage space is also required for tools, as well as the lubricants, fluids, cleaning solvents, etc. which soon become necessary.

Sometimes waste oil and fluids, drained from the engine or cooling system during normal maintenance or repairs, present a disposal problem. To avoid pouring them on the ground or into a sewage system, pour the used fluids into large containers, seal them with caps and take them to an authorized disposal site or recycling center. Plastic jugs, such as old antifreeze containers, are ideal for this purpose.

Always keep a supply of old newspapers and clean rags available. Old towels are excellent for mopping up spills. Many mechanics use rolls of paper towels for most work because they are readily available and disposable. To help keep the area under the vehicle clean, a large cardboard box can be cut open and flattened to protect the garage or shop floor.

Whenever working over a painted surface, such as when leaning over a fender to service something under the hood, always cover it with an old blanket or bedspread to protect the finish. Vinyl covered pads, made especially for this purpose, are available at auto parts stores.

Booster battery (jump) starting

Observe these precautions when using a booster battery to start a vehicle:

a) Before connecting the booster battery, make sure the ignition switch is in the Off position.

b) Turn off the lights, heater and other electrical loads.

c) Your eyes should be shielded. Safety goggles are a good idea.

d) Make sure the booster battery is the same voltage as the dead one in the vehicle.

e) The two vehicles MUST NOT TOUCH each other!

f) Make sure the transmission is in Neutral (manual) or Park (automatic).

g) If the booster battery is not a maintenance-free type, remove the vent caps and lay a cloth over the vent holes.

Connect the red jumper cable to the positive (+) terminals of each battery.

Connect one end of the black jumper cable to the negative (-) terminal of the booster battery. The other end of this cable should be connected to a good ground on the vehicle to be started, such as a bolt or bracket on the engine block (see illustration). Make sure the cable will not come into contact with the fan, drivebelts or other moving parts of the engine.

Start the engine using the booster battery, then, with the engine running at idle speed, disconnect the jumper cables in the reverse order of connection.

Make the booster battery cable connections in the numerical order shown (note that the negative cable of the booster battery is NOT attached to the negative terminal of the dead battery).

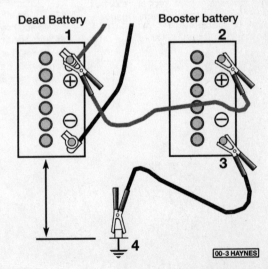

Make the booster battery cable connections in the numerical order shown (note that the negative cable of the booster battery is NOT attached to the negative terminal of the dead battery)

Jacking and towing

Jacking

The jack supplied with the vehicle should only be used for raising the vehicle when changing a tire or placing jackstands under the frame. **Warning:** *Never work under the vehicle or start the engine while this jack is being used as the only means of support.*

The vehicle should be on level ground with the hazard flashers on, the wheels blocked, the parking brake applied and the transmission in Park (automatic) or Reverse (manual). If a tire is being changed, pry off the hubcap (if equipped) and loosen the lug nuts one-half turn, leaving them in place until the wheel is raised off the ground.

Place the jack under the vehicle in the indicated position **(see illustrations)**. Oper- ate the jack with a slow, smooth motion until the wheel is raised off the ground. Remove the lug nuts, pull off the wheel, install the spare and thread the lug nuts back on with the beveled sides facing in. Tighten them snugly, but wait until the vehicle is lowered to tighten them completely. Note that some spare tires are designed for temporary use only - don't exceed the recommended speed, mileage or other restrictions accompanying the spare.

Lower the vehicle, remove the jack and tighten the nuts (if loosened or removed) in a criss-cross pattern.

Towing

These vehicles should *not* be towed with all four wheels on the ground. The front or rear wheels should be placed on a dolly. Do not exceed 35 mph or tow the vehicle farther than 50 miles.

Equipment specifically designed for towing should be used and should be attached to the main structural members of the vehicle, not the bumper or brackets.

Safety is a major consideration when towing and all applicable state and local laws must be obeyed. A safety chain must be used for all towing.

While towing, the parking brake should be released and the transmission and (if equipped) transfer case must be in Neutral. The steering must be unlocked (ignition switch in the Off position). Remember that power steering and power brakes will not work with the engine off.

The front jacking point is located directly behind the front wheel. When raising the vehicle . . .

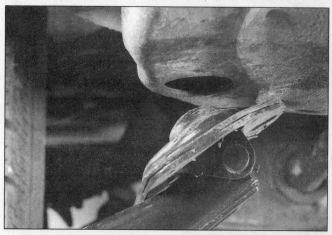

. . . make sure the jack head securely engages with the hole in the frame (on the rear jacking point, the hole for the jack is in the leaf spring hanger

Automotive chemicals and lubricants

A number of automotive chemicals and lubricants are available for use during vehicle maintenance and repair. They include a wide variety of products ranging from cleaning solvents and degreasers to lubricants and protective sprays for rubber, plastic and vinyl.

Cleaners

Carburetor cleaner and choke cleaner is a strong solvent for gum, varnish and carbon. Most carburetor cleaners leave a dry-type lubricant film which will not harden or gum up. Because of this film it is not recommended for use on electrical components.

Brake system cleaner is used to remove grease and brake fluid from the brake system, where clean surfaces are absolutely necessary. It leaves no residue and often eliminates brake squeal caused by contaminants.

Electrical cleaner removes oxidation, corrosion and carbon deposits from electrical contacts, restoring full current flow. It can also be used to clean spark plugs, carburetor jets, voltage regulators and other parts where an oil-free surface is desired.

Demoisturants remove water and moisture from electrical components such as alternators, voltage regulators, electrical connectors and fuse blocks. They are non-conductive, non-corrosive and non-flammable.

Degreasers are heavy-duty solvents used to remove grease from the outside of the engine and from chassis components. They can be sprayed or brushed on and, depending on the type, are rinsed off either with water or solvent.

Lubricants

Motor oil is the lubricant formulated for use in engines. It normally contains a wide variety of additives to prevent corrosion and reduce foaming and wear. Motor oil comes in various weights (viscosity ratings) from 0 to 50. The recommended weight of the oil depends on the season, temperature and the demands on the engine. Light oil is used in cold climates and under light load conditions. Heavy oil is used in hot climates and where high loads are encountered. Multi-viscosity oils are designed to have characteristics of both light and heavy oils and are available in a number of weights from 5W-20 to 20W-50.

Gear oil is designed to be used in differentials, manual transmissions and other areas where high-temperature lubrication is required.

Chassis and wheel bearing grease is a heavy grease used where increased loads and friction are encountered, such as for wheel bearings, balljoints, tie-rod ends and universal joints.

High-temperature wheel bearing grease is designed to withstand the extreme temperatures encountered by wheel bearings in disc brake equipped vehicles. It usually contains molybdenum disulfide (moly), which is a dry-type lubricant.

White grease is a heavy grease for metal-to-metal applications where water is a problem. White grease stays soft under both low and high temperatures (usually from -100 to +190-degrees F), and will not wash off or dilute in the presence of water.

Assembly lube is a special extreme pressure lubricant, usually containing moly, used to lubricate high-load parts (such as main and rod bearings and cam lobes) for initial start-up of a new engine. The assembly lube lubricates the parts without being squeezed out or washed away until the engine oiling system begins to function.

Silicone lubricants are used to protect rubber, plastic, vinyl and nylon parts.

Graphite lubricants are used where oils cannot be used due to contamination problems, such as in locks. The dry graphite will lubricate metal parts while remaining uncontaminated by dirt, water, oil or acids. It is electrically conductive and will not foul electrical contacts in locks such as the ignition switch.

Moly penetrants loosen and lubricate frozen, rusted and corroded fasteners and prevent future rusting or freezing.

Heat-sink grease is a special electrically non-conductive grease that is used for mounting electronic ignition modules where it is essential that heat is transferred away from the module.

Sealants

RTV sealant is one of the most widely used gasket compounds. Made from silicone, RTV is air curing, it seals, bonds, waterproofs, fills surface irregularities, remains flexible, doesn't shrink, is relatively easy to remove, and is used as a supplementary sealer with almost all low and medium temperature gaskets.

Anaerobic sealant is much like RTV in that it can be used either to seal gaskets or to form gaskets by itself. It remains flexible, is solvent resistant and fills surface imperfections. The difference between an anaerobic sealant and an RTV-type sealant is in the curing. RTV cures when exposed to air, while an anaerobic sealant cures only in the absence of air. This means that an anaerobic sealant cures only after the assembly of parts, sealing them together.

Thread and pipe sealant is used for sealing hydraulic and pneumatic fittings and vacuum lines. It is usually made from a Teflon compound, and comes in a spray, a paint-on liquid and as a wrap-around tape.

Chemicals

Anti-seize compound prevents seizing, galling, cold welding, rust and corrosion in fasteners. High-temperature ant-seize, usually made with copper and graphite lubricants, is used for exhaust system and exhaust manifold bolts.

Anaerobic locking compounds are used to keep fasteners from vibrating or working loose and cure only after installation, in the absence of air. Medium strength locking compound is used for small nuts, bolts and screws that may be removed later. High-strength locking compound is for large nuts, bolts and studs which aren't removed on a regular basis.

Oil additives range from viscosity index improvers to chemical treatments that claim to reduce internal engine friction. It should be noted that most oil manufacturers caution against using additives with their oils.

Gas additives perform several functions, depending on their chemical makeup. They usually contain solvents that help dissolve gum and varnish that build up on carburetor, fuel injection and intake parts. They also serve to break down carbon deposits that form on the inside surfaces of the combustion chambers. Some additives contain upper cylinder lubricants for valves and piston rings, and others contain chemicals to remove condensation from the gas tank.

Miscellaneous

Brake fluid is specially formulated hydraulic fluid that can withstand the heat and pressure encountered in brake systems. Care must be taken so this fluid does not come in contact with painted surfaces or plastics. An opened container should always be resealed to prevent contamination by water or dirt.

Weatherstrip adhesive is used to bond weatherstripping around doors, windows and trunk lids. It is sometimes used to attach trim pieces.

Undercoating is a petroleum-based, tar-like substance that is designed to protect metal surfaces on the underside of the vehicle from corrosion. It also acts as a sound-deadening agent by insulating the bottom of the vehicle.

Waxes and polishes are used to help protect painted and plated surfaces from the weather. Different types of paint may require the use of different types of wax and polish. Some polishes utilize a chemical or abrasive cleaner to help remove the top layer of oxidized (dull) paint on older vehicles. In recent years many non-wax polishes that contain a wide variety of chemicals such as polymers and silicones have been introduced. These non-wax polishes are usually easier to apply and last longer than conventional waxes and polishes.

Conversion factors

Length (distance)

Inches (in)	X	25.4	= Millimetres (mm)	X 0.0394	= Inches (in)
Feet (ft)	X	0.305	= Metres (m)	X 3.281	= Feet (ft)
Miles	X	1.609	= Kilometres (km)	X 0.621	= Miles

Volume (capacity)

Cubic inches (cu in; in³)	X	16.387	= Cubic centimetres (cc; cm³)	X 0.061	= Cubic inches (cu in; in³)
Imperial pints (Imp pt)	X	0.568	= Litres (l)	X 1.76	= Imperial pints (Imp pt)
Imperial quarts (Imp qt)	X	1.137	= Litres (l)	X 0.88	= Imperial quarts (Imp qt)
Imperial quarts (Imp qt)	X	1.201	= US quarts (US qt)	X 0.833	= Imperial quarts (Imp qt)
US quarts (US qt)	X	0.946	= Litres (l)	X 1.057	= US quarts (US qt)
Imperial gallons (Imp gal)	X	4.546	= Litres (l)	X 0.22	= Imperial gallons (Imp gal)
Imperial gallons (Imp gal)	X	1.201	= US gallons (US gal)	X 0.833	= Imperial gallons (Imp gal)
US gallons (US gal)	X	3.785	= Litres (l)	X 0.264	= US gallons (US gal)

Mass (weight)

Ounces (oz)	X	28.35	= Grams (g)	X 0.035	= Ounces (oz)
Pounds (lb)	X	0.454	= Kilograms (kg)	X 2.205	= Pounds (lb)

Force

Ounces-force (ozf; oz)	X	0.278	= Newtons (N)	X 3.6	= Ounces-force (ozf; oz)
Pounds-force (lbf; lb)	X	4.448	= Newtons (N)	X 0.225	= Pounds-force (lbf; lb)
Newtons (N)	X	0.1	= Kilograms-force (kgf; kg)	X 9.81	= Newtons (N)

Pressure

Pounds-force per square inch (psi; lbf/in²; lb/in²)	X	0.070	= Kilograms-force per square centimetre (kgf/cm²; kg/cm²)	X 14.223	= Pounds-force per square inch (psi; lbf/in²; lb/in²)
Pounds-force per square inch (psi; lbf/in²; lb/in²)	X	0.068	= Atmospheres (atm)	X 14.696	= Pounds-force per square inch (psi; lbf/in²; lb/in²)
Pounds-force per square inch (psi; lbf/in²; lb/in²)	X	0.069	= Bars	X 14.5	= Pounds-force per square inch (psi; lbf/in²; lb/in²)
Pounds-force per square inch (psi; lbf/in²; lb/in²)	X	6.895	= Kilopascals (kPa)	X 0.145	= Pounds-force per square inch (psi; lbf/in²; lb/in²)
Kilopascals (kPa)	X	0.01	= Kilograms-force per square centimetre (kgf/cm²; kg/cm²)	X 98.1	= Kilopascals (kPa)

Torque (moment of force)

Pounds-force inches (lbf in; lb in)	X	1.152	= Kilograms-force centimetre (kgf cm; kg cm)	X 0.868	= Pounds-force inches (lbf in; lb in)
Pounds-force inches (lbf in; lb in)	X	0.113	= Newton metres (Nm)	X 8.85	= Pounds-force inches (lbf in; lb in)
Pounds-force inches (lbf in; lb in)	X	0.083	= Pounds-force feet (lbf ft; lb ft)	X 12	= Pounds-force inches (lbf in; lb in)
Pounds-force feet (lbf ft; lb ft)	X	0.138	= Kilograms-force metres (kgf m; kg m)	X 7.233	= Pounds-force feet (lbf ft; lb ft)
Pounds-force feet (lbf ft; lb ft)	X	1.356	= Newton metres (Nm)	X 0.738	= Pounds-force feet (lbf ft; lb ft)
Newton metres (Nm)	X	0.102	= Kilograms-force metres (kgf m; kg m)	X 9.804	= Newton metres (Nm)

Vacuum

Inches mercury (in. Hg)	X	3.377	= Kilopascals (kPa)	X 0.2961	= Inches mercury
Inches mercury (in. Hg)	X	25.4	= Millimeters mercury (mm Hg)	X 0.0394	= Inches mercury

Power

Horsepower (hp)	X	745.7	= Watts (W)	X 0.0013	= Horsepower (hp)

Velocity (speed)

Miles per hour (miles/hr; mph)	X	1.609	= Kilometres per hour (km/hr; kph)	X 0.621	= Miles per hour (miles/hr; mph)

Fuel consumption*

Miles per gallon, Imperial (mpg)	X	0.354	= Kilometres per litre (km/l)	X 2.825	= Miles per gallon, Imperial (mpg)
Miles per gallon, US (mpg)	X	0.425	= Kilometres per litre (km/l)	X 2.352	= Miles per gallon, US (mpg)

Temperature

Degrees Fahrenheit = (°C x 1.8) + 32

Degrees Celsius (Degrees Centigrade; °C) = (°F - 32) x 0.56

*It is common practice to convert from miles per gallon (mpg) to litres/100 kilometres (l/100km), where mpg (Imperial) x l/100 km = 282 and mpg (US) x l/100 km = 235

Safety first!

Regardless of how enthusiastic you may be about getting on with the job at hand, take the time to ensure that your safety is not jeopardized. A moment's lack of attention can result in an accident, as can failure to observe certain simple safety precautions. The possibility of an accident will always exist, and the following points should not be considered a comprehensive list of all dangers. Rather, they are intended to make you aware of the risks and to encourage a safety conscious approach to all work you carry out on your vehicle.

Essential DOs and DON'Ts

DON'T rely on a jack when working under the vehicle. Always use approved jackstands to support the weight of the vehicle and place them under the recommended lift or support points.

DON'T attempt to loosen extremely tight fasteners (i.e. wheel lug nuts) while the vehicle is on a jack - it may fall.

DON'T start the engine without first making sure that the transmission is in Neutral (or Park where applicable) and the parking brake is set.

DON'T remove the radiator cap from a hot cooling system - let it cool or cover it with a cloth and release the pressure gradually.

DON'T attempt to drain the engine oil until you are sure it has cooled to the point that it will not burn you.

DON'T touch any part of the engine or exhaust system until it has cooled sufficiently to avoid burns.

DON'T siphon toxic liquids such as gasoline, antifreeze and brake fluid by mouth, or allow them to remain on your skin.

DON'T inhale brake lining dust - it is potentially hazardous (see *Asbestos* below).

DON'T allow spilled oil or grease to remain on the floor - wipe it up before someone slips on it.

DON'T use loose fitting wrenches or other tools which may slip and cause injury.

DON'T push on wrenches when loosening or tightening nuts or bolts. Always try to pull the wrench toward you. If the situation calls for pushing the wrench away, push with an open hand to avoid scraped knuckles if the wrench should slip.

DON'T attempt to lift a heavy component alone - get someone to help you.

DON'T rush or take unsafe shortcuts to finish a job.

DON'T allow children or animals in or around the vehicle while you are working on it.

DO wear eye protection when using power tools such as a drill, sander, bench grinder, etc. and when working under a vehicle.

DO keep loose clothing and long hair well out of the way of moving parts.

DO make sure that any hoist used has a safe working load rating adequate for the job.

DO get someone to check on you periodically when working alone on a vehicle.

DO carry out work in a logical sequence and make sure that everything is correctly assembled and tightened.

DO keep chemicals and fluids tightly capped and out of the reach of children and pets.

DO remember that your vehicle's safety affects that of yourself and others. If in doubt on any point, get professional advice.

Asbestos

Certain friction, insulating, sealing, and other products - such as brake linings, brake bands, clutch linings, torque converters, gaskets, etc. - may contain asbestos. Extreme care must be taken to avoid inhalation of dust from such products, since it is hazardous to health. If in doubt, assume that they do contain asbestos.

Fire

Remember at all times that gasoline is highly flammable. Never smoke or have any kind of open flame around when working on a vehicle. But the risk does not end there. A spark caused by an electrical short circuit, by two metal surfaces contacting each other, or even by static electricity built up in your body under certain conditions, can ignite gasoline vapors, which in a confined space are highly explosive. Do not, under any circumstances, use gasoline for cleaning parts. Use an approved safety solvent.

Always disconnect the battery ground (-) cable at the battery before working on any part of the fuel system or electrical system. Never risk spilling fuel on a hot engine or exhaust component. It is strongly recommended that a fire extinguisher suitable for use on fuel and electrical fires be kept handy in the garage or workshop at all times. Never try to extinguish a fuel or electrical fire with water.

Fumes

Certain fumes are highly toxic and can quickly cause unconsciousness and even death if inhaled to any extent. Gasoline vapor falls into this category, as do the vapors from some cleaning solvents. Any draining or pouring of such volatile fluids should be done in a well ventilated area.

When using cleaning fluids and solvents, read the instructions on the container carefully. Never use materials from unmarked containers.

Never run the engine in an enclosed space, such as a garage. Exhaust fumes contain carbon monoxide, which is extremely poisonous. If you need to run the engine, always do so in the open air, or at least have the rear of the vehicle outside the work area.

If you are fortunate enough to have the use of an inspection pit, never drain or pour gasoline and never run the engine while the vehicle is over the pit. The fumes, being heavier than air, will concentrate in the pit with possibly lethal results.

The battery

Never create a spark or allow a bare light bulb near a battery. They normally give off a certain amount of hydrogen gas, which is highly explosive.

Always disconnect the battery ground (-) cable at the battery before working on the fuel or electrical systems.

If possible, loosen the filler caps or cover when charging the battery from an external source (this does not apply to sealed or maintenance-free batteries). Do not charge at an excessive rate or the battery may burst.

Take care when adding water to a non maintenance-free battery and when carrying a battery. The electrolyte, even when diluted, is very corrosive and should not be allowed to contact clothing or skin.

Always wear eye protection when cleaning the battery to prevent the caustic deposits from entering your eyes.

Household current

When using an electric power tool, inspection light, etc., which operates on household current, always make sure that the tool is correctly connected to its plug and that, where necessary, it is properly grounded. Do not use such items in damp conditions and, again, do not create a spark or apply excessive heat in the vicinity of fuel or fuel vapor.

Secondary ignition system voltage

A severe electric shock can result from touching certain parts of the ignition system (such as the spark plug wires) when the engine is running or being cranked, particularly if components are damp or the insulation is defective. In the case of an electronic ignition system, the secondary system voltage is much higher and could prove fatal.

Troubleshooting

Contents

Symptom	Section

Engine and performance
Alternator light fails to come on when key is turned on 13
Alternator light stays on 12
Battery will not hold a charge... 11
Engine backfires... 18
Engine diesels (continues to run) after being turned off............ 21
Engine hard to start when cold 4
Engine hard to start when hot 5
Engine lacks power 17
Engine 'lopes' while idling or idles erratically............................. 8
Engine misses at idle speed.. 9
Engine misses throughout driving speed range........................ 14
Engine rotates but will not start 2
Engine stalls 16
Engine starts but stops immediately 7
Engine surges while holding accelerator steady 19
Engine will not rotate when attempting to start 1
Excessive fuel consumption... 24
Excessively high idle speed 10
Excessive oil consumption... 23
Fuel odor 25
Hesitation or stumble during acceleration 15
Low oil pressure 22
Miscellaneous engine noises 26
Pinging or knocking engine sounds when engine
    is under load 20
Starter motor noisy or engages roughly....................................... 6
Starter motor operates without turning engine 3

Cooling system
Abnormal coolant loss.. 31
Corrosion... 33
External coolant leakage 29
Internal coolant leakage 30
Overcooling 28
Overheating 27
Poor coolant circulation 32

Clutch
Clutch pedal stays on floor when disengaged 39
Clutch slips (engine speed increases with no increase in
    vehicle speed) 35
Fails to release (pedal pressed to the floor - shift lever does
    not move freely in and out of Reverse) 34
Grabbing (chattering) as clutch is engaged 36
Squeal or rumble with clutch disengaged (pedal depressed)........ 38
Squeal or rumble with clutch engaged (pedal released) 37

Manual transmission
Difficulty engaging gears.. 45
Noise occurs while shifting gears... 46
Noisy in all gears 41
Noisy in Neutral with engine running.. 40
Noisy in one particular gear 42
Oil leaks... 44
Slips out of gear 43

Automatic transmission
Engine will start in gears other than Park or Neutral................... 50

Symptom	Section

Fluid leakage 47
General shift mechanism problems 48
Transmission slips, shifts rough, is noisy or has no drive in
    forward or Reverse gears 51
Transmission will not downshift with the accelerator pedal
    pressed to the floor... 49

Driveshaft
Knock or clunk when transmission is under initial load (just
    after transmission is put into gear) 53
Leaks at transmission or transfer case end of driveshaft 52
Metallic grating sound consistent with vehicle speed 54
Scraping noise 56
Vibration 55
Whining or whistling noise 57

Axle(s) and differential(s)
Knocking sound when starting, shifting gears or accelerating
    after coasting 59
Noise - same when in drive as when vehicle is coasting............. 58
Noise when turning 60
Oil leaks... 62
Vibration 61

Transfer case (4WD models)
Difficult shifting... 64
Gear jumping out of mesh 63
Noise 65

Brakes
Brake pedal feels spongy when depressed 69
Brake pedal pulsates during brake application........................... 72
Brakes drag (indicated by sluggish engine performance or
    wheels being very hot after driving) 73
Excessive brake pedal travel 68
Excessive effort required to stop vehicle 70
Noise (high-pitched squeal or rattle) 67
Pedal travels to the floor with little resistance............................ 71
Rear brakes lock up under heavy brake application 75
Rear brakes lock up under light brake application 74
Vehicle pulls to one side during braking 66

Suspension and steering
Excessively stiff steering 80
Excessive pitching and/or rolling around
    corners or during braking 78
Excessive play in steering 81
Excessive tire wear (not specific to one area)............................ 87
Excessive tire wear on inside edge 89
Excessive tire wear on outside edge.. 88
Lack of power assistance 82
Miscellaneous noises 86
Noisy power steering pump 85
Shimmy, shake or vibration.. 77
Steering effort not the same in both directions (power system) 84
Steering wheel fails to return to straight-ahead position 83
Tire tread worn in one place... 90
Vehicle pulls to one side 76
Wandering or general instability 79

This Section provides an easy reference guide to the more common problems that may occur during the operation of your vehicle. Various symptoms and their probable causes are grouped under headings denoting components or systems, such as Engine, Cooling system, etc. They also refer to the Chapter and/or Section that deals with the problem.

Remember that successful troubleshooting isn't a mysterious 'black art' practiced only by professional mechanics, it's simply the result of knowledge combined with an intelligent, systematic approach to a problem. Always use a process of elimination starting with the simplest solution and working through to the most complex - and never overlook the obvious. Anyone can run the gas tank dry or leave the lights on overnight, so don't assume that you're exempt from such oversights.

Finally, always establish a clear idea why a problem has occurred and take steps to ensure that it doesn't happen again. If the electrical system fails because of a poor connection, check all other connections in the system to make sure they don't fail as well. If a particular fuse continues to blow, find out why - don't just go on replacing fuses. Remember, failure of a small component can often be indicative of potential failure or incorrect functioning of a more important component or system.

Engine and performance

1 Engine will not rotate when attempting to start

1   Battery terminal connections loose or corroded. Check the cable terminals at the battery; tighten cable clamp and/or clean off corrosion as necessary (see Chapter 1).
2   Battery discharged or faulty. If the cable ends are clean and tight on the battery posts, turn the key to the On position and switch on the headlights or windshield wipers. If they won't run, the battery is discharged.
3   Automatic transmission not engaged in park (P) or Neutral (N) or neutral safety switch faulty (see Chapter 7B).
4   On manual transmissions, clutch pedal not depressed or clutch start switch malfunctioning (see Chapter 7A).
5   Broken, loose or disconnected wires in the starting circuit. Inspect all wires and connectors at the battery, starter solenoid and ignition switch (on steering column).
6   Starter motor pinion jammed in flywheel ring gear. If manual transmission, place transmission in gear and rock the vehicle to manually turn the engine. Remove starter (Chapter 5) and inspect pinion and flywheel (Chapter 2) at earliest convenience.
7   Starter solenoid faulty (Chapter 5).
8   Starter motor faulty (Chapter 5).
9   Ignition switch faulty (Chapter 12).

10   Engine seized. Try to turn the crankshaft with a large socket and breaker bar on the pulley bolt.

2 Engine rotates but will not start

1   Fuel tank empty.
2   Battery discharged (engine rotates slowly). Check the operation of electrical components as described in previous Section.
3   Battery terminal connections loose or corroded. See previous Section.
4   Fuel not reaching carburetor or fuel injector(s). Check for clogged fuel filter or lines and defective fuel pump. Also make sure the tank vent lines aren't clogged (Chapter 4).
5   Choke not operating properly (Chapter 1).
6   Faulty distributor components. Check the cap and rotor (Chapter 1).
7   Low cylinder compression. Check as described in Chapter 2.
8   Valve clearances not properly adjusted (Chapter 1 or 2).
9   Water in fuel. Drain tank and fill with new fuel.
10   Defective ignition coil (Chapter 5).
11   Dirty or clogged carburetor jets or fuel injector(s). Carburetor out of adjustment. Check the float level (Chapter 4).
12   Wet or damaged ignition components (Chapters 1 and 5).
13   Worn, faulty or incorrectly gapped spark plugs (Chapter 1).
14   Broken, loose or disconnected wires in the starting circuit (see previous Section).
15   Loose distributor (changing ignition timing). Turn the distributor body as necessary to start the engine, then adjust the ignition timing as soon as possible (Chapter 1).
16   Broken, loose or disconnected wires at the ignition coil or faulty coil (Chapter 5).
17   Timing chain failure or wear affecting valve timing (Chapter 2).

3 Starter motor operates without turning engine

1   Starter pinion sticking. Remove the starter (Chapter 5) and inspect.
2   Starter pinion or flywheel/driveplate teeth worn or broken. Remove the inspection cover and inspect.

4 Engine hard to start when cold

1   Battery discharged or low. Check as described in Chapter 1.
2   Fuel not reaching the carburetor or fuel injector(s). Check the fuel filter, lines and fuel pump (Chapters 1 and 4).
3   Choke inoperative (Chapters 1 and 4).
4   Defective spark plugs (Chapter 1).

5 Engine hard to start when hot

1   Air filter dirty (Chapter 1).
2   Fuel not reaching carburetor or fuel injector(s) (see Section 4). Check for a vapor lock situation, brought about by clogged fuel tank vent lines.
3   Bad engine ground connection.
4   Choke sticking (Chapter 1).
5   Defective pick-up coil in distributor (Chapter 5).
6   Float level too high (Chapter 4).

6 Starter motor noisy or engages roughly

1   Pinion or flywheel/driveplate teeth worn or broken. Remove the inspection cover on the left side of the engine and inspect.
2   Starter motor mounting bolts loose or missing.

7 Engine starts but stops immediately

1   Loose or damaged wire harness connections at distributor, coil or alternator.
2   Intake manifold vacuum leaks. Make sure all mounting bolts/nuts are tight and all vacuum hoses connected to the manifold are attached properly and in good condition.
3   Insufficient fuel flow (see Chapter 4).

8 Engine 'lopes' while idling or idles erratically

1   Vacuum leaks. Check mounting bolts at the intake manifold for tightness. Make sure that all vacuum hoses are connected and in good condition. Use a stethoscope or a length of fuel hose held against your ear to listen for vacuum leaks while the engine is running. A hissing sound will be heard. A soapy water solution will also detect leaks. Check the intake manifold gasket surfaces.
2   Leaking EGR valve or plugged PCV valve (see Chapters 1 and 6).
3   Air filter clogged (Chapter 1).
4   Fuel pump not delivering sufficient fuel (Chapter 4).
5   Leaking head gasket. Perform a cylinder compression check (Chapter 2).
6   Timing chain worn (Chapter 2).
7   Camshaft lobes worn (Chapter 2).
8   Valve clearance out of adjustment (Chapter 1 or 2). Valves burned or otherwise leaking (Chapter 2).
9   Ignition timing out of adjustment (Chapter 1).
10   Ignition system not operating properly (Chapters 1 and 5).
11   Thermostatic air cleaner not operating properly (Chapter 1 or 6).

12   Choke not operating properly (Chapters 1 and 4).
13   Dirty or clogged injector(s). Carburetor dirty, clogged or out of adjustment. Check the float level (Chapter 4).
14   Idle speed out of adjustment (Chapter 1).
15   Throttle Position Sensor (TPS) faulty (Chapter 6).

9   Engine misses at idle speed

1   Spark plugs faulty or not gapped properly (Chapter 1).
2   Faulty spark plug wires (Chapter 1).
3   Wet or damaged distributor components (Chapter 1).
4   Short circuits in ignition, coil or spark plug wires.
5   Sticking or faulty emissions systems (see Chapter 6).
6   Clogged fuel filter and/or foreign matter in fuel. Remove the fuel filter (Chapter 1) and inspect.
7   Vacuum leaks at intake manifold or hose connections. Check as described in Section 8.
8   Incorrect idle speed (Chapter 1).
9   Incorrect ignition timing (Chapter 1).
10   Low or uneven cylinder compression. Check as described in Chapter 2.
11   Choke not operating properly (Chapter 1).
12   Clogged or dirty fuel injector(s) (Chapter 4).
13   Throttle Position Sensor (TPS) faulty (Chapter 6).
14   Possible Programmable Read-Only Memory (PROM) problem (Chapter 6).

10   Excessively high idle speed

1   Sticking throttle linkage (Chapter 4).
2   Choke opened excessively at idle (Chapter 4).
3   Idle speed incorrectly adjusted (Chapter 1).
4   Valve clearances incorrectly adjusted (Chapter 1 or 2).
5   Vacuum leaks. Check as described in Section 8.

11   Battery will not hold a charge

1   Alternator drivebelt defective or not adjusted properly (Chapter 1).
2   Battery cables loose or corroded (Chapter 1).
3   Alternator not charging properly (Chapter 5).
4   Loose, broken or faulty wires in the charging circuit (Chapter 5).
5   Short circuit causing a continuous drain on the battery.
6   Battery defective internally.

12   Alternator light stays on

1   Fault in alternator or charging circuit (Chapter 5).
2   Alternator drivebelt defective or not properly adjusted (Chapter 1).

13   Alternator light fails to come on when key is turned on

1   Faulty bulb (Chapter 12).
2   Defective alternator (Chapter 5).
3   Fault in the printed circuit, dash wiring or bulb holder (Chapter 12).

14   Engine misses throughout driving speed range

1   Fuel filter clogged and/or impurities in the fuel system. Check fuel filter (Chapter 1) or clean system (Chapter 4).
2   Faulty or incorrectly gapped spark plugs (Chapter 1).
3   Incorrect ignition timing (Chapter 1).
4   Cracked distributor cap, disconnected distributor wires or damaged distributor components (Chapter 1).
5   Defective spark plug wires (Chapter 1).
6   Emissions system components faulty (Chapter 6).
7   Low or uneven cylinder compression pressures. Check as described in Chapter 2.
8   Weak or faulty ignition coil (Chapter 5).
9   Weak or faulty ignition system (Chapter 5).
10   Vacuum leaks at intake manifold or vacuum hoses (see Section 8).
11   Dirty or clogged carburetor or fuel injector(s) (Chapter 4).
12   Leaky EGR valve (Chapter 6).
13   Carburetor out of adjustment (Chapter 4).
14   Idle speed out of adjustment (Chapter 1).

15   Hesitation or stumble during acceleration

1   Ignition timing incorrect (Chapter 1).
2   Ignition system not operating properly (Chapter 5).
3   Dirty or clogged carburetor or fuel injector(s) (Chapter 4).
4   Low fuel pressure. Check for proper operation of the fuel pump and for restrictions in the fuel filter and lines (Chapter 4).
5   Carburetor out of adjustment (Chapter 4).

16   Engine stalls

1   Idle speed incorrect (Chapter 1).

2   Fuel filter clogged and/or water and impurities in the fuel system (Chapter 1).
3   Choke not operating properly (Chapter 1).
4   Damaged or wet distributor cap and wires.
5   Emissions system components faulty (Chapter 6).
6   Faulty or incorrectly gapped spark plugs (Chapter 1). Also check the spark plug wires (Chapter 1).
7   Vacuum leak at the carburetor, intake manifold or vacuum hoses. Check as described in Section 8.

17   Engine lacks power

1   Incorrect ignition timing (Chapter 1).
2   Excessive play in distributor shaft. At the same time check for faulty distributor cap, wires, etc. (Chapter 1).
3   Faulty or incorrectly gapped spark plugs (Chapter 1).
4   Air filter dirty (Chapter 1).
5   Faulty ignition coil (Chapter 5).
6   Brakes binding (Chapters 1 and 9).
7   Automatic transmission fluid level incorrect, causing slippage (Chapter 1).
8   Clutch slipping (Chapter 8).
9   Fuel filter clogged and/or impurities in the fuel system (Chapters 1 and 4).
10   EGR system not functioning properly (Chapter 6).
11   Use of sub-standard fuel. Fill tank with proper octane fuel.
12   Low or uneven cylinder compression pressures. Check as described in Chapter 2.
13   Air leak at carburetor or intake manifold (check as described in Section 8).
14   Dirty or clogged carburetor jets or malfunctioning choke (Chapters 1 and 4).
15   Throttle Position Sensor (TPS) faulty (Chapter 6).

18   Engine backfires

1   EGR system not functioning properly (Chapter 6).
2   Ignition timing incorrect (Chapter 1).
3   Thermostatic air cleaner system not operating properly (Chapter 1 or 6).
4   Vacuum leak (refer to Section 8).
5   Valve clearances incorrect (Chapter 1 or 2).
6   Damaged valve springs or sticking valves (Chapter 2).
7   Intake air leak (see Section 8).
8   Carburetor float level out of adjustment (Chapter 4).

19   Engine surges while holding accelerator steady

1   Intake air leak (see Section 8).

2   Fuel pump not working properly (Chapter 4).
3   Throttle Position Sensor (TPS) faulty (Chapter 6).
4   Possible Programmable Read-Only Memory (PROM) problem (Chapter 6).

20 Pinging or knocking engine sounds when engine is under load

1   Incorrect grade of fuel. Fill tank with fuel of the proper octane rating.
2   Ignition timing incorrect (Chapter 1).
3   Carbon build-up in combustion chambers. Remove cylinder head(s) and clean combustion chambers (Chapter 2).
4   Incorrect spark plugs (Chapter 1).
5   If you have a 1986 model with a 2.5L engine, the cause of pinging when the accelerator is slightly depressed may be hardened lubricant in the tiny vacuum orifice in the EGR valve. Try removing the vacuum hose and probing the EGR orifice with a piece of wire or a pin.
6   Possible Programmable Read-Only Memory (PROM) problem (Chapter 6).

21 Engine diesels (continues to run) after being turned off

1   Idle speed too high (Chapter 1).
2   Ignition timing incorrect (Chapter 1).
3   Incorrect spark plug heat range (Chapter 1).
4   Intake air leak (see Section 8).
5   Carbon build-up in combustion chambers. Remove the cylinder head(s) and clean the combustion chambers (Chapter 2).
6   Valves sticking (Chapter 2).
7   Valve clearance incorrect (Chapter 1 or 2).
8   EGR system not operating properly (Chapter 6).
9   Fuel shut-off solenoid not operating properly (carbureted models only) (Chapter 4).
10   Check for causes of overheating (Section 27).

22 Low oil pressure

1   Improper grade of oil.
2   Oil pump worn or damaged (Chapter 2).
3   Engine overheating (refer to Section 27).
4   Clogged oil filter (Chapter 1).
5   Clogged oil strainer (Chapter 2).
6   Oil pressure gauge not working properly (Chapter 2).

23 Excessive oil consumption

1   Loose oil drain plug.
2   Loose bolts or damaged oil pan gasket (Chapter 2).

3   Loose bolts or damaged front cover gasket (Chapter 2).
4   Front or rear crankshaft oil seal leaking (Chapter 2).
5   Loose bolts or damaged rocker arm cover gasket (Chapter 2).
6   Loose oil filter (Chapter 1).
7   Loose or damaged oil pressure switch (Chapter 2).
8   Pistons and cylinders excessively worn (Chapter 2).
9   Piston rings not installed correctly on pistons (Chapter 2).
10   Worn or damaged piston rings (Chapter 2).
11   Intake and/or exhaust valve oil seals worn or damaged (Chapter 2).
12   Worn valve stems.
13   Worn or damaged valves/guides (Chapter 2).

24 Excessive fuel consumption

1   Dirty or clogged air filter element (Chapter 1).
2   Incorrect ignition timing (Chapter 1).
3   Incorrect idle speed (Chapter 1).
4   Low tire pressure or incorrect tire size (Chapter 10).
5   Fuel leakage. Check all connections, lines and components in the fuel system (Chapter 4).
6   Choke not operating properly (Chapter 1).
7   Dirty or clogged carburetor jets or fuel injector(s) (Chapter 4).

25 Fuel odor

1   Fuel leakage. Check all connections, lines and components in the fuel system (Chapter 4).
2   Fuel tank overfilled. Fill only to automatic shut-off.
3   Charcoal canister filter in Evaporative Emissions Control system clogged (Chapter 1).
4   Vapor leaks from Evaporative Emissions Control system lines (Chapter 6).

26 Miscellaneous engine noises

1   A strong dull noise that becomes more rapid as the engine accelerates indicates worn or damaged crankshaft bearings or an unevenly worn crankshaft. To pinpoint the trouble spot, remove the spark plug wire from one plug at a time and crank the engine over. If the noise stops, the cylinder with the removed plug wire indicates the problem area. Replace the bearing and/or service or replace the crankshaft (Chapter 2).
2   A similar (yet slightly higher pitched) noise to the crankshaft knocking described in the previous paragraph, that becomes more rapid as the engine accelerates, indicates

worn or damaged connecting rod bearings (Chapter 2). The procedure for locating the problem cylinder is the same as described in Paragraph 1.
3   An overlapping metallic noise that increases in intensity as the engine speed increases, yet diminishes as the engine warms up indicates abnormal piston and cylinder wear (Chapter 2).To locate the problem cylinder, use the procedure described in Paragraph 1.
4   A rapid clicking noise that becomes faster as the engine accelerates indicates a worn piston pin or piston pin hole. This sound will happen each time the piston hits the highest and lowest points in the stroke (Chapter 2). The procedure for locating the problem piston is described in Paragraph 1.
5   A metallic clicking noise coming from the water pump indicates worn or damaged water pump bearings or pump. Replace the water pump with a new one (Chapter 3).
6   A rapid tapping sound or clicking sound that becomes faster as the engine speed increases indicates "valve tapping" or improperly adjusted valve clearances. This can be identified by holding one end of a section of hose to your ear and placing the other end at different spots along the rocker arm cover. The point where the sound is loudest indicates the problem valve. Adjust the valve clearance (Chapter 1 or 2). If the problem persists, you likely have a collapsed hydraulic valve lifter or other damaged valve train component. Changing the engine oil and adding a high viscosity oil treatment will sometimes cure a stuck lifter problem. If the problem still persists, the lifters, pushrods and rocker arms must be removed for inspection (see Chapter 2).
7   A steady metallic rattling or rapping sound coming from the area of the timing chain cover indicates a worn, damaged or out-of-adjustment timing chain. Service or replace the chain and related components (Chapter 2).

Cooling system

27 Overheating

1   Insufficient coolant in system (Chapter 1).
2   Drivebelt defective or not adjusted properly (Chapter 1).
3   Radiator core blocked or radiator grille dirty and restricted (Chapter 3).
4   Thermostat faulty (Chapter 3).
5   Fan not functioning properly (Chapter 3).
6   Radiator cap not maintaining proper pressure. Have cap pressure tested by gas station or repair shop.
7   Ignition timing incorrect (Chapter 1).
8   Defective water pump (Chapter 3).
9   Improper grade of engine oil.
10   Inaccurate temperature gauge (Chapter 12).

11   On 1987 and later models with a serpentine drivebelt and a reverse-rotating water pump, if overheating occurs after the water pump has been replaced, suspect it may be the result of an earlier-type normal-rotating pump being installed instead of a reverse-rotating type.

28   Overcooling

1   Thermostat faulty (Chapter 3).
2   Inaccurate temperature gauge (Chapter 12).

29   External coolant leakage

1   Deteriorated or damaged hoses. Loose clamps at hose connections (Chapter 1).
2   Water pump seals defective. If this is the case, water will drip from the weep hole in the water pump body (Chapter 3).
3   Leakage from radiator core or header tank. This will require the radiator to be professionally repaired (see Chapter 3 for removal procedures).
4   Engine drain plugs or water jacket freeze plugs leaking (see Chapters 1 and 2).
5   Leak from coolant temperature switch (Chapter 3).
6   Leak from damaged gaskets or small cracks (Chapter 2).
7   Damaged head gasket. This can be verified by checking the condition of the engine oil as noted in Section 30.

30   Internal coolant leakage

Note: *Internal coolant leaks can usually be detected by examining the oil. Check the dipstick and inside the rocker arm cover for water deposits and an oil consistency like that of a milkshake.*
1   Leaking cylinder head gasket. Have the system pressure tested or remove the cylinder head (Chapter 2) and inspect.
2   Cracked cylinder bore or cylinder head. Dismantle engine and inspect (Chapter 2).
3   Loose cylinder head bolts (tighten as described in Chapter 2).

31   Abnormal coolant loss

1   Overfilling system (Chapter 1).
2   Coolant boiling away due to overheating (see causes in Section 27).
3   Internal or external leakage (see Sections 29 and 30).
4   Faulty radiator cap. Have the cap pressure tested.
5   Cooling system being pressurized by engine compression. This could be due to a cracked head or block or leaking head gasket(s).

32   Poor coolant circulation

1   Inoperative water pump. A quick test is to pinch the top radiator hose closed with your hand while the engine is idling, then release it. You should feel a surge of coolant if the pump is working properly (Chapter 3).
2   Restriction in cooling system. Drain, flush and refill the system (Chapter 1). If necessary, remove the radiator (Chapter 3) and have it reverse flushed or professionally cleaned.
3   Loose water pump drivebelt (Chapter 1).
4   Thermostat sticking (Chapter 3).
5   Insufficient coolant (Chapter 1).

33   Corrosion

1   Excessive impurities in the water. Soft, clean water is recommended. Distilled or rainwater is satisfactory.
2   Insufficient antifreeze solution (refer to Chapter 1 for the proper ratio of water to antifreeze).
3   Infrequent flushing and draining of system. Regular flushing of the cooling system should be carried out at the specified intervals as described in (Chapter 1).

Clutch

Note: *All clutch related service information is located in Chapter 8, unless otherwise noted.*

34   Fails to release (pedal pressed to the floor - shift lever does not move freely in and out of Reverse)

1   Clutch contaminated with oil. Remove clutch plate and inspect.
2   Clutch plate warped, distorted or otherwise damaged.
3   Diaphragm spring fatigued. Remove clutch cover/pressure plate assembly and inspect.
4   Broken or stretched clutch cable or broken cable self-adjusting mechanism (1982 and 1983 models).
5   Damaged release linkage.
6   Leakage of fluid from clutch hydraulic system (1984 and later models). Inspect master cylinder, slave cylinder and connecting lines.
7   Air in clutch hydraulic system (1984 and later models). Bleed the system.
8   Insufficient pedal stroke. Check and adjust as necessary.
9   Piston seal in slave cylinder deformed or damaged.
10   Lack of grease on pilot bushing.

35   Clutch slips (engine speed increases with no increase in vehicle speed)

1   Worn or oil soaked clutch plate.
2   Clutch plate not broken in. It may take 30 or 40 normal starts for a new clutch to seat.
3   Diaphragm spring weak or damaged. Remove clutch cover/pressure plate assembly and inspect.
4   Flywheel warped (Chapter 2).
5   Debris in master cylinder preventing the piston from returning to its normal position.
6   Clutch hydraulic line damaged.

36   Grabbing (chattering) as clutch is engaged

1   Oil on clutch plate. Remove and inspect. Repair any leaks.
2   Worn or loose engine or transmission mounts. They may move slightly when clutch is released. Inspect mounts and bolts.
3   Worn splines on transmission input shaft. Remove clutch components and inspect.
4   Warped pressure plate or flywheel. Remove clutch components and inspect.
5   Diaphragm spring fatigued. Remove clutch cover/pressure plate assembly and inspect.
6   Clutch linings hardened or warped.
7   Clutch lining rivets loose.

37   Squeal or rumble with clutch engaged (pedal released)

1   Improper pedal adjustment. Adjust pedal free play.
2   Release bearing binding on transmission shaft. Remove clutch components and check bearing. Remove any burrs or nicks, clean and relubricate before reinstallation.
3   Pilot bushing worn or damaged.
4   Clutch rivets loose.
5   Clutch plate cracked.
6   Fatigued clutch plate torsion springs. Replace clutch plate.

38   Squeal or rumble with clutch disengaged (pedal depressed)

1   Worn or damaged release bearing.
2   Worn or broken pressure plate diaphragm fingers.

39   Clutch pedal stays on floor when disengaged

1   Binding cable or cable self-adjusting mechanism (1982 and 1983 models).

2   Binding linkage or release bearing. Inspect linkage or remove clutch components as necessary.

Manual transmission

Note: *All manual transmission service information is located in Chapter 7, unless otherwise noted.*

40   Noisy in Neutral with engine running

1   Input shaft bearing worn.
2   Damaged main drive gear bearing.
3   Insufficient transmission oil (Chapter 1).
4   Transmission oil in poor condition. Drain and fill with proper grade oil. Check old oil for water and debris (Chapter 1).
5   Noise can be caused by variations in engine torque. Change the idle speed and see if noise disappears.

41   Noisy in all gears

1   Any of the above causes, and/or:
2   Worn or damaged output gear bearings or shaft.

42   Noisy in one particular gear

1   Worn, damaged or chipped gear teeth.
2   Worn or damaged synchronizer.

43   Slips out of gear

1   Transmission loose on clutch housing.
2   Stiff shift lever seal.
3   Shift linkage binding.
4   Broken or loose input gear bearing retainer.
5   Dirt between clutch lever and engine housing.
6   Worn linkage.
7   Damaged or worn check balls, fork rod ball grooves or check springs.
8   Worn mainshaft or countershaft bearings.
9   Loose engine mounts (Chapter 2).
10   Excessive gear end play.
11   Worn synchronizers.

44   Oil leaks

1   Excessive amount of lubricant in transmission (see Chapter 1 for correct checking procedures). Drain lubricant as required.
2   Rear oil seal or speedometer oil seal damaged.
3   To pinpoint a leak, first remove all built-up dirt and grime from the transmission.

Degreasing agents and/or steam cleaning will achieve this. With the underside clean, drive the vehicle at low speeds so the air flow will not blow the leak far from its source. Raise the vehicle and determine where the leak is located.

45   Difficulty engaging gears

1   Clutch not releasing completely.
2   Loose or damaged shift linkage. Make a thorough inspection, replacing parts as necessary.
3   Insufficient transmission oil (Chapter 1).
4   Transmission oil in poor condition. Drain and fill with proper grade oil. Check oil for water and debris (Chapter 1).
5   Worn or damaged striking rod.
6   Sticking or jamming gears.

46   Noise occurs while shifting gears

1   Check for proper operation of the clutch (Chapter 8).
2   Faulty synchronizer assemblies. Measure baulk (syncro) ring-to-gear clearance. Also, check for wear or damage to baulk rings or any parts of the synchromesh assemblies.

Automatic transmission

Note: *Due to the complexity of the automatic transmission, it's difficult for the home mechanic to properly diagnose and service. For problems other than the following, the vehicle should be taken to a reputable mechanic.*

47   Fluid leakage

1   Automatic transmission fluid is a deep red color, and fluid leaks should not be confused with engine oil which can easily be blown by air flow to the transmission.
2   To pinpoint a leak, first remove all built-up dirt and grime from the transmission. Degreasing agents and/or steam cleaning will achieve this. With the underside clean, drive the vehicle at low speeds so the air flow will not blow the leak far from its source. Raise the vehicle and determine where the leak is located. Common areas of leakage are:

a) *Fluid pan: tighten mounting bolts and/or replace pan gasket as necessary (Chapter 1).*
b) *Rear extension: tighten bolts and/or replace oil seal as necessary.*
c) *Filler pipe: replace the rubber oil seal where pipe enters transmission case.*
d) *Transmission oil lines: tighten fittings where lines enter transmission case and/or replace lines.*

e) *Vent pipe: transmission overfilled and/or water in fluid (see checking procedures, Chapter 1).*
f) *Speedometer or Vehicle Speed Sensor (VSS) connector: replace the seals at the adapter where this component attaches to the transmission or transfer case.*

3   On 1985 and 1986 models with the 700-R4 transmission, if repeated efforts fail to solve a fluid leak, it may be necessary to install a new pump body.

48   General shift mechanism problems

Chapter 7 deals with checking and adjusting the shift linkage on automatic transmissions. Common problems which may be caused by out of adjustment linkage are:

a) *Engine starting in gears other than P (park) or N (Neutral).*
b) *Indicator pointing to a gear other than the one actually engaged.*
c) *Vehicle moves with transmission in P (Park) position.*

49   Transmission will not downshift with the accelerator pedal pressed to the floor

Chapter 7 deals with adjusting the TV linkage to enable the transmission to downshift properly.

50   Engine will start in gears other than Park or Neutral

Chapter 7 deals with adjusting the Neutral safety switch used with automatic transmissions.

51   Transmission slips, shifts rough, is noisy or has no drive in forward or Reverse gears

1   There are many probable causes for the above problems, but the home mechanic should concern himself only with one possibility; fluid level.
2   Before taking the vehicle to a shop, check the fluid level and condition as described in Chapter 1. Add fluid, if necessary, or change the fluid and filter if needed. If problems persist, have a professional diagnose the transmission.

Driveshaft

Note: *Refer to Chapter 8, unless otherwise specified, for service information.*

52 Leaks at transmission or transfer case end of driveshaft

Defective transmission or transfer case seal. See Chapter 7 for the replacement procedure. As this is done, check the splined yoke for burrs or roughness that could damage the new seal. Remove burrs with a fine file or whetstone.

53 Knock or clunk when transmission is under initial load (just after transmission is put into gear)

1   Loose or disconnected suspension components or transmission mount. Check all mounting bolts and bushings (Chapters 7 and 10).
2   Loose driveshaft bolts. Inspect all bolts and nuts and tighten them securely.
3   Worn or damaged universal joint bearings. Replace driveshaft (Chapter 8).
4   Worn sleeve yoke and mainshaft spline.

54 Metallic grating sound consistent with vehicle speed

Pronounced wear in the universal joint bearings. Replace U-joints or driveshafts, as necessary.

55 Vibration

Note: *Before blaming the driveshaft, make sure the tires are perfectly balanced and perform the following test.*
1   Install a tachometer inside the vehicle to monitor engine speed as the vehicle is driven. Drive the vehicle and note the engine speed at which the vibration (roughness) is most pronounced. Now shift the transmission to a different gear and bring the engine speed to the same point.
2   If the vibration occurs at the same engine speed (rpm) regardless of which gear the transmission is in, the driveshaft is NOT at fault since the driveshaft speed varies.
3   If the vibration decreases or is eliminated when the transmission is in a different gear at the same engine speed, refer to the following probable causes.
4   Bent or dented driveshaft. Inspect and replace as necessary.
5   Undercoating or built-up dirt, etc. on the driveshaft. Clean the shaft thoroughly.
6   Worn universal joint bearings. Replace the U-joints or driveshaft as necessary.
7   Driveshaft and/or companion flange out of balance. Check for missing weights on the shaft. Remove driveshaft and reinstall 180-degrees from original position, then recheck. Have the driveshaft balanced if problem persists.

8   Loose driveshaft mounting bolts/nuts.
9   Defective center bearing, if so equipped.
10   Worn transmission rear bushing (Chapter 7).

56 Scraping noise

Make sure nothing is rubbing against the driveshaft as it's turning.

57 Whining or whistling noise

.   Defective center bearing, if so equipped.

Axle(s) and differential(s)
Note: *For differential servicing information, refer to Chapter 8, unless otherwise specified.*

58 Noise - same when in drive as when vehicle is coasting

1   Road noise. No corrective action available.
2   Tire noise. Inspect tires and check tire pressures (Chapter 1).
3   Wheel bearings loose, worn or damaged (Chapters 1 and 8).
4   Insufficient differential oil (Chapter 1).
5   Defective differential.

59 Knocking sound when starting, shifting gears or accelerating after coasting

1   Defective or incorrectly adjusted differential.
2   On 4WD models, a knocking sound from the front when accelerating after coasting often indicates a defective front inner CV joint. Check for worn or damaged boots and repair as necessary (Chapter 8).

60 Noise when turning

1   Defective differential.
2   On 4WD models, a clicking noise from the front when turning often indicates a defective front outer CV joint. Check for worn or damaged boots and repair as necessary (Chapter 8).

61 Vibration

1   See probable causes under Driveshaft. Proceed under the guidelines listed for the driveshaft. If the problem persists, check the

rear wheel bearings by raising the rear of the vehicle and spinning the wheels by hand. Listen for evidence of rough (noisy) bearings. Also check for bearing play by trying to move the axle flange up and down. If there's noticeable movement, the bearing is probably bad. Remove and inspect (Chapter 8).
2   On 4WD models, shudder or vibration from the front end during acceleration indicates one of the following:
a) *Excessive inner CV joint angle. Check and correct as necessary (Chapter 8).*
b) *Worn or damaged CV joints. Repair or replace as necessary (Chapter 8).*
c) *Sticking inner CV joint assembly. Correct or replace as necessary (Chapter 8).*

62 Oil leaks

1   Pinion oil seal damaged (Chapter 8).
2   Axleshaft oil seals damaged (Chapter 8).
3   Differential cover leaking. Tighten mounting bolts or replace the gasket as required.
4   Loose filler or drain plug on differential (Chapter 1).
5   Clogged or damaged breather on differential.

Transfer case (4WD models)
Note: *Refer to Chapters 7C and 8 for 4WD system service and repair information.*

63 Gear jumping out of mesh

1   Incorrect control lever free play (Chapter 7C).
2   Interference between the control lever and the console.
3   Play or fatigue in the transfer case mounts.
4   Internal wear or incorrect adjustments.

64 Difficult shifting

1   Lack of oil.
2   Internal wear, damage or incorrect adjustment.

65 Noise

1   Lack of oil in transfer case.
2   Noise in 4H and 4L, but not in 2H indicates cause is in the front differential or front axle.
3   Noise in 2H, 4H and 4L indicates cause is in rear differential or rear axle.
4   Noise in 2H and 4H but not in 4L, or in 4L only, indicates internal wear or damage in transfer case.

Brakes

Note: *Before assuming a brake problem exists, make sure the tires are in good condition and inflated properly, the front end alignment is correct and the vehicle is not loaded with weight in an unequal manner. All service procedures for the brakes are included in Chapter 9, unless otherwise noted.*

66 Vehicle pulls to one side during braking

1   Defective, damaged or oil contaminated brake pad on one side. Inspect as described in Chapter 1. Refer to Chapter 9 if replacement is required.
2   Excessive wear of brake pad material or disc on one side. Inspect and repair as necessary.
3   Loose or disconnected front suspension components. Inspect and tighten all bolts securely (Chapters 1 and 10).
4   Defective caliper assembly. Remove caliper and inspect for stuck piston or damage.
5   Brake pad to rotor adjustment needed. Inspect automatic adjusting mechanism for proper operation.
6   Scored or out of round rotor.
7   Loose caliper mounting bolts.
8   Incorrect wheel bearing adjustment.

67 Noise (high-pitched squeal or rattle)

1   Front brake pads worn out (high-pitched squeal). This noise comes from the wear sensor rubbing against the disc. Replace pads with new ones immediately!
2   Glazed or contaminated pads (high-pitched squeal).
3   Dirty or scored rotor (high-pitched squeal).
4   Bent support plate.
5   Outer brake pad loose on caliper.

68 Excessive brake pedal travel

1   Partial brake system failure. Inspect entire system (Chapter 1) and correct as required.
2   Insufficient fluid in master cylinder. Check (Chapter 1) and add fluid - bleed system if necessary.
3   Air in system. Bleed system.
4   Excessive lateral rotor play.
5   Brakes out of adjustment. Check the operation of the automatic adjusters.
6   Defective proportioning valve. Replace valve and bleed system.

69 Brake pedal feels spongy when depressed

1   Air in brake lines. Bleed the brake system.

2   Deteriorated rubber brake hoses. Inspect all system hoses and lines. Replace parts as necessary.
3   Master cylinder mounting nuts loose. Inspect master cylinder bolts (nuts) and tighten them securely.
4   Master cylinder faulty.
5   Incorrect shoe or pad clearance.
6   Defective check valve. Replace valve and bleed system.
7   Clogged reservoir cap vent hole.
8   Deformed rubber brake lines.
9   Soft or swollen caliper seals.
10   Poor quality brake fluid. Bleed entire system and fill with new approved fluid.

70 Excessive effort required to stop vehicle

1   Power brake booster not operating properly.
2   Excessively worn linings or pads. Check and replace if necessary.
3   One or more caliper pistons seized or sticking. Inspect and rebuild as required.
4   Brake pads or linings contaminated with oil or grease. Inspect and replace as required.
5   New pads or linings installed and not yet seated. It'll take a while for the new material to seat against the rotor or drum.
6   Worn or damaged master cylinder or caliper assemblies. Check particularly for frozen pistons.
7   Also see causes listed under Section 69.

71 Pedal travels to the floor with little resistance

Little or no fluid in the master cylinder reservoir caused by leaking caliper piston(s) or loose, damaged or disconnected brake lines. Inspect entire system and repair as necessary.

72 Brake pedal pulsates during brake application

1   Wheel bearings damaged, worn or out of adjustment (Chapter 1).
2   Caliper not sliding properly due to improper installation or obstructions. Remove and inspect.
3   Rotor (disc) not within specifications. Remove the rotor and check for excessive lateral runout and parallelism. Have the rotors resurfaced or replace them with new ones. Also make sure that all rotors are the same thickness.
4   Out of round rear brake drums. Remove the drums and have them turned or replace them with new ones.

73 Brakes drag (indicated by sluggish engine performance or wheels being very hot after driving)

1   Output rod adjustment incorrect at the brake pedal.
2   Obstructed master cylinder compensator. Disassemble master cylinder and clean.
3   Master cylinder piston seized in bore. Overhaul master cylinder.
4   Caliper assembly in need of overhaul.
5   Brake pads or shoes worn out.
6   Piston cups in master cylinder or caliper assembly deformed. Overhaul master cylinder.
7   Rotor (disc) not within specifications (Section 72).
8   Parking brake assembly will not release or is adjusted too tight.
9   Clogged brake lines.
10   Wheel bearings out of adjustment (Chapter 1).
11   Brake pedal height improperly adjusted.
12   Wheel cylinder needs overhaul.
13   Improper shoe to drum clearance. Adjust as necessary.

74 Rear brakes lock up under light brake application

1   Tire pressures too high.
2   Tires excessively worn (Chapter 1).
3   Proportioning section of combination valve defective.

75 Rear brakes lock up under heavy brake application

1   Tire pressures too high.
2   Tires excessively worn (Chapter 1).
3   Front brake pads contaminated with oil, mud or water. Clean or replace the pads.
4   Front brake pads excessively worn.
5   Defective master cylinder or caliper assembly.
6   Proportioning section of combination valve defective.

Suspension and steering

Note: *All service procedures for the suspension and steering systems are included in Chapter 10, unless otherwise noted.*

76 Vehicle pulls to one side

1   Tire pressures uneven (Chapter 1).
2   Defective tire (Chapter 1).
3   Excessive wear in suspension or steering components (Chapter 1).

4   Front end alignment incorrect.
5   Front brakes dragging. Inspect as described in Section 73.
6   Wheel bearings improperly adjusted (Chapter 1).
7   Wheel lug nuts loose.

77   Shimmy, shake or vibration

1   Tire or wheel out of balance or out of round. Have them balanced on the vehicle.
2   Loose, worn or out of adjustment wheel bearings (Chapter 1).
3   Shock absorbers and/or suspension components worn or damaged. Check for worn bushings in the upper and lower links.
4   Wheel lug nuts loose.
5   Incorrect tire pressures.
6   Excessively worn or damaged tire.
7   Loosely mounted steering gear housing.
8   Steering gear improperly adjusted.
9   Loose, worn or damaged steering components.
10   Damaged idler arm.
11   Worn balljoint.

78   Excessive pitching and/or rolling around corners or during braking

1   Defective shock absorbers. Replace as a set.
2   Broken or weak springs and/or suspension components.
3   Worn or damaged stabilizer bar or bushings.

79   Wandering or general instability

1   Improper tire pressures.
2   Worn or damaged upper and lower link or tension rod bushings.
3   Incorrect front end alignment.
4   Worn or damaged steering linkage or suspension components.
5   Improperly adjusted steering gear.
6   Out of balance wheels.
7   Loose wheel lug nuts.
8   Worn rear shock absorbers.
9   Fatigued or damaged rear leaf springs.

80   Excessively stiff steering

1   Lack of lubricant in power steering fluid reservoir, where appropriate (Chapter 1).
2   Incorrect tire pressures (Chapter 1).
3   Lack of lubrication at balljoints (Chapter 1).
4   Front end out of alignment.
5   Steering gear out of adjustment or lacking lubrication.

6   Improperly adjusted wheel bearings.
7   Worn or damaged steering gear.
8   Interference of steering column with turn signal switch.
9   Low tire pressures.
10   Worn or damaged balljoints.
11   Worn or damaged steering linkage.
12   See also Sections 79 and 82.

81   Excessive play in steering

1   Loose wheel bearings (Chapter 1).
2   Excessive wear in suspension bushings (Chapter 1).
3   Steering gear improperly adjusted.
4   Incorrect front end alignment.
5   Steering gear mounting bolts loose.
6   Worn steering linkage.

82   Lack of power assistance

1   Steering pump drivebelt faulty or not adjusted properly (Chapter 1).
2   Fluid level low (Chapter 1).
3   Hoses or pipes restricting the flow. Inspect and replace parts as necessary.
4   Air in power steering system (this is usually accompanied by a groaning noise from the system as the steering wheel is turned). Bleed the system as described in Chapter 10.
5   Defective power steering pump.

83   Steering wheel fails to return to straight-ahead position

1   Incorrect front end alignment.
2   Tire pressures low.
3   Steering gears improperly engaged.
4   Steering column out of alignment.
5   Worn or damaged balljoint.
6   Worn or damaged steering linkage.
7   Improperly lubricated idler arm.
8   Insufficient lubricant in steering gear.
9   Lack of fluid in power steering pump.

84   Steering effort not the same in both directions (power system)

1   Leaks in steering gear.
2   Clogged fluid passage in steering gear.

85   Noisy power steering pump

1   Insufficient fluid in pump or air in the system. Add fluid and bleed the system, as described in Chapter 10.
2   Clogged hoses or oil filter in pump.
3   Loose pulley.

4   Improperly adjusted drivebelt (Chapter 1).
5   Defective pump.

86   Miscellaneous noises

1   Improper tire pressures.
2   Insufficiently lubricated balljoint or steering linkage.
3   Loose or worn steering gear, steering linkage or suspension components.
4   Defective shock absorber.
5   Defective wheel bearing.
6   Worn or damaged suspension bushings.
7   Damaged spring.
8   Loose wheel lug nuts.
9   Worn or damaged rear axleshaft spline.
10   Worn or damaged rear shock absorber mounting bushing.
11   Incorrect rear axle end play.
12   See also causes of noises at the rear axle and driveshaft.

87   Excessive tire wear (not specific to one area)

1   Incorrect tire pressures.
2   Tires out of balance. Have them balanced on the vehicle.
3   Wheels damaged. Inspect and replace as necessary.
4   Suspension or steering components worn (Chapters 1 and 10).

88   Excessive tire wear on outside edge

1   Incorrect tire pressure.
2   Excessive speed in turns.
3   Front end alignment incorrect (excessive toe-in).

89   Excessive tire wear on inside edge

1   Incorrect tire pressure.
2   Front end alignment incorrect (toe-out).
3   Loose or damaged steering components (Chapter 1).

90   Tire tread worn in one place

1   Tires out of balance. Have them balanced on the vehicle.
2   Damaged or buckled wheel. Inspect and replace if necessary.
3   Defective tire.

Notes

Chapter 1
Tune-up and routine maintenance

Contents

	Section
Air filter and PCV filter replacement	31
Automatic transmission fluid and filter change	26
Battery check and maintenance	5
Brake check	13
Carburetor choke check	14
Carburetor/TBI fastener torque check	21
Chassis lubrication	10
Check engine light	See Chapter 6
Clutch pedal freeplay check and adjustment (1982 and 1983 models only)	24
Cooling system check	7
Cooling system servicing (draining, flushing and refilling)	29
Differential lubricant change	25
Drivebelt check and adjustment	6
Early Fuel Evaporation (EFE) system check (carbureted and TBI-equipped models only	22
Engine idle speed check and adjustment (carbureted models only)	15
Engine oil and filter change	16
Evaporative Emissions Control (EEC) system filter replacement	34
Exhaust Gas Recirculation (EGR) valve check	33
Exhaust system check	11

	Section
Fluid level checks	4
Fuel filter replacement	18
Fuel system check	17
Ignition timing check and adjustment	35
Introduction and routine maintenance schedule	1
Manual transmission lubricant change	27
Positive Crankcase Ventilation (PCV) valve replacement	32
Spark plug replacement	36
Spark plug wires, distributor cap and rotor check and replacement	37
Suspension and steering check	12
Thermo-controlled Air Cleaner (TAC) check (carbureted and TBI models only)	20
Throttle linkage check	19
Tire and tire pressure checks	3
Tire rotation	23
Transfer case lubricant change	28
Tune-up general information	2
Underbody flushing	39
Underhood hose check and replacement	8
Valve clearance adjustment (1.9 liter engine only)	38
Wheel bearing check and repack (2WD models only)	30
Windshield wiper blade inspection and replacement	9

Specifications

Recommended lubricants and fluids

Note: *Listed here are manufacturer recommendations at the time this manual was written. Manufacturers occasionally upgrade their fluid and lubricant specifications, so check with your local auto parts store for current recommendations.*

Engine oil type	API grade SG, SG/CC or SG/CD multigrade and fuel efficient oil
Engine oil viscosity	See accompanying chart
Automatic transmission fluid	Dexron II or IIE ATF
Manual transmission lubricant	Dexron II or IIE ATF

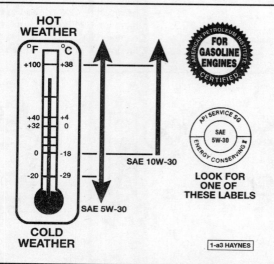

HOT WEATHER

FOR GASOLINE ENGINES

AMERICAN PETROLEUM INSTITUTE CERTIFIED

°F   °C
+100   +38

+40   +4
+32   0

0   -18

-20   -29

SAE 10W-30

SAE 5W-30

COLD WEATHER

API SERVICE SG
SAE 5W-30
ENERGY CONSERVING II

LOOK FOR ONE OF THESE LABELS

RECOMMENDED SAE VISCOSITY GRADE ENGINE OILS

For best fuel economy and cold starting, select the lowest SAE viscosity grade oil for the expected temperature range

1-a3 HAYNES

Recommended lubricants and fluids (continued)

Transfer case lubricant .... Dexron II or IIE ATF
Differential lubricant (standard or locking) .... SAE 80W-90 GL-5 gear lubricant
Chassis grease .... NLGI No. 2 chassis grease
Engine coolant .... 50/50 mixture of water and ethylene glycol-based antifreeze
Brake fluid .... DOT-3 brake fluid
Clutch fluid .... DOT-3 brake fluid
Power steering fluid .... GM power steering fluid or equivalent
Manual steering gear lubricant .... GM lubricant 4673M or equivalent
Wheel bearing grease .... NLGI No. 2 moly-base wheel bearing grease

General

Engine idle speed .... Refer to the *Vehicle Emission Control Information* label in the engine compartment
Radiator pressure cap rating .... 15 psi
Valve clearances (1.9L engine)
    Intake... 0.006 inch
    Exhaust.. 0.010 inch

Capacities*

Engine oil (with filter change)
    Four-cylinder engines... 3.5 quarts
    V6 engines
      2.8L.. 4.5 quarts
      4.3L.. 5 quarts
Cooling system
    Four-cylinder engines
      1.9L and 2.0L.. 10 quarts
      2.5L.. 11 quarts
    V6 engine
      2.8L.. 10.5 quarts
      4.3L.. 13.5 quarts
Automatic transmission
    180C... 3 pints
    200C... 7 pints
    700R4, 4L60 and 4L60-E .... 10 pints
Manual transmission
    4-speed.. 1.3 quarts
    5-speed.. 2.2 quarts
Transfer case
    NP 207... 2.3 quarts
    NP 231, 233.. 2.2 pints

All capacities approximate. Add as necessary to bring to appropriate level.

Ignition system

Spark plug type and gap*
    Type
      1.9L engine .... Champion RN12YC or equivalent
      2.0L engine .... Champion RV12YC or equivalent
      2.5L engine .... Champion RV15YC6 or equivalent
      2.8L engine .... Champion RV12YC or equivalent
      4.3L engine .... Champion RV15YC or equivalent

**FIRING ORDER
1-6-5-4-3-2**

1987 and earlier 4.3L V6

**FIRING ORDER
1-6-5-4-3-2**

1988 and later 4.3L V6

24070-1 specs HAYNES

2.0L L4

1.9L L4

2.5L L4

2.8L V6

Cylinder location and distributor rotation

The blackened terminal shown on the distributor cap indicates the Number One spark plug wire position

Spark plug type and gap*
  Gap
    1.9L engine .... 0.045 inch
    2.0L engine .... 0.035 inch
    2.5L engine .... 0.060 inch
    2.8L engine .... 0.045 inch
    4.3L engine .... 0.035 inch
*Refer to the Vehicle Emission Control Information label in the engine compartment; use the information there if it differs from that listed here
Firing order
  Four-cylinder engines 1-3-4-2
  V6 engine
    2.8L 1-2-3-4-5-6
    4.3L 1-6-5-4-3-2
Ignition timing .... Refer to the *Vehicle Emission Control Information* label
                                                in the engine compartment

Brakes
Brake pad wear limit .... 1/3 inch
Brake shoe wear limit .... 1/16 inch

Torque specifications   **Ft-lbs** (unless otherwise indicated)
Brake caliper mounting bolts .... See Chapter 9
Engine oil drain plug 20
Wheel lug nuts .... 90 to 100
Manual transmission check/fill plug .... 15 to 25
Manual transmission drain plug .... 15 to 25
Automatic transmission pan bolts .... 120 to 180 in-lbs
Carburetor bolts .... 84 to 132 in-lbs
Throttle body nuts .... 144 in-lbs
Rocker arm shaft nut (1.9L engine) 16
Carburetor-mounted fuel filter nut .... 108 to 180 in-lbs
Spark plugs .... 84 to 180 in-lbs

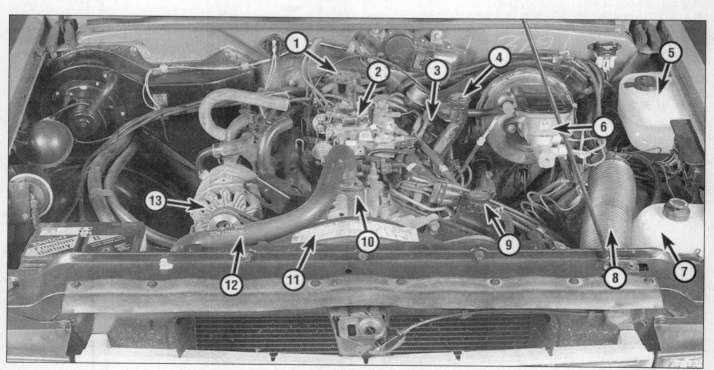

Engine compartment component layout - 2.8L V6 (carbureted)

1	Distributor	6	Brake fluid reservoir	10	Thermostat housing
2	Carburetor	7	Coolant overflow reservoir	11	Vehicle Emission Control Information (VECI) label
3	PCV valve	8	Air cleaner duct (air cleaner removed for clarity)	12	Upper radiator hose
4	Engine oil filler cap	9	Power steering fluid reservoir	13	Alternator
5	Windshield washer fluid reservoir				

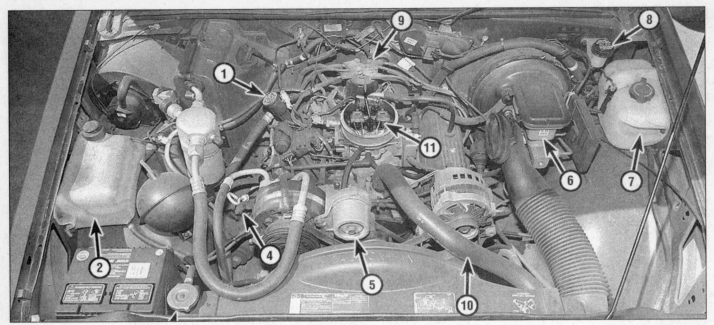

Engine compartment component layout - 2.8L V6 (TBI)

1	Engine oil filler cap	5	Serpentine drivebelt tensioner	9	Distributor
2	Coolant overflow reservoir	6	Brake fluid reservoir	10	Upper radiator hose
3	Radiator cap	7	Windshield washer fluid reservoir	11	TBI unit
4	Engine oil dipstick	8	Clutch master cylinder reservoir		

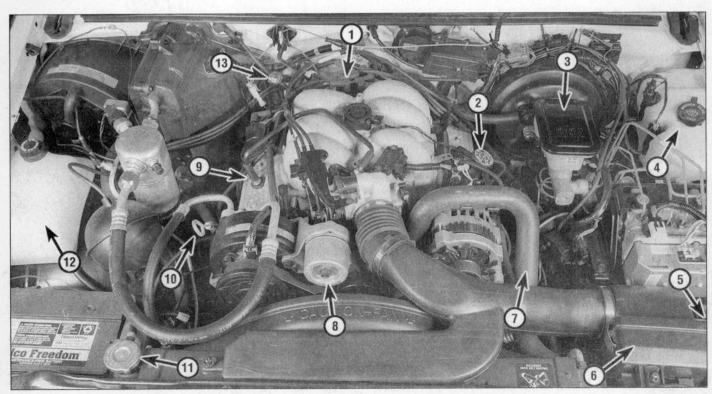

Engine compartment component layout - 4.3L V6 (CPI fuel injection)

1	Distributor	6	Air cleaner housing	11	Radiator cap
2	Engine oil filler cap	7	Upper radiator hose	12	Coolant reservoir
3	Brake fluid reservoir	8	Serpentine drivebelt tensioner	13	Automatic transmission fluid dipstick
4	Windshield washer fluid reservoir	9	PCV valve		
5	Oil filter adapter	10	Engine oil dipstick		

Typical engine compartment underside components (2WD)

1 Idler arm grease fitting
2 Drivebelt
3 Steering knuckle
4 Balljoint grease fitting
5 Fuel filter (fuel-injected models)
6 Transmission
7 Engine oil drain plug
8 Exhaust system
9 Balljoint grease fitting
10 Shock absorber
11 Tie-rod end grease fitting

Typical engine compartment underside components (4WD)

1 Shock absorber	5 Driveaxle boot	9 Front differential
2 Lower radiator hose	6 Fuel filter (fuel-injected models)	10 Automatic transmission fluid pan
3 Drivebelt	7 Exhaust system	11 Engine oil pan
4 Tie-rod	8 Transfer case	

Typical rear underside components

1	Rear shock absorber	3	Driveshaft rear universal joint	5	Fuel filter
2	Exhaust system	4	Fuel tank	6	Rear drum brake

1   Introduction and routine maintenance schedule

This Chapter was designed to help the home mechanic maintain his (or her) vehicle for peak performance, economy, safety and long life.

On the following pages you will find a maintenance schedule along with Sections which deal specifically with each item on the schedule. Included are visual checks, adjustments and item replacements.

Servicing your vehicle using the time/mileage maintenance schedule and the sequenced Sections will give you a planned program of maintenance. Keep in mind that it is a full plan, and maintaining only a few items at the specified intervals will not give you the same results.

You will find as you service your vehicle that many of the procedures can, and should, be grouped together, due to the nature of the job at hand. Examples of this are as follows:

If the vehicle is fully raised for a chassis lubrication, for example, this is the ideal time for the following checks: manual transmission lubricant, rear axle lubricant, exhaust system, suspension, steering and the fuel system.

If the wheels are removed, as during a routine tire rotation, go ahead and check the brakes and wheel bearings at the same time.

If you must borrow or rent a torque wrench, it is a good idea to service the spark plugs, repack (or replace) the wheel bearings and check the carburetor mounting bolt torque all in the same day to save time and money.

The first step of this or any maintenance plan is to prepare yourself before the actual work begins. Read through the appropriate Sections for all work that is to be performed before you begin. Gather together all necessary parts and tools. If it appears that you could have a problem during a particular job, don't hesitate to seek advice from your local auto parts store or dealer service department.

Chevy S-10, GMC S-15 and Oldsmobile Bravada Routine maintenance intervals

The following recommendations are given with the assumption that the vehicle owner will be doing the maintenance or service work (as opposed to having a dealer service department do the work). The following are factory maintenance recommendations; however, subject to the preference of the individual owner, in the interest of keeping his or her vehicle in peak condition at all times and with the vehicle's ulti-

mate resale in mind, many of these operations may be performed more often. We encourage such owner initiative.

When the vehicle is new, it should be serviced initially by a factory authorized dealer service department to protect the factory warranty. In most cases the initial maintenance check is done at no cost to the owner.

Every 250 miles or weekly, whichever comes first

Check the tires and tire pressures (Section 3)
Check the engine oil level (Section 4)
Check the engine coolant level (Section 4)
Check the windshield washer fluid level (Section 4)

Every 6000 miles or 6 months, whichever comes first

Check the automatic transmission fluid level (Section 4)
Check the power steering fluid level (Section 4)
Check the brake master cylinder fluid level (Section 4)
Check the manual transmission lubricant level (Section 4)
Check the rear axle lubricant level (Section 4)
Check and service the battery (Section 5)
Check and adjust (if necessary) the engine drivebelts (Section 6)
Check the cooling system (Section 7)
Check and replace (if necessary) the underhood hoses (Section 8)
Check and replace (if necessary) the windshield wiper blades (Section 9)
Lubricate the chassis components (Section 10)
Check the exhaust system (Section 11)
Check the steering and suspension components (Section 12)
Check the disc brake pads (Section 13)
Check the brake system (Section 13)
Change the engine oil and oil filter (Section 16)
Rotate the tires (Section 23)
Check the clutch pedal freeplay (Section 24)
Change the differential lubricant (if the vehicle is used to pull a trailer (Section 25)

Every 12000 miles or 12 months, whichever comes first

Check the drum brake linings (Section 13)
Check the parking brake (Section 13)
Check the operation of the choke (Section 14)
Check and adjust (if necessary) the engine idle speed (Section 15)

Check the fuel system components (Section 17)
Replace the fuel filter (Section 18)
Check the throttle linkage (Section 19)
Check the Thermo-controlled Air Cleaner (TAC) for proper operation (Section 20)
Check the EFE system (Section 22)
Change the differential lubricant (Section 25)
Check the operation of the EGR valve (Section 33)
Check and adjust (if necessary) the valve clearance (1.9 liter engine only) (Section 38)

Every 18000 miles or 18 months, whichever comes first

Check the torque of the carburetor mounting bolts (Section 21)
Change the automatic transmission fluid and filter (if driven mainly in heavy city traffic in hot-climate regions, in hilly or mountainous areas, or for frequent trailer pulling) (Section 26)
Drain, flush and refill the cooling system (Section 29)
Check and repack the front wheel bearings (perform this procedure whenever brake pads are replaced, regardless of maintenance interval) (Section 30)

Every 24000 miles or 24 months, whichever comes first

Lubricate the clutch cross-shaft (Section 10)
Change the rear differential lubricant (if driven under severe conditions, see 12000 or 18000 mile interval) (Section 25)
Change the automatic transmission fluid (if driven under severe conditions, see 18000 mile interval) (Section 26)
Replace the air filter and PCV filter (Section 31)
Replace the PCV valve (Section 32)
Check the EGR system (Section 33)
Check the EEC emissions system and replace the canister filter (Section 34)
Check and adjust (if necessary) the ignition timing (Section 35)
Replace the spark plugs (Section 36)
Check the spark plug wires, distributor cap and rotor (Section 37)
Check the engine compression (Chapter 2, Part F)

2   Tune-up general information

The term "tune-up" is loosely used for any general operation that puts the engine back in its proper running condition. A tune-up is not a specific operation, but rather a combination of individual operations, such as replacing the spark plugs, adjusting the idle speed, setting the ignition timing, etc.

If, from the time the vehicle is new, the routine maintenance schedule (see Section 1) is followed closely and frequent checks are made of fluid levels and high wear items, as suggested throughout this manual, the engine will be kept in relatively good running

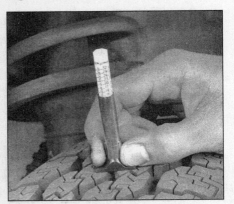

3.2 Use a tire tread depth indicator to monitor tire wear - they are available at auto parts stores and service stations and cost very little

condition and the need for additional tune-ups will be minimized.

More likely than not, however, there will be times when the engine is running poorly due to lack of regular maintenance. This is even more likely if a used vehicle (which has not received regular and frequent maintenance checks) is purchased. In such cases, an engine tune-up will be needed outside of the regular routine maintenance intervals.

The following series of operations are those most often needed to bring a generally poor running engine back into a proper state of tune.

Minor tune-up

*Clean, inspect and test the battery
    (Section 5)
Check all engine-related fluids (Section 4)
Check the engine compression
    Chapter 2, Part F)
Check and adjust the drivebelts
    (Section 6)
Replace the spark plugs (Section 36)
Inspect the distributor cap and rotor
    (Section 37)
Inspect the spark plug and coil wires
    (Section 37)
Check and adjust the idle speed
    (Section 15)
Check and adjust the fuel/air mixture
    (carbureted models only) (see
    underhood VECI label)
Replace the fuel filter (Section 18)
Check the PCV valve (Section 32)
Check the cooling system (Section 7)*

Major tune-up

All items listed under Minor tune-up plus . . .

*Check the EGR system (Chapter 6)
Check the ignition system (Chapter 5)
Check the charging system (Chapter 5)
Check the fuel system (Section 17)
Check and adjust the ignition timing
    (Section 35)*

3   Tire and tire pressure checks

Refer to illustrations 3.2, 3.3, 3.4a, 3.4b and 3.8

1   Periodic inspection of the tires may spare you the inconvenience of being stranded with a flat tire. It can also provide you with vital information regarding possible problems in the steering and suspension systems before major damage occurs.

2   The original tires on this vehicle are equipped with 1/2-inch wide bands that will appear when tread depth reaches 1/16-inch, indicating the tires are worn out. Tread wear can be monitored with a simple, inexpensive device known as a tread depth indicator **(see illustration)**.

3   Note any abnormal tread wear **(see illustration)**. Tread pattern irregularities such as cupping, flat spots and more wear on one side than the other are indications of front end alignment and/or balance problems. If any of these conditions are noted, take the vehicle to a tire shop or service station to correct the problem.

UNDERINFLATION

**INCORRECT TOE-IN
OR EXTREME CAMBER**

CUPPING

Cupping may be caused by:

• Underinflation and/or mechanical
  irregularities such as out-of-balance
  condition of wheel and/or tire,
  and bent or damaged wheel.
• Loose or worn steering tie-rod
  or steering idler arm.
• Loose, damaged or worn front
  suspension parts.

OVERINFLATION

**FEATHERING DUE
TO MISALIGNMENT**

3.3 This chart will help you determine the condition of the tires, the probable cause(s) of abnormal wear and the corrective action necessary

3.4a If a tire loses air on a steady basis, check the valve core first to make sure it's snug (special inexpensive wrenches are commonly available at auto parts stores)

3.4b If the valve core is tight, raise the corner of the vehicle with the low tire and spray a soapy water solution onto the tread as the tire is turned slowly - leaks will cause small bubbles to appear

3.8 To extend the life of the tires, check the air pressure at least once a week with an accurate gauge (don't forget the spare!)

4   Look closely for cuts, punctures and embedded nails or tacks. Sometimes a tire will hold air pressure for a short time or leak down very slowly after a nail has embedded itself in the tread. If a slow leak persists, check the valve stem core to make sure it's tight **(see illustration)**. Examine the tread for an object that may have embedded itself in the tire or for a "plug" that may have begun to leak (radial tire punctures are repaired with a plug that's installed in a puncture). If a puncture is suspected, it can be easily verified by spraying a solution of soapy water onto the puncture area **(see illustration)**. The soapy solution will bubble if there's a leak. Unless the puncture is unusually large, a tire shop or service station can usually repair the tire.

5   Carefully inspect the inner sidewall of each tire for evidence of brake fluid leakage. If you see any, inspect the brakes immediately.

6   Correct air pressure adds miles to the lifespan of the tires, improves mileage and enhances overall ride quality. Tire pressure cannot be accurately estimated by looking at a tire, especially if it's a radial. The correct tire pressures are located on a label on the inside of the glove box door. A tire pressure gauge is essential. Keep an accurate gauge in the vehicle. The pressure gauges attached to the nozzles of air hoses at gas stations are often inaccurate.

7   Always check tire pressure when the tires are cold. Cold, in this case, means the vehicle has not been driven over a mile in the three hours preceding a tire pressure check. A pressure rise of four to eight pounds is not uncommon once the tires are warm.

8   Unscrew the valve cap protruding from the wheel or hubcap and push the gauge firmly onto the valve stem **(see illustration)**. Note the reading on the gauge and compare the figure to the recommended tire pressure shown on the placard on the driver's side door pillar. Be sure to reinstall the valve cap to keep dirt and moisture out of the valve stem mechanism. Check all four tires and, if

necessary, add enough air to bring them up to the recommended pressure.

9   Don't forget to keep the spare tire inflated to the specified pressure (refer to your owner's manual or the tire sidewall). Note that the pressure recommended for the compact spare is higher than for the tires on the vehicle.

4   Fluid level checks

1   There are a number of components on a vehicle which rely on the use of fluids to perform their job. During normal operation of the vehicle, these fluids are used up and must be replenished before damage occurs. See *Recommended lubricants and fluids* at the front of this Chapter for the specific fluid to be used when addition is required. When checking fluid levels, it is important to have the vehicle on a level surface.

Engine oil

Refer to illustrations 4.4a, 4.4b and 4.6

2   The engine oil level is checked with a dipstick which is located at the side of the

4.4a The engine oil dipstick is located on the side of the engine

engine block. The dipstick travels through a tube and into the oil pan to the bottom of the engine.

3   The oil level should be checked preferably before the vehicle has been driven, or about 5 minutes after the engine has been shut off. If the oil is checked immediately after driving the vehicle, some of the oil will remain in the upper engine components, producing an inaccurate reading on the dipstick.

4   Pull the dipstick from the tube **(see illustration)** and wipe all the oil from the end with a clean rag. Insert the clean dipstick all the way back into the oil pan and pull it out again. Observe the oil at the end of the dipstick **(see illustration)**. At its highest point, the level should be between the Add and Full marks.

5   It takes approximately one quart of oil to raise the level from the Add mark to the Full mark on the dipstick. Do not allow the level to drop below the Add mark as engine damage due to oil starvation may occur. On the other hand, do not overfill the engine by adding oil above the Full mark since it may result in oil-fouled spark plugs, oil leaks or oil seal failures.

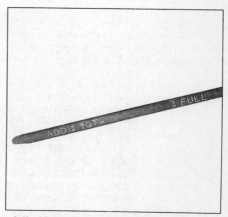

4.4b Maintain the oil level between ADD to FULL marks on the dipstick

4.6 The oil filler cap is clearly marked

4.9a The fluid level on the coolant reservoir should be kept between the FULL HOT and FULL COLD (or ADD) marks when the engine is at normal operating temperature

4.9b When the engine is completely cool, check the coolant level in the radiator - when it is hot check it only at the coolant reservoir

6   Oil is added to the engine after removing a twist-off cap located on the rocker arm cover or through a raised tube near the front of the engine **(see illustration)**. The cap should be marked "Engine oil" or "Oil." A funnel will reduce spills as the oil is poured in.

7   Checking the oil level can also be an important preventative maintenance step. If you find the oil level dropping abnormally, it is an indication of oil leakage or internal engine wear which should be corrected. If there are water droplets in the oil, or if it is milky looking, component failure is indicated and the engine should be checked immediately. The condition of the oil can also be checked along with the level. With the dipstick removed from the engine, take your thumb and index finger and wipe the oil up the dipstick, looking for small dirt or metal particles which will cling to the dipstick. This is an indication that the oil should be drained and fresh oil added (see Section 16).

Engine coolant

Refer illustrations 4.9a and 4.9b

8   All vehicles covered by this manual are equipped with a pressurized coolant recovery system which makes coolant level checks very easy. A clear or white coolant reservoir attached to the inner fender panel is connected by a hose to the radiator cap. As the engine heats up during operation, coolant is forced from the radiator, through the connecting tube and into the reservoir. As the engine cools, the coolant is automatically drawn back into the radiator to keep the level correct.

9   The coolant level should be checked when the engine is hot. Merely observe the level of fluid in the reservoir, which should be at or near the Full Hot mark on the side of the reservoir **(see illustration)**. If the system is completely cool, also check the level in the radiator by removing the cap **(see illustration)**.

10   **Warning:** *Under no circumstances should either the radiator cap or the coolant recovery reservoir cap be removed when the system is hot, because escaping steam and scalding liquid could cause serious personal*

injury. In the case of the radiator cap, wait until the system has cooled completely, then wrap a thick cloth around the cap and turn it to the first stop. If any steam escapes, wait until the system has cooled further, then remove the cap. The coolant recovery cap may be removed carefully after it is apparent that no further "boiling' is occurring in the recovery tank.

11   If only a small amount of coolant is required to bring the system up to the proper level, regular water can be used. However, to maintain the proper antifreeze/water mixture in the system, both should be mixed together to replenish a low level. High-quality antifreeze offering protection to minus 20-degrees F should be mixed with water in the proportion specified on the container. Do not allow antifreeze to come in contact with your skin or painted surfaces of the vehicle. Flush contacted areas immediately with plenty of water.

12   Coolant should be added to the reservoir until it reaches the Full Cold mark.

13   As the coolant level is checked, note the condition of the coolant. It should be relatively clear. If it is brown or a rust color, the system should be drained, flushed and refilled (see Section 29).

14   If the cooling system requires repeated additions to maintain the proper level, have the radiator cap checked for proper sealing ability. Also check for leaks in the system (cracked hoses, loose hose connections, leaking gaskets, etc.).

Windshield washer fluid

Refer to illustration 4.15

15   Fluid for the windshield washer system is located in a plastic reservoir **(see illustration)**. The level in the reservoir should be maintained at the Full mark, except during periods when freezing temperatures are expected, at which times the fluid level should be maintained no higher than 3/4 full to allow for expansion should the fluid freeze.

The use of an additive such as windshield washer fluid (available at auto parts stores) will help lower the freezing point of the fluid and will result in better cleaning of the windshield surface. Do not use antifreeze because it will cause damage to the vehicle's paint.

16   Also, to help prevent icing in cold weather, warm the windshield with the defroster before using the washer.

Battery electrolyte

Refer to illustration 4.17

17   All vehicles with which this manual is concerned are equipped with a battery which is permanently (except for vent holes) and has no filler caps. Water does not have to be added to these batteries at any time. If a maintenance-type battery is installed, the caps on the top of the battery should be removed periodically to check for a low water level **(see illustration)**. This is most critical during the warm summer months.

Brake fluid and clutch fluid

Refer to illustration 4.19

18   The master cylinder is mounted directly on the firewall (manual brake models) or on the front of the power booster unit (power

4.15 Flip up the cap to add windshield washer fluid to the reservoir

4.17 Remove the cell caps to check the water level in the battery - if the level is low, add distilled water only

4.19 The brake fluid reservoir is easily checked by looking through the reservoir housing - the level must be above the MIN marks

brake models in the engine compartment. The clutch cylinder used on later manual transmissions is mounted adjacent to it.

19   The fluid inside the reservoir is readily visible and should be above the MIN marks on the reservoirs **(see illustration)**

20   If a low level is indicated, be sure to wipe the top of the reservoir cover with a clean rag, to prevent contamination of the brake system, before lifting the cover.

21   When adding fluid, pour it carefully into the reservoir, taking care not to spill any onto surrounding painted surfaces. Be sure the specified fluid is used, since mixing different types of brake fluid can cause damage to the system. See *Recommended lubricants and fluids* or your owner's manual.

22   At this time the fluid and master cylinder can be inspected for contamination. Normally, the brake system will not need periodic draining and refilling, but if rust deposits, dirt particles or water droplets are seen in the fluid, the system should be dismantled, drained and refilled with fresh fluid.

23   After filling the reservoir to the proper level, make sure the lid is properly seated to prevent fluid leakage and/or system pressure loss.

24   The brake fluid in the master cylinder will drop slightly as the brake shoes or pads at each wheel wear down during normal operation. If the master cylinder requires repeated replenishing to keep it at the proper level, this is an indication of leakage in the brake system, which should be corrected immediately. Check all brake lines and connections, along with the wheel cylinders and booster (see Section 13 for more information).

25   If upon checking the master cylinder fluid level you discover one or both reservoirs empty or nearly empty, the brake system should be bled (see Chapter 9).

Manual transmission lubricant

Refer to illustration 4.26

26   Manual transmissions do not have a dipstick. The fluid level is checked with the engine cold by removing a plug from the side of the transmission case. Locate the plug and use a rag to clean the plug and the area around it, then remove it with a wrench **(see illustration)**.

27   If lubricant immediately starts leaking out, thread the plug back into the transmission because the level is all right. If there is no leakage, completely remove the plug and

place your little finger inside the hole. The lubricant level should be just at the bottom of the plug hole.

28   If the transmission needs more lubricant, use a syringe to squeeze the appropriate lubricant into the plug hole until the level is correct.

29   Thread the plug back into the transmission and tighten it securely.

30   Drive the vehicle a short distance, then check to make sure the plug is not leaking.

Automatic transmission fluid

Refer to illustrations 4.33 and 4.37

31   The level of the automatic transmission fluid should be carefully maintained. Low fluid level can lead to slipping or loss of drive, while overfilling can cause foaming and loss of fluid.

32   With the parking brake set, start the engine, then move the shift lever through all the gear ranges, ending in Park. The fluid level must be checked with the vehicle level and the engine running at idle. **Note:** *Incorrect fluid level readings will result if the vehicle has just been driven at high speeds for an extended period, in hot weather in city traffic, or if it's been pulling a trailer.* If any of these conditions apply, wait until the fluid has cooled (about 30 minutes).

33   Locate the dipstick at the rear of the engine compartment on the passenger's side and pull it out of the filler tube **(see illustration)**.

34   Carefully touch the end of the dipstick to determine if the fluid is cool (about room temperature), or warm or hot (uncomfortable to the touch).

35   Wipe the fluid from the dipstick and push it back into the filler tube until the cap seats.

36   Pull the dipstick out again and note the fluid level.

37   If the fluid felt cool, the level should be 1/8 to 3/8-inch below the ADD mark **(see illustration)**. The two dimples below the ADD mark indicate this range.

38   If the fluid felt warm, the level should be close to the ADD mark (just above or below it).

4.26 Use a wrench to unscrew the fill plug on the side of the transmission

4.33 The automatic transmission dipstick (arrow) is located at the rear of the engine compartment

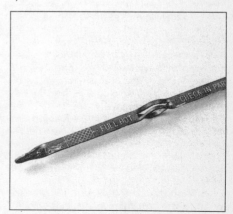

4.37 When checking the automatic transmission fluid level be sure to note the fluid temperature

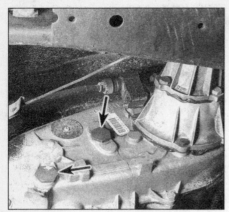

4.43 Location of the transfer case drain (lower arrow) and filler (upper arrow) plugs

4.46a The front differential fill plug is located on the face of the housing - use a wrench to remove it

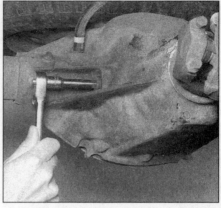

4.46b Use a 1/2-inch-drive socket extension to remove the rear differential fill plug

39 If the fluid felt hot, the level should be at the FULL mark.

40 Add just enough of the recommended fluid to fill the transmission to the proper level. It takes about one pint to raise the level from the ADD mark to the FULL mark with a hot transmission, so add the fluid a little at a time and keep checking the level until it is correct.

41 The condition of the fluid should also be checked along with the level. If the fluid at the end of the dipstick is a dark reddish-brown color, or if the fluid has a burnt smell, the transmission fluid should be changed. If you are in doubt about the condition of the fluid, purchase some new fluid and compare the two for color and smell.

Transfer case lubricant (4WD models)

Refer to illustration 4.43

42 The transfer case lubricant level should be checked at the same time as the manual transmission and differentials.

43 Remove the filler plug and determine whether or not the lubricant level is even with the bottom of the filler hole **(see illustration)**.

44 Fill the transfer case and, if so equipped, the reduction unit to the proper level with the specified lubricant. Replace the filler plugs, drive the vehicle and check for leaks.

Differential lubricant

Refer to illustrations 4.46a and 4.46b

45 Like the manual transmission and transfer case, the front and rear differentials have an inspection and fill plug which must be removed to check the level.

46 Remove the plug, which is located on the side of the differential carrier **(see illustrations)**.

47 Use your little finger to reach inside the housing to feel the level of the lubricant. It should be at the bottom of the plug hole.

48 If such is not the case, add the proper lubricant to the carrier through the plug hole. A syringe or a small funnel can be used for this.

49 Tighten the plug securely and check for leaks after the first few miles of driving.

Power steering fluid

Refer to illustration 4.55

50 Unlike manual steering, the power steering system relies on fluid which may, over a period of time, require replenishing.

51 The reservoir for the power steering pump will be located near the front of the engine and can be mounted on either the left or right side.

52 For the check, the front wheels should be pointed straight ahead and the engine should be off.

53 Use a clean rag to wipe off the reservoir cap and the area around the cap. This will help prevent any foreign matter from entering the reservoir during the check.

54 Make sure the engine is at normal operating temperature.

55 Remove the dipstick **(see illustration)**, wipe it off with a clean rag, reinsert it, then withdraw it and read the fluid level. The level should be between the Add and Full Hot marks.

56 If additional fluid is required, pour the specified type directly into the reservoir using a funnel to prevent spills.

57 If the reservoir requires frequent fluid additions, all power steering hoses, hose connections, the power steering pump and the steering box should be carefully checked for leaks.

5 Battery check and maintenance

Refer to illustrations 5.1 and 5.3

Warning: *Certain precautions must be followed when checking and servicing the battery. Hydrogen gas, which is highly flammable, is always present in the battery cells, so keep lighted tobacco and all other open flames and sparks away from the battery. The electrolyte in the battery cells is actually dilute sulfuric acid, which will cause injury if splashed on your skin or in your eyes. It will also ruin clothes and painted surfaces. When removing the battery cables, always detach the negative cable first and hook it up last!*

1 Battery maintenance is an important

procedure which will help ensure that you're not stranded because of a dead battery. Several tools are required for this procedure **(see illustration)**.

2 The external condition of the battery should be monitored periodically for damage such as a cracked case or cover.

3 Check the tightness of the battery cable clamps to ensure good electrical connections and check the entire length of each cable for cracks and frayed conductors **(see illustration)**.

4 If corrosion (visible as white, fluffy deposits) is evident, remove the cables from the terminals, clean them with a battery brush and reinstall the cables. Corrosion can be kept to a minimum by applying a layer of petroleum jelly or grease to the terminals and cable clamps after they are assembled.

5 Make sure that the rubber protector (if so equipped) over the positive terminal is not torn or missing. It should completely cover the terminal.

6 Make sure that the battery carrier is in good condition and that the hold-down clamp bolts are tight. If the battery is removed from the carrier, make sure that no parts remain in the bottom of the carrier when the battery is reinstalled. When reinstalling the hold-down clamp bolts, do not overtighten them.

4.55 Wipe off the area around the power steering fluid reservoir before removing the dipstick

5.1 Tools and materials required for battery maintenance

1 **Face shield/safety goggles** - *When removing corrosion with a brush, the acidic particles can easily fly up into your eyes*
2 **Rubber gloves** - *Another safety item to consider when servicing the battery; remember that's acid inside the battery!*
3 **Battery terminal/cable cleaner** - *This wire brush cleaning tool will remove all traces of corrosion from the battery and cable*
4 **Treated felt washers** - *Placing one of these one each terminal, directly under the cable end, will help prevent corrosion (be sure to get the correct type for side terminal batteries)*
5 **Baking soda** - *A solution of baking soda and water can be used to neutralize corrosion*
6 **Petroleum jelly** - *A layer of this on the battery terminal bolts will help prevent corrosion*

7 Corrosion on the hold-down components, battery case and surrounding areas may be removed with a solution of water and baking soda, but take care to prevent any solution from coming in contact with your eyes, skin or clothes, as it contains acid. Protective gloves should be worn. Thoroughly wash all cleaned areas with plain water.

8 Any metal parts of the vehicle damaged by corrosion should be covered with a zinc-based primer, then painted after the affected areas have been cleaned and dried.

9 Further information on the battery, charging and jump-starting can be found in Chapter 5.

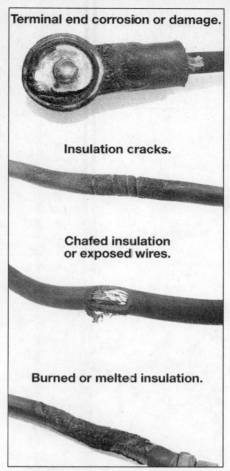

5.3 Typical battery cable problems

Terminal end corrosion or damage.

Insulation cracks.

Chafed insulation or exposed wires.

Burned or melted insulation.

6 Drivebelt check and adjustment

Refer to illustrations 6.3, 6.4a, 6.4b, 6.5, 6.7a, 6.7b, 6.10

1 The drivebelts, or V-belts as they are sometimes called, are located at the front of the engine and play an important role in the overall operation of the vehicle and its components. Due to their function and material make-up, the belts are prone to failure after a period of time and should be inspected and adjusted periodically to prevent major engine damage.

2 The number of belts used on a particular vehicle depends on the accessories installed. Drivebelts are used to turn the generator/alternator, air injection (smog) pump, power steering pump, water pump, fan and air-conditioning compressor. Depending on the pulley arrangement, a single belt may be used to drive more than one of these components.

3 1987 and later models use a single serpentine drivebelt in place of multiple V-belts. A serpentine belt requires no adjustment, as this is taken care of by a spring-loaded tensioner pulley. The belt should be replaced when the wear indicator on the tensioner reaches its maximum travel **(see illustration)**. Inspect the belt for missing ribs, fraying and

6.3 The arrow mark on the tensioner must be within the marked range - if it isn't t, the belt is stretched and must be replaced

other signs of abnormal wear.

4 With the engine off, open the hood and locate the various belts at the front of the engine. Using your fingers (and a flashlight, if necessary), move along the belts checking for cracks and separation of the belt plies. Also check for fraying and glazing, which gives the belt a shiny appearance **(see illustrations)**. Both sides of the belt should be

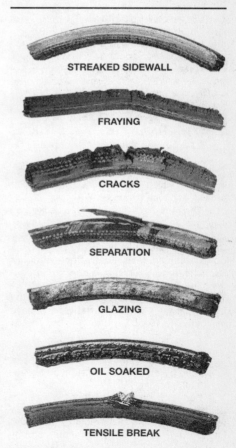

STREAKED SIDEWALL

FRAYING

CRACKS

SEPARATION

GLAZING

OIL SOAKED

TENSILE BREAK

6.4a Here are some of the more common problems associated with drivebelts (check the belts very carefully to prevent an untimely breakdown)

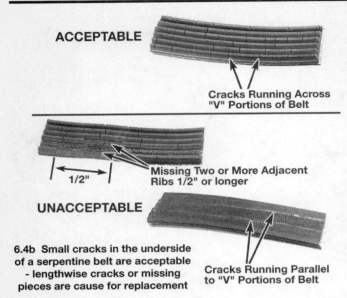

ACCEPTABLE

Cracks Running Across
"V" Portions of Belt

1/2"

UNACCEPTABLE

Missing Two or More Adjacent
Ribs 1/2" or longer

**6.4b Small cracks in the underside
of a serpentine belt are acceptable
- lengthwise cracks or missing
pieces are cause for replacement**

Cracks Running Parallel
to "V" Portions of Belt

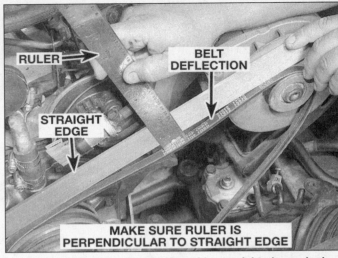

RULER

BELT
DEFLECTION

STRAIGHT
EDGE

MAKE SURE RULER IS
PERPENDICULAR TO STRAIGHT EDGE

6.5 Measuring drivebelt deflection with a straightedge and ruler

**6.7a Loosen the component pivot
bolt (arrow) . . .**

**6.7b . . . then the adjustment bolt before
moving the component**

**6.10 Rotate the tensioner
counterclockwise to release the belt**

inspected, which means you will have to twist the belt to check the underside.

5   The tension of each belt is checked by pushing on the belt at a distance halfway between the pulleys. Push firmly with your thumb and see how much the belt moves down (deflects) **(see illustration)**. A rule of thumb is that if the distance from pulley center-to-pulley center is between 7 and 11 inches, the belt should deflect 1/4-inch. If the belt is longer and travels between pulleys spaced 12 to 16 inches apart, the belt should deflect 1/2-inch.

6   If it is necessary to adjust the belt tension, either to make the belt tighter or looser, it is done by moving the belt-driven accessory on the bracket.

7   For each component there will be an adjustment or strap bolt and a pivot bolt **(see illustrations)**. Both bolts must be loosened slightly to enable you to move the component.

8   After the two bolts have been loosened, move the component away from the engine (to tighten the belt) or toward the engine (to loosen the belt). Hold the accessory in posi-

tion and check the belt tension. If it is correct, tighten the two bolts until just snug, then recheck the tension. If it is all right, tighten the bolts.

9   It will often be necessary to use some sort of pry bar to move the accessory while the belt is adjusted. If this must be done to gain the proper leverage, be very careful not to damage the component being moved or the part being pried apart.

10   When replacing the serpentine belt (used on later models), use a 1/2-inch drive breaker bar to rotate the tensioner counterclockwise to release the belt tension **(see illustration)**. Make sure the new belt is routed correctly (refer to the label in the engine compartment). Also, the belt must completely engage the grooves in the pulleys.

7   Cooling system check

Refer to illustration 7.4

1   Many major engine failures can be attributed to a faulty cooling system. If the vehicle is equipped with an automatic trans-

mission, the cooling system also plays an important role in prolonging its life.

2   The cooling system should be checked with the engine cold. Do this before the vehicle is driven for the day or after it has been shut off for at least three hours.

3   Remove the radiator cap and thoroughly clean the cap (inside and out) with clean water. Also clean the filler neck on the radiator. All traces of corrosion should be removed.

4   Carefully check the upper and lower radiator hoses along with the smaller diameter heater hoses. Inspect each hose along its entire length, replacing any hose which is cracked, swollen or shows signs of deterioration. Cracks may become more apparent if the hose is squeezed **(see illustration)**.

5   Also make sure that all hose connections are tight. A leak in the cooling system will usually show up as white or rust colored deposits on the areas adjoining the leak.

6   Use compressed air or a soft brush to remove bugs, leaves, etc. from the front of the radiator or air-conditioning condenser. Be careful not to damage the delicate cooling

Check for a chafed area that could fail prematurely.

Check for a soft area indicating the hose has deteriorated inside.

Overtightening the clamp on a hardened hose will damage the hose and cause a leak.

Check each hose for swelling and oil-soaked ends. Cracks and breaks can be located by squeezing the hose.

7.4 Hoses, like drivebelts, have a habit of failing at the worst possible time - to prevent the inconvenience of a blown radiator or heater hose, inspect them carefully as shown here

fins or cut yourself on them.

7　Finally, have the cap and system pressure tested. If you do not have a pressure tester, most gas stations and repair shops will do this for a minimal change.

8 Underhood hose check and replacement

General

1　**Warning:** *Replacement of air conditioning hoses must be left to a dealer service department or air conditioning shop that has the equipment to depressurize the system safely. Never remove air conditioning components or hoses until the system has been depressurized.*

2　High temperatures in the engine compartment can cause the deterioration of the rubber and plastic hoses used for engine, accessory and emission systems operation. Periodic inspection should be made for cracks, loose clamps, material hardening and leaks. Information specific to the cooling system hoses can be found in Section 7.

3　Some, but not all, hoses are secured to the fittings with clamps. Where clamps are used, check to be sure they haven't lost their tension, allowing the hose to leak. If clamps aren't used, make sure the hose has not expanded and/or hardened where it slips over the fitting, allowing it to leak.

Vacuum hoses

4　It's quite common for vacuum hoses, especially those in the emissions system, to be color coded or identified by colored stripes molded into them. Various systems require hoses with different wall thicknesses, collapse resistance and temperature resistance. When replacing hoses, be sure the new ones are made of the same material.

5　Often the only effective way to check a hose is to remove it completely from the vehicle. If more than one hose is removed, be sure to label the hoses and fittings to ensure correct installation.

6　When checking vacuum hoses, be sure to include any plastic T-fittings in the check. Inspect the fittings for cracks and the hose where it fits over the fitting for distortion, which could cause leakage.

7　A small piece of vacuum hose (1/4-inch inside diameter) can be used as a stethoscope to detect vacuum leaks. Hold one end of the hose to your ear and probe around vacuum hoses and fittings, listening for the "hissing" sound characteristic of a vacuum leak. **Warning:** *When probing with the vacuum hose stethoscope, be very careful not to come into contact with moving engine components such as the drivebelt, cooling fan, etc.*

Fuel hoses

Warning: *There are certain precautions which must be taken when inspecting or servicing fuel system components. Work in a well ventilated area and do not allow open flames (cigarettes, appliance pilot lights, etc.) or bare light bulbs near the work area. Mop up any spills immediately and do not store fuel soaked rags where they could ignite. If you spill any fuel on your skin, rinse it off immediately with soap and water. When you perform any kind of work on the fuel system, wear safety glasses and have a Class B type fire extinguisher on hand. On vehicles equipped with fuel injection, the fuel system is under pressure, so if any fuel lines are to be disconnected, the pressure in the system must be relieved first (see Chapter 4 for more information).*

8　Check all rubber fuel lines for deterioration and chafing. Check especially for cracks in areas where the hose bends and just before fittings, such as where a hose attaches to the fuel filter.

9　High quality fuel line, usually identified by the word *Fluroelastomer* printed on the hose, should be used for fuel line replacement. Never, under any circumstances, use unreinforced vacuum line, clear plastic tubing or water hose for fuel lines.

10　Spring-type clamps are commonly used on fuel lines. These clamps often lose their tension over a period of time, and can be "sprung" during removal. Replace all spring-type clamps with screw clamps whenever a hose is replaced.

Metal lines

11　Sections of metal line are often used for fuel line between the fuel pump and carburetor or fuel injection unit. Check carefully to be sure the line has not been bent or crimped and that cracks have not started in the line.

12　If a section of metal fuel line must be replaced, only seamless steel tubing should be used, since copper and aluminum tubing don't have the strength necessary to withstand normal engine vibration.

13　Check the metal brake lines where they enter the master cylinder and brake proportioning unit (if used) for cracks in the lines or loose fittings. Any sign of brake fluid leakage calls for an immediate thorough inspection of the brake system.

9 Windshield wiper blade inspection and replacement

Refer to illustration 9.4

1　The windshield wiper and blade assembly should be inspected periodically for damage, loose components and cracked or worn blade elements.

2　Road film can build up on the wiper blades and affect their efficiency so they should be washed regularly with a mild detergent solution.

3　The action of the wiping mechanism can loosen the bolts, nuts and fasteners so they should be checked and tightened, as necessary, at the same time the wiper blades are checked.

4　If the wiper blade elements are cracked, worn or warped, they should be replaced

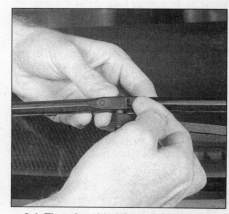

9.4 The wiper blade assembly can be removed by lifting the release lever, the sliding the assembly off the pin

1

10.1 Materials required for chassis and body lubrication

1   *Engine oil - Light engine oil in a can like this can be used for door and hood hinges*
2   *Graphite spray - Used to lubricate lock cylinders*
3   *Grease - Grease, in a variety of types and weights, is available for use in a grease gun. Check the Specifications for your requirements*
4   *Grease gun - A common grease gun, shown here with a detachable hose and nozzle, is needed for chassis lubrication. After use, clean it thoroughly*

10.2a Upper and lower balljoint and steering arm grease fittings (arrows)

10.2b Steering idler arm grease fitting (arrow)

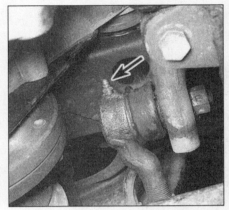

10.2c Relay rod grease fitting (arrow)

with new ones. The wiper blade assemblies are equipped with release levers. Pull the lever up and slide the old wiper blade assembly off the wiper arm pin **(see illustration)**. Install the new blade by positioning it over the wiper arm pin and pressing on it until it snaps into place.

5   The wiper blade element is locked in place at either end of the wiper blade assembly by a spring-loaded retainer and metal tabs. To remove the element, use a screwdriver to slide the blade under the element near the tabs and rotate the screwdriver, then slide the element up, out of the tabs.

6   To install, slide the element into the retaining tabs, lining up the slot in the element with the tabs, and snap the element into place.

7   Snap the blade assembly into place on the wiper arm pin.

10   Chassis lubrication

Refer to illustrations 10.1, 10.2a, 10.2b and 10.2c

1   Refer to the *Recommended lubricants and fluids* at the front of this Chapter to obtain the necessary grease, etc. You'll also need a grease gun **(see illustration)**.

2   Refer to the accompanying illustrations for the locations of the various grease fittings **(see illustrations)**. Look under the vehicle to find these components and determine if grease fittings or solid plugs are installed. If there are plugs, remove them with a wrench and buy grease fittings which will thread into the component. A dealer or auto parts store will be able to supply replacement fittings. Straight, as well as angled, fittings are available.

3   For easier access under the vehicle, raise it with a jack and place jackstands under the frame. Make sure the vehicle is securely supported by the stands.

4   Before proceeding, force a little of the grease out of the nozzle to remove any dirt from the end of the gun. Wipe the nozzle clean with a rag.

5   With the grease gun and plenty of clean rags, crawl under the vehicle and begin lubricating the components.

6   Wipe the grease fitting nipple clean and push the nozzle firmly over the fitting nipple. Squeeze the trigger on the grease gun to force grease into the component. **Note:** *The lower control arm balljoints (one for each front wheel) should be lubricated until the rubber reservoir is firm to the touch. Do not pump too much grease into these fittings as it could rupture the reservoir. For all other*

suspension and steering fittings, continue pumping grease into the nipple until grease seeps out of the joint between the two components. If the grease seeps out around the grease gun nozzle, the nipple is clogged or the nozzle is not seated on the fitting nipple. Reseure the gun nozzle to the fitting and try again. If necessary, replace the fitting.

7   Wipe the excess grease from the components and the grease fitting. Follow the procedures for the remaining fittings.

8   While you are under the vehicle, clean and lubricate the parking brake cable, along with the cable guides and levers. This can be done by smearing some of the chassis grease onto the cable and its related parts with your fingers.

9   Lower the vehicle to the ground for the remaining body lubrication process.

10   Open the hood and smear a little chassis grease on the hood latch mechanism. If the hood has an inside release, have an assistant pull the release knob from inside the vehicle as you lubricate the cable at the latch.

11   Lubricate all the hinges (door, hood, hatch) with a few drops of light engine oil to keep them in proper working order.

12   Finally, the key lock cylinders can be lubricated with spray-on graphite which is available at auto parts stores.

11.2 A broken hanger bracket here will cause noise and lead to further exhaust system damage

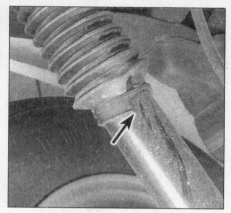

12.3 Check for signs of oil leaks in this area of each shock absorber

13.6 The front disc brake pads can be checked easily by looking through the inspection window in each caliper

11 Exhaust system check

Refer to illustration 11.2

1   With the engine cold (at least three hours after the vehicle has been driven), check the complete exhaust system from its starting point at the engine to the end of the tailpipe. This should be done on a hoist where unrestricted access is available.

2   Check the pipes and connections for signs of leakage and/or corrosion indicating a potential failure. Make sure that all brackets and hangers are in good condition and tight **(see illustration)**.

3   At the same time, inspect the underside of the body for holes, corrosion, open seams, etc. which may allow exhaust gases to enter the passenger compartment. Seal all body openings with silicone or body putty.

4   Rattles and other noises can often be traced to the exhaust system, especially the mounts and hangers. Try to move the pipes, muffler and catalytic converter (if so equipped). If the components can come in contact with the body or driveline parts, secure the exhaust system with new mounts.

5   This is also an ideal time to check the running condition of the engine by inspecting inside the very end of the tailpipe. The exhaust deposits here are an indication of engine state-of-tune. If the pipe is black and sooty or coated with white deposits, the engine is in need of a tune-up (including a thorough carburetor inspection and adjustment).

12 Suspension and steering check

Refer to illustration 12.3

1   Whenever the front of the vehicle is raised for service, it is a good idea to visually check the suspension and steering components for wear.

2   Indications of a fault in these systems are excessive play in the steering wheel before the front wheels react, excessive sway

around corners, body movement over rough roads or binding at some point as the steering wheel is turned.

3   Before the vehicle is raised for inspection, test the shock absorbers by pushing down to rock the vehicle at each corner. If you push down and the vehicle does not come back to a level position within one or two bounces, the shocks are worn and must be replaced. As this is done, check for squeaks and strange noises coming from the suspension components. Also check the shocks for oil leakage **(see illustration)**. Information on suspension components can be found in Chapter 10.

4   Now raise the front end of the vehicle and support it firmly on jackstands placed under the frame rails. Because of the work to be done, make sure the vehicle cannot fall from the stands.

5   Grab the top and bottom of the front tire with your hands and rock the tire/wheel on the spindle. On 2WD models, if there is movement of more than 0.005 inch, the wheel bearings should be serviced (see Section 30).

6   Crawl under the vehicle and check for loose bolts, broken or disconnected parts and deteriorated rubber bushings on all suspension and steering components. Look for grease or fluid leaking from around the steering box. Check the power steering hoses and connections for leaks. Check the balljoints for wear. On 4WD models, push on the front driveaxle Constant Velocity (CV) joint boots to check for damage and leaking grease.

7   Have an assistant turn the steering wheel from side-to-side and check the steering components for free movement, chafing and binding. If the steering does not react with the movement of the steering wheel, try to determine where the slack is located.

13 Brake check

Warning: *The dust created by the brake system may contain asbestos, which is harmful to your health. Never blow it out with com-*

pressed air and don't inhale any of it. An approved filtering mask should be worn when working on the brakes.

Note: *For detailed illustrations of the brake system,* see Chapter 9.

1   The brakes should be inspected every time the wheels are removed or whenever a defect is suspected. Indications of a potential brake system defect are: the vehicle pulls to one side when the brake pedal is depressed; noises coming from the brakes when they are applied; excessive brake pedal travel; pulsating pedal; and leakage of fluid, usually seen on the inside of the tire or wheel.

Disc brakes

Refer to illustration 13.6

2   The front disc brakes can be visually checked without removing any parts except the wheels.

3   Raise the vehicle and place it securely on jackstands. Remove the wheels (see *Jacking and towing* at the front of the manual, if necessary).

4   The disc brake calipers, which contain the pads, are now visible. There is an outer pad and an inner pad in each caliper. All pads should be inspected.

5   The inner pads on the front wheels are equipped with a wear sensor. This is a small, bent piece of metal which is visible from the inner side of the brake caliper. When the pads wear to the danger limit, the metal sensor rubs against the disc and makes a screeching sound.

6   Check the pad thickness by looking at each end of the caliper and through the inspection hole in the caliper body **(see illustration)**. If the wear sensor clip is very close to the disc, or if the lining material is 1/8-inch or less in thickness, the pads should be replaced. Keep in mind that the lining material is riveted or bonded to a metal backing shoe and the metal portion is not included in this measurement.

7   Since it will be difficult, if not impossible, to measure the exact thickness of the remaining lining material, remove the pads for

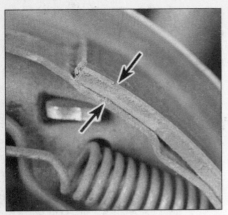

13.13 Measure the brake shoe lining thickness from the outer surface of the lining to the metal shoe

further inspection or replacement if you are in doubt as to the quality of the pad.

8   Before installing the wheels, check for leakage around the brake hose connections leading to the caliper and damage (cracking, splitting, etc.) to the brake hose. Replace the hose or fittings as necessary, (see Chapter 9).

9   Also check the condition of the disc. Look for scoring, gouging and burnt spots. If these conditions exist, the hub/disc assembly should be removed for servicing (see Chapter 9).

Drum brakes

Refer to illustration 13.13

10   Using a scribe or chalk, mark the drum, hub and backing plate so it can be reinstalled in the same position.

11   Pull the brake drum off the axle and brake assembly. If this proves difficult, make sure the parking brake is released, then squirt some penetrating oil around the center hub area. Allow the oil to soak in and again try to pull the drum off. Then, if the drum cannot be pulled off, the brake shoes will have to be adjusted in. This is done by first removing the lanced knock-out in the backing plate with a hammer and chisel. With the lanced area punched in, pull the lever off the sprocket and then use a small screwdriver to turn the adjuster wheel, which will move the shoes away from the drum.

12   Clean the brake assembly with brake system cleaner and allow the residue to drip into a pan.

13   Note the thickness of the lining material on both the front and rear brake shoes **(see illustration)**. If the material has worn away to within 1/16-inch of the recessed rivets or metal backing, the shoes should be replaced. If the linings look worn, but you are unable to determine their exact thickness, compare them with a new set at an auto parts store. The shoes should also be replaced if they are cracked, glazed (shiny surface) or contaminated with brake fluid.

14   Check to see that all the brake assembly springs are connected and in good condition.

15   Check the brake components for signs of fluid leakage. With your finger, carefully pry back the rubber cups on the wheel cylinder located at the top of the brake shoes. Any leakage is an indication that the wheel cylinders should be overhauled immediately (see Chapter 9). Also check the hoses and connections for signs of leakage.

16   Wipe the inside of the drum with a clean rag and denatured alcohol. Again, be careful not to breathe the dangerous asbestos dust.

17   Check the inside of the drum for cracks, scores, deep scratches and hard spots which will appear as small discolored areas. If imperfections cannot be removed with fine emery cloth, the drum must be taken to a machine shop for resurfacing.

18   After the inspection process, if all parts are found to be in good condition, reinstall the brake drum (using a rubber plug if the lanced knock-out was removed). Install the wheel and lower the vehicle to the ground.

Parking brake

19   The easiest way to check the operation of the parking brake is to park the vehicle on a steep hill with the parking brake set and the transmission in Neutral. If the parking brake cannot prevent the vehicle from rolling, it is in need of adjustment (see Chapter 9).

14   Carburetor choke check

Refer to illustration 14.3

1   The choke only operates when the engine is cold, so this check should be performed before the vehicle has been started for the day.

2   Open the hood and remove the top plate of the air cleaner assembly. It is usually held in place by a wing nut. If any vacuum hoses must be disconnected, make sure you tag them to ensure reinstallation in their original positions. Place the top plate and wing nut aside, out of the way of moving engine components.

3   Look at the top of the carburetor at the center of the air cleaner housing. You will notice a flat plate at the carburetor opening

14.3 The choke plate is easily checked once the air cleaner is removed

(see illustration).

4   Have an assistant press the accelerator pedal to the floor. The plate should close completely. Start the engine while you observe the plate at the carburetor. **Warning:** *Do not position your face directly over the carburetor, because the engine could backfire and cause serious burns.* When the engine starts, the choke plate should open slightly.

5   Allow the engine to continue running at an idle speed. As the engine warms up to operating temperature, the plate should slowly open, allowing more air to enter through the top of the carburetor.

6   After a few minutes, the choke plate should be all the way open to the vertical position.

7   You will notice that the engine speed corresponds with the plate opening. With the plate completely closed, the engine should run at a fast idle. As the plate opens, the engine speed will decrease.

8   If a malfunction is detected during the above checks, see Chapter 4 for specific information related to adjusting and servicing the choke components.

15   Engine idle speed check and adjustment (carbureted models only)

Refer to illustration 15.4

1   Engine idle speed is the speed at which the engine operates when no accelerator pedal pressure is applied. This speed is critical to the performance of the engine itself, as well as many engine sub-systems.

2   A hand-held tachometer must be used when adjusting the idle speed to get an accurate reading. The exact hook-up for these meters varies with the manufacturer, so follow the particular directions included with the meter.

3   Since these models were equipped with many different carburetors in the time period covered by this manual, and each has its own peculiarities when setting idle speed, it would be impractical to cover all types in this Section. Chapter 4 contains information on each individual carburetor used. The carburetor used on your particular engine can be found in the Specifications Section of Chapter 4. However, all vehicles covered in this manual have a *Vehicle Emission Control Information* label in the engine compartment, usually placed near the top of the radiator. The printed instructions for setting idle speed can be found on the label, and should be followed since it is for your particular engine.

4   Basically, for most applications, the idle speed is set by turning an adjustment screw located at the side of the carburetor **(see illustration)**. Turning the screw changes the position of the throttle valve in the carburetor. This screw may be on the linkage itself or may be part of the idle stop solenoid. Refer to the *Vehicle Emission Control Information* label or Chapter 4.

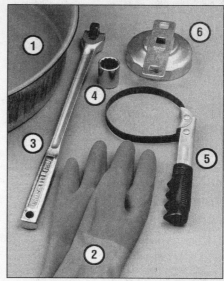

15.4 Be sure to turn only the idle speed adjustment screw (Rochester 2SE carburetor shown)

16.3 These tools are required when changing the engine oil and filter

1   **Drain pan** - It should be fairly shallow in depth, but wide to prevent spills
2   **Rubber gloves** - When removing the drain plug and filter, you will get oil on your hands (the gloves will prevent burns)
3   **Breaker bar** - Sometimes the oil drain plug is tight, and a long breaker bar is needed to loosen it
4   **Socket** - To be used with the breaker bar or a ratchet (must be the correct size to fit the drain plug - six-point preferred)
5   **Filter wrench** - This is a metal band-type wrench, which requires clearance around the filter to be effective
6   **Filter wrench** - This type fits on the bottom of the filter and can be turned with a ratchet or breaker bar (different-size wrenches are available for different types of filters)

5   Once you have located the idle speed screw, experiment with different length screwdrivers until the adjustments can easily be made without coming into contact with hot or moving engine components.

6   Follow the instructions on the *Emission Control Information* label, which may include disconnecting certain vacuum or electrical connections. To plug a vacuum hose after disconnecting it, insert a properly sized metal rod into the opening or thoroughly wrap the open end with tape to prevent any vacuum loss through the hose.

7   If the air cleaner is removed, the vacuum hose to the snorkel should be plugged.

8   Make sure the parking brake is firmly set and the wheels blocked to prevent the vehicle from rolling. This is especially true if the transmission is to be in Drive. An assistant inside the vehicle pushing on the brake pedal is the safest method.

9   For all applications, the engine must be completely warmed-up to operating temperature, which will automatically render the choke fast idle inoperative.

10   Turn the idle speed screw in or out, as required, until the idle speed listed in the Specifications is obtained.

16   Engine oil and filter change

Refer to illustrations 16.3, 16.9, 16.14a, 16.14b and 16.18

1   Frequent oil changes are the most important preventive maintenance procedures that can be done by the home mechanic. As engine oil ages, it becomes diluted and contaminated, which leads to premature engine wear.

2   Although some sources recommend oil filter changes every other oil change, we feel that the minimal cost of an oil filter and the relative ease with which it is installed dictate that a new filter be installed every time the oil is changed.

3   Gather together all necessary tools and materials before beginning this procedure **(see illustration)**.

4   You should have plenty of clean rags and newspapers handy to mop up any spills. Access to the underside of the vehicle is greatly improved if the vehicle can be lifted on a hoist, driven onto ramps or supported by jackstands. **Warning:** *Do not work under a vehicle which is supported only by a bumper, hydraulic or scissors-type jack.*

5   If this is your first oil change, get under the vehicle and familiarize yourself with the locations of the oil drain plug and the oil filter. The engine and exhaust components will be warm during the actual work, so note how they are situated to avoid touching them when working under the vehicle.

6   Warm the engine to normal operating temperature. If the new oil or any tools are needed, use this warm-up time to gather everything necessary for the job. The correct type of oil for your application can be found in *Recommended lubricants and fluids* at the beginning of this Chapter.

7   With the engine oil warm (warm engine oil will drain better and more built-up sludge will be removed with it), raise and support the vehicle. Make sure it's safely supported!

8   Move all necessary tools, rags and newspapers under the vehicle. Set the drain pan under the drain plug. Keep in mind that the oil will initially flow from the pan with some force; position the pan accordingly.

9   Being careful not to touch any of the hot exhaust components, use a wrench to remove the drain plug near the bottom of the oil pan **(see illustration)**. Depending on how hot the oil is, you may want to wear gloves while unscrewing the plug the final few turns.

10   Allow the old oil to drain into the pan. It may be necessary to move the pan as the oil flow slows to a trickle.

11   After all the oil has drained, wipe off the drain plug with a clean rag. Small metal particles may cling to the plug and would immediately contaminate the new oil.

12   Clean the area around the drain plug opening and reinstall the plug. Tighten the plug securely with the wrench. If a torque wrench is available, use it to tighten the plug.

13   Move the drain pan into position under the oil filter.

14   On most models the oil filter is located

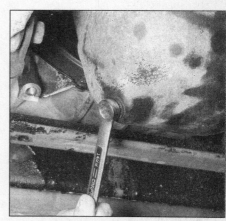

16.9 The oil drain plug is located at the bottom of the pan and should be removed with a socket or box-end wrench - DO NOT use an open-end wrench, as the corners on the bolt can be easily rounded off

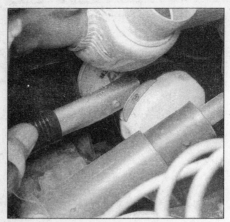

16.14a Use a strap-type oil filter wrench to loosen the filter - if access makes removal difficult, other types of filter wrenches are available - most filters are like this one which is on the engine

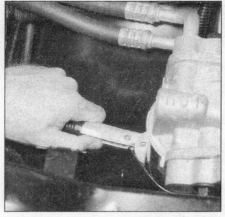

16.14b On some later models the oil filter is mounted in the left front corner of the engine compartment (it's necessary to remove the air cleaner housing for access)

16.18 Lubricate the oil filter gasket with clean engine oil before installing the filter on the engine

17.4 Check the seal around the fuel tank gasket - it's crucial that there is no air leak here

underneath the engine. On some later V6 models, the oil filter is mounted remotely in the drivers side front corner of the engine compartment and it will be necessary to remove the air cleaner assembly (see Section 31). Use the filter wrench to loosen the oil filter **(see illustrations)**. Chain or metal band filter wrenches may distort the filter canister, but it doesn't matter since the filter will be discarded anyway.

15   Completely unscrew the old filter. Be careful; it's full of oil. Empty the oil inside the filter into the drain pan.

16   Compare the old filter with the new one to make sure they're the same type.

17   Use a clean rag to remove all oil, dirt and sludge from the area where the oil filter mounts to the engine. Check the old filter to make sure the rubber gasket isn't stuck to the engine. If the gasket is stuck to the engine (use a flashlight if necessary), remove it.

18   Apply a light coat of clean oil to the rubber gasket on the new oil filter **(see illustration)**.

19   Attach the new filter to the engine, following the tightening directions printed on the filter canister or packing box. Most filter manufacturers recommend against using a filter wrench due to the possibility of over-tightening and damage to the seal.

20   Remove all tools, rags, etc. from under the vehicle, being careful not to spill the oil in the drain pan, then lower the vehicle.

21   Move to the engine compartment and locate the oil filler cap.

22   Add the new oil through the filler opening. Use a funnel if necessary.

23   Pour four quarts of fresh oil into the engine. Wait a few minutes to allow the oil to drain into the pan, then check the level on the oil dipstick (see Section 4 if necessary). If the oil level is above the ADD mark, start the engine and allow the new oil to circulate.

24   Run the engine for only about a minute and then shut it off. Immediately look under the vehicle and check for leaks at the oil pan

drain plug and around the oil filter. If either is leaking, tighten with a bit more force.

25   With the new oil circulated and the filter now completely full, recheck the level on the dipstick and add more oil as necessary.

26   During the first few trips after an oil change, make it a point to check frequently for leaks and proper oil level.

27   The old oil drained from the engine cannot be reused in its present state and should be disposed of. Oil reclamation centers, auto repair shops and gas stations will normally accept the oil, which can be refined and used again. After the oil has cooled it can be drained into a suitable container (capped plastic jugs, topped bottles, milk cartons, etc.) for transport to one of these disposal sites.

17   Fuel system check

Refer to illustration 17.4

Warning: *Gasoline is extremely flammable, so take extra precautions when you work on any part of the fuel system. Don't smoke or allow open flames or bare light bulbs near the work area, and don't work in a garage where a natural gas-type appliance (such as a water heater or clothes dryer) with a pilot light is present. If you spill any fuel on your skin, rinse it off immediately with soap and water. When you perform any kind of work on the fuel system, wear safety glasses and have a Class B type fire extinguisher on hand.*

1   The fuel system is under pressure, so if any fuel lines are to be disconnected, the fuel system pressure must first be relieved (fuel-injected models only - see Chapter 4). Plug all disconnected fuel lines immediately after disconnection to prevent the tank from emptying itself.

2   The fuel system is most easily checked with the vehicle raised on a hoist so the components underneath the vehicle are readily visible and accessible.

3   If the smell of gasoline is noticed while driving or after the vehicle has been in the

sun, the system should be thoroughly inspected immediately.

4   Remove the gas filler cap and check for damage, corrosion and an unbroken sealing imprint on the gasket **(see illustration)**. Replace the cap with a new one, if necessary.

5   With the vehicle raised, inspect the gas tank and filler neck for punctures, cracks and other damage. The connection between the filler neck and the tank is especially critical. Sometimes a rubber filler neck will leak due to loose clamps or deteriorated rubber, problems a home mechanic can usually rectify. **Warning:** *Do not, under any circumstances, try to repair a fuel tank yourself (except rubber components). A welding torch or any open flame can easily cause the fuel vapors to explode if the proper precautions are not taken.*

6   Carefully check all rubber hoses and metal lines leading away from the fuel tank. Check for loose connections, deteriorated hoses, crimped lines and other damage. Follow the lines up to the front of the vehicle, carefully inspecting them all the way. Repair or replace damaged sections as necessary.

7   If a fuel odor is still evident after the inspection, check the Evaporative Emissions Control (EEC) system (see Section 34).

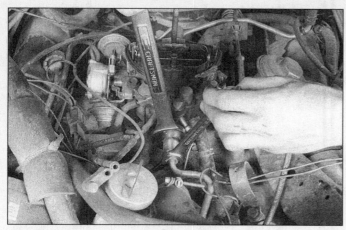

18.6 Two wrenches are required to loosen the carburetor fuel line inlet nut

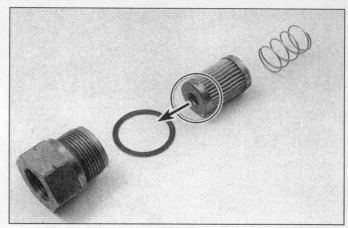

18.8 Component layout of the carburetor mounted fuel filter

1

18 Fuel filter replacement

Warning: *Gasoline is extremely flammable, so take extra precautions when you work on any part of the fuel system. Don't smoke or allow open flames or bare light bulbs near the work area, and don't work in a garage where a natural gas-type appliance (such as a water heater or clothes dryer) with a pilot light is present. If you spill any fuel on your skin, rinse it off immediately with soap and water. When you perform any kind of work on the fuel system, wear safety glasses and have a Class B type fire extinguisher on hand.*

Carbureted models

Refer to illustrations 18.6 and 18.8

1   On these models the fuel filter is located inside the fuel inlet nut at the carburetor. It's made of either pleated paper or porous bronze and cannot be cleaned or reused.

2   The job should be done with the engine cold (after sitting at least three hours). The necessary tools include open-end wrenches to fit the fuel line nuts. Flare nut wrenches (which wrap around the nut) should be used if available. In addition, you have to obtain the replacement filter (make sure it's for your specific vehicle and engine) and some clean rags.

3   Remove the air cleaner assembly. If vacuum hoses must be disconnected, be sure to note their positions and/or tag them to ensure that they are reinstalled correctly.

4   Follow the fuel line from the fuel pump to the point where it enters the carburetor. In most cases the fuel line will be metal all the way from the fuel pump to the carburetor.

5   Place some rags under the fuel inlet fittings to catch spilled fuel as the fittings are disconnected.

6   With the proper size wrench, hold the fuel inlet nut immediately next to the carburetor body. Now loosen the fitting at the end of the metal fuel line. Make sure the fuel inlet nut next to the carburetor is held securely while the fuel line is disconnected **(see illustration)**.

7   After the fuel line is disconnected, move it aside for better access to the inlet nut. Don't crimp the fuel line.

8   Unscrew the fuel inlet nut, which was previously held steady. As this fitting is drawn away from the carburetor body, be careful not to lose the thin washer-type gasket on the nut or the spring, located behind the fuel filter. Also pay close attention to how the filter is installed **(see illustration)**.

9   Compare the old filter with the new one to make sure they're the same length and design.

10   Reinstall the spring in the carburetor body.

11   Place the filter in position (a gasket is usually supplied with the new filter) and tighten the nut. Make sure it's not cross-threaded. Tighten it securely, but be careful not to overtighten it as the threads can strip easily, causing fuel leaks. Reconnect the fuel line to the fuel inlet nut, again using caution to avoid cross-threading the nut. Use a back-up wrench on the fuel inlet nut while tightening the fuel line fitting.

12   Start the engine and check carefully for leaks. If the fuel line fitting leaks, disconnect it and check for stripped or damaged threads. If the fuel line fitting has stripped threads, remove the entire line and have a repair shop install a new fitting. If the threads look all right, purchase some thread sealing tape and wrap the threads with it. Inlet nut repair kits are available at most auto parts stores to overcome leaking at the fuel inlet nut.

Fuel-injected models

Refer to illustration 18.15

Warning: *See Chapter 4 and relieve the fuel system pressure before proceeding.*

13   Fuel-injected engines employ an in-line fuel filter. The filter is located under the vehicle.

14   With the engine cold, place a container, newspapers or rags under the fuel filter.

15   Use wrenches to disconnect the fuel lines and detach the filter from the frame **(see illustration)**.

16   Install the new filter by reversing the

18.15 Use two wrenches to detach the fuel lines from the filter

removal procedure. Make sure the arrow on the filter points toward the engine, not the fuel tank. Tighten the fittings securely, but don't cross-thread them.

19 Throttle linkage check

1   There are no adjustments for the linkage itself, but periodic maintenance is necessary to assure its proper function.

2   Remove the air cleaner (carbureted and TBI only) so the entire linkage is visible.

3   Check the entire length of the cable to make sure that it is not binding.

4   Check all nylon bushings for wear, replacing them with new ones as necessary.

5   Lubricate the cable mechanisms with engine oil at the pivot points.

20 Thermo-controlled Air Cleaner (TAC) check (carbureted and TBI models only)

Refer to illustrations 20.3 and 20.5

1   All engines are equipped with a thermo-

20.3 Make sure the TAC hot air hose isn't loose or torn

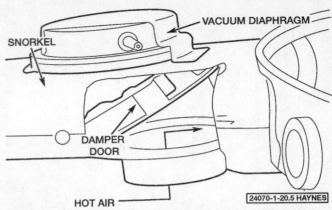

20.5 The thermo-controlled air cleaner improves driveability and emissions when the engine is cold

statically controlled air cleaner which draws air to the carburetor or fuel injection from different locations, depending upon engine temperature.

2   This is a simple visual check; however, if access is limited, a small mirror may have to be used.

3   Open the hood and locate the damper door inside the air cleaner assembly. It will be located inside the long snorkel of the metal air cleaner housing. Make sure that the flexible air hose is securely attached and undamaged **(see illustration)**.

4   If there is a flexible air duct attached to the end of the snorkel, leading to an area behind the grille, disconnect it at the snorkel. This will enable you to look through the end of the snorkel and see the damper door inside.

5   The check should be done when the engine and outside air are cold. Start the engine and look through the snorkel at the damper door, which should move to a closed position **(see illustration)**. With the damper door closed, air cannot enter through the end of the snorkel, but instead enters the air cleaner through the flexible duct attached to the exhaust manifold.

6   As the engine warms up to operating temperature, the damper door should open to allow air through the snorkel end. Depending on ambient temperature, this may take 10 to 15 minutes. To speed this up you can reconnect the snorkel air duct, drive the vehicle and then check to see if the damper door is completely open.

7   If the thermo-controlled air cleaner is not operating properly, see Chapter 6 for more information.

21   Carburetor/TBI unit fastener torque check

Refer to illustration 21.4

1   The carburetor or Throttle Body Injection (TBI) unit is attached to the top of the intake manifold by four nuts or bolts. These fasteners can sometimes work loose from vibration and temperature changes during normal engine operation and cause a vacuum leak.

2   To properly tighten the mounting nuts/bolts, a torque wrench is necessary. If you do not own one, they can usually be rented on a daily basis.

3   Remove the air cleaner assembly, tag-

ging each hose to be disconnected with a piece of numbered tape to make reassembly easier.

4   Locate the mounting nuts/bolts at the base of the carburetor or TBI unit. Decide what special tools or adapters will be necessary, if any, to tighten the fasteners with a socket and the torque wrench **(see illustration)**.

5   Tighten the nuts/bolts to the torque listed in this Chapter's Specifications. Do not overtighten them, as the threads could strip.

6   If you suspect that a vacuum leak exists at the bottom of the carburetor or TBI unit, obtain a length of hose about the diameter of fuel hose. Start the engine and place one end of the hose next to your ear as you probe around the base with the other end. You will hear a hissing sound if a leak exists.

7   If, after the nuts/bolts are properly tightened, a vacuum leak still exists, the carburetor or TBI unit must be removed and a new gasket installed. See Chapter 4 for more information.

8   After tightening the fasteners, reinstall the air cleaner and return all hoses to their original positions.

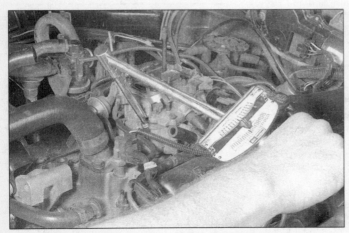

21.4 A socket extension and universal joint will probably be needed to tighten the carburetor/TBI unit bolt or nuts

22.2 The EFE temperature switch usually screws into the intake manifold in the vicinity of the thermostat

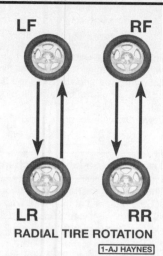

RADIAL TIRE ROTATION

1-AJ HAYNES

23.2 The tire rotation pattern for these vehicles

22 Early Fuel Evaporation (EFE) system check (carbureted and TBI-equipped models only)

Refer to illustration 22.2

1   The EFE system improves cold engine driveability and, by reducing the time that the choke is closed, exhaust emissions levels. The system utilizes a ceramic heater grid located between the carburetor/TBI base and intake manifold. This electrically heated unit improves vaporization of the air/fuel mixture during engine warm-up.

2   To check the EFE, disconnect the wires at the EFE temperature switch **(see illustration)**.

3   Connect a 12-volt test light across the connector terminals of the wire leads. If the test light glows when the ignition switch is turned on (engine off), the EFE system is working properly.

4   If the test light does not glow, see Chapter 6 for further tests and information concerning the EFE system.

23 Tire rotation

Refer to illustration 23.2

1   The tires should be rotated at the specified intervals and whenever uneven wear is noticed. Since the vehicle will be raised and the tires removed anyway, this is a good time to check the brakes (see Section 13) and/or repack the wheel bearings (see Section 30). Read over these Sections if this is to be done at the same time.

2   Refer to the **accompanying illustration** of the "preferred" and "optional" tire rotation patterns. Do not include "Temporary Use Only" spare tires in the rotation sequence **(see illustration)**.

3   Refer to the information in *Jacking and towing* at the front of this manual for the proper procedures to follow when raising the vehicle and changing a tire; however, if the

brakes are to be checked, do not apply the parking brake as stated. Make sure the tires are blocked to prevent the vehicle from rolling.

4   Preferably, the entire vehicle should be raised at the same time. This can be done on a hoist or by jacking up each corner and then lowering the vehicle onto jackstands placed under the frame rails. Always use four jackstands and make sure the vehicle is firmly supported.

5   After rotation, check and adjust the tire pressures as necessary and be sure to check the lug nut tightness.

24 Clutch pedal freeplay check and adjustment (1982 and 1983 models only)

Note: *The information which follows applies to 1982 and 1983 models with cable-actuated clutch assemblies.*

1   If your vehicle is equipped with a manual transmission, it is important to have the clutch reeplay properly adjusted. Basically, freeplay is the distance the clutch pedal moves before all play in the linkage is removed and the clutch begins to disengage. It is measured at the pedal pad. Slowly depress the pedal and determine how far it moves before resistance is felt.

2   There is only one linkage adjustment to compensate for all normal clutch wear.

3   Lift the clutch pedal all the way up to the stop. Now depress the pedal slowly several times (to make sure the pawl engages completely with the detent teeth on the self-adjusting ratchet).

4   See Chapter 8 for further clutch service information.

25 Differential lubricant change

1   Some differentials can be drained by removing a drain plug, while on others it is necessary to remove the cover plate on the differential housing. Because of this, be sure to buy a new gasket at the same time the gear lubricant is purchased.

2   Move a drain pan (at least five-pint capacity), rags, newspapers and wrenches under the vehicle.

3   On four-wheel drive models, a suction pump will be needed to remove the lubricant from the front differential. Remove the filler plug and insert the flexible suction hose. Work the hose down to the bottom of the differential housing and pump the lubricant out.

4   Fill the front differential with the specified lubricant to the base of the fill plug hole. Install the fill plug and tighten it securely.

5   On rear differentials, remove the bolts on the lower half of the differential cover plate. Use the upper bolts to keep the cover loosely attached to the differential. Allow the lubricant to drain into the drain pan, then completely remove the cover.

6   Using a lint-free rag, clean the inside of the cover and accessible areas of the differ-

ential housing. As this is done, check for chipped gears and metal particles in the lubricant, indicating the differential should be more thoroughly inspected and/or repaired.

7   Thoroughly clean the gasket mating surface on the cover and the differential housing. Use a gasket scraper or putty knife to remove all traces of the old gasket material.

8   Apply a thin film of RTV-type gasket sealant to the cover flange and then press a new gasket into position on the cover. Make sure the bolt holes align properly.

9   Place the cover on the differential housing and install the bolts. Tighten the bolts a little at a time, working across the cover in a diagonal fashion until all bolts are tight.

10   Remove the fill plug on the side of the differential housing and fill the housing with the proper lubricant until the level is at the bottom of the plug hole.

11   Securely install the plug.

26 Automatic transmission fluid and filter change

1   At the specified time intervals, the transmission fluid should be changed and the filter replaced with a new one. Since there is no drain plug, the transmission oil pan must be removed from the bottom of the transmission to drain the fluid.

2   Before draining, purchase the specified transmission fluid (see *Recommended lubricants and fluids*) and a new filter. The necessary gaskets should be included with the filter; if not, purchase an oil pan gasket and a strainer-to-valve body gasket.

3   Other tools necessary for this job include jackstands to support the vehicle in a raised position, a wrench to remove the oil pan bolts, a standard screwdriver, a drain pan capable of holding at least eight pints, newspapers and clean rags.

4   The fluid should be drained immediately after the vehicle has been driven. This will remove any built-up sediment better than if the fluid were cold. Because of this, it may be wise to wear protective gloves (fluid temperature can exceed 350-degrees F in a hot transmission).

5   After it has been driven to warm up the fluid, raise the vehicle and place it on jackstands for access underneath. Make sure it is firmly supported by the four stands placed under the frame rails.

6   Move the necessary equipment under the vehicle, being careful not to touch any of the hot exhaust components.

7   Remove the keeper at the rear of the transmission selector cable assembly.

8   Remove the clip that retains the transmission selector cable to the transmission selector lever.

9   Remove the cable from the selector lever.

10   Remove the cable housing from the transmission selector cable bracket.

11   Remove the selector cable bracket. To avoid confusion when reinstalling the transmission pan, note that the bolts retaining the

1

cable bracket are a different size than those retaining the pan.

12   Place the drain pan under the transmission oil pan and remove the oil pan bolts along the rear and sides of the pan. Loosen, but do not remove, the bolts at the front of the pan.

13   Carefully pry the pan down at the rear, allowing the hot fluid to drain into the container. If necessary, use a screwdriver to break the gasket seal at the rear of the pan; however, do not damage the pan or transmission in the process.

14   Support the pan and remove the remaining bolts at the front. Lower the pan and drain the remaining fluid into the container. As this is done, check the fluid for metal particles, which may be an indication of internal failure.

15   Now visible on the bottom of the transmission is the filter/strainer held in place by two screws.

16   Remove the two screws, the filter and the gasket.

17   Thoroughly clean the transmission oil pan with solvent. Inspect it for metal particles and foreign matter. Dry it with compressed air if available. It is important that all remaining gasket material is removed from the oil pan mounting flange. Use a gasket scraper or putty knife for this.

18   Clean the filter mounting surface on the valve body. Again, this surface should be smooth and free of any leftover gasket material.

19   Clean the screen assembly with solvent, then dry it thoroughly (use compressed air, if available). Paper or felt-type filters should be replaced with new ones.

20   Place the new filter into position, with a new gasket between it and the transmission valve body. Install the two mounting screws and tighten them securely.

21   Apply a light bead of gasket sealant around the oil pan mounting surface, with the sealant to the inside of the bolt holes. Press the new gasket into place on the pan, making sure all bolt holes line up.

22   Lift the pan up to the bottom of the transmission and install the mounting bolts. Tighten the bolts in a diagonal fashion, working around the pan. Using a torque wrench, tighten the bolts to the torque listed in this Chapter's Specifications.

23   Lower the vehicle.

24   Open the hood and remove the transmission fluid dipstick from the guide tube.

25   Since fluid capacities vary between the various transmission types, it is best to add a little fluid at a time, continually checking the level with the dipstick. Allow the fluid time to drain into the pan. Add fluid until the level just registers on the end of the dipstick (use a funnel to prevent spills).

26   With the selector lever in Park, apply the parking brake and start the engine without depressing the accelerator pedal (if possible). Do not race the engine at a high speed; run it at slow idle only.

27   Depress the brake pedal and shift the transmission through each gear. Place the selector back into Park and check the level on the dipstick (with the engine still idling). Look under the vehicle for leaks around the transmission oil pan mating surface.

28   Add more fluid through the dipstick tube until the level on the dipstick is 1/4-inch below the Add mark on the dipstick. Do not allow the fluid level to go above this point, as the transmission would then be overfull, necessitating the removal of the pan to drain the excess fluid.

29   Push the dipstick firmly back into the tube and drive the vehicle to reach normal operating temperature (15 miles of highway driving or its equivalent in the city). Park on a level surface and check the fluid level on the dipstick with the engine idling and the transmission in Park. The level should now be at the Full mark on the dipstick. If not, add more fluid as necessary to bring the level up to this point. Again, do not overfill.

27   Manual transmission lubricant change

Refer to illustration 27.3

1   The manual transmission lubricant should be drained and replaced at the specified intervals. Drive the vehicle to bring the transmission lubricant to operating temperature.

2   Raise the vehicle and support it securely. Before beginning this job, you will need:

> *A wrench to remove the transmission plug*
> *A drain pan of at least six-quart capacity*
> *An adequate supply of the specified lubricant*
> *Jackstands to support the vehicle in a raised position*
> *Newspapers and clean rags*

3   Place the drain pan under the drain plug and remove the fill plug **(see illustration)**.

4   Remove the drain plug and allow the transmission lubricant to drain into the pan.

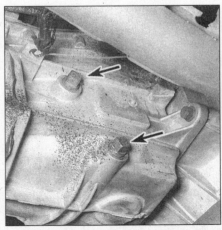

27.3 Fill and drain plug locations (arrows)

Inspect the lubricant for signs of contamination and metal particles, which could indicate a malfunction in the transmission.

5   Install the fill plug and fill the transmission with the specified lubricant (see *Recommended lubricants and fluids*) to the bottom of the fill plug hole. Install the fill plug and tighten it securely.

6   Lower the vehicle, drive it and check for leaks.

28   Transfer case lubricant change

1   The transfer case lubricant should be drained and replaced at the same time as the manual transmission (see Section 27).

2   Follow the procedures in Steps 2 and 3 of Section 27.

3   Remove the drain plug and allow the lubricant to run into the pan **(see illustration 4.43)**.

4   Inspect the lubricant for clues as to the condition of the transfer case, such as metal particles, water and other contamination.

5   Install the drain plug.

6   Fill the transfer case to just below the fill hole with the specified lubricant and install the plug. Tighten it securely.

7   Lower the vehicle, test drive it and check for leaks.

29   Cooling system servicing (draining, flushing and refilling)

Refer to illustration 29.6

Warning: *Do not allow antifreeze to come in contact with your skin or painted surfaces of the vehicle. Rinse off spills immediately with plenty of water. Antifreeze is highly toxic if ingested. Never leave antifreeze lying around in an open container or in puddles on the floor; children and pets are attracted by it's sweet smell and may drink it. Check with local authorities about disposing of used antifreeze. Many communities have collection centers which will see that antifreeze is disposed of safely.*

29.6 The drain plug (arrow) is located at the lower corner of the radiator on most models

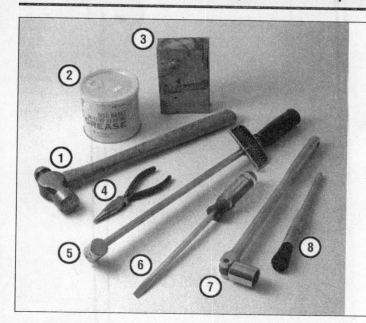

30.1 Tools and materials needed for front wheel bearing maintenance

1   *Hammer - A common hammer will do just fine*
2   *Grease - High-temperature grease that is formulated specially for front wheel bearings should be used*
3   *Wood block - If you have a scrap piece of 2x4, it can be used to drive the new seal into the hub*
4   *Needle-nose pliers - Used to straighten and remove the cotter pin in the spindle*
5   *Torque wrench - This is very important in this procedure; if the bearing is too tight, the wheel won't turn freely - if it's too loose, the wheel will "wobble" on the spindle. Either way, it could mean extensive damage*
6   *Screwdriver - Used to remove the seal from the hub (a long screwdriver is preferred)*
7   *Socket/breaker bar - Needed to loosen the nut on the spindle if it's extremely tight*
8   *Brush - Together with some clean solvent, this will be used to remove old grease from the hub and spindle*

1   Periodically, the cooling system should be drained, flushed and refilled to replenish the antifreeze mixture and prevent formation of rust and corrosion, which can impair the performance of the cooling system and ultimately cause engine damage.

2   At the same time the cooling system is serviced, all hoses and the radiator cap should be inspected and replaced if defective (see Section 7).

3   Since antifreeze is a corrosive and poisonous solution, be careful not to spill any of the coolant mixture on the vehicle's paint or your skin. If this happens, rinse immediately with plenty of clean water.

4   With the engine cold, remove the radiator cap.

5   Move a large container under the radiator to catch the coolant as it is drained.

6   Drain the radiator. Most models are equipped with a drain plug at the bottom **(see illustration)**. If this drain has excessive corrosion and cannot be turned easily, or if the radiator is not equipped with a drain, disconnect the lower radiator hose to allow the coolant to drain. Be careful that none of the solution is splashed on your skin or into your eyes.

7   If accessible, remove the two engine drain plugs. There is one plug on each side of the engine about halfway back, on the lower edge near the oil pan rail. These will allow the coolant to drain from the engine itself.

8   Disconnect the hose from the coolant reservoir and remove the reservoir. Flush it out with clean water.

9   Place a garden hose in the radiator filler neck at the top of the radiator and flush the system until the water runs clear at all drain points.

10   In severe cases of contamination or clogging of the radiator, remove it (see Chapter 3) and reverse flush it. This involves simply inserting a hose in the bottom radiator outlet to allow the clear water to run against the normal flow, draining through the top. A radiator repair shop should be consulted if further cleaning or repair is necessary.

11   When the coolant is regularly drained and the system refilled with the correct antifreeze/water mixture, there should be no need to use chemical cleaners or descalers.

12   To refill the system, reconnect the radiator hoses and install the drain plugs securely in the engine. Special thread-sealing tape (available at auto parts stores) should be used on the drain plugs. Install the reservoir and the overflow hose where applicable.

13   Fill the radiator to the base of the filler neck and then add more coolant to the reservoir until it reaches the mark.

14   Run the engine until normal operating temperature is reached and, with the engine idling, add coolant up to the Full Hot level. Install the radiator cap so that the arrows are in alignment with the overflow hose. Install the reservoir cap.

15   Always refill the system with a mixture of high quality antifreeze and water in the proportion called for on the antifreeze container or in your owner's manual. Chapter 3 also contains information on antifreeze mixtures.

16   Keep a close watch on the coolant level and the various cooling system hoses during the first few miles of driving. Tighten the hose clamps and/or add more coolant as necessary.

30   Wheel bearing check and repack (2WD models only)

Refer to illustrations 30.1 30.6, 30.7a, 30.7b, 30.8a, 30.8b, 30.9, 30.10, 30.11, 30.15, 30.16, 30.19, 30.20, 30.21a, 30.21b, 30.26 and 30.27

Note: *Front wheel bearings on 4WD models do not require periodic maintenance (see Chapter 8 for servicing).*

1   In most cases, the front wheel bearings will not need servicing until the brake pads

30.6 Removing the wheel bearing dust cap

are changed. However, these bearings should be checked whenever the front wheels are raised for any reason. Several items including a torque wrench and special grease, are required for this procedure **(see illustration)**.

2   With the vehicle securely supported on jackstands, spin the wheel and check for noise, rolling resistance and freeplay.

3   Grab the top of the tire with one hand and the bottom of the tire with the other. Move the tire in-and-out on the spindle. If it moves more than 0.005-inch, the bearings should be checked and then repacked with grease or replaced if necessary.

4   To remove the bearings for replacement or repacking, begin by removing the hub cap and wheel.

5   Remove the disc brake caliper and support it with a piece of wire (see Chapter 9).

6   Pry the dust cap out of the hub using a screwdriver or hammer and chisel **(see illustration)**. The cap is located at the center of the hub.

30.7a Use a screwdriver to straighten the ends of the cotter pin . . .

30.7b . . . then pull the pin out with needle-nose pliers

30.8a Remove the spindle nut . . .

30.8b . . . and the washer

30.9 Pull the hub out to dislodge it, then remove the outer wheel bearing

30.10 Lift the hub assembly off the spindle

7   Use needle-nose pliers or a screwdriver to straighten the bent ends of the cotter pin and then pull the cotter pin out of the locking nut **(see illustrations)**. Discard the cotter pin and use a new one during reassembly.

8   Remove the spindle nut and washer from the end of the spindle **(see illustrations)**.

9   Pull the hub assembly out slightly and then push it back into its original position. This should force the outer bearing off the spindle enough so that it can be removed with your fingers **(see illustration)**. Remove the outer bearing, noting how it is installed on the end of the spindle **(see illustration)**.

10   Now the hub assembly can be pulled off the spindle **(see illustration)**.

11   On the rear side of the hub, use a screwdriver to pry out the inner bearing lip seal **(see illustration)**. As this is done, note the direction in which the seal is installed.

12   The inner bearing can now be removed from the hub, again noting how it is installed.

13   Use solvent to remove all traces of the

30.11 Use a large screwdriver to pry the seal out of the hub

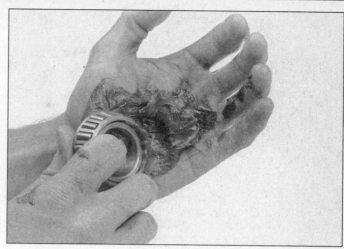

30.15 Work the grease into the rollers from the back side of the bearing

30.16 Apply a thin coat of grease to the spindle, especially to the area where the seal rides

30.19 Use a plastic hammer to tap the seal evenly into place

old grease from the bearings, hub and spindle. A small brush may prove useful; however, make sure no bristles from the brush embed themselves inside the bearing rollers. Allow the parts to air dry.

14   Carefully inspect the bearings for cracks, heat discoloration, bent rollers, etc. Check the bearing races inside the hub for cracks, scoring and uneven surfaces. If the bearing races are defective, the hubs should be taken to a machine shop with the facilities to remove the old races and press new ones in.

15   Use an approved high-temperature front wheel bearing grease to pack the bearings. Work the grease completely into the bearings, forcing it between the rollers, cone and cage (see illustration).

16   Apply a thin coat of grease to the spindle at the outer bearing seat, inner bearing seat, shoulder and seal seat (see illustration).

17   Put a small quantity of grease on the inner side of each bearing race inside the hub. Using your finger, form a dam at these points to provide extra grease availability and

30.20 Install the outer bearing

to keep thinned grease from flowing out of the bearing.

18   Place the grease-packed inner bearing into the rear of the hub and put a little more grease on the outside of the bearing.

19   Place a new seal over the inner bearing

and tap the seal with a hammer until it is flush with the hub (see illustration).

20   Carefully place the hub assembly onto the spindle and push the grease-packed outer bearing into position (see illustration).

21   Install the washer and spindle nut.

30.21a Line up the tab with the groove and press the washer into place

30.21b Use a torque wrench to tighten the spindle nut slightly

30.26 Line up the nut slot with the hole in the spindle and insert a new cotter pin

30.27 Pry the ends of the cotter pin over with a screwdriver

Tighten the nut only slightly (12 ft-lbs of torque) (see illustrations).

22   Spin the hub in a forward direction to seat the bearings and remove any grease or burrs which could cause excessive bearing play later.

23   Put a little grease on the outside of the outer bearing to provide extra grease availability.

24   Now check to see that the tightness of the spindle nut is still 12 ft-lbs.

25   Loosen the spindle nut until it is just loose, no more.

26   Using your hand (not a wrench of any kind), tighten the nut until it is snug. Install a new cotter pin through the hole in the spindle and spindle nut (see illustration). If the nut slots do not line up, loosen the nut slightly until they do. From the hand-tight position, the nut should not be loosened more than one-half flat to install the cotter pin.

27   Bend the ends of the new cotter pin until they are flat against the nut (see illustration). Cut off any extra length which could interfere with the dust cap.

28   Install the dust cap, tapping it into place

with a rubber mallet.

29   Place the brake caliper near the rotor and carefully remove the wood spacer. Slide the caliper over the disc. Tighten the caliper mounting bolts to the torque listed in the Chapter 9 Specifications.

30   Install the wheel and tighten the lug nuts securely.

31   Grab the top and bottom of the tire and check the bearings in the same manner as described at the beginning of this Section.

32   Lower the vehicle to the ground and tighten the lug nuts to the torque listed in this Chapter's Specifications. Install the hub cap, using a rubber mallet to seat it.

---

31   Air filter and PCV filter replacement

Refer to illustrations 31.2, 31.13a, 31.13b, 31.15 and 31.16

Carbureted and TBI models

1   At the specified intervals, the air filter

and PCV filter should be replaced with new ones. A thorough program of preventative maintenance would call for the two filters to be inspected between changes.

2   The air filter is located inside the air cleaner housing on the top of the engine. The filter is generally replaced by removing the wing nut at the top of the air cleaner assembly and lifting off the top plate (see illustration). If vacuum hoses are connected to the plate, note their positions and disconnect them.

3   While the top plate is off, be careful not to drop anything down into the carburetor or TBI unit.

4   Lift the air filter element out of the housing.

5   To check the filter, hold it up to strong sunlight or place a flashlight or droplight on the inside of the filter. If you can see light coming through the paper element, the filter is all right. Check all the way around the filter.

6   Wipe out the inside of the air cleaner housing with a clean rag.

7   Place the old filter (if in good condition) or the new filter into the air cleaner housing.

31.2 Remove the wingnut (arrow) and lift out the top plate for access to the air and PCV filters

31.13a Detach the two housing clips

31.13b Separate the cover from the housing

31.15 Lift the filter out

Make sure it seats properly in the bottom of the housing.

8   Connect any disconnected vacuum hoses to the top plate and reinstall the plate.

9   The PCV filter is also located inside the air cleaner housing. Remove the top plate and air filter as described previously, then locate the PCV filter on the side of the housing.

10   Remove the retaining clip from the outside of the housing, then remove the PCV filter.

11   Install a new PCV filter, then reinstall the retaining clip, air filter, top plate and any hoses that were disconnected.

Central Port Injection (CPI) models

12   Disconnect the air hose from the filter housing.

13   Remove the two plastic wingnuts and lift the housing up for access, then detach the clips (see illustrations).

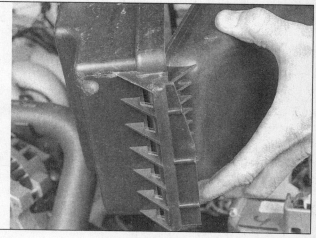
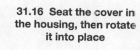
31.16 Seat the cover in the housing, then rotate it into place

14   Separate the housing halves.

15   Lift the filter out of the housing, noting the direction in which it's installed (see illustration).

16   Installation is the reverse of removal. When reinstalling the cover, hook the end in the housing and rotate it into position (see illustration).

32.1 On 2.8L V6 engines, the PCV valve (arrow) is located in the left valve cover

34.3 The EEC canister (arrow) is located in the front corner of the engine compartment on most models

32   Positive Crankcase Ventilation (PCV) valve replacement

Refer to illustration 32.1

1   The PCV valve is located in the valve cover or intake manifold **(see illustration)**. A hose connected to the valve runs to either the carburetor or TBI unit or the intake manifold.

2   When purchasing a replacement PCV valve, make sure it is for your particular vehicle, model year and engine size.

3   Pull the valve (with hose attached) from the rubber grommet in the valve cover or manifold.

4   Loosen the retaining clamp and pull the PCV valve from the end of the hose, noting its installed position and direction.

5   Compare the old valve with the new one to make sure they are the same.

6   Push the new valve into the end of the hose until it is seated and reinstall the clamp.

7   Inspect the rubber grommet for damage and replace it with a new one, if faulty.

8   Push the PCV valve and hose securely into position.

9   More information on the PCV system can be found in Chapter 6.

33   Exhaust Gas Recirculation (EGR) valve check

1   The EGR valve is located on the intake manifold, adjacent to the carburetor. Most of the time when a problem develops in this emissions system, it is due to a stuck or corroded EGR valve.

2   With the engine cold to prevent burns, reach under the EGR valve and manually push on the diaphragm. Using moderate pressure, you should be able to press the diaphragm up and down within the housing. **Note:** *Some models use a sealed valve, which makes this check impossible.*

3   If the diaphragm does not move or moves only with much effort, replace the EGR valve with a new one. If in doubt about the quality of the valve, compare the free movement of your EGR valve with a new valve.

4   See Chapter 6 for more information on the EGR system.

34   Evaporative Emissions Control (EEC) system filter replacement

Refer to illustration 34.3

1   The function of the Evaporative Emissions Control System is to draw fuel vapors from the tank and carburetor or TBI unit, store them in a charcoal canister and then burn them during normal engine operation.

2   The filter at the bottom of the charcoal canister should be replaced at the specified intervals. If, however, a fuel odor is detected, the canister, filter and system hoses should immediately be inspected.

3   To replace the filter, locate the canister at the front of the engine compartment. It will have between three and six hoses running out of the top **(see illustration)**.

4   Mark the hoses with tape to simplify reinstallation, then disconnect them from the canister.

5   Remove the two bolts which secure the bottom of the canister to the body.

6   Turn the canister upside-down and pull the old filter from the bottom of the canister.

7   Push the new filter into the bottom of the canister, making sure it is seated all the

way around.

8   Place the canister back into position and tighten the two mounting bolts. Connect the various hoses if disconnected.

9   The EEC is explained in more detail in Chapter 6.

35   Ignition timing check and adjustment

Refer to illustrations 35.4 and 35.5

Note: *It is imperative that the procedures included on the Vehicle Emissions Control Information label be followed when adjusting the ignition timing. The label will include all information concerning preliminary steps to be performed before adjusting the timing, as well as the timing specifications.*

1   Locate the VECI label under the hood and read through and perform all preliminary instructions concerning ignition timing.

2   Locate the timing mark pointer plate located beside the crankshaft pulley. The 0 mark represents top dead center (TDC). The pointer plate will be marked in either one or two-degree increments and should have the proper timing mark for your particular engine noted. If not, count back from the 0 mark the correct number of degrees BTDC, as noted on the VECI label, and mark the plate.

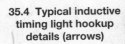
35.4 Typical inductive timing light hookup details (arrows)

35.5 Move the timing light close enough to the marks (arrow) so they can be seen clearly, but watch out for the fan!

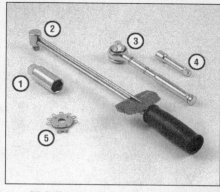

36.2 Tools required for changing spark plugs

1

3   Locate the notch on the crankshaft balancer of pulley and mark it with chalk or a dab of paint so it will be visible under the timing light.

4   With the ignition off, connect the pickup lead of the timing light to the number one spark plug wire (see illustration). Do not pierce the wire or attempt to insert a wire between the boot and the wire. Connect the timing light power leads according to the manufacturer's instructions. Note: Some engines incorporate a magnetic timing probe hole for use with special electronic timing equipment. Consult the manufacturer's instructions for proper use of this equipment.

5   Start the engine, aim the timing light at the timing mark by the crankshaft pulley and note which timing mark the notch on the pulley is lining up with (see illustration).

6   If the notch is not lining up with the correct mark, loosen the distributor hold-down bolt and rotate the distributor until the notch is lined up with the correct timing mark.

7   Retighten the hold-down bolt and recheck the timing.

8   Turn off the engine and disconnect the timing light. Reconnect the number one spark plug wire, if removed.

36   Spark plug replacement

Refer to illustrations 36.2, 36.5a, 36.5b, 36.6 and 36.10

1   The spark plugs are located on each side of V6 engines and on the left (driver's) side of four-cylinder engines. They may or may not be easily accessible for removal. If the vehicle is equipped with air-conditioning or power steering, some of the plugs may be tricky to remove. Special extension or swivel tools may be necessary. Make a survey under the hood to determine if special tools will be needed.

2   In most cases, the tools necessary for spark plug replacement include a spark plug socket which fits onto a ratchet (spark plug sockets are padded inside to prevent damage to the porcelain insulators on the new plugs), various extensions and a gap gauge to check and adjust the gaps on the new

plugs (see illustration). A special plug wire removal tool is available for separating the wire boots from the spark plugs, but it isn't absolutely necessary. A torque wrench should be used to tighten the new plugs.

3   The best approach when replacing the spark plugs is to purchase the new ones in advance, adjust them to the proper gap and replace them one at a time. When buying the new spark plugs, be sure to obtain the correct plug type for your particular engine. This information can be found on the Vehicle Emission Control Information label located under the hood, in the owner's manual and in this Chapter's Specifications. If differences exist between the plug specified on the emissions label and in this Chapter's Specifications or the owner's manual, assume that the emissions label is correct.

4   Allow the engine to cool completely before attempting to remove any of the plugs. While you're waiting for the engine to cool, check the new plugs for defects and adjust the gaps.

5   The gap is checked by inserting the proper thickness gauge between the electrodes at the tip of the plug (see illustration). The gap between the electrodes should be the same as the one specified on the Vehicle

1   Spark plug socket - This will have special padding inside to protect the spark plug's porcelain insulator

2   Torque wrench - Although not mandatory, using this tool is the best way to ensure the plugs are tightened properly

3   Ratchet - Standard hand tool to fit the spark plug socket

4   Extension - Depending on model and accessories, you may need special extensions and universal joints to reach one or more of the plugs

5   Spark plug gap gauge - This gauge for checking the gap comes in a variety of styles. Make sure the gap for your engine is included

Emissions Control Information label or listed in this Chapter's Specifications. The wire should just slide between the electrodes with a slight amount of drag. If the gap is incorrect, use the adjuster on the gauge body to bend the curved side electrode slightly until the proper gap is obtained (see illustration). If the side electrode is not exactly over the center electrode, bend it with the adjuster until it is. Check for cracks in the porcelain insulator (if any are found, the plug should not be used).

36.5a Spark plug manufacturers recommend using a wire-type gauge when checking the gap - if the wire does not slide between the electrodes with a slight drag, adjustment is required

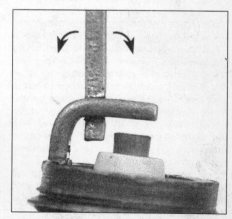

36.5b To change the gap, bend the side electrode only, as indicated by the arrows, and be very careful not to crack or chip the porcelain insulator surrounding the center electrode

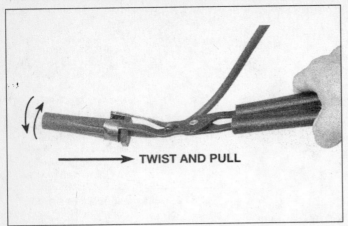

36.6 When removing the spark plug wires, pull only on the boot and twist it back-and-forth

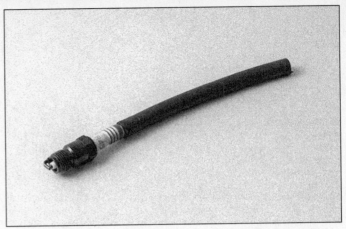

36.10 A length of snug-fitting rubber hose will save time and prevent damaged threads when installing the spark plugs

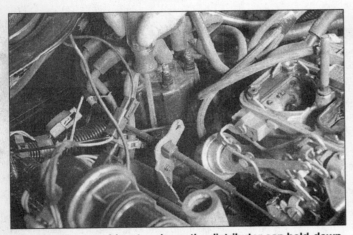

37.3 Use a screwdriver to release the distributor cap hold-down latches - the spark plug wire ring has already been removed for clarity

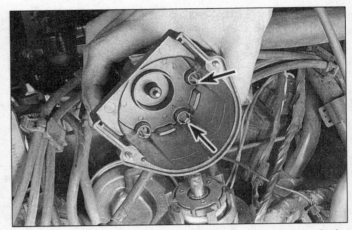

37.4 Inspect the inside of the cap, especially the metal terminals (arrows) for corrosion and wear

6   With the engine cool, remove the spark plug wire from one spark plug. Pull only on the boot at the end of the wire - do not pull on the wire. A plug wire removal tool should be used if available **(see illustration)**.

7   If compressed air is available, use it to blow any dirt or foreign material away from the spark plug hole. A common bicycle pump will also work. The idea here is to eliminate the possibility of debris falling into the cylinder as the spark plug is removed.

8   Place the spark plug socket over the plug and remove it from the engine by turning it in a counterclockwise direction.

9   Compare the spark plug to those shown in the photos on the inside back cover of this manual to get an indication of the general running condition of the engine.

10   Thread one of the new plugs into the hole until you can no longer turn it with your fingers, then tighten it with a torque wrench (if available) or the ratchet. It might be a good idea to slip a short length of rubber hose over the end of the plug to use as a tool to thread it into place **(see illustration)**. The hose will grip the plug well enough to turn it, but will start to slip if the plug begins to cross-thread

in the hole - this will prevent damaged threads and the accompanying repair costs.

11   Before pushing the spark plug wire onto the end of the plug, inspect it following the procedures outlined in Section 37.

12   Attach the plug wire to the new spark plug, again using a twisting motion on the boot until it's seated on the spark plug.

13   Repeat the procedure for the remaining spark plugs, replacing them one at a time to prevent mixing up the spark plug wires.

37 Spark plug wires, distributor cap and rotor check and replacement

Refer to illustrations 37.3, 37.4 and 37.7

1   Begin this procedure by making a visual check of the spark plug wires while the engine is running. In a darkened garage (make sure there is ventilation) start the engine and observe each plug wire. Be careful not to come into contact with any moving engine parts. If there is a break in the wire, you will see arcing or a small spark at the damaged area. If arcing is noticed, make a note to obtain new wires, then allow the

engine to cool and check the distributor cap and rotor.

2   Disconnect the negative cable from the battery. At the distributor, disconnect the ECM connector and coil wire.

3   Remove the distributor cap by placing a screwdriver on the slotted head of each latch. Press down on the latch and turn it 180-degrees to release the hooked end at the bottom **(see illustration)**. On some engines, due to restricted working room, a stubby screwdriver will work best. With all latches disengaged, separate the cap from the distributor with the spark plug wires still attached. **Note:** *Some caps use screws instead of latches.*

4   Inspect the cap for cracks and other damage. Closely examine the contacts on the inside of the cap for excessive corrosion **(see illustration)**. Slight erosion or pitting is normal. Deposits on the contacts may be removed with a small file.

5   If the inspection reveals damage to the cap, make a note to obtain a replacement for your particular engine, then examine the rotor.

6   The rotor is visible, with the cap

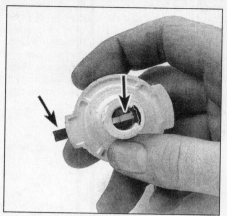

37.7 Check the distributor rotor contacts (arrows) for wear and burn marks

38.7 To adjust the valve clearance, loosen the adjuster lock nut with a box-end wrench and back off the adjuster screw with a screwdriver. Carefully tighten the adjuster screw until you feel a slight drag when withdrawing the feeler gauge, then tighten the adjuster locknut while still holding the adjuster screw with a screwdriver

1

removed, at the top of the distributor shaft. It is held in place by two screws. Remove the screws and the rotor.

7 Inspect the rotor for cracks and other damage. Carefully check the condition of the metal contact at the top of the rotor for excessive burning and pitting **(see illustration)**.

8 If it is determined that a new rotor is required, make a note to that effect. If the rotor and cap are in good condition, reinstall them at this time. Note that the rotor has two raised pegs on the bottom and that it has a wide slot and a narrow slot. Make sure that the slots are correctly aligned and that the pegs are firmly seated when the rotor is installed.

9 If the cap must be replaced, do not reinstall it. Leave it off the distributor with the wires still connected.

10 If the spark plug wires are being replaced, now is the time to obtain a new set, along with a new cap and rotor as determined in the checks above. Purchase a wire set for your particular engine, pre-cut to the proper size, with the rubber boots already installed.

11 If the spark plug wires passed the check in Step 1, they should be checked further as follows.

12 Examine the wires one at a time to avoid mixing them up.

13 Disconnect the plug wire from the spark plug. A removal tool can be used for this, or you can grab the rubber boot, twist slightly and then pull the wire free. Do not pull on the wire itself, only on the rubber boot.

14 Inspect inside the boot for corrosion, which will look like a white crusty powder. Some models use a conductive white silicone lubricant which should not be mistaken for corrosion.

15 Now push the wire and boot back onto the end of the spark plug. It should be a tight fit on the plug end. If not, remove the wire and use pliers to carefully crimp the metal connector inside the wire boot until the fit is snug.

16 Now, using a clean rag, clean the entire length of the wire. Remove all built-up dirt

and grease. As this is done, check for burns, cracks and any other form of damage. Bend the wires in several places to ensure that the conductive wire inside has not hardened.

17 Next, the wires should be checked at the distributor cap in the same manner. On four-cylinder engines, remove the wire from the cap by pulling on the boot, again examining the wires one at a time, and reinstalling each one after examination. Apply new silicone lubricant before reinstallation. On some V6 engines, the distributor boots are connected to a circular retaining ring attached to the distributor cap. Release the locking tabs, turn the ring upside down and check all wire boots at the same time.

18 If the wires appear to be in good condition, reinstall the retaining ring (V6 engines) and make sure that all wires are secure at both ends. If the cap and rotor are also in good condition, the check is finished. Reconnect the wires at the distributor and at the battery.

19 If it was determined in Steps 12 through 17 that new wires are required, obtain them at this time, along with a new cap and rotor if so determined in the checks above.

20 Attach the rotor to the distributor. Make sure that the carbon brush is properly installed in the cap, as a wide gap between the carbon brush and the rotor will cause rotor burn-through and/or damage to the distributor cap.

21 If new wires are being installed, replace them one at a time. **Note:** *It is important to replace the wires one at a time, noting the routing as each wire is removed and installed, to maintain the correct firing order.*

22 Attach the cap to the distributor, reconnecting all wires disconnected in Step 2, then reconnect the battery cable.

38 Valve clearance adjustment (1.9 liter engine only)

Refer to illustration 38.7

1 Tag and remove the emissions hoses from the valve cover. Remove the valve cover.

2 Before adjusting the valves, check the

tightness of the rocker shaft bracket nuts with a torque wrench. Tighten them to the torque listed in this Chapter's Specifications if necessary.

3 Position the number 1 piston at top dead center (TDC) on the compression stroke. To do this, first number each spark plug wire, then remove all of the spark plugs from the engine.

4 Locate the number 1 cylinder spark plug wire and trace it back to the distributor. Write a number 1 on the distributor body directly below the terminal where the number 1 spark plug wire attaches to the distributor cap. Do this for the number 4 cylinder as well, then remove the cap and wires from the distributor.

5 Slip a wrench or socket over the large bolt at the front of the crankshaft and slowly turn it in a clockwise direction until the groove in the crankshaft pulley is aligned with the 0 (zero) on the timing mark tag. The rotor should be pointing directly at the number 1 you made on the distributor body. If it is not, turn the crankshaft one more complete revolution (360-degrees) in a clockwise direction. If the rotor is now pointing at the number 1 on the distributor body, then the number 1 piston is at TDC on the compression stroke. With the crankshaft in this position, the valves on the following cylinders can be checked and adjusted:

No. 1 cylinder...... Intake and exhaust
No. 2 cylinder...... Intake
No. 3 cylinder...... Exhaust

6 Insert an appropriate size feeler gauge between the valve stem and the adjusting screw. If the feeler gauge fits with a slight drag, then the clearance is correct and no adjustment is required. Be sure to use the correct feeler gauge, as the intake and exhaust valves require different clearances for proper engine operation.

7 If the feeler gauge will not fit between the valve stem and adjusting screw or if it is loose, loosen the adjusting screw locknut and carefully tighten or loosen the adjusting screw until you can feel a slight drag on the feeler gauge as it is withdrawn **(see illustration)**.

8   Hold the adjusting screw with a wrench to keep it from turning and tighten the locknut securely.

9   Turn the crankshaft 360-degrees and align the rotor with the number 4 on the distributor. With the crankshaft in this position, the valves on the following cylinders can be checked and adjusted:

No. 2 cylinder...... Exhaust
No. 3 cylinder...... Intake
No. 4 cylinder...... Intake and exhaust

10   Install the valve cover (use a new gasket) and tighten the mounting bolts evenly and securely.

11   Install the distributor cap and spark plugs, then hook up the spark plug wires and the various hoses and vacuum lines.

12   Start the engine and check for oil leakage between the valve cover and the cylinder head.

39   Underbody flushing

1   At least every spring, the underbody should be flushed with plain water to remove corrosive materials picked up from road surfaces. Materials used for ice and snow removal and dust control will cause premature rusting of the underbody sheet metal.

2   Be sure to thoroughly clean areas where mud and other debris can collect. Areas with large deposits of sediment should be presoaked before being flushed.

Chapter 2 Part A
1.9L four-cylinder engine

Contents

	Section
Air filter and PCV filter replacement	See Chapter 1
Camshaft - removal and installation	10
Check engine light	See Chapter 6
Compression check	See Chapter 1
Cylinder head - removal and installation	11
Drivebelt check and adjustment	See Chapter 1
Engine mounts - check and replacement	2
Engine oil and filter change	See Chapter 1
Engine oil level check	See Chapter 1
Engine overhaul - general information	See Chapter 2F
Engine removal - methods and precautions	See Chapter 2F
Exhaust manifold - removal and installation	6
Flywheel/driveplate and rear main oil seal - replacement	12

	Section
General information	1
Intake manifold - removal and installation	5
Oil pan - removal and installation	3
Oil pump - removal and installation	4
Spark plug replacement	See Chapter 1
Timing cover and chain - removal and installation	9
Timing cover seal - replacement	8
Top Dead Center (TDC) for number one piston - locating	See Chapter 2C
Valve cover and valve train components - removal, inspection and installation	7
Water pump - removal and installation	See Chapter 3

Specifications

General

Cylinder numbering (front-to-rear)	1-2-3-4
Firing order	1-3-4-2
Rocker shaft runout limit	0.0079 inch
Rocker shaft diameter	
Standard	0.8071 inch
Service limit	0.8012 inch
Rocker shaft-to-rocker arm clearance limit	0.0078 inch
Timing chain wear measurement (forty links)	
Standard	15 inches
Service limit	15.16 inches
Surface warpage limit	
Intake manifold-to-cylinder head	0.0157 inch
Exhaust manifold-to-cylinder head	0.0156 inch

Torque specifications

	Ft-lbs (unless otherwise indicated)
Rocker shaft bracket nuts	16
Camshaft sprocket bolt	58
Cylinder head bolts (see illustration 11.23)	72
Crankshaft pulley bolt	87
Flywheel/driveplate bolts	76
Oil pan mounting bolts	48 in-lbs
Valve cover nuts	48 in-lbs
Timing cover mounting bolts	18
Exhaust manifold mounting nuts	16

0757H

Cylinder numbering and distributor rotation direction for the 1.9L four-cylinder engine

The blackened terminal shown on the distributor cap indicates the Number One spark plug wire position

3.5 Apply a thin coat of RTV sealant to these locations (arrows) before installing the oil pan gasket

4.2 To remove the oil pump assembly from the engine, remove the pump and pick-up tube mounting bolts

1   General information

The Isuzu engine used in these models is equipped with a forged crankshaft supported by five main bearings, with the number three bearing used as the thrust bearing. An overhead camshaft directly operates the rocker arms, and periodic valve lash adjustment is required. An automatic adjuster tensions the timing chain.

The Sections in this Part of Chapter 2 are devoted to "in-vehicle" repair procedures for the Isuzu 1.9 liter engine. All information concerning engine block and cylinder head servicing can be found in Part F of this Chapter.

The repair procedures included in this Part are based on the assumption that the engine is still installed in the vehicle. Therefore, if this information is being used during a complete engine overhaul - with the engine already out of the vehicle and on a stand - many of the steps included here will not apply.

The Specifications included in this Part of Chapter 2 apply only to the engine and procedures found here. For Specifications regarding engines other than the Isuzu, see Part B, C, etc. Part F of Chapter 2 contains the Specifications necessary for engine block and cylinder head rebuilding.

2   Engine mounts - check and replacement

1   Engine mounts seldom require attention, but broken or deteriorated mounts should be replaced immediately or the added strain placed on the driveline components may cause damage or wear.

Check

2   During the check, the engine must be raised slightly to remove the weight from the mounts.
3   Raise the vehicle and support it securely on jackstands, then position a jack under the engine oil pan. Place a large block of wood between the jack head and the oil pan, then carefully raise the engine just enough to take the weight off the mounts. **Warning:** *DO NOT place any part of your body under the engine when it's supported only by a jack!*
4   Check the mounts to see if the rubber is cracked, hardened or separated from the metal plates Sometimes the rubber will split right down the center.
5   Check for relative movement between the mount plates and the engine or frame (use a large screwdriver or pry bar to attempt to move the mounts). If movement is noted, lower the engine and tighten the mount fasteners.
6   Rubber preservative should be applied to the mounts to slow deterioration.

Replacement

Front mounts

7   Disconnect the negative battery cable.
8   Remove the air filter assembly.
9   Remove the upper fan shroud (see Chapter 3).
10   Remove the safety wire from the engine mount bolt and remove the engine mount retaining nut from the connecting stud.
11   Raise the engine with a jack (position a block of wood underneath the oil pan). Make sure that the engine mounts do not bind as the engine is raised off the insulator assembly.
12   Remove the mount-to-engine bracket.
13   Remove the engine mount.
14   Installation is the reverse of removal.

Rear mount

15   Disconnect the negative battery cable.
16   Remove the retaining nut and bolt from the engine mount.
17   Place a jack under the transmission extension housing and raise the transmission until the mount can be removed from the frame crossmember.
18   Installation is the reverse of removal.

3   Oil pan - removal and installation

Refer to illustration 3.5
Note: *The engine must be removed from the*
vehicle before the oil pan can be removed.

1   Remove the engine as described in Part F of this Chapter.
2   Remove the oil pan retaining bolts and nuts and separate the oil pan from the engine block. Do not damage the gasket sealing surfaces.
3   Remove the dipstick guide tube from the intake manifold and oil pan.
4   Clean the oil pan and block sealing surfaces. Inspect the gasket sealing surfaces for distortion due to overtightening of the bolts. Repair with a wood block and hammer as necessary.
5   Before installing the oil pan, apply a thin coat of RTV sealant to the locations shown **(see illustration)**.
6   Attach the new oil pan gasket to the oil pan. Make sure that all the holes are properly aligned.
7   Attach the dipstick guide tube and oil pan to the engine block.
8   Starting at the center of the pan and working out to the corners, tighten the retaining bolts and nuts to the torque listed in this Chapter's Specifications.
9   Install the engine (Chapter 2F).

4   Oil pump - removal and installation

Refer to illustration 4.2
1   Remove the oil pan (see Section 3).
2   Remove the mounting bolts from the oil pump and oil pump pick-up tube **(see illustration)**.
3   Remove the oil pump. The oil pump is not rebuildable and must be replaced as a unit.
4   Installation is the reverse of removal.

5   Intake manifold - removal and installation

Removal

1   Drain the coolant from the radiator and engine block (see Chapter 1). The cooling sys-

tem must be completely drained before removing the intake manifold or coolant will flow into the cylinders when the manifold is removed.

2   Remove the air cleaner assembly.

3   Disconnect the upper radiator hose from the front of the intake manifold.

4   Disconnect the vacuum hose from the intake manifold.

5   Disconnect the heater hoses from the rear of the intake manifold and from the connector under the dashboard.

6   Disconnect the accelerator cable from the carburetor.

7   Disconnect the vacuum hose from the distributor and disconnect the thermo-unit wiring at the connector.

8   Disconnect the carburetor automatic choke and solenoid wiring at the connectors.

9   Disconnect the PCV hose from the valve cover.

10   Remove the bolt that attaches the oil dipstick guide tube to the intake manifold.

11   Disconnect the EGR pipe from the EGR valve adapter.

12   Disconnect the AIR vacuum hose from the three-way joint.

13   Remove the eight retaining nuts and separate the intake manifold from the cylinder head.

14   Check the manifold for cracks and damage. Replace it if necessary.

15   Scrape away all traces of gasket material from the manifold-to-cylinder head surfaces. Wipe the surfaces clean with a rag soaked in lacquer thinner or acetone.

16   Using a straightedge and a feeler gauge, check the cylinder head mating surface of the manifold for distortion and compare it to the Specifications. If the manifold is distorted beyond the specified limit, a machine shop should be able to correct the condition with a surface grinder.

Installation

17   Installation is the reverse of removal. Be sure to use a new gasket. Tighten the mounting bolts in four or five increments, working from the center of the manifold out in a criss-cross pattern.

6   Exhaust manifold - removal and installation

Note: *Before beginning, see the Warning below. Also, exhaust system fasteners are often difficult to remove because of the heating/cooling cycles they are subjected to. It's a good idea to apply penetrating oil to the exhaust manifold mounting nuts and to the exhaust manifold-to-pipe nuts or bolts and let it soak in for several minutes before attempting to remove the fasteners.*

1   Disconnect the negative battery cable.

2   Raise the vehicle and support it securely on jackstands.

3   Disconnect the exhaust pipe from the exhaust manifold.

4   Disconnect the EGR pipe from the

exhaust manifold.

5   Lower the vehicle.

6   Remove the air cleaner mounting bolts. Loosen the air cleaner clamp bolts.

7   Lift the air cleaner slightly and remove the hot air hose.

8   Remove the air-conditioning compressor adjustment brackets and relocate the compressor, if equipped, without disconnecting the refrigerant lines (see Chapter 3). **Warning:** *Do not disconnect or in any way damage the pressurized refrigerant lines. If necessary, have the system depressurized by a professional.*

9   Remove the power steering pump adjustment bracket and unbolt the pump, if equipped (see Chapter 10). Set it aside without disconnecting the power steering lines. Keep the pump level so fluid doesn't spill.

10   Remove the four mounting bolts from the manifold cover and remove the manifold cover.

11   Remove the seven mounting nuts from the exhaust manifold and remove the exhaust manifold.

12   Scrape away all traces of gasket material from the cylinder head-to-exhaust manifold surfaces. Wipe the surfaces clean with a rag soaked in lacquer thinner or acetone.

13   Check the exhaust manifold for cracks and damage. Replace it if necessary.

14   Using a straightedge and a feeler gauge, measure the cylinder head mating surface of the exhaust manifold for distortion and compare it to the Specifications. If the manifold is warped beyond the specified limit, a machine shop should be able to correct the condition with a surface grinder.

15   Installation is the reverse of removal. Be sure to use a new gasket.

16   Tighten the exhaust manifold nuts a little at a time, in sequence, starting with the inner nuts and working out. Finally, tighten the exhaust manifold nuts to the torque listed in this Chapter's Specifications.

17   If depressurized, have the air conditioning system evacuated, recharged and leak tested by the shop that depressurized it.

7   Valve cover and valve train components - removal, inspection and installation

Removal

Note: *Before beginning this procedure, see the Warning below.*

1   Disconnect the negative battery cable.

2   Remove the air cleaner assembly.

3   Disconnect the spark plug wires from the routing bracket on the valve cover and secure them out of the way.

4   Disconnect the evaporator pipe at the air injection manifold and at the engine lift bracket. **Warning:** *Do not disconnect or in any way damage the air conditioning refrigerant lines. If necessary, have the system depressurized by a professional.*

5   Remove the valve cover retaining nuts

and washers and remove the valve cover.

6   Loosen the rocker shaft bracket nuts a little at a time in sequence, beginning with the outer brackets and working toward the center.

7   Remove the retaining nuts from the rocker shaft brackets.

8   The valve train components can be disassembled by removing the spring from the rocker arm shaft and then removing the rocker arm brackets and rocker arms. To remove the valve springs, retainers and seals, see Chapter 2B, Section 8.

Inspection

9   Inspect the rocker shafts for runout. Support the shaft on V-blocks at the ends and position a dial indicator at the center of the shaft. Turn the shaft slowly and then note the amount of runout shown on the dial indicator. Replace the rocker shaft if it is not within the specified limits.

10   Use a micrometer to measure the shaft diameter at the four rocker arm locations. Replace the shaft if it is less than the specified diameter.

11   Using a telescoping gauge, measure the inside diameter of the rocker arms. Compare this measurement to the rocker shaft diameter at the corresponding rocker arm location. If the clearance exceeds the specified limits, replace the rocker shaft or rocker arms as necessary.

12   Check the valve contact area of the rocker arms for step wear and scoring. Replace the rocker arm(s) if there is considerable step wear or scoring.

Installation

Refer to illustrations 7.14 and 7.19

13   Apply liberal amounts of engine oil to the rocker shaft, rocker arms and valve stems.

14   Install the longer shaft on the exhaust valve side and the short rocker shaft on the intake side. The alignment marks on the shafts should face up and towards the front of the engine **(see illustration)**.

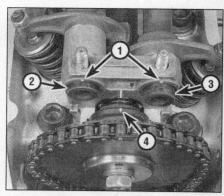

7.14 The non-interchangeable rocker shafts have alignment marks for correct installation

1   Shaft alignment marks
2   Short shaft
3   Long shaft
4   Camshaft sprocket alignment marks

7.19 When tightening the rocker shaft bracket nuts, hold the rocker arm springs in place to prevent spring damage

8.9 A seal driver or a large piece of pipe, is needed to install a new timing cover seal without removing the cover

15   Install the rocker shaft brackets and rocker arms. Make sure that the cylinder number on the upper face of the brackets points to the front of the engine.

16   Align the mark on the number one rocker shaft bracket with the marks on the intake and exhaust side rocker shafts. The rocker shaft on the exhaust side should extend past the outer face of the number one rocker shaft bracket farther than on the intake side.

17   Place the rocker shaft springs in position between the rocker shaft brackets and rocker arms.

18   Make sure that the punch marks are still aligned properly and then install the rocker shaft bracket assembly on the cylinder head studs. Align the mark on the camshaft with the mark on the number one rocker shaft bracket.

19   While holding the rocker arm springs with an adjustable wrench to prevent damage to the springs (see illustration), tighten the rocker shaft bracket nuts to the torque listed in this Chapter's Specifications.

20   Adjust the valves as described in Chapter 1.

21   The rest of installation is the reverse of removal. If depressurized, have the air conditioning system evacuated, recharged and leak tested by the shop that depressurized it.

8   Timing cover seal - replacement

Refer to illustration 8.9

1   Disconnect the negative battery cable.
2   Drain the cooling system (see Chapter 1).
3   Remove the engine fan.
4   Disconnect the upper and lower radiator hoses.
5   Remove the radiator mounting bolts and carefully remove the radiator (see Chapter 3).
6   Remove the engine drivebelts.
7   Remove the crankshaft pulley bolt and remove the pulley assembly.
8   Pry out the timing cover seal with a large screwdriver.
9   Use a seal driver or a large piece of pipe to install the new seal (see illustration).
10   Align the groove in the crankshaft pulley with the crankshaft key and install the pulley

assembly. Install the washer and crankshaft pulley bolt and tighten the bolt to the torque listed in this Chapter's Specifications.
11   The rest of installation is the reverse of removal.

9   Timing cover and chain - removal and installation

Refer to illustrations 9.6a, 9.6b, 9.16, 9.26, 9.29, 9.31 and 9.32

1   Remove the engine as described in Part F of this Chapter.
2   Remove the valve cover as described in Section 7.
3   Remove the bolt from the EGR pipe clamp at the rear of the cylinder head.
4   Remove the engine drivebelts.
5   Remove the distributor (see Chapter 5), if not already done.
6   Lock the timing chain tensioner automatic adjuster shoe in the fully retracted position by depressing the adjuster lock lever with a screwdriver (see illustrations).
7   Remove the timing sprocket-to-camshaft

9.6a To release tension on the timing chain, pivot the lock lever and push the adjuster shoe in

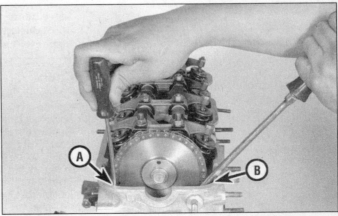

9.6b Use two screwdrivers for retracting the timing chain tensioner - pivot the tensioner lock lever (screwdriver A), pry the tensioner foot into the tensioner body (with screwdriver B), then pivot the lever back to hold the tensioner in place

9.16 You'll need a puller to remove the crankshaft timing sprocket

9.26 With the camshaft timing sprocket mark at top dead center, position the crankshaft sprocket and chain timing marks as shown

bolt and remove the sprocket and the fuel pump drive cam. Keep the sprocket on the chain damper and tensioner. Do not remove the sprocket from the chain at this time.

8   Remove the oil pan (see Section 3).

9   Remove the retaining bolt from the oil pick-up tube and unthread the pick-up tube from the oil pump.

10   Remove the crankshaft pulley (see Section 8).

11   Remove the timing cover mounting bolts and separate the timing cover from the engine.

12   Remove the cylinder head mounting bolts in a criss-cross sequence, starting with the outer bolts (see Section 11).

13   Remove the cylinder head, intake manifold and exhaust manifold as an assembly.

14   Scrape away all traces of gasket material from the timing cover and engine block sealing surfaces.

15   Inspect the timing cover for cracks, leakage and deterioration. If necessary, the seal can be pried out and a new seal installed.

16   Check the timing sprockets for wear and damage. If the timing sprocket must be replaced, a puller **(see illustration)** will be needed.

17   Check the timing chain for wear by stretching it with an approximate pull of 22 pounds. Measure the length of 40 links on one side of the chain and compare your measurement to the dimensions listed in this Chapter's Specifications. Replace the chain if the links exceed the specified length or if the chain shows signs of excessive wear.

18   Remove the mounting bolt from the timing chain tensioner and remove the tensioner. Make sure that the shoe becomes locked when the shoe is pushed in with the lock lever released.

19   Make sure that the lock releases when the shoe is pushed in. Replace the tensioner assembly if it does not operate properly or if the rack teeth show excessive wear.

20   Inspect the tensioner pin in the engine block for wear and damage. If replacement is

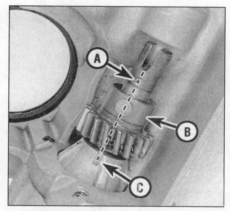

9.29 Align the marks on the oil pump pinion gear as shown when installing the timing cover

A   Center of the dowel pin
B   Punch mark
C   Alignment mark

necessary, the pin can be removed with locking pliers.

21   If a new tensioner pin is being installed, lubricate it with clean engine oil before installation. Start the pin into the block and place the chain tensioner over the pin. Place the E-clip on the pin and carefully tap the pin into the block until the clip just clears the tensioner.

22   Inspect the tensioner guide for wear and damage. Make sure that the lower oil jet is not clogged. If necessary, remove the mounting bolts and clean or replace the guides as needed.

23   If the crankshaft timing sprocket is being replaced, install the sprocket and pinion gear (groove side toward the front) on the crankshaft and align the key grooves with the crankshaft key. Drive the sprocket into position using a large section of pipe.

24   Turn the crankshaft so that the key is toward the cylinder head.

25   Reinstall the head (see Section 11).

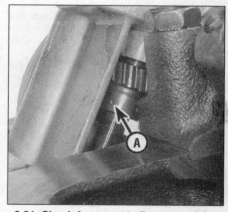

9.31 Check for correct alignment of the oil pump pinion gear by sighting between the rear of the timing cover and the engine block

A   Punch mark

26   Install the timing chain by aligning the chain mark plate with the crankshaft sprocket **(see illustration)**. Next, install the camshaft sprocket with the timing mark at the top as shown and the triangular mark on the sprocket aligned with the marked plate on the chain.

27   Install the timing chain tensioner. Release the lock by depressing the tensioner shoe by hand and then make sure that the chain is properly tensioned.

28   Use a new gasket when installing the timing cover.

29   Align the punch mark on the oil pump drive gear with the oil filter side of the cover. Next, align the center of the dowel pin with the alignment mark on the oil pump case **(see illustration)**.

30   Install the timing cover by engaging the pinion gear with the oil pump drive gear in the crankshaft.

31   Make sure that the punch mark on the oil pump drive gear can be viewed through the clearance area between the front cover and the engine block **(see illustration)**.

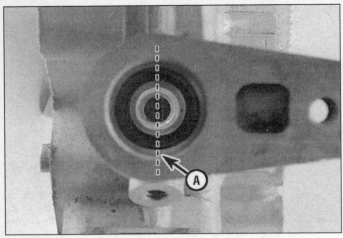

9.32 The centerline of the oil pump shaft (A) should be parallel to the front face of the engine block

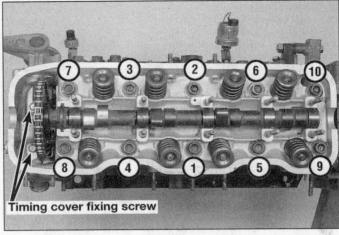

Timing cover fixing screw

11.23 Cylinder head bolt tightening sequence (1.9L engine)

32   Check to be sure that the slot at the end of the oil pump shaft is parallel to the face of the engine block and offset forward **(see illustration)**.

33   Install the timing cover bolts and tighten them to the torque listed in this Chapter's Specifications.

34   The rest of the installation procedure is the reverse of removal. Check the ignition timing after the installation is complete. If depressurized, have the air conditioning system evacuated, recharged and leak tested by the shop that depressurized it.

10   Camshaft - removal and installation

1   Remove the valve cover (see Section 7).

2   Remove the number 4 spark plug.

3   Place your finger over the spark plug hole while turning the crankshaft with a wrench on the pulley bolt at the front of the engine.

4   When you feel compression, continue turning the crankshaft slowly until the timing mark on the crankshaft pulley is aligned with the 0 of the engine timing indicator on the front cover.

5   Remove the distributor (see Chapter 5). Do not rotate the crankshaft again until the distributor has been reinstalled.

6   Remove the fuel pump mounting bolts and remove the fuel pump.

7   Remove the rocker arm, shaft and bracket assembly (see Section 7).

8   Lock the automatic adjuster in the fully retracted position and disconnect the camshaft sprocket from the camshaft (see Steps 13 and 14 in Section 11.)

9   Remove the camshaft.

10   Refer to Part F of this Chapter for camshaft inspection procedures.

11   Apply liberal amounts of clean engine oil to the camshaft and cylinder head journals before installation.

12   Install the camshaft.

13   Install the rocker arm, shaft and bracket assembly (see Section 7).

14   Make sure that the mark on the number one rocker shaft bracket aligns with the mark on the camshaft and that the timing mark on the crankshaft pulley aligns with the top dead center mark on the front cover.

15   While keeping the chain and sprocket together, attach the timing sprocket to the camshaft by aligning it with the pin on the camshaft.

16   Install the fuel pump drive cam, washer and sprocket bolt.

17   Remove the half-moon seal at the front of the cylinder head and tighten the sprocket bolt to the torque listed in this Chapter's Specifications. Replace the half-moon seal in the cylinder head.

18   Install the distributor.

19   Release the lock on the timing chain tensioner by depressing the shoe with a screwdriver. Make sure that the timing chain is at the proper tension.

20   Check to be sure that the rotor and mark on the distributor housing line up when the number four cylinder is in the firing position.

21   Install the distributor cap. Install the valve cover (see Section 7).

11   Cylinder head - removal and installation

Refer to illustration 11.23

Note: *Before beginning, see the* **Warning** *below.*

1   Remove the valve cover (see Section 7).

2   Remove the bolt from the EGR pipe clamp at the rear of the cylinder head.

3   Raise the vehicle and support it securely on jackstands.

4   Disconnect the exhaust pipe at the exhaust manifold.

5   Lower the vehicle.

6   Drain the cooling system, including the

engine block (see Chapter 1).

7   Disconnect the heater hoses at the intake manifold and at the front of the cylinder head.

8   Unbolt the air-conditioning compressor without disconnecting the refrigerant lines (see Chapter 3). **Warning:** *Do not disconnect or in any way damage the refrigerant lines. If necessary, have the system depressurized by a professional.* Also unbolt the power steering pump and brackets, if equipped (see Chapter 10) and set the pump aside, keeping it level so fluid doesn't spill. Do not disconnect the power steering lines.

9   Disconnect the accelerator linkage and fuel line at the carburetor (see Chapter 4).

10   Disconnect all electrical wires, spark plug wires and vacuum lines from the cylinder head.

11   Remove the distributor (see Chapter 5).

12   Remove the fuel pump mounting bolts and remove the fuel pump.

13   Lock the shoe on the automatic adjuster in the fully retracted position by depressing the lock lever with a screwdriver and prying the tensioner foot back **(see illustrations 9.6a and 9.6b)**.

14   Remove the camshaft sprocket bolt and remove the sprocket and fuel pump drive cam from the camshaft. Keep the sprocket on the chain damper and tensioner - DO NOT remove the sprocket from the chain. **Caution:** *Make sure the chain is kept tight (suspending the camshaft sprocket from a piece of rope may help) so it does not fall off the crankshaft sprocket, and do not disturb the crankshaft while the camshaft sprocket is disconnected.*

15   Disconnect the AIR hose and check valve at the air injection manifold.

16   Remove the upper timing cover bolts which thread into the cylinder head.

17   Remove the cylinder head mounting bolts in a criss-cross sequence, starting with the outer bolts.

18   With the aid of an assistant, remove the cylinder head, intake manifold and exhaust

12.13 You can pry out and replace the rear main oil seal (2) without removing the seal retainer (1)

manifold as an assembly.

19   Scrape away all traces of gasket material from the cylinder head and engine block mating surfaces. Cylinder head inspection procedures can be found in Part F of this Chapter.

20   Before installing the cylinder head, make sure that the mounting bolt threads, engine block threads and both gasket surfaces are clean and free of any foreign matter.

21   Install a new gasket over the dowel pin ("top" side up).

22   With the aid of an assistant, carefully install the cylinder head assembly.

23   Apply oil to the threaded portion of the cylinder head bolts and install the bolts. Tighten the cylinder head bolts a little at a time in the sequence shown **(see illustration)** until you reach the torque listed in this Chapter's Specifications.

24   The rest of the installation procedure is the reverse of removal. Refer to Section 9 for timing chain installation procedures.

25   If depressurized, have the air conditioning system evacuated, recharged and leak tested by the shop that depressurized it.

12   Flywheel/driveplate and rear main oil seal - replacement

Flywheel/driveplate removal and installation

Removal

1   Remove the starter motor mounting bolts and separate the starter motor from the engine. Lay the starter motor to one side or wire the motor to a frame member.

2   Remove the transmission (see Chapter 7).

3   On models with a manual transmission, remove the clutch cover and pressure plate assembly (see Chapter 8).

4   Use a center-punch to make alignment marks on the flywheel/driveplate and crankshaft to ensure correct alignment during reinstallation.

5   Remove the bolts that secure the flywheel/driveplate to the crankshaft. If the crankshaft turns, wedge a screwdriver through the starter opening to jam the flywheel.

6   Remove the flywheel/driveplate from the crankshaft. Since the flywheel is fairly heavy, be sure to support it while removing the last bolt.

7   Clean the flywheel to remove grease and oil. Inspect the surface for cracks, rivet grooves, burned areas and score marks. Light scoring can be removed with emery cloth. Check for cracked and broken ring gear teeth. Lay the flywheel on a flat surface and use a straightedge to check for warpage.

8   Clean and inspect the mating surfaces of the flywheel/driveplate and the crankshaft. If the rear main oil seal is leaking, replace it before reinstalling the flywheel/driveplate (see below).

Installation

9   Position the flywheel/driveplate against the crankshaft. Be sure to align the marks made during removal. Note that some engines have an alignment dowel or staggered bolt holes to ensure correct installation. Before installing the bolts, apply thread locking compound to the threads.

10   Wedge a screwdriver through the starter motor opening to keep the flywheel/driveplate from turning as you tighten the bolts to the torque listed in this Chapter's Specifications.

11   The remainder of installation is the reverse of the removal procedure.

Oil seal replacement

Refer to illustration 12.13

12   Remove the flywheel or driveplate (see above).

13   On models with an automatic transmission, remove the driveplate cover. Using a large screwdriver, carefully pry the old seal out of the retainer **(see illustration)**. Be very careful not to nick or scratch the crankshaft or seal bore in the engine or the new seal will leak.

14   Before installing the replacement seal, fill the groove between the seal lips with grease. Also, lubricate the seal lips with clean engine oil.

15   Position the seal in the retainer and drive it into place using a section of large pipe and a hammer. The pipe should be slightly smaller in diameter than the outside diameter of the seal.

16   The rest of the installation procedure is the reverse of removal.

2A

Notes

Chapter 2 Part B
2.0L four-cylinder engine

Contents

	Section			Section
Air filter replacement... See Chapter 1		General information..		1
Camshaft - removal and installation	15	Hydraulic lifters - removal, inspection and installation		11
Check engine light.. See Chapter 6		Intake manifold - removal and installation		5
Compression check.. See Chapter 1		Oil pan - removal and installation..		3
Crankshaft pulley, hub and front oil seal - removal		Oil pump - removal, inspection and installation............................		4
and installation...	12	Spark plug replacement .... See Chapter 1		
Cylinder head - removal and installation.............................	10	Timing chain and sprockets - inspection, removal		
Drivebelt check and adjustment..................... See Chapter 1		and installation...		14
Engine mounts - check and replacement	2	Timing chain cover - removal and installation.............................		13
Engine oil and filter change .... See Chapter 1		Top Dead Center (TDC) for number 1		
Engine oil level check .... See Chapter 1		piston - locating... See Chapter 2C		
Engine overhaul - general information.......................... See Chapter 2F		Valve cover - removal and installation..		7
Engine removal - methods and precautions .... See Chapter 2F		Valve lash - adjustment...		9
Exhaust manifold - removal and installation	6	Valve train components - replacement (cylinder head installed) ...		8
Flywheel/driveplate and rear main bearing oil seal - removal		Water pump - removal and installation .... See Chapter 3		
and installation...	16			

Specifications

General

Cylinder numbers (front-to-rear)...	1-2-3-4
Firing order	1-3-4-2

Torque specifications

	Ft-lbs (unless otherwise indicated)
Oil pan bolts..	72 in-lbs
Oil screen support bolt	37
Oil pump-to-block bolts	22
Oil pump cover bolts..	120 in-lbs
Crankshaft pulley hub bolts...	160
Flywheel/driveplate-to-crankshaft bolts	44
Intake manifold-to-cylinder head bolts/nuts..............................	29
Exhaust manifold-to-cylinder head bolts....................................	44
Timing chain cover-to-block bolts	
Long bolts	15 to 22
Short bolts..	72 to 108 in-lbs
Cylinder head bolts (see illustration 10.29)	85
Valve cover nuts	120 in-lbs
Valve cover bolts	36 in-lbs
Camshaft thrust plate-to-block bolts	84 in-lbs

**Cylinder location and
distributor rotation**

*The blackened terminal shown
on the distributor cap indicates
the Number One spark plug
wire position*

1   General information

The 2.0L engine utilizes a cast iron crankshaft supported by five main bearings, with the number four bearing used as the thrust bearing. Hydraulic lifters and hollow pushrods activate rocker arms which operate on stud-mounted pivots.

The Sections in this Part of Chapter 2 are devoted to "in-vehicle" repair procedures for the 2.0 liter four-cylinder engine. All information concerning engine block and cylinder head servicing can be found in Part F of this Chapter.

The repair procedures included in this Part are based on the assumption that the engine is still installed in the vehicle. Therefore, if this information is being used during a complete overhaul - with the engine already out of the vehicle and on a stand - many of the steps included here will not apply.

The Specifications included in this Part of Chapter 2 apply only to the engine and procedures found here. For Specifications regarding engines other than the 2.0 liter four-cylinder, see Part A, C, D, etc. Part F of this Chapter contains the Specifications necessary for engine block and cylinder head rebuilding.

2   Engine mounts - check and replacement

Follow the procedure in Chapter 2A, note that distributor or EGR component damage can result from raising the engine higher than necessary to replace a mount. Check for interference between the rear of the engine and the cowl panel while raising the engine.

3   Oil pan - removal and installation

2WD models

Removal

1   Disconnect the negative battery cable.
2   Remove the engine (see Chapter 2, Part F).
3   Remove the oil pan mounting bolts and separate the oil pan from the engine. If the pan sticks to the engine block, tap the pan with a rubber mallet or a block of wood and a hammer to break the gasket seal.

Installation

4   Before installation, clean the oil pan sealing surfaces on the engine block and oil pan with a scraper, then wipe them clean with a rag soaked in lacquer thinner or acetone. Inspect the gasket sealing surfaces on the pan for distortion. Repair with a wood block and hammer if necessary.
5   Before installing the oil pan apply a thin coat of RTV-type sealant to both ends of the new rear oil pan seal. Do not let the sealant extend beyond the tabs of the seal. Install the

seal firmly into the rear main bearing cap.
6   Apply a uniform bead of RTV-type sealant (about 1/8-inch diameter) to the oil pan side rails. The bead should run between the bolt holes and to the inside edge of each bolt hole. Do not apply sealant to the rear oil pan seal mating surface.
7   Apply a thin bead of RTV-type sealant to the timing cover mating surface on the oil pan. Make sure that the sealant meets the beads on the oil pan side rails.
8   Immediately attach the oil pan to the engine block, taking care not to smear the sealant.
9   Tighten the mounting bolts, working from the center of the pan out, to the torque listed in this Chapter's Specifications.

4WD models

Removal

10   Disconnect the negative battery cable.
11   Remove the starter front brace bolt.
12   Support the engine with a hoist. Remove the motor mount through bolts.
13   Raise the vehicle, support it on jackstands, and remove the front splash shield.
14   Remove the brake and fuel line clip retaining bolts.
15   Remove the crossmember bolts, and, rotating the crossmember around the lines, lower it from beneath the truck.
16   Drain the engine oil (see Chapter 1).
17   Remove the starter mounting bolts.
18   Disconnect the steering damper (if equipped) at the frame.
19   Scribe the idler arm location, then disconnect the idler arm and steering gear from the frame (see Chapter 10).
20   Disconnect the front axle at the frame (see Chapter 10).
21   Disconnect the front driveshaft at the front differential (see Chapter 8).
22   Slide the differential forward.
23   Remove the oil pan bolts and raise the engine just enough to remove the pan. If the pan sticks to the engine block, tap the pan with a rubber mallet or a block of wood and a hammer to break the gasket seal.

Installation

24   Before installation clean the oil pan sealing surfaces on the engine block and oil pan with a scraper, then wipe them clean with a rag soaked in lacquer thinner or acetone. Inspect the gasket sealing surfaces on the pan for distortion. Repair with a wood block and hammer if necessary.
25   Apply a thin coat of RTV-type sealant to both ends of the new rear oil pan seal. Do not let the sealant extend beyond the tabs of the seal. Install the seal firmly into the rear main bearing cap.
26   Apply a uniform bead of RTV-type sealant (about 1/8-inch diameter) to the oil pan side rails. The bead should run between the bolt holes and to the inside edge of each bolt hole. Do not apply sealant to the rear oil pan seal mating surface.
27   Apply a thin bead of RTV-type sealant to

the timing cover mating surface on the oil pan. Make sure that the sealant meets the beads on the oil pan side rails.
28   Immediately attach the oil pan to the engine block, taking care not to smear the sealant.
29   Tighten the mounting bolts, working from the center of the pan out, to the torque listed in this Chapter's Specifications.
30   Reverse the removal procedures for the remainder of the installation.

4   Oil pump - removal, inspection and installation

Removal

1   Remove the oil pan (see Section 3).
2   Remove the oil pump mounting bolt.
3   Remove the pump and extension shaft.

Inspection

4   To disassemble the pump for inspection, first remove the cover attaching bolts and the cover. Mark the gear teeth so that the gears can be reassembled with the same teeth indexing.
5   Remove the idler gear, drive gear and shaft from the pump body.
6   Remove the pressure regulator valve retaining pin.
7   Remove the pressure regulator spring and valve.
8   If the pick-up screen and pipe assembly need replacing, it is possible to remove the pipe and press the replacement in (with sealant). However, it is recommended that anyone without experience in this operation consult a GM dealer before proceeding.
9   Clean all parts with solvent. Allow to air dry or, if available, use compressed air.
10   Inspect the pump body and cover for cracks and signs of excessive wear.
11   Inspect the pump gears for damage or excessive wear.
12   If the pump gears or body are damaged and worn, the entire oil pump assembly will have to be replaced. The pump gears and body are not available separately. **Note:** *Because of the difficulty in accessing the oil pump, and because a faulty oil pump can quickly ruin an otherwise good engine, we recommend the oil pump be routinely replaced whenever it is removed.*
13   Inspect the drive gear shaft and the pressure regulator valve for any looseness where they fit into the oil pump body.
14   Finally, before reassembling the oil pump, check to make sure that the oil pump shaft retainer is not split. Replace it if necessary.
15   Install the pressure regulator valve, spring and retaining pin.
16   Install the drive gear and shaft in the oil pump body.
17   Install the idler gear in the pump body. Use the alignment marks to position the gears as they were before disassembly.
18   Install a new cover gasket.

19 Install the pump cover and tube brace and tighten the bolts to the torque listed in this Chapter's Specifications.

20 Turn the pump drive shaft by hand to make sure the components are meshing smoothly.

Installation

21 Attach the pump and extension shaft with retainer to the rear main bearing cap. While aligning the pump with the two dowel pins at the bottom of the main bearing cap, align the top end of the hexagon extension shaft with the hexagon lower end of the distributor drive gear.

22 Install the pump mounting bolt and tighten it to the torque listed in this Chapter's Specifications.

23 Install the oil pan (see Section 3).

5 Intake manifold - removal and installation

Warning: *Allow the engine to cool completely before following this procedure.*

1 Disconnect the negative battery cable.

2 Remove the air cleaner assembly, tagging each hose to be disconnected with a piece of numbered tape to simplify reinstallation.

3 Remove the distributor cap (see Chapter 1).

4 Raise the vehicle and support it securely on jackstands.

5 Remove the middle right-hand bellhousing bolt from the engine block. Move the wiring harness out of the way.

6 Remove the distributor hold-down nut and clamp. Mark the distributors's relation to the engine before removing the nut so it can be returned to the same position if it's accidentally disturbed (see Chapter 5).

7 Disconnect the primary wires at the coil.

8 Remove the fuel pump mounting bolts (see Chapter 4). It is not necessary to disconnect the fuel line; the fuel pump can hang in place.

9 Lower the vehicle.

10 Disconnect the fuel delivery line, accelerator cable and necessary wires and vacuum hoses (see Chapter 4).

11 Remove the carburetor (see Chapter 4).

12 Drain the cooling system (see Chapter 1).

13 Disconnect the fuel vapor harness pipes from the cylinder head.

14 Remove the vacuum pipe bolt from the rear of the cylinder head and disconnect the adjacent vacuum hoses.

15 Disconnect the heater hose and bypass hose from the intake manifold.

16 Disconnect the remaining hoses and wires from the intake manifold.

17 Remove the retaining nuts and bolts from the intake manifold.

18 Remove the intake manifold and gasket. Scrape away all traces of gasket material from the intake manifold mating surfaces on the manifold and cylinder head. Wipe the sur- faces clean with a rag soaked in lacquer thinner or acetone.

19 Installation is the reverse of removal. Be sure to use a new gasket. Tighten the retaining nuts/bolts, a little at a time, to the torque listed in this Chapter's Specifications.

6 Exhaust manifold - removal and installation

Warning: *Allow the engine to cool completely before following this procedure.*
Note: *The exhaust manifold-to-cylinder head bolts and the manifold-to-exhaust pipe bolts will be easier to remove if you first apply penetrating oil to their threads and let it soak in for several minutes.*

1 Disconnect the negative battery cable.

2 Remove the air cleaner assembly, tagging each hose to be disconnected with a piece of numbered tape to simplify reinstallation.

3 Raise the vehicle and support it securely on jackstands.

4 Remove the exhaust pipe mounting bolts from the manifold and disconnect the exhaust pipe from the manifold.

5 Remove the AIR hose, AIR pipe bracket bolt and dipstick tube bracket.

6 Remove the fuel vapor harness pipes from the left and right side of the engine.

7 Remove the exhaust manifold mounting bolts and remove the exhaust manifold.

8 Inspect the exhaust manifold for cracks. If a replacement exhaust manifold is going to be installed, remove the AIR injection manifold and exhaust manifold seal. Transfer the parts to the new manifold.

9 Scrape away all traces of gasket material from the exhaust manifold mating surfaces on the exhaust manifold and cylinder head. Wipe the surfaces clean with a rag soaked in lacquer thinner or acetone.

10 Clean all manifold-related threads before installation. A wire brush can be used on the manifold mounting bolts while a tap works well when cleaning the cylinder head bolt holes.

11 Installation is the reverse of removal. Tighten all bolts to the torque listed in this Chapter's Specifications.

7 Valve cover - removal and installation

1 Remove the air cleaner assembly, tagging each hose to be disconnected with a piece of numbered tape to simplify installation.

2 Disconnect the throttle cable, making careful note of the exact locations of the cable components and hardware to ensure correct reinstallation (see Chapter 4).

3 Disconnect the fuel vapor hoses from the harness pipes on both sides of the engine. Remove the retaining bolts from the harness pipes and remove the harness pipes.

4 Remove the valve cover bolts.

5 Remove the valve cover. **Note:** *If the cover sticks to the cylinder head, use a block of wood and a hammer to dislodge it. If the cover still will not come loose, pry on it carefully, but do not distort the sealing flange surface.*

6 Prior to installation of the cover, clean all dirt, oil and old gasket material from the sealing surfaces of the cover and cylinder head with a scraper and degreaser. Check the cover mounting flange for distortion, particularly around the bolt holes. Straighten the flange, if necessary, with a hammer and block of wood.

7 Apply a continuous 1/8-inch (5 mm) diameter bead of RTV-type sealant to the sealing flange of the cover. Be sure to apply the sealant to the edge of the cover inside of the bolt holes.

8 Place the valve cover on the cylinder head while the sealant is still wet and install the mounting bolts. Tighten the bolts a little at a time to the torque listed in this Chapter's Specifications.

9 Complete the installation by reversing the removal procedure.

8 Valve train components - replacement (cylinder head installed)

Refer to illustration 8.6
Note: *If you're working on a 1.9L engine, remove the rocker arms and shafts (see Section 7 in Chapter 2A) and begin this procedure at* Step 3.

1 Remove the valve cover (see Section 7).

2 If only the pushrod is to be replaced, loosen the rocker arm nut enough to allow the rocker arm to be rotated away from the pushrod. Pull the pushrod out of the hole in the cylinder head. If the rocker arm is to be removed, remove the rocker arm nut and pivot and lift off the rocker arm.

3 If the valve spring is to be removed, remove the spark plug from the affected cylinder. Also remove both pushrods for the cylinder being worked on.

4 There are two methods that will allow the valve to remain in place while the valve spring is removed. If you have access to compressed air, install an air hose adapter (available at many auto parts stores, but the screw-in adapter for many compression gauges also works) in the spark plug hole. When air pressure is applied to the adapter, the valves will be held in place by the pressure. **Warning:** *When applying air pressure, stay away from engine components that normally move when the engine is in operation - the piston will be forced to the bottom of its stroke by the air pressure, rotating the crankshaft.*

5 If you do not have access to compressed air, bring the piston of the affected cylinder to a point approximately 45-degrees before Top Dead Center (TDC) on the com-

pression stroke (see Chapter 2C). Feed a long piece of 1/4-inch nylon cord in through the spark plug hole until it fills the combustion chamber. Be sure to leave the end of the cord hanging out of the spark plug hole so it can be removed easily. Rotate the crankshaft with a wrench (in the normal direction of rotation) until slight resistance is felt.

6   Use a valve spring compressor to compress the spring. Remove the keepers with small needle-nose pliers or a magnet **(see illustration)**. **Note:** *A couple of different types of tools are available for compressing the valve springs with the head in place. One type, shown here, grips the lower spring coils and presses on the retainer as the knob is turned, while the other type utilizes the rocker arm stud and nut for leverage (this last type cannot be used on the 1.9L engine). Both types work very well, although the lever type is usually less expensive.*

7   Remove the retainer, cup shield, O-ring seal, spring, spring damper (if so equipped) and valve stem oil seal (if so equipped).

8   Inspection procedures for valve train components are covered in Section 10 of this Chapter (2.0L engines) or Section 7 of Chapter 2A (1.9L engine) and in Chapter 2, Part F.

9   Installation of the valve train components is the reverse of the removal procedure. Always use new valve stem oil seals whenever the spring keepers have been disturbed. On 2.0L engines, prior to installing the rocker arms, coat the bearing surfaces of the arms and rocker arm pivots with moly-based grease or engine assembly lube. On both engines, be sure to adjust the valve lash (see Section 9 [2.0L engine] or Chapter 1 [1.9L engine]).

---

9   Valve lash - adjustment

Note: *The 2.0L engine does not require periodic lash adjustment; it should only be required after valve train disassembly or as an attempt to silence tapping noises coming from the valve cover area (see Section 11 to isolate the noise). If adjustment does not silence the tapping, the problem is most likely a bad lifter (see Section 11).*

1   Disconnect the cable from the negative battery terminal.

2   If the valve cover is still on the engine, remove it (see Section 7).

3   If the valve train components have been serviced just prior to this procedure, make sure that the components are completely reassembled.

4   Rotate the crankshaft until the number one piston is at Top Dead Center (TDC) on the compression stroke (see Chapter 2C for the preferred method). Since the valve cover is off, another method of locating TDC is possible. Place your fingers on the number one cylinder rocker arms as the timing marks line up at the crankshaft pulley. If the rocker arms are not moving, the number one piston is at TDC. If they move as the timing marks line

8.6 Once the spring is compressed, the keepers can be removed with a small magnet or needle-nose pliers (a magnet is preferred to prevent dropping the keepers)

up, the number four piston is at TDC.

5   Back off the rocker arm nut until play is felt at the pushrod, then turn it back in just until all play is removed. This can be determined by rotating the pushrod while tightening the nut. Just when drag is felt at the pushrod, all lash has been removed. Now tighten the nut an additional 1-1/2 turns.

6   Adjust the number one and two cylinder intake valves and the number one and three cylinder exhaust valves with the crankshaft in this position, using the method just described.

7   Rotate the crankshaft until the number four piston is at TDC on the compression stroke (one complete revolution) and adjust the number three and four cylinder intake valves and the number two and four cylinder exhaust valves.

8   Install the valve covers (see Section 7).

---

10   Cylinder head - removal and installation

Warning: *Allow the engine to cool to room temperature before following this procedure.*

Removal

1   Remove the intake manifold (see Section 5).

2   Remove the exhaust manifold (see Section 6).

3   Remove the bolts that secure the alternator bracket to the cylinder head.

4   If so equipped, unbolt the air conditioning compressor and swing it out of the way for clearance (see Chapter 3). **Caution:** *Do not disconnect any of the air conditioning lines unless the system has been depressurized by a dealer or repair shop, because personal injury may occur. Disconnection of the lines should not be necessary in this case.*

5   Disconnect all electrical and vacuum lines from the cylinder head. Be sure to label the lines to simplify reinstallation.

6   Remove the upper radiator hose.

7   Remove the heater hoses.

8   Disconnect the spark plug wires and remove the spark plugs (see Chapter 1). Be sure to label the plug wires to simplify reinstallation.

9   Remove the distributor (see Chapter 5).

10   Remove the valve cover (see Section 7).

11   When disassembling the valve mechanisms, keep all of the components separate so they can be reinstalled in their original positions. A cardboard box or rack, numbered to correspond to the engine cylinders, can be used for this purpose.

12   Remove each of the rocker arm nuts and separate the rocker arms and pivots from the cylinder head.

13   Remove the pushrods.

14   Remove the upper fan shroud.

15   Remove the four mounting bolts from the fan and remove the fan.

16   Remove the air diverter valve from its mounting bracket.

17   Remove the air pump mounting bolts and remove the pump. Remove the upper air pump bracket.

18   Disconnect and plug the fuel line at the fuel pump.

19   Loosen each of the cylinder head mounting bolts one turn at a time until they can be removed. Note the length and position of each bolt to ensure correct reinstallation.

20   Lift the head off of the engine. If it is stuck to the engine block, do not attempt to pry it free, as you could damage the sealing surfaces. Instead, use a hammer and block of wood to tap the head and break the gasket seal. Place the head on a block of wood to prevent damage to the gasket surface.

21   Remove the cylinder head gasket.

22   Refer to Chapter 2, Part F for cylinder head disassembly and valve service procedures.

Installation

Refer to illustration 10.29

23   If a new cylinder head is being installed, transfer all external parts from the old cylinder head to the new one.

24   If not already done, use a scraper to thoroughly clean the gasket surfaces on the cylinder head and the engine block. Do not gouge or otherwise damage the gasket surfaces. Wipe the surfaces clean with a rag soaked in lacquer thinner or acetone.

25   To get the proper torque readings, the threads of the head bolts must be clean. This also applies to the threaded holes in the engine block. Run a tap through the holes to ensure that they are clean.

26   Place the gasket in position over the engine block dowel pins. Many gaskets are marked to indicate which side goes up. Be sure the holes in the gasket line up with the holes in the engine block and head.

27   Carefully lower the cylinder head onto the engine, over the dowel pins and the gasket.

28 Coat the threads of each cylinder head bolt and the point at which the head and the bolt meet with a sealing compound and install the bolts finger tight. Do not tighten any of the bolts at this time.

29 Tighten each of the bolts a little at a time in the sequence shown (see illustration). Continue tightening in this sequence until the bolts are tightened to the torque listed in this Chapter's Specifications. As a final check, work around the head in a front-to-rear sequence to make sure none of the bolts have been left out of the sequence.

30 The remaining installation steps are the reverse of removal.

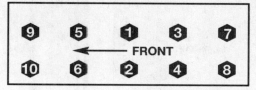

10.29 The cylinder head mounting bolts must be tightened in the sequence shown

24070-2b-10.29 HAYNES

11 Hydraulic lifters - removal, inspection and installation

1 A noisy valve lifter can be isolated when the engine is idling. Place a length of hose or tubing near the position of each valve while listening at the other end of the tube. Another method is to remove the valve cover and, with the engine idling, place a finger on each of the valve spring retainers, one at a time. When you find the noisy lifter, it will be evident from the shock felt at the retainer as the valve seats.

2 Common causes of noisy valve lifters are incorrect valve lash adjustment (see Section 9) or a piece of dirt trapped between the plunger and the lifter body. If adjustment fails to cure the problem, proceed as follows.

3 Remove the valve cover (see Section 7).

4 Loosen the rocker arm nut and rotate the rocker arm away from the pushrod.

5 Remove the pushrod.

6 To remove the lifter, a special hydraulic lifter removal tool should be used. These are commonly available at auto parts stores or automotive tool and equipment suppliers. If such a tool is not available, you may try removing the lifters with a scribe with a bent end - position the point of the scribe under the wire lifter retainer. A magnet may also work.

7 The lifters should be kept separate for reinstallation in their original positions. Inspect the lifters as described in Chapter 2F before deciding whether or not to disassemble and repair them.

8 To disassemble a valve lifter, hold the plunger down with a pushrod and then extract the retainer spring with a small screwdriver.

9 Remove the pushrod seat and the metering valve.

10 Remove the plunger, ball check valve and plunger spring. Remove the ball check valve and spring by prying them out with a small screwdriver.

11 Clean the lifter components with solvent and dry them with compressed air. Examine the internal components for wear and check the ball carefully for flat spots.

12 If the lifters are worn, they must be replaced with new ones and the camshaft

must be replaced as well (see Chapter 2, Part F). If the lifters were contaminated with dirt, they can be reinstalled - they may operate normally.

13 Reassembly should be done in the following manner:
   a) Place the ball check valve on the small hole in the bottom of the plunger.
   b) Insert the ball check spring into the seat in the valve retainer and place the retainer over the ball so that the spring rests on the ball. Using a small screwdriver, carefully press the retainer into position in the plunger
   c) Place the plunger spring over the ball retainer, invert the lifter body and slide it over the spring and plunger. Make sure the oil holes in the body and plunger line up.
   d) Fill the assembly with 10-weight oil. Place the metering valve and pushrod seat in position, press down on the seat and install the retainer spring.

14 When installing the lifters, make sure they are replaced in their original bores and coat them with moly-based grease or engine assembly lube.

15 The remaining installation steps are the reverse of removal.

12 Crankshaft pulley, hub and front oil seal - removal and installation

Refer to illustration 12.5

1 Remove the cable from the negative battery terminal.

2 Loosen the accessory drivebelt tension adjusting bolts, as necessary, and remove the drivebelts. Tag each belt as it is removed

to simplify reinstallation.

3 With the parking brake applied and the shifter in Park (automatic) or in gear (manual) to prevent the engine from turning over, remove the crank pulley bolts. A breaker bar will probably be necessary, since the bolts are very tight.

4 Mark the position of the pulley in relation to the hub. Remove the bolts and separate the pulley from the hub.

5 Remove the hub center bolt, then, using a puller, remove the hub from the crankshaft (see illustration).

6 Carefully pry the oil seal out of the front cover with a large screwdriver. Be careful not to distort the cover.

7 Install the new seal with the helical lip toward the rear of the engine. Drive the seal into place using a seal installation tool or a large socket. If there is enough room, a block of wood and hammer can also be used.

8 Apply a thin layer of clean multi-purpose grease to the seal contact surface of the hub.

9 Position the pulley hub on the crankshaft and slide it through the seal until it bottoms against the crankshaft gear. Note that the slot in the hub must be aligned with the Woodruff key in the end of the crankshaft. The hub-to-crankshaft bolt can be used to press the hub into position.

10 Install the crank pulley on the hub, noting the alignment marks made during removal. The pulley-to-hub bolts should be coated with a thread locking compound whenever they are removed and installed.

11 Tighten the hub-to-crankshaft and pulley-to-hub bolts to the torque listed in this Chapter's Specifications.

12 The remaining installation steps are the reverse of removal. Tighten the drivebelts to the proper tension (see Chapter 1).

2B

12.5 To remove the crankshaft pulley hub, you'll need a puller like this

14.2 The timing marks on the crankshaft and camshaft sprockets must be up as shown before removing the timing chain and sprockets

16.5 Carefully pry the rear main oil seal out of the block with a small screwdriver - make sure you don't nick or gouge the seal bore or damage the crankshaft

13 Timing chain cover - removal and installation

1   Remove the crankshaft pulley and hub (see Section 12).
2   Remove the water pump (see Chapter 3).
3   Remove the oil pan-to-timing gear cover bolts.
4   Using a scraper and degreaser, remove all dirt and old gasket material from the sealing surfaces of the timing gear cover, engine block and oil pan.
5   Replace the front oil seal by carefully prying it out of the timing gear cover with a large screwdriver. Do not distort the cover.
6   Install the new seal with the helical lip towards the inside of the cover. Drive the seal into place using a seal installation tool or a large socket and hammer. A block of wood will also work.
7   Apply a thin (2 mm) bead of RTV sealant to the timing gear cover-to-engine block mating surface.
8   Apply a slightly thicker (3 mm) bead of RTV sealant to the oil pan mating surface of the timing cover.
9   Insert the crankshaft hub through the cover seal and place the cover in position on the block, sliding the hub onto the nose of the crankshaft.
10   Install the oil pan-to-cover bolts and partially tighten them.
11   Install the bolts that secure the cover to the block, then tighten all of the mounting bolts, including the pan bolts, to the correct torque values listed this Chapter's Specifications.
12   Complete installation by reversing the removal procedure.

14 Timing chain and sprockets - inspection, removal and installation

Refer to illustration 14.2
1   Remove the timing chain cover (see

Section 13).
2   Align the marks on the camshaft and crankshaft sprockets **(see illustration)**. Do not attempt to remove any of the timing chain components until these marks are properly aligned.
3   Remove the chain tensioner and damper.
4   Remove the camshaft sprocket center bolt and lift off the cam sprocket and chain.
5   Inspect the camshaft and crankshaft sprockets, timing chain and chain tensioner for excessive or unusual wear. Failure to replace worn components can result in erratic engine performance, loss of power and decreased gas mileage. If any one component requires replacement all related components, including both sprockets and the chain, must be replaced.
6   A special puller is required to remove the crankshaft sprocket from the crankshaft should replacement of the timing chain assembly be required.
7   Replacement of the camshaft and crankshaft sprockets and timing chain is the reverse of removal. Make sure the timing marks on the camshaft and crankshaft sprockets line up and coat the thrust face of the camshaft sprocket with moly-base lubricant or assembly lube.
8   Before reinstalling the chain tensioner, the spring loading unit must be "cocked". After compressing the spring, a cotterkey or nail is inserted through the small hole in the tensioner provided for the purpose, holding the spring compressed until the tensioner unit is installed. After bolting the tensioner in place remove the pin, releasing the spring.
9   Lubricate the chain with engine oil and reinstall the timing chain cover as previously outlined.

15 Camshaft - removal and installation

1   Remove the cable from the negative battery terminal.

2   Drain the coolant from the radiator (see Chapter 1).
3   Remove the radiator (see Chapter 3).
4   If equipped with air conditioning, remove the condenser (see Chapter 3). **Caution:** *The air conditioning system must be discharged by an air conditioning system technician before the condenser can be removed. Under no circumstances should this be attempted by the home mechanic, as personal injury may result.*
5   Remove the water pump (see Chapter 3).
6   Mark the distributor for proper alignment before removal (see Chapter 5).
7   Remove the fuel pump (see Chapter 4).
8   Remove the distributor hold-down nut and clamp.
9   Remove the distributor.
10   Remove the rocker arms and pushrods (see Section 8).
11   Remove the rocker arm studs and pushrod guide plates.
12   Remove the lifters (see Section 11).
13   Remove the timing cover and timing chain (see Sections 13 and 14).
14   Remove the camshaft thrust plate.
15   Carefully support the camshaft (use both hands) and slide it out of the block, being careful that none of the lobes nick or scratch the camshaft bearings. A long bolt can be threaded into the end of the camshaft to use as a handle when pulling out the camshaft.
16   Inspect the camshaft (see Chapter 2, Part F). Whenever a new camshaft is installed, we recommend a complete new set of valve lifters be installed at the same time, along with new oil and a new oil filter.
17   Prior to reinstalling the camshaft coat each of the lobes and journals with engine assembly lube.
18   Slide the camshaft into the engine block, again being extra careful not to damage the bearings.
19   Install the camshaft thrust plate and tighten the mounting bolts to the torque listed in this Chapter's Specifications.

20   Complete the installation by reversing the removal procedure, referring to the appropriate Sections or Chapters.

21   Have the air conditioning system evacuated, recharged and leak tested by the shop that discharged it.

16   Flywheel/driveplate and rear main bearing oil seal - removal and installation

Refer to illustration 16.5

1   If your engine is equipped with a one-piece (360-degree) rear main seal, identified by a mark on the engine, the seal can be replaced without removing the oil pan or crankshaft. If there is no mark on the engine, you must first remove the oil pan and rear main bearing cap (but the transmission stays in place). See Chapter 2D for the procedure.

2   Remove the transmission (see Chapter 7).

3   If equipped with a manual transmission, remove the clutch pressure plate and disc (see Chapter 8).

4   Mark the relationship of the flywheel/driveplate to the crankshaft. Remove the flywheel/driveplate mounting bolts and separate it from the crankshaft. The flywheel is fairly heavy, so support it securely when removing the last bolt.

5   Using a screwdriver or prybar, carefully remove the oil seal from the block **(see illustration)**. It is very important here not; to damage the crankshaft surface or seal bore while prying with the tool.

6   Check the seal bore for nicks or scratches and carefully file if necessary.

7   A special tool is available to install the replacement oil seal. Check with your local auto parts store. Slide the seal on the mandril until the dust lip bottoms squarely against the collar of the tool.

8   Align the dowel pin of the tool with the dowel pin hole in the crankshaft and attach the tool to the crankshaft by hand-tightening the attaching bolts.

9   Turn the handle of the tool until the collar bottoms against the case, seating the seal.

10   Loosen the tool handle and remove the attaching bolts. Remove the special tool.

11   Check the seal and make sure that it is seated squarely in the bore.

12   Install the flywheel/driveplate and tighten the bolts to the torque listed in this Chapter's Specifications.

13   If equipped with a manual transmission, install the clutch disc and pressure plate (see Chapter 8).

14   Install the transmission (see Chapter 7).

2B

Notes

Chapter 2 Part C
2.5L four-cylinder engine

Contents

	Section
Camshaft, timing gears and bearings - removal, inspection and installation	15
Crankshaft front oil seal - replacement	12
Crankshaft pulley and hub - removal and installation	11
Cylinder compression check	See Chapter 2F
Cylinder head - removal and installation	10
Drivebelt check, adjustment and replacement	See Chapter 1
Engine mounts - replacement	21
Engine oil and filter change	See Chapter 1
Engine overhaul - general information	See Chapter 2F
Engine - removal and installation	See Chapter 2F
Exhaust manifold - removal and installation	9
Flywheel/driveplate - removal and installation	19
General information	1
Hydraulic lifters - removal, inspection and installation	7

	Section
Intake manifold - removal and installation	8
Oil pan - removal and installation	17
Oil pump - removal and installation	18
Oil pump driveshaft - removal and installation	16
Pushrod cover - removal and installation	5
Rear main oil seal - replacement	20
Repair operations possible with the engine in the vehicle	2
Rocker arms and pushrods - removal, inspection and installation	6
Spark plug replacement	See Chapter 1
Timing gear cover - removal and installation	14
Top Dead Center (TDC) for number 1 piston - locating	13
Valve cover - removal and installation	3
Valve springs, retainers and seals - replacement	4
Water pump - removal and installation	See Chapter 3

Specification

General
Cylinder numbers (front-to-rear) 1-2-3-4
Firing order 1-3-4-2

Camshaft
Lobe lift (intake and exhaust) .... 0.398 inch
Bearing journal diameter .... 1.869 inches
Bearing oil clearance .... 0.0007 to 0.0027 inch
Gear/thrust plate end clearance .... 0.0015 to 0.0050 inch

Torque specifications
Cylinder head bolts **(see illustration 10.26)**

Ft-lbs (unless otherwise indicated)

1985 and earlier 85
1986 and 1987
  Step 1 18
  Step 2
    All but bolt 9 22
    Bolt 9 29
  Step 3
    All but bolt 9 .... Turn an additional 120 degrees
    Bolt 9 .... Turn an additional 90 degrees
1988 and later
  Step 1 18
  Step 2
    All but bolt 9 26
    Bolt 9 18
  Step 3 (all bolts) .... Turn an additional 90 degrees

Cylinder location and distributor rotation

The blackened terminal shown on the distributor cap indicates the Number One spark plug wire position

Torque specifications (continued)

Ft-lbs (unless otherwise indicated)

Intake manifold-to-cylinder head bolts
1985	29
1986 (see illustration 8.15)	
Bolts 1, 2 and 6...	28
Bolts 3, 4 and 5...	25
Bolt 7	37
1987 on	25

Exhaust manifold bolts
1985	44
1986 on (see illustration 9.13)	
Bolts 1, 2 and 3...	36
Bolts 4, 5, 6 and 7..	32

Flywheel-to-crankshaft bolts
1985	44
1986	55
1987 on	65

Driveplate-to-crankshaft bolts
1985	44
1986 on	55
Crankshaft pulley hub-to-crankshaft bolt.....................................	160
Lifter guide retainer-to-block stud..	90 in-lbs

Oil pan bolts
1985	75 in-lbs
1986 on	90 in-lbs
Oil pick-up tube bracket nut..	37
Oil pump-to-block bolts	22
Pushrod cover nuts	90 in-lbs

Rocker arm bolts
1985 and 1986	20
1987 on	24

Valve cover bolts
1985 and 1986	72 in-lbs
1987 on	48 in-lbs
Timing gear cover bolts	90 in-lbs
Camshaft thrust plate bolts	90 in-lbs

1   General information

This Part of Chapter 2 is devoted to in-vehicle repair procedures for the 2.5 liter four-cylinder engine. Information concerning engine removal and installation, as well as engine block and cylinder head overhaul, is in Part F of this Chapter.

The following repair procedures are based on the assumption that the engine is installed in the vehicle. If the engine has been removed from the vehicle and mounted on a stand, many of the steps included in this Part of Chapter 2 will not apply.

The Specifications included in this Part of Chapter 2 apply only to the engine and procedures in this Part. The Specifications necessary for rebuilding the block and cylinder head are found in Part F.

2   Repair operations possible with the engine in the vehicle

Many major repair operations can be accomplished without removing the engine from the vehicle.

Clean the engine compartment and the exterior of the engine with some type of pressure washer before any work is done. A clean engine will make the job easier and will help keep dirt out of the internal areas of the engine.

Depending on the components involved, it may be necessary to remove the hood to improve access to the engine as repairs are performed (see Chapter 11 if necessary).

If vacuum, exhaust, oil or coolant leaks develop, indicating a need for gasket or seal replacement, the repairs can generally be made with the engine in the vehicle. The intake and exhaust manifold gaskets, oil pan gasket and cylinder head gasket are all accessible with the engine in place.

Exterior engine components such as the intake and exhaust manifolds, the oil pan (and the oil pump), the water pump, the starter motor, the alternator, the distributor and the fuel injection system can be removed for repair with the engine in place.

Since the cylinder head can be removed without pulling the engine, valve component servicing can also be accomplished with the engine in the vehicle.

In extreme cases caused by a lack of necessary equipment, repair or replacement of piston rings, pistons, connecting rods and rod bearings is possible with the engine in the vehicle. However, this practice is not recommended because of the cleaning and preparation work that must be done to the components involved.

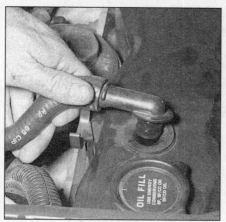

3.3 The PCV valve can be pulled out of the rubber grommet in the valve cover (leave the hose attached to the valve)

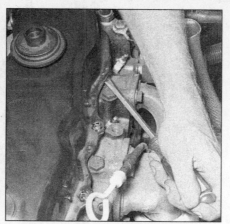

3.8 The valve cover is sealed with RTV - if you have to pry it off the head, try to avoid bending the flange

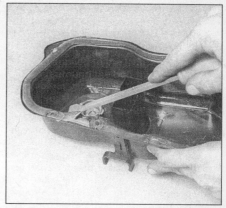

3.9 Remove the old sealant from the valve cover flange and the cylinder head with a gasket scraper, then clean the mating surfaces with lacquer thinner or acetone

2C

3   Valve cover - removal and installation

Refer to illustrations 3.3, 3.8, 3.9, 3.10a and 3.10b

1   Disconnect the negative battery cable from the battery, then remove the air cleaner assembly.

2   Unbolt the dipstick and oil filler tubes at the water outlet.

3   Remove the PCV valve from the valve cover **(see illustration)**.

4   Label each spark plug wire before removal to ensure that all wires are reinstalled correctly, then remove the wires from the plugs (see Chapter 1). Detach the wires and retaining clips from the valve cover.

5   Remove the EGR valve (see Chapter 6).

6   Detach the vacuum rail at the intake manifold and water outlet.

7   Remove the valve cover bolts.

8   Remove the valve cover. If it sticks to the head, use a soft-face hammer or a block of wood and a hammer to dislodge it. If the cover still won't come loose, pry on it carefully

at several points until the seal is broken, but don't distort the cover flange **(see illustration)**. **Note:** *If you bend the cover, straighten it with a block of wood and a hammer.*

9   Prior to reinstallation, remove all dirt, oil and old gasket material from the cover and cylinder head with a scraper **(see illustration)**. Clean the mating surfaces with lacquer thinner or acetone.

10   Apply a continuous 3/16-inch (5 mm) diameter bead of RTV sealant to the flange on the cover. Be sure the sealant is applied to the inside of the bolt holes **(see illustrations)**. **Note:** *Don't get the sealant in the bolt holes in the head or damage to the head may occur.*

11   Place the valve cover on the cylinder head while the sealant is still wet and install the mounting bolts. Tighten the bolts a little at a time until the torque listed in this Chapter's Specifications is reached.

12   Complete the installation by reversing the removal procedure.

13   Start the engine and check for oil leaks at the valve cover-to-head joint.

4   Valve springs, retainers and seals - replacement

Refer to illustrations 4.4, 4.8a, 4.8b, 4.16 and 4.17

Note: *Broken valve springs and defective valve stem seals can be replaced without removing the cylinder head. Two special tools and a compressed air source are normally required to perform this operation, so read through this Section carefully and rent or buy the tools before beginning the job. If compressed air isn't available, a length of nylon rope can be used to keep the valves from falling into the cylinder during this procedure.*

1   Remove the valve cover (see Section 3).

2   Remove the spark plug from the cylinder which has the defective component. If all of the valve stem seals are being replaced, all of the spark plugs should be removed.

3   Turn the crankshaft until the piston in the affected cylinder is at top dead center on the compression stroke (see Section 13 for instructions). If you're replacing all of the

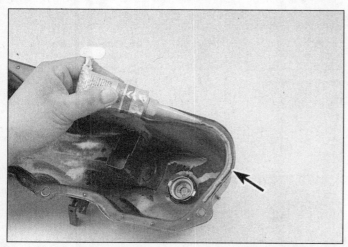

3.10a Apply a continuous 3/16-in diameter bead of RTV sealant (arrow) to the valve cover flange

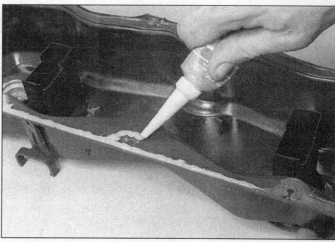

3.10b Make sure the sealant is applied to the INSIDE of the bolt holes or oil will leak out around the bolt threads

valve stem seals, begin with cylinder number one and work on the valves for one cylinder at a time. Move from cylinder-to-cylinder following the firing order sequence (1-3-4-2).

4   Thread an adapter into the spark plug hole and connect an air hose from a compressed air source to it **(see illustration)**. Most auto parts stores can supply the air hose adapter. **Note:** *Many cylinder compression gauges utilize a screw-in fitting that may work with your air hose quick-disconnect fitting.*

5   Remove the bolt, pivot ball and rocker arm for the valve with the defective part and pull out the pushrod. If all of the valve stem seals are being replaced, all of the rocker arms and pushrods should be removed (see Section 6).

6   Apply compressed air to the cylinder. The valves should be held in place by the air pressure. If the valve faces or seats are in poor condition, leaks may prevent the air pressure from retaining the valves - see the alternative procedure below.

7   If you don't have access to compressed air, an alternative method can be used. Position the piston at a point just before TDC on the compression stroke, then feed a long piece of nylon rope through the spark plug hole until it fills the combustion chamber. Be sure to leave the end of the rope hanging out of the engine so it can be removed easily. Use a large breaker bar and socket to rotate the crankshaft in the normal direction of rotation until slight resistance is felt.

8   Stuff shop rags into the cylinder head holes above and below the valves to prevent parts and tools from falling into the engine, then use a valve spring compressor to compress the spring **(see illustration)**. Remove the keepers with small needle-nose pliers or a magnet **(see illustration)**. **Note:** *A couple of different types of tools are available for compressing the valve springs with the head*

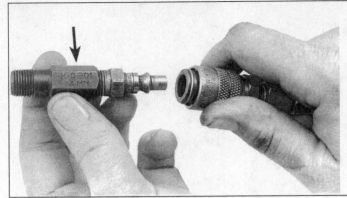

4.4 This is what the air hose adapter that threads into the spark plug holes looks like - they're commonly available from auto parts stores

in place. One type grips the lower spring coils and presses on the retainer as the knob is turned, while the other type, shown here, utilizes the rocker arm bolt for leverage. Both types work very well, although the lever type is usually less expensive.

9   Remove the valve stem O-ring seal, spring retainer, shield and valve spring, then remove the umbrella type guide seal, if equipped (the O-ring seal will most likely be hardened and will probably break when removed, so plan on installing a new one each time the original is removed). **Note:** *If air pressure fails to hold the valve in the closed position during this operation, the valve face or seat is probably damaged. If so, the cylinder head will have to be removed for additional repair operations.*

10   Wrap a rubber band or tape around the top of the valve stem so the valve will not fall into the combustion chamber, then release the air pressure. **Note:** *If a rope was used instead of air pressure, turn the crankshaft slightly in the direction opposite normal rotation.*

11   Inspect the valve stem for damage. Rotate the valve in the guide and check the end for eccentric movement, which would indicate that the valve is bent.

12   Move the valve up-and-down in the guide and make sure it doesn't bind. If the valve stem binds, either the valve is bent or

the guide is damaged. In either case, the head will have to be removed for repair.

13   Reapply air pressure to the cylinder to retain the valve in the closed position, then remove the tape or rubber band from the valve stem. If a rope was used instead of air pressure, rotate the crankshaft in the normal direction of rotation until slight resistance is felt.

14   Lubricate the valve stem with engine oil and install a new umbrella type guide seal, if used.

15   Install the spring and shield in position over the valve.

16   Install the valve spring retainer. Compress the valve spring and carefully install the new O-ring seal in the lower groove of the valve stem. Make sure the seal isn't twisted - it must lie perfectly flat in the groove **(see illustration)**.

17   Position the keepers in the upper groove. Apply a small dab of grease to the inside of each keeper to hold it in place if necessary **(see illustration)**. Remove the pressure from the spring tool and make sure the keepers are seated. Check the seals with a vacuum pump (see Chapter 2, Part F).

18   Disconnect the air hose and remove the adapter from the spark plug hole. If a rope was used in place of air pressure, pull it out of the cylinder.

19   Install the rocker arm(s) and pushrod(s)

4.8a A lever-type valve spring compressor is used to compress the spring and remove the keepers to replace valve seals or springs with the head installed

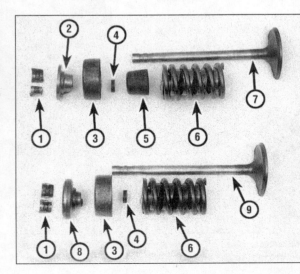

4.8b Exploded view of a valve and related components (later models are slightly different)

1	Keeper
2	Retainer
3	Oil shield
4	O-ring oil seal
5	Umbrella seal
6	Damper
7	Spring
8	Intake valve
9	Rotator
10	Exhaust valve

4.16 Make sure the O-ring seal under the retainer is seated in the groove and not twisted before installing the keepers

4.17 Keepers don't always stay in place, so apply a small dab of grease to each one as shown here before installation - it'll hold them in place on the valve stem as the spring is released

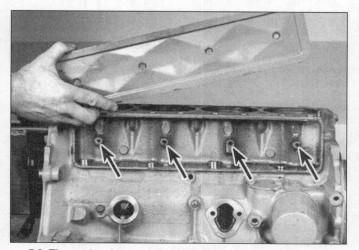

5.9 The pushrod cover is held in place with four studs/nuts

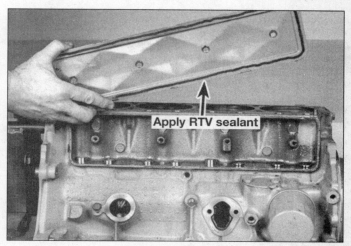

Apply RTV sealant

5.12 The pushrod cover is sealed with RTV - no gasket is required

(see Section 6).

20   Install the spark plug(s) and hook up the wire(s).

21   Install the valve cover (see Section 3).

22   Start and run the engine, then check for oil leaks and unusual sounds coming from the valve cover area.

5   Pushrod cover - removal and installation

Refer to illustrations 5.9, 5.12 and 5.13

1   Disconnect the negative cable from the battery.

2   Remove the air cleaner assembly (see Chapter 4).

3   Remove the alternator and brackets (see Chapter 5).

4   Remove the intake manifold-to-block brace.

5   Drain the cooling system (see Chapter 1).

6   Detach the lower radiator and heater hoses.

7   Remove the oil pressure sending unit.

8   Detach the wiring harness brackets from the cover.

9   Remove the four pushrod cover nuts **(see illustration)**. Flip one nut over so the washer faces out and reinstall it on the long inner stud. Put a second nut on the stud with the washer facing in. Put two 6 mm nuts on the shorter stud. Jam them together with two wrenches. Unscrew the studs by turning the inner nuts until the cover breaks free.

10   Remove the pushrod cover. **Caution:** *Careless prying may damage the sealing surface of the cover. If you bend the cover during removal, place it on a flat surface and straighten it with a soft-face hammer.*

11   Remove all traces of old gasket material with a scraper, then clean the mating surfaces with lacquer thinner or acetone.

12   Apply a continuous 3/16-inch diameter bead of RTV sealant to the mating surface of the pushrod cover **(see illustration)**.

13   Install new rubber pushrod cover seals **(see illustration)**.

14   Install the cover while the sealant is still wet. Make sure the semicircular cutout in the edge of the pushrod cover is facing down.

15   Tighten the nuts gradually until they're snug, then tighten them to the torque listed in

5.13 Don't forget to install new rubber sealing washers around the pushrod cover mounting studs or oil will leak past the studs

this Chapter's Specifications.

16   The remaining installation steps are the reverse of removal.

17   Start and run the engine, then check for oil and coolant leaks.

6.3 Remove the rocker bolts, pivot balls and arms

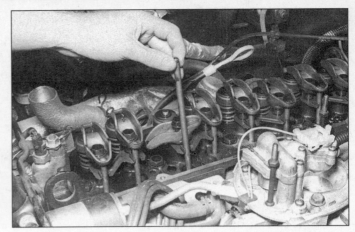

6.4a If you're just removing the pushrod(s), loosen the rocker arm bolt, rotate the rocker arm to one side and lift out the pushrod

6   Rocker arms and pushrods - removal, inspection and installation

Refer to illustrations 6.3, 6.4a, 6.4b and 6.5

Removal

1   Detach the valve cover from the cylinder head (see Section 3).
2   Beginning at the front of the cylinder head, loosen the rocker arm bolts. **Note:** *If the pushrods are the only items being removed, rotate the rocker arms to one side so the pushrods can be lifted out.*
3   Remove the bolts, the rocker arms and the pivot balls **(see illustration)** and store them in marked containers (they must be reinstalled in their original locations).
4   Remove the pushrods and store them separately to make sure they don't get mixed up during installation **(see illustrations)**.
5   If the pushrod guides must be removed for any reason, make sure they're marked so they can be reinstalled in their original locations **(see illustration)**.

Inspection

6   Check each rocker arm for wear, cracks and other damage, especially where the pushrods and valve stems contact the rocker arm faces.
7   Make sure the hole at the pushrod end of each rocker arm is open.
8   Check each rocker arm pivot area for wear, cracks and galling. If the rocker arms are worn or damaged, replace them with new ones and use new pivot balls as well.
9   Inspect the pushrods for cracks and excessive wear at the ends. Roll each pushrod across a piece of plate glass to see if it's bent (if it wobbles, it's bent).

Installation

10   Lubricate the lower ends of the pushrods with clean engine oil or moly-base grease and install them in their original locations. Make sure each pushrod seats completely in the lifter socket.
11   Apply moly-base grease to the ends of the valve stems and the upper ends of the pushrods before positioning the rocker arms

and installing the bolts.
12   Set the rocker arms in place, then install the pivot balls and bolts. Apply moly-base grease to the pivot balls to prevent damage to the mating surfaces before engine oil pressure builds up. Tighten the bolts to the torque listed in this Chapter's Specifications.

7   Hydraulic lifters - removal, inspection and installation

Removal

Refer to illustrations 7.7a, 7.7b, 7.8 and 7.9

1   A noisy valve lifter can be isolated when the engine is idling. Place a length of hose or tubing near the position of each valve while listening at the other end. Or remove the valve cover and, with the engine idling, place a finger on each of the valve spring retainers, one at a time. If a valve lifter is defective, it'll be evident from the shock felt at the retainer as the valve seats.
2   The most likely cause of a noisy valve lifter is a piece of dirt trapped between the

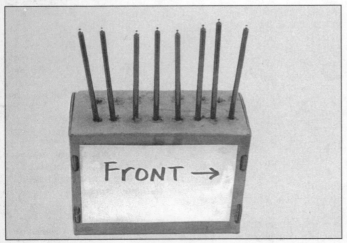

6.4b If more than one pushrod is being removed, store them in a perforated cardboard box to prevent mix-ups during the installation - note the label indicating the front of the engine

6.5 If they're removed, make sure the pushrod guides (arrows) are kept in order also

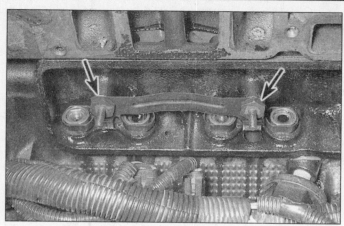

7.7a Pushrod cover stud locknuts (arrows) - manifold removed for clarity

7.7b Remove the lifter guide - if you're removing more than one guide, keep them in order to prevent mix-ups during installation

plunger and the lifter body.

3   Remove the valve cover (see Section 3).

4   Loosen both rocker arm bolts at the cylinder with the noisy lifter and rotate the rocker arms away from the pushrods.

5   Remove the pushrod guides and pushrods (see Section 6).

6   Remove the pushrod cover (see Section 5).

7   Remove the lifter guide retainer by

7.8 On engines that haven't become sticky with sludge and varnish, the lifters can usually be removed by hand

unscrewing the locknuts on the pushrod cover studs. Remove the lifter guide (see illustrations).

8   There are several ways to extract a lifter from its bore. A special removal tool is available, but isn't always necessary. On newer engines without a lot of varnish buildup, lifters can often be removed with a small magnet or even with your fingers (see illustration). A scribe can also be used to pull the lifter out of the bore. Caution: Don't use pliers of any type to remove a lifter unless you intend to replace it with a new one - they will damage the precision machined and hardened surface of the lifter, rendering it useless.

9   Store the lifters in a clearly labeled box to insure their reinstallation in the same lifter bores (see illustration).

Inspection

Refer to illustrations 7.11a and 7.11b

10   Clean the lifters with solvent and dry them thoroughly without mixing them up.

11   Check each lifter wall, pushrod seat and roller for scuffing, score marks and uneven wear. Check the rollers for wear and damage. Make sure the rollers turn freely without excessive play (see illustration). If the lifter walls are damaged or worn (which isn't very

likely), inspect the lifter bores in the engine block as well. If the pushrod seats (see illustration) are worn, check the pushrod ends.

12   Used roller lifters can be reinstalled with a new camshaft if the lifters are in good condition. The original camshaft can be used if new lifters are installed, provided the cam lobes are in good condition.

Installation

13   The used lifters must be installed in their original bores. Coat them with moly-base grease or engine assembly lube.

14   Lubricate the bearing surfaces of the lifter bores with engine oil.

15   Install the lifter(s) in the lifter bore(s). Note: Make sure that the oil orifice is facing toward the front of the engine.

16   Install the lifter guide(s) and retainer(s).

17   Install the pushrods, pushrod guides, rocker arms and rocker arm retaining bolts (see Section 6). Caution: Make sure that each pair of lifters is on the base circle of the camshaft; that is, with both valves closed, before tightening the rocker arm bolts.

18   Tighten the rocker arm bolts to the torque listed in this Chapter's Specifications.

19   Install the pushrod cover (see Section 5).

20   Install the valve cover (see Section 3).

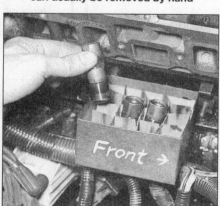

7.9 If you're removing more than one lifter, keep them in order in a clearly labeled box

7.11a The roller on the bottom of the lifter must turn freely - check for wear and excessive play as well

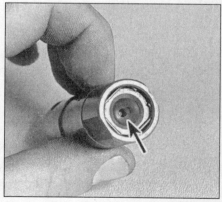

7.11b Check the pushrod seat (arrow) in the top of each lifter for wear

2C

8   Intake manifold - removal and installation

Refer to illustrations 8.10 and 8.15

1   Disconnect the cable from the negative battery terminal.
2   Remove the air cleaner assembly (see Chapter 4).
3   Remove the PCV valve and hose.
4   Drain the cooling system (see Chapter 1).
5   Detach the fuel lines, vacuum lines and wire leads from the fuel injection assembly (see Chapter 4). When disconnecting the fuel line be prepared to catch some fuel, then plug the line to prevent contamination.
6   After noting how it's installed, disconnect the fuel injection throttle linkage. Disconnect the cruise control and TVS linkage (if so equipped).
7   Tag and disconnect all remaining vacuum lines and wires hooked to components on the manifold. Remove the coolant hoses from the manifold.
8   Remove the ignition coil. Unbolt the alternator and bracket and set it aside (see Chapter 5).
9   Remove the mounting bolts and separate the manifold from the cylinder head. Don't pry between the manifold and head, as damage to the gasket sealing surfaces may result.
10   Remove the old gasket **(see illustration)**.
11   If a new manifold is being installed,

8.10 Remove the old intake manifold gasket with a scraper - don't leave any material on the mating surfaces

transfer all components still attached to the old manifold to the new one.
12   Before installing the manifold, clean the cylinder head and manifold gasket surfaces with lacquer thinner or acetone. All gasket material and sealing compound must be removed prior to installation.
13   Apply a thin coat of RTV sealant to the intake manifold and cylinder head mating surfaces. Make certain that the sealant will not spread into the air or coolant passages when the manifold is installed.
14   Place a new gasket on the manifold, hold the manifold in position against the cylinder head and install the mounting bolts finger tight.
15   Tighten the mounting bolts a little at a time in the correct sequence **(see illustration)** until they're all at the torque listed in this Chapter's Specifications.
16   Install the remaining components in the reverse order of removal.
17   Fill the radiator with coolant, start the engine and check for leaks.

9   Exhaust manifold - removal and installation

Refer to illustration 9.13

1   Remove the cable from the negative battery terminal.
2   Remove the air cleaner assembly (see Chapter 4).
3   Remove the heat stove pipe at the exhaust manifold.
4   Raise the vehicle and support it securely on jackstands.
5   Disconnect the oxygen sensor.
6   Label the four spark plug wires, then disconnect them and secure them out of the way.
7   Disconnect the exhaust pipe from the exhaust manifold. You may have to apply penetrating oil to the fastener threads, as they are usually corroded. The exhaust pipe can be hung from the frame with a piece of wire.
8   Remove the rear air conditioning compressor bracket.
9   Remove the exhaust manifold end bolts first, then remove the center bolts and separate the exhaust manifold from the engine.
10   Remove the exhaust manifold gasket.
11   Before installing the manifold, clean the

gasket mating surfaces on the cylinder head and manifold. All old gasket material and carbon deposits must be removed. Check the bolt threads for damage.
12   Place a new exhaust manifold gasket in position on the cylinder head, then place the manifold in position and install the mounting bolts finger tight.
13   Tighten the mounting bolts a little at a time in the correct sequence **(see illustration)** until all of the bolts are at the torque listed in this Chapter's Specifications.
14   Reconnect the exhaust pipe and reinstall the air conditioning compressor bracket.
15   Lower the vehicle.
16   Install the remaining components in the reverse order of removal.
17   Start the engine and check for exhaust leaks between the manifold and cylinder head and between the manifold and exhaust pipe.

10   Cylinder head - removal and installation

Removal

Refer to illustrations 10.15, 10.16 and 10.17

1   Disconnect the negative cable from the battery.
2   Drain the cooling system (see Chapter 1).
3   Remove the air cleaner assembly (see Chapter 4).
4   Remove the throttle, cruise control and Throttle Valve (TV) cables (as equipped).
5   Remove the dipstick tube and thermostat housing.
6   Remove the alternator and brackets (see Chapter 5).
7   Unbolt the air conditioner compressor and swing it out of the way for clearance. **Caution:** *Don't disconnect any of the air conditioning lines unless the system has been depressurized by a dealer service department or other repair shop.*
8   Disconnect all wires and vacuum hoses from the cylinder head and manifold. Be sure to label them to simplify reinstallation. Detach the fuel lines from the TBI unit (see Chapter 4).
9   Remove the upper radiator, water pump bypass and heater hoses.
10   Disconnect the spark plug wires and remove the spark plugs. Be sure to label the plug wires to simplify reinstallation.

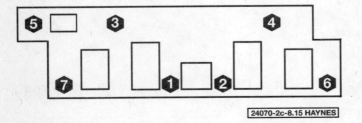

24070-2c-8.15 HAYNES

8.15 Intake manifold bolt TIGHTENING sequence

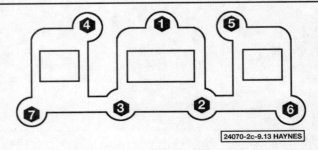

24070-2c-9.13 HAYNES

9.13 Exhaust manifold bolt TIGHTENING sequence

10.15 To avoid mixing up the head bolts, use a new gasket to transfer the bolt hole pattern to a piece of cardboard, then punch holes to accept the bolts . . .

10.16 . . . and push each head bolt through the matching hole in the cardboard

2C

11   Remove the valve cover (see Section 3).

12   Remove the pushrods (see Section 6).

13   Remove the ignition coil (see Chapter 5).

14   Raise the vehicle and support it securely on jackstands, then unbolt the exhaust pipe from the manifold.

15   Using a new head gasket, outline the cylinders and bolt pattern on a piece of cardboard **(see illustration)**. Be sure to indicate the front of the engine for reference. Punch holes at the bolt locations.

16   Loosen the cylinder head mounting bolts in 1/4-turn increments until they can be removed by hand. Store the bolts in the cardboard holder as they're removed - this will ensure that they are reinstalled in their original locations **(see illustration)**.

17   Lift the head off the engine. If it's stuck, pry on it only at the overhang on the thermostat end of the head **(see illustration)**. **Caution:** *If you pry on the head anywhere else, damage to the gasket surface may result.*

18   Place the head on a block of wood to prevent damage to the gasket surface. See Part F for cylinder head disassembly and valve service procedures.

Installation

Refer to illustrations 10.23 and 10.26

19   If a new cylinder head is being installed, transfer all external parts from the old cylinder head to the new one.

20   The mating surfaces of the cylinder head and block must be perfectly clean when the head is installed. It's also a good idea to have the head checked for distortion (warpage) and cracks by an automotive machine shop.

21   Use a gasket scraper to remove all traces of carbon and old gasket material, then clean the mating surfaces with lacquer thinner or acetone. If there's oil on the mating surfaces when the head is installed, the gasket may not seal correctly and leaks may develop. Use a vacuum cleaner to remove any debris that falls into the cylinders.

22   Check the block and head mating surfaces for nicks, deep scratches and other damage. If damage is slight, it can be

10.17 If the head is stuck, pry it up at the overhang just behind and below the thermostat housing

removed with a file; if it's excessive, machining may be the only alternative.

23   Use a tap of the correct size to chase the threads in the head bolt holes. Mount each bolt in a vise and run a die down the threads to remove corrosion and restore the threads. Dirt, corrosion, sealant and damaged threads will affect critical head bolt torque readings.

24   Position the new gasket over the dowel pins in the block, then carefully position the head on the block without disturbing the gasket.

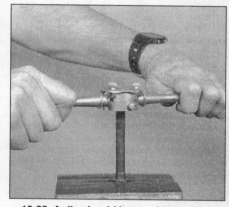

10.23 A die should be used to remove sealant and corrosion from the head bolt threads prior to installation

25   Coat the threads and the undersides of the heads of cylinder head bolt numbers 9 and 10 with Teflon pipe thread sealant and install the bolts finger tight **(see illustration 10.26)**.

26   Tighten each of the bolts a little at a time in the sequence shown to the torque listed in this Chapter's Specifications **(see illustration)**.

27   The remaining installation steps are the reverse of removal.

28   Change the oil and filter, run the engine and check for leaks.

10.26 The cylinder head bolts must be tightened in three stages to the torque listed in this Chapter's Specifications, using the numerical sequence shown here

A   Apply sealing compound to the threads and undersides of the heads of bolts 9 and 10

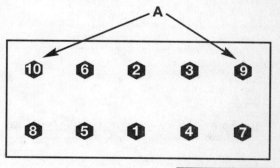

24070-2c-10.25 HAYNES

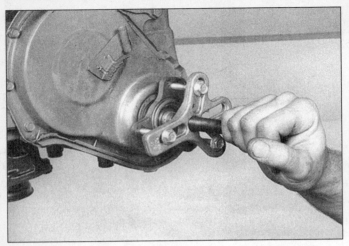

11.6 Use a puller to remove the hub from the crankshaft

11.9 Use the pulley hub bolt to press the hub onto the crankshaft

11   Crankshaft pulley and hub - removal and installation

Refer to illustrations 11.6 and 11.9

1   Remove the cable from the negative battery terminal.

2   Remove the drivebelts (see Chapter 1). Tag each belt as it's removed to simplify reinstallation.

3   Raise the vehicle and place it securely on jackstands.

4   If your vehicle is equipped with a manual transmission, apply the parking brake and put the transmission in gear to prevent the engine from turning over, then remove the crankshaft pulley bolts. If your vehicle is equipped with an automatic transmission, it may be necessary to remove the starter motor (see Chapter 5) and immobilize the starter ring gear with a large screwdriver while an assistant loosens the pulley bolts.

5   To loosen the crankshaft hub retaining bolt, install a bolt in one of the pulley bolt holes. Attach a breaker bar, extension and socket to the hub retaining bolt and immobilize the hub by wedging a large screwdriver between the bolt and the socket. Remove the hub retaining bolt.

6   Remove the crankshaft hub. Use a puller if necessary **(see illustration)**.

7   Replace the front oil seal, if necessary (see Section 12).

8   Apply a thin layer of multi-purpose grease to the seal contact surface of the hub.

9   Slide the pulley hub onto the crankshaft until it bottoms against the crankshaft timing gear. Note that the slot in the hub must be aligned with the Woodruff key in the end of the crankshaft. The hub retaining bolt can also be used to press the hub into position **(see illustration)**.

10   Tighten the hub-to-crankshaft bolt to the torque listed in this Chapter's Specifications.

11   Install the crankshaft pulley on the hub. Use Locktite on the bolt threads.

12   Install the drivebelts (see Chapter 1).

12   Crankshaft front oil seal - replacement

Note: *The front seal can be replaced with the timing gear cover in place. However, due to the limited amount of room available, you may conclude that the procedure would be easier if the cover were removed from the engine first. If so, see Section 14 for the cover removal and installation procedure.*

Timing gear cover in place

Refer to illustration 12.2

1   Disconnect the negative battery cable from the battery, then remove the crankshaft pulley hub (see Section 11).

2   Note how the seal is installed - the new one must face the same direction! Carefully pry the oil seal out of the cover with a seal puller or a large screwdriver **(see illustration)**. Be very careful not to distort the cover or scratch the crankshaft!

3   Apply clean engine oil or multi-purpose grease to the outer edge of the new seal, then install it in the cover with the lip (open

12.2 The crankshaft front seal can be removed in the vehicle with a seal removal tool or a large screwdriver (V6 engine shown, four-cylinder similar)

end) facing IN. Drive the seal into place with a large socket and a hammer (if a large socket isn't available, a piece of pipe will also work). Make sure the seal enters the bore squarely and stop when the front face is flush with the cover.

4   Install the pulley hub (see Section 11).

Timing gear cover removed

Refer to illustrations 12.6, 12.8a and 12.8b

5   Remove the timing gear cover (see Section 14).

6   Using a large screwdriver, pry the old seal out of the cover **(see illustration)**. Be careful not to distort the cover or scratch the wall of the seal bore. If the engine has accumulated a lot of miles, apply penetrating oil to the seal-to-cover joint and allow it to soak in before attempting to remove the seal.

7   Clean the bore to remove any old seal material and corrosion. Support the cover on a block of wood and position the new seal in the bore with the lip (open end) of the seal facing IN. A small amount of oil applied to the outer edge of the new seal will make installation easier - don't overdo it!

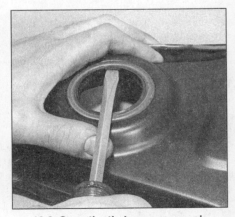

12.6 Once the timing gear cover is removed, place it on a flat surface and gently pry the old seal out with a large screwdriver

12.8a Clean the bore, then apply a small mount of oil to the outer edge of the new seal and drive it squarely into the opening with a large socket . . .

12.8b . . . or block of wood and a hammer - don't damage the seal in the process!

8   Drive the seal into the bore with a large socket and hammer until it's completely seated **(see illustration)**. Select a socket that's the same outside diameter as the seal. A section of pipe or even a block of wood can be used if a socket isn't available) **(see illustration)**.

9   Reinstall the timing gear cover.

13   Top Dead Center (TDC) for number 1 piston - locating

Refer to illustrations 13.4 and 13.5

1   Top Dead Center (TDC) is the highest point in the cylinder that each piston reaches as it travels up-and-down when the crankshaft turns. Each piston reaches TDC on the compression stroke and again on the exhaust stroke, but TDC generally refers to piston position on the compression stroke.

The timing marks on the pulley installed on the front of the crankshaft are referenced to the number one piston at TDC on the compression stroke.

2   Positioning the piston(s) at TDC is an essential part of many procedures such as rocker arm removal, camshaft and timing gear removal and distributor removal.

3   In order to bring any piston to TDC, the crankshaft must be turned using one of the methods outlined below. When looking at the front of the engine, normal crankshaft rotation is clockwise. **Warning:** *Before beginning this procedure, be sure to place the transmission in Neutral and unplug the distributor wire harness connector to disable the ignition system.*

a) *The preferred method is to turn the crankshaft with a large socket and breaker bar attached to the crankshaft pulley hub bolt threaded into the front of the crankshaft.*

b) *A remote starter switch, which may save some time, can also be used. Attach the*

switch leads to the S (switch) and B (battery) terminals on the starter motor. Once the piston is close to TDC, use a socket and breaker bar (see previous paragraph).

c) *If an assistant is available to turn the ignition switch to the Start position in short bursts, you can get the piston close to TDC without a remote starter switch. Use a socket and breaker bar (see Paragraph a) to complete the procedure.*

4   Note the position of the terminal for the number one spark plug wire on the distributor cap **(see illustration)**. Use a felt-tip pen or chalk to make a mark on the distributor body directly under the terminal. Remove the screws, detach the cap from the distributor and set it aside.

5   Turn the crankshaft (see Paragraph 3 above) until the notch in the crankshaft pulley is aligned with the 0 on the timing plate (located at the front of the engine) **(see illustration)**.

6   Look at the distributor rotor - it should be pointing directly at the mark you made on the distributor body. If the rotor is pointing at the terminal for the number four spark plug, the number one piston is at TDC on the exhaust stroke.

7   To get the piston to TDC on the compression stroke, turn the crankshaft one complete turn (360-degrees) clockwise. The rotor should now be pointing at the mark on the distributor. When the rotor is pointing at the number one spark plug wire terminal in the distributor cap and the ignition timing marks are aligned, the number one piston is at TDC on the compression stroke.

8   After the number one piston has been positioned at TDC on the compression stroke, TDC for any of the remaining pistons can be located by turning the crankshaft 180-degrees at a time and following the firing order (1-3-4-2).

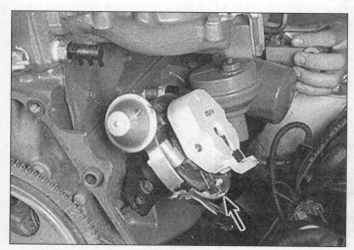

13.4 After you locate the number 1 spark plug wire terminal on the distributor cap, make a mark (arrow) on the distributor body directly under the terminal (2.5L engine shown, but the principle applies to other engines)

13.5 Turn the crankshaft until the notch in the drivebelt pulley (lower arrow) is directly opposite the zero mark on the timing plate (upper arrow)

14.9 Timing gear cover bolt locations

15.3 When checking the camshaft lobe lift, the dial indicator plunger must be positioned directly in line with the pushrod

14 Timing gear cover - removal and installation

Refer to illustration 14.9

1   Detach the cable from the negative terminal of the battery.
2   Remove the power steering reservoir (if equipped). Be prepared to catch the fluid in a drain pan.
3   Remove the upper fan shroud (see Chapter 3).
4   Remove the drivebelts (see Chapter 1).
5   Detach the fan and drivebelt pulley.
6   Disconnect and unbolt the alternator and brackets (see Chapter 5).
7   Raise the front of the vehicle and support it on jackstands. Apply the parking brake. Drain the coolant (see Chapter 1), then detach the lower radiator hose from the water pump.
8   Remove the crankshaft pulley and hub (see Section 11).
9   Remove the timing gear cover-to-block bolts **(see illustration)**.
10   Remove the cover by carefully prying it off. The cover is sealed with RTV, so it may be stuck to the block. The flange between the cover and oil pan may be bent during removal. Try to minimize damage to the flange or it may be too distorted to be straightened.
11   Use a scraper to remove all old sealant from the cover, oil pan and block, then clean the mating surfaces with lacquer thinner or acetone.
12   Check the cover flanges for distortion, particularly around the bolt holes. If necessary, place the cover on a block of wood and use a hammer to flatten and restore the mating surfaces.
13   Apply a 3/8-inch wide by 3/16-inch thick bead of RTV sealant to the timing gear cover flange that mates with the oil pan. Apply a 1/4-inch wide by 1/8-inch thick bead to the cover-to-block flange.
14   Apply a dab of sealant to the joints between the oil pan and the engine block.

15   Place the cover in position and loosely install a couple of mounting bolts.
16   Install the crankshaft hub to center the cover (see Section 11). Be sure to lubricate the seal contact surface of the hub.
17   Install the remaining mounting bolts and tighten them to the torque listed in this Chapter's Specifications.
18   Install the crankshaft pulley, then hook up the lower radiator hose.
19   Lower the vehicle.
20   Refill the cooling system (see Chapter 1).
21   Install the components removed to gain access to the cover.
22   Reattach the cable to the negative terminal of the battery.
23   Start the engine and check for oil leaks at the seal.

15 Camshaft, timing gears and bearings - removal, inspection and installation

Camshaft lobe lift check

Refer to illustration 15.3

1   In order to determine the extent of cam lobe wear, the lobe lift should be checked prior to camshaft removal. Remove the valve cover (see Section 3).
2   Position the number one piston at TDC on the compression stroke (see Section 13).
3   Beginning with the number one cylinder valves, loosen the rocker arm bolts and pivot the rocker arms to the side. Mount a dial indicator on the engine and position the plunger against the first pushrod. The plunger should be directly in line with the pushrod **(see illustration)**.
4   Zero the dial indicator, then very slowly turn the crankshaft in the normal direction of rotation (clockwise when looking at the front of the engine) until the indicator needle stops and begins to move in the opposite direction. The point at which it stops indicates maximum cam lobe lift.

5   Record this figure for future reference, then reposition the piston at TDC on the compression stroke.
6   Move the dial indicator to the remaining number one cylinder pushrod and repeat the check. Be sure to record the results for each valve.
7   Repeat the check for the remaining valves. Since each piston must be at TDC on the compression stroke for this procedure, work from cylinder-to-cylinder following the firing order sequence. Turn the crankshaft 180-degrees when moving from one cylinder to the next.
8   After the check is complete, compare the results to the Specifications. If camshaft lobe lift is less than specified, cam lobe wear has occurred and a new camshaft should be installed.

Removal

Refer to illustration 15.24

9   Disconnect the negative battery cable from the battery.
10   Place a drain pan under the power steering reservoir.
11   Detach the power steering reservoir from the fan shroud and drain the fluid.
12   Remove the radiator (see Chapter 3).
13   Remove the drivebelts (see Chapter 1).
14   Detach the fan and drivebelt pulley (see Chapter 3).
15   Remove the air cleaner assembly.
16   Remove the pushrod cover (see Section 5).
17   Remove the EGR valve (see Chapter 6).
18   Tag and disconnect the vacuum hoses at the intake manifold and thermostat housing.
19   Remove the pushrods and lifters.
20   Detach the timing gear cover (see Section 14).
21   Remove the distributor (see Chapter 5) and the oil pump driveshaft (see Section 16).
22   Remove the headlight bezels, the grille and the bumper filler panel (see Chapter 11).
23   Remove the air conditioning condenser baffles. Unbolt the condenser and support it

15.24 Turn the camshaft until the holes in the gear are aligned with the thrust plate bolts, then remove them with a ratchet and socket

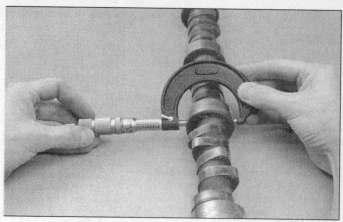

15.28 The camshaft bearing journal diameters are checked to pinpoint excessive wear and out-of-round conditions

2C

out of the way - don't disconnect the refrigerant lines!

24   Turn the crankshaft until the holes in the camshaft gear are aligned with the thrust plate bolts, then remove the bolts **(see illustration)**.

25   Carefully pull the camshaft and gear assembly out of the block. **Caution:** *To avoid damage to the camshaft bearings as the lobes pass over them, support the camshaft near the block as it's withdrawn.*

26   The crankshaft gear should slide off the crankshaft without a great deal of resistance.

Inspection

Refer to illustration 15.28

Camshaft

27   After the camshaft has been removed from the engine, cleaned with solvent and dried, inspect the bearing journals for uneven wear, pitting and evidence of seizure. If the journals are damaged, the bearing inserts in the block are probably damaged as well. Both the camshaft and bearings will have to be replaced.

28   If the journals are in good condition, measure the bearing journals with a microm-

eter to determine their sizes and whether or not they're out-of-round. The inside diameter of each bearing can be measured with a telescoping gauge and micrometer. Subtract each cam journal diameter from the corresponding bearing inside diameter to obtain the bearing oil clearance.

29   Compare the clearance for each bearing to the Specifications. If it's excessive for any of the bearings, have new bearings installed by an automotive machine shop.

30   Check the camshaft lobes for heat discoloration, score marks, chipped areas, pitting and uneven wear. If the lobes are in good condition and if the lobe lift measurements are as specified, the camshaft can be reused.

Gears

31   Check the camshaft drive and driven gears for cracks, missing teeth and excessive wear. If the teeth are highly polished, pitted and galled, or if the outer hardened surface of the teeth is flaking off, new parts will be required. If one gear is worn or damaged, replace both gears as a set. Never install one new and one used gear.

32   Check the thrust plate clearance with a feeler gauge and compare it to the Specifica-

tions. If it's less than the minimum specified, the spacer ring should be replaced. If it's excessive, the thrust plate must be replaced. In either case, the gear will have to be pressed off the camshaft, so take the parts to an automotive machine shop.

Bearing replacement

33   Camshaft bearing replacement requires special tools and expertise that place it outside the scope of the home mechanic. Take the block to an automotive machine shop to ensure that the job is done correctly.

Installation

Refer to illustrations 15.34 and 15.36

34   Lubricate the camshaft bearing journals and cam lobes with camshaft assembly lube **(see illustration)**.

35   Slide the camshaft into the engine. Support the cam near the block and be careful not to scrape or nick the bearings.

36   Install the gear on the end of the crankshaft (if not already done). Don't forget the Woodruff key and don't hammer the gear onto the shaft. Align the timing marks on the gears as the gears mesh **(see illustration)**.

37   Line up the access holes in the gear with

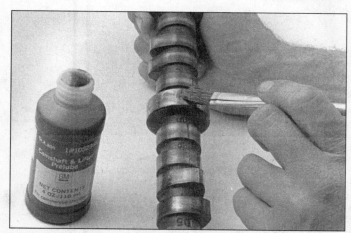

15.34 Be sure to prelube the bearing journals and lobes prior to camshaft installation

15.36 Align the timing marks as shown here when installing the camshaft

16.3 The oil pump driveshaft retainer plate is located on the engine block, just below the pushrod cover and just above the oil filter

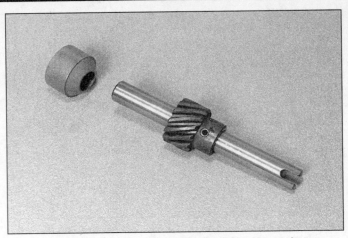

16.6 Inspect the oil pump driveshaft, gear and bushing for wear and damage

the thrust plate holes and the bolt holes in the block. Apply non-hardening thread locking compound to the threads, then install the thrust plate bolts and tighten them to the torque listed in this Chapter's Specifications.
38 The remaining installation steps are the reverse of removal.

16 Oil pump driveshaft - removal and installation

Refer to illustrations 16.3, 16.6 and 16.7
1 Disconnect the cable from the negative terminal of the battery.
2 Raise the vehicle and support it on jack-stands.
3 Remove the oil pump driveshaft retainer plate bolts **(see illustration)**.
4 Remove the oil pump driveshaft and bushing with a magnet.
5 Clean the mating surfaces of the block and retainer plate with lacquer thinner or ace-tone.
6 Check the bushing and driveshaft for

wear **(see illustration)**. Replace them if they're worn or damaged.
7 Install the bushing and oil pump drive-shaft in the block. The shaft driven gear must mesh with the camshaft drive gear and the slot in the lower end of the shaft must mate with the oil pump gear tang **(see illustration)**.
8 Apply a 1/16-inch bead of RTV sealant to the retainer plate so it completely seals around the oil pump driveshaft hole in the block.
9 Install the retainer plate and tighten the mounting bolts securely.

17 Oil pan - removal and installation

1 Disconnect the cable from the negative battery terminal.
2 Disconnect the radiator fan shroud.
3 Raise the vehicle and support it securely on jackstands.
4 Drain the engine oil and remove the oil filter (see Chapter 1).
5 Remove the engine strut rods.

6 Disconnect the exhaust pipe at the manifold and remove the catalytic converter and exhaust pipe.
7 Remove the starter (see Chapter 5) and the bellhousing dust cover.
8 Remove the engine mount through bolts. Raise the engine with a jack and block it up in a safe position.
9 Remove the bolts and detach the oil pan. Don't pry between the block and pan or damage to the sealing surfaces may result and oil leaks could develop. If the pan is stuck, dislodge it with a block of wood and a hammer.
10 Use a scraper to remove all traces of sealant from the pan and block, then clean the mating surfaces with lacquer thinner or acetone.
11 Apply a 3/16-inch wide by 1/8-inch thick bead of RTV sealant to the oil pan flange. Make the bead 3/8-inch wide by 3/16-inch thick between the bolt holes at the rear end of the pan. Apply a 1/8-inch bead of sealant to the block at the rear main bearing cap joints and the timing gear cover joints.
12 Install the oil pan and tighten the

16.7 If the slotted oil pump driveshaft is properly mated with the oil pump gear tang, the top of the bushing will be flush with the retainer plate mounting surface

18.2 Remove the oil pump flange mounting bolts and the pick-up tube bracket nut

19.2 A large screwdriver wedged in the starter ring gear teeth or one of the holes in the driveplate can be used to keep the flywheel/driveplate from turning as the mounting bolts are removed

19.3 Don't lose the shim used on automatic transmission equipped vehicles

2C

mounting bolts to the torque listed in this Chapter's Specifications. Start at the center of the pan and work out toward the ends in a spiral pattern.

13   The remainder of installation is reverse of removal.

14   Lower the vehicle.

15   Install a new filter and add oil to the engine.

16   Reconnect the negative battery cable.

17   Start the engine and check for leaks.

18   Oil pump - removal and installation

Refer to illustration 18.2

1   Remove the oil pan (see Section 17).

2   Remove the two oil pump mounting bolts and the pick-up tube bracket nut from the main bearing cap bolt **(see illustration)**.

3   Detach the oil pump and pick-up assembly from the block.

4   If the pump is defective, replace it with a new one. If the engine is being completely overhauled, install a new oil pump - don't reuse the original or attempt to rebuild it.

5   To install the pump, turn the shaft so the gear tang mates with the slot on the lower end of the oil pump driveshaft. The oil pump should slide easily into place over the oil pump driveshaft lower bushing. If it doesn't, pull it off and turn the tang until it's aligned with the pump driveshaft slot.

6   Install the pump mounting bolts and the tube bracket nut. Tighten them to the torque listed in this Chapter's Specifications.

7   Reinstall the oil pan (see Section 17).

8   Add oil, run the engine and check for leaks.

19   Flywheel/driveplate - removal and installation

Refer to illustrations 19.2 and 19.3

1   Remove the transmission (see Chapter 7). If your vehicle has a manual transmission, the pressure plate and clutch will also have to be removed (see Chapter 8).

2   Jam a large screwdriver in the starter ring gear or driveplate hole to keep the crankshaft from turning, then remove the mounting bolts **(see illustration)**. Since it's

fairly heavy, support the flywheel as the last bolt is removed.

3   Pull straight back on the flywheel/driveplate to detach it from the crankshaft. Note the shim installed between the driveplate and crankshaft on vehicles equipped with an automatic transmission **(see illustration)**.

4   On manual transmission equipped vehicles, check the pilot bushing and replace it if necessary (see Chapter 8).

5   Installation is the reverse of removal. Be sure to align the hole in the flywheel/driveplate with the dowel pin in the crankshaft. Use Locktite on the bolt threads and tighten them to the torque listed in this Chapter's Specifications in a criss-cross pattern.

20   Rear main oil seal - replacement

Refer to illustrations 20.5 and 20.8

1   The rear main bearing oil seal can be replaced without removing the oil pan or crankshaft.

2   Remove the transmission (see Chapter 7).

3   If equipped with a manual transmission, remove the pressure plate and clutch disc (see Chapter 8).

4   Remove the flywheel or driveplate (see Section 19).

5   Using a seal removal tool or a large screwdriver, carefully pry the seal out of the block **(see illustration)**. Don't scratch or nick the crankshaft in the process.

6   Clean the bore in the block and the seal contact surface on the crankshaft. Check the crankshaft surface for scratches and nicks that could damage the new seal lip and cause oil leaks. If the crankshaft is damaged, the only alternative is a new or different crankshaft.

7   Apply a light coat of engine oil or multi-purpose grease to the outer edge of the new seal. Lubricate the seal lip with moly-base grease.

8   Press the new seal into place. The seal

20.5 Carefully pry the oil seal out with a screwdriver - don't nick or scratch the crankshaft or the new seal will be damaged and leaks will develop lip must face toward the front of the engine. If the special tool isn't available, carefully work the seal lip over the end of the crankshaft and tap the seal in with a hammer and punch until it's seated in the bore **(see illustration)**.

9   Install the flywheel or driveplate.

10   If equipped with a manual transmission, reinstall the clutch disc and pressure plate.

11   Reinstall the transmission (see Chapter 7).

21   Engine mounts - replacement

Warning: *Improper lifting methods or devices are hazardous and could result in severe injury or death. DO NOT place any part of your body under the engine/transmission when it's supported only by a jack. Failure of the lifting device could result in serious injury or death.*

1   If the rubber mounts have hardened, cracked or separated from the metal backing plates, they must be replaced. This operation

may be carried out with the engine/transmission still in the vehicle.

2   Disconnect the negative cable from the battery.

3   Raise the front of the vehicle and support it securely on jackstands.

4   Support the engine with a jack. Position a block of wood between the jack head and the oil pan.

5   Remove the engine mount-to-chassis bolts.

6   Remove the mount-to-engine support bracket bolts. It's not necessary to detach the support bracket from the engine.

7   Raise the engine just enough to clear the bracket, then remove the engine mount.

8   Place the new mount in position.

9   Install the mount-to-engine support bracket bolts and tighten them securely.

10   Tighten the mount-to-chassis bolts securely.

11   Remove the jack.

12   Remove the jackstands and lower the vehicle.

20.8 Tap around the outer edge of the new seal with a hammer and punch to seat it squarely in the bore

Chapter 2 Part D
2.8L V6 engine

Contents

	Section
Air filter replacement	See Chapter 1
Camshaft - removal and installation	16
CHECK ENGINE light	See Chapter 6
Crankcase front cover - removal and installation	13
Compression check	See Chapter 2F
Cylinder heads - removal and installation	8
Drivebelt check and adjustment	See Chapter 1
Engine mounts - replacement	17
Engine oil and filter change	See Chapter 1
Engine overhaul - general information	See Chapter 2F
Engine removal - methods and precautions	See Chapter 2F
Engine repairs possible with the engine in the vehicle	See Chapter 2F
Exhaust manifolds - removal and installation	7
Flywheel/driveplate - removal and installation	See Chapter 2E
Front cover oil seal - replacement	14

	Section
General information	1
Hydraulic lifters - removal, inspection and installation	5
Intake manifold - removal and installation	4
Oil pan - removal and installation	9
Oil pump - removal and installation	10
Rear main bearing oil seal - replacement	11
Spark plug replacement	See Chapter 1
Timing chain and sprockets - inspection, removal and installation	15
Top Dead Center (TDC) for number 1 piston - locating	See Chapter 2E
Valve covers - removal and installation	2
Valve lash - adjustment	6
Valve train components - replacement (cylinder head installed)	3
Vibration damper - removal and installation	12
Water pump - removal and installation	See Chapter 3

2D

Specifications

General

Cylinders
Right bank (passenger's side, front-to-rear)	1-3-5
Left bank (driver's side, front-to-rear)	2-4-6
Firing order	1-2-3-4-5-6

Torque specifications

Ft-lbs (unless otherwise indicated)

Camshaft sprocket bolts	18
Rear camshaft cover bolts	84 in-lbs
Cylinder head bolts	68
Connecting rod cap nuts	37
Crankshaft pulley bolts	25
Vibration damper hub bolt	75
Engine mounting bracket bolts	80
Engine strut bracket	35
Exhaust manifold mounting bolts	25
Flywheel/driveplate mounting bolts	50
Front cover mounting bolts	
Small	15
Large	25
Intake manifold mounting bolts/nuts	23
Oil pan mounting bolts	
Small	84 in-lbs
Large	18
Oil pump mounting bolt	30
Oil pump cover bolts	96 in-lbs
Rear lifting bracket bolt	25
Valve cover bolts	96 in-lbs
Rocker arm studs	45
Strut bracket assembly nut and bolt	35
Timing chain tensioner bolts	15

Note: Refer to Chapter 2, Part F for additional specifications.

Cylinder location and distributor rotation

The blackened terminal shown on the distributor cap indicates the Number One spark plug wire position

0761H

1.1a 2.8L V6 engine front view

A   *Vacuum break diaphragm*
B   *Thermal vacuum switch*
C   *Intake manifold*
D   *Coolant temperature sending unit*
E   *Fuel pump*

1.1b 2.8L V6 engine left side view

A   *Water pump*
B   *Timing chain cover*
C   *PCV valve*
D   *Oil pressure sending unit*
E   *Vibration damper*
F   *Engine drivebelt pulley*

1   General information

Refer to illustrations 1.1a, 1.1b, 1.1c and 1.1d

The 2.8L V6 engine **(see illustrations)** uses a cast-iron crankshaft supported by four main bearings (the number three bearing is the thrust bearing). Hydraulic lifters and hollow pushrods actuate rocker arms which operate on stud-mounted ball pivots.

The Sections in this Part of Chapter 2 are devoted to "in-vehicle" repair procedures for the 2.8L V6 engine. Chapter 2, Part F includes the removal and installation procedures for all engines. All information concerning engine block and cylinder head servicing can be found in Part F of this Chapter.

The repair procedures included in this Part are based on the assumption that the engine is still installed in the vehicle. Therefore, if this information is being used during a complete engine overhaul - with the engine already out of the vehicle and on a stand - many of the steps included here will not apply.

The Specifications included in this Part of Chapter 2 apply only to the engine and procedures found here. For Specifications regarding engines other than the 2.8L V6, see Part A, B, C or E. The Specifications necessary for engine block and cylinder head rebuilding procedures are contained in Part F of Chapter 2.

2   Valve covers - removal and installation

Right side

1   Disconnect the cable from the negative battery terminal.
2   Remove the air cleaner assembly, tagging each hose to be disconnected with a piece of numbered tape to simplify reinstallation.
3   Remove the bolts retaining the air management valve/coil bracket.
4   Disconnect the wires and hoses that would interfere with the removal of the valve covers, tagging them as they are disconnected.
5   Disconnect the carburetor controls at the carburetor, then remove them from the support bracket.
6   Remove the valve cover bolts.
7   Remove the valve cover. **Note:** *If the cover sticks to the cylinder head, use a block of wood and a rubber hammer to dislodge it. If the cover still will not come loose, pry on it carefully, but do not distort the sealing flange surface.*
8   Before installing the cover, clean all dirt, oil and old gasket material from the sealing surfaces of the cover and cylinder head with a scraper and degreaser.
9   Apply a continuous 3/16-inch (5 mm) diameter bead of RTV-type sealant to the

flange of the cover. Be sure to apply the sealant around the inside of the bolt holes.
10   Place the valve cover on the cylinder head while the sealant is still wet and install the mounting bolts. Tighten the bolts a little at a time to the torque listed in this Chapter's Specifications.
11   Complete the installation by reversing the removal procedure.

Left side

12   Disconnect the cable from the negative battery terminal.
13   Disconnect the hoses at the PCV valve and label them.
14   Remove the air cleaner assembly, tagging each hose to be disconnected with a piece of numbered tape to simplify reinstallation.
15   Disconnect all other wires and hoses that would interfere with the removal of the valve cover, tagging them as they are disconnected.
16   Remove the three way hose bracket from the front of the cover and set the assembly aside.
17   Remove the valve cover bolts.
18   Disconnect the fuel line at the carburetor, plugging the fitting at the carburetor and the disconnected fuel line to prevent leakage and contamination.
19   Follow Steps 7 through 11 in this Section.

1.1c 2.8L V6 engine rear view

A   *Deceleration valve*
B   *EGR valve*
C   *AIR pump output pipe*

1.1d 2.8L V6 engine right side view

A   *Ignition coil*
B   *AIR management valve*
C   *Soft plug (also called a core plug or freeze plug)*

2D

3   Valve train components - replacement (cylinder head installed)

Refer to illustration 3.2

1   Remove the valve cover(s) (see Section 2).

2   If only the pushrod is to be replaced, loosen the rocker nut enough to allow the rocker arm to be rotated away from the pushrod **(see illustration)**. Pull the pushrod out of the hole in the cylinder head.

3   If the rocker arm is to be removed, remove the rocker arm nut and pivot and lift off the rocker arm.

4   If the valve spring is to be removed,

3.2 To remove the pushrods, simply loosen the rocker arm nuts, rotate the rocker arms out of the way and pull out the pushrods

remove the spark plug from the affected cylinder.

5   There are two methods that will allow the valve to remain in place while the valve spring is removed. If you have access to compressed air, install an air hose adapter (available at many auto parts stores; also, the screw-in fitting from a cylinder compression gauge may work) in the spark plug hole. When air pressure is applied to the adapter, the valves will be held in place by the pressure. **Warning:** *Stay away from components that move when the engine is running. The piston will be forced down by air pressure, rotating the crankshaft.*

6   If you do not have access to compressed air, bring the piston of the affected cylinder to a point approximately 45-degrees before Top Dead Center on the compression stroke (see Chapter 2E). Feed a long piece of 1/4-inch nylon cord in through the spark plug hole until it fills the combustion chamber. Be sure to leave the end of the cord hanging out of the spark plug hole so it can be removed easily. Rotate the crankshaft with a wrench (in the normal direction of rotation) until slight resistance is felt.

7   Stuff shop rags into the cylinder head holes above and below the valves to prevent parts and tools from falling into the engine, then use a valve spring compressor to compress the spring/retainer assembly. Remove the keepers with small needle-nose pliers or a magnet. **Note:** *A couple of different types of tools are available for compressing valve springs with the head in place. One type grips the lower coils and presses on the retainer as the knob is turned, while the other type utilizes the rocker arm stud and nut for leverage.*

Both types work very well, although the lever type is usually less expensive.

8   Remove the retainer, cup shield, O-ring seal, spring, spring damper (if so equipped) and valve stem oil seal (if so equipped).

9   The threaded rocker arm studs may be replaced by simply removing the damaged one and replacing it with a new one. Be sure to reinstall the pushrod guide (if so equipped) under the stud nut and tighten the nut to the torque listed in this Chapter's Specifications.

10   Inspection procedures for the hydraulic lifters are detailed in Section 5. Procedures regarding other valve train components are detailed in Chapter 2, Part F.

11   Installation of the valve train components is the reverse of the removal procedure. Always use new valve stem oil seals whenever the spring keepers have been disturbed. Before installing the rocker arms, coat the bearing surfaces of the arms and pivots with moly-based grease or engine assembly lube. Be sure to adjust the valve lash (see Section 6).

4   Intake manifold - removal and installation

Refer to illustrations 4.12, 4.20 and 4.35

1   If the vehicle is equipped with air-conditioning, carefully examine the routing of the hoses and the mounting of the compressor. You may be able to remove the intake manifold without disconnecting the system. If you are in doubt, take the vehicle to a dealer or air conditioning specialist to have the system depressurized. Do not, under any circum-

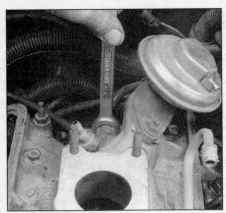

4.12 The power brake tube fitting is located at the rear of the intake manifold

4.20 Use a screwdriver to remove a stubborn heater hose from the intake manifold fitting

4.35 Recommended TIGHTENING sequence for the intake manifold bolts

stances, disconnect the hoses while the system is under pressure.

2   Disconnect the cable from the negative battery terminal.

3   Drain the coolant from the radiator (see Chapter 1).

4   Remove the air cleaner assembly, tagging each hose to be disconnected with a piece of numbered tape to simplify reinstallation.

5   Label and disconnect all electrical wires and vacuum hoses at the carburetor.

6   Disconnect the fuel line at the carburetor. Be prepared to catch some fuel, then plug the fuel line to prevent contamination.

7   Disconnect the throttle cable, making careful note of how it was installed.

8   Disconnect the spark plug wires at the spark plugs (see Chapter 1).

9   Disconnect the wires at the coil, again using numbered pieces of tape to label them.

10   Remove the distributor cap and the attached spark plug wires (see Chapter 5).

11   Remove the distributor (see Chapter 5).

12   Remove the power brake fitting from the rear of the manifold **(see illustration)**.

13   Remove the power brake tube mounting bracket from the manifold boss.

14   Move the power brake tube/hose aside so it will not interfere with the removal of the manifold.

15   Remove the three way hose bracket from the front of the left valve cover.

16   Remove the mounting bolts from the left valve cover, then remove the cover.

17   Remove the AIR management valve/coil mounting bracket assembly bolts from the right cylinder head, disconnect the AIR management hose and remove the assembly.

18   Remove the bolts from the right valve cover, then remove the cover.

19   Remove the upper radiator hose from the manifold.

20   Disconnect the heater hose at the manifold **(see illustration)**.

21   Disconnect the vacuum lines from the TVS switch at the front of the manifold.

22   Label and remove the remaining vacuum hoses from the rear of the manifold.

23   Loosen the air conditioning compressor

pivot bolt and remove the adjusting bolt, if equipped. Remove the compressor drivebelt and rotate the compressor out of the way without disconnecting the refrigerant hoses - if possible - (see Chapter 3). **Warning:** *Do not, under any circumstances, disconnect the hoses while the system is under pressure.*

24   Remove the electrical connector from the coolant switch at the front of the manifold.

25   Make sure that all wires, vacuum hoses and coolant hoses that would interfere with manifold removal have been disconnected.

26   If the manifold is to be replaced with a new one, the external components remaining on the manifold must be removed for transfer to the new manifold. These components may be removed either before or after the manifold has been separated from the engine. These components include:

> *The carburetor studs or bolts*
> *The coolant switch*
> *The EGR valve (use a new gasket when installing)*
> *The emissions system TVS valve*

27   Loosen the manifold bolts in a sequence opposite to the one used for tightening them **(see illustration 4.35)**. Remove the manifold bolts.

28   Separate the manifold from the engine. Do not pry between the mating surfaces because it could damage them. Tap the manifold with a hammer and wooden block to loosen it if necessary.

29   If a new manifold is being installed, transfer the external components from the old manifold to the new one.

30   Before installing the manifold, place clean, lint-free rags in the engine cavity and clean the engine block, cylinder head and manifold gasket surfaces with a scraper. All gasket material and sealant must be removed prior to installation. Remove all dirt and gasket remnants from the engine cavity.

31   Clean the gasket sealing surfaces with degreaser, then apply a 3/16-inch (5 mm) diameter bead of RTV-type sealant to the engine block gasket surfaces only.

32   Install the new intake gaskets on the

cylinder heads. Notice that the gaskets are marked *Right* and *Left*. Be sure to use the correct gasket on each cylinder head.

33   Hold the gaskets in place by extending the bead of RTV up about 1/4-inch onto the gasket ends. The new gaskets will have to be cut so they can be installed behind the pushrods.

34   Carefully lower the intake manifold into position, making sure that you do not disturb the gaskets.

35   Install the intake manifold mounting bolts/nuts and tighten them following the proper sequence **(see illustration)**. Tighten the bolts a little at a time until they are all at the torque listed in this Chapter's Specifications.

36   Install the remaining components in the reverse order of removal.

37   Fill the radiator with coolant, start the engine and check for leaks. Adjust the ignition timing and idle speed as necessary (see Chapter 1). If depressurized, have the air conditioning system evacuated, recharged and leak tested by the shop that depressurized it.

5   Hydraulic lifters - removal, inspection and installation

Refer to illustration 5.7

1   A noisy hydraulic lifter can be isolated when the engine is idling. Place a length of hose or tubing near the position of each valve while listening at the other end of the tube. Another method is to remove the valve cover and, with the engine idling, place a finger on each of the valve spring retainers, one at a time. If a valve lifter is defective, it will be evident from the shock felt at the retainer as the valve seats.

2   Assuming that adjustment is correct (see Section 6), the most likely cause of a noisy valve lifter is a piece of dirt trapped between the plunger and the lifter body.

5.7 Use a scribe to remove the lifters

6.5 Rotate each pushrod as you tighten the rocker arm nut to determine the point at which freeplay is completely eliminated - when you feel drag on the pushrod, all play has been removed; now turn the nut in an extra 3/4 turn

3   Remove the valve covers (see Section 2).

4   Remove the intake manifold (see Section 4).

5   Loosen the rocker arm nut and rotate the rocker arm away from the pushrod.

6   Remove the pushrod.

7   To remove the lifter, a special hydraulic lifter removal tool (available at many auto parts stores) should be used, or a scribe can be positioned at the top of the lifter and used to force the lifter up **(see illustration)**. Do not use pliers or other tools on the outside of the lifter body, as they will damage the finished surface and render the lifter useless.

8   The lifters should be kept separate for reinstallation in their original positions.

9   To dismantle a valve lifter, hold the plunger down with a pushrod and then extract the retainer spring with a small screwdriver.

10   Remove the pushrod seat and the metering valve.

11   Remove the plunger, ball check valve and plunger spring. Remove the ball check valve and spring by prying them out with a small screwdriver.

12   Clean the lifter components with solvent and dry them with compressed air. Examine the internal components for wear and check the ball carefully for flat spots. Refer to Chapter 2, Part F, for additional lifter (and camshaft) inspection procedures.

13   If the lifters are worn, they must be replaced with new ones and the camshaft must be replaced as well (see Chapter 2, Part F). If the lifters were contaminated with dirt, they can be reinstalled - they may operate normally.

14   Reassembly should be done in the following manner:

a)   *Place the ball check valve on the small hole in the bottom of the plunger.*

b)   *Insert the ball check valve spring into the seat in the retainer and place the retainer over the ball so that the spring rests on the ball. Using a small screwdriver, care-*

fully press the retainer into position in the plunger.

c)   *Place the plunger spring over the ball retainer, invert the lifter body and slide it over the spring and plunger. Make sure the oil holes in the body and plunger line up.*

d)   *Fill the assembly with 10-weight oil. Place the metering valve and pushrod seat in position, press down on the seat and install the retainer spring.*

15   When installing the lifters, make sure they are replaced in their original bores and coat them with moly-based grease or engine assembly lube.

16   The remaining installation steps are the reverse of removal.

6   Valve lash - adjustment

Refer to illustration 6.5

1   Disconnect the cable from the negative battery terminal.

2   If the valve covers are still on the engine, refer to Section 2 and remove them.

3   If the valve train components have been serviced just prior to this procedure, make sure that the components are completely reassembled.

4   Rotate the crankshaft until the number one piston is at top dead center (TDC) on the compression stroke (see Chapter 2E). To make sure that you do not mix up the TDC positions of the number one and four pistons, check the position of the rotor in the distributor to see which terminal it is pointing at. Another method is to place your fingers on the number one rocker arms as the timing marks line up at the crankshaft pulley. If the rocker arms are not moving, the number one piston is at TDC. If they move as the timing marks line up, the number four piston is at TDC.

5   Back off the rocker arm nut until play is

felt at the pushrod, then turn it back in until all play is just removed. This can be determined by rotating the pushrod while tightening the nut **(see illustration)**. Just when drag is felt at the pushrod, all lash has been removed. Now turn the nut in an additional 3/4 turn.

6   Adjust the number one, five and six cylinder intake valves and the number one, two and three cylinder exhaust valves, with the crankshaft in this position, using the method just described.

7   Rotate the crankshaft until the number four piston is at TDC on the compression stroke and adjust the number two, three and four cylinder intake valves and the number four, five and six cylinder exhaust valves.

8   Install the valve covers (see Section 2).

7   Exhaust manifolds - removal and installation

Note: *The exhaust manifold and manifold-to-pipe fasteners will be easier to remove if you apply penetrating oil to them and allow it to soak in for several minutes.*

Right side

Refer to illustration 7.7

1   Remove the cable from the negative battery terminal.

2   Raise the front of the vehicle and support it securely on jackstands.

Block the rear wheels to keep the vehicle from rolling.

3   Remove the bolts attaching the exhaust pipe to the exhaust manifold, then separate the pipe from the manifold.

4   Remove the jackstands and lower the vehicle.

5   Disconnect the air management hose at the check valve.

6   Disconnect the spark plug wires from the spark plugs, labeling them as they are disconnected to simplify installation.

2D

7.7 Locations of the three upper exhaust manifold bolts (right side shown, left similar)

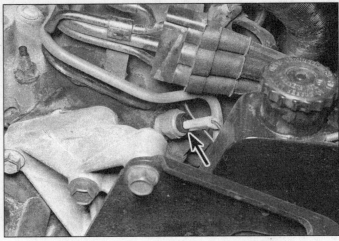

8.11 Location of the coolant temperature sending unit

7   Remove the exhaust manifold mounting bolts **(see illustration)** and separate the manifold from the engine.

8   Installation is the reverse of the removal procedure. Before installing the manifold, be sure to thoroughly clean the mating surfaces on the manifold and cylinder head. Install a new gasket and torque the bolts to the torque listed in this Chapter's Specifications.

Left side

9   Disconnect the cable from the negative battery terminal.

10   Raise the front of the vehicle and place it securely on jackstands. Block the rear wheels to keep the vehicle from rolling.

11   Remove the bolts retaining the exhaust pipe to the manifold, then disconnect the pipe from the manifold.

12   Remove the four bolts and one nut accessible at the rear of the manifold.

13   Remove the jackstands and lower the vehicle.

14   Remove the air cleaner assembly, labeling all hoses.

15   Disconnect the hoses leading to the air management valve.

16   Disconnect and label any wires that will interfere with the removal of the manifold.

17   Remove the power steering pump bracket from the cylinder head. Loosen the pump adjusting bracket bolt and remove the pump drivebelt from the pulley first. After removing the bracket from the cylinder head, place the steering pump assembly aside, out of the way. Don't disconnect the hoses, and keep the pump upright so fluid doesn't spill.

18   Remove the remaining manifold bolts and separate the manifold and heat shield from the engine.

19   Installation is the reverse of the removal procedure. Be sure to thoroughly clean the cylinder head and manifold surfaces before installing the manifold. Use a new gasket and tighten the bolts to the torque listed in this Chapter's Specifications.

8   Cylinder heads - removal and installation

Left side

Refer to illustrations 8.9, 8.11, 8.12 and 8.13

1   Remove the intake manifold (see Section 4).

2   Raise the vehicle and place it securely on jackstands.

3   Drain the cooling system (see Chapter 1), including the engine block. The engine block drain plugs are located to the rear of the engine mounts (the plug on the left side is just above the oil filter).

4   Disconnect the exhaust pipe from the exhaust manifold.

5   Remove the oil dipstick tube assembly from the side of the engine.

6   Remove the jackstands and lower the vehicle.

7   **Note:** *Steps 8 through 11 are to be followed if the head is to be replaced with a new one. These Steps may be performed either before or after the head has been removed. In the accompanying illustrations, the procedures were performed before the head was removed.*

8   Remove the exhaust manifold (see Section 7).

9   Remove the power steering pump bracket from the side of the cylinder head.

10   Remove the air conditioning compressor bracket from the front of the cylinder head, if equipped.

11   Remove the coolant temperature sending unit from the front of the cylinder head **(see illustration)**.

12   Loosen the rocker arm nuts enough to allow removal of the pushrods, then remove the pushrods **(see illustration)**.

13   Loosen the head bolts in a sequence opposite to the one used for tightening them **(see illustration 8.19)**.

14   Remove the cylinder head. To break the gasket seal, use a long screwdriver or pry bar

under the cast "ears" of the cylinder head **(see illustration)**. Be sure not to damage the cylinder head sealing surface.

15   If a new cylinder head is being installed, attach the components previously removed from the old head. Before installing the cylinder head, the gasket surfaces of both the head and the engine block must be clean and free of nicks and scratches. Also, the threads in the block and on the head bolts must be completely clean, as any dirt remaining in the threads will affect bolt torque.

16   Place the gasket in position over the locating dowels, with the note "This Side Up" visible.

17   Position the cylinder head over the gasket.

18   Coat the cylinder head bolts with Teflon pipe thread sealant and install the bolts.

19   Tighten the bolts in the proper sequence **(see illustration)** to the torque listed in this Chapter's Specifications. Work up to the final torque in three steps.

20   Install the pushrods, making sure the lower ends are in the lifter seats, place the rocker arm ends over the pushrods and loosely install the rocker arm nuts.

21   The remaining installation steps are the

8.12 When removing the pushrods, be sure to store them separately to ensure reinstallation in their original positions

8.14 Don't damage the cylinder head sealing surface when breaking the gasket loose with a screwdriver or pry bar

8.19 TIGHTENING sequence for the cylinder head bolts

reverse of those for removal. Before installing the valve covers, adjust the valve lash (see Section 6).

Right side

22   Remove the intake manifold (see Section 4).
23   Raise the vehicle and place it securely on jackstands.
24   Drain the cooling system, including the engine block (see Chapter 1). The engine block drain plugs are located to the rear of the engine mounts (the plug on the left side is just above the oil filter).
25   Disconnect the exhaust pipe from the exhaust manifold.
26   Remove the jackstands and lower the vehicle.
27   Remove the alternator from the alternator bracket, then remove the bracket from the head.
28   Remove the lifting "eye" from the rear of the head (necessary only if the head is to be replaced with a new one).
29   Remove the exhaust manifold (if the head is to be replaced with a new one).
30   Loosen the rocker arm nuts sufficiently to allow removal of the pushrods, then remove the pushrods.
31   Loosen the head bolts in a sequence opposite to the one used for tightening them (see illustration 8.19).
32   Remove the cylinder head. To break the gasket seal, insert a bar into one of the exhaust ports, then carefully lift on the tool.
33   Install the head (see Steps 15 through 21).

9   Oil pan - removal and installation

Note: *On 2WD vehicles, due to the close proximity of the frame crossmember to the oil pan, the engine must be removed to remove the oil pan. Refer to Chapter 2F and then follow Steps 23 through 26.*
1   On four-wheel drive vehicles, disconnect the negative battery cable.
2   Remove the oil dipstick.
3   Raise the vehicle and support it securely on jackstands.

4   Remove the undervehicle splash shield.
5   Remove the front axle shield.
6   Remove the transfer case shield.
7   Disconnect the brake lines from the clips on the crossmember.
8   Remove the number two crossmember.
9   If equipped with an automatic transmission, remove the converter hanger bolts and disconnect the exhaust pipe clamp at the converter. Disconnect the exhaust pipes at the manifolds and slide the pipes to the rear.
10   Disconnect the front driveshaft at the drive pinion (see Chapter 8).
11   Disconnect the engine braces at the flywheel cover and loosen the braces attached to the engine block.
12   Remove the starter motor wires and mounting bolts. Remove the starter motor.
13   Disconnect the steering shock absorber at the frame bracket.
14   Remove the steering gear mounting bolts (see Chapter 10).
15   Scribe a line indicating the position of the idler arm bracket and remove the idler arm mounting bolts (see Chapter 10).
16   Pull the steering gear and linkage forward.
17   On the right side, remove the differential housing mounting bolts from the mounting bracket. On the left side, remove the mounting bolts from the frame.
18   Move the differential housing forward.
19   Remove the through bolts from the engine mounts.
20   Drain the oil (see Chapter 1).
21   Raise the engine with a floor jack.
Warning: *Keep your hands and other parts of your body out of areas where they'd be hurt if the engine falls off the jack.*
22   Unbolt and remove the oil pan. If the pan sticks to the block, dislodge it with a rubber mallet.
23   Before installing the pan, make sure that the sealing surfaces on the pan, block and timing cover are clean and free of oil. If the old pan is being reinstalled, make sure that all sealant has been removed from the pan sealing flange and from the blind attaching holes.
24   With all the sealing surfaces clean, place a 1/8-inch bead of RTV-type sealant on the oil pan sealing flange.

25   Install all bolts finger tight before tightening any bolts. Tighten the pan bolts to the torque listed in this Chapter's Specifications. On 4WD models, you'll have to lower the engine first.
26   The rest of installation is the reverse of removal.

10   Oil pump - removal and installation

1   Remove the oil pan (see Section 9).
2   Remove the pump-to-rear main bearing cap bolt and separate the pump and extension shaft from the engine.
3   To install the pump, move it into position and align the top end of the hexagonal extension shaft with the hexagonal socket in the lower end of the distributor drive gear. The distributor drives the oil pump, so it is essential that this alignment is correct.
4   Install the oil pump-to-rear main bearing cap bolt and tighten it to the torque listed in this Chapter's Specifications.
5   Reinstall the oil pan.

11   Rear main bearing oil seal - replacement

Note 1: *1985 and later models are equipped with a one-piece rear main oil seal. Refer to Chapter 2A for the seal replacement procedure.*
Note 2: *The following procedure describes replacing the rear main bearing oil seal with the engine installed in the vehicle. If this method does not repair a rear main seal oil leak, remove the engine and the crankshaft and install a service replacement one-piece rear main seal (available at most auto parts stores) following the instructions provided with the seal kit.*

1982 and 1983 models

Refer to illustrations 11.3a, 11.3b, 11.5 and 11.10
Note: *Special tools, as noted in the Steps which follow, are required for this procedure.*

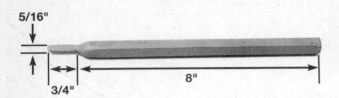

5/16"

3/4"

8"

11.3a Grind a piece of 1/2-inch diameter brass or aluminum rod to these dimensions as a rear seal driver

11.3b Drive each end of the seal into the groove until it feels tightly packed

They are available from your dealer or may in some cases be rented from an auto parts store or tool rental shop.

1   Although the crankshaft must be removed to install a new seal, the upper portion of the seal can be repaired with the crankshaft in place.

2   Remove the oil pan and oil pump (see Sections 9 and 10). Remove the rear main bearing cap (see Chapter 2F).

3   Using a special seal driver tool, drive the old seal gently back into the groove, packing it tightly **(see illustrations)**. It will pack in to a depth of 1/4 to 3/4-inch.

4   Repeat the procedure on the other end of the seal.

5   Measure the amount that the seal was driven up into the groove on one side and add 1/16-inch. Remove the old seal from the main bearing cap. Use the main bearing cap as a fixture and cut off a piece of the old seal to the predetermined length. Repeat this process for the other side **(see illustration)**.

6   Place a drop of sealant on each end of these pieces and pack them into the upper groove to fill the gap made previously.

7   Trim the remaining material perfectly flush with the block.

8   Be careful not to harm the bearing surface. If necessary, place a thin piece of shim stock between the seal and the crankshaft (to protect the crankshaft) and trim the seal against the shim stock.

9   Install a new seal in the main bearing cap.

10   Apply a thin, even coat of anaerobic-type gasket sealant to the areas of the engine block that mate with the rear main bearing

cap **(see illustration). Caution:** *Do not get any sealant on the bearing or seal faces.*

11   Tighten the rear main bearing cap bolts to the torque specified in Chapter 2, Part F.

12   Install the oil pump and oil pan.

1984 models

Refer to illustrations 11.17, 11.20 and 11.21

13   Always service both halves of the rear main oil seal. While replacement of this seal is much easier with the engine removed from the vehicle, the job can be done with the engine in place.

14   Remove the oil pan and oil pump as described previously in this Chapter (see Section 9).

15   Remove the rear main bearing cap from the engine.

16   Using a screwdriver, pry the lower half of the oil seal from the bearing cap.

17   To remove the upper half of the seal, use a small hammer and a brass pin punch to roll the seal around the crankshaft journal. Tap one end of the seal with the hammer and punch (be careful not to strike the crankshaft) until the other end of the seal protrudes enough to pull the seal out with pliers **(see illustration)**.

18   Remove all sealant and foreign material from the main bearing cap. Do not use an abrasive cleaner for this.

19   Inspect the components for nicks, scratches and burrs at all sealing surfaces. Remove any defects with a fine file or deburring tool.

20   Apply a very thin coat of RTV-type gas-

11.5 Measure the amount that the seal has been driven up into the groove - here a small screwdriver was used with a sleeve of masking tape (arrow) to serve as a depth indicator

ket sealant to the outer surface of the upper seal **(see illustration)**. Do not get any sealant on the seal lips.

11.10 Apply anaerobic sealant to the areas shown, but don't get sealant in the grooves or on the seal (1984 models)

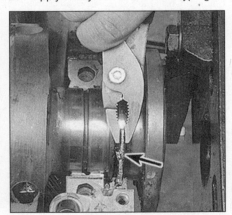

11.17 Drive in one end of the upper seal half until the other end protrudes, then pull the seal (arrow) all the way out with a pair of pliers

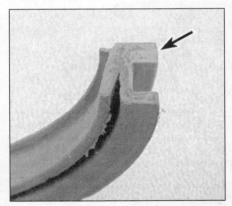

11.20 A very thin coat of RTV-type gasket sealant should be applied to the area shown on 1984 and 1985 rear main bearing seals (avoid getting sealant on the seal lips)

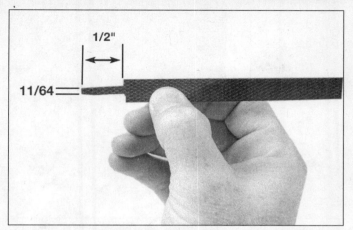

11.21 A "shoehorn" guide for the rear seal can be made from a thin piece of plastic, brass or shim stock

12.6 You'll need a puller to remove the crankshaft vibration damper

21   A small plastic installation tool should be included in the purchase of the rear main oil seal. If not, fabricate one from an old feeler gauge, a thin piece of plastic or shim stock **(see illustration)**.

22   With the upper half of the seal positioned so that the seal lip faces toward the front of the engine and the small dust lip faces toward the flywheel, install the seal by rolling it around the crankshaft using the installation tool as a "shoehorn" for protection.

23   Apply sealing compound as described in Step 20 to the other half of the seal and install it in the bearing cap.

24   Apply a film of anaerobic sealant to the cap between the rear main oil seal end and oil pan rear seal groove **(see illustration 11.10)**. Be sure to keep the sealant off the rear main oil seal and bearing and out of the drain slot.

25   Just before installing the cap, apply a light coat of multi-purpose grease to the crankshaft surface that will contact the seal.

26   Install the rear main bearing cap and tighten the bolts to the torque specified in Chapter 2, Part F.

27   Install the oil pump and oil pan.

12   Vibration damper - removal and installation

Refer to illustration 12.6

1   Remove the hose from the retaining strap atop the radiator shroud by releasing the end of the strap from the underside of the shroud with pliers. Move the hose to the side, out of the way.

2   Remove the bolts and separate the upper radiator shroud from the radiator.

3   Remove the cooling fan from the fan pulley.

4   Loosen the accessory drivebelt adjusting bolts as necessary, then remove the drivebelts, tagging each one as it is removed to simplify reinstallation.

5   Remove the bolts from the crankshaft

13.6a Locations of the remaining front cover mounting bolts (the bottom two bolts and top bolt aren't visible in this illustration)

pulley and the damper center bolt. (a screwdriver can be used to lock the starter ring gear on the flywheel), then remove the pulley.

6   Attach a puller to the damper **(see illustration)**. Draw the damper off the crankshaft, being careful not to drop it as it breaks free. A common gear puller should not be used to draw the damper off, as it may separate the outer portion of the damper from the hub. Use only a puller which bolts to the hub.

7   Before installing the damper, coat the front cover seal area (on the damper) with moly-based grease.

8   Place the damper in position over the key on the crankshaft. Make sure the damper keyway lines up with the key.

9   Using a damper installation tool (available at most auto parts stores) push the damper onto the crankshaft. The special tool distributes the pressure evenly around the hub.

10   Remove the installation tool and install the damper retaining bolt. Tighten the bolt to the torque listed in this Chapter's Specifications.

11   Follow the removal procedure in the

13.6b Some of the timing cover bolts pass through the oil pan

reverse order for the remaining components.

12   Adjust the drivebelts (see Chapter 1).

13   Crankcase front cover - removal and installation

Refer to illustrations 13.6a and 13.6b

1   Remove the water pump as described in Chapter 3.

2   If equipped with air conditioning, remove the compressor from the mounting bracket and secure it out of the way (see Chapter 3). In most cases you can relocate the compressor without disconnecting the hoses. **Warning:** *Do not disconnect any of the air conditioning system hoses without having the system depressurized by a GM dealer or air conditioning technician.*

3   Remove the compressor mounting bracket.

4   Remove the vibration damper (see Section 12).

5   Disconnect the lower radiator hose at the front cover.

6   Remove the front cover mounting bolts and separate the cover from the engine **(see illustrations)**.

7   Clean all oil, dirt and old gasket material from the sealing surfaces of the front cover and engine block. Replace the front cover oil seal (see Section 14).

8   Apply a continuous 3/32-inch (2 mm) bead of anaerobic sealant to both mating surfaces of the front cover, except the cover-to-block mating surface, where the cover engages the oil pan lip. Apply RTV-type sealant to the cover-to-oil pan area. Also apply anaerobic sealant to the areas surrounding the coolant passages.

9   Place the front cover in position on the engine block and install the mounting bolts. Tighten the bolts to the torque listed in this Chapter's Specifications.

10   The remaining installation procedures are the reverse of removal.

14   Front cover oil seal - replacement

With front cover installed on engine

1   With the vibration damper removed (see Section 12), pry the old seal out of the crankcase front cover with a large screwdriver. Be very careful not to damage the surface of the crankshaft.

2   Place the new seal in position with the open end of the seal (seal lip) toward the inside of the cover.

3   Drive the seal into the cover until it is seated. A section of large-diameter pipe or a large socket can be used as a seal driver if the proper driver is not available.

4   Be careful not to distort the front cover.

With front cover removed from engine

Refer to illustrations 14.7 and 14.9

5   This method is preferred, as the cover can be supported while the old seal is removed and the new one is installed.

6   Remove the crankcase front cover (see

14.7 Lay the front cover on a pair or wood blocks and knock out the old seal with a punch

Section 13).

7   Using a large screwdriver, pry the old seal out of the bore from the front of the cover. Alternatively, support the cover and drive the seal out from the rear **(see illustration)**. Be careful not to damage the cover.

8   With the front of the cover facing up, place the new seal in position with the open end of the seal toward the inside of the cover.

9   Using a wooden block and hammer, drive the new seal into the cover until it is completely seated **(see illustration)**.

10   If the cover was removed, install it by reversing the removal procedure.

15   Timing chain and sprockets - inspection, removal and installation

Refer to illustrations 15.8, 15.9, 15.10 and 15.12

1   Disconnect the cable from the negative battery terminal.

2   Remove the vibration damper (see Section 12).

14.9 Use a wood block and a hammer to install the new front cover seal

3   Remove the crankcase front cover (see Section 13).

4   Before removing the chain and sprockets, visually inspect the teeth on the sprockets for signs of wear and the chain for looseness.

5   If either or both sprockets show any signs of wear (edges on the teeth of the camshaft sprocket not "square," bright or blue areas on the teeth of either sprocket, chipping, pitting, etc.), they should be replaced with new ones. Wear in these areas is very common. Failure to replace a worn timing chain may result in erratic engine performance, loss of power and lowered gas mileage.

6   If any one component requires replacement, all related components should be replaced as well.

7   If it is determined that the timing components require replacement, proceed as follows:

8   Turn the engine over until the marks on the camshaft and crankshaft sprockets are in exact alignment **(see illustration)**. At this point the number one and four pistons will be at top dead center with the number four pis-

15.8 The camshaft and crankshaft sprocket timing marks should be aligned before you remove the timing sprockets and chain

15.9 Use a screwdriver to hold the camshaft sprocket in place while you loosen the mounting bolts

15.10 You'll need a puller to remove the crankshaft sprocket

15.12 Lubricate the thrust surface of the camshaft sprocket

ton in the firing position (verify by checking the position of the rotor in the distributor). Do not attempt to remove either sprocket or the timing chain until this is done and do not turn the crankshaft or camshaft after the sprockets/chain are removed.

9   Remove the three camshaft sprocket retaining bolts **(see illustration)** and lift the camshaft sprocket and timing chain off the front of the engine. It may be necessary to tap the sprocket with a soft-faced hammer to dislodge it.

10   If it is necessary to remove the crankshaft sprocket, it can be withdrawn from the crankshaft with a special puller **(see illustration)**.

11   Attach the crankshaft sprocket to the crankshaft using a piece of pipe and a bolt and washer from the puller set.

12   Lubricate the thrust (rear) surface of the camshaft sprocket with moly-based grease or engine assembly lube **(see illustration)**. Install the timing chain over the camshaft sprocket with slack in the chain hanging down over the crankshaft sprocket.

13   With the timing marks aligned, slip the chain over the crankshaft sprocket and then draw the camshaft sprocket into place with

the three retaining bolts. Do not hammer or attempt to drive the camshaft sprocket into place, as it could dislodge the welch plug at the rear of the engine.

14   With the chain and both sprockets in place, check again to ensure that the timing marks on the two sprockets are properly aligned. If not, remove the camshaft sprocket and move it until the marks align.

15   Lubricate the chain with engine oil and install the remaining components in the reverse order of removal.

16   Camshaft - removal and installation

Refer to illustrations 16.11 and 16.13

1   Remove the cable from the negative battery terminal.

2   Drain the oil from the crankcase (see Chapter 1).

3   Drain the coolant from the radiator (see Chapter 1).

4   Remove the radiator (see Chapter 3).

5   If equipped with air conditioning, remove the condenser (see Chapter 3). **Warning:** *The air conditioning system must be dis-*

charged by an air conditioning technician before the condenser can be removed. Under no circumstances should this be attempted by the home mechanic, as personal injury may result.

6   Remove the valve lifters (see Section 5).

7   Remove the crankcase front cover (see Section 13).

8   Remove the fuel pump and pushrod (see Chapter 4).

9   Remove the timing chain and camshaft sprocket (see Section 15).

10   Install a long bolt in one of the camshaft bolt holes to be used as a handle to pull on and support the camshaft.

11   Carefully draw the camshaft out of the engine block **(see illustration)**. Do this very slowly to avoid damage to the camshaft bearings as the lobes pass over the bearing surfaces. Always support the camshaft with one hand near the engine block.

12   Refer to Chapter 2, Part F, for the camshaft inspection procedures.

13   Prior to installing the camshaft, coat each of the lobes and journals with camshaft assembly lube **(see illustration)**.

14   Slide the camshaft into the engine block, again taking extra care not to damage

16.11 Use a hooked wire to support the camshaft during removal

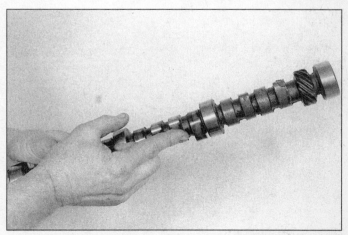

16.13 Be sure to apply camshaft assembly lube to the camshaft lobes and bearing journals before you install the camshaft

the bearings.

15   Install the camshaft sprocket and timing chain (see Section 15).

16   Install the remaining components in the reverse order of removal by referring to the appropriate Chapter or Section.

17   Adjust the valve lash (see Section 6).

18   Have the air conditioning system (if so equipped), evacuated, recharged and leak tested by the shop that discharged it.

17   Engine mounts - replacement with engine in vehicle

1   If the mounts have become hard, split or separated from the metal backing, they must be replaced. This operation may be carried out with the engine/transmission still in the vehicle.

Front mount

2   Remove the through-bolt and nut.

3   Remove the upper fan shroud.

4   Raise the engine slightly using a hoist or jack with a wood block under the oil pan, then remove the mount and bracket assembly from the crossmember. **Warning:** *Keep your hands and other body parts out of areas where they'd be hurt if the engine were to fall off the jack or hoist.*

5   Position the new mount, install the through-bolt and nut, then tighten all the bolts to the torque listed in this Chapter's Specifications.

Rear mount

Refer to illustration 17.6

6   Remove the crossmember-to-mount bolts **(see illustration)**, then raise the transmission slightly with a jack. **Warning:** *Keep your hands and other body parts cut of areas where they'd be hurt if the transmission were to fall off the jack.*

7   Remove the mount-to-transmission bolts, followed by the mount.

8   Install the new mount, lower the trans-

17.6 Mounting bolt locations for the rear engine mount

mission and align the crossmember-to-mount bolts.

9   Tighten all the bolts to the torque listed in this Chapter's Specifications.

Chapter 2 Part E
4.3L V6 engine

Contents

	Section
Balancer shaft - removal and installation (1992 and later VIN W engines)	12
Camshaft, bearings and lifters - removal, inspection and installation	11
Crankshaft oil seals - replacement	15
Cylinder compression check	See Chapter 2F
Cylinder heads - removal and installation	8
Drivebelt check, adjustment and replacement	See Chapter 1
Engine mounts - check and replacement	17
Engine oil and filter change	See Chapter 1
Engine overhaul - general information	See Chapter 2F
Engine - removal and installation	See Chapter 2F
Exhaust manifolds - removal and installation	6
Flywheel/driveplate - removal and installation	16

	Section
General information	1
Intake manifold - removal and installation	5
Oil pan - removal and installation	13
Oil pump - removal and installation	14
Repair operations possible with the engine in the vehicle	2
Rocker arms and pushrods - removal, inspection and installation	7
Spark plug replacement	See Chapter 1
Timing cover, chain and sprockets - removal and installation	10
Top Dead Center (TDC) for number 1 piston - locating	9
Valve covers - removal and installation	3
Valve spring, retainer and seals - replacement	4
Water pump - removal and installation	See Chapter 3

2E

Specifications

General

Cylinder numbers (front-to-rear)	
Left (driver's) side	1-3-5
Right side	2-4-6
Firing order	1-6-5-4-3-2
Displacement	262 cubic inches

Camshaft

Bearing journal	
Diameter	1.8682 to 1.8692 inches
Out-of-round limit	0.001 inch
Lobe lift	
Intake	0.357 inch
Exhaust	0.390 inch
Endplay	0.004 to 0.012 inch
Balancer shaft (1992 and later VIN W engine)	
Rear bearing journal outside diameter	1.4309 to 1.4215 in

Torque specifications

	Ft-lbs (unless otherwise indicated)
Valve cover bolts	90 in-lbs
Intake manifold bolts	
TBI models	36
CPI models	
Initial torque	35
Final torque	
All bolts except bolt A	35
Bolt A	41
Exhaust manifold bolts	
Center bolts	26
All others	20

**FIRING ORDER
1-6-5-4-3-2**

1987 and earlier 4.3L V6

The blackened terminal shown on the distributor cap indicates the Number One spark plug wire position

Cylinder location and distributor rotation

**FIRING ORDER
1-6-5-4-3-2**

1988 and later 4.3L V6

24070-1 specs HAYNES

Torque specifications (continued)

Ft-lbs (unless otherwise indicated)

Cylinder head bolts*	
Step 1	25
Step 2	45
Step 3	65
Timing chain cover bolts..	120 in-lbs
Camshaft sprocket bolts	18
Balancer shaft (1992 and later VIN W engine)	
Retainer bolts	120 in-lbs
Driven gear bolt	15 plus an additional 35-degrees rotation
Drive gear retaining stud	144 in-lbs
Rocker arm nut (1992 and later VIN W engine)	20
Vibration damper bolt	70
Lifter guide retainer bolts..	145 in-lbs
Oil pan	
Bolts/studs	100 in-lbs
Nuts	200 in-lbs
Oil pump bolt	65
Rear main bearing cap bolts..	80
Rear main oil seal housing bolts..................................	135 in-lbs
Flywheel bolts..	65
Driveplate bolts..	55

*Use Permatex number 2 on the bolt threads

1   General information

This Part of Chapter 2 is devoted to in-vehicle repair procedures for the 4.3L V6 engine. All information concerning engine removal and installation and engine block and cylinder head overhaul can be found in Part F of this Chapter.

The VIN W V6 engine introduced in 1992 is very similar to the other V6 engines in this Chapter, except it is equipped with a balancer shaft and has the Central Port Injection (CPI) fuel injection system. You can identify this engine by its unique intake plenum assembly. If there's any doubt as to whether or not you have this engine, refer to the Vehicle Identification Number (VIN) that is located on the forward edge of the dashboard on the driver's side. The VIN is visible from outside the vehicle, through the windshield. If the eighth position in the alpha-numeric code is a W, you have the VIN W engine.

The following repair procedures are based on the assumption that the engine is installed in the vehicle. If the engine has been removed from the vehicle and mounted on a stand, many of the steps outlined in this Part of Chapter 2 will not apply.

The Specifications included in this Part of Chapter 2 apply only to the procedures contained in this Part. Part F of Chapter 2 contains the Specifications necessary for cylinder head and engine block rebuilding.

2   Repair operations possible with the engine in the vehicle

Many major repair operations can be accomplished without removing the engine from the vehicle.

Clean the engine compartment and the exterior of the engine with some type of pressure washer before any work is done. It will make the job easier and help keep dirt out of the internal areas of the engine.

Remove the hood, if necessary, to improve access to the engine as repairs are performed (see Chapter 11 if necessary).

If vacuum, exhaust, oil or coolant leaks develop, indicating a need for gasket or seal replacement, the repairs can generally be made with the engine in the vehicle. The intake and exhaust manifold gaskets, timing cover gasket, oil pan gasket, crankshaft oil seals and cylinder head gaskets are all accessible with the engine in place.

Exterior engine components, such as the intake and exhaust manifolds, the oil pan (and the oil pump), the water pump, the starter motor, the alternator, the distributor and the fuel system components can be removed for repair with the engine in place.

Since the cylinder heads can be removed without pulling the engine, valve component servicing can also be accomplished with the engine in the vehicle. Replacement of the timing chain and sprockets is also possi-

ble with the engine in the vehicle.

In extreme cases caused by a lack of necessary equipment, repair or replacement of piston rings, pistons, connecting rods and rod bearings is possible with the engine in the vehicle. However, this practice is not recommended because of the cleaning and preparation work that must be done to the components involved.

3   Valve covers - removal and installation

Removal

1   Disconnect the negative cable from the battery.

2   Remove the air cleaner assembly (see Chapter 4).

3   Remove the heat stove tube, if so equipped (see Chapter 4).

Right side

Refer to illustrations 3.4, 3.6 and 3.10

4   Detach the wiring harness from the clip **(see illustration)**, then separate the tube from the valve cover.

5   Disconnect the crankcase ventilation pipe from the valve cover.

6   Working in the passenger compartment, remove the diverter valve, bracket and hoses **(see illustration)**. Refer to Chapter 6 if necessary.

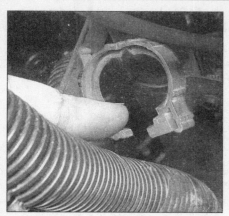

3.4 Unclip the wiring harness to make room for valve cover removal

3.6 The diverter valve (arrow) is mounted near the rear of the right valve cover

3.10 The valve cover bolts require a T-30 Torx bit for removal

7 Remove the spark plug wire bracket from the right cylinder head.
8 Remove the ignition coil (see Chapter 5).
9 Finish unclipping the wire harness at the valve cover and move it aside.
10 Use a T-30 TORX bit to remove the valve cover bolts, then detach the cover from the head (see illustration). Note: *If the cover is stuck to the head, bump one end with a block of wood and a hammer to jar it loose. If that doesn't work, try to slip a flexible putty knife between the head and cover to break the gasket seal. Don't pry at the cover-to-head joint or damage to the sealing surfaces may occur (leading to oil leaks in the future).*

Left side

Refer to illustrations 3.13 and 3.14
11 Unbolt the cruise control servo and bracket (if equipped) and set it aside (see illustration 5.8, if necessary).
12 Remove the air conditioning compressor rear brace (if so equipped) (see illustration 5.6, if necessary).
13 Detach the power brake booster vacuum line from the intake manifold (see illustration).
14 Remove the PCV valve (see illustration).
15 Remove the spark plug wire bracket from the cylinder head.
16 Detach the accelerator/TV (kickdown) cable bracket from the manifold.
17 Use a T-30 TORX bit to remove the valve cover bolts, then detach the cover from the head. Note: *If the cover is stuck to the head, bump one end with a block of wood and a hammer to jar it loose. If that doesn't work, try to slip a flexible putty knife between the head and cover to break the gasket seal. Don't pry at the cover-to-head joint or damage to the sealing surfaces may occur (leading to oil leaks in the future).*

Installation

18 The mating surfaces of each cylinder head and valve cover must be perfectly clean when the covers are installed. Use a gasket scraper to remove all traces of sealant and old gasket material, then clean the mating surfaces with lacquer thinner or acetone. If there's sealant or oil on the mating surfaces when the cover is installed, oil leaks may develop.
19 Clean the mounting bolt threads with a die to remove any corrosion and restore damaged threads. Make sure the threaded holes in the head are clean - run a tap into them to remove corrosion and restore damaged threads.
20 The gaskets should be mated to the covers before the covers are installed. Apply a thin coat of RTV sealant to the cover flange, then position the gasket inside the cover lip and allow the sealant to set up so the gasket adheres to the cover. If the sealant isn't allowed to set, the gasket may fall out of the cover as it's installed on the engine.
21 Carefully position the cover on the head and install the bolts.
22 Tighten the bolts in three or four steps to the torque listed in this Chapter's Specifications.
23 The remaining installation steps are the reverse of removal.
24 Start the engine and check carefully for oil leaks as the engine warms up.

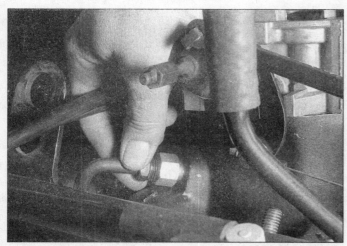

3.13 Unscrewing the power brake booster vacuum line fitting

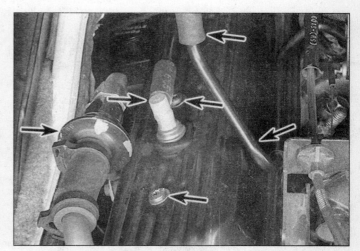

3.14 Rear view of left valve cover showing the vacuum brake booster line, the PCV valve, the AIR check valve and tube and the valve cover mounting bolts (arrows)

4   Valve spring, retainer and seals - replacement

Refer to illustrations 4.4, 4.8a, 4.8b, 4.9, 4.16 and 4.17

Note: *Broken valve springs and defective valve stem seals can be replaced without removing the cylinder heads. Two special tools and a compressed air source are normally required to perform this operation, so read through this Section carefully and rent or buy the tools before beginning the job. If compressed air isn't available, a length of nylon rope can be used to keep the valves from falling into the cylinder during this procedure.*

1   Remove the valve cover from the cylinder head (see Section 3). If all of the valve stem seals are being replaced, remove both valve covers.

2   Remove the spark plug from the cylinder which has the defective component. If all of the valve stem seals are being replaced, all of the spark plugs should be removed.

3   Turn the crankshaft until the piston in the affected cylinder is at top dead center on the compression stroke (see Section 9). If you are replacing all of the valve stem seals, begin with cylinder number one and work on the valves for one cylinder at a time. Move from cylinder-to-cylinder following the firing order sequence (1-6-5-4-3-2).

4   Thread an adapter into the spark plug hole **(see illustration)** and connect an air hose from a compressed air source to it. Most auto parts stores can supply the air hose adapter. **Note:** *Many cylinder compression gauges utilize a screw-in fitting that may work with your air hose quick-disconnect fitting.*

5   Remove the nut, pivot ball and rocker arm for the valve with the defective part and pull out the pushrod. If all the valve stem seals are being replaced, all of the rocker arms and pushrods should be removed (see Section 7).

6   Apply compressed air to the cylinder.

4.4 Use compressed air, if available, to hold the valves closed when the springs are removed - the air hose adapter (arrow) threads into the spark plug hole and accepts the hose from the compressor

The valves should be held in place by the air pressure. If the valve faces or seats are in poor condition, leaks may prevent air pressure from retaining the valves - refer to the alternative procedure below.

7   If you don't have access to compressed air, an alternative method can be used. Position the piston at a point approximately 45-degrees (1/8-turn) before TDC on the compression stroke, then feed a long piece of nylon rope through the spark plug hole until it fills the combustion chamber. Be sure to leave the end of the rope hanging out of the engine so it can be removed easily. Use a large breaker bar and socket to rotate the crankshaft in the normal direction of rotation until slight resistance is felt.

8   Stuff shop rags into the cylinder head holes above and below the valves to prevent parts and tools from falling into the engine, then use a valve spring compressor to compress the spring/damper assembly. Remove the keepers with small needle-nose pliers or a magnet **(see illustration). Note:** *A couple*

4.8a Once the spring is depressed, the keepers can be removed with a small magnet or needle-nose pliers (a magnet is preferred to prevent dropping the keepers)

of different types of tools are available for compressing the valve springs with the head in place. One type, shown here, grips the lower spring coils and presses on the retainer as the knob is turned, while the other type utilizes the rocker arm stud and nut for leverage **(see illustration).** *Both types work very well, although the lever type is less expensive.*

9   Remove the spring retainer or rotator, oil shield and valve spring assembly, then remove the valve stem O-ring seal and the umbrella-type guide seal (the O-ring seal will most likely be hardened and will probably break when removed, so plan on installing a new one each time the original is removed) **(see illustration). Note:** *If air pressure fails to hold the valve in the closed position during this operation, the valve face and/or seat is*

4.8b The stamped steel lever-type valve spring compressor is much less expensive than the type that grips the spring coils

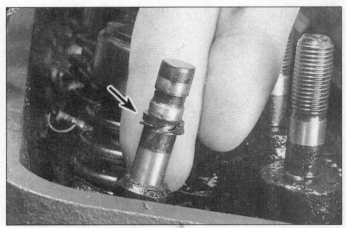

4.9 The O-ring seal (arrow) should be replaced with a new one each time the keepers and retainer are removed

4.16 Make sure the O-ring seal under the retainer is seated in the groove and not twisted before installing the keepers

4.17 Apply a small dab of grease to each keeper as shown here before installation - it will hold them in place on the valve stem as the spring is released

5.6 Rear of air conditioning compressor showing brace attached to intake manifold stud (arrow) (throttle body removed for clarity)

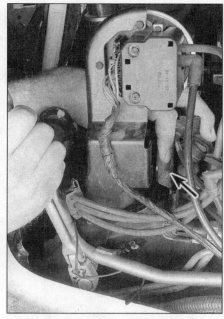

5.8 Arrow points to optional cruise control servo bracket bolt location - socket wrench is on lower bracket mounting bolt

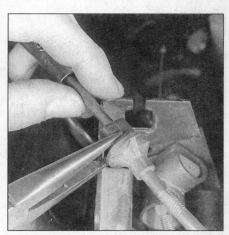

5.9 Pinch the cable tabs together to get them out of the bracket (cable removed for clarity)

probably damaged. If so, the cylinder head will have to be removed for additional repair operations.

10 Wrap a rubber band or tape around the top of the valve stem so the valve won't fall into the combustion chamber, then release the air pressure. **Note:** *If a rope was used instead of air pressure, turn the crankshaft slightly in the direction opposite normal rotation.*

11 Inspect the valve stem for damage. Rotate the valve in the guide and check the end for eccentric movement, which would indicate that the valve is bent.

12 Move the valve up-and-down in the guide and make sure it doesn't bind. If the valve stem binds, either the valve is bent or the guide is damaged. In either case, the head will have to be removed for repair.

13 Reapply air pressure to the cylinder to retain the valve in the closed position, then remove the tape or rubber band from the valve stem. If a rope was used instead of air pressure, rotate the crankshaft in the normal direction of rotation until slight resistance is felt.

14 Lubricate the valve stem with engine oil and install a new umbrella-type guide seal.

15 Install the spring/damper assembly and shield in position over the valve.

16 Install the valve spring retainer or rotator. Compress the valve spring assembly and carefully install the new O-ring seal in the lower groove of the valve stem. Make sure the seal isn't twisted - it must lie perfectly flat in the groove **(see illustration)**.

17 Position the keepers in the upper groove. Apply a small dab of grease to the inside of each keeper to hold it in place if necessary **(see illustration)**. Remove the pressure from the spring tool and make sure the keepers are seated.

18 Disconnect the air hose and remove the adapter from the spark plug hole. If a rope was used in place of air pressure, rotate the crankshaft counterclockwise and pull it out of the cylinder.

19 Install the rocker arm(s) and pushrod(s) (see Section 7).

20 Install the valve cover(s) (see Section 3).

21 Install the spark plug(s) and hook up the wire(s).

22 Start and run the engine, then check for oil leaks and unusual sounds coming from the valve cover area.

5 Intake manifold - removal and installation

Removal

Refer to illustrations 5.6, 5.8, 5.9, 5.10 and 5.15

1 Disconnect the negative cable from the battery.

2 Remove the upper fan shroud.

3 Remove the air cleaner assembly (TBI models) or air intake tube (CPI models) (see Chapter 4).

4 Drain the radiator (see Chapter 1).

5 Disconnect the upper radiator and heater hoses at the front of the engine.

6 Remove the rear brace from the air conditioning compressor **(see illustration)**.

7 Remove the spark plug wires, coil and distributor (see Chapters 1 and 5).

8 Remove the cruise control servo and brackets, if so equipped **(see illustration)**.

9 Remove the throttle, cruise control and TV cables from the bracket(s) on the manifold **(see illustration)**.

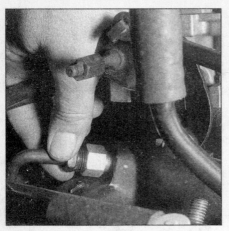

5.10 The vacuum brake booster line-to-intake manifold fitting is to the left of the throttle body

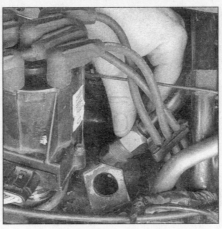

5.15 Disconnect the coolant tube at the manifold and set it aside

5.18 After covering the lifter valley, use a gasket scraper to remove all traces of sealant and old gasket material from the head and manifold mating surfaces

5.19a The bolt hole threads must be clean and dry to ensure accurate torque readings when the manifold mounting bolts are installed

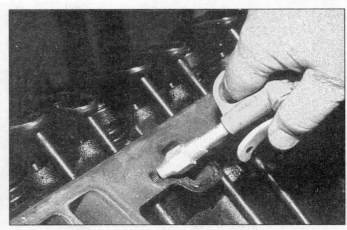

5.19b Clean the bolt holes with compressed air, but be careful - wear safety goggles!

10   Detach the vacuum brake booster line from the manifold **(see illustration)**.

11   On models equipped with CPI fuel injection, remove the air intake plenum (see Chapter 4).

12   Unbolt the alternator bracket at the manifold and push it aside.

13   Label and disconnect the fuel lines, vacuum hoses/pipes and wires at the manifold and TBI unit or CPI unit (see Chapter 4).

14   On TBI models, unbolt the fuel line from the rear of the cylinder head. It may be necessary to keep the stud from turning with vise-grip pliers.

15   Remove the coolant tube from the right side of the manifold **(see illustration)**.

16   Loosen the manifold mounting bolts in 1/4-turn increments until they can be removed by hand.

17   The manifold will probably be stuck to the cylinder heads and force may be required to break the gasket seal. A large pry bar can be positioned under the cast-in lug near the left front mounting bolt to pry up the front of the manifold, but make sure all bolts have been removed first! **Caution:** *Don't pry*

between the block and manifold or the heads and manifold or damage to the gasket sealing surfaces may occur, leading to vacuum leaks.

Installation

Refer to illustrations 5.18, 5.19a, 5.19b, 5.20, 5.21, 5.22, 5.23, 5.25a and 5.25b

Note: *The mating surfaces of the cylinder heads, block and manifold must be perfectly clean when the manifold is installed. Gasket removal solvents in aerosol cans are available at most auto parts stores and may be helpful when removing old gasket material that's stuck to the heads and manifold (since the manifold is made of aluminum, aggressive scraping can cause damage). Be sure to follow the directions printed on the container.*

18   Use a gasket scraper to remove all traces of sealant and old gasket material, then clean the mating surfaces with lacquer thinner or acetone. If there's old sealant or oil on the mating surfaces when the manifold is installed, oil or vacuum leaks may develop. When working on the heads and block, cover the lifter valley with shop rags to keep debris out of the engine **(see illustration)**. Use a

vacuum cleaner to remove any gasket material that falls into the intake ports in the heads.

19   Use a tap of the correct size to chase the threads in the bolt holes, then use compressed air (if available) to remove the debris from the holes **(see illustrations)**. **Warning:** *Wear safety glasses or a face shield to protect your eyes when using compressed air! Remove excessive carbon deposits and corrosion from the exhaust, EGR and coolant passages in the heads and manifold.*

20   Apply a 3/16-inch wide bead of RTV sealant to the front and rear manifold mating surfaces of the block **(see illustration)**. Make sure the beads extend up the heads 1/2-inch on each side.

21   Apply a thin coat of RTV sealant around the coolant passage holes on the cylinder head side of the new intake manifold gaskets **(see illustration)**.

22   Position the gaskets on the cylinder heads, with the ears at each end overlapping the bead of RTV sealant on the head. The upper side of each gasket will have a THIS SIDE UP label stamped into it to ensure correct installation **(see illustration)**.

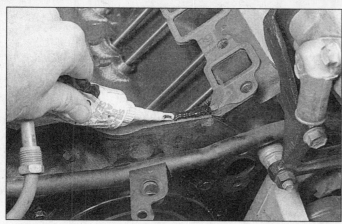

5.20 Apply a bead of RTV sealant to the ridges at the front and rear of the block

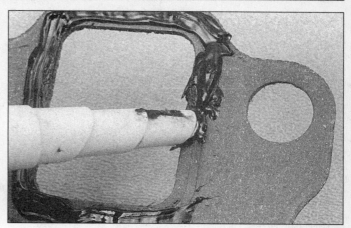

5.21 RTV sealant should be used around the coolant passage holes in the new intake manifold gaskets

5.22 Be sure to install the gaskets with the marks UP!

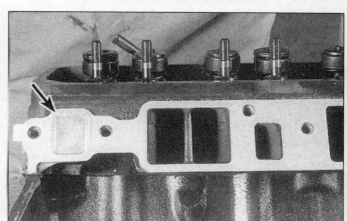

5.23 Make sure the gaskets are installed with the blocked off holes at the rear!

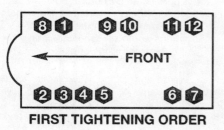

FIRST TIGHTENING ORDER

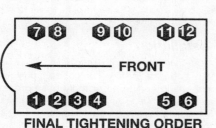

FINAL TIGHTENING ORDER

24070-2e-5.25a HAYNES

5.25a Intake manifold bolt tightening sequence (TBI models)

23 Make sure all intake port openings, coolant passage holes and bolt holes are aligned correctly. **Note:** *Be sure the gaskets are installed with the blocked off coolant passages at the rear of the engine* (**see illustration**). *Some gaskets may have small tabs which must be bent over until they're flush with the rear surface of each head.*

24 Carefully set the manifold in place while the sealant is still wet. **Caution:** *Don't disturb the gaskets and don't move the manifold fore-and-aft after it contacts the sealant on the block.*

25 Following the recommended sequence, install the bolts and tighten them to the torque listed in this Chapter's Specifications (**see illustrations**). Work up to the final torque in two stages and note that two differ-ent tightening sequences must be followed, one for each stage.

26 The remaining installation steps are the reverse of removal. Start the engine and check carefully for oil and coolant leaks at the intake manifold joints.

---

6   Exhaust manifolds - removal and installation

Removal

Refer to illustrations 6.7 and 6.10

1 Disconnect the negative battery cable from the battery.

2 Raise the vehicle and support it securely on jackstands.

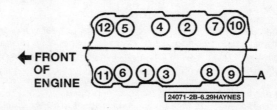

← FRONT OF ENGINE

24071-2B-6.29HAYNES

5.25b Intake manifold bolt tightening sequence (CPI models) - on the final pass, bolt A must be tightened an additional amount (see this Chapter's Specifications)

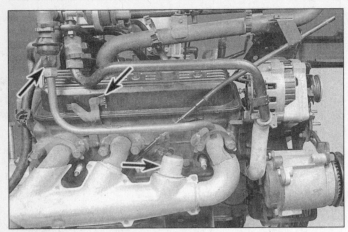

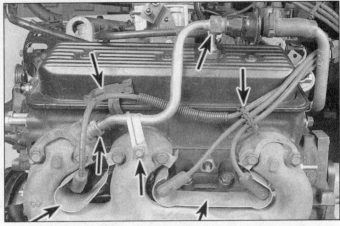

6.7 Right side exhaust manifold mounting details showing the AIR system check valve, spark plug wire bracket and heat stove pipe mount (arrows) (engine removed for clarity)

6.10 Left side exhaust manifold mounting details showing the spark plug wire brackets, heat shields, AIR system check valve, AIR tube-to-manifold fitting and AIR tube bracket bolt (arrows) (engine removed for clarity)

3   Working under the vehicle, apply penetrating oil to the exhaust pipe-to-manifold studs and nuts (they're usually rusty).
4   Remove the nuts holding the exhaust pipe(s) to the manifold(s). In extreme cases you may have to heat them with a propane or acetylene torch in order to loosen them.

Right side manifold

5   On TBI models, remove the air cleaner assembly (see Chapter 4).
6   Remove the heat stove pipe.
7   Release the hose clamp and separate the hose from the AIR system check valve **(see illustration)**.
8   Detach the spark plug wires from the plugs and brackets and position them out of the way (see Chapter 1).

Left side manifold

9   Unplug the oxygen sensor wire (see Chapter 6).
10   Detach the spark plug wires from the plugs and brackets and position them out of the way **(see illustration)**.
11   Unscrew the fitting at the manifold, release the hose clamp and detach the hose from the AIR system check valve, then remove the bracket bolt and detach the AIR tube and check valve as an assembly.

Both manifolds

12   Bend the lock tabs back, then remove the mounting bolts and separate the manifold from the head. The heat shields on the left side manifold will come off after the bolts are removed.

Installation

13   Check the manifold for cracks and make sure the bolt threads are clean and undamaged. The manifold and cylinder head mating surfaces must be clean before the manifolds are reinstalled - use a gasket scraper to remove all carbon deposits.
14   Position the manifold, tab washers and heat shields (if equipped) on the head and install the mounting bolts.
15   When tightening the mounting bolts, work from the center to the ends and be sure to use a torque wrench. Tighten the bolts in three equal steps until the torque listed in this Chapter's Specifications is reached.
16   The remaining installation steps are the reverse of removal.
17   Start the engine and check for exhaust leaks.

7   Rocker arms and pushrods - removal, inspection and installation

Removal

Refer to illustration 7.4

1   Detach the valve cover(s) from the cylinder head(s) (see Section 3).
2   Beginning at the front of one cylinder head, loosen and remove the rocker arm stud nuts. Store them separately in marked containers to ensure that they will be reinstalled in their original locations. **Note:** *If the pushrods are the only items being removed, loosen each nut just enough to allow the rocker arms to be rotated to the side so the pushrods can be lifted out.*
3   Lift off the rocker arms and pivot balls and store them in the marked containers with the nuts (they must be reinstalled in their original locations).
4   Remove the pushrods and store them separately to make sure they don't get mixed up during installation **(see illustration)**.

Inspection

5   Check each rocker arm for wear, cracks and other damage, especially where the pushrods and valve stems contact the rocker arm faces.
6   Make sure the hole at the pushrod end of each rocker arm is open.
7   Check each rocker arm pivot area for

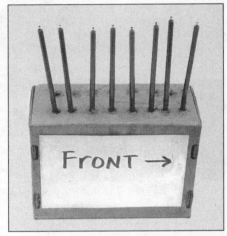

7.4 A perforated cardboard box can be used to store the pushrods to ensure that they're reinstalled in their original locations - note the label indicating the front of the engine

wear, cracks and galling. If the rocker arms are worn or damaged, replace them with new ones and use new pivot balls as well.
8   Inspect the pushrods for cracks and excessive wear at the ends. Roll each pushrod across a piece of plate glass to see if it's bent (if it wobbles, it's bent).

Installation

Refer to illustrations 7.10 and 7.11

9   Lubricate the lower end of each pushrod with clean engine oil or moly-base grease and install them in their original locations. Make sure each pushrod seats completely in the lifter.
10   Apply moly-base grease to the ends of the valve stems and the upper ends of the pushrods before positioning the rocker arms over the studs **(see illustration)**.
11   Set the rocker arms in place, then install the pivot balls and nuts. Apply moly-base

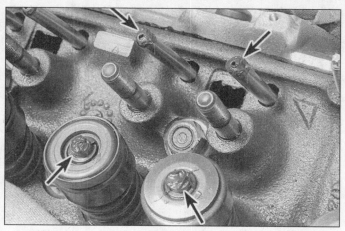

7.10 The ends of the pushrods and the valve stems should be lubricated with moly-base grease prior to installation of the rocker arms

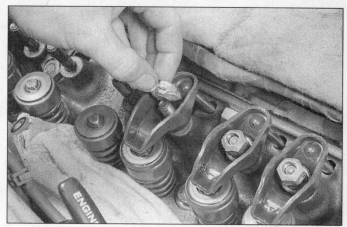

7.11 Moly-base grease applied to the pivot balls will ensure adequate lubrication until oil pressure builds up when the engine is started

2E

grease to the pivot balls to prevent damage to the mating surfaces before engine oil pressure builds up **(see illustration)**. Be sure to install each nut with the flat side against the pivot ball.

Valve adjustment (all except 1992 and later VIN W engines)

Refer to illustration 7.13

Note: *On 1992 and later VIN W engines, there are no provisions for valve adjustment. The rocker arm studs have a positive stop shoulder for the rocker arm. After valve service, tighten the rocker arm nuts to the torque listed in this Chapter's Specifications. Unless there have been machining operations that significantly altered the valve lash, the adjustment should be correct.*

12   Bring the number one piston to top dead center on the compression stroke (see Section 9).

13   Tighten the rocker arm nuts (number one cylinder only) until all play is removed at the pushrods. This can be determined by rotating each pushrod between your thumb and index finger as the nut is tightened **(see illustration)**. At the point where a slight drag is just felt as you spin the pushrod, all lash has been removed.

14   Tighten each nut an additional 3/4-turn to center the lifters. Valve adjustment for cylinder number one is now complete.

15   Turn the crankshaft 120-degrees in the normal direction of rotation until the next piston in the firing order (number six) is at TDC on the compression stroke. The distributor rotor should be pointing in the direction of terminal number six on the cap (see Section 9 for additional information).

16   Repeat the procedure described in Steps 13 and 14 for the number six cylinder valves.

17   Turn the crankshaft another 120-degrees and adjust the number five cylinder valves. Continue turning the crankshaft 120-degrees at a time and adjust both valves for each cylinder before proceeding. Follow the

7.13 Rotate each pushrod as the rocker arm nut is tightened to determine the point at which all play is removed, then tighten each nut an additional 3/4-turn

firing order sequence (a cylinder number illustration is also included in the Specifications.

18   Install the valve covers (see Section 3). Start the engine, listen for unusual valvetrain noises and check for oil leaks at the valve cover joints.

---

8   Cylinder heads - removal and installation

Caution: *The engine must be completely cool when the heads are removed. Failure to allow the engine to cool off could result in head warpage.*

Removal

1   Remove the intake manifold (see Section 5).

2   Remove the valve cover (see Section 3).

3   Remove the pushrods (see Section 7).

4   Raise and support the vehicle on jackstands.

8.13 To avoid mixing up the head bolts, use a new gasket to transfer the bolt hole pattern to a piece of cardboard, then punch holes to accept the bolts

Left (driver's side) cylinder head

5   Remove the air conditioning and power steering pump drivebelts, if equipped (see Chapter 1).

6   Unbolt the power steering pump and lay it aside. Leave the hoses connected (see Chapter 10).

7   Remove the air conditioning compressor, idler pulley and bracket, if equipped (see Chapter 3).

8   Remove the exhaust manifold (see Section 6).

9   Proceed to Step 13.

Right cylinder head

10   Remove the engine ground wire and electrical harness at the rear of the head.

11   Remove the diverter valve assembly (see Chapter 6).

12   Remove the alternator (see Chapter 5).

Both cylinder heads

Refer to illustration 8.13

13   Using a new head gasket, outline the cylinders and bolt pattern on a piece of card-

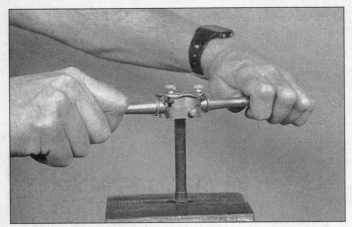

8.20   A die should be used to remove sealant and corrosion from the head bolt threads prior to installation

8.21a Locating dowels (arrows) are used to position the head gaskets on the block

board **(see illustration)**. Be sure to indicate the front of the engine for reference. Punch holes at the bolt locations.

14   Loosen the head bolts in 1/4-turn increments until they can be removed by hand. Work from bolt-to-bolt in a pattern that's the

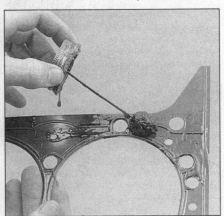

8.21b Steel gaskets should be coated with a sealant such as K&W copper Coat before installation

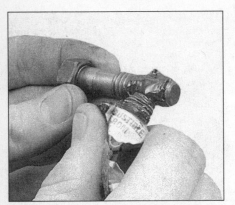

8.23   The head bolts MUST be coated with a non-hardening sealant (such as Permatex no. 2) before they're installed - coolant will leak past the bolts if this isn't done

reverse of the tightening sequence shown in illustration 8.24. **Note:** *Don't overlook the row of bolts on the lower edge of each head, near the spark plug holes.* Store the bolts in the cardboard holder as they're removed; this will ensure that the bolts are reinstalled in their original holes.

15   Lift the head(s) off the engine. If resistance is felt, DO NOT pry between the head and block as damage to the mating surfaces will result. To dislodge the head, place a block of wood against the end of it and strike the wood block with a hammer. Store the heads on blocks of wood to prevent damage to the gasket sealing surfaces.

16   Cylinder head disassembly and inspection procedures are covered in detail in Chapter 2, Part F.

Installation

Refer to illustrations 8.20, 8.21a, 8.21b, 8.23 and 8.24

17   The mating surfaces of the cylinder heads and block must be perfectly clean when the heads are installed.

18   Use a gasket scraper to remove all traces of carbon and old gasket material, then clean the mating surfaces with lacquer thinner or acetone. If there's oil on the mating surfaces when the heads are installed, the gaskets may not seal correctly and leaks may develop. When working on the block, cover the lifter valley with shop rags to keep debris

out of the engine. Use a vacuum cleaner to remove any debris that falls into the cylinders.

19   Check the block and head mating surfaces for nicks, deep scratches and other damage. If damage is slight, it can be removed with a file - if it's excessive, machining may be the only alternative.

20   Use a tap of the correct size to chase the threads in the head bolt holes. Mount each bolt in a vise and run a die down the threads to remove corrosion and restore the threads **(see illustration)**. Dirt, corrosion, sealant and damaged threads will affect torque readings.

21   Position the new gaskets over the dowel pins in the block **(see illustration)**. **Note:** *If a steel gasket is used, apply a thin, even coat of sealant such as K&W Copper Coat to both sides prior to installation* **(see illustration)**. *Steel gaskets must be installed with the raised bead UP. The composition gasket must be installed dry - don't use sealant.*

22   Carefully position the heads on the block without disturbing the gaskets.

23   Before installing the head bolts, coat the threads with a non-hardening sealant such as Permatex no. 2 **(see illustration)**.

24   Install the bolts in their original locations and tighten them finger tight. Follow the recommended sequence and tighten the bolts in several steps to the torque listed in this Chapter's Specifications **(see illustration)**.

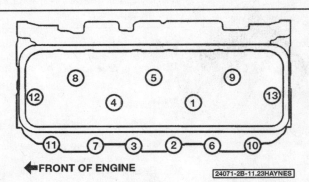

8.24 Cylinder head bolt tightening sequence

◄ **FRONT OF ENGINE**

24071-2B-11.23HAYNES

9.4a Make a mark on the distributor housing directly below the number 1 spark plug wire terminal (arrow)

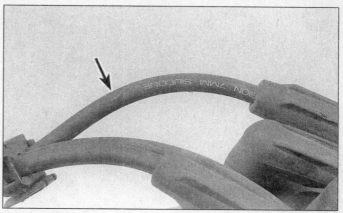

9.4b The spark plug wires are numbered to correspond to their respective cylinders (arrow)

9.6a Turn the crankshaft until the line on the vibration damper is directly opposite the zero mark on the timing plate as shown here

9.6b The vibration damper has two marks - the first one that approaches the timing plate can be disregarded, while the second mark (arrow) is the one that's used to locate TDC

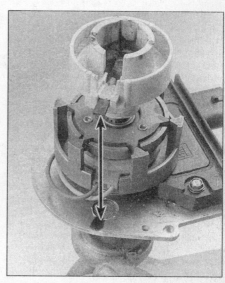

9.7 If the rotor is pointing directly at the mark on the distributor housing, as shown here, the number one piston is at TDC on the compression stroke

25 The remaining installation steps are the reverse of removal.

26 Change the engine oil and filter (see Chapter 1), then start the engine and check carefully for oil and coolant leaks.

9 Top Dead Center (TDC) for number 1 piston - locating

Refer to illustrations 9.4a, 9.4b, 9.6a, 9.6b and 9.7

1 Top Dead Center (TDC) is the highest point in the cylinder that each piston reaches as it travels up-and-down when the crankshaft turns. Each piston reaches TDC on the compression stroke and again on the exhaust stroke, but TDC generally refers to piston position on the compression stroke. The timing marks on the vibration damper installed on the front of the crankshaft are referenced to the number one piston at TDC on the compression stroke.

2 Positioning the piston(s) at TDC is an essential part of many procedures such as rocker arm removal, valve adjustment, timing

chain and sprocket replacement and distributor removal.

3 In order to bring any piston to TDC, the crankshaft must be turned using one of the methods outlined below. When looking at the front of the engine, normal crankshaft rotation is clockwise. **Warning:** *Before beginning this procedure, be sure to place the transmission in Neutral and unplug the electrical connector(s) at the distributor to disable the ignition system.*

a) *The preferred method is to turn the crankshaft with a large socket and breaker bar attached to the vibration damper bolt threaded into the front of the crankshaft.*

b) *A remote starter switch, which may save some time, can also be used. Attach the switch leads to the S (switch) and B (battery) terminals on the starter motor. Once the piston is close to TDC, use a socket and breaker bar as described in the previous paragraph.*

c) *If an assistant is available to turn the ignition switch to the Start position in short bursts, you can get the piston*

close to TDC without a remote starter switch. Use a socket and breaker bar as described in Paragraph a) to complete the procedure.

4 Make a mark on the distributor housing directly below the number one spark plug wire terminal on the distributor cap **(see illustration)**. **Note:** *The terminal numbers are marked on the spark plug wires near the distributor* **(see illustration)**.

5 Remove the distributor cap (see Chapter 1).

6 Turn the crankshaft (see Step 3 above) until the line on the vibration damper is aligned with the zero mark on the timing plate **(see illustrations)**. The timing plate and vibration damper are located low on the front of the engine, near the pulley that turns the drivebelt.

7 The rotor should now be pointing directly at the mark on the distributor housing **(see illustration)**. If it isn't, the piston is at TDC on the exhaust stroke.

2E

10.2 The vibration damper bolt (arrow) is usually very tight, so use a six-point socket and a breaker bar to loosen it (the three other bolts hold the pulley to the vibration damper)

10.4 Use the recommended puller to remove the vibration damper - if a puller that applies force to the outer edge is used, the damper will be damaged!

8   To get the piston to TDC on the compression stroke, turn the crankshaft one complete turn (360-degrees) clockwise. The rotor should now be pointing at the mark. When the rotor is pointing at the number one spark plug wire terminal in the distributor cap (which is indicated by the mark on the housing) and the ignition timing marks are aligned, the number one piston is at TDC on the compression stroke.

9   After the number one piston has been positioned at TDC on the compression stroke, TDC for any of the remaining cylinders can be located by turning the crankshaft 120-degrees at a time and following the firing order (see the Specifications at the beginning of this Chapter).

---

10   Timing cover, chain and sprockets - removal and installation

---

Removal

Refer to illustrations 10.2, 10.4, 10.5 and 10.6

1   Refer to Chapter 3 and remove the water pump.

2   Remove the bolts and separate the crankshaft drivebelt pulley from the vibration damper **(see illustration)**.

3   Position the number *four* piston at TDC on the compression stroke (see Section 9). **Caution:** *Once this has been done, DO NOT turn the crankshaft until the timing chain and sprockets have been reinstalled!*

4   Remove the bolt from the front of the crankshaft, then use a puller to detach the vibration damper **(see illustration). Caution:** *Don't use a puller with jaws that grip the outer edge of the damper. The puller must be the type shown in the illustration that utilizes bolts to apply force to the damper hub only.*

5   Remove the bolts and separate the timing chain cover from the block. It may be stuck - if so, use a putty knife or screwdriver to break the gasket seal **(see illustration).**

10.5 A putty knife or screwdriver can be used to break the timing chain cover-to-block seal, but be careful when prying it off as damage to the cover may result

The cover is easily distorted, so be very careful when prying it off.

6   Remove the three bolts (all except VIN W) or two bolts and one nut (VIN W) from the end of the camshaft **(see illustration)**, then detach the camshaft sprocket and chain as an assembly. **Note:** *On VIN W engines, the balancer shaft drive gear will stay attached to the camshaft and the driven gear will stay attached to the balancer shaft. The sprocket on the crankshaft can be removed with a two- or three-jaw puller, but be careful not to damage the threads in the end of the crankshaft.* **Note:** *If the timing chain cover oil seal has been leaking,* refer to Section 15 *and install a new one.*

Installation

Refer to illustration 10.10

7   Use a gasket scraper to remove all

10.6 Remove the three bolts from the end of the camshaft (arrows)

traces of old gasket material and sealant from the cover and engine block. Stuff a shop rag into the opening at the front of the oil pan to keep debris out of the engine. Clean the cover and block sealing surfaces with lacquer thinner or acetone.

8   Check the cover flange for distortion, particularly around the bolt holes. If necessary, place the cover on a block of wood and use a hammer to flatten and restore the gasket surface.

9   If new parts are being installed, be sure to align the keyway in the crankshaft sprocket with the Woodruff key in the end of the crankshaft. Press the sprocket onto the crankshaft with the vibration damper bolt, a large socket and some washers or tap it gently into place until it's completely seated. **Caution:** *If resistance is encountered, DO NOT hammer the sprocket onto the crankshaft. It may eventually move onto the shaft, but it may be cracked in the process and fail later, causing extensive engine damage.*

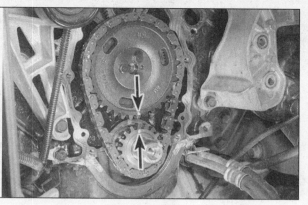

10.10 With the number four piston at TDC on the compression stroke and the timing marks on the cam and crankshaft sprockets in the 6 and 12 o'clock positions, a straight line should pass through the camshaft timing mark, the center of the camshaft, the crankshaft timing mark and the center of the crankshaft as shown here

10   Loop the new chain over the camshaft sprocket, then turn the sprocket until the timing mark is in the 6 o'clock position. Mesh the chain with the crankshaft sprocket and position the camshaft sprocket on the end of the cam. If necessary, turn the camshaft so the dowel pin fits into the sprocket hole with the timing mark in the 6 o'clock position. When correctly installed, the marks on the sprockets will be aligned as shown (see illustration). Note: The number four piston must be at TDC on the compression stroke as the chain and sprockets are installed (see Step 3 above).
11   Apply Loctite to the camshaft sprocket bolt threads, then install and tighten them to the torque listed in this Chapter's Specifications. Lubricate the chain with clean engine oil.
12   Check the oil pan-to-block joints to make sure that all excess sealant is removed.
13   Apply RTV sealant to the U-shaped channel on the bottom of the cover.
14   Apply a thin layer of RTV sealant to both sides of the new gasket, then position it on the engine block (the dowel pins and sealant will hold it in place).
15   Since the oil pan seal in the bottom of the cover must be compressed in order to position the cover over the dowel pins and thread the bolts into the block, the cover is nearly impossible to install unless the oil pan is removed first. It can be done, but it's very difficult and frustrating. If the front three bolts on each side of the oil pan are removed, the oil pan can be pried down slightly, allowing

the cover to be installed. Squirt some RTV sealant into the gap between the pan and the block. If difficulty is encountered, it may be necessary to remove the oil pan.
16   Install the timing chain cover and tighten the bolts to the torque listed in this Chapter's Specifications. If the front of the oil pan was pried down, install the bolts and tighten them to the torque listed in this Chapter's Specifications.
17   Lubricate the oil seal contact surface of the vibration damper hub with moly-base grease or clean engine oil, then install the damper on the end of the crankshaft. The keyway in the damper must be aligned with the Woodruff key in the crankshaft nose. If the damper cannot be seated by hand, slip a large washer over the bolt, install the bolt and tighten it to push the damper into place. Remove the large washer and tighten the bolt to the torque listed in this Chapter's Specifications.
18   The remaining installation steps are the reverse of removal.

11   Camshaft, bearings and lifters - removal, inspection and installation

Camshaft lobe lift check

Refer to illustration 11.3
1   In order to determine the extent of cam

lobe wear, the lobe lift should be checked prior to camshaft removal. Remove the valve covers (see Section 3).
2   Position the number one piston at TDC on the compression stroke (see Section 9).
3   Beginning with the number one cylinder valves, loosen the rocker arm nuts and pivot the rocker arms out of the way. Mount a dial indicator on the engine and position the plunger against the top of the first pushrod. The plunger should be directly in line with the pushrod (see illustration).
4   Zero the dial indicator, then very slowly turn the crankshaft in the normal direction of rotation until the indicator needle stops and begins to move in the opposite direction. The point at which it stops indicates maximum cam lobe lift.
5   Record this figure for future reference, then reposition the piston at TDC on the compression stroke.
6   Move the dial indicator to the remaining number one cylinder pushrod and repeat the check. Be sure to record the results for each valve.
7   Repeat the check for the remaining valves. Since each piston must be at TDC on the compression stroke for this procedure, work from cylinder-to-cylinder following the firing order sequence.
8   After the check is complete, compare the results to this Chapter's Specifications. If camshaft lobe lift is less than specified, cam lobe wear has occurred and a new camshaft should be installed.

Removal

Refer to illustrations 11.10a, 11.10b, 11.10c and 11.12
9   Refer to the appropriate Sections and remove the intake manifold, the rocker arms, the pushrods and the timing chain and camshaft sprocket. The radiator should be removed as well (see Chapter 3).
10   Before removing the lifters, arrange to store them in a clearly labeled box to ensure that they're reinstalled in their original locations. Remove the lifter retainer and guides (see illustrations). Remove the lifters and store them where they won't get dirty (see

11.3 When checking the camshaft lobe lift, the dial indicator plunger must be positioned directly above the pushrod

11.10a The guide plate is held in place by two bolts (arrows)

2E

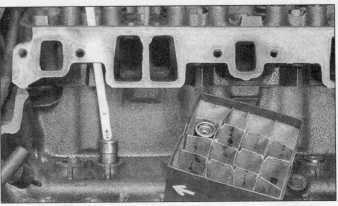

11.10b **The lifter guides slip over the lifters**

11.10c **The lifters on an engine that has accumulated many miles may have to be removed with a special tool - be sure to store the lifters in an organized manner to make sure they are reinstalled in their original locations**

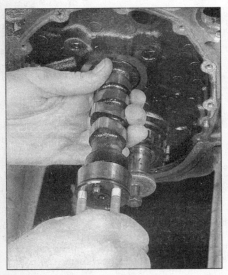

11.13 **Long bolts can be threaded into the camshaft bolt holes to provide a handle for removal and installation of the camshaft - support the cam near the blocks as it's withdrawn**

11.19 **After the camshaft is in place, turn it until the dowel pin (arrow) is in the 3 o'clock position as shown here**

illustration). DO NOT attempt to withdraw the camshaft with the lifters in place.

11   There are several ways to extract the lifters from the bores. A special tool designed to grip and remove lifters is manufactured by many tool companies and is widely available, but it may not be required in every case. On newer engines without a lot of varnish buildup, the lifters can often be removed with a small magnet or even with your fingers. A machinist's scribe with a bent end can be used to pull the lifters out by positioning the point under the retainer ring in the top of each lifter. **Caution:** *Don't use pliers to remove the lifters unless you intend to replace them with new ones (along with the camshaft). The pliers will damage the precision machined and hardened lifters, rendering them useless.*

12   On VIN W engines, remove the balancer shaft drive and driven gears (see Section 12).

13   Thread two 6-inch long 5/16-18 bolts into two of the camshaft sprocket bolt holes to use as a handle when removing the camshaft from the block **(see illustration)**.

14   Carefully pull the camshaft out. Support the cam near the block so the lobes don't nick or gouge the bearings as it's withdrawn.

Inspection

15   Inspect the camshaft, bearings and lifters (see Chapter 2, Part C). The illustrations in Part C also pertain to the 4.3L V6 engine.

Bearing replacement

16   Camshaft bearing replacement requires special tools and expertise that place it outside the scope of the home mechanic. Take the block to an automotive machine shop to ensure that the job is done correctly.

Installation

Refer to illustration 11.19

17   Lubricate the camshaft bearing journals and cam lobes with camshaft assembly lube.

18   Slide the camshaft into the engine. Support the cam near the block and be careful not to scrape or nick the bearings.

19   Turn the camshaft until the dowel pin is

in the 3 o'clock position **(see illustration)**.

20   On VIN W engines, install the balancer shaft drive and driven gears (see Section 12).

21   Install the timing chain and sprockets (see Section 10).

22   Lubricate the lifters with clean engine oil and install them in the block. If the original lifters are being reinstalled, be sure to return them to their original locations. (The old lifters can be used even if a new camshaft has been installed, provided they are in good condition).

23   The remaining installation steps are the reverse of removal.

24   Before starting and running the engine, change the oil and install a new oil filter (see Chapter 1).

---

12   Balancer shaft - removal and installation (1992 and later VIN W engines)

Removal

1   Remove the air cleaner assembly and air intake duct.

2   Remove the timing cover, chains and sprockets (see Section 10).

12.22 Make sure the balancer shaft timing marks on both the drive and driven gears are aligned

3 Remove the hood latch (see Chapter 11).
4 Remove the intake manifold (see Section 5).
5 Remove the radiator grille and headlight bezels (see Chapter 11).
6 Remove the radiator and its support braces, then remove the air conditioning condenser - if equipped - (see Chapter 3).
7 Remove the radiator support crossover.
8 Remove the retaining stud and the balancer shaft drive gear from the camshaft.
9 Remove the retaining bolt and the balancer shaft driven gear.
10 Remove the two bolts securing the balancer shaft retainer and remove the retainer.
11 Unbolt and remove the lifter retainer (see illustration 11.10a).
12 Using a soft-faced mallet, carefully tap the balancer shaft out of the block.

Inspection

13 After the balancer shaft has been removed from the engine, cleaned with solvent and dried, inspect the rear bearing journal for uneven wear, pitting and evidence of seizure. If the journal is damaged, the rear bearing in the block is probably damaged as well. The bearing will have to be replaced.
14 Check the balancer drive and driven gears for cracks, missing teeth and excessive wear. If the teeth are highly polished, pitted or galled, or if the outer hardened surface of the teeth is flaking off, new parts will be required. If one gear is worn or damaged, replace both gears as a set. Never install one new gear and one used gear.

Bearing replacement

15 Balancer shaft bearing replacement requires special tools and expertise that place it outside the scope of the home mechanic. Take the engine block to a dealer service department or an automotive machine shop to ensure that the job is done correctly.

Installation

Refer to illustration 12.22
16 Lubricate the balancer shaft bearing journals with engine assembly lube.
17 Slide the balancer shaft into the engine.

Support the balancer near the block and be careful not to scrape or nick the bearing. It may be necessary to gently tap on the shaft with a soft-face mallet.
18 Install the balance shaft retainer and two bolts and tighten them to the torque listed in this Chapter's Specifications.
19 Install the lifter retainer and bolts, then tighten the bolts to the torque listed in this Chapter's Specifications.
20 Rotate the balancer shaft by hand to make sure there is sufficient clearance between the balancer shaft and the lifter retainer. Replace the lifter retainer if necessary.
21 Install the balancer shaft driven gear and tighten the bolt to the torque listed in this Chapter's Specifications.
22 Rotate the camshaft so that, with the drive gear temporarily installed, the timing mark is straight up at the 12 o'clock position (see illustration). Remove the drive gear.
23 Rotate the balancer shaft until the timing mark is facing straight down at the 6 o'clock position (see illustration 12.22).
24 Install the balancer drive gear onto the camshaft and install the retaining stud, then tighten it to the torque listed in this Chapter's Specifications.
25 Install the timing chain, sprockets and cover (see Section 10).

13 Oil pan - removal and installation

Note: *On 2WD models it is necessary to remove the engine from the vehicle to perform this procedure (see Chapter 2F). On 4WD models, the front differential housing must be unbolted, moved forward and supported (see Chapter 8) and the engine must be unbolted from the mounts and raised with an engine hoist to provide the necessary clearance for oil pan removal.*

Removal

1 Disconnect the negative battery cable from the battery, then refer to Chapter 1 and drain the oil.
2 Remove the starter motor (see Chapter 5).
3 Remove the cover from the lower part of

the bellhousing.
4 Separate the exhaust pipes from the manifolds, if not already done.
5 Remove the oil pan mounting bolts/nuts. Most models are equipped with a reinforcement strip on each side of the oil pan which may come loose after the bolts/nuts are removed.
6 Carefully separate the pan from the block. Don't pry between the block and pan or damage to the sealing surfaces may result and oil leaks could develop. You may have to turn the crankshaft slightly to maneuver the front of the pan past the crank counterweights.

Installation

7 Clean the gasket sealing surfaces with lacquer thinner or acetone. Make sure the bolt holes in the block are clean.
8 Check the oil pan flange for distortion, particularly around the bolt holes. If necessary, place the pan on a block of wood and use a hammer to flatten and restore the gasket surface.
9 The rubber gasket should be checked carefully and replaced with a new one if damage is noted. Apply a small amount of RTV sealant to the corners of the semi-circular cutouts at both ends of the pan, then attach the rubber gasket to the pan.
10 Carefully position the pan against the block and install the bolts/nuts finger tight (don't forget the reinforcement strips, if used). Tighten the bolts/nuts in three steps to the torque listed in this Chapter's Specifications. Start at the center of the pan and work out toward the ends in a spiral pattern.
11 The remaining steps are the reverse of removal. **Caution:** *Don't forget to refill the engine with oil before starting it (see Chapter 1).*
12 Start the engine and check carefully for oil leaks at the oil pan.

14 Oil pump - removal and installation

1 Remove the oil pan (see Section 12).
2 While supporting the oil pump, remove the pump-to-rear main bearing cap bolt. On some models, the oil pan baffle must be removed first, since it's also held in place by the pump mounting bolt.
3 Lower the pump and remove it along with the pump driveshaft.
4 If a new oil pump is installed, make sure the pump driveshaft is mated with the shaft inside the pump.
5 Position the pump on the engine and make sure the slot in the upper end of the driveshaft is aligned with the tang on the lower end of the distributor shaft. The distributor drives the oil pump, so it is absolutely essential that the components mate properly.
6 Install the mounting bolt and tighten it to the torque listed in this Chapter's Specifications.
7 Install the oil pan.

2E

15.2 The crankshaft front oil seal can be removed in the vehicle with a seal removal tool (shown here) or a large screwdriver

15.4 Installing the front crankshaft oil seal using a deep socket

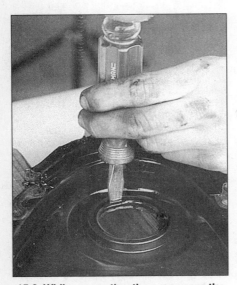

15.6 While supporting the cover near the seal bore, drive the old seal out from the inside with a hammer and punch or screwdriver

15   Crankshaft oil seals - replacement

Front seal - timing chain cover in place

Refer to illustrations 15.2 and 15.4

1   Remove the vibration damper (see Section 10).

2   Carefully pry the seal out of the cover with a seal removal tool or a large screwdriver **(see illustration)**. Be careful not to distort the cover or scratch the wall of the seal bore. If the engine has accumulated a lot of miles, apply penetrating oil to the seal-to-cover joint and allow it to soak in before attempting to pull the seal out.

3   Clean the bore to remove any old seal material and corrosion. Position the new seal in the bore with the open end of the seal facing IN. A small amount of oil applied to the outer edge of the new seal will make installation easier.

4   Apply a light film of grease to the lip of the seal. Drive the seal into the bore with a seal driver or a large socket and hammer until

it's completely seated **(see illustration)**. Select a socket that's the same outside diameter as the seal (a section of pipe can be used if a socket isn't available).

5   Reinstall the vibration damper.

Front seal - timing chain cover removed

Refer to illustrations 15.6 and 15.8

6   Use a punch or screwdriver and hammer to drive the seal out of the cover from the back side. Support the cover as close to the seal bore as possible **(see illustration)**. Be careful not to distort the cover or scratch the wall of the seal bore. If the engine has accumulated a lot of miles, apply penetrating oil to the seal-to-cover joint on each side and allow it to soak in before attempting to drive the seal out.

7   Clean the bore to remove any old seal material and corrosion. Support the cover on blocks of wood and position the new seal in the bore with the open end of the seal facing IN. A small amount of oil applied to the outer edge of the new seal will make installation easier.

8   Drive the seal into the bore with a large

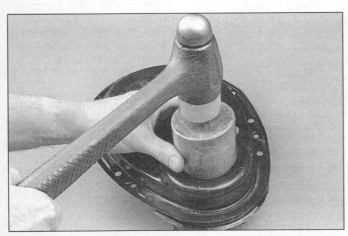

15.8 Clean the bore, then apply a small amount of oil to the outer edge of the seal and drive it squarely into the opening with a large socket and hammer - DO NOT damage the seal in the process!

15.10 To remove the rear main seal from the housing, insert the tip of the screwdriver into each notch and pry the seal out

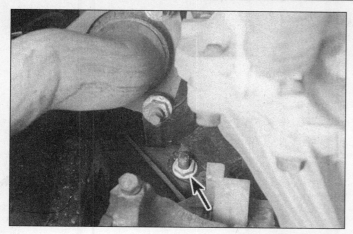
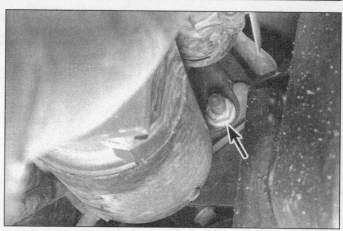

17.7 Left and right engine mount through-bolts

socket and hammer until it's completely seated **(see illustration)**. Select a socket that's the same outside diameter as the seal (a section of pipe can be used if a socket isn't available). Install the timing chain cover.

Rear main oil seal

Refer to illustrations 15.10 and 15.13

9   Remove the transmission (see Chapter 7).

10   The old seal can be removed from the housing by inserting a screwdriver into the notches provided and prying it out **(see illustration)**. Be sure to note how far it's recessed into the housing bore before removing it; the new seal will have to be recessed an equal amount. Be very careful not to scratch or otherwise damage the bore in the housing or oil leaks could develop.

11   Check the seal contact surface very carefully for scratches and nicks that could damage the new seal lip and cause oil leaks. If the crankshaft is damaged, the only alternative is a new or different crankshaft.

12   Make sure the housing is clean, then apply a thin coat of engine oil to the outer edge of the new seal. Apply multi-purpose grease to the seal lips. The seal must be pressed squarely into the housing bore, so hammering it into place is not recommended. If your don't have access to a special installer tool, unbolt the seal housing from the block. Sandwich the housing and seal between two smooth pieces of wood and press the seal into place with the jaws of a large vise. The pieces of wood must be thick enough to distribute the force evenly around the entire circumference of the seal. Work slowly and make sure the seal enters the bore squarely.

13   The seal lips must be lubricated with clean engine oil or multi-purpose grease

before the seal/housing is slipped over the crankshaft and bolted to the block. Use a new gasket - no sealant is required - and make sure the dowel pins are in place before installing the housing **(see illustration)**.

14   Tighten the nuts/screws a little at a time until they're all snug.

16   Flywheel/driveplate - removal and installation

1   Remove the transmission (see Chapter 7). If your vehicle has a manual transmission, remove the pressure plate and clutch (see Chapter 8).

2   Jam a large screwdriver in the starter ring gear to keep the crankshaft from turning, then remove the mounting bolts. Since it's fairly heavy, support the flywheel as the last bolt is removed.

3   Pull straight back on the flywheel/driveplate to detach it from the crankshaft.

4   Installation is the reverse of removal. The driveplate must be mounted with the torque converter pads facing the transmission. Be sure to align the hole in the flywheel/driveplate with the dowel pin in the crankshaft. Use non-hardening thread locking compound on the bolt threads and tighten them to the torque listed in this Chapter's Specifications in a criss-cross pattern.

17   Engine mounts - check and replacement

Refer to illustration 17.7

1   Engine mounts seldom require attention, but broken or deteriorated mounts

should be replaced immediately or the added strain placed on the driveline components may cause damage.

Check

2   During the check, the engine must be raised slightly to remove the weight from the mounts.

3   Raise the vehicle and support it securely on jackstands, then position the jack under the engine oil pan. Place a large block of wood between the jack head and the oil pan, then carefully raise the engine just enough to take the weight off the mounts.

4   Check the mounts to see if the rubber is cracked, hardened or separated from the metal plates. Sometimes the rubber will split right down the center. Rubber preservative or WD-40 should be applied to the mounts to slow deterioration.

5   Check for relative movement between the mount plates and the engine or frame (use a large screwdriver or pry bar to attempt to move the mounts). If movement is noted, lower the engine and tighten the mount fasteners.

Replacement

6   Disconnect the negative battery cable from the battery, then raise the vehicle and support it securely on jackstands.

7   Remove the nut and withdraw the mount through-bolt from the frame bracket **(see illustration)**.1

8   Raise the engine slightly, then remove the mount-to-frame bolts and detach the mount.

9   Installation is the reverse of removal. Use thread locking compound on the mount bolts and be sure to tighten them securely.

2E

Notes

Chapter 2 Part F
General engine overhaul procedures

Contents

	Section
Camshaft, lifters and bearings - inspection and bearing replacement	16
Crankshaft - inspection	18
Crankshaft - installation and main bearing oil clearance check	22
Crankshaft - removal	13
Cylinder compression check	2
Cylinder head - cleaning and inspection	9
Cylinder head - disassembly	8
Cylinder head - reassembly	11
Engine block - cleaning	14
Engine block - inspection	15
Engine overhaul - disassembly sequence	6
Engine overhaul - general information	3
Engine overhaul - reassembly sequence	24

	Section
Engine rebuilding alternatives	4
Engine - removal and installation	7
Engine removal - methods and precautions	5
General information	1
Initial start-up and break-in after overhaul	26
Main and connecting rod bearings - inspection	19
Piston/connecting rod assembly - inspection	17
Piston/connecting rod assembly - installation and bearing oil clearance check	23
Piston/connecting rod assembly - removal	12
Piston rings - installation	20
Pre-oiling engine after overhaul (V6 engine only)	25
Rear main oil seal - installation	21
Valves - servicing	10

2F

Specifications

Four-cylinder engines

Isuzu 1.9L engine

General

Bore and stroke	3.43 x 3.23 inches
Oil pressure	10 psi at 500 rpm; 30 to 50 psi at 2000 rpm
Compression pressure	Lowest reading cylinder must be at least 70-percent of highest reading cylinder (100 psi minimum)

Cylinder head and valvetrain

Cylinder head warpage limit	0.006 inch
Valve spring free length	
Standard	1.894 inches
Service limit	1.833 inches
Valve spring pressure and length (intake and exhaust)	51 to 60 lbs at 1.614 inches
Valve stem diameter (service limit)	
Intake	0.3102 inch
Exhaust	0.3091 inch
Stem-to-guide clearance	
Standard	
Intake	0.0009 to 0.0022 inch
Exhaust	0.0015 to 0.0031 inch
Service limit	
Intake	0.01298 inch
Exhaust	0.0097 inch
Valve head thickness (service limit)	
Intake	0.0315 inch
Exhaust	0.0394 inch

Four-cylinder engines

Isuzu 1.9L engine (continued)

Crankshaft and connecting rods

Crankshaft endplay	0.0117 inch
Connecting rod endplay (side clearance)	0.0137 inch
Main bearing journal diameter	
Standard	2.2016 to 2.2022 inches
Service limit	2.1555 inches
Main bearing oil clearance	
Standard	0.0008 to 0.0025 inch
Service limit	0.0046 inch

Crankshaft and connecting rods

Connecting rod bearing journal diameter	
Standard	1.9262 to 1.9268 inches
Service limit	1.8799 inch
Connecting rod bearing oil clearance	
Standard	0.0007 to 0.0030 inch
Service limit	0.0046 inch
Crankshaft journal taper/out-of-round limit	0.00028 inch

Engine block

Cylinder bore diameter	3.43 inches
Taper limit	0.0026 inch

Piston and rings

Piston ring side clearance	0.0059
Compression ring end gap	0.014 to 0.020
Oil ring end gap	0.008 to 0.035

2.0L engine

General

Bore and stroke	3.50 x 3.15 inches
Oil pressure	10 psi at 500 rpm; 30 to 50 psi at 2000 rpm
Compression pressure	Lowest reading cylinder must be at least 70-percent of highest reading cylinder (100 psi minimum)

Cylinder head and valvetrain

Cylinder head warpage limit	0.006 inch
Valve face angle	45-degrees
Valve seat angle	46-degrees
Stem-to-guide clearance	
Intake	0.0011 to 0.0026 inch
Exhaust	0.0014 to 0.003 inch
Valve seat width	
Intake	0.049 to 0.059
Exhaust	0.063 to 0.075
Valve spring installed height	No less than 1.60 inches
Valve spring pressure and length (intake and exhaust)	
Valve closed	1.6 inches at 73 to 81 lbs
Valve open	1.33 inches at 176 to 188 lbs

Crankshaft and connecting rods

Crankshaft endplay	0.002 to 0.008 inch
Connecting rod endplay (side clearance)	0.004 to 0.015 inch
Main bearing journal diameter	
Nos. 1 through 4	2.4945 to 2.4954 inches
No. 5	2.4937 to 2.4946 inch
Main bearing oil clearance	
1983	
Nos. 1 through 4	0.001 to 0.023 inch
No. 5	0.0018 to 0.0031 inch
1984	
No. 1 through 4	0.0006 to 0.0019 inch
No. 5	0.014 to 0.0027 inch
Connecting rod bearing journal diameter	1.9983 to 1.9994 inches
Connecting rod bearing oil clearance	0.0001 to 0.0031 inch
Crankshaft journal taper/out-of-round limit	0.0002 inch

Engine block
Cylinder bore diameter ....   3.50 inches
Out-of-round limit ....   0.001 inch
Taper limit ....   0.001 inch

Pistons and rings
Compression ring side clearance ....   0.001 to 0.003 inch
Oil ring side clearance ....   0.008 inch
Compression ring end gap ....   0.01 to 0.02 inch
Oil ring end gap ....   0.02 to 0.06 inch

Camshaft
Lobe lift (intake and exhaust)..   0.26 inch
Bearing journal diameter..   1.867 to 1.869 inches
Bearing oil clearance ....   0.001 to 0.004 inch

2.5L engine

General
Bore and stroke ....   4 00 x 3.00 inches
Oil pressure..   36 to 41 psi at 2000 rpm
Compression pressure ....   140 psi at 160 rpm

Cylinder head and valvetrain
Head warpage limit ....   0.006 inch
Valve face angle..   45-degrees
Valve seat angle
    1985 and 1986 ....   45-degrees
    1987 on 46-degrees
Minimum valve margin width ....   1/32 inch
Valve stem-to-guide clearance
    Intake..   0.001 to 0.0027 inch
    Exhaust...   0.001 to 0.0027 inch
Valve seat width
    Intake..   0.035 to 0.075 inch
    Exhaust
        1985 and 1986 ....   0.058 to 0.097 inch
        1987 on ....   0.085 to 0.105 inch
Valve spring free length ....   1.78 inches
Valve spring installed height
    1985 and 1986 ....   1.690 inches
    1987 on ....   1.440 inches
Valve spring pressure and length (intake and exhaust)
    Valve closed
        1985 and 1986 ....   78 to 86 lbs at 1.66 inches
        1987 on ....   71 to 78 lbs at 1.44 inches
    Valve open
        1985 and 1986 ....   170 to 180 lbs at 1.26 inches
        1987 on ....   158 to 170 lbs at 1.040 inches

Crankshaft and connecting rods
Crankshaft endplay..   0.0035 to 0.0085 inch
Connecting rod endplay (side clearance) ....   0.006 to 0.022 inch
Main bearing journal diameter..   2.300 inches
Main bearing oil clearance ....   0.0005 to 0.0022 inch
Connecting rod journal diameter ....   2.000 inches
Connecting rod bearing oil clearance.............................   0.0005 to 0.0026 inch
Crankshaft journal taper/out-of-round limit ....   0.005 inch

Engine block
Cylinder bore diameter ....   4.0 inches
Out-of-round limit ....   0.001 inch
Taper limit ....   0.005 inch

Pistons and rings
Piston-to-bore clearance
    1985
        Top of bore ....   0.0025 to 0.0033 inch
        Bottom of bore..   0.0017 to 0.0041 inch
    1986 on ....   0.0014 to 0.0022 inch

2F

2.5L engine

Pistons and rings (continued)

Ring side clearance

Top compression ring

1985 .... 0.0015 to 0.003 inch

1986 on .... 0.002 to 0.003 inch

Second compression ring

1985 .... 0.0015 to 0.003 inch

1986 on .... 0.001 to 0.003 inch

Oil ring .... 0.015 to 0.055 inch

Compression ring end gap .... 0.010 to 0.020 inch

Oil ring end gap

1985 .... 0.015 to 0.055 inch

1986 on .... 0.020 to 0.060 inch

V6 engines

2.8L engine

General

Bore and stroke .... 3.50 x 3.00 inches

Oil pressure.. 10 psi at 500 rpm; 50 to 55 psi at 2000 rpm

Compression pressure .... Lowest reading cylinder must be at least 70-percent
of highest reading cylinder (100 psi minimum)

Cylinder head and valvetrain

Cylinder head warpage limit .... 0.006 inch

Valve face angle... 45-degrees

Valve seat angle... 46-degrees

Valve seat runout .... 0.002 inch maximum

Stem-to-guide clearance .... 0.001 to 0.0028 inch

Valve seat width

Intake.. 0.049 to 0.059 inch

Exhaust... 0.063 to 0.075 inch

Valve spring installed height .... 1.57 inches

Valve spring free length .... 1.91 inches

Valve spring pressure and length (intake and exhaust)

Valve closed .... 1.57 inch at 87.9 lbs

Valve open... 1.18 inch at 194.9 lbs

Crankshaft and connecting rods

Crankshaft endplay... 0.002 to 0.007 inch

Connecting rod endplay (side clearance)............................ 0.006 to 0.017 inch

Main bearing journal diameter

1982 (all)... 2.4937 to 2.4946 inches

1983 on (1, 2 and 4).. 2.4937 to 2.4946 inches

1983 on (3 only)... 2.4932 to 2.4941 inches

Main bearing oil clearance

1982 (all)... 0.0017 to 0.0030 inch

1983 on (all).. 0.0016 to 0.0032 inch

Connecting rod bearing journal diameter .... 1.9983 to 1.9994 inches

Connecting rod bearing oil clearance.................................. 0.0012 to 0.0037 inch

Crankshaft journal taper/out-of-round limit.......................... 0.0002 inch

Engine block

Cylinder bore diameter .... 3.504 to 3.507 inches

Out-of-round limit .... 0.0008 inch

Taper limit... 0.0003 inch

Pistons and rings

Compression ring side clearance

Top ring .... 0.0019 to 0.0028 inch

Second ring .... 0.0016 to 0.0037 inch

Oil ring side clearance.. 0.0078 inch

Piston-to-bore clearance... 0.0017 to 0.0027 inch

Piston pin diameter... 0.90526 to 0.90557 inch

Pin-to-piston clearance .... 0.00026 to 0.00036 inch

Pin-to-rod clearance (press fit) .... 0.00074 to 0.00203 inch (press)

Piston ring end gap

Top ring .... 0.0098 to 0.0196 inch

Second ring .... 0.0098 to 0.0196 inch

Oil ring .... 0.020 to 0.055 inch

Camshaft

Lobe lift	
Intake	0.231 inch
Exhaust	0.262 inch
Bearing journal diameter	1.868 to 1.870 inches
Bearing oil clearance	0.001 to 0.004 inch

4.3L V6 engine

General

Bore and stroke	4.000 x 3.480 inches
Oil pressure	10 psi at 500 rpm; 30 to 55 psi at 2000 rpm
Compression pressure	Lowest reading cylinder must be at least 70-percent of highest reading cylinder (100 psi minimum)

Engine block

Cylinder bore diameter	3.9995 to 4.0025 inches
Taper limit	0.001 inch
Out-of-round limit	0.002 inch

Pistons and rings

Piston-to-cylinder bore clearance	
Standard	0.0007 to 0.0017 inch
Service limit	0.0027 inch
Piston ring-to-groove side clearance	
Standard	
Compression rings	0.0012 to 0.0032 inch
Oil control ring	0.002 to 0.007 inch
Service limit	
Compression rings	0.0033 inch
Oil control ring	0.008 inch
Piston ring end gap	
Standard	
Top compression ring	0.010 to 0.020 inch
Second compression ring	0.010 to 0.025 inch
Oil control ring	0.015 to 0.055 inch
Service limit	
Top compression ring	0.030 inch
Second compression ring	0.035 inch
Oil control ring	0.065 inch
Piston pin	
Diameter	0.9270 to 0.9273 inch
Pin-to-piston clearance limit	0.001 inch
Pin-to-rod interference fit	0.0008 to 0.0016 inch

Crankshaft and connecting rods

Main journal	
Diameter	
No. 1 journal	2.4484 to 2.4493 inches
No. 2 and 3 journals	2.4481 to 2.4490 inches
No. 4 journal	2.4479 to 2.4488 inches
Taper limit	0.001 inch
Out-of-round limit	0.001 inch
Main bearing oil clearance	
Standard	
No. 1 journal	0.0008 to 0.0020 inch
No. 2 and 3 journals	0.0011 to 0.0023 inch
No. 4 journal	0.0017 to 0.0032 inch
Service limit	
No. 1 journal	0.001 to 0.0015 inch
No. 2 and 3 journals	0.001 to 0.0025 inch
No. 4 journal	0.0025 to 0.0035 inch
Connecting rod journal	
Diameter	2.2487 to 2.2497 inches
Taper limit	0.001 inch
Out-of-round limit	0.001 inch
Connecting rod bearing oil clearance	
Standard	0.0013 to 0.0035 inch
Service limit	0.0035 inch
Connecting rod endplay (side clearance)	0.006 to 0.014 inch
Crankshaft endplay	0.002 to 0.006 inch

2F

4.3L V6 engine

Cylinder head and valvetrain

Head warpage limit...	0.003 inch per 6 inch span/0.006 inch overall
Valve seat angle..	46-degrees
Valve seat width	
Intake..	1/32 to 1/16 (0.0313 to 0.0625) inch
Exhaust...	1/16 to 3/32 (0.0625 to 0.0938) inch
Valve seat runout limit	0.002 inch
Valve face angle..	45-degrees
Minimum valve margin width..	1/32 inch
Valve stem-to-guide clearance	
Standard..	0.0010 to 0.0027 inch
Service limit	
Intake	0.0037 inch
Exhaust	0.0047 inch
Valve spring free length	2.030 inches
Valve spring damper (inner spring) free length	1.860 inches
Valve spring installed height	
Intake..	1-23/32 (1.7188) inches
Exhaust...	1-19/32 (1.5938) inches
Valve spring pressure and length (intake and exhaust)	
Closed	76 to 84 lbs. at 1.70 inches
Open..	194 to 206 lbs. at 1.25 inches

Torque specifications

Ft-lbs

1.9L engine*

Main bearing cap bolts	72
Connecting rod cap nuts	43

*Note: *Refer to Part A for additional torque specifications*

2.0L engine*

Main bearing cap bolts	70
Connecting rod cap nuts	32

*Note: *Refer to Part B for additional torque specifications*

2.5L engine*

Main bearing cap bolts	70
Connecting rod cap nuts	32
Oil pump-to-block bolts	22
Oil pick-up tube bracket nut..	37

*Note: *Refer to Part C for additional torque specifications*

2.8L V6 engine*

Main bearing cap bolts	70
Connecting rod cap nuts	37

*Note: *Refer to Part D for additional torque specifications*

4.3L V6*

Rocker arm studs	50
Main bearing cap bolts	80
Connecting rod cap nuts	45
Oil pump bolts	65

*Note: *Refer to Part E for additional torque specifications*

2.3 If your engine has a coil-in-cap distributor, disconnect the wire from the BAT terminal on the distributor cap when checking the compression

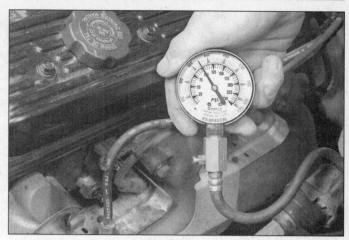

2.4 A compression gauge with a threaded fitting for the plug hole is preferred over the type that requires hand pressure to maintain the seal

1 General information

Included in this portion of Chapter 2 are the general overhaul procedures for the cylinder head(s) and internal engine components. The information ranges from advice concerning preparation for an overhaul and the purchase of replacement parts to detailed, step-by-step procedures covering removal and installation of internal engine components and the inspection of parts.

The following Sections have been written based on the assumption that the engine has been removed from the vehicle. For information concerning in-vehicle engine repair, as well as removal and installation of the external components necessary for the overhaul, see Part A, B, C, D or E of Chapter 2 (depending on engine type).

The Specifications included here in Part F are only those necessary for the inspection and overhaul procedures which follow. Refer to Part A, B, C, D or E for additional Specifications related to the various engines covered in this manual.

2 Cylinder compression check

Refer to illustrations 2.3 and 2.4

1   A compression check will tell you what mechanical condition the upper end (pistons, rings, valves, head gaskets) of your engine is in. Specifically, it can tell you if the compression is down due to leakage caused by worn piston rings, defective valves and seats or a blown head gasket. **Note:** *The engine must be at normal operating temperature and the battery must be fully charged for this check. Also, if the engine is equipped with a carburetor, the choke valve must be all the way open to get an accurate compression reading (if the engine's warm, the choke should already be open).*

2   Begin by cleaning the area around the spark plugs before you remove them (compressed air should be used, if available, otherwise a small brush or even a bicycle tire pump will work). The idea is to prevent dirt from getting into the cylinders as the compression check is being done. Remove all of the spark plugs from the engine (see Chapter 1).

3   If the vehicle is fuel-injected, remove the fuel pump relay or unplug the electrical connector to the fuel pump. If the ignition coil is an integral part of the distributor cap, disconnect the wire from the BAT terminal on the cap **(see illustration)**. If the ignition coil is mounted separately, unplug the coil-to-distributor wire harness at the distributor.

4   With the compression gauge in the number one spark plug hole **(see illustration)**, depress the accelerator pedal all the way to the floor to open the throttle valve. Crank the engine over at least four compression strokes and watch the gauge. The compression should build up quickly in a healthy engine. Low compression on the first stroke, followed by gradually increasing pressure on successive strokes, indicates worn piston rings. A low compression reading on the first stroke, which doesn't build up during successive strokes, indicates leaking valves or a blown head gasket (a cracked head could also be the cause). Record the highest gauge reading obtained.

5   Repeat the procedure for the remaining cylinders and compare the results to the Specifications.

6   Add some engine oil (about three squirts from a plunger-type oil can) to each cylinder, through the spark plug hole, and repeat the test.

7   If the compression increases after the oil is added, the piston rings are definitely worn. If the compression doesn't increase significantly, the leakage is occurring at the valves or head gasket. Leakage past the valves may be caused by burned valve seats and/or faces or warped, cracked or bent valves.

8   If two adjacent cylinders have equally low compression, there's a strong possibility that the head gasket between them is blown. The appearance of coolant in the combustion chambers or the crankcase would verify this condition.

9   If the compression is unusually high, the combustion chambers are probably coated with carbon deposits. If that's the case, the cylinder head(s) should be removed and decarbonized.

10   If compression is way down or varies greatly between cylinders, it would be a good idea to have a leak-down test performed by an automotive repair shop. This test will pinpoint exactly where the leakage is occurring and how severe it is.

3 Engine overhaul - general information

Refer to illustration 3.4

It is not always easy to determine when, or if, an engine should be completely overhauled, as a number of factors must be considered.

High mileage is not necessarily an indication that an overhaul is needed while low mileage, on the other hand, does not preclude the need for an overhaul. Frequency of servicing is probably the single most important consideration. An engine that has regular (and frequent) oil and filter changes, as well as other required maintenance, will most likely give many thousands of miles of reliable service. Conversely, a neglected engine may require an overhaul very early in its life.

Excessive oil consumption is an indication that piston rings and/or valve guides are in need of attention (make sure that oil leaks are not responsible before deciding that the rings and guides are bad). Have a cylinder compression or leak-down test performed by an experienced tune-up mechanic to determine for certain the extent of the work required.

2F

3.4 The oil pressure gauge can be checked by attaching the gauge to the fitting block near the distributor (V6 engine shown) - on four-cylinder models the fitting is located near the oil filter)

If the engine is making obvious knocking or rumbling noises, the connecting rod and/or main bearings are probably at fault. Check the oil pressure with a gauge **(see illustration)**, installed in place of the oil pressure sending unit. Compare your readings with the values listed in this Chapter's Specifications. If it is extremely low, the bearings and/or oil pump are probably worn out.

Loss of power, rough running, excessive valvetrain noise and high fuel consumption rates may also point to the need for an overhaul (especially if they are all present at the same time). If a complete tune-up does not remedy the situation, major mechanical work is the only solution.

An engine overhaul generally involves restoring the internal parts to the specifications of a new engine. During an overhaul, the piston rings are replaced and the cylinder walls are reconditioned (rebored and/or honed). If a rebore is done, then new pistons are also required. The main and connecting rod bearings are replaced with new ones and, if necessary, the crankshaft may be reground to restore the journals. Generally, the valves are serviced as well, since they're usually in less-than-perfect condition at this point. While the engine is being overhauled, rebuild other components such as the carburetor, the distributor, the starter and the alternator. The end result will be a like-new engine that will give as many trouble-free miles as the original.

Before beginning the engine overhaul, read through the entire procedure to familiarize yourself with the scope and requirements of the job. Overhauling an engine is not that difficult, but it is time consuming. Plan on the vehicle being tied up for a minimum of two weeks, especially if parts must be taken to an automotive machine shop for repair or reconditioning. Check on availability of parts and make sure that any necessary special tools and equipment are obtained in advance. Most work can be done with typical shop hand tools, although a number of precision measuring tools are required for inspecting parts to determine if they must be replaced.

Often a reputable automotive machine shop will handle the inspection of parts and offer advice concerning reconditioning and replacement. **Note:** *Always wait until the engine has been completely disassembled and all components, especially the engine block, have been inspected before deciding what service and repair operations must be performed by an automotive machine shop.* Since the block's condition will be the major factor to consider when determining whether to overhaul the original engine or buy a rebuilt one, never purchase parts or have machine work done on other components until the block has been thoroughly inspected. As a general rule, time is the primary cost of an overhaul, so it does not pay to install worn or sub-standard parts.

As a final note, to ensure maximum life and minimum trouble from a rebuilt engine, everything must be assembled with care in a spotlessly clean environment.

4   Engine rebuilding alternatives

The do-it-yourselfer is faced with a several options when performing an engine overhaul. The decision to replace the block, piston/connecting rod assemblies and crankshaft depends on a number of factors, with the number one consideration being the condition of the block. Other factors are cost, access to machine shop facilities, parts availability, time required to complete the project and experience.

Some of the rebuilding alternatives include:

Individual parts - If the inspection procedures reveal that the engine block and most engine components are in reusable condition, purchasing individual parts may be the most economical alternative. The block, crankshaft and piston/connecting rod assemblies should all be inspected carefully. Even if the block shows little wear, the cylinder bores should receive a finish hone; a job for an automotive machine shop.

Master kit (crankshaft kit) - This rebuild package usually consists of a reground crankshaft and a matched set of pistons and connecting rods. The pistons will already be installed on the connecting rods. Piston rings and the necessary bearings may or may not be included in the kit. These kits are commonly available for standard cylinder bores, as well as for engine blocks which have been bored to a regular oversize.

Short block - A short block consists of an engine block with a crankshaft and piston/connecting rod assemblies already installed. All new bearings are incorporated and all clearances will be correct. Depending on where the short block is purchased, a guarantee may be included. The existing camshaft, valvetrain components, cylinder head(s) and external parts can be bolted to the short block with little or no machine shop work necessary.

Long block - A long block consists of a short block plus an oil pump, oil pan, cylinder head(s), valve cover(s), camshaft and valve-train components, timing gears or sprockets and chain and timing gear/chain cover. All components are installed with new bearings, seals and gaskets incorporated throughout. The installation of manifolds and external parts is all that is necessary. Some form of guarantee is usually included with the purchase.

Give careful thought to which alternative is best for you and discuss the situation with local automotive machine shops, auto parts stores or dealership partsmen before ordering or purchasing replacement parts.

5   Engine removal - methods and precautions

If it has been decided that an engine must be removed for overhaul or major repair work, certain preliminary steps should be taken.

Locating a suitable work area is extremely important. A shop is, of course, the most desirable place to work. Adequate work space along with storage space for the vehicle is very important. If a shop or garage is not available, at the very least a flat, level, clean work surface made of concrete or asphalt is required.

Cleaning the engine compartment and engine prior to removal will help keep tools clean and organized.

An engine hoist or A-frame will also be necessary. Make sure that the equipment is rated in excess of the combined weight of the engine and its accessories. Safety is of primary importance, considering the potential hazards involved in lifting the engine out of the vehicle.

If the engine is being removed by a novice, a helper should be available. Advice and aid from someone more experienced would also be helpful. There are many instances when one person cannot simultaneously perform all of the operations required when lifting the engine out of the vehicle.

Plan the operation ahead of time. Arrange for or obtain all of the tools and equipment you will need prior to beginning the job. Some of the equipment necessary to perform engine removal and installation safely and with relative ease are (in addition to an engine hoist) a heavy-duty floor jack, complete sets of wrenches and sockets as described in the front of this manual, wooden blocks and plenty of rags and cleaning solvent for mopping up the inevitable spills. If the hoist is to be rented, make sure that you arrange for it in advance and perform beforehand all of the operations possible without it. This will save you money and time.

Plan for the vehicle to be out of use for a considerable amount of time. A machine shop will be required to perform some of the work which the do-it-yourselfer cannot accomplish due to a lack of special equipment. These shops often have a busy schedule so it would be wise to consult them before removing the engine in order to accurately estimate the amount of time required to rebuild or repair components that may need work.

Always use extreme caution when removing and installing the engine; serious injury can result from careless actions. Plan ahead. Take your time and a job of this nature, although major, can be accomplished successfully.

6 Engine overhaul - disassembly sequence

1 It is much easier to disassemble and work on the engine if it is mounted on a portable engine stand. These stands can often be rented for a reasonable fee from an equipment rental yard. Before the engine is mounted on a stand, the flywheel/driveplate should be removed from the engine (see Chapter 8).

2 If a stand is not available, it is possible to disassemble the engine with it blocked up on a sturdy workbench or on the floor. Be extra careful not to tip or drop the engine when working without a stand.

3 If you are going to obtain a rebuilt engine, all external components must come off first in order to be transferred to the replacement engine (just as they will if you are doing a complete engine overhaul yourself). These include:

Alternator and brackets
Emissions control components
Distributor, spark plug wires and spark plugs
Thermostat and housing cover
Water pump
Carburetor, TBI unit or CPI unit
Intake/exhaust manifolds
Oil filter
Fuel pump
Engine mounts
Flywheel/driveplate

Note: *When removing the external components from the engine, pay close attention to details that may be helpful or important during installation. Note the installed position of gaskets, seals, spacers, pins, washers, bolts and other small items.*

4 If you are obtaining a short block (which consists of the engine block, crankshaft, pistons and connecting rods all assembled), then the cylinder heads, oil pan and oil pump will have to be removed also. See *Engine rebuilding alternatives* for additional information regarding the different possibilities to be considered.

5 If you are planning a complete overhaul, the engine must be disassembled and the internal components removed in the following order:

Valve cover(s)
Cylinder head(s) and pushrods/valve gear
Valve lifters
Timing chain/gear cover
Timing chain/sprockets or gears
Camshaft
Oil pan
Oil pump
Piston/connecting rod assemblies
Crankshaft

6 Before beginning the disassembly and overhaul procedures, make sure the following items are available:

Common hand tools
Small cardboard boxes or plastic bags for storing parts
Gasket scraper
Ridge reamer
Vibration damper puller
Micrometers
Small hole gauges
Telescoping gauges
Dial indicator set
Valve spring compressor
Cylinder surfacing hone
Piston ring groove cleaning tool
Electric drill motor
Tap and die set
Wire brushes
Cleaning solvent

7 Engine - removal and installation

Refer to illustrations 7.16, 7.17, 7.20, 7.22, 7.38 and 7.40

Note 1: *The following sequence of operations does not necessarily need to be performed in the order given. It is, rather, a checklist of everything that must be disconnected or removed before the engine can be lifted out of the vehicle. If a component mentioned does not apply to your particular vehicle, simply move on to the next step. It is very important that all linkages, electrical wiring, hoses and cables are removed or disconnected before attempting to lift the engine out of the vehicle. It should also be noted that the "S" series vehicles are fitted with both metric and standard size fasteners. Therefore, both types of tools will be needed for this operation.*

Note 2: *On 4WD models with a 2.8L V6 engine and a manual transmission, it is necessary to remove the transmission from the vehicle to provide adequate clearance for engine removal. Refer to Chapter 7 Part A for the transmission removal procedure, then ignore any Steps here which do not apply.*

1 Disconnect the negative battery cable.
2 Disconnect the underhood light.
3 Scribe very light lines on the underside of the hood, around the hood mounting bracket, so the hood can be installed in the same position.
4 Unbolt the hood and, with the aid of an assistant, remove the hood from the vehicle (see Chapter 11).
5 Remove the air cleaner assembly (See Chapter 4).
6 Drain the cooling system (see Chapter 3).

7.16 To gain working clearance, the front body mounts must be removed (most models) to allow the body to be raised off the chassis

7.17 Location of the right side middle body mount bolt

7 Drain the engine oil (see Chapter 1).
8 Remove the upper radiator hose.
9 Remove the upper fan shroud (see Chapter 3).
10 Disconnect the automatic transmission oil cooler lines, if equipped.
11 Remove the lower radiator hose.
12 Unbolt the radiator mounting bolts and carefully remove the radiator (see Chapter 3).
13 Remove the four mounting bolts from the fan. Remove the fan, and if equipped, remove the fan clutch (see Chapter 3).
14 Unbolt the air-conditioning compressor, if equipped, and lay it to the side out of the way (see Chapter 3). **Warning:** *Do not disconnect any of the air conditioning lines unless the system has been depressurized by a dealer service department or air-conditioning technician, as personal injury may occur.*
15 Due to the inaccessibility of the top bellhousing bolts on these vehicles, it is necessary to raise the body off the chassis to gain adequate working clearance.
16 Remove the two front body mount bolts located behind the front bumper **(see illustration)**.
17 Remove the two middle body mount bolts located behind the door pillars **(see illustration)**.

2F

7.20 Spacer blocks are used to hold the body off the chassis

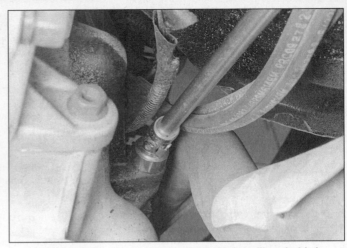

7.22 A socket extension and universal joint will probably be needed to remove the upper bellhousing bolts

18   Loosen the two rear body mount bolts.
19   Remove the front bumper mounting bolts and remove the front bumper.
20   Position a jack and a wood block under the front crossbrace. Raise the body off of the chassis just enough to insert a 2x4 wood block between the crossbrace and the frame rail on each side **(see illustration)**.
21   Lower the jack.
22   Remove the two upper bellhousing-to-engine bolts **(see illustration)**.
23   Disconnect the AIR pump hoses at the pump fittings and at the AIR injection manifold. Remove the hoses.
24   Remove the exhaust pipe mounting bolts from the exhaust manifold(s).
25   On V6-equipped models, remove the upper mounting bolts from the right side exhaust manifold.
26   Remove the lower mounting bolts from the right side exhaust manifold (V6 engines). It may be necessary to raise the vehicle (be sure to support it securely on jackstands) to gain access to the lower manifold bolts.
27   Remove the electrical connectors from the starter motor and remove the starter lead clamp located at the right front corner of the oil pan. Position the wiring out of the way.
28   Remove the starter motor mounting bolts and remove the starter motor (see Chapter 5).
29   Disconnect the clutch cable at the clutch actuating lever (if equipped).
30   Remove the alternator electrical connectors.
31   Disconnect the alternator wiring harness from the two harness clamps and position the harness out of the way.
32   Remove the electrical connector from the diverter valve.
33   Remove the diverter valve from the mounting bracket on the valve cover.
34   Disconnect all electrical connections from the carburetor or fuel injection unit.
35   Disconnect the vacuum hose from the intake manifold fitting located just below the secondary choke pulloff. Disconnect the vac-

uum brake hose from the filter, and any other manifold vacuum hoses which would later interfere with engine removal.
36   Disconnect the throttle cable from the carburetor throttle lever and from the cable routing bracket on the valve cover.
37   Remove the spark plug wires from the spark plugs.
38   Remove the distributor cap along with the spark plug wires. Disconnect the distributor electrical connector **(see illustration)**.
39   Disconnect the fuel vapor hose three-way connector at the front of the engine. Remove the vapor hose harness clip from the power steering bracket and position the hoses out of the way.
40   Remove the electrical connector from the coolant temperature sending unit at the front of the engine **(see illustration)**.
41   Remove the torque converter cover. Remove the torque converter-to-driveplate bolts (see Chapter 7 Part B).
42   Remove the four remaining bellhousing-to-engine bolts.
43   Position a moveable jack (floor jack or transmission jack) under the transmission oil pan using a block of wood as an insulator.

Support the transmission securely.
44   Attach the hoist lifting chains to the lifting brackets on the engine. There is one bracket at the front of the engine and one at the rear, diagonally opposite the front one. Make sure the chain is looped properly through the engine brackets and secured with bolts and nuts through the chain links. The hook on the lifting hoist should be at the center of the engine.
45   Raise the engine slightly and then pull it forward to clear the input shaft (manual transmission). Where an automatic transmission is involved, keep the torque converter pushed well to the rear to retain engagement of the converter tangs with the oil pump inside the transmission.
46   Carefully lift the engine straight up and out of the engine compartment, continually checking clearances around it.
47   The transmission should remain supported by the floor jack or wood blocks while the engine is out.
48   Attach the engine to an engine stand.
49   Refer to other Sections in this Chapter for further disassembly and rebuilding procedures.

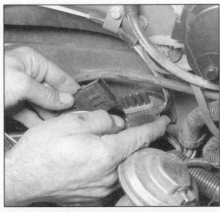

7.38 Disconnect the distributor electrical connector

7.40 Location of the electrical connector for the coolant temperature sending unit

8.1 A small plastic bag, with an appropriate label, can be used to store the valvetrain components so they can be kept together and reinstalled in the correct guide

8.3a Use a valve spring compressor to compress the springs, then remove the keepers from the valve stem

8.3b If the valve won't pull through the guide, deburr the edge of the stem end and the area around the top of the keeper groove with a file

8 Cylinder head - disassembly

Refer to illustrations 8.1, 8.3a and 8.3b
Note: *New and rebuilt cylinder heads are commonly available for most engines at dealerships and auto parts stores. Due to the fact that some specialized tools are necessary for the disassembly and inspection procedures, and replacement parts may not be readily available, it may be more practical and economical for the home mechanic to purchase a replacement head (or heads) rather than taking the time to disassemble, inspect and recondition the original head(s).*

1   Cylinder head disassembly involves removal and disassembly of the intake and exhaust valves and their related components. If they are still in place, remove the nuts or bolts and pivot balls, then separate the rocker arms from the cylinder head. Label the parts or store them separately so they can be reinstalled in their original locations **(see illustration)**.

2   Before the valves are removed, arrange to label and store them, along with their related components, so they can be kept separate and reinstalled in the same valve guides they are removed from.

3   Compress the valve spring on the first valve with a spring compressor and remove the keepers **(see illustration)**. Carefully release the valve spring compressor and remove the retainer (or rotator), the shield (if so equipped), the springs, the valve guide seal and/or O-ring seal, the spring seat and the valve from the head. If the valve binds in the guide (won't pull through), push it back into the head and deburr the area around the keeper groove with a fine file or whetstone **(see illustration)**.

4   Repeat the procedure for the remaining valves. Remember to keep together all the parts for each valve so they can be reinstalled in the same locations.

5   Once the valves have been removed and safely stored, the head should be thoroughly cleaned and inspected. If a complete

engine overhaul is being done, finish the engine disassembly procedures before beginning the cylinder head cleaning and inspection process.

9 Cylinder head - cleaning and inspection

1   Thorough cleaning of the cylinder head and related valvetrain components, followed by a detailed inspection, will enable you to decide how much valve service work must be done during the engine overhaul.

Cleaning

2   Scrape away all traces of old gasket material and sealing compound from the head gasket, intake manifold and exhaust manifold sealing surfaces.

3   Remove any built-up scale around the coolant passages.

4   Run a stiff wire brush through the oil holes to remove any deposits that may have formed in them.

5   It is a good idea to run an appropriate size tap into each of the threaded holes to remove any corrosion and thread sealant that may be present. If compressed air is available, use it to clear the holes of debris produced by this operation.

6   Clean the exhaust and intake manifold stud threads in a similar manner with an appropriate size die. Clean the rocker arm pivot bolt or stud threads with a wire brush.

7   Next, clean the cylinder head with solvent and dry it thoroughly. Compressed air will speed the drying process and ensure that all holes and recessed areas are clean. **Note:** *Decarbonizing chemicals are available and may prove very useful when cleaning cylinder heads and valvetrain components. They are very caustic and should be used with caution. Be sure to follow the instructions on the container.*

8   Clean the rocker arms, pivot balls and pushrods with solvent and dry them thoroughly. Compressed air will speed the drying process and can be used to clean out the oil

passages.

9   Clean all the valve springs, keepers, retainers, rotators, shields and spring seats with solvent and dry them thoroughly. Do the components from one valve at a time to avoid mixing up the parts.

10   Scrape off any heavy deposits that may have formed on the valves, then use a motorized wire brush to remove deposits from the valve heads and stems. Again, make sure the valves do not get mixed up.

Inspection

Cylinder head

Refer to illustrations 9.12, 9.14a and 9.14b

11   Inspect the head very carefully for cracks, evidence of coolant leakage and other damage. If cracks are found, a new cylinder head should be obtained.

12   Using a straightedge and feeler gauges, check the head gasket mating surface for warpage **(see illustration)**. If the head is warped beyond the limits given in the Specifications, it can be resurfaced at an automotive machine shop.

9.12 Check the cylinder head gasket surface for warpage by trying to slip a feeler gauge under the straightedge (see the Specifications to the maximum warpage allowed and use a feeler gauge of that thickness)

2F

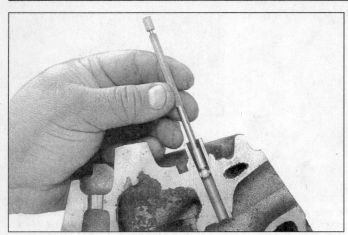

9.14a Use a small hole gauge to determine the inside diameter of
the valve guides (the gauge is then measured with a micrometer)

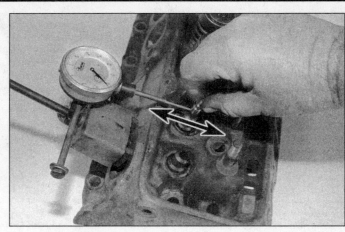

9.14b A dial indicator can also be used to determine the valve
stem-to-guide clearance (move the valve stem as
indicated by the arrows)

13   Examine the valve seats in each of the combustion chambers. If they are pitted, cracked or burned, the head will require valve service that is beyond the scope of the home mechanic.

14   Measure the inside diameters of the valve guides **(see illustration)**, at both ends and the center of each guide, with a small hole gauge and a 0-to-1-inch micrometer. Record the measurements for future reference. These measurements, along with the valve stem diameter measurements, will enable you to compute the valve stem-to-guide clearances. These clearances, when compared to the Specifications, will be one factor that will determine the extent of valve service work required. The guides are measured at the ends and at the center to determine if they are worn in a bell-mouth pattern (more wear at the ends). If they are, guide reconditioning or replacement is necessary. As an alternative, use a dial indicator to measure the lateral movement of each valve stem with the valve in the guide and approximately 1/16-inch off the seat **(see illustration)**. The

reading must be divided by two to obtain the actual clearance.

Rocker arm components

15   Check the rocker arm faces (that contact the pushrod ends and valve stems) for pits, wear and rough spots. Check the pivot contact areas as well.

16   Inspect the pushrod ends for scuffing and excessive wear. Roll the pushrod on a flat surface, such as a piece of glass, to determine if it is bent.

17   Any damaged or excessively worn parts must be replaced with new ones.

Valves

Refer to illustrations 9.18, 9.19 and 9.20

18   Carefully inspect each valve face for cracks, pits and burned spots **(see illustration)**. Check the valve stem and neck for cracks. Rotate the valve and check for any obvious indication that it is bent. Check the end of the stem for pits and excessive wear. The presence of any of these conditions indicates the need for valve service by a properly equipped professional.

19   Measure the width of the valve margin **(see illustration)** on each valve and compare it to the Specifications. Any valve with a mar-

gin narrower than specified will have to be replaced with a new one.

20   Measure the valve stem diameter **(see illustration)**. By subtracting the stem diameter from the corresponding valve guide diameter, the valve stem-to-guide clearance is obtained. Compare the results to the Specifications. If the stem-to-guide clearance is greater than specified, the guides will have to be reconditioned and new valves may have to be installed, depending on the condition of the old ones.

Valve components

Refer to illustrations 9.21a, 9.21b and 9.22

21   Check the ends of each valve spring for wear and pitting. Measure the free length **(see illustration)** and compare it to the Specifications. Any springs that are shorter than specified have sagged and should not be reused. Stand the spring on a flat surface and check it for squareness **(see illustration)**.

22   Check the spring retainers or rotators and keepers for obvious wear and cracks **(see illustration)**. Any questionable parts should be replaced with new ones, as extensive damage will occur in the event of failure during engine operation.

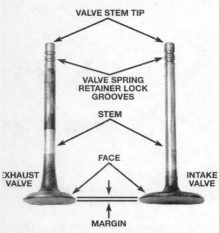

9.18a Check for valve wear at the
points shown here

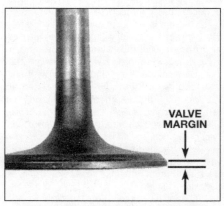

9.19 The margin width on each valve
must be as specified (if no margin exists,
the valve must be replaced)

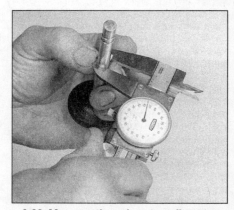

9.20 Measure the valve stem diameter
at three points

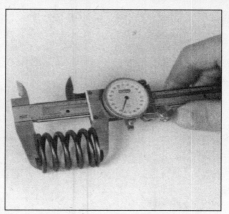

9.21a Measure the free length of each valve spring with a dial or vernier caliper

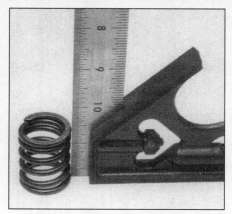

9.21 Check each valve spring for squareness

9.22 The exhaust valve rotators can be checked by turning the inner and outer sections in opposite directions - feel for smooth movement and excessive play

23 If the inspection process indicates that the valve components are in generally poor condition and worn beyond the limits specified, which is usually the case in an engine that is being overhauled, reassemble the valves in the cylinder head and refer to Section 10 for valve servicing recommendations.

24 If the inspection turns up no excessively worn parts, and if the valve faces and seats are in good condition, the valvetrain components can be reinstalled in the cylinder head without major servicing. Refer to the appropriate Section for cylinder head reassembly procedures.

10 Valves - servicing

1 Because of the complex nature of the job and the special tools and equipment needed, servicing of the valves, the valve seats and the valve guides (commonly known as a "valve job") is best left to a professional.

2 The home mechanic can remove and disassemble the head, do the initial cleaning and inspection, then reassemble and deliver the head to a dealer service department or a reputable automotive machine shop for the actual valve servicing.

3 The dealer service department or automotive machine shop will remove the valves and springs, recondition or replace the valves and valve seats, recondition the valve guides, check and replace the valve springs, spring retainers or rotators and keepers (as necessary), replace the valve seals with new ones, reassemble the valve components and make sure the installed spring height is correct. The cylinder head gasket surface will also be resurfaced if it is warped.

4 After the valve job has been performed by a professional, the head will be in like-new condition. When the head is returned, be sure to clean it again, very thoroughly (before installation on the engine), to remove any metal particles and abrasive grit that may still be present from the valve service or head resurfacing operations. Use compressed air, if available, to blow out all the oil holes and passages.

11 Cylinder head - reassembly

Refer to illustrations 11.3, 11.5, 11.6, 11.8 and 11.9

1 Regardless of whether or not a head was sent to an automotive repair shop for valve servicing, make sure it's clean before beginning reassembly.

2 If a head was sent out for valve servicing, the valves and related components will already be in place. Begin the reassembly procedure with Step 8.

3 Install new seals on each of the intake valve guides. Using a hammer and a deep socket or seal installation tool, gently tap each seal into place until it's completely seated on the guide **(see illustration)**. Don't twist or cock the seals during installation or they won't seal properly on the valve stems. The umbrella-type seals (if used) are installed over the valves after the valves are in place.

4 Beginning at one end of the head, lubricate and install the first valve. Apply moly-base grease or clean engine oil to the valve stem.

5 Drop the spring seat or shim(s) over the valve guide and set the valve springs, shield

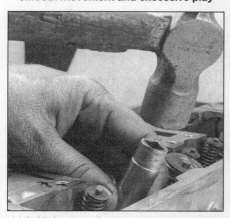

11.3 Make sure the new valve stem seals are seated against the tops of the valve guide

and retainer (or rotator) in place **(see illustration)**.

6 Compress the springs with a valve spring compressor and carefully install the O-ring oil seal in the lower groove of the valve stem. Make sure the seal isn't twisted - it

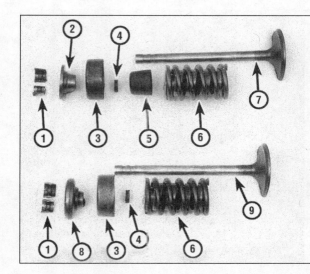

11.5 V6 engine valves and related components - exploded view

1   *Keeper*
2   *Retainer*
3   *Oil shield*
4   *O-ring oil seal*
5   *Umbrella seal*
6   *Damper*
7   *Spring*
8   *Intake valve*
9   *Rotator*
10   *Exhaust valve*

2F

11.6 Make sure the O-ring seal under the retainer is seated in the groove and not twisted before installing the keepers

11.8 A special adapter and vacuum pump are required to check the O-ring valve stem seals for leaks

11.9 Be sure to check the valve spring installed height (the distance from the top of the seat/shims to the top of the shield)

must lie perfectly flat in the groove **(see illustration)**. Position the keepers in the upper groove, then slowly release the compressor and make sure the keepers seat properly. Apply a small dab of grease to each keeper to hold it in place if necessary.

7   Repeat the procedure for the remaining valves. Be sure to return the components to their original locations - don't mix them up!

8   Once all the valves are in place in both heads, the valve stem O-ring seals must be checked to make sure they don't leak. This procedure requires a vacuum pump and special adapter available at most auto parts stores. The adapter is positioned on each valve retainer or rotator and vacuum is applied with the hand pump **(see illustration)**. If the vacuum can't be maintained, the seal is leaking and must be checked/replaced before the head is installed on the engine.

9   Check the installed valve spring height with a ruler graduated in 1/32-inch increments or a dial caliper. If the head was sent out for service work, the installed height should be correct (but don't assume that it is). The measurement is taken from the top of

each spring seat or shim(s) to the top of the oil shield (or the bottom of the retainer/rotator - the two points are the same) **(see illustration)**. If the height is greater than specified, shims can be added under the springs to correct it. **Caution:** *Do not, under any circumstances, shim the springs to the point where the installed height is less than specified.*

10   Apply moly-base grease to the rocker arm faces and the pivot balls, then install the rocker arms and pivots on the cylinder head studs. Thread the nuts on three or four turns only (when the heads are installed on a V6 engine, the nuts will be tightened following a specific procedure).

12 Piston/connecting rod assembly - removal

Refer to illustrations 12.2, 12.6 and 12.8

1   Prior to removal of the piston/connecting rod assemblies, the engine should be positioned upright.

2   Using a ridge reamer, completely re-

move the ridge at the top of each cylinder (follow the manufacturer's instructions provided with the ridge reaming tool) **(see illustration)**. Failure to remove the ridge before attempting to remove the piston/connecting rod assemblies will result in piston breakage.

3   After all of the cylinder wear ridges have been removed, turn the engine upside-down.

4   Before the connecting rods are removed, check the endplay as follows. Mount a dial indicator with its stem in line with the crankshaft and touching the side of the number one cylinder connecting rod cap.

5   Push the connecting rod forward, as far as possible, and zero the dial indicator. Next, push the connecting rod all the way to the rear and check the reading on the dial indicator. The distance that it moves is the endplay. If the endplay exceeds the service limit, a new connecting rod will be required. Repeat the procedure for the remaining connecting rods.

6   An alternative method is to slip feeler gauges between the connecting rod and the crankshaft throw until the play is removed **(see illustration)**. The endplay is then equal to the thickness of the feeler gauge(s).

7   Check the connecting rods and connecting rod caps for identification marks. If they are not plainly marked, identify each rod and cap using a small punch to make the appropriate number of indentations to indicate the cylinders they are associated with.

8   Loosen each of the connecting rod cap nuts approximately 1/2-turn. Remove the number one connecting rod cap and bearing insert. Do not drop the bearing insert out of the cap. Slip a short length of plastic or rubber hose over each connecting rod cap bolt (to protect the crankshaft journal and cylinder wall when the piston is removed) **(see illustration)** and push the connecting rod/piston assembly out through the top of the engine. Use a wooden tool to push on the upper bearing insert in the connecting rod. If resistance is felt, double-check to make sure that all of the ridge was removed from the cylinder.

12.2 A special tool is required to remove the ridge from the top of each cylinder (do it before removing the piston)

12.6 Checking connecting rod endplay with a feeler gauge

12.8 To prevent damage to the crankshaft journals and cylinder walls, slip sections of hose over the rod bolts before removing the pistons

13.1 Checking crankshaft endplay with a dial indicator

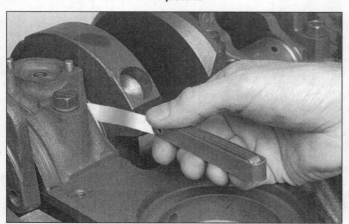

13.3 Checking crankshaft endplay with a feeler gauge

13.4a Mark the bearing caps with a center-punch before removing them

9   Repeat the procedure for the remaining cylinders. After removal, reassemble the connecting rod caps and bearing inserts in their respective connecting rods and install the cap nuts finger tight. Leaving the old bearing inserts in place until reassembly will help prevent the connecting rod bearing surfaces from being accidentally nicked or gouged.

13 Crankshaft - removal

Refer to illustrations 13.1, 13.3, 13.4a, and 13.4b

1   Before the crankshaft is removed, check the endplay as follows. Mount a dial indicator with the stem in line with the crankshaft and just touching one of the crank throws **(see illustration)**.
2   Push the crankshaft all the way to the rear and zero the dial indicator. Next, pry the crankshaft to the front as far as possible and check the reading on the dial indicator. The distance that it moves is the endplay. If it is greater than specified, check the crankshaft thrust surfaces for wear. If no wear is apparent, new main bearings should correct the endplay.

13.4b The arrow on the main bearing cap indicates the front of the engine

3   If a dial indicator is not available, feeler gauges can be used. Gently pry or push the crankshaft all the way to the front of the engine. Slip feeler gauges between the crankshaft and the front face of the thrust main bearing **(see illustration)** to determine the clearance (which is equivalent to crankshaft endplay).
4   Loosen each of the main bearing cap bolts 1/4 of a turn at a time until they can be

removed by hand. Check the main bearing caps to see if they are marked as to their locations. They are usually numbered consecutively (beginning with 1) from the front of the engine to the rear. If they are not, mark them with number stamping dies or a center-punch **(see illustration)**. Most main bearing caps have a cast-in arrow, which points to the front of the engine **(see illustration)**.
5   Gently tap the caps with a soft-faced

14.1a A hammer and large punch can be used to drive the freeze plugs into the block

14.1b Using pliers to remove a freeze plug from the block

hammer, then separate them from the engine block. If necessary, use the main bearing cap bolts as levers to remove the caps. Try not to drop the bearing insert if it comes out with the cap.

6   Carefully lift the crankshaft out of the engine. It is a good idea to have an assistant available, since the crankshaft is quite heavy. With the bearing inserts in place in the engine block and in the main bearing caps, return the caps to their respective locations on the engine block and tighten the bolts finger tight.

14 Engine block - cleaning

Refer to illustrations 14.1a, 14.1b and 14.10

1   Remove the freeze plugs from the engine block. To do this, knock one side of the plugs into the block with a hammer and punch, then grasp them with large pliers and pull them back through the holes **(see illustrations)**.

2   Using a gasket scraper, remove all traces of gasket material from the engine block. Be very careful not to nick or gouge the gasket sealing surfaces.

3   Remove the main bearing caps and separate the bearing inserts from the caps and the engine block. Tag the bearings according to which cylinder they were removed from (and whether they were in the cap or the block) and set them aside.

4   Using a wrench of the appropriate size, remove the threaded oil gallery plugs from the front and back of the block.

5   If the engine is extremely dirty, it should be taken to an automotive machine shop to be steam cleaned or hot tanked. Any bearings left in the block (such as the camshaft bearings) will be damaged by the cleaning process, so plan on having new ones installed while the block is at the machine shop.

6   After the block is returned, clean all oil holes and oil galleries one more time (brushes for cleaning oil holes and galleries are available at most auto parts stores). Flush the passages with warm water until the water runs clear, dry the block thoroughly and wipe all machined surfaces with a light, rust-preventative oil. If you have access to compressed air, use it to speed the drying process and to blow out all the oil holes and galleries.

7   If the block is not extremely dirty or sludged up, you can do an adequate cleaning job with warm soapy water and a stiff brush. Take plenty of time and do a thorough job. Regardless of the cleaning method used, be very sure to thoroughly clean all oil holes and galleries, dry the block completely and coat all machined surfaces with light oil.

8   The threaded holes in the block must be clean to ensure accurate torque readings during reassembly. Run the proper size tap into each of the holes to remove any rust, corrosion, thread sealant or sludge and to restore any damaged threads. If possible, use compressed air to clear the holes of debris produced by this operation. Now is a good time to thoroughly clean the threads on the head bolts and the main bearing cap bolts as well.

9   Reinstall the main bearing caps and tighten the bolts finger tight.

10   After coating the sealing surfaces of the new freeze plugs with a good quality gasket sealant, install them in the engine block **(see illustration)**. Make sure they are driven in straight and seated properly or leakage could result. Special tools are available for this purpose, but equally good results can be obtained using a large socket (with an outside diameter that will just slip into the soft plug) and a large hammer.

11   If the engine is not going to be reassembled right away, cover it with a large plastic trash bag to keep it clean.

15 Engine block - inspection

Refer to illustrations 15.4a, 15.4b, 15.4c, 15.7a and 15.7b

1   Thoroughly clean the engine block as described in Section 14 and double-check to make sure that the ridge at the top of each cylinder has been completely removed.

2   Visually check the block for cracks, rust and corrosion. Look for stripped threads in the threaded holes. It is also a good idea to have the block checked for hidden cracks by an automotive machine shop that has the special equipment to do this type of work. If defects are found, have the block repaired, if possible, or replaced.

3   Check the cylinder bores for scuffing and scoring.

4   Using the appropriate precision measur-

14.10 A large socket on an extension can be used to drive the new freeze plugs into their bores

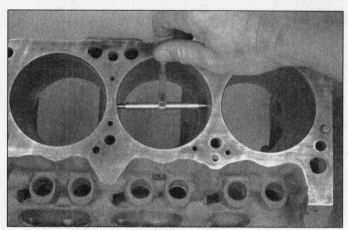

15.4a A telescoping gauge can be used to determine the cylinder bore diameter

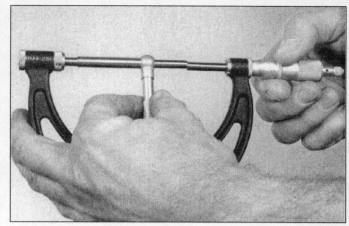

15.4b The gauge is then measured with a micrometer to determine the bore size in inches

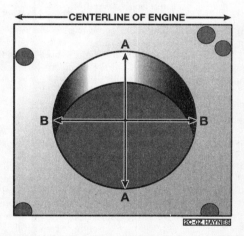

15.4c Measure the diameter of each cylinder at a right angle to the engine centerline (A), and parallel to the engine centerline (B) - out-of-round is the difference between A and B; taper is the difference between the diameter at the top of the cylinder and the diameter at the bottom of the cylinder

15.7a A "bottle brush" type cylinder hone is the easiest to use and will give the best results

2F

ing tools, measure each cylinder's diameter at the top (just under the ridge), center and bottom of the cylinder bore, parallel to the crankshaft axis **(see illustrations)**. Next, measure each cylinder's diameter at the same three locations across the crankshaft axis. Compare the results to the Specifications. If the cylinder walls are badly scuffed or scored, or if they are out-of-round or tapered beyond the limits given in the Specifications, have the engine block rebored and honed at an automotive machine shop. If a rebore is done, oversize pistons and rings will be required as well.

5   If the cylinders are in reasonably good condition and not worn to the outside of the limits, and if the piston-to-cylinder clearances can be maintained properly, then they do not have to be rebored; honing is all that is necessary.

6   Before honing the cylinders, install the main bearing caps (without the bearings) and tighten the bolts to the torque listed in this Chapter's Specifications.

7   To perform the honing operation, you will need the proper size flexible hone, plenty of light oil or honing oil, some rags and an electric drill motor. Mount the hone in the drill motor and slip the hone into the first cylinder **(see illustration)**. Lubricate the cylinder thoroughly, turn on the drill and move the hone up and down in the cylinder at a pace which will produce a fine crosshatch pattern on the cylinder walls, with the cross-hatch lines intersecting at approximately a 60-degree angle **(see illustration)**. Be sure to use plenty of lubricant and do not take off any more material than is absolutely necessary to produce the desired finish. Do not withdraw the hone from the cylinder while it is running. Instead, shut off the drill and continue moving the hone up and down in the cylinder until it comes to a complete stop, then manually turn the drill chuck in the normal direction of rotation and withdraw the hone. Wipe the oil out of the cylinder and repeat the procedure on the remaining cylinders. Remember, do not remove too much material from the cylinder wall. If you do not have the tools or do not desire to perform the honing operation,

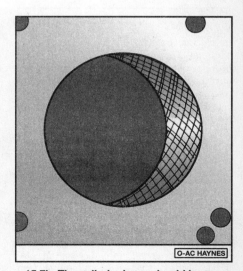

15.7b The cylinder hone should leave a cross-hatch pattern with the lines intersecting at approximately a 60-degree angle

16.3 A dial indicator can be mounted as shown here to check the camshaft lobe lift

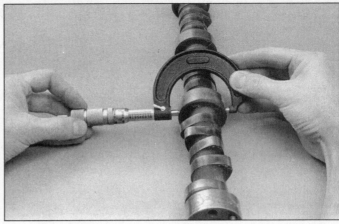

16.9 The camshaft bearing journal diameter is subtracted from the bearing inside diameter to obtain the oil clearance, which must be as specified

most automotive machine shops will do it for a reasonable fee.

8   After the honing job is complete, chamfer the top edges of the cylinder bores with a small file so the rings will not catch when the pistons are installed.

9   Next, the entire engine block must be thoroughly washed again with warm, soapy water to remove all traces of the abrasive grit produced during the honing operation. Be sure to run a brush through all oil holes and galleries and flush them with running water. After rinsing, dry the block and apply a coat of light rust preventative oil to all machined surfaces. Wrap the block in a plastic trash bag to keep it clean and set it aside until reassembly.

16 Camshaft, lifters and bearings - inspection and bearing replacement

Camshaft

Refer to illustrations 16.3 and 16.9

1   The most critical camshaft inspection procedure is lobe lift measurement, which must be done before the engine is disassembled.

2   Remove the valve cover(s), then remove the nuts/bolts and separate the rocker arms and ball pivots from the cylinder head(s).

3   Beginning with the number one (1) cylinder, mount a dial indicator with the stem resting on the end of, and directly in line with, the exhaust valve pushrod **(see illustration)**.

4   Rotate the crankshaft very slowly in the direction of rotation until the lifter is on the heel of the cam lobe. At this point the pushrod will be at its lowest position.

5   Zero the dial indicator, then very slowly rotate the crankshaft in the direction of rotation until the pushrod is at its highest position. Note and record the reading on the dial indicator, then compare it to the lobe lift specifications.

6   Repeat the procedure for each of the

remaining valves. Note that intake and exhaust valves may have different lobe lift specifications.

7   If the lobe lift measurements are not as specified, a new camshaft should be installed.

8   After the camshaft has been removed from the engine, cleaned with solvent and dried, inspect the bearing journals for uneven wear, pitting and evidence of seizure. If the journals are damaged, the bearing inserts in the block are probably damaged as well. Both the camshaft and bearings will have to be replaced with new ones. Measure the inside diameter of each camshaft bearing and record the results (take two measurements, 90-degrees apart, at each bearing).

9   Measure the bearing journals with a micrometer **(see illustration)** to determine if they are excessively worn or out-of-round. If they are more than 0.001-inch out-of-round, the camshaft should be replaced with a new one. Subtract the bearing journal diameter(s) from the corresponding bearing inside diameter measurement to obtain the oil clearance. If it is excessive, new bearings must be installed.

10   Check the camshaft lobes for heat dis-

coloration, score marks, chipped areas, pitting and uneven wear. If the lobes are in good condition and if the lobe lift measurements (Steps 1 through 7) were as specified, the camshaft can be reused.

Lifters

Refer to illustration 16.12

Note: *If the vehicle is equipped with roller lifters,* refer to Chapter 2 Part C *for the inspection procedure.*

11   Clean the lifters with solvent and dry them thoroughly without mixing them up.

12   Check the lifter wall, pushrod seat and foot for scuffing, score marks and uneven wear. Each lifter foot (the surface that rides on the cam lobe) must be slightly convex - if they are concave **(see illustration)**, the lifters and camshaft must be replaced with new ones. If the lifter walls are damaged or worn (which is not very likely), inspect the lifter bores in the engine block as well. If the pushrod seats are worn, check the pushrod ends.

13   If new lifters are being installed, a new camshaft must also be installed. If a new camshaft is installed, then use new lifters as well. Never install used lifters unless the orig-

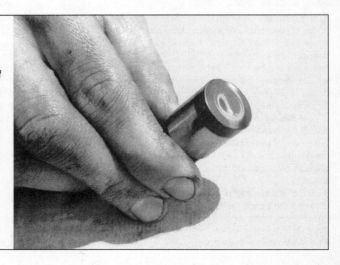

16.12 If the bottom of any of the lifters is worn concave, scratched or galled, they should all be replaced with new ones

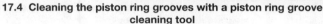

17.4 Cleaning the piston ring grooves with a piston ring groove cleaning tool

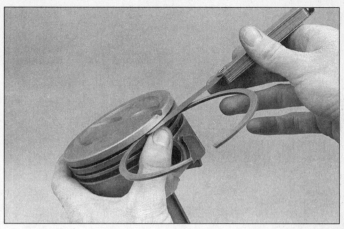

17.10 Checking the piston ring side clearance with a feeler gauge

inal camshaft is used and the lifters can be installed in their original locations.

Bearing replacement

14 Camshaft bearing replacement requires special tools and expertise that place it outside the scope of the do-it-yourselfer. Take the block to an automotive machine shop to ensure that the job is done correctly.

17 Piston/connecting rod assembly - inspection

Refer to illustrations 17.4, 17.10 and 17.11

1 Before the inspection process can be carried out, the piston/connecting rod assemblies must be cleaned and the original piston rings removed from the pistons. **Note:** *Always use new piston rings when the engine is reassembled.*

2 Using a piston ring installation tool, carefully remove the rings from the pistons. Do not nick or gouge the pistons in the process.

3 Scrape all traces of carbon from the top (or crown) of the piston. A hand-held wire brush or a piece of fine emery cloth can be used once the majority of the deposits have been scraped away. Do not, under any circumstances, use a wire brush mounted in a drill motor to remove deposits from the pistons. The piston material is soft and will be eroded away by the wire brush.

4 Use a piston ring groove cleaning tool to remove any carbon deposits from the ring grooves. If a tool is not available, a piece broken off the old ring will do the job. Be very careful to remove only the carbon deposits. Do not remove any metal and do not nick or scratch the sides of the ring grooves **(see illustration)**.

5 Once the deposits have been removed, clean the piston/rod assemblies with solvent and dry them thoroughly. Make sure that the oil hole in the big end of the connecting rod and the oil return holes in the back sides of the ring grooves are clear.

6 If the pistons are not damaged or worn excessively, and if the engine block is not rebored, new pistons will not be necessary. Normal piston wear appears as even vertical wear on the piston thrust surfaces and slight looseness of the top ring n its groove. New piston rings, on the other hand, should always be used when an engine is rebuilt.

7 Carefully inspect each piston for cracks around the skirt, at the pin bosses and at the ring lands.

8 Look for scoring and scuffing on the thrust faces of the skirt, holes in the piston crown and burned areas at the edge of the crown. If the skirt is scored or scuffed, the engine may have been suffering from overheating and/or abnormal combustion, which caused excessively high operating temperatures. The cooling and lubrication systems should be checked thoroughly. A hole in the piston crown, an extreme to be sure, is an indication that abnormal combustion (preignition) was occurring. Burned areas at the edge of the piston crown are usually evidence of spark knock (detonation). If any of the above problems exist, the causes must be corrected or the damage will occur again.

9 Corrosion of the piston (evidenced by pitting) indicates that coolant is leaking into the combustion chamber and/or the crankcase. Again, the cause must be corrected or the problem may persist in the rebuilt engine.

10 Measure the piston ring side clearance by laying a new piston ring in each ring groove and slipping a feeler gauge in beside it **(see illustration)**. Check the clearance at three or four locations around each groove. Be sure to use the correct ring for each groove; they are different. If the side clearance is greater than specified, new pistons will be used.

11 Check the piston-to-bore clearance by measuring the bore (see Section 15) and the piston diameter **(see illustration)**. Make sure that the pistons and bores are correctly matched. Measure the piston across the skirt, on the thrust faces (at a 90-degrees angle to the piston pin), directly in line with the center of the pin hole. Subtract the piston diameter from the bore diameter to obtain the clearance. If it is greater than specified, the block will have to be rebored and new pistons and rings installed. Check the piston-to-rod clearance by twisting the piston and rod in opposite directions. Any noticeable play

2F

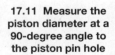
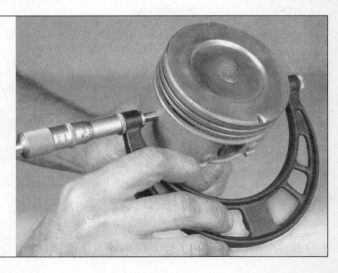

17.11 Measure the piston diameter at a 90-degree angle to the piston pin hole

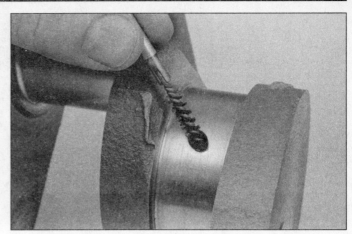

18.1 The oil holes should be chamfered so sharp edges don't gouge or scratch the new bearings

18.2 Use a wire or stiff plastic bristle brush to clean the oil passages in the crankshaft

18.4 Rubbing a penny lengthwise on each journal will reveal its condition - if copper rubs off and is embedded in the crankshaft, the journals should be reground

18.6 Measure the diameter of each crankshaft journal at several points to detect taper and out-of-round conditions

indicates that there is excessive wear, which must be corrected. The piston/connecting rod assemblies should be taken to an automotive machine shop to have new piston pins installed and the pistons and connecting rods rebored.

12   If the pistons must be removed from the connecting rods, such as when new pistons must be installed, or if the piston pins have too much play in them, they should be taken to an automotive machine shop. While they are there, it would be convenient to have the connecting rods checked for bend and twist, as automotive machine shops have special equipment for this purpose. Unless new pistons or connecting rods must be installed, do not disassemble the pistons from the connecting rods.

13   Check the connecting rods for cracks and other damage. Temporarily remove the rod caps, lift out the old bearing inserts, wipe the rod and cap bearing surfaces clean and inspect them for nicks, gouges and scratches. After checking the rods, replace the old bearings, slip the caps into place and tighten the nuts finger tight.

18   Crankshaft - inspection

Refer to illustrations 18.1, 18.2, 18.4, 18.6 and 18.8

1   Remove all burrs from the crankshaft oil holes with a stone, file or scraper **(see illustration)**.

2   Clean the crankshaft with solvent and dry it with compressed air (if available). **Warning:** *Wear eye protection when using compressed air.* Be sure to clean the oil holes with a stiff brush **(see illustration)** and flush them with solvent.

3   Check the main and connecting rod bearing journals for uneven wear, scoring, pits and cracks.

4   Rub a penny across each journal several times **(see illustration)**. If a journal picks up copper from the penny, it's too rough and must be reground.

5   Check the rest of the crankshaft for cracks and other damage. It should be magnafluxed to reveal hidden cracks - an automotive machine shop will handle the procedure.

6   Using a micrometer, measure the diameter of the main and connecting rod journals and compare the results to this Chapter's Specifications **(see illustration)**. By measuring the diameter at a number of points around each journal's circumference, you'll be able to determine whether or not the journal is out-of-round. Take the measurement at each end of the journal, near the crank throws, to determine if the journal is tapered.

7   If the crankshaft journals are damaged, tapered, out-of-round or worn beyond the limits given in the Specifications, have the crankshaft reground by an automotive machine shop. Be sure to use the correct size bearing inserts if the crankshaft is reconditioned.

8   Check the oil seal journals at each end of the crankshaft for wear and damage. If the seal has worn a groove in the journal, or if it's nicked or scratched **(see illustration)**, the new seal may leak when the engine is reassembled. In some cases, an automotive machine shop may be able to repair the journal by pressing on a thin sleeve. If repair isn't feasible, a new or different crankshaft should

18.8 If the seals have worn grooves in the crankshaft journals, or if the seal contact surfaces are nicked or scratched, the new seals will leak

be installed.

9   Refer to Section 19 and examine the main and rod bearing inserts.

19 Main and connecting rod bearings - inspection

Refer to illustration 19.1

1   Even though the main and connecting rod bearings should be replaced with new ones during the engine overhaul, the old bearings should be retained for close examination, as they may reveal valuable information about the condition of the engine **(see illustration)**.

2   Bearing failure occurs mainly because of lack of lubrication, the presence of dirt or other foreign particles, overloading the engine and corrosion. Regardless of the cause of bearing failure, it must be corrected before the engine is reassembled to prevent it from happening again.

3   When examining the bearings, remove them from the engine block, the main bearing caps, the connecting rods and the rod caps and lay them out on a clean surface in the same general position as their location in the engine. This will enable you to match any noted bearing problems with the corresponding crankshaft journal.

4   Dirt and other foreign particles get into the engine in a variety of ways. If may be left in the engine during assembly, or it may pass through filters or breathers. It may get into the oil, and from there into the bearings. Metal chips from machining operations and normal engine wear are often present. Abrasives are sometimes left in engine components after reconditioning, especially when parts are not thoroughly cleaned using the proper cleaning methods. Whatever the source, these foreign objects often end up embedded in the soft bearing material and are easily recognized. Large particles will not embed in the bearing and will score or gouge the bearing and shaft. The best prevention for this cause of bearing failure is to clean all parts thoroughly and keep everything spotlessly clean during engine assembly. Fre-

quent and regular engine oil and filter changes are also recommended.

5   Lack of lubrication (or lubrication breakdown) has a number of interrelated causes. Excessive heat (which thins the oil), overloading (which squeezes the oil from the bearing face) and oil leakage or throw-off (from excessive bearing clearances, worn oil pump or high engine speeds) all contribute to lubrication breakdown. Blocked oil passages, which usually are the result of misaligned oil holes in a bearing shell, will also oil-starve a bearing and destroy it. When lack of lubrication is the cause of bearing failure, the bearing material is wiped or extruded from the steel backing of the bearing. Temperatures may increase to the point where the steel backing turns blue from overheating.

6   Driving habits can have a definite effect on bearing life. Full-throttle, low-speed operation (or "lugging' the engine) puts very high loads on bearings, which tends to squeeze out the oil film. These loads cause the bearings to flex, which produces fine cracks in the bearing face (fatigue failure). Eventually the bearing material will loosen in pieces and tear away from the steel backing. Short-trip driving leads to corrosion of bearings because insufficient engine heat is produced to drive off the condensed water and corrosive gases. These products collect in the engine oil, forming acid and sludge. As the oil is carried to the engine bearings, the acid attacks and corrodes the bearing material.

7   Incorrect bearing installation during engine assembly will lead to bearing failure as well. Tight-fitting bearings leave insufficient bearing oil clearance and will result in oil starvation. Dirt or foreign particles trapped behind a bearing insert result in high spots on the bearing which lead to failure.

2F

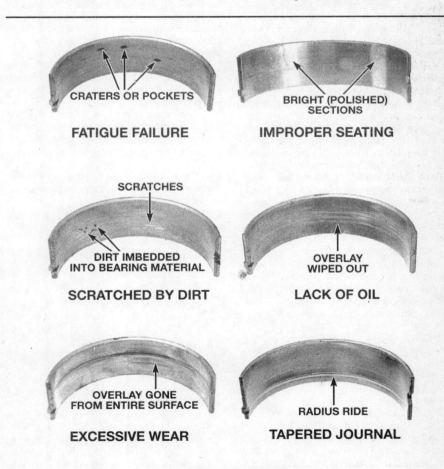

19.1 Typical bearing failures

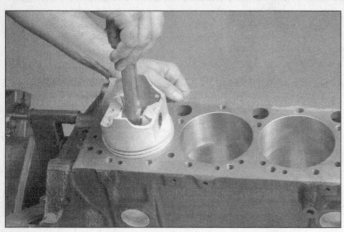

20.3a Use the piston to square up the ring in the cylinder prior to checking the ring end gap

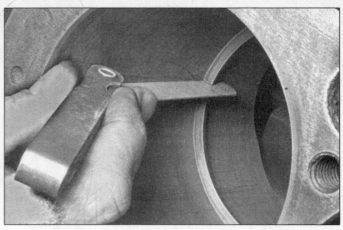

20.3b Measure the ring end gap with a feeler gauge

20 Piston rings - installation

Refer to illustrations 20.3a, 20.3b, 20.9a, 20.9b and 20.12

1   Before installing the new piston rings, the ring end gaps must be checked. It is assumed that the piston ring side clearance has been checked and verified correct (see Section 17).

2   Lay out the piston/connecting rod assemblies and the new ring sets so the ring sets will be matched with the same piston and cylinder during the end gap measurement and engine assembly.

3   Insert the top (number one) ring into the first cylinder and square it up with the cylinder walls by pushing it in with the top of the piston **(see illustration)**. The ring should be near the bottom of the cylinder at the lower limit of ring travel. To measure the end gap, slip a feeler gauge between the ends of the ring **(see illustration)**. Compare the measurement to the Specifications.

4   If the gap is larger or smaller than specified, double-check to make sure that you

have the correct rings before proceeding.

5   If the gap is too small, it must be enlarged or the ring ends may come in contact with each other during engine operation, which can cause serious damage to the engine. The end gap can be increased by filing the ring ends very carefully with a fine file. Mount the file in a vise equipped with soft jaws, slip the ring over the file with the ends contacting the file face and slowly move the ring to remove material from the ends. When performing this operation, file only from the outside in.

6   Excessive end gap is not critical unless it is greater than 0.040-inch (1 mm). Again, double-check to make sure you have the correct rings for your engine.

7   Repeat the procedure for each ring that will be installed in the first cylinder and for each ring in the remaining cylinders. Remember to keep rings, pistons and cylinders matched up.

8   Once the ring end gaps have been checked/corrected, the rings can be installed on the pistons.

9   The oil control ring (lowest one on the piston) is installed first. It is composed of

three separate components. Slip the spacer expander into the groove **(see illustration)**, then install the upper side rail. Do not use a piston ring installation tool on the oil ring side rails, as they may be damaged. Instead, place one end of the side rail into the groove between the spacer expander and the ring land, hold it firmly in place and slide a finger around the piston while pushing the rail into the groove **(see illustration)**. Next, install the lower side rail in the same manner.

10   After the three oil ring components have been installed, check to make sure that both the upper and lower side rails can be turned smoothly in the ring groove.

11   The number two (middle) ring is installed next. It should be stamped with a mark so it can be readily distinguished from the top ring. **Note:** *Always follow the instructions printed on the package that the new rings are in - different manufacturers may require different approaches. Do not mix up the top and middle rings, as they have different cross-sections.*

12   Use a piston ring installation tool and make sure that the identification mark is facing the top of the piston, then slip the ring into the middle groove on the piston **(see**

20.9a Installing the spacer/expander in the oil control ring groove

20.9b DO NOT use a piston ring installation tool when installing the oil ring side rails

20.12 Installing the compression rings with the special tool - the mark (arrow) must face *up*

22.10 Lay the Plastigage strips (arrow) on the main bearing journals, parallel to the crankshaft centerline

2F

illustration). Do not expand the ring any more than is necessary to slide it over the piston.

13   Finally, install the number one (top) ring in the same manner. Make sure the identifying mark is facing up.

14   Repeat the procedure for the remaining pistons and rings. Be careful not to confuse the number one and number two rings.

21 Rear main oil seal - installation

Note: *On 1984 and earlier 2.8L V6 engines, install a service replacement one-piece rear main seal (available at most auto parts stores) following the instructions provided with the seal kit.*

Refer to Chapter 2 Part A, B, C, D or E, depending on engine type, for the seal installation procedure.

22 Crankshaft - installation and main bearing oil clearance check

Refer to illustrations 22.10 and 22.14

1   Crankshaft installation is generally one of the first steps in engine reassembly; it is assumed at this point that the engine block and crankshaft have been cleaned, inspected and repaired or reconditioned. **Note:** *On models without a one-piece (360-degree) neoprene seal, refer to Section 21 and install the rear main oil seal sections before proceeding.*

2   Position the engine with the bottom facing up.

3   Remove the main bearing cap bolts and lift out the caps. Lay them out in the proper order to help ensure that they are installed correctly.

4   If they are still in place, remove the old bearing inserts from the block and the main bearing caps. Wipe the main bearing surfaces of the block and caps with a clean, lint-free cloth (they must be kept spotlessly clean).

5   Clean the back sides of the new main bearing inserts and lay one bearing half in each main bearing saddle in the block. Lay the other bearing half from each bearing set in the corresponding main bearing cap. Make sure the tab on the bearing insert fits into the recess in the block or cap. Also, the oil holes in the block and cap must line up with the oil holes in the bearing insert. Do not hammer the bearing into place and do not nick or gouge the bearing faces. No lubrication should be used at this time.

6   The flanged thrust bearing must be installed in the number three cap and saddle on 2.8L V6 and 1.9 liter four-cylinder engines, the number four cap and saddle on 2.0 liter four-cylinder engines, and the rear cap and saddle on 2.5L four-cylinder engines and 4.3L V6 engines.

7   Clean the faces of the bearings in the block and the crankshaft main bearing journals with a clean, lint-free cloth. Check or clean the oil holes in the crankshaft, as any dirt here can only go one way - straight through the new bearings.

8   Once you are certain that the crankshaft is clean, carefully lay it in position (an assistant would be very helpful here) in the main bearings with the counterweights lying sideways.

9   Before the crankshaft can be permanently installed, the main bearing oil clearance must be checked.

10   Trim several pieces of the appropriate type of Plastigage (so they are slightly shorter than the width of the main bearings) and place one piece on each crankshaft main bearing journal, parallel with the journal axis **(see illustration)**. Do not lay them across the oil holes.

11   Clean the faces of the bearings in the caps and install the caps in their respective positions (do not mix them up) with the arrows pointing toward the front of the engine. Do not disturb the Plastigage.

12   Starting with the center main and working out toward the ends, tighten the main bearing cap bolts, in three steps, to the torque listed in this Chapter's Specifications. Do not rotate the crankshaft at any time during this operation.

22.14 Compare the width of the crushed Plastigage to the scale on the envelope to determine the main bearing oil clearance (always take the measurement at the widest point of the Plastigage); be sure to use the correct scale - standard and metric ones are included

13   Remove the bolts and carefully lift off the main bearing caps. Keep them in order. Do not disturb the Plastigage or rotate the crankshaft. If any of the main bearing caps are difficult to remove, tap them gently from side-to-side with a soft-faced hammer to loosen them.

14   Compare the width of the crushed Plastigage on each journal to the scale printed on the Plastigage container to obtain the main bearing oil clearance **(see illustration)**. Check the Specifications to make sure it is correct.

15   If the clearance is not correct, double-check to make sure you have the right size bearing inserts. Also, make sure that no dirt or oil was between the bearing inserts and the main bearing caps or the block when the clearance was measured.

16   Carefully scrape all traces of the Plastigage material off the main bearing journals and/or the bearing faces. Do not nick or scratch the bearing faces.

17   Carefully lift the crankshaft out of the

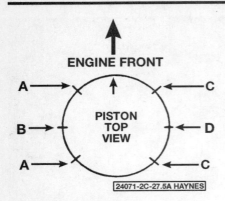

ENGINE FRONT

PISTON TOP VIEW

24071-2C-27.5A HAYNES

23.5 Ring end gap positions

A   Oil ring rail gaps
B   Second compression ring gap
C   Oil ring spacer gap (position in-between marks)
D   Top compression ring gap

engine. Clean the bearing faces in the block, then apply a thin, uniform layer of clean, high-quality moly-based grease or engine assembly lube to each of the bearing faces. Be sure to coat the thrust flange faces as well as the journal face of the thrust bearing.

18   Lubricate the rear main oil seal (where it contacts the crankshaft) with moly-based grease or engine assembly lube. Note that on four-cylinder engines the oil seal is installed after the crankshaft is in place.

19   If you are working on a 2.8L V6 or 2.0L four-cylinder engine, refer to Section 21 and apply anaerobic-type gasket sealant to the rear main bearing cap or block as described there. Make sure the crankshaft journals are clean, then lay it back in place in the block. Clean the faces of the bearings in the caps, then apply a thin, uniform layer of clean, moly-based grease to each of the bearing faces and install the caps in their respective positions with the arrows pointing toward the front of the engine. Install the bolts and tighten them to the torque listed in this Chap-

ter's Specifications, starting with the center main and working out toward the ends. Work up to the final torque in three steps.

20   Rotate the crankshaft a number of times by hand and check for any obvious binding.

21   The final step is to check the crankshaft endplay. This can be done with a feeler gauge or a dial indicator set. Refer to Section 13 for the procedure.

23   Piston/connecting rod assembly - installation and bearing oil clearance check

Refer to illustrations 23.5, 23.10, 23.12 and 23.14

1   Before installing the piston/connecting rod assemblies, the cylinder walls must be perfectly clean, the top edge of each cylinder must be chamfered, and the crankshaft must be in place.

2   Remove the connecting rod cap from the end of the number one connecting rod. Remove the old bearing inserts and wipe the bearing surfaces of the connecting rod and cap with a clean, lint-free cloth (they must be kept spotlessly clean).

3   Clean the back side of the new upper bearing half, then lay it in place in the connecting rod. Make sure that the tab on the bearing fits into the recess in the rod. Do not hammer the bearing insert into place and be very careful not to nick or gouge the bearing face. Do not lubricate the bearing at this time.

4   Clean the back side of the other bearing insert and install it in the rod cap. Again, make sure the tab on the bearing fits into the recess in the cap, and do not apply any lubricant. It is critically important that the mating surfaces of the bearing and connecting rod are perfectly clean and oil-free when they are assembled.

5   Position the piston ring gaps as shown **(see illustration)**, then slip a section of plastic or rubber hose over the connecting rod cap bolts.

6   Lubricate the piston and rings with clean engine oil and attach a piston ring compressor to the piston. Leave the skirt protruding about 1/4-inch to guide the piston into the cylinder. The rings must be compressed as far as possible.

7   Rotate the crankshaft until the number one connecting rod journal is as far from the number one cylinder as possible (bottom dead center), and apply a uniform coat of engine oil to the cylinder walls.

8   With the notch on top of the piston facing to the front of the engine, gently place the piston/connecting rod assembly into the number one cylinder bore and rest the bottom edge of the ring compressor on the engine block. Tap the top edge of the ring compressor to make sure it is contacting the block around its entire circumference.

9   Clean the number one connecting rod journal on the crankshaft and the bearing faces in the rod.

10   Carefully tap on the top of the piston with the end of a wooden hammer handle **(see illustration)** while guiding the end of the connecting rod into place on the crankshaft journal. The piston rings may try to pop out of the ring compressor just before entering the cylinder bore, so keep some downward pressure on the ring compressor. Work slowly, and if any resistance is felt as the piston enters the cylinder, stop immediately. Find out what is hanging up and fix it before proceeding. Do not, for any reason, force the piston into the cylinder, as you will break a ring and/or the piston.

11   Once the piston/connecting rod assembly is installed, the connecting rod bearing oil clearance must be checked before the rod cap is permanently bolted in place.

12   Cut a piece of the appropriate type Plastigage slightly shorter than the width of the connecting rod bearing and lay it in place on the number one connecting rod journal, parallel with the journal axis (it must not cross the oil hole in the journal) **(see illustration)**.

13   Clean the connecting rod cap bearing face, remove the protective hoses from the

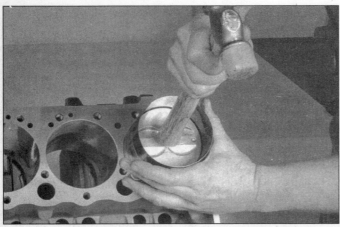

23.10 If resistance is encountered when tapping the piston/connecting rod assembly into the block, stop immediately and make sure the rings are fully compressed

23.12 Position the Plastigage strip on the bearing journal, parallel to the journal axis

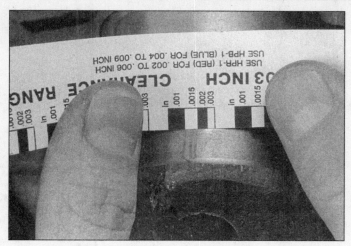

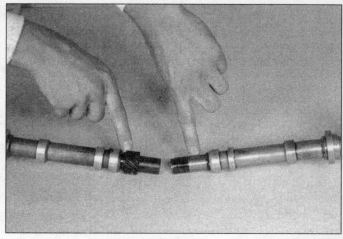

23.14 The crushed Plastigage is compared to the scale printed on the container to obtain the bearing oil clearance

25.3 The pre-oil tool (right) has the gear and advance weights ground off

2F

connecting rod bolts and gently install the rod cap in place. Make sure the mating mark on the cap is on the same side as the mark on the connecting rod. Install the nuts and tighten them to the torque listed in this Chapter's Specifications, working up to it in three steps. Do not rotate the crankshaft at any time during this operation.

14   Remove the rod cap, being very careful not to disturb the Plastigage. Compare the width of the crushed Plastigage to the scale printed on the Plastigage container to obtain the oil clearance **(see illustration)**. Compare it to the Specifications to make sure the clearance is correct. If the clearance is not correct, double-check to make sure that you have the correct size bearing inserts. Also, recheck the crankshaft connecting rod journal diameter and make sure that no dirt or oil was between the bearing inserts and the connecting rod or cap when the clearance was measured.

15   Carefully scrape all traces of the Plastigage material off the rod journal and/or bearing face (be very careful not to scratch the bearing - use your fingernail or a piece of hardwood). Make sure the bearing faces are perfectly clean, then apply a uniform layer of engine assembly lube to both of them. You will have to push the piston into the cylinder to expose the face of the bearing insert in the connecting rod; be sure to slip the protective hoses over the rod bolts first.

16   Slide the connecting rod back into place on the journal, remove the protective hoses from the rod cap bolts, install the rod cap and tighten the nuts to the torque listed in this Chapter's Specifications. Again, work up to the torque in three steps.

17   Repeat the entire procedure for the remaining piston/connecting rod assemblies. Keep the back sides of the bearing inserts and the inside of the connecting rod and cap perfectly clean when assembling them. Make sure you have the correct piston for the cylinder and that the notch, arrow or F on the piston faces to the front of the engine when the

piston is installed. Remember, use plenty of oil to lubricate the piston before installing the ring compressor and cap. Also, when installing the rod caps for the final time, be sure to lubricate the bearing faces adequately.

18   After all the piston/connecting rod assemblies have been properly installed, rotate the crankshaft a number of times by hand and check for any obvious binding.

19   As a final step, the connecting rod endplay must be checked. Refer to Section 12 for the procedure to follow. Compare the measured endplay to the Specifications to make sure it is correct.

24   Engine overhaul - reassembly sequence

1   Before beginning engine reassembly, make sure you have all the necessary new parts, gaskets and seals as well as the following items on hand:

> Common hand tools
> A 1/2-inch drive torque wrench
> Piston ring installation tool
> Piston ring compressor
> Short lengths of rubber or plastic hose to fit over connecting rod bolts
> Plastigage
> Feeler gauges
> A fine-tooth file
> New, clean engine oil
> Engine assembly lube
> RTV-type gasket sealant
> Anaerobic-type gasket sealant
> Thread locking compound

2   In order to save time and avoid problems, engine reassembly must be done in the following order.

> Rear main oil seal (engines with two-piece seal only)
> Crankshaft and main bearings
> Rear main oil seal (engines with one-piece seal)

> Piston rings
> Piston/connecting rod assemblies
> Oil pump
> Oil pan
> Camshaft
> Timing chain/sprockets or gears
> Timing chain/gear cover
> Valve lifters
> Cylinder head(s) and pushrods
> Intake and exhaust manifolds
> Oil filter
> Pre-oil the engine (V6 engine only - Section 25)
> Valve cover(s)
> Fuel pump
> Water pump
> Flywheel/driveplate
> Carburetor
> Thermostat and housing cover
> Distributor, spark plug wires and spark plugs
> Emissions control components
> Alternator

25   Pre-oiling engine after overhaul (V6 engine only)

Refer to illustrations 25.3, 25.4 and 25.5

1   After an overhaul it is a good idea to pre-oil the engine before it is installed and initially started. This will reveal any problems with the lubrication system at a time when corrections can be made easily and without major engine damage. Pre-oiling the engine will also allow the parts to be lubricated thoroughly in a normal fashion, but without the heavy loads associated with the combustion process placed upon them.

2   The engine should be assembled completely with the exception of the distributor and the valve covers.

3   A modified distributor will be needed for this procedure. This pre-oil tool is a distributor body with the bottom gear ground off and the advance weight assembly removed from the top of the shaft **(see illustration)**.

25.4 A drill motor connected to the modified distributor drives the oil pump

25.5 Oil and assembly lube will spurt out of the holes in the rocker arms if the lubrication system is functioning properly

4   Place the pre-oiler into the distributor shaft access hole at the rear of the intake manifold and make sure the bottom of the shaft mates with the oil pump. Clamp the modified distributor into place just as you would an ordinary distributor. Now attach an electric drill motor to the top of the shaft **(see illustration)**.

5   With the oil filter installed, all oil ways plugged (oil-pressure sending unit at rear of block) and the crankcase full of oil as shown on the dipstick, rotate the pre-oiler with the drill. Make sure the rotation is in a clockwise direction. Soon, oil should start to flow from the rocker arms, signifying that the oil pump and lubrication system are functioning properly. It may take two or three minutes for oil to flow to all of the rocker arms **(see illustration)**. Allow the oil to circulate through the engine for a few minutes, then shut off the drill motor.

6   Check for oil leaks at the filter and all gasket and seal locations.

7   Remove the pre-oil tool, then install the distributor and valve covers.

26 Initial start-up and break-in after overhaul

1   Once the engine has been properly installed in the vehicle, double-check the engine oil and coolant levels.

2   On fuel-injected models, remove the fuel injection fuse from the fuse block.

3   With the spark plugs out of the engine and the coil high-tension wire grounded to the engine block, crank the engine over until oil pressure registers on the gauge (if so equipped) or until the oil light goes off.

4   Install the spark plugs, hook up the plug wires and the coil high-tension wire.

5   Make sure the carburetor choke plate is closed, then start the engine. It may take a few moments for the gasoline to reach the carburetor, but the engine should start without a great deal of effort.

6   As soon as the engine starts, it should be set at a fast idle (to ensure proper oil circulation) and allowed to warm up to normal operating temperature. While the engine is warming up, make a thorough check for oil and coolant leaks.

7   Shut the engine off and recheck the engine oil and coolant levels. Also, check the ignition timing and the engine idle speed (see Chapter 1) and make any necessary adjustments.

8   Drive the vehicle to an area with minimum traffic, accelerate at full throttle from 30 to 50 mph, then allow the vehicle to slow to 30 mph with the throttle closed. Repeat the procedure 10 or 12 times. This will load the piston rings and cause them to seat properly against the cylinder walls. Check again for oil and coolant leaks.

9   Drive the vehicle gently for the first 500 miles (no sustained high speeds) and keep a constant check on the oil level. It is not unusual for an engine to use oil during the break-in period.

10   At approximately 500 to 600 miles, change the oil and filter, retorque the cylinder head bolts and recheck the valve clearances (if applicable).

11   For the next few hundred miles, drive the vehicle normally. Do not pamper it or abuse it.

12   After 2000 miles, change the oil and filter again and consider the engine fully broken in.

Chapter 3
Cooling, heating and air conditioning systems

Contents

	Section
Air conditioning accumulator - removal and installation	12
Air conditioning and heater control assembly - removal and installation	16
Air conditioning compressor - removal and installation	13
Air conditioning condenser - removal and installation	14
Air conditioning orifice tube screen - removal and installation	15
Air conditioning system - check and maintenance	11
Antifreeze - general information	2
Coolant temperature sending unit - check and replacement	8
Cooling system check	See Chapter 1
Cooling system servicing - draining, flushing and refilling	See Chapter 1

	Section
Drivebelt check and adjustment	See Chapter 1
Engine cooling fan and clutch - check and replacement	4
Fluid level checks	See Chapter 1
General information	1
Heater blower motor - removal and installation	9
Heater core - removal and installation	10
Radiator - removal, servicing and installation	5
Thermostat - check and replacement	3
Underhood hose check and replacement	See Chapter 1
Water pump - check	6
Water pump - removal and installation	7

Component location

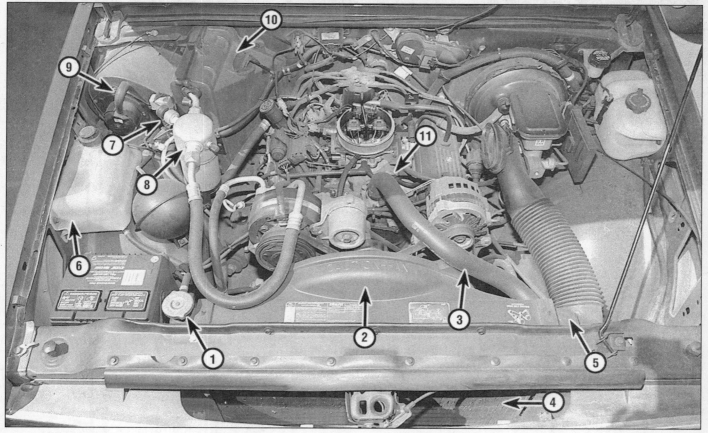

1	Radiator cap	4	Condenser	7	A/C pressure switch	10	Evap. housing/case
2	Fan shroud	5	Radiator	8	Accumulator	11	Thermostat housing
3	Upper radiator hose	6	Coolant recovery bottle	9	Blower motor		

Specifications

Cooling system
Operating pressure.. 14 to 17 psi
Coolant capacity.. See Chapter 1

Refrigerant capacity (approximate)
Through 1987 .... 40 ounces
1988 on .... 56 ounces

Torque specifications   **Ft-lbs** (unless otherwise specified)
Fan-to-water pump bolts.. 20
Fan clutch-to-fan bolts
   2.5L four-cylinder and 2.8L V6 engines .... 108 in-lbs
   4.3L V6 engine.. 25
   All others .... 132 to 192 in-lbs
Water pump bolts 15
Water outlet (thermostat housing) bolts 25
Coolant temperature sending unit 20

1 General information

The cooling system is conventional in design, utilizing a cross-flow radiator, an engine driven water pump and a thermostat controlled coolant flow. Some models are equipped with a fan clutch, which allows the fan to draw air through the radiator at lower speeds. At higher speeds the fan is not needed for cooling, so the clutch automatically lowers the fan speed and reduces the engine power required for fan operation.

The water pump is mounted on the front of the engine and is driven by a belt from the pulley mounted on the front of the crankshaft. The belt is also used to drive other components.

The heater utilizes the heat produced by the engine and absorbed by the coolant to warm the interior of the vehicle. It is manually controlled from inside by the driver or passenger.

Air conditioning is optional equipment. All components of the system are mounted in the engine compartment and the system is driven by a belt from the pulley mounted on the front of the crankshaft.
Output of the system is controlled from inside the vehicle.

2 Antifreeze - general information

Warning: *Don't allow antifreeze to come in contact with your skin or the painted surfaces of the vehicle. Flush contacted areas immediately with plenty of water. Don't store new coolant or leave old coolant lying around where it's easily accessible to children and pets - they're attracted by its sweet smell. Ingestion of even a small amount can be fatal. Wipe up the garage floor and drip pan coolant spills immediately. Keep antifreeze containers covered and repair leaks in your cooling system immediately. Antifreeze is flammable - be sure to read the precautions on the container. Check with local authorities about disposing of used antifreeze. Most communities have collection centers which will see that antifreeze is disposed of safely.*

The cooling system should be filled with a water/ethylene glycol based antifreeze solution, which will prevent freezing down to at least -20-degrees F at all times. It also provides protection against corrosion and increases the coolant boiling point.

The cooling system should be drained, flushed and refilled at least every other year (see Chapter 1). The use of antifreeze solutions for periods of longer than two years is likely to cause damage and encourage the formation of rust and scale in the system.

Before adding antifreeze to the system, check all hose connections and retorque the cylinder head bolts. Antifreeze tends to search out and leak through very minute openings.

The exact mixture of antifreeze-to-water which you should use depends on the relative weather conditions. The mixture should contain at least 50 percent antifreeze, but should never contain more than 70 percent antifreeze.

3 Thermostat - check and replacement

Warning 1: *Don't allow antifreeze to come in contact with your skin or the painted surfaces of the vehicle. Flush contacted areas immediately with plenty of water. Don't store new coolant or leave old coolant lying around where it's easily accessible to children and pets - they're attracted by its sweet smell. Ingestion of even a small amount can be fatal. Wipe up the garage floor and drip pan coolant spills immediately. Keep antifreeze containers covered and repair leaks in your cooling system immediately. Antifreeze is flammable - be sure to read the precautions on the container.*
Warning 2: *The engine must be completely cool before beginning this procedure.*
Note: *Don't drive the vehicle without a thermostat! The computer will stay in open loop and emissions and fuel economy will suffer.*

On-vehicle check
1 Before condemning the thermostat, check the coolant level, drivebelt tension and temperature gauge (or light) operation.
2 If the engine takes a long time to warm up, the thermostat is probably stuck open. Replace the thermostat.
3 If the engine runs too hot, check the temperature of the upper radiator hose. If the hose isn't hot, the thermostat is probably stuck shut. Replace the thermostat.
4 If the upper radiator hose is hot, it means the coolant is circulating and the thermostat is open. Refer to the *Troubleshooting* section for the cause of overheating. Keep in mind that a thermostat can be stuck half-open and still cause overheating. In this case, the hose would still be hot. The best way to identify this condition is with a bench test (see below).
5 If an engine has been overheated, you may find damage such as leaking head gaskets, scuffed pistons and warped or cracked heads.

Replacement
1.9L four-cylinder engine
6 Drain the cooling system until the level is below the thermostat by opening the petcock at the bottom of the radiator (see Chapter 1).

3.26 A typical thermostat assembly (2.5L shown, 2.0L similar)

3.27a If the old thermostat gasket is made of RTV-type sealant, it may be necessary to scrape away some of the excess sealant

Close the petcock when enough coolant has drained.

7 Label and disconnect the PCV hose, ECS hose, AIR hose and TCA hose (from the hot idle compensator to the intake manifold).

8 Remove the two air cleaner mounting bolts and loosen the clamp bolt. Lift the air cleaner from the carburetor and disconnect the TCA hose from the thermo sensor on the air cleaner snorkel. On California models there will be two additional emissions hoses to label and disconnect. Remove the air cleaner.

9 Disconnect the upper radiator hose from the water outlet.

10 Remove the two water outlet mounting bolts and separate the outlet from the intake manifold.

11 Remove the thermostat from the thermostat housing.

12 Before installing the thermostat, clean the gasket sealing surfaces on the water outlet and the thermostat housing. Use a scraper for large deposits, then wipe them clean with a rag soaked in lacquer thinner or acetone.

13 Install the replacement thermostat in the thermostat housing.

14 Apply a thin coat of RTV sealant to both sides of the new gasket and install the gasket on the thermostat housing.

15 Install the water outlet and tighten the bolts to the torque listed in this Chapter's Specifications.

16 Install the upper radiator hose.

17 Fill the cooling system with the proper antifreeze/water mixture (see Chapter 1).

18 Run the engine with the radiator cap removed until the upper radiator hose is hot (thermostat open).

19 With the engine idling, add coolant to the radiator until the level reaches the bottom of the filler neck.

20 Install the radiator cap, making sure the arrows on the cap line up with the radiator overflow tube.

2.0L and 2.5L four-cylinder engines

Refer to illustrations 3.26, 3.27a, 3.27b, 3.28, 3.29 and 3.30

21 Refer to the **Warnings** at the beginning of this procedure.

22 Disconnect the negative battery cable.

23 Drain the cooling system until the level is below the thermostat (see Chapter 1).

24 Remove the steel vacuum pipes from the intake manifold to gain adequate working clearance.

25 Disconnect the upper radiator hose from the thermostat cover.

26 Remove the two thermostat cover mounting bolts and separate the cover from the thermostat housing **(see illustration)**.

27 Remove the thermostat from the thermostat housing. It may be necessary to scrape away some excess sealant to break the bond **(see illustrations)**.

28 Before installation, use a gasket scraper or putty knife to carefully remove all traces of the old gasket from the thermostat housing and the engine sealing surface **(see illustration)**. Do not allow the gasket pieces to drop down into the intake manifold. Wipe the surfaces clean with a rag soaked in lacquer thinner or acetone.

29 Apply a 1/8-inch bead of RTV sealant to the thermostat cover-to-engine sealing sur-

3

3.27b The thermostat can then be lifted from the housing

3.28 Make sure that the thermostat housing and cover sealing surfaces are completely free of old sealant and gasket material

3.29 A 1/8-inch bead of RTV-type sealant must be applied to the thermostat cover or thermostat housing sealing surface on V6 and 2.0L/2.5L four-cylinder engines

3.30 A torque wrench should be used when tightening the thermostat housing bolts because of the soft threads in the aluminum intake manifold

face **(see illustration)** and place the thermostat into the recess.

30   Immediately place the thermostat housing with sealant and a new gasket into position and tighten the bolts to the torque listed in this Chapter's Specifications **(see illustration)**.

31   Where applicable, install the alternator brace and/or the TVS switch and vacuum hoses.

32   Connect the upper radiator hose and tighten the clamp securely.

33   Reinstall the air cleaner.

34   To complete the installation, refer to Steps 17 through 20.

V6 engines

Refer to illustration 3.39

35   Refer to the **Warnings** at the beginning of this procedure.

36   Disconnect the cable from the negative battery terminal.

37   Drain the cooling system until the level is below the thermostat (see Step 3).

38   Disconnect the upper radiator hose from the thermostat housing.

39   Remove the thermostat housing bolts

and the housing **(see illustration)**. If the present gasket is made of RTV-type sealant, it may be necessary to scrape away some excess sealant to break the bond.

40   The thermostat can now be lifted out. Note how the thermostat is positioned in the recess, as it must be replaced in the same position.

41   Refer to Steps 28 through 30.

42   Connect the upper radiator hose and tighten the hose clamp securely.

43   To complete the installation, refer to Steps 17 through 20.

Bench-testing the thermostat

44   The best way to check the operation of the thermostat is with it removed from the engine. In most cases, if the thermostat is suspect, it is more economical to simply buy and install a replacement thermostat, as they are not very costly.

45   Remove the thermostat (see above).

46   Inspect the thermostat for excessive corrosion or damage. Replace it with a new one if either of these conditions is noted.

47   Place the thermostat in hot water (25 degrees above the temperature stamped on

the thermostat). When submerged the valve should open all the way.

48   Next, remove the thermostat using a piece of bent wire and place it in water which is 10 degrees below the temperature on the thermostat. At this temperature the thermostat valve should close completely.

49   Reinstall the thermostat if it operates properly. If it does not, purchase a new thermostat of the same temperature rating.

4   Engine cooling fan and clutch - check and replacement

Check

1   Many, but not all engines are equipped with thermostatically controlled fan clutches.

2   Begin the clutch check with a lukewarm engine (start it when cold and let it run for two minutes only).

3   Remove the key from the ignition switch for safety purposes.

4   Turn the fan blades and note the resistance. There should be moderate resistance, depending on temperature.

3.39 A typical V6 thermostat (4.3L model shown, typical)

4.10a The fan is attached to the clutch assembly or water pump hub with four nuts or bolts (arrow)

4.10b Engine cooling fan assembly, two of four nuts shown

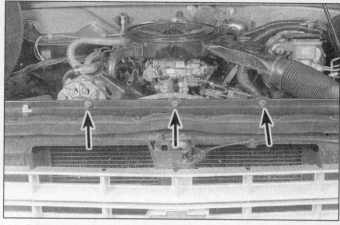

5.8 Location of the upper radiator shroud mounting bolts

5   Drive the vehicle until the engine is warmed up. Shut it off and remove the key.
6   Turn the fan blades and again note the resistance. There should be a noticeable increase in resistance.
7   If the fan clutch fails this check or is locked up solid, replacement is indicated. If excessive fluid is leaking from the hub or lateral play over 1/4-inch is noted, replace the fan clutch.
8   If any fan blades are bent, don't straighten them! The metal will be weakened and blades could fly off during engine operation. Replace the fan with a new one.

5.9 Location of the upper shroud-to-lower shroud attaching bolts

Replacement

Refer to illustrations 4.10a and 4.10b
9   Remove the upper fan shroud.
10   Remove the fasteners holding the fan assembly to the water pump hub **(see illustrations)**.
11   Detach the fan and clutch assembly.
12   Unbolt the fan from the clutch (if equipped).
13   Installation is the reverse of removal.
14   Tighten all fasteners to the specified torque.

5   Radiator - removal, servicing and installation

Refer to illustrations 5.8 and 5.9
Warning: *The engine must be completely cool before beginning this procedure.*

Removal

1   Refer to **Warning** 1 in Section 2.
2   Disconnect the cable from the negative battery terminal.
3   Drain the radiator (see Chapter 1 if necessary).
4   Disconnect the upper and lower radiator hoses from the radiator.
5   On vehicles equipped with an automatic transmission, disconnect the fluid cooler lines at the radiator and immediately plug the lines.

Caution: *Do not disconnect the air-conditioning refrigerant lines (if equipped) leading to the condenser unit in front of the radiator.*
6   If equipped with air-conditioning, remove the air-conditioning hose from the retaining clip.
7   Remove the clamp securing the coolant reservoir hose to the radiator outlet. On V6 models, remove the hose from the upper radiator shroud retainers. Disconnect the coolant reservoir hose from the radiator.
8   Remove the bolts securing the top of the upper radiator shroud to the metal support **(see illustration)**.
9   Remove the bolts securing the upper radiator shroud to the lower shroud **(see illustration)**.
10   Pull straight up on the radiator and shroud assembly and remove it from the vehicle.

Servicing

11   Carefully examine the radiator for evidence of leaks or damage. It is recommended that any necessary repairs be performed by a radiator repair shop.
12   With the radiator removed, brush accumulations of insects and leaves from the fins and examine and replace, if necessary, any hoses or clamps which have deteriorated.

13   The radiator can be flushed as described in Chapter 1.
14   Check the pressure rating of the radiator cap and have it tested by a service station.
15   If you are installing a new radiator, transfer the fittings from the old unit to the new one.

Installation

16   Installation is the reverse of the removal procedure. When setting the radiator in the chassis, make sure the bottom of the radiator is seated correctly in the two bottom cradles secured to the radiator support.
17   After installing the radiator, refill it with the proper coolant mixture (see Chapter 1), then start the engine and check for leaks.
18   If equipped with an automatic transmission, check the transmission fluid level (see Chapter 1).

6   Water pump - check

Refer to illustration 6.4
1   A failure in the water pump can cause overheating and serious engine damage (the pump will not circulate coolant through the engine).

3

6.4 The water pump weep hole (arrow) will drip coolant when the seal for the pump shaft bearing fails

7.4 Mark the drivebelts before removing them to ensure reinstallation on the correct pulleys

7.7 On some models, various brackets and/or accessories must be removed before the water pump can be detached (4.3L V6 shown)

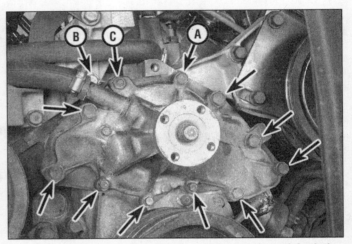

7.10a On 2.8L V6 engines in which stud C goes through both the timing cover and the water pump, remove the water pump mounting bolts (arrows) after using bolt A to attach the tool mentioned in the text to the right cylinder head

2   There are three ways to check the operation of the water pump while it is installed on the engine. If the pump is defective, it should be replaced with a new or rebuilt unit.

3   With the engine at normal operating temperature, squeeze the upper radiator hose. If the water pump is working properly a pressure surge will be felt as the hose is released.

4   Water pumps are equipped with a "weep" or vent hole **(see illustration)**. If a pump seal failure occurs, small amounts of coolant will leak from the weep holes. In most cases it will be necessary to use a flashlight from under the vehicle to see evidence of leakage from this point on the pump body.

5   If the water pump shaft bearings fail there may be a squealing sound emitted from the front of the engine while it is running. Shaft wear can be felt if the water pump pulley is forced up and down. Do not mistake drivebelt slippage (which also causes a squealing sound) for water pump failure.

7   Water pump - removal and installation

Refer to illustrations 7.4, 7.7, 7.10a, 7.10b, 7.10c and 7.10d

Warning: *The engine must be completely cool before beginning this procedure.*

1   Refer to **Warning** 1 in Section 2.

2   Disconnect the cable from the negative battery terminal.

3   Drain the cooling system (see Chapter 1 if necessary).

4   Mark the accessory drivebelts with white paint to simplify installation **(see illustration)**.

5   On V6 models, remove the upper fan shroud (see Section 5 if necessary).

6   Remove the accessory drivebelts (alternator, air conditioning compressor, AIR system pump, power steering pump, as applicable) by loosening the pivot and adjusting bolts and pushing the accessory toward the

engine (see Chapter 1, if necessary).

7   On some engines it may be necessary to remove one or more accessories and/or brackets to gain access to the water pump **(see illustration)**. Refer to the appropriate Chapter(s) for removal details.

8   Remove the bolts retaining the fan to the fan pulley hub, then separate the fan and pulley hub from the water pump.

9   Disconnect the heater and lower radiator hoses from the water pump.

10   Remove the water pump mounting bolts **(see illustrations)** and separate the water pump from the engine. **Caution:** *On 1986 and earlier 2.8L V6 engines, the water pump bolts hold the timing cover to the block. Removal of the water pump may break the gasket seal and allow coolant into the oil. To prevent this, secure the timing cover to the block with a clamping device before removing the water pump.*

11   Prior to installing the water pump remove all old gasket material and sealant

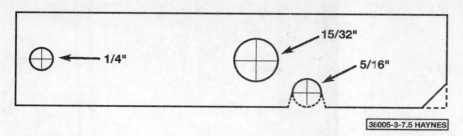

7.10b Here's a template for the 2.8L V6 timing chain cover, shown in actual size

7.10c Here's the holder bolted in place on the right cylinder head (this applies to 1986 and earlier models only). Note the 1/4 x 1-inch bolt inserted at the left side of the holder and secured with a nut - it serves as a spacer

left rear corner of the cylinder head on 2.0L engines, at the front of the left cylinder head on 2.8L V6 engines and on the side of the left cylinder head on 4.3L V6 engines. The sending unit on the 1.9L four-cylinder engine is located at the front of the intake manifold. On the 2.5L four-cylinder, it's located on the side of the block, above the distributor. If a temperature gauge is included in the instrument cluster the temperature sending unit is replaced by a transducer.

Check

2   If overheating occurs, check the coolant level in the system and then make sure that the wiring between the light or gauge and the sending unit is secure.
3   When the ignition switch is turned On and the starter motor is turning, the indicator light should be on (overheated engine indication). If the light is not on, the bulb may be burned out, the ignition switch may be faulty or the circuit may be open.
4   As soon as the engine starts the light should go out and remain out unless the engine overheats. Failure of the light to go out may be due to grounded wiring between the light and the sending unit, a defective sending unit or a faulty ignition switch.

Replacement

5   If the sending unit is to be replaced, apply thread sealant to the replacement unit, drain the coolant below the level of the sending unit, unscrew the old unit from the cylinder head with a six-point socket and install the replacement unit. Make sure that the engine is cool before removing the defective sending unit. There may be some coolant loss, so check the level after the replacement has been installed.

from the gasket sealing surfaces. Clean the threaded holes in the block as well. Wipe the mating surfaces clean with a rag soaked in lacquer thinner or acetone.
12   Installation is the reverse of the removal procedure.
13   If a new water pump is being installed transfer the heater hose fitting from the old pump to the new one.
14   On 2.0L four-cylinder engines use a new gasket or RTV-type sealant when installing the pump.
15   On V6 engines use a new gasket(s) when installing the pump.
16   Tighten the bolts to the torque listed in this Chapter's Specifications after coating the threads with RTV-type sealant to prevent leaks. Follow a crisscross pattern and work up to the final torque in three steps.
17   Adjust all drivebelts (see Chapter 1).

18   Connect the negative battery cable and fill the radiator with a mixture of antifreeze and water. Start the engine and allow it to idle until the upper radiator hose gets hot. Check for leaks. With the engine hot, fill the radiator with more coolant mixture until the level is at the bottom of the filler neck. Install the radiator cap and check the coolant level periodically during the first few miles of driving.

8   Coolant temperature sending unit - check and replacement

Refer to illustration 8.1
1   The coolant temperature indicator system is composed of a light mounted in the instrument panel and a coolant temperature sending unit **(see illustration)** located at the

9   Heater blower motor - removal and installation

Refer to illustrations 9.2 and 9.6
1   Disconnect the cable from the negative battery terminal.

7.10d Engine water pump mounting bolt locations (4.3L V6)

8.1 Typical coolant temperature sending unit (arrow)

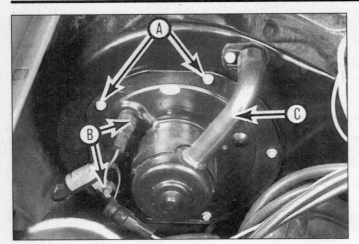

9.2 To remove the heater blower motor, remove the mounting bolts (A - 6 total), the motor and resistor wire (B) and the cooling tube (C)

9.6 Remove the nut (arrow) to separate the cage from the blower motor shaft

2   Working in the engine compartment, disconnect the wires at the lower blower motor and resistor **(see illustration)**.
3   Disconnect the blower motor cooling tube.
4   On some models it may be necessary to disconnect the radio capacitor to allow removal of the blower motor.
5   Remove the blower motor mounting bolts and separate the motor/cage assembly from the case.
6   While holding the cage, remove the cage retaining nut and slide the cage off the motor shaft **(see illustration)**.
7   Installation is the reverse of the removal procedure.

10   Heater core - removal and installation

1   Disconnect the negative battery cable.
2   Drain the coolant from the radiator (see Chapter 1).
3   From inside the passenger compartment, remove the mounting bolts from the modular duct and remove the duct from the dashboard side of the firewall.
4   Disconnect the heater hoses at the heater core and plug the core tubes.
5   Remove the four mounting screws from the heater core and remove the core.
6   Installation is the reverse of removal.

11   Air conditioning system - check and maintenance

Refer to illustration 11.9
Warning: *The air conditioning system is under high pressure. Do not loosen any hose fittings or remove any components until after the system has been discharged by a dealer service department, automotive air conditioning shop or service station. After the system has been discharged, residual pressure may*

still remain - be sure to wear eye protection when loosening line fittings!
1   The following maintenance steps should be performed on a regular basis to ensure that the air conditioner continues to operate at peak efficiency.

a) *Check the tension of the drivebelt and adjust it if necessary (Chapter 1).*
b) *Check the condition of the hoses. Look for cracks, hardening and deterioration.* **Warning:** *Don't replace air conditioning hoses until the system has been discharged by a dealer service department or repair shop.*
c) *Check the fins of the condenser for leaves, bugs and any other foreign material. A soft brush and compressed air can be used to remove them.*
d) *Maintain the correct refrigerant charge.*

2   The system should be run for about 10 minutes at least once a month. This is particularly important during the winter months because long term non-use can cause hardening and failure of the seals.
3   Because of the complexity of the air conditioning system and the special equipment necessary to service it, troubleshooting and repairs should be done by a professional mechanic. The most common cause of poor cooling is low refrigerant charge. If a noticeable drop in system cooling ability occurs, the following procedure will help pinpoint the cause.
4   Warm the engine to normal operating temperature.
5   The hood and doors should be open.
6   Operate the air conditioning mode control.
7   Move the temperature selector lever to the coolest position.
8   Turn the fan control to the High position.
9   With the compressor engaged, feel the evaporator inlet pipe between the orifice and the evaporator. Put your other hand on the surface of the accumulator can **(see illustration)**.

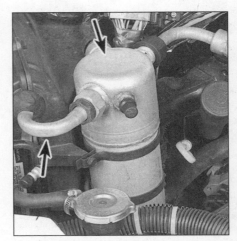

11.9 To determine if the refrigerant level is adequate, feel the evaporator inlet pipe with one hand and the surface of the accumulator (arrows) with the other and note the temperature of each

10   If both surfaces feel about the same temperature and if both feel a little cooler than the surrounding air, the refrigerant level is probably okay. The problem is elsewhere.
11   If the inlet pipe has frost accumulation or feels cooler than the accumulator surface, the refrigerant charge is low.
12   If a low refrigerant charge is suspected, take your vehicle to a dealer or automotive air conditioning shop for service by a certified air conditioning technician.

12   Air conditioning accumulator - removal and installation

Refer to illustrations 12.3 and 12.4
Warning: *The air conditioning system is under high pressure. Do not loosen any hose fittings or remove any components until after the system has been discharged by a dealer*

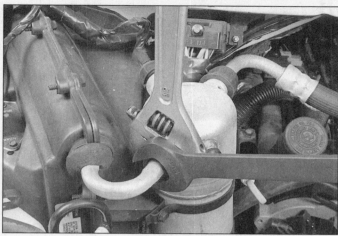

12.3 Use a back-up wrench when loosening/tightening the air conditioning line fittings (accumulator shown)

12.4 The accumulator is held in place with two brackets - loosen the bolts to withdraw it

13.5 Detach the wire harness and ground wire (arrows) before you remove the compressor drivebelt and mounting bolts (arrows)

13.6 Typical rear view of a compressor (V6 engine shown) - remove the manifold bolt, brace bolt and mounting bolts (arrows)

3

service department, automotive air conditioning shop or service station. After the system has been discharged, residual pressure may still remain - be sure to wear eye protection when loosening line fittings!

1 Have the system discharged.
2 Disconnect the negative battery cable from the battery.
3 Disconnect the accumulator inlet and outlet lines **(see illustration)**. Immediately cap the open lines.
4 Loosen the bolts and lift the accumulator out of the bracket **(see illustration)**. Pour the oil out of the accumulator into a measuring cup, noting the amount.
5 Pour an equal amount of fresh 525 viscosity refrigerant oil into the new accumulator, plus an additional two ounces.
6 Use new O-rings lubricated with refrigerant oil during installation.
7 Installation is the reverse of removal.
8 Have the system evacuated and recharged by an air conditioning shop or service station.

13 Air conditioning compressor - removal and installation

Refer to illustrations 13.5 and 13.6
Warning: *The air conditioning system is under high pressure. Do not loosen any hose fittings or remove any components until after the system has been discharged by a dealer service department, automotive air conditioning shop or service station. After the system has been discharged, residual pressure may still remain - be sure to wear eye protection when loosening line fittings!*

1 Have the system discharged.
2 Disconnect the negative battery cable from the battery.
3 Remove the engine cover (Chapter 11).
4 Remove the drivebelt (Chapter 1).
5 Detach the wire harness from the compressor **(see illustration)**.
6 Unbolt the refrigerant hose manifold from the compressor and cap all the fittings **(see illustration)**.

7 Unbolt the compressor and remove it from the vehicle.
8 Installation is the reverse of removal. See Chapter 1 and adjust the drivebelt. If the compressor is being replaced, drain the oil into a measuring cup and add the same amount of 525 viscosity refrigerant oil to the new compressor, plus two ounces.
9 Have the system evacuated and recharged by an air conditioning shop or service station.

14 Air conditioning condenser - removal and installation

Refer to illustrations 14.5a and 14.5b
Warning: *The air conditioning system is under high pressure. Do not loosen any hose fittings or remove any components until after the system has been discharged by a dealer service department, automotive air conditioning shop or service station. After the system has been discharged, residual pressure may*

14.5a Disconnect the refrigerant lines (left line shown) before lifting out the condenser

14.5b Be sure to use a back-up wrench on the stationary fitting to prevent twisting the tubing

15.2 The orifice tube screen is located inside this tube, which is taped over to seal out dirt (radiator removed for clarity)

still remain - be sure to wear eye protection when loosening line fittings!

1   Have the system discharged.

2   Disconnect the negative battery cable from the battery.

3   Remove the grille (see Chapter 11).

4   Remove the radiator tie bar support (if equipped) and horns.

5   Disconnect the refrigerant lines from the condenser (one fitting is located just in front of and slightly below the brake master cylinder and the other is located in front of the accumulator on the passenger side of the vehicle) **(see illustrations)**. Use a back-up wrench to prevent twisting the tubing.

6   Carefully lift the condenser out of the vehicle. Don't lose the rubber mounting pads. Store it upright so the oil won't run out.

7   Cap all open fittings to keep dirt and moisture out.

8   Installation is the reverse of removal. If you're replacing the condenser, drain the oil

out of it into a measuring cup and record the amount. The amount drained, plus one ounce, must be replaced during recharging. Use 525 viscosity refrigerant oil.

9   Have the system evacuated, recharged and leak tested by an air conditioning shop or service station.

15 Air conditioning orifice tube screen - removal and installation

Refer to illustration 15.2

Warning: *The air conditioning system is under high pressure. Do not loosen any hose fittings or remove any components until after the system has been discharged by a dealer service department, automotive air conditioning shop or service station. After the system has been discharged, residual pressure may still remain - be sure to wear eye protection when loosening line fittings!*

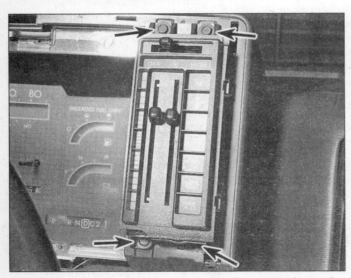

16.3 Air conditioner/heater control mounting screws (arrows)

16.4a The cable (arrow) can be detached after you remove the press-on retainer from the arm

Note: *The orifice tube screen is a filtering device that may clog and cause insufficient cooling. It can be removed and cleaned or replaced if necessary.*

1   Have the system discharged.

2   Disconnect the refrigerant line at the evaporator inlet and remove the orifice tube screen from the inlet tube **(see illustration)**.

3   Installation is the reverse of removal. Be sure to install the end marked "shorter screen end" first.

4   Have the system evacuated, recharged and leak tested by an air conditioning shop or service station.

16   Air conditioning and heater control assembly - removal and installation

Refer to illustrations 16.3, 16.4a and 16.4b

1   Disconnect the negative battery cable from the battery.

2   Remove the trim ring around the instru-

16.4b Air conditioning/heater control assembly

A   *Electrical connector*

B   *Vacuum harness*

ment cluster.

3   Remove the screws and pull the control assembly out of the dashboard **(see illustration)**.

4   Disconnect the control cable, vacuum hoses and wire harnesses **(see illustrations)**.

5   Installation is the reverse of removal.

3

Notes

Chapter 4
Fuel and exhaust systems

Contents

	Section
Carburetor - removal and installation	7
Carburetor (DCH340 and DFP340) - overhaul and adjustment	9
Carburetor (E2SE and 2SE) - overhaul and adjustment	8
Central Port Injection (CPI) - general information and CPI unit removal and installation	15
Engine idle speed check and adjustment	See Chapter 1
Exhaust system check	See Chapter 1
Exhaust system components - removal and installation	16
Fuel filter replacement	See Chapter 1
Fuel injection system - general information	10
Fuel line - repair and replacement	4

	Section
Fuel pressure relief procedure	2
Fuel pump/fuel pressure - check	14
Fuel pump - removal and installation	3
Fuel system check	See Chapter 1
Fuel tank - removal and installation	5
Fuel tank - repair	6
General information	1
Model 300 Throttle Body Injection (TBI) - overhaul	11
Model 700 Throttle Body Injection (TBI) - overhaul	12
Model 220 Throttle Body Injection (TBI) - overhaul	13
Thermo-controlled Air Cleaner (TAC) - check	See Chapter 1
Throttle linkage check	See Chapter 1

4

Specifications

General

Fuel pressure	
TBI	9 to 13 psi
CPI	54 to 62 psi
Non-adjustable TPS output check (TBI models only)	
Model 300 and 700	less than 1.25 volt
Model 220	less than 1.00 volt
Minimum idle speed adjustment (TBI models only)	
Model 700	650 rpm ± 25 rpm
Model 220	
Manual transmission	600 to 650 rpm
Automatic transmission	500 to 550 rpm

Rochester 2SE and E2SE carburetors

1982 models

Float adjustment, all	7/16-inch
Fast idle cam (choke rod) adjustment, all	22-degrees
Primary vacuum break adjustment	
Carburetor numbers 17082348 and 17082350	26-degrees
All others	28-degrees
Air valve rod link adjustment, all	1-degree
Secondary vacuum break adjustment	
Carburetor numbers 17082353 and 17082355	35-degrees
All others	32-degrees
Unloader adjustment	
Carburetor numbers 17082353 and 17082355	30-degrees
All others	35-degrees

Rochester 2SE and E2SE carburetors (continued

1983 models

Float adjustment
    Carburetor numbers: 13/32-inch
        17083356
        17083357
        17083358
        17083359
    Carburetor numbers: 1/8-inch
        17083368
        17083370
        17083450
        17083451
        17083452
        17083453
        17083454
        17083455
        17083456
        17083650
    Carburetor numbers: 1/4-inch
        17083630
        17083631
        17083632
        17083633
        17083634
        17083635
        17083636
Air valve spring adjustment
    Carburetor number 17083650 .... 1/2 turn
    All others .... 1 turn
Choke coil lever adjustment, all .... 0.085 inch
Fast idle cam (choke rod) adjustment
    Carburetor numbers: 22-degrees
        17083356
        17083357
        17083358
        17083359
        17083368
        17083370
    All others 28-degrees
Primary vacuum break adjustment
    Carburetor numbers: 25-degrees
        17083356
        17083357
        17083358
        17083359
        17083368
        17083370
    All others 27-degrees
Air valve rod link adjustment, all 1-degree
Secondary vacuum break adjustment, all 35-degrees
Unloader adjustment
    Carburetor numbers: 30-degrees
        17083356
        17083357
        17083358
        17083359
        17083368
        17083370
    All others 45-degrees

1984 models

Float adjustment
    Carburetor numbers: 9/32-inch
        17084356
        17084357
        17084358
        17084359
        17084632

17084633
17084635
17084636
Carburetor numbers: 1/8-inch
   17084368
   17084370
   17084542
Carburetor numbers: 5/32-inch
   17084360
   17084362
   17084364
   17084366
   17084534
   17084535
   17084537
   17084538
   17084540
Carburetor numbers: 7/16-inch
   17084390
   17084391
   17084392
   17084393
All others 11/32-inch
Air valve spring adjustment
Carburetor numbers: .... 3/4 turn
   17084356
   17084357
   17084358
   17084359
   17084368
   17084370
Carburetor numbers: .... 1/2 turn
   17084534
   17084535
   17084537
   17084538
   17084540
   17084542
   17084632
   17084633
   17084635
   17084636
All others .... 1 turn
Coil choke lever adjustment .... 0.085 inch
Fast idle cam (choke rod) adjustment
Carburetor numbers: 22-degrees
   17084348
   17084349
   17084350
   1708435l
   17084352
   17084353
   17084354
   17084355
   17084356
   17084357
   17084358
   17084359
   17084360
   17084362
   17084364
   17084366
   17084368
   17084370
Carburetor numbers: 15-degrees
   17084410
   17084412
   17084425
   17084427
   17084430

4

1984 models

Fast idle cam (choke rod) adjustment (continued)
    Carburetor numbers (continued): 15-degrees
        17084431
        17084434
        17084435
        17084560
        17084562
        17084569
    All others 28-degrees

Primary vacuum break adjustment
    Carburetor numbers: 26-degrees
        17084425
        17084427
        17084430
        17084431
        17084434
        17084435
    Carburetor numbers: 30-degrees
        17084348
        17084349
        17084350
        17084351
        17084352
        17084353
        17084354
        17084355
        17084360
        17084362
        17084364
        17084366
        17084390
        17084391
        17084392
        17084393
    All others 25-degrees
Air valve rod link adjustment, all 1-degree

Secondary vacuum break adjustment
    Carburetor numbers: 30-degrees
        17084356
        17084357
        17084358
        17084359
        17084368
        17084370
    Carburetor numbers: 38-degrees
        17084390
        17084391
        17084392
        17084393
        17084410
        17084412
        17084430
        17084431
        17084434
        17084435
    All others 35-degrees

Unloader adjustment
    Carburetor numbers: 30-degrees
        17084356
        17084357
        17084358
        17084359
        17084368
        17084370
    Carburetor numbers: 38-degrees
        17084390
        17084391
        17084392
        17084393

17084560
17084562
17084569
Carburetor numbers:.. 40-degrees
17084348
17084349
17084350
17084351
17084352
17084353
17084354
17084355
17084360
17084362
17084364
17084366
17084425
17084427
All others 45-degrees

1985 models
Float adjustment
Carburetor numbers 1/8-inch
17085356
17085358
17085368
Carburetor numbers 5/32-inch
17085348
17085350
17085352
17085354
17085360
17085362
17085364
17085366
17085372
17085374
17085452
17085453
17085458
Carburetor numbers 9/32-inch
17085357
17085359
17085369
17085371
Carburetor numbers 11/32-inch
17085351
17085355
17085363
17085367
Air valve spring adjustment
Carburetor numbers 1/2-turn
17085452
17085453
17085458
Carburetor numbers 3/4-turn
17085372
17085374
All others .... 1 turn
Fast idle cam (choke rod) adjustment
Carburetor numbers 28-degrees
17085452
17085453
17085458
All others 22-degrees
Primary vacuum break adjustment
Carburetor numbers 30-degrees
17085352
17085354
17085355

1985 models (continued)

Primary vacuum break adjustment (continued)

    Carburetor numbers (continued) 30-degrees
        17085364
        17085366
        17085367
    Carburetor numbers 32-degrees
        17085348
        17085350
        17085357
        17085360
        17085362
        17085363
        17085372
        17085374
    All others 25-degrees

Secondary vacuum break adjustment

    Carburetor numbers 34-degrees
        17085352
        17085354
        17085355
        17085364
        17085366
        17085367
    Carburetor numbers 35-degrees
        17085452
        17085453
        17085458
    Carburetor numbers 36-degrees
        17085348
        17085350
        17085351
        17085360
        17085362
        17085363
        17085372
        17085374
    All others 30-degrees

Unloader adjustment

    Carburetor numbers 45-degrees
        17085452
        17085453
        17085458
    Carburetor numbers 30-degrees
        17085356
        17085357
        17085358
        17085359
        17085368
        17085369
        17085370
        17085371
    All others 40-degrees

Hitachi DCH340/DFP340 carburetors

Float level (dry) 21/64-inch
Float drop (needle valve stroke) 0.059-inch
Choke unloader 3/32-inch
Vacuum break adjustment .... 3/32 to 7/64-inch

Torque specifications

	F-lbs (unless otherwise indicated)
CPI air intake plenum fasteners..	124 in-lbs
Throttle Body components	
TBI fuel meter cover screws..	28 in-lbs
TBI IAC valve...	156 in-lbs
TBI mounting bolts...	120 to 180 in-lbs
TBI mounting stud..	36 to 72 in-lbs
TBI mounting nut..	120 to 180 in-lbs
TBI fuel line fittings...	17
Carburetor components	
Carburetor mounting nuts...	156 in-lbs
Fuel inlet nut-to-carburetor..	18
Carburetor fuel line-to-inlet nut.................................	24
Fuel pump mounting bolts...	15

Component location

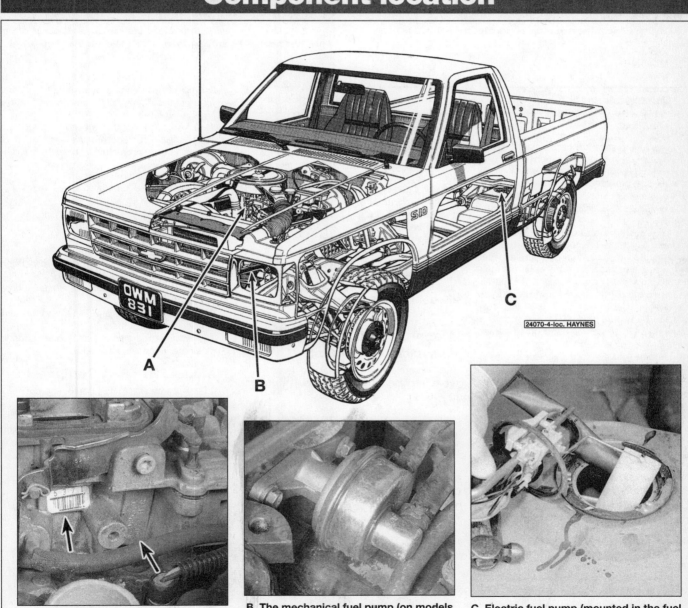

OWM 831

S10

24070-4-loc. HAYNES

A

B

C

A Typical Rochester E2SE carburetor number stamping and I.D. tag

B The mechanical fuel pump (on models so equipped) is bolted to the side of the engine block

C Electric fuel pump (mounted in the fuel tank) and level sending unit

4

2.12 Disconnect the electrical connector from the fuel pump relay (arrow)

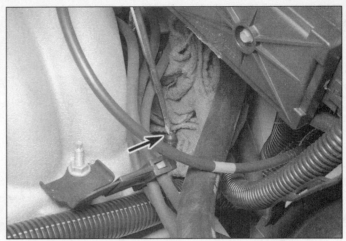

2.13 Use a screwdriver to bleed the remaining fuel out of the fuel line fitting - be sure to absorb the fuel with the shop towel

1   General information

Fuel system

The fuel system on carbureted models consists of a fuel tank, mechanical fuel pump, fuel feed, return and vapor lines between the tank and the carburetor, an in-line fuel filter, air cleaner assembly and either a Model E2SE, 2SE, DCH340 or DFP340 carburetor.

Fuel systems on fuel-injected models include a fuel tank, electrically operated fuel pump inside the tank, fuel pump relay, fuel feed, return and vapor lines between the tank and the throttle body, an in-line fuel filter, air cleaner assembly and either a Model 300 or 700 (single injector) or 220 (twin injector) Throttle Body Injection (TBI) system. The Model 300 TBI system is used on all earlier four-cylinder engines and the Model 700 system is used on later four-cylinder engines. The Model 220 is used on all V6 engines. 1992 models with a 4.3L V6 engine are equipped with a Central Port Injection (CPI) system (see Section 15 for details).

Exhaust system

The exhaust system, which is similar for both four-cylinder and V6 powered models, includes an exhaust manifold fitted with an oxygen sensor, the exhaust pipe itself, a catalytic converter and a muffler. The exhaust system is supported by several rubber mountings, which permit some movement of the exhaust system but do not permit transfer of noise and vibration into the passenger compartment.

The catalytic converter is an emission control device added to the exhaust system to reduce hydrocarbon and carbon monoxide pollutants from the exhaust gas stream.

2   Fuel pressure relief procedure

Warning: *Gasoline is extremely flammable, so take extra precautions when you work on any part of the fuel system. Do not smoke or allow open flames or bare light bulbs near the work area, and don't work in a garage where a natural gas-type appliance (such as a water heater or clothes dryer) with a pilot light is present. If you spill any fuel on your skin, rinse it off immediately with soap and water. When you perform any kind of work on the fuel system, wear safety glasses and have a Class B type fire extinguisher on hand.*

1   Before servicing any component on a fuel-injected vehicle it is necessary to relieve the fuel pressure to minimize the risk of fire or personal injury.

Model 300 TBI (earlier four-cylinder engine)

2   Remove the fuse marked Fuel Pump from the fuse block in the passenger compartment.

3.4 Remove the fuel pump mounting bolts (arrows)

3   Crank the engine over. It will start and run until the fuel supply remaining in the fuel lines is depleted.
4   After the engine stops, engage the starter again for another three seconds to assure that any remaining pressure is dissipated.
5   Turn the ignition to Off.
6   Replace the fuel pump fuse.

Model 700 TBI (later four-cylinder engines)

7   Place the transmission in Park (automatic) or Neutral (manual), set the parking brake and block the drive wheels.
8   Detach the three terminal electrical connector at the fuel tank.
9   Start the engine and allow it to run until it stops for lack of fuel.
10   Engage the starter for three seconds to dissipate fuel pressure in lines.

Model 220 TBI (V6 engines)

11   The Model 220 TBI contains a constant

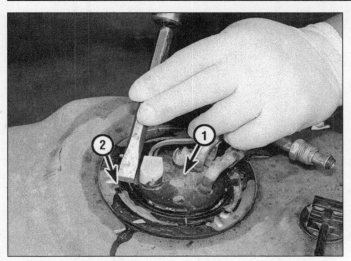

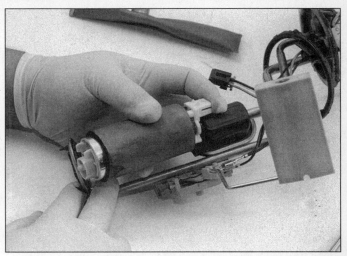

3.15 To remove the fuel pump and sender (1), turn the lock ring (2) counterclockwise, then lift the pump/sender assembly out

3.19 Separating the fuel pump from the support

bleed feature in the pressure regulator that relieves pressure. No special procedure is required to relieve the fuel pressure.

Central Port Injection (CPI) - 4.3L V6 engine

Refer to illustrations 2.12 and 2.13

12   CPI systems are equipped with a special fitting built into the fuel line at the rear of the air intake plenum. Connect a fuel pressure gauge equipped with a bleed-off valve to the fitting. If the tool is not available, disconnect the fuel pump relay **(see illustration)** and crank the engine over.

13   Place a shop towel around the fitting **(see illustration)** and bleed the remaining fuel out of the fuel line by placing the tip of a screwdriver on the valve. Be careful not to let the fuel spray into the engine compartment.

---

3 Fuel pump - removal and installation

Warning: *Gasoline is extremely flammable, so take extra precautions when you work on any part of the fuel system. Do not smoke or allow open flames or bare light bulbs near the work area, and don't work in a garage where a natural gas-type appliance (such as a water heater or clothes dryer) with a pilot light is present. If you spill any fuel on your skin, rinse it off immediately with soap and water. When you perform any kind of work on the fuel system, wear safety glasses and have a Class B type fire extinguisher on hand.*

Mechanical pump (carbureted models)

Refer to illustration 3.4

1   The fuel pump is a sealed unit and cannot be rebuilt.

2   To remove the pump, first isolate the battery by disconnecting the negative battery cable.

3   Detach the fuel inlet hose, the outlet line and the vapor return hose (if equipped). Hold the fitting on the pump with a back-up wrench as the outlet line is disconnected. Also, if possible, use a flare-nut wrench on the fuel line fitting.

4   Remove the two mounting bolts and detach the fuel pump **(see illustration)**. As the pump is removed, the pushrod may fall out - be sure to retrieve it.

5   Remove the gasket and mounting plate.

6   Remove all traces of old gasket and sealant with a scraper, then clean the block mounting surface with lacquer thinner or acetone.

7   Apply a dab of heavy grease to the pushrod to hold it in place as the pump is installed.

8   Position the new gasket, the mounting plate and the pump on the block, then install the bolts and tighten them to the torque listed in this Chapter's Specifications.

9   Reattach the inlet hose, the outlet line and the vapor return hose to the pump. Be sure to tighten the fitting on the outlet line and the clamps on the hoses securely.

10   Start the engine and check for fuel leaks at the hose and line connections.

Electric pump (fuel-injected models)

Refer to illustrations 3.15 and 3.19

11   Relieve the fuel pressure (see Section 2).

12   Disconnect the cable from the negative battery terminal.

13   Remove the fuel tank (see Section 5).

14   The fuel pump/sending unit assembly is located inside the fuel tank. It is held in place by a cam lock ring mechanism consisting of an inner ring with three locking cams and an outer ring with three tangs. The outer ring is

welded to the tank and can't be turned.

15   To unlock the fuel pump/sending unit assembly, turn the inner ring counterclockwise until the locking cams are free of the tangs **(see illustration). Warning:** *If the rings are locked together too tightly to release them by hand, gently knock them loose with a hammer and a brass drift. Do not use a steel punch to knock the lock rings loose - a spark could cause an explosion!*

16   Extract the fuel pump/sending unit assembly from the fuel tank. **Caution:** *The fuel level float and sending unit are delicate. Do not bump them against the tank during removal or the accuracy of the sending unit may be affected.*

17   Inspect the condition of the rubber gasket around the mouth of the lock ring mechanism. If it is dried, cracked or deteriorated, replace it.

18   Inspect the strainer on the lower end of the fuel pump **(see illustration)**. If it is dirty, remove it, clean it with a suitable solvent and blow it out with compressed air. If it is too dirty to be cleaned, replace it.

19   If it is necessary to separate the fuel pump and sending unit, remove the pump from the sending unit by pulling the fuel pump assembly into the rubber connector and sliding the pump away from the bottom support **(see illustration)**. Care should be taken to prevent damage to the rubber insulator and fuel strainer during removal. After the pump assembly is clear of the bottom support, pull it out of the rubber connector.

20   Insert the fuel pump/sending unit assembly into the fuel tank.

21   Turn the inner lock ring clockwise until the locking cams are fully engaged by the retaining tangs. **Note:** *If you have installed a new O-ring type rubber gasket, it may be necessary to push down on the inner lock ring until the locking cams slide under the retaining tangs.*

22   Install the fuel tank (see Section 5).

4

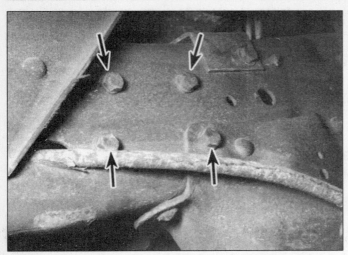

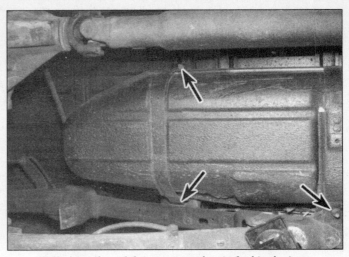

5.8a Location of the fuel tank mounting bolts which must be removed from the frame rail

5.8b Location of the crossmember to fuel tank strap mounting bolts

4 Fuel line - repair and replacement

Warning: *Gasoline is extremely flammable, so take extra precautions when you work on any part of the fuel system. Do not smoke or allow open flames or bare light bulbs near the work area, and don't work in a garage where a natural gas-type appliance (such as a water heater or clothes dryer) with a pilot light is present. If you spill any fuel on your skin, rinse it off immediately with soap and water. When you perform any kind of work on the fuel system, wear safety glasses and have a Class B type fire extinguisher on hand.*

1   If a section of metal fuel line must be replaced, only brazed, seamless steel tubing should be used, since copper or aluminum does not have enough durability to withstand normal operating vibrations.

2   If only one section of a metal fuel line is damaged on carbureted or TBI-equipped models, it can be cut out and replaced with a piece of rubber hose. Be sure to use only reinforced fuel resistant hose, identified by the word "Fluroelastomer" on the hose. The inside diameter of the hose should match the outside diameter of the metal line. The rubber hose should be cut four inches longer than the section it's replacing, so there are two inches of overlap between the rubber and metal line at either end of the section. Hose clamps should be used to secure both ends of the repaired section. **Note:** *CPI systems operate at higher pressures and only factory replacement parts should be used.*

3   If a section of metal line longer than six inches is being removed, use a combination of metal tubing and rubber hose so the hose lengths will be no longer than ten inches.

4   Never use rubber hose within four inches of any part of the exhaust system or within ten inches of the catalytic converter.

5   When replacing clamps, make sure the replacement clamp is identical to the one being replaced, as different clamps are used depending on location.

5 Fuel tank - removal and installation

Refer to illustrations 5.8a and 5.8b
Warning: *Gasoline is extremely flammable, so take extra precautions when you work on any part of the fuel system. Do not smoke or allow open flames or bare light bulbs near the work area, and don't work in a garage where a natural gas-type appliance (such as a water heater or clothes dryer) with a pilot light is present. If you spill any fuel on your skin, rinse it off immediately with soap and water. When you perform any kind of work on the fuel system, wear safety glasses and have a Class B type fire extinguisher on hand.*

1   Disconnect the cable from the negative battery terminal.

2   Remove the filler cap from the fuel tank.

3   Drain all fuel from the tank into a clean container. Since there are no drain plugs on the fuel tank and there is a restriction in the filler neck which prevents siphoning, the fuel will have to be drained through the line which feeds fuel from the tank to the fuel pump. **Warning:** *Use a siphoning kit, available at most auto parts stores. Do not start the siphoning process with your mouth - serious personal injury could result.*

4   Raise the vehicle and support it securely on jackstands.

5   Disconnect the fuel gauge wire at the body wiring harness and the ground strap wire at the fuel tank reinforcement.

6   Disconnect the tank ventilator hose, fuel vapor hose and fuel feed and return hoses from the sender unit by loosening the hose clamps and pulling the hoses off the fittings.

7   Support the tank with a floor jack and wood block.

8   Remove the fuel tank strap support bolts from the frame rail **(see illustrations)**.

9   Lower the jack to remove the tank.

10   Installation is the reverse of removal.

11   When the installation is complete, carefully check all lines, hoses and fittings for leaks.

7.3 Removing the fuel vapor hose

7.5 All wires and hoses should be moved out of the way before carburetor removal

7.6 Needle-nose pliers work well when removing the cable retaining circlip from the throttle linkage

6   Fuel tank - repair

1   Any repairs to the fuel tank or filler neck should be carried out by a professional who has experience in this critical and potentially dangerous work. Even after cleaning and flushing of the fuel system, explosive fumes can remain and ignite during repair of the tank.

2   If the fuel tank is removed from the vehicle, it should not be placed in an area where sparks or open flames could ignite the fumes coming out of the tank. Be especially careful inside garages where a natural gas-type appliance is located, because the pilot light could cause an explosion.

7   Carburetor - removal and installation

Refer to illustrations 7.3, 7.5 and 7.6

Warning: *Gasoline is extremely flammable, so take extra precautions when you work on any part of the fuel system. Do not smoke or allow open flames or bare light bulbs near the work area, and don't work in a garage where a natural gas-type appliance (such as a water heater or clothes dryer) with a pilot light is present. If you spill any fuel on your skin, rinse it off immediately with soap and water. When you perform any kind of work on the fuel system, wear safety glasses and have a Class B type fire extinguisher on hand.*

1   Disconnect the negative battery cable from the battery.

2   Label the air cleaner hoses and remove the air cleaner.

3   On V6 models, remove the mounting bolt from the three-way connector on the left valve cover. Remove the fuel vapor hose from the carburetor **(see illustration)**, and disconnect the coolant sensor wire. Place the hose and wire out of the way.

4   Label and remove all vacuum hoses from the carburetor.

5   Detach all wires from the carburetor and position them out of the way **(see illustration)**.

6   Disconnect the throttle return spring and accelerator linkage **(see illustration)**.

7   Disconnect the downshift cable (automatic transmission only).

8   Remove the carburetor mounting nuts and/or bolts and separate the carburetor from the manifold.

9   Remove the gasket and/or EFE insulator.

10   Installation is the reverse of the removal procedure, but the following points should be noted:

a) *By filling the carburetor bowl with fuel, the initial start-up will be easier and less drain on the battery will occur.*

b) *New gaskets should be used.*

c) *Idle speed and mixture settings should be checked and, if necessary, adjusted.*

d) *Be sure to tighten the carburetor mounting nuts/bolts to the torque listed in this Chapter's Specifications.*

8   Carburetor (E2SE and 2SE) - overhaul and adjustment

Warning: *Gasoline is extremely flammable, so take extra precautions when you work on any part of the fuel system. Do not smoke or allow open flames or bare light bulbs near the work area, and don't work in a garage where a natural gas-type appliance (such as a water heater or clothes dryer) with a pilot light is present. If you spill any fuel on your skin, rinse it off immediately with soap and water. When you perform any kind of work on the fuel system, wear safety glasses and have a Class B type fire extinguisher on hand.*

Note: *Carburetor overhaul is an involved procedure that requires some experience. Because of running production changes, some details of the unit overhauled here may not exactly match those of your carburetor, although the home mechanic with previous experience should be able to detect the differences and modify the procedure.*

Disassembly

Refer to illustrations 8.3a through 8.3ag and 8.6

1   Before disassembling the carburetor, purchase a carburetor rebuild kit for your particular model (the model number will be found on a metal tag at the side of the carburetor or stamped into the carburetor body). This kit will have all the necessary replacement parts for the overhaul procedure.

2   It will be necessary to have a relatively large, clean workbench to lay out all of the parts as they are removed. Many of the parts are very small and can be lost easily if the work space is cluttered.

3   Carburetor disassembly is illustrated in the following step-by-step illustration sequence to make the operation as easy as possible. Work slowly through the procedure and if at any point you feel the reassembly of a certain component may prove confusing, stop and make a rough sketch or apply identification marks. The time to think about reassembling the carburetor is when it is being taken apart **(see illustrations)**.

4   The final step in disassembly involves the idle mixture needle. It is recessed in the throttle body and sealed with a hardened steel plug. The plug should not be removed unless the needle requires replacement or normal cleaning procedures fail to clean the idle mixture passages. If the idle mixture needle must be removed, proceed as follows.

5   Secure the throttle body in a vise so it is inverted with the manifold side up. Use blocks of wood to cushion the throttle body.

4

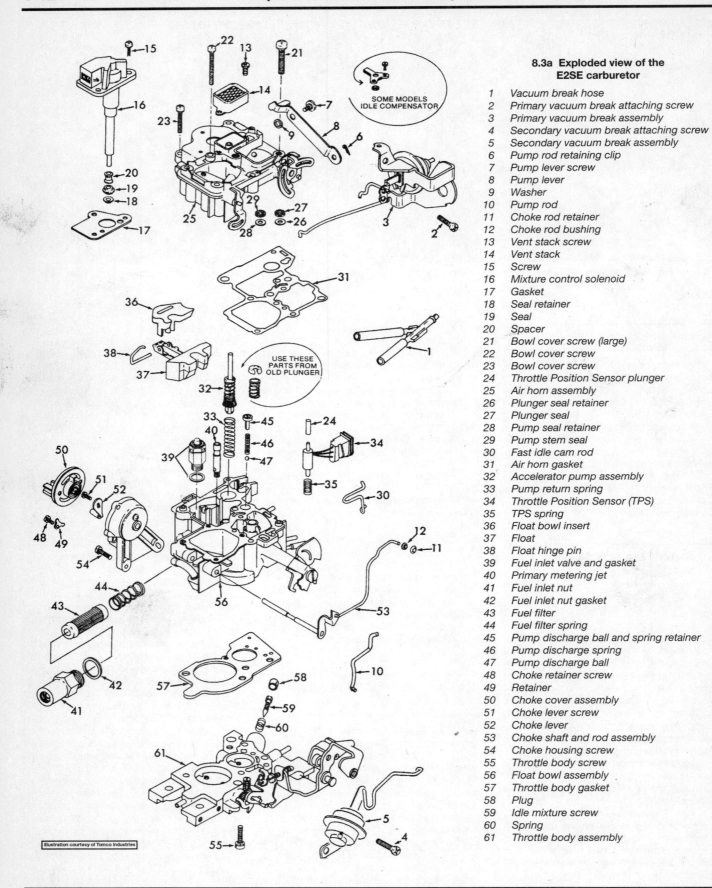

SOME MODELS
IDLE COMPENSATOR

USE THESE
PARTS FROM
OLD PLUNGER

Illustration courtesy of Tomco Industries

**8.3a Exploded view of the
E2SE carburetor**

1 Vacuum break hose
2 Primary vacuum break attaching screw
3 Primary vacuum break assembly
4 Secondary vacuum break attaching screw
5 Secondary vacuum break assembly
6 Pump rod retaining clip
7 Pump lever screw
8 Pump lever
9 Washer
10 Pump rod
11 Choke rod retainer
12 Choke rod bushing
13 Vent stack screw
14 Vent stack
15 Screw
16 Mixture control solenoid
17 Gasket
18 Seal retainer
19 Seal
20 Spacer
21 Bowl cover screw (large)
22 Bowl cover screw
23 Bowl cover screw
24 Throttle Position Sensor plunger
25 Air horn assembly
26 Plunger seal retainer
27 Plunger seal
28 Pump seal retainer
29 Pump stem seal
30 Fast idle cam rod
31 Air horn gasket
32 Accelerator pump assembly
33 Pump return spring
34 Throttle Position Sensor (TPS)
35 TPS spring
36 Float bowl insert
37 Float
38 Float hinge pin
39 Fuel inlet valve and gasket
40 Primary metering jet
41 Fuel inlet nut
42 Fuel inlet nut gasket
43 Fuel filter
44 Fuel filter spring
45 Pump discharge ball and spring retainer
46 Pump discharge spring
47 Pump discharge ball
48 Choke retainer screw
49 Retainer
50 Choke cover assembly
51 Choke lever screw
52 Choke lever
53 Choke shaft and rod assembly
54 Choke housing screw
55 Throttle body screw
56 Float bowl assembly
57 Throttle body gasket
58 Plug
59 Idle mixture screw
60 Spring
61 Throttle body assembly

8.3b Location of carburetor identification
number (arrow)

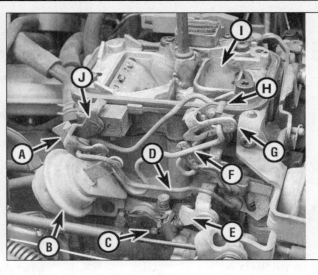

**8.3c E2SE carburetor
choke system**

A   Intermediate choke
lever
B   Secondary vacuum
break unit
C   Fast idle screw
D   Air valve rod
E   Fast idle cam
F   Intermediate choke
link
G   Vacuum break
lever
H   Choke lever
I   Choke valve
J   Air valve lever

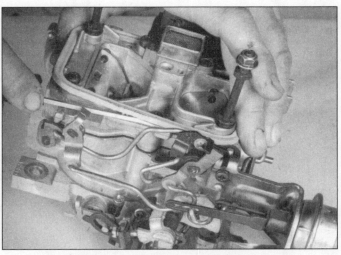

8.3d Remove the gasket from the top of the air horn

8.3e Removing the fuel inlet nut, fuel filter and spring

4

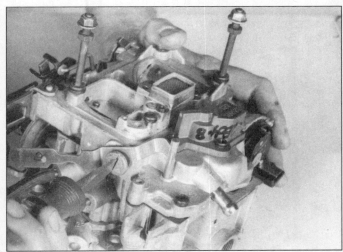

8.3f Remove the pump lever attaching screw

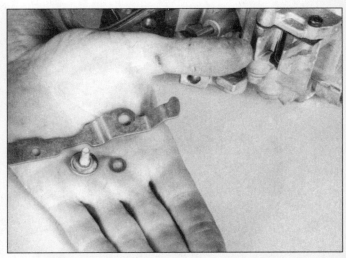

8.3g Disconnect the pump rod from the pump lever
and remove the pump lever

8.3h Disconnect the primary vacuum break diaphragm
hose from the throttle body

8.3i Remove the screws that retain the idle speed
solenoid/vacuum break diaphragm bracket

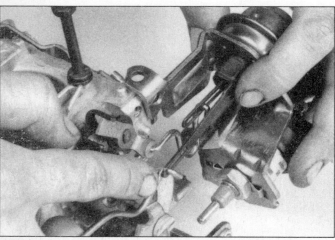

8.3j Lift off the idle speed solenoid/vacuum break diaphragm
assembly and disconnect the air valve link from the vacuum break
plunger (repeat this step for the secondary vacuum break
assembly, disconnecting the link from the slot in the choke lever)

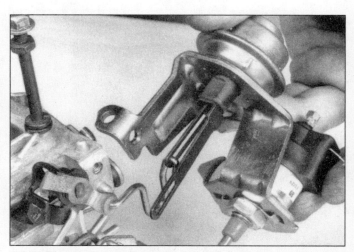

8.3k Disconnect the vacuum break and air valve links from the
levers - it is not necessary to disconnect the links from the
vacuum break plungers unless either the rods or the
vacuum break units are being replaced

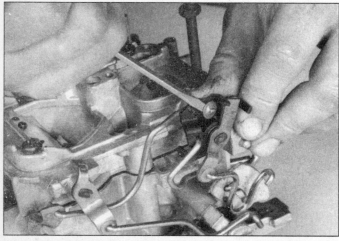

8.3l Pry off the clip that retains the intermediate choke link to the
choke lever and separate the link from the lever

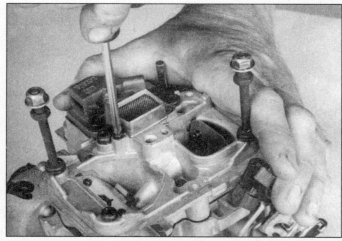

8.3m Remove the screws that retain the vent/screen assembly to
the air horn and lift off the assembly

8.3n Remove the screws that retain the mixture control solenoid and, using a slight twisting motion, lift the solenoid out of the air horn

8.3o Remove the screws securing the air horn to the float bowl, noting their lengths and positions to simplify installation

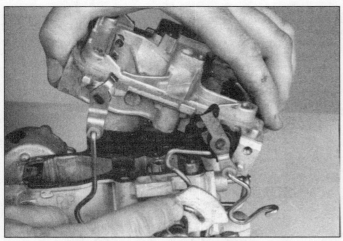

8.3p Rotate the fast idle cam up, lift off the air horn and disconnect the fast idle cam link from the fast idle cam

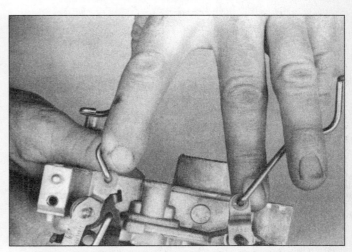

8.3q The links attached to the air horn need not be removed unless their replacement or removal is required to service other components

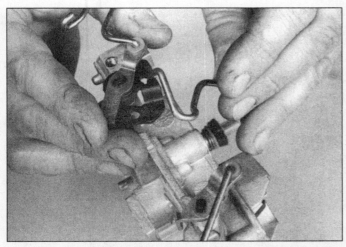

8.3r Disengage the fast idle cam link from the choke lever and save the bushing for reassembly

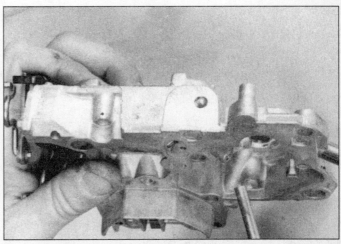

8.3s Remove the pump plunger from the air horn or the pump well in the float bowl

4

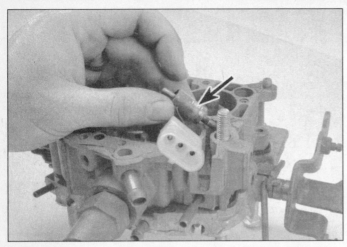

8.3t TPS removal on the E2SE carburetors (push up from the bottom of the electrical connector and remove the TPS and connector assembly from the float bowl - also, remove the spring from the bottom of the float bowl)

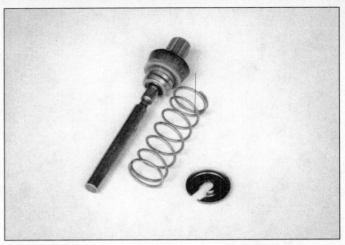

8.3u Compress the pump plunger spring and separate the spring retainer clip and spring from the piston

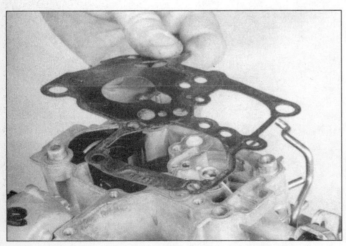

8.3v Remove the air horn gasket from the float bowl

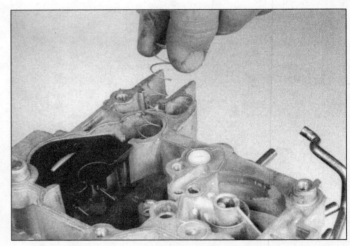

8.3w Remove the pump return spring from the pump well

8.3x Remove the plastic filler block that covers the float valve

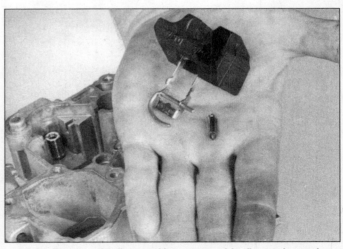

8.3y Remove the float and lever assembly, float valve and stabilizing spring (if used) by pulling up on the hinge pin

8.3z Remove the float valve seat and gasket (left) and the extended metering jet (right) from the float bowl

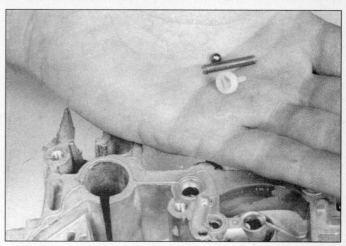

8.3aa Using needle-nose pliers, pull out the white plastic retainer and remove the pump discharge spring and check ball (do not pry on the retainer to remove it)

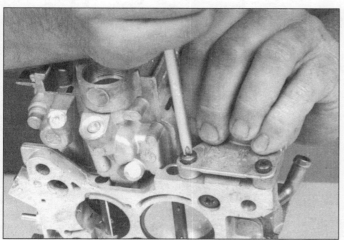

8.3ab Remove the screws that retain the choke housing to the throttle body

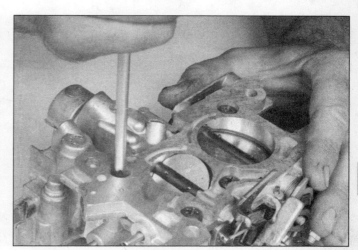

8.3ac Remove the screws that retain the float bowl to the throttle body

4

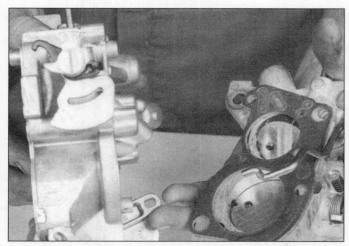

8.3ad Separate the float bowl from the throttle body

8.3ae Carefully file the heads off the pop rivets that retain the choke cover to the choke housing, remove the cover and tap out the remainder of the rivets

8.3af Remove the choke coil lever screw and lift out the lever

8.3ag Remove the intermediate shaft and lever assembly by sliding it out the lever side of the float bowl

8.6 The idle mixture screws on the E2SE carburetor are concealed behind two plugs - carefully cut where indicated (arrow), then knock the plug out

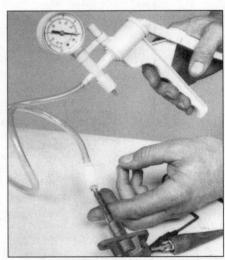

8.22 Attaching a hand-held vacuum pump to the end of the mixture control solenoid

6   Locate the idle mixture needle and plug. It should be marked by an indented locator point on the underside of the throttle body. Using a hacksaw, make two parallel cuts in the throttle body on either side of the locator mark. The cuts should be deep enough to touch the steel plug, but should not extend more than 1/8-inch beyond the dimples on either side of the plug **(see illustration)**.

7   Position a flat punch at a point near the ends of the saw marks. Holding it at a 45-degree angle, drive it into the throttle body until the casting breaks away, exposing the steel plug.

8   Use a center punch to make an indentation in the steel plug. Holding it at a 45-degree angle, drive the plug from the throttle body casting. **Note:** *If the plug breaks apart, be sure to remove all of the pieces.*

9   Use a 3/16-inch deep socket to remove the idle mixture needle and spring from the throttle body.

Cleaning and inspection

Refer to illustration 8.22

10   Clean the air horn, float bowl, throttle body and related components with clean solvent and blow them out with compressed air. A can of compressed air can be used if an air compressor is not available. Do not use a piece of wire for cleaning the jets and passages.

11   The idle speed solenoid, mixture control solenoid, Throttle Position Sensor, electric choke, pump plunger, diaphragm, plastic filler block and other electrical, rubber and plastic parts should not be immersed in carburetor cleaner because they will harden, swell or distort.

12   Make sure all fuel passages, jets and other metering components are free of burrs and dirt.

13   Inspect the upper and lower surfaces of the air horn, float bowl and throttle body for damage. Be sure all material has been removed.

14   Inspect all lever holes and plastic bushings for excessive wear and an out-of-round condition and replace them if necessary.

15   Inspect the float valve and seat for dirt, deep wear grooves and scoring and replace it if necessary.

16   Inspect the float valve pull clip for proper installation and adjust it if necessary.

17   Inspect the float, float arms and hinge pin for distortion and binding and correct or replace as necessary.

18   Inspect the rubber cup on the pump plunger for excessive wear and cracks.

19   Check the choke valve and linkage for excessive wear, binding and distortion and correct or replace as necessary.

20   Inspect the choke vacuum diaphragm for leaks and replace if necessary.

21   Check the choke valve for freedom of movement.

22   Check the mixture control solenoid in the following manner.

a) *Connect one end of a jumper wire to either end of the solenoid connector and the other end to the positive terminal of the battery.*

b) *Connect another jumper wire between the other terminal of the solenoid connector and the negative terminal of the battery.*

c) *Remove the rubber seal and retainer from the end of the solenoid stem and attach a hand-held vacuum pump to it* **(see illustration)**.

8.25 Installing the gasket on the bottom of the float bowl

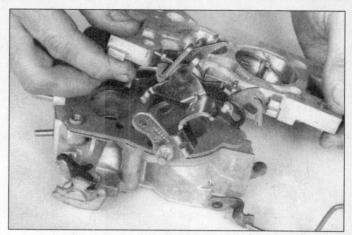

8.26a Mounting the throttle body on the float bowl

8.26b Installing the throttle body-to-float bowl attaching screws

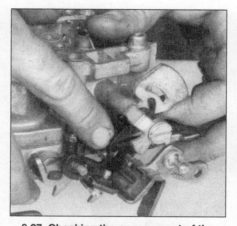

8.27 Checking the engagement of the lockout tang in the secondary lockout lever

8.28a Attaching the choke housing to the throttle body

4

d) With the solenoid fully energized (lean position), apply at least 25 in-Hg of vacuum and time the leak-down rate from 20 to 15 in-Hg. The leak-down rate should not exceed 5 in-Hg in five seconds. If leakage exceeds that amount, replace the solenoid.

e) To check if the solenoid is sticking in the down position, again apply about 25 in-Hg of vacuum to it, then disconnect the jumper lead to the battery and watch the pump gauge reading. It should fall to zero in less than one second.

Reassembly

Refer to illustrations 8.25, 8.26a, 8.26b, 8.27, 8.28a, 8.28b, 8.30, 8.31, 8.32, 8.35, 8.36, 8.37, 8.38, 8.39, 8.40, 8.42, 8.43, 8.44, 8.49, 8.50, 8.52, 8.53, 8.56, 8.57, 8.58a, 8.58b, 8.62 and 8.64a through 8.64j

23 Before reassembling the carburetor, compare all old and new gaskets back-to-back to make sure they match perfectly. Check especially that all the necessary holes are present and in the proper positions in the new gaskets.

24 If the idle mixture needle and spring

have been removed, reinstall them by lightly seating the needle, then back it off three turns. This will provide a preliminary idle mixture adjustment. Final idle mixture adjustment must be made on the vehicle. Proper adjustment must be done using special emission sensing equipment, making it impractical for the home mechanic. To have the mixture settings checked or readjusted, take your vehicle to a dealer service department or other qualified mechanic with the proper equipment.

25 Install a new gasket on the bottom of the float bowl **(see illustration)**.

26 Mount the throttle body on the float bowl so it is properly installed over the locating dowels on the bowl **(see illustration)**, reinstall the screws and tighten them evenly and securely **(see illustration)**. Be sure that the steps on the fast idle cam face toward the fast idle screw on the throttle lever when installed.

27 Inspect the linkage to make sure that the lockout tang properly engages in the slot of the secondary lockout lever and that the linkage moves freely without binding **(see illustration)**.

28 Attach the choke housing to the throttle

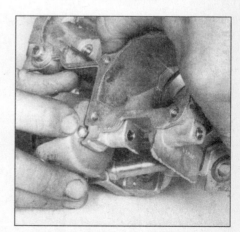

8.28b The lug at the rear of the choke housing should sit in the bowl recess

body, making sure the locating lug on the rear of the housing sits in the recess in the float bowl **(see illustrations)**.

29 Install the intermediate choke shaft and lever assembly in the float bowl by pushing it through from the throttle lever side.

30 Position the intermediate choke lever in

8.30 Install the thermostatic coil lever so it is in the 12 o'clock position when the intermediate choke lever is facing up

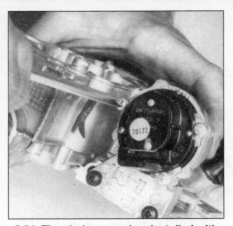

8.31 The choke cover is reinstalled with the self-tapping screws supplied in the overhaul kit

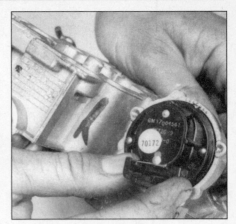

8.32 Be sure the notch in the choke cover is aligned with the raised casting projection on the housing cover flange

8.35 Installing the main metering jet

8.36 Installing the float valve seat assembly

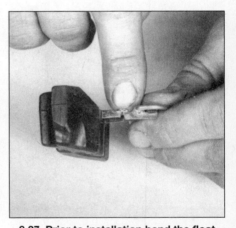

8.37 Prior to installation bend the float arm up slightly at the point shown

the up position and install the thermostatic coil lever on the end sticking into the choke housing. The coil lever is properly aligned when the coil pick-up tang is in the 12 o'clock position **(see illustration)**. Install the screw in the end of the intermediate shaft to secure the coil lever.

31   Three self-tapping screws supplied in the overhaul kit are used in place of the original pop rivets to secure the choke cover and coil assembly to the choke housing. Thread the screws into the housing, making sure they start easily and are properly aligned, then remove them **(see illustration)**.

32   Place the fast idle screw on the highest step of the fast idle cam, then install the choke cover on the housing, aligning the notch in the cover with the raised casting projection on the housing cover flange **(see illustration)**. When installing the cover, be sure the coil pick-up tang engages the inside choke lever. **Note:** *The thermostatic coil tang is formed so that it will completely encircle the coil pick-up lever. Make sure the lever is inside of the tang when installing the cover.*

33   With the choke cover in place, install the

self-tapping screws and tighten them securely.

34   Install the pump discharge check ball and spring in the passage next to the float chamber, then place a new plastic retainer in the hole so that its end engages the spring and tap it lightly into place until the retainer top is flush with the bowl surface.

35   Install the main metering jet in the bottom of the float chamber **(see illustration)**.

36   Install the float valve seat assembly and gasket **(see illustration)**.

37   To make float level adjustments easier, bend the float arm up slightly at the notch before installing the float **(see illustration)**.

38   Install the float valve onto the float arm by sliding the lever under the pull clip **(see illustration)**. Install the float assembly by aligning the valve and seat and the float retaining pin and locating channels in the float bowl.

39   To adjust the float level, hold the float pin firmly in place, push down on the float arm at the outer end and see if the top of the float is the specified distance from the float bowl surface **(see illustration)**. Bend the float

arm as necessary to achieve the proper measurement by pushing down on the pontoon. See the Specifications at the beginning of this Chapter for the proper float level for your vehicle.

40   Install the plastic filler block over the

8.38 Installing the float retaining pin in the float lever

8.39 Measuring the float level

8.40 Installing the plastic filler block

8.42 Installing a new air horn gasket on the float bowl

8.43 Installing the pump return spring in the pump well

45   If used, remove the old pump plunger seal and retainer and the old TPS plunger seal and retainer from the air horn. Install new seals and retainers in both locations and lightly stake both seal retainers in three (3) places other than the original staking locations.

46   Install the fast idle cam rod in the lower hole of the choke lever.

47   If so equipped, apply a light coat of silicone grease or engine oil to the TPS plunger and push it through the seal in the air horn so that about one-half of the plunger extends above the seal.

48   Before installing the air horn, apply a light coat of silicone grease or engine oil to the pump plunger stem to aid in slipping it through the seal in the air horn.

49   Rotate the fast idle cam to the Up position so it can be engaged with the lower end of the fast idle cam rod **(see illustration)**. While holding down on the pump plunger assembly, carefully lower the air horn onto the float bowl and guide the pump plunger stem through the seal.

50   Install the air horn retaining screws and washers, making sure the different length screws are inserted into their respective holes, then tighten them in the sequence

4

float valve so that it is flush with the float bowl surface **(see illustration)**.

41   If the carburetor is equipped with a Throttle Position Sensor, install the TPS return spring in the bottom of the well in the float bowl. Then install the TPS and connector assembly by aligning the groove in the electrical connector with the slot in the float bowl. When properly installed, the assembly

should sit below the float bowl surface.

42   Install a new air horn gasket on the float bowl **(see illustration)**.

43   Install the pump return spring in the pump well **(see illustration)**.

44   Reassemble the pump plunger assembly, lubricate the plunger cap with a thin coat of engine oil and install the pump plunger in the pump well **(see illustration)**.

8.44 Installing the pump plunger in the pump well

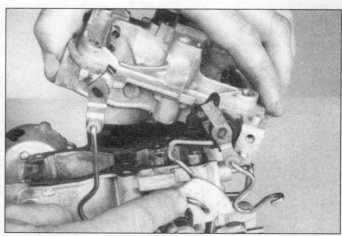

8.49 Engage the fast idle cam link in the fast idle cam prior to installation of the air horn

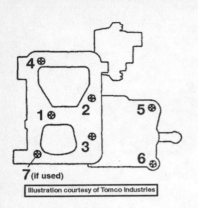

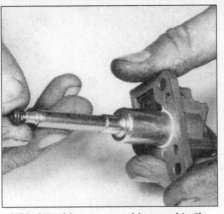

8.50 Recommended air horn screw tightening sequence for E2SE carburetor

Illustration courtesy of Tomco Industries

8.52 Attaching a new rubber seal to the mixture control solenoid

8.53 Using a hammer and a hollow tool to tap the seal retainer onto the mixture control solenoid stem

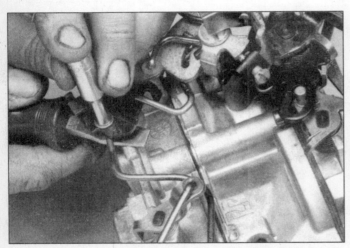

8.56 Attaching a retaining clip to the intermediate choke rod to secure it to the choke lever

8.57 Installing the idle speed solenoid/vacuum break diaphragm assembly

illustrated **(see illustration)**.

51   If so equipped, install a new seal in the recess of the float bowl and attach the hot idle compensator valve.

52   Install a new rubber seal on the end of the mixture control solenoid stem until it is up against the boss on the stem **(see illustration)**.

53   Using a 3/16-inch socket and a hammer **(see illustration)**, drive the retainer over the mixture control solenoid stem just far enough to retain the rubber seal, while leaving a slight clearance between them for seal expansion.

54   Apply a light coat of engine oil to the rubber seal and, using a new gasket, install the mixture control solenoid in the air horn. Use a slight twisting motion while installing the solenoid to help the rubber seal slip into the recess.

55   Install the vent/screen assembly on the air horn.

56   Install a plastic bushing in the hole in the choke lever, with the small end facing out, then, with the intermediate choke lever at the 12 o'clock position, install the intermediate choke rod in the bushing. Install a new retaining clip on the end of the rod. Use a broad

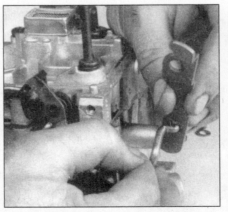

8.58a Engaging the pump rod with the pump rod lever

flat-blade screwdriver and a 3/16-inch socket **(see illustration)**. Make sure the clip is not seated tightly against the bushing and that the linkage moves freely.

57   Reattach the primary and secondary vacuum break links and install the vacuum break and idle speed solenoid assemblies

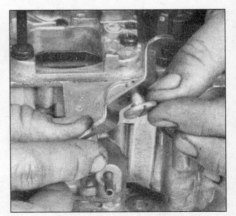

8.58b Inserting the pump rod mounting screw through the pump rod prior to installation

(see illustration).

58   Engage the pump rod with the pump rod lever **(see illustration)**, install a new retaining clip on the pump rod and install the pump lever on the air horn with the washer between the lever and the air horn **(see illustration)**.

8.62 Installing a new gasket on top of the air horn

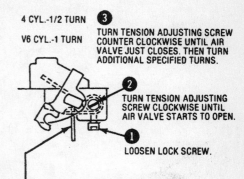

4 CYL.-1/2 TURN
V6 CYL.-1 TURN

3 TURN TENSION ADJUSTING SCREW COUNTER CLOCKWISE UNTIL AIR VALVE JUST CLOSES. THEN TURN ADDITIONAL SPECIFIED TURNS.

2 TURN TENSION ADJUSTING SCREW CLOCKWISE UNTIL AIR VALVE STARTS TO OPEN.

1 LOOSEN LOCK SCREW.

NOTE: USE LITHIUM BASE GREASE TO LUBRICATE AIR VALVE SHAFT PIN.

Illustration courtesy of Tomco Industries

8.64a E2SE carburetor air valve spring adjustment procedure

59 Reconnect the vacuum break hoses.
60 Install the fuel filter with the hole facing toward the inlet nut.
61 Place a new gasket on the inlet nut and install and tighten it securely. Take care not to over tighten the nut, as it could damage the gasket, leading to a fuel leak.
62 Install a new gasket on the top of the air horn **(see illustration)**.
63 Check that all linkage hook-ups have been made and that they do not bind.
64 Adjust the external linkage **(see illustrations)**.

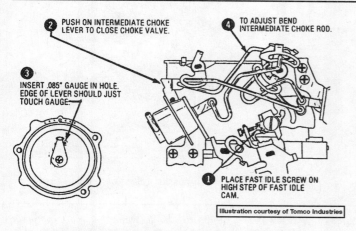

2 PUSH ON INTERMEDIATE CHOKE LEVER TO CLOSE CHOKE VALVE.

4 TO ADJUST BEND INTERMEDIATE CHOKE ROD.

3 INSERT .085" GAUGE IN HOLE. EDGE OF LEVER SHOULD JUST TOUCH GAUGE.

1 PLACE FAST IDLE SCREW ON HIGH STEP OF FAST IDLE CAM.

Illustration courtesy of Tomco Industries

8.64b E2SE carburetor choke coil lever adjustment procedure (typical)

1 ROTATE DEGREE SCALE UNTIL ZERO (0) IS OPPOSITE POINTER.

2 CHOKE VALVE HELD COMPLETELY CLOSED. PLACE MAGNET SQUARELY ON TOP OF CHOKE VALVE.

3 ROTATE BUBBLE UNTIL IT IS CENTERED.

4 ROTATE SCALE SO THAT DEGREE SPECIFIED FOR ADJUSTMENT IS OPPOSITE POINTER.

5 FOLLOW NUMERICAL OUTLINE IN MAKING ADJUSTMENT.

CAUTION: PLACE CARBURETOR ON HOLDING FIXTURE SO THAT IT WILL REMAIN IN SAME POSITION WHEN GAUGE IS IN PLACE.

GAUGE: J-26701 KENT MOORE TOOL
BT-7704 BORROUGHS TOOL

Illustration courtesy of Tomco Industries

ANGLE GAUGE: BASIC ADJUSTMENT
CONTINUE NUMERICAL OUTLINE IN EACH ADJUSTMENT USING DEGREE SETTING.

8.64c Measuring the E2SE carburetor choke valve angle with an angle gauge

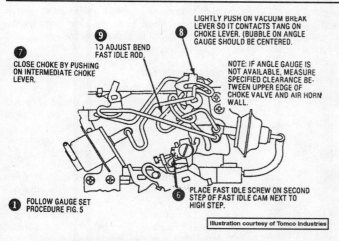

7 CLOSE CHOKE BY PUSHING ON INTERMEDIATE CHOKE LEVER.

10 TO ADJUST BEND FAST IDLE ROD.

8 LIGHTLY PUSH ON VACUUM BREAK LEVER SO IT CONTACTS TANG ON CHOKE LEVER. (BUBBLE ON ANGLE GAUGE SHOULD BE CENTERED.

NOTE: IF ANGLE GAUGE IS NOT AVAILABLE, MEASURE SPECIFIED CLEARANCE BETWEEN UPPER EDGE OF CHOKE VALVE AND AIR HORN WALL.

1 FOLLOW GAUGE SET PROCEDURE FIG. 5

6 PLACE FAST IDLE SCREW ON SECOND STEP OF FAST IDLE CAM NEXT TO HIGH STEP.

Illustration courtesy of Tomco Industries

8.64d E2SE carburetor choke rod fast idle cam adjustment procedure

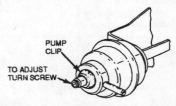

PUMP CLIP

TO ADJUST TURN SCREW

1. REMOVE VACUUM BREAK ASSY. AND CAREFULLY GRIND OFF ADJUSTMENT SCREW CAP.
2. FOLLOW PRI. OR SEC. VAC. BREAK ADJUSTMENT PROCEDURE.
3. ON PRIMARY SIDE MAKE SURE VAC. DIAPHRAGM IS FULLY SEATED. BEND AIR VALVE ROD TO OBTAIN A SLIGHT CLEARANCE BETWEEN ROD AND END OF SLOT. (FOLLOW PRI. VAC. BREAK ADJ. WITH AIR VALVE ROD. ADJ.)
4. ON DELAY MODELS, PLUG AIR BLEED HOLE WITH A VERAJET TYPE PUMP PLUNGER CUP.
5. TO ADJUST USE A 1/8" HEX WRENCH TO TURN SCREW IN REAR COVER UNTIL BUBBL EIS CENTERED. (REMOVE CUP AFTER ADJUSTMENT.)
6. SEAL ADJ. SCREW WITH A SEALER. (SUCH AS A SILICONE SEALANT RTV RUBBER OR EQUIVALENT.)

Illustration courtesy of Tomco Industries

8.64e E2SE carburetor vacuum break adjustment details

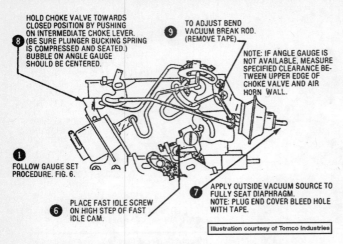

**8.64f E2SE carburetor primary vacuum break adjustment
procedure for models with dual vacuum break units**

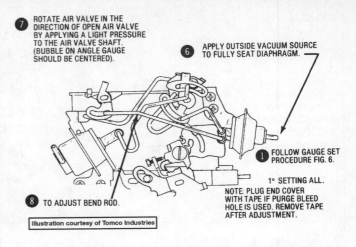

8.64g E2SE carburetor air valve link adjustment procedure

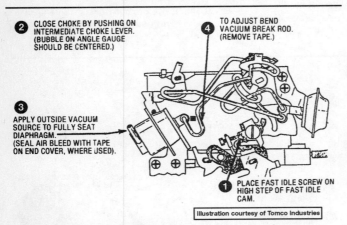

**8.64h E2SE carburetor secondary vacuum break
adjustment procedure**

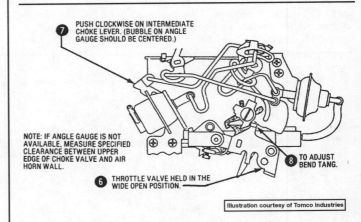

8.64i E2SE carburetor unloader adjustment procedure

9 Carburetor (DCH340/DFP340) - overhaul and adjustment

Warning: Gasoline is extremely flammable, so take extra precautions when you work on any part of the fuel system. Do not smoke or allow open flames or bare light bulbs near the work area, and don't work in a garage where a natural gas-type appliance (such as a water heater or clothes dryer) with a pilot light is present. If you spill any fuel on your skin, rinse it off immediately with soap and water. When you perform any kind of work on the fuel system, wear safety glasses and have a Class B type fire extinguisher on hand.

Note: Carburetor overhaul is an involved procedure that requires some experience. The home mechanic without much experience should have the overhaul done by a dealer service department or repair shop. Because of running production changes, some details of the unit overhauled here may not exactly match those of your carburetor, although the home mechanic with previous experience should be able to detect the differences and modify the procedure.

Disassembly

Refer to illustration 9.2

1 Remove the two throttle return springs.
2 Disconnect the accelerator pump lever **(see illustration)**.
3 Remove the choke lead connector mounting bracket from the carburetor.
4 Disconnect the switch vent valve wire.
5 Disconnect the choke connecting rod from the fast idle lever by removing the circlip.
6 Disconnect the vacuum hose from the choke chamber. Remove the four screws from the choke chamber assembly and remove the assembly.
7 Remove the circlip retaining the vacuum

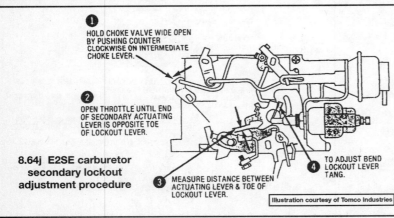

**8.64j E2SE carburetor
secondary lockout
adjustment procedure**

9.2 Exploded view of the Hitachi DCH340 carburetor

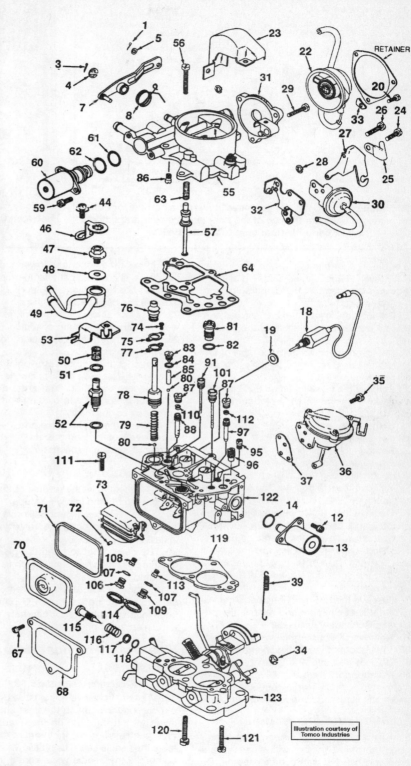

1 Cotter pin	64 Not used
2 Screw and lockwasher	65 Not used
3 Cotter pin	66 Not used
4 Accelerator pump lever retainer	67 Screw
	68 Level gauge cover
5 Washer	69 Not used
6 Not used	70 Level gauge
7 Accelerator pump lever	71 Level gauge seal
8 Pump lever spring	72 Float collar
9 Not used	73 Float
10 Not used	74 Screw and lockwasher
11 Not used	
12 Screw and lockwasher	75 Accelerator pump plate
13 Coasting valve solenoid	
14 O-ring	76 Pump plate boot
15 Not used	77 Pump plate gasket
16 Not used	78 Accelerator pump
17 Not used	79 Pump return spring
18 Anti-dieseling solenoid	
19 Gasket	80 Pump intake check ball
20 Screw	
21 Not used	81 Power valve assembly
22 Choke cover assembly	
23 Choke linkage cover	82 Power valve gasket
24 Screw and lockwasher	
25 Wire clamp	83 Pump discharge needle plug
26 Screw and lockwasher	
27 Cable bracket	84 Gasket
28 Retainer	85 Pump discharge needle
29 Choke housing screw	
30 Vacuum break (primary)	86 Primary slow air bleed jet
31 Choke cover housing	
32 Bracket	87 Plug
33 Spacer	88 Primary slow jet
34 E-clip	89 Not used
35 Screw and lockwasher	90 Not used
36 Secondary vacuum break	91 Primary main air bleed jet
	92 Not used
37 Gasket	93 Not used
38 Not used	94 Not used
39 Spring	95 Coasting air bleed jet
40 Cotter pin	
41 Not used	96 Coasting jet
42 Not used	97 Secondary slow jet
43 Not used	
44 Not used	98 Not used
45 Not used	99 Not used
46 Banjo bolt lock	100 Not used
47 Banjo bolt	101 Secondary main air bleed jet
48 Sealing washer	
49 Banjo fitting	102 Not used
50 Fuel inlet screen	103 Not used
51 Sealing washer	104 Not used
52 Fuel inlet valve and gasket	105 Not used
	106 Primary main jet plug
53 Banjo fitting stop bracket	
54 Not used	107 Gasket
55 Air horn assembly	108 Primary main jet
56 Screw and lockwasher	109 Secondary main jet plug
57 Power piston assembly	
58 Not used	110 Primary slow jet spring
59 Screw and lockwasher	111 Screw and lockwasher
60 Bowl vent solenoid	112 Secondary slow jet spring
61 O-ring	
62 O-ring	113 Secondary main jet
63 Power piston spring	

114 Plugs	119 Throttle body gasket
115 Idle mixture screw	120 Screw and lockwasher
116 Spring	121 Screw and lockwasher
117 Washer	122 Bowl assembly
118 Seal	123 Throttle body assembly

4

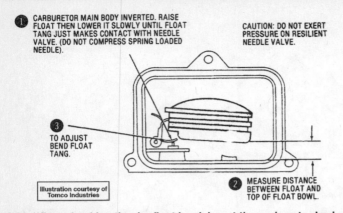

9.32 When checking the dry float level, invert the carburetor body and measure between the top of the float and the roof of the float bowl; bend the float tang to adjust the level

9.33 To check the float drop adjustment, invert the carburetor body, raise the float against its stop and measure the gap between the float tang and the needle valve; bend the float stop tang to change the gap

break diaphragm plunger to the secondary throttle lever. Remove the diaphragm assembly screws and remove the diaphragm from the carburetor.

8   Remove the float chamber screws and separate the float chamber from the throttle chamber.

9   Remove the screws from the base of the accelerator pump and remove the accelerator pump assembly.

10   Remove the fuel inlet fitting and strainer. Be careful not to distort the strainer during removal.

11   Using a six-point socket, remove the float needle valve.

12   Remove the three screws from the float bowl cover and remove the cover. Carefully remove the float and float collar.

13   Remove the jets from the top of the float chamber.

14   Remove the injector weight plug and the injector weight and check ball. On California models there will also be a spring.

15   Using a screwdriver, remove the power valve from the base of the float chamber (be sure that the screwdriver blade fits the valve head snugly).

16   Remove the two main jet plugs from the top of the float chamber and remove the primary and secondary main jets.

17   Remove the primary slow air bleed jet from the bottom of the choke chamber.

18   Do not remove the primary throttle valve, secondary throttle valve or choke valve. Also, on California models, do not remove the slow and main actuators.

Cleaning and inspection

19   Clean the choke chamber, float chamber and throttle chamber with clean solvent and blow them out with compressed air. Do not use a piece of wire for cleaning the jets and passages.

20   Do not immerse any rubber or plastic parts in solvent because they will harden, swell or distort.

21   Make sure all fuel passages, jets and other metering components are free of burrs and dirt.

22   Inspect the upper and lower surfaces of the choke chamber, float chamber and throttle chamber for damage. Be sure all gasket material has been removed.

23   Inspect all lever holes for excessive wear and an out-of-round condition.

24   Inspect the fuel inlet strainer for corrosion and damage.

25   Inspect the rubber cup on the pump plunger for excessive wear or cracks.

26   Inspect the float, float arms and float collar for distortion and binding and correct or replace as necessary.

27   Check the choke valve and linkage for excessive wear, binding and distortion and correct or replace as necessary.

Reassembly

28   Reassembly is the reverse of disassembly, but refer to the following steps:

29   On all vehicles except California models, be careful not to bend the valve rod when installing the power valve.

30   Be careful not to bend the piston connecting rod when reassembling the accelerator pump.

31   If the main actuator was removed, be sure to apply grease to the O-ring before installation and tighten it carefully to avoid damaging the O-ring.

Float level and float drop adjustment

Refer to illustrations 9.32 and 9.33

32   The dry float level is adjusted by holding the carburetor body so the float chamber is inverted. Lift the float off the needle valve, then gently lower it until the float tang contacts the needle valve. Don't allow the float to compress the needle valve spring. Measure the distance between the top of the float and the top of the float bowl **(see illustration)**. The clearance should be 21/64-inch. If it isn't, bend the float tang to change the float level.

33   The float drop is checked by measuring the stroke of the needle valve. Invert the float chamber and raise the float completely. Measure the clearance between the fully seated

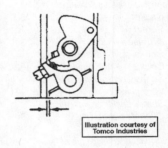

9.36 Primary throttle valve clearance is measured with the fast idle screw on the highest step of the fast idle cam (choke completely closed)

valve stem and the float tang **(see illustration)**. A number 53 drill bit works well for this procedure (the specified clearance is 1.5 mm). The drill bit should just fit between the tang of the raised float and the valve stem - do not force it!

Primary throttle valve adjustment

Refer to illustration 9.36

34   Close the choke valve completely.

35   Turn the throttle stop screw all the way in.

36   Measure the clearance between the throttle valve and the wall of the throttle valve chamber **(see illustration)**. Again, a drill bit will work well as a gauge. Use a number 54 or 55 drill bit for vehicles equipped with manual transmissions. A number 51, 52 or 53 bit will work for vehicles equipped with automatic transmissions.

37   If necessary, adjust the throttle valve opening by turning the fast idle screw.

Secondary throttle valve adjustment

Refer to illustration 9.38

38   The secondary throttle valve should begin to open when the primary throttle valve

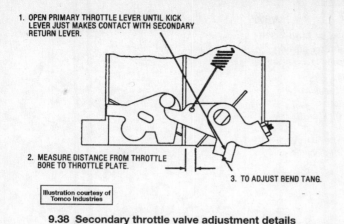

1. OPEN PRIMARY THROTTLE LEVER UNTIL KICK LEVER JUST MAKES CONTACT WITH SECONDARY RETURN LEVER.

2. MEASURE DISTANCE FROM THROTTLE BORE TO THROTTLE PLATE.

3. TO ADJUST BEND TANG.

Illustration courtesy of Tomco Industries

9.38 Secondary throttle valve adjustment details

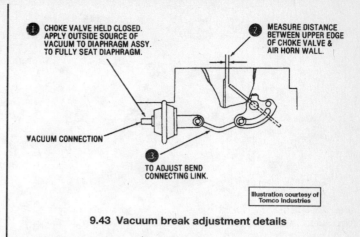

1. CHOKE VALVE HELD CLOSED. APPLY OUTSIDE SOURCE OF VACUUM TO DIAPHRAGM ASSY. TO FULLY SEAT DIAPHRAGM.

2. MEASURE DISTANCE BETWEEN UPPER EDGE OF CHOKE VALVE & AIR HORN WALL.

VACUUM CONNECTION

3. TO ADJUST BEND CONNECTING LINK.

Illustration courtesy of Tomco Industries

9.43 Vacuum break adjustment details

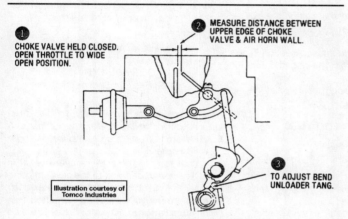

1. CHOKE VALVE HELD CLOSED. OPEN THROTTLE TO WIDE OPEN POSITION.

2. MEASURE DISTANCE BETWEEN UPPER EDGE OF CHOKE VALVE & AIR HORN WALL.

3. TO ADJUST BEND UNLOADER TANG.

Illustration courtesy of Tomco Industries

9.46 Choke unloader adjustment details

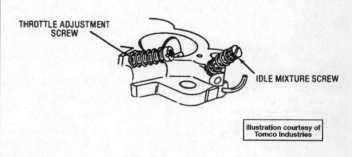

THROTTLE ADJUSTMENT SCREW

IDLE MIXTURE SCREW

Illustration courtesy of Tomco Industries

9.51 Throttle adjustment and idle mixture screws

4

opens to an angle of 47-degrees. Using a drill bit as a gauge, measure the clearance between the center of the primary throttle valve and the throttle chamber wall when the return plate is brought into contact with the kick lever **(see illustration)**. Standard clearance is 0.24 to 0.30 inches (6.1 to 7.6 mm).

39   If necessary, adjust the opening point of the secondary throttle valve by bending the kick lever where it comes into contact with the return plate.

Kick lever adjustment

40   Close the primary throttle valve by turning the throttle adjustment screw out (count the turns for future reference).

41   Loosen the locknut on the kick lever screw and turn the screw until it comes into contact with the return plate. Tighten the lock screw.

42   Reset the throttle adjustment screw.

Vacuum break adjustment

Refer to illustration 9.43

43   Connect a hand-held vacuum pump to the fitting on the vacuum servo **(see illustration)**.

44   Actuate the throttle and close the choke valve, then apply vacuum and measure the distance between the choke valve and the air horn wall. The clearance should be approximately 3/32 to 7/64-inch. If not, bend the connecting link to change the clearance.

Choke unloader adjustment

Refer to illustration 9.46

45   Hold the choke valve closed and rotate the throttle valve to the wide-open position.

46   Measure the clearance between the choke valve and the air horn wall **(see illustration)**. The clearance should be approximately 3/32-inch. If not, bend the unloader tang as necessary to achieve the desired clearance.

Idle mixture and idle speed adjustment

Refer to illustration 9.51

47   As a preliminary adjustment, turn the idle mixture screw in completely then back it out 1-1/2 turns.

48   Connect a tachometer in accordance with the tool manufacturer's instructions.

49   Start the engine and allow it to reach normal operating temperature.

50   Check and, if necessary, adjust the ignition timing (see Chapter 1).

51   Turn the throttle adjustment screw to achieve an engine speed of 850 rpm (Federal) or 900 rpm (California) **(see illustration)**.

52   Turn the idle mixture screw to obtain the highest possible rpm and the smoothest idle.

53   Repeat Step 51, then turn the idle mixture screw clockwise to adjust the engine speed to 800 rpm (Federal) or 900 +/- 50 rpm (California).

54   If the vehicle is equipped with air conditioning, turn the air conditioning on to MAX and turn the blower to HI. Open the throttle far enough to actuate the idle speed-up solenoid, then release the throttle. Turn the idle speed-up solenoid adjusting screw to achieve an engine speed of 900 rpm.

10   Fuel injection system - general information

Refer to illustrations 10.2a and 10.2b

Electronic fuel injection provides optimum air/fuel mixture ratios at all stages of combustion and offers better throttle response characteristics than carburetion. It also enables the engine to run at the leanest possible air/fuel mixture ratio, greatly reducing exhaust gas emissions.

Three types of Throttle Body Injection

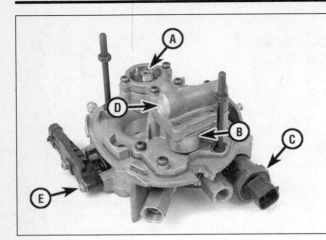

10.2a   Typical Model 300 TBI unit on earlier four-cylinder engines

A   Fuel injector
B   Fuel pressure regulator
C   Idle Air Control (IAC) valve
D   Fuel meter cover
E   Throttle Position Sensor (TPS)

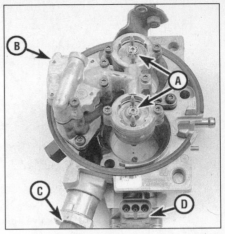

10.2b   Typical Model 220 TBI unit on V6 powered vehicles

A   Fuel injectors
B   Fuel pressure regulator (under fuel meter cover)
C   Idle Air Control (IAC) valve
D   Throttle Position Sensor (TPS)

(TBI) units are employed on the vehicles covered by this manual **(see illustrations)**. The Model 300 is used on earlier four-cylinder engines; the Model 700 is used on later vehicles with four-cylinder engines. The Model 220 is used on V6 engines.

Both the 300 and the 700 are single injector designs. All fuel injected V6 engines with Throttle Body Injection utilize the Model 220 twin-injector model.

Although they differ somewhat in design, there is very little difference in function between these three TBI units.

All three TBI systems are controlled by an Electronic Control Module (ECM), which monitors engine performance and adjusts the air/fuel mixture accordingly during all engine operating conditions.

An electric fuel pump located in the fuel tank with the fuel gauge sending unit pumps fuel to the TBI unit through the fuel feed line and an in-line fuel filter. A pressure regulator in the TBI keeps fuel available to the injector(s) at a constant pressure between 9 and 13 psi. Fuel in excess of injector needs is returned to the fuel tank by a separate line.

11   Model 300 Throttle Body Injection (TBI) - overhaul

Refer to illustrations 11.5, 11.7, 11.8a, 11.8b, 11.10, 11.11, 11.17, 11.18, 11.19, 11.25, 11.26 and 11.35

Warning: *Gasoline is extremely flammable, so take extra precautions when you work on any part of the fuel system. Do not smoke or allow open flames or bare light bulbs near the work area, and don't work in a garage where a natural gas-type appliance (such as a water heater or clothes dryer) with a pilot light is present. If you spill any fuel on your skin, rinse it off immediately with soap and water. When you perform any kind of work on the fuel system, wear safety glasses and have a Class B type fire extinguisher on hand.*

Note: *Because of its relative simplicity, a throttle body assembly does not need to be removed from the intake manifold nor completely disassembled for component replace-*

ment. However, for the sake of clarity, the following procedures are shown with the TBI unit removed from the vehicle.
1   Relieve the fuel pressure (see Section 2).
2   Detach the cable from the negative terminal of the battery.
3   Remove the air cleaner housing assembly, adapter and gaskets.

Fuel meter cover and fuel injector

Disassembly
4   Remove the injector electrical connector (on top of the TBI) by squeezing the two tabs together and pulling straight up.
5   Unscrew the fuel meter cover retaining screws and lockwashers securing the fuel meter cover to the fuel meter body. Note the location of the two short screws **(see illustration)**.
6   Remove the fuel meter cover. **Caution:** *Do not immerse the fuel meter cover in solvent. It might damage the pressure regulator diaphragm and gasket.*
7   The fuel meter cover contains the fuel pressure regulator, which is pre-set and plugged at the factory. If a malfunction occurs, it cannot be serviced, and must be replaced as a complete assembly. **Warning:**

Do not remove the screws securing the pressure regulator to the fuel meter cover **(see illustration)**. *It has a large spring inside under heavy compression.*
8   With the old fuel meter cover gasket in place to prevent damage to the casting, carefully pry the injector from the fuel meter body with a screwdriver until it can be lifted free **(see illustrations)**. **Caution:** *Use care in removing the injector to prevent damage to the electrical connector terminals, the injector fuel filter, the O-ring and the nozzle.*
9   The fuel meter body should be removed from the throttle body if it needs to be cleaned. To remove it, remove the fuel feed and return line fittings and the Torx screws that attach the fuel meter body to the throttle body.
10   Remove the old gasket from the fuel meter cover and discard it. Remove the large O-ring and steel back-up washer from the upper counterbore of the fuel meter body

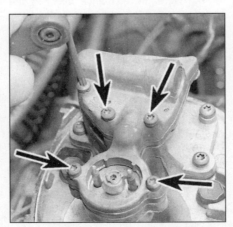

11.5 Remove the fuel metering screws (arrows) (Model 300 unit shown)

11.7 The fuel pressure regulator is installed in the fuel meter cover and pre-adjusted by the factory - do not remove the four retaining screws (arrows) or you may damage the regulator

11.8a The best way to remove the fuel injector is to pry on it with a screwdriver, using a second screwdriver as a fulcrum

11.8b Note the position of the terminals on top and the dowel pin on the bottom of the injector in relation to the fuel meter cover when you lift the injector out of the cover

11.10 Remove the large O-ring and steel washer from the injector cavity

injector cavity **(see illustration)**. Clean the fuel meter body thoroughly in solvent and blow dry.

11   Remove the small O-ring from the nozzle end of the injector. Carefully rotate the injector fuel filter back and forth and remove the filter from the base of the injector **(see illustration)**. Gently clean the filter in solvent and allow it to drip dry. It is too small and delicate to dry with compressed air.
Caution: *The fuel injector itself is an electrical component. Do not immerse it in any type of cleaning solvent.*

12   The fuel injector is not serviceable. If it is malfunctioning, replace it as an assembly.

Reassembly

13   Install the clean fuel injector nozzle filter on the end of the fuel injector with the larger end of the filter facing the injector so that the filter covers the raised rib at the base of the injector. Use a twisting motion to position the filter against the base of the injector.

14   Lubricate a new small O-ring with automatic transmission fluid. Push the O-ring

onto the nozzle end of the injector until it presses against the injector fuel filter.

15   Insert the steel backup washer in the top counterbore of the fuel meter body injector cavity.

16   Lubricate a new large O-ring with automatic transmission fluid and install it directly over the backup washer. Be sure that the O-ring is seated properly in the cavity and is flush with the top of the fuel meter body casting surface. **Caution:** *The back-up washer and large O-ring must be installed before the injector or improper seating of the large O-ring could cause fuel to leak.*

17   Install the injector in the cavity in the fuel meter body, aligning the raised lug on the injector base with the cast-in notch in the fuel meter body cavity. Push straight down on the injector with both thumbs **(see illustration)** until it is fully seated in the cavity. **Note:** *The electrical terminals of the injector should be approximately parallel to the throttle shaft.*

18   Install a new fuel outlet passage gasket

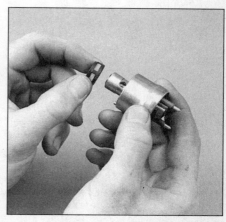

11.11 Gently rotate the fuel injector filter back and forth and carefully pull it off the nozzle

on the fuel meter cover and a new fuel meter cover gasket on the fuel meter body **(see illustration)**.

11.17 Make sure that the lug is aligned with the notch in the bottom of the fuel injector cavity

11.18 Position the fuel outlet passage gasket (A) and the fuel meter cover gasket (B) properly

4

19 Install a new dust seal into the recess on the fuel meter body (see illustration).
20 Install the fuel meter cover onto the fuel meter body, making sure that the pressure regulator dust seal and cover gaskets are in place.
21 Apply non-hardening thread locking compound to the threads of the fuel meter cover attaching screws. Install the screws (the two short screws go next to the injector) and tighten them securely.
22 Plug in the electrical connector to the injector.
23 Install the air cleaner.

Idle Air Control (IAC) valve

Removal

24 Unplug the electrical connector at the IAC valve.
25 Remove the IAC valve with a wrench on the hex surface only (see illustration).

Installation

26 Before installing a new IAC valve, measure the distance the valve is extended (see illustration). The measurement should be made from the motor housing to the end of the cone. The distance should be no greater than 1-1/8 inch. If the cone is extended too far, damage may occur to the valve when it is installed.
27 Identify the replacement IAC valve as either a Type I (with a collar at the electric terminal end) or a Type II (without a collar). If the measured dimension "A" is greater than 1-1/8 inch, the distance must be reduced as follows:
Type I - Exert firm pressure on the valve to retract it (a slight side-to-side movement may be helpful) (see illustration 13.41a).
Type II - Compress the retaining spring of the valve while turning the valve in a clockwise direction (see illustration 13.41b). Return the spring to its original position with the straight portion of the spring aligned with the flat surface of the valve.
28 Install the new IAC valve to the throttle

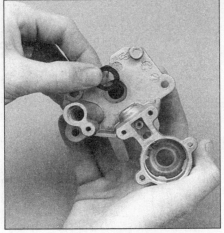

11.19 Install a new dust seal into the recess of the fuel meter body

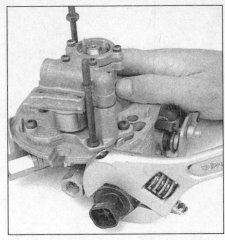

11.25 Remove the IAC valve with a large wrench, but be careful - it's a delicate device

body. Use the new gasket supplied with the assembly.
29 Plug in the electrical connector.
30 Install the air cleaner.
31 Start the engine and allow it to reach normal operating temperature. The Electronic Control Module (ECM) will reset the idle speed when the vehicle is driven above 35 mph.

Throttle Position Sensor (TPS)

32 The Throttle Position Sensor (TPS) is connected to the throttle shaft on the TBI unit. As the throttle valve angle is changed (as the accelerator pedal is moved), the output of the TPS also changes. At a closed throttle position, the output of the TPS is below 1.25-volts. As the throttle valve opens, the output increases so that, at wide-open throttle, the output voltage is approximately 5-volts.
33 A broken or loose TPS can cause intermittent bursts of fuel from the injector and an unstable idle, because the ECM thinks the throttle is moving. A problem in any of the

TPS circuits will set either a Code 21 or 22 (see Chapter 6, Section 3).
34 The TPS is not adjustable. The ECM uses the reading at idle for the zero reading. If the TPS malfunctions, it is replaced as a unit.
35 Unscrew the two Torx screws (see illustration) and remove the TPS.
36 Install the new TPS. **Note:** *Make sure that the tang on the lever is properly engaged with the stop on the TBI.*
37 Install the air cleaner assembly.
38 Attach the cable to the negative terminal of the battery.
39 With the ignition switch on and the engine off, check for fuel leaks.

---

12 Model 700 Throttle Body Injection (TBI) - overhaul

Refer to illustrations 12.5, 12.6, 12.32, 12.33, 12.51 and 12.62
Warning: *Gasoline is extremely flammable,*

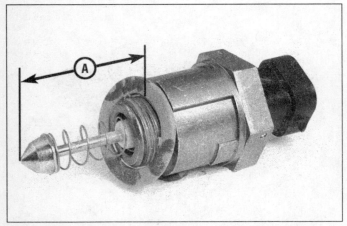

11.26 Distance A should be less than 1-1/8 inch - if it isn't, determine what kind of IAC valve you have and adjust it accordingly

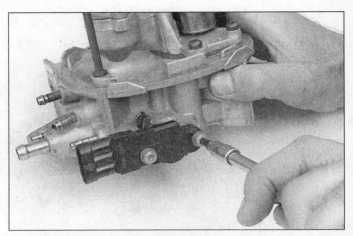

11.35 The Throttle Position Sensor (TPS) is mounted to the side of the TBI with two Torx screws

12.5 Remove the injector retaining screw and retainer

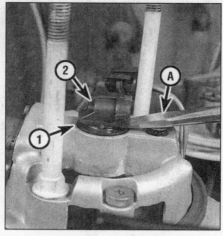

12.6 To remove the fuel injector unit (2) from the fuel meter body (1), insert a screwdriver (A) under the fuel injector flange and pry the injector loose

so take extra precautions when you work on any part of the fuel system. Do not smoke or allow open flames or bare light bulbs near the work area, and don't work in a garage where a natural gas-type appliance (such as a water heater or clothes dryer) with a pilot light is present. If you spill any fuel on your skin, rinse it off immediately with soap and water. When you perform any kind of work on the fuel system, wear safety glasses and have a Class B type fire extinguisher on hand.

Note: *Because of its relative simplicity, the throttle body does not need to be removed from the intake manifold or disassembled for component replacement. However, for the sake of clarity, the following procedures are shown with the TBI removed from the vehicle.*

1   Relieve the fuel pressure (see Section 2).
2   Detach the cable from the negative terminal of the battery.
3   Remove the air cleaner housing assembly, adapter and gaskets.

Fuel injector

4   Unplug the electrical connector from the fuel injector.
5   Remove the injector retainer screw and retainer **(see illustration)**.
6   To remove the fuel injector assembly, place a screwdriver blade under the ridge and carefully pry it out **(see illustration)**.
7   Remove the upper and lower O-rings from the injector and from the fuel injector cavity and discard them.
8   Inspect the fuel injector filter for evidence of dirt and contamination. If present, look for the presence of dirt in the fuel lines and the fuel tank.
9   Lubricate new upper and lower O-rings with transmission fluid and install them on the injector. Make sure that the upper O-ring is in the groove and the lower one is flush up against the filter.
10   To install the injector assembly, push it straight into the fuel injector cavity. Be sure that the electrical connector end on the injector is facing in the general direction of the

cut-out in the fuel meter body for the wire grommet. **Note:** *If you are installing a new injector, be sure to replace the old unit with an identical part. Injectors from other models will fit in the Model 700 TBI assembly but are calibrated for different flow rates.*
11   Using thread locking compound on the retainer attaching screw, install the injector retainer and tighten the retaining screw.
12   Install the air cleaner housing assembly, adapter and gaskets.
13   With the engine off and the ignition on, check for fuel leaks.

Fuel pressure regulator

14   Remove the four pressure regulator attaching screws while keeping the pressure regulator compressed. **Caution:** *The pressure regulator contains a large spring under heavy compression. Use care when removing the screws to prevent personal injury.*
15   Remove the pressure regulator cover assembly.
16   Remove the pressure regulator spring, seat, and the pressure regulator diaphragm.
17   Using a magnifying glass, if necessary, inspect the pressure regulator seat in the fuel meter body cavity for pitting, nicks or irregularities. If any damage is present, the entire

fuel body casting must be replaced.
18   Install the new pressure regulator diaphragm assembly. Make sure it is seated in the groove in the fuel meter body.
19   Install the regulator spring seat and spring into the cover assembly.
20   Install the cover assembly over the diaphragm while aligning the mounting holes. **Caution:** *Use care while installing the pressure regulator to prevent misalignment and possible leaks.*
21   While maintaining pressure on the regulator spring, install the four screw assemblies that have been coated with thread locking compound.
22   Reconnect the negative battery cable. With the engine off and the ignition on, check for fuel leaks.

Throttle Position Sensor (TPS)

23   Unplug the electrical connector from the TPS.
24   Remove the two TPS attaching screws and remove the TPS from the throttle body.
25   With the throttle valve closed, install the TPS on the throttle shaft. Rotate it counterclockwise to align the mounting holes.
26   Install the two TPS attaching screws.
27   Install the air cleaner housing assembly, adapter and gaskets.
28   Attach the cable to the negative terminal of the battery. **Note:** *See non-adjustable TPS output check at end of this Section.*

Idle Air Control (IAC) valve

29   Unplug the electrical connector from the IAC valve and remove the IAC valve mounting screws and the IAC valve.
30   Remove the O-ring from the IAC valve and discard it.
31   Clean the IAC valve seating surfaces on the throttle body to assure proper sealing of the new O-ring and proper contact of the IAC valve flange.
32   Before installing a new IAC valve, measure the distance between the tip of the valve pintle and the flange mounting surface when the pintle is fully extended **(see illustration)**. If dimension "A" is greater than 1-1/8 inches, it must be reduced to prevent damage to the valve.
33   To retract the IAC valve, grasp the IAC valve as shown and exert firm pressure with

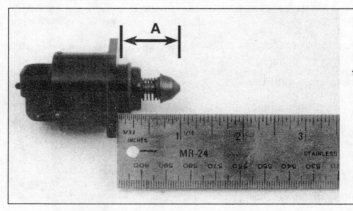

12.32 Measuring the pintle extension on a flange-type IAC valve

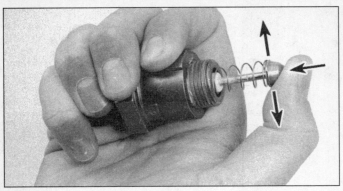

12.33 To adjust the IAC valve pintle, grasp it as shown and, using a side-to-side motion with your thumb, press it firmly down into the valve

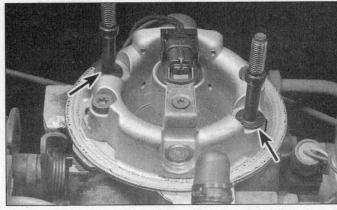

12.51 Remove the throttle body mounting studs (arrows)

12.62 To gain access to the factory sealed idle stop screw, remove the plug (arrow) by piercing it with an awl, then levering it loose

your thumb, using a slight side-to-side movement on the valve pintle **(see illustration)**.

34   Lubricate a new O-ring with transmission fluid and install it on the IAC valve.

35   Install the IAC valve to the throttle body. Coat the IAC valve attaching screws with thread locking compound. Install and tighten them securely. Plug in the IAC valve electrical connector.

36   Install the air cleaner housing assembly, adapter and gaskets.

37   Attach the cable to the negative terminal of the battery.

38   Start the engine, allow it to reach operating temperature, then take the vehicle for a drive. When the engine reaches normal operating temperature the ECM will set the proper idle speed.

Tube module assembly

39   Remove the tube module assembly attaching screws and remove the tube module.

40   Remove the tube module gasket and discard it. Clean any old gasket material from the surface of the throttle body to insure proper sealing of the new gasket.

41   Install the new tube module gasket.

42   Install the tube module and tighten the screws securely..

43   Install the air cleaner housing assembly, adapter and gaskets.

Fuel meter assembly

44   Remove the TBI unit (see Step 50).

45   Remove the two fuel meter body attaching screws and washers and remove the fuel meter assembly from the throttle body.

46   If you are installing a new fuel meter, remove the fuel pressure regulator and the fuel outlet nut and transfer them to the new fuel meter.

47   Remove the fuel meter body-to-throttle body gasket and discard it.

48   Install a new fuel meter-to-throttle body gasket. Match the cutout portions of the gasket with the openings in the throttle body.

49   Install the fuel meter onto the throttle body and tighten the attaching screws.

Throttle body assembly

50   Unplug the electrical connectors from

the fuel injector, IAC and TPS.

51   Remove the two throttle body mounting studs **(see illustration)**.

52   Remove and discard the throttle body-to-intake manifold gasket. Place the TBI assembly on a clean work surface.

53   Remove the fuel injector, fuel meter assembly, TPS, IAC valve and the tube module.

54   Install the new tube module assembly, IAC valve and TPS on the new throttle body assembly.

55   Install a new fuel meter body-to-throttle body gasket.

56   Install the fuel meter assembly and fuel injector.

57   Install a new throttle body-to-intake manifold gasket and install the throttle body assembly on the intake manifold. Tighten the mounting studs to the specified torque.

Minimum idle speed adjustment

Note: *This adjustment should be performed only when the throttle body assembly has been replaced. The engine should be at normal operating temperature before making the adjustment.*

58   Plug any vacuum line ports as required (see the VECI label).

59   With the IAC valve connected, ground the diagnostic terminal of the ALDL connector **(see illustration 14.6)**.

60   Turn the ignition on but do not start the engine. Wait at least 30 seconds to allow the IAC valve pintle to extend and seat in the throttle body. Unplug the IAC valve electrical connector.

61   Remove the ground jumper from the diagnostic terminal and start the engine.

62   The throttle stop screw used for regulating minimum idle speed is adjusted at the factory. The screw is covered with a plug to discourage unauthorized adjustments. To remove the plug, pierce it with an awl **(see illustration)**, then apply leverage.

63   With the transmission in Neutral (manual) or Park (automatic), adjust the idle stop screw to obtain the specified rpm.

64   Turn the ignition off and reconnect the IAC valve electrical connector, unplug any

plugged vacuum line ports and install the air cleaner housing assembly, adapter and gaskets.

Non-adjustable TPS output check

Note: *This check should be performed only when the throttle body or the throttle position sensor has been replaced or after the minimum idle speed has been adjusted.*

65   Connect a digital voltmeter from center terminal "B" to outside terminal "A" of the TPS connector.

66   With the ignition on and the engine stopped, the TPS voltage should be as listed in the Specifications. If the voltage is greater than specified, replace the TPS.

13   Model 220 Throttle Body Injection (TBI) - overhaul

Refer to illustrations 13.6, 13.7, 13.14, 13.16, 13.21, 13.22, 13.23, 13.24, 13.25, 13.37, 13.41a, 13.41b, 13.41c, 13.50, 13.52, 13.65 and 13.66

Warning: *Gasoline is extremely flammable,*

13.6   Carefully peel away the old fuel meter outlet passage gasket and fuel meter cover gasket with a razor blade

13.7   Never remove the four pressure regulator screws (arrows) from the fuel meter cover

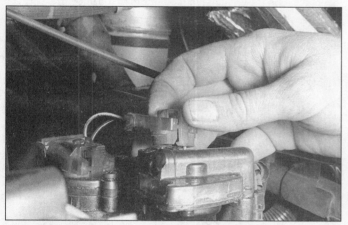

13.14   To remove either injector electrical connector, squeeze the two tabs on each connector and lift straight up

13.16   To remove an injector, slip the tip of a flat-bladed screwdriver under the lip of the lug on top of the injector and, using another screwdriver as a fulcrum, carefully pry the injector up and out

4

so take extra precautions when you work on any part of the fuel system. Do not smoke or allow open flames or bare light bulbs near the work area, and don't work in a garage where a natural gas-type appliance (such as a water heater or clothes dryer) with a pilot light is present. If you spill any fuel on your skin, rinse it off immediately with soap and water. When you perform any kind of work on the fuel system, wear safety glasses and have a Class B type fire extinguisher on hand.

Note: *Because of its relative simplicity, the throttle body assembly does not need to be removed from the intake manifold or disassembled for component replacement. However, for the sake of clarity, the following procedures are shown with the TBI assembly removed from the vehicle.*

1   Relieve system fuel pressure (see Section 2).
2   Detach the cable from the negative terminal of the battery.
3   Remove the air cleaner housing assembly, adapter and gaskets.

Fuel meter cover/fuel pressure regulator assembly

Note: *The fuel pressure regulator is housed in*

the fuel meter cover. Whether you are replacing the meter cover or the regulator itself, the entire assembly must be replaced. The regulator must not be removed from the cover.
4   Unplug the electrical connectors to the fuel injectors.
5   Remove the long and short fuel meter cover screws **(see illustration)** and remove the fuel meter cover.
6   Remove the fuel meter outlet passage gasket, cover gasket and pressure regulator seal. Carefully remove any old gasket material that is stuck with a razor blade **(see illustration)**. **Caution:** *Do not attempt to re-use either of these gaskets.*
7   Inspect the cover for dirt, foreign material and casting warpage. If it is dirty, clean it with a clean shop rag soaked in solvent. Do not immerse the fuel meter cover in cleaning solvent - it could damage the pressure regulator diaphragm and gasket. **Warning:** *Do not remove the four screws* **(see illustration)** *securing the pressure regulator to the fuel meter cover. The regulator contains a large spring under compression which, if accidentally released, could cause injury. Disassembly might also result in a fuel leak between the diaphragm and the regulator housing. The new fuel meter cover assembly will include a*

new pressure regulator.
8   Install the new pressure regulator seal, fuel meter outlet passage gasket and cover gasket.
9   Install the fuel meter cover using Loctite 262 or equivalent on the screws. **Note:** *The short screws go next to the injectors.*
10   Attach the electrical connectors to both injectors.
11   Attach the cable to the negative terminal of the battery.
12   With the engine off and the ignition on, check for leaks around the gasket and fuel line couplings.
13   Install the air cleaner, adapter and gaskets.

Fuel injector(s)

14   To unplug the electrical connectors from the fuel injectors, squeeze the plastic tabs and pull straight up **(see illustration)**.
15   Remove the fuel meter cover/pressure regulator assembly. **Note:** *Do not remove the fuel meter cover assembly gasket - leave it in place to protect the casting from damage during injector removal.*
16   Use two screwdrivers **(see illustration)** to pry out the injector(s).

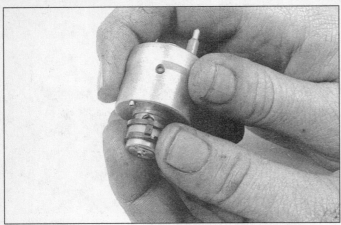

13.21 Slide the new filter onto the nozzle of the fuel injector

13.22 Lubricate the lower O-ring with transmission fluid then place it on the shoulder in the bottom of the injector cavity

13.23 Place the steel back-up washer on the shoulder near the top of the injector cavity

13.24 Lubricate the upper O-ring with transmission fluid then install it on top of the steel washer

13.25 Make sure that the lug is aligned with the notch in the bottom of the fuel injector cavity

17   Remove the upper (larger) and lower (smaller) O-rings and filter from the injector(s).
18   Remove the steel backup washer from the top of each injector cavity.
19   Inspect the fuel injector filters for evidence of dirt and contamination. If present, check for the presence of dirt in the fuel lines and fuel tank.
20   Be sure to replace the fuel injector with an identical part. Injectors from other models can fit in the Model 220 TBI assembly but are calibrated for different flow rates.
21   Slide the new filter into place on the nozzle of the injector **(see illustration)**.
22   Lubricate the new lower (smaller) O-ring with automatic transmission fluid and place it on the small shoulder at the bottom of the fuel injector cavity in the fuel meter body **(see illustration)**.
23   Install the steel back-up washer in the injector cavity **(see illustration)**.
24   Lubricate the new upper (larger) O-ring with automatic transmission fluid and install it on top of the steel back-up washer **(see illustration)**. **Note:** *The backup washer and the large O-ring must be installed before the injector. If they aren't, improper seating of the large O-ring could cause fuel leakage.*
25   To install an injector, align the raised lug on the injector base with the notch in the fuel meter body cavity **(see illustration)**. Push down on the injector until it is fully seated in the fuel meter body. **Note:** *The electrical terminals should be parallel with the throttle shaft.*
26   Install the fuel meter cover assembly and gasket.
27   Attach the cable to the negative terminal of the battery.
28   With the engine off and the ignition on, check for fuel leaks.
29   Attach the electrical connectors to the fuel injectors.
30   Install the air cleaner housing assembly, adapter and gaskets.

Throttle Position Sensor (TPS)

31   Remove the two TPS attaching screws and retainers and remove the TPS from the throttle body.
32   If you intend to re-use the same TPS, do not attempt to clean it by soaking it in any liquid cleaner or solvent. The TPS is a delicate electrical component and can be damaged by solvents.
33   Install the TPS on the throttle body while lining up the TPS lever with the TPS drive lever.

13.37 The IAC valve can be removed with an adjustable wrench or a 1-1/4 inch wrench

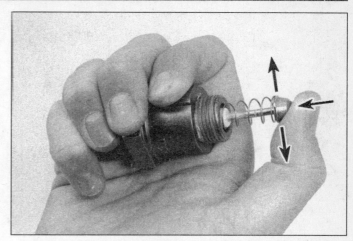

13.41a To adjust an IAC valve with a collar, retract the valve pintle by exerting firm pressure while using a slight side-to-side movement on the pintle

13.41b To adjust an IAC valve without a collar, compress the valve retaining spring while turning the valve clockwise . . .

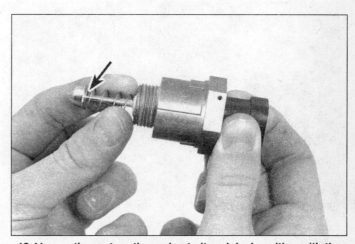

13.41c . . . then return the spring to its original position with the straight portion aligned in the slot under the flat surface of the valve

34   Install the two TPS attaching screws and retainers.

35   Install the air cleaner housing assembly, adapter and gaskets.

36   Attach the cable to the negative terminal of the battery. **Note:** *See the non-adjustable TPS output check at end of this section.*

Idle Air Control (IAC) valve

37   Unplug the electrical connector from the IAC valve and remove the IAC valve **(see illustration)**.

38   Remove and discard the old IAC valve gasket. Clean any old gasket material from the surface of the throttle body assembly to insure proper sealing of the new gasket.

39   All pintles in IAC valves on Model 220 TBI units have the same dual taper. However, the pintles on some units have a 12 mm diameter and the pintles on others have a 10 mm diameter. A replacement IAC valve must have the appropriate pintle taper and diameter for proper seating of the valve in the throttle body.

40   Measure the distance between the tip of the pintle and the housing mounting surface with the pintle fully extended **(see illustration 12.32)**. If dimension "A" is greater than 1-1/8 inches, it must be reduced to prevent damage to the valve.

41   If the pintle must be adjusted, determine whether your valve is a Type I (collar around the electrical terminal) or a Type II (no collar around the electrical terminal).

a) *To adjust the pintle of an IAC valve with a collar, grasp the valve and exert firm pressure on the pintle with the thumb. Use a slight side-to-side movement on the pintle as you press it in with your thumb* **(see illustration)**.

b) *To adjust the pintle of an IAC valve without a collar, compress the retaining spring while turning the pintle clockwise* **(see illustration)**. *Return the spring end to its original position with the straight portion aligned in the slot under the flat surface of the valve* **(see illustration)**.

42   Install the IAC valve and tighten it to the

specified torque. Attach the electrical connector.

43   Install the air cleaner housing assembly, adapter and gaskets.

44   Attach the cable to the negative terminal of the battery.

45   Start the engine and allow it to reach operating temperature, then turn it off. No adjustment of the IAC valve is required after installation. The IAC valve is reset by the ECM when the engine is turned off.

Fuel meter body assembly

46   Unplug the electrical connectors from the fuel injectors.

47   Remove the fuel meter cover/pressure regulator assembly, fuel meter cover gasket, fuel meter outlet gasket and pressure regulator seal.

48   Remove the fuel injectors.

49   Unscrew the fuel inlet and return line threaded fittings, detach the lines and remove the O-rings.

50   Remove the fuel inlet and outlet nuts

13.50   Remove the fuel inlet and outlet nuts from the fuel meter body

13.52   Once the fuel inlet and outlet nuts are off, pull the fuel meter body straight up to separate it from the throttle body

13.65   When disconnecting the fuel feed and return lines from the fuel inlet and outlet nuts, be sure to use a backup wrench to prevent damage to the lines

13.66   To remove the Model 220 throttle body from the intake manifold, remove the three bolts (arrows)

and gaskets from the fuel meter body assembly **(see illustration)**. Note the locations of the nuts to ensure proper reassembly. The inlet nut has a larger passage than the outlet nut.

51   Remove the gasket from the inner end of each fuel nut.

52   Remove the fuel meter body-to-throttle body attaching screws and remove the fuel meter body from the throttle body **(see illustration)**.

53   Install the new throttle body-to-fuel meter body gasket. Match the cut-out portions in the gasket with the openings in the throttle body.

54   Install the fuel meter body on the throttle body. Coat the fuel meter body-to-throttle body attaching screws with thread locking compound before installing them.

55   Install the fuel inlet and outlet nuts, with new gaskets, in the fuel meter body and tighten the nuts to the specified torque. Install the fuel inlet and return line threaded fittings with new O-rings. Use a backup wrench to prevent the nuts from turning.

56   Install the fuel injectors.

57   Install the fuel meter cover/pressure regulator assembly.

58   Attach the cable to the negative terminal of the battery.

59   Attach the electrical connectors to the fuel injectors.

60   With the engine off and the ignition on, check for leaks around the fuel meter body, the gasket and around the fuel line nuts and threaded fittings.

61   Install the air cleaner housing assembly, adapters and gaskets.

Throttle body assembly

62   Unplug all electrical connectors - the IAC valve, TPS and fuel injectors. Detach the grommet with the wires from the throttle body.

63   Detach the throttle linkage, return spring(s), transmission control cable (automatics) and, if equipped, cruise control.

64   Clearly label, then detach, all vacuum hoses.

65   Using a backup wrench, detach the inlet and outlet fuel line nuts **(see illustration)**. Remove the fuel line O-rings from the nuts

and discard them.

66   Remove the TBI mounting bolts **(see illustration)** and lift the TBI unit from the intake manifold. Remove and discard the TBI manifold gasket.

67   Place the TBI unit on a holding fixture available at most auto parts stores. **Note:** *If you don't have a holding fixture, and decide to place the TBI directly on a work bench surface, be extremely careful when servicing it. The throttle valve can be easily damaged.*

68   Remove the fuel meter body-to-throttle body attaching screws and separate the fuel meter body from the throttle body.

69   Remove the throttle body-to-fuel meter body gasket and discard it.

70   Remove the TPS.

71   Invert the throttle body on a flat surface for greater stability and remove the IAC valve.

72   Clean the throttle body assembly in a cold immersion cleaner. Clean the metal parts thoroughly and blow dry with compressed air. Be sure that all fuel and air passages are free of dirt or burrs. **Caution:** *Do not place the TPS, IAC valve, pressure regulator diaphragm, fuel injectors or other com-*

ponents containing rubber in the solvent or cleaning bath. *If the throttle body requires cleaning, soaking time in the cleaner should be kept to a minimum. Some models have throttle shaft dust seals that could lose their effectiveness by extended soaking.*

73   Inspect the mating surfaces for damage that could affect gasket sealing. Inspect the throttle lever and valve for dirt, binds, nicks and other damage.

74   Invert the throttle body on a flat surface for stability and install the IAC valve and the TPS.

75   Install a new throttle body-to-fuel meter body gasket and place the fuel meter body assembly on the throttle body assembly. Coat the fuel meter body-to-throttle body attaching screws with thread locking compound and tighten them securely.

76   Install the TBI unit and tighten the mounting bolts to the specified torque. Use a new TBI-to-manifold gasket.

77   Install new O-rings on the fuel line nuts. Install the fuel line and outlet nuts by hand to prevent stripping the threads. Using a backup wrench, tighten the nuts to the specified torque once they have been correctly threaded into the TBI unit.

78   Attach the vacuum hoses, throttle linkage, return spring(s), transmission control cable (automatics) and, if equipped, cruise control cable. Attach the grommet, with wire harness, to the throttle body.

79   Plug in all electrical connectors, making sure that the connectors are fully seated and latched.

80   Check to see if the accelerator pedal is free by depressing the pedal to the floor and releasing it with the engine off.

81   Connect the negative battery cable, and, with the engine off and the ignition on, check for leaks around the fuel line nuts.

82   Adjust the minimum idle speed and check the TPS output (see Steps 84 through 93).

83   Install the air cleaner housing assembly, adapter and gaskets.

Minimum idle speed adjustment

Note: *This adjustment should be performed only when the throttle body has been replaced. The engine should be at normal operating temperature before making the adjustment.*

84   Remove the air cleaner housing assembly, adapter and gaskets.

85   Plug any vacuum ports as required by the VECI label.

86   With the IAC valve connected, ground the diagnostic terminal of the ALDL connector **(see illustration 14.6).** Turn on the ignition but do not start the engine. Wait at least 30 seconds to allow the IAC valve pintle to extend and seat in the throttle body. Disconnect the IAC valve electrical connector. Remove the ground from the diagnostic terminal and start the engine.

87   Remove the idle stop screw plug by first

piercing it with an awl, then applying leverage.

88   Adjust the idle stop screw to obtain the specified rpm in neutral (manual) or in Drive (automatic).

89   Turn the ignition off and reconnect the IAC valve electrical connector.

90   Unplug any plugged vacuum line ports.

91   Install the air cleaner housing assembly, adapter and new gaskets.

Non-adjustable TPS output check

Note: *This check should be performed only when the throttle body or the TPS has been replaced or after the minimum idle speed has been adjusted.*

92   Connect a digital voltmeter from the TPS connector center terminal "B" to outside terminal "A" (you'll have to fabricate jumpers for terminal access).

93   With the ignition on and the engine off, TPS voltage should be less than the specified voltage. If it's more than the specified voltage, check the minimum idle speed before replacing the TPS.

14   Fuel pump/fuel pressure - check

Warning: *Gasoline is extremely flammable, so take extra precautions when working on any part of the fuel system. Don't smoke or allow open flames or bare light bulbs in or near the work area, and don't work in a garage where a natural gas-type appliance (such as a water heater or clothes dryer) with a pilot light is present. If you spill fuel on your skin, rinse it off immediately with soap and water. Have a Class B fire extinguisher on hand.*
Note: *In order to perform the fuel pressure test, you will have to obtain a fuel pressure gauge and adapter set for the TBI/CPI system.*

Preliminary inspection

1   If the fuel system fails to deliver the proper amount of fuel, or any fuel at all, to the carburetor/throttle body injection/central point injection system, inspect it as follows.

2   Always make certain there's fuel in the tank.

3   With the engine running, check for leaks at the threaded fittings at both ends of the fuel lines (see Chapter 1). Tighten any loose connections. Inspect all hoses for flat spots and kinks which would restrict the flow of fuel.

Pressure check

Refer to illustration 14.6

4   Relieve fuel system pressure (see Section 2).

5   Disconnect the fuel feed hose at the inlet fitting on the carburetor/TBI unit. **Note:** *On CPI systems, connect the fuel pressure gauge to the special fuel pressure connection on the fuel rail near the rear of the plenum. On all others, attach a fuel pressure gauge using a T-fitting.*

6   With the ignition off, connect a fused jumper wire from the positive battery terminal to the fuel pump test terminal (terminal G of the ALDL on CPI equipped models) **(see illustration).** On other models the test terminal is a single wire connector located near the fuel pump relay or in the ECM harness. Note the pressure reading.

7   If the pressure is within specifications, no further testing is necessary.

8   If the pressure is higher than specified, check for a restricted fuel return line. If the line is okay, replace the fuel pressure regulator on the throttle body.

9   If the pressure was less than specified, slowly pinch the fuel return line and note the pressure. If the pressure increases, replace the pressure regulator. If there isn't any pressure, check for a plugged fuel filter, plugged fuel pump inlet filter or restricted fuel line.

10   After testing is complete, relieve the fuel pressure and remove the fuel gauge.

11   If no problems are found with any of the above listed components, check the fuel pump (see below).

Fuel pump check

12   If you suspect a problem with the fuel pump, verify that it actually runs. Have an assistant turn the ignition switch to On while you listen at the fuel tank - you should hear a whirring sound from the pump.

13   If the pump doesn't run (makes no

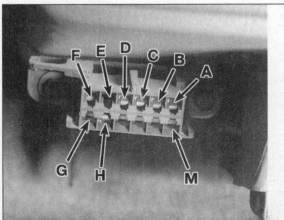

14.6 The Assembly Line Data Link (ALDL) terminal identification

A   Ground
B   Diagnostic terminal
C   AIR (if used)
D   Check Engine light (if used)
E   Serial data (special tool required - do not use)
F   TCC (if used)
G   Fuel pump (if used)
H   Brake sense speed input
M   Serial data (four-cylinder engine only, special tool required - do not use)

15.6   Central Port Injection (CPI) details

1	*Poppet nozzle*	5	*Fuel line access fitting*
2	*Distributor*	6	*Return fuel line*
3	*Fuel pressure regulator*	7	*Inlet fuel line*
4	*Central Port Injection unit*	8	*Fuel inlet and return line clip*

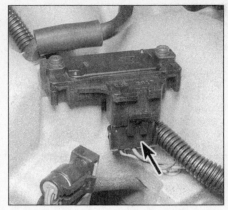

15.10 Disconnect the MAP sensor electrical connector

sound), proceed to the next Step.

14   Check the fuel pump fuse located in the engine compartment. If the fuse is good, proceed to Step 17. If the fuse is blown, replace the fuse and see if the pump works. If the pump still doesn't work, go to the next Step.

15   With the ignition off, apply 12-volts to the fuel pump test terminal (see Step 6) and listen for the sound that indicates the fuel pump is running.

16   If the pump runs, check the fuel pump relay. If the pump does not run, check for an open circuit between the relay and the fuel pump.

Fuel pump relay check

17   To test the fuel pump relay, start the engine and let it idle at normal operating temperature, then disconnect the fuel pump relay (see Section 3). If the engine stops, the oil pressure switch is faulty.

18   If the engine keeps on running, reconnect the relay and turn off the ignition. Using a test light, probe the fuel pump test terminal. If the light does not come on, the fuel pump circuit is okay. If the test light comes on, the oil pressure switch is bad.

15   Central Port Injection (CPI) - general information and CPI unit removal and installation

General information

Refer to illustration 15.6

1   The function of the Central Port Injection (CPI) unit is to control fuel delivery to the engine. The CPI system is controlled by the Electronic Control Module (ECM) located in the passenger compartment. The ECM is the control center of the Computer Command Control system (CCCS).

2   The ECM monitors voltage from several sensors to determine how much fuel the engine needs. When the key is first turned "ON", the ECM turns on the fuel pump relay for two seconds and the fuel pump builds up pressure to the CPI unit. The ECM monitors the Coolant Temperature Sensor (CTS), the Intake Air Temperature Sensor (IATS), Throttle Position Sensor (TPS) and Manifold Absolute Pressure (MAP) sensor and then determines the proper air/fuel ratio for starting.

3   The fuel control system has an electric fuel pump, located in the fuel tank on the fuel gauge sending unit. The pump provides pressure above the regulated pressure needed by the CPI injector.

4   The intake manifold is designed with an upper and lower manifold assembly. The upper manifold is a variable-tuned split-plenum design that also includes an intake manifold tuning valve, MAP sensor and a throttle valve attached to the plenum.

5   The throttle valve is used to control air flow into the engine and consequently engine output. During engine idle, the throttle valve is almost completely closed and air flow control is handled by the Idle Air Control (IAC) valve.

6   Most of the CPI components are housed directly under the air intake plenum **(see illustration on following page)**. In order to service the CPI unit, it will be necessary to remove the air intake plenum from the intake manifold. The pressure regulator assembly consists of a fuel meter body, gasket seal, fuel pressure regulator, fuel injector and six poppet nozzles with fuel tubes. The CPI unit is not repairable and must be replaced as an assembly if found to be defective. Be sure to contact a dealer service department for any service contracts or warranties that might cover the repair of the fuel system before attempting it on your own.

7   The CPI system has a low gain fuel pressure regulator to maintain pressure at the fuel injector through a range of fuel recirculation rates from the in-tank fuel pump. With the ignition "ON" and the engine NOT running, the fuel pressure should be 54 to 62 psi. Fuel enters the fuel meter body through the inlet line and flows directly into the injector cavity. When the ECM de-energizes the injector solenoid, fuel is recirculated through the pressure regulator. Fuel pressure applied to the regulator diaphragm acts against the spring force and opens the valve from its seat. This allows fuel to return to the fuel tank by way of the fuel meter body outlet and the return line. When the ECM energizes the injector solenoid, the armature lifts off the six fuel tube seats and delivers fuel through the fuel meter body out to the six poppet nozzles.

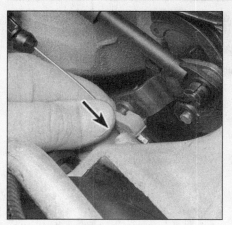

15.11a Push the TV cable forward and off the throttle valve

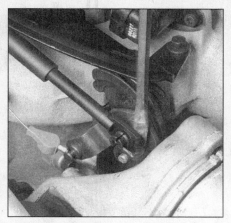

15.11b Carefully pry the cruise control cable off the throttle valve

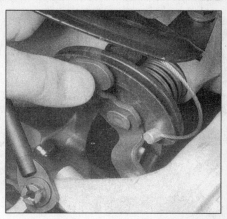

15.11c While pulling the throttle back, lift the accelerator cable from the notch on the throttle valve

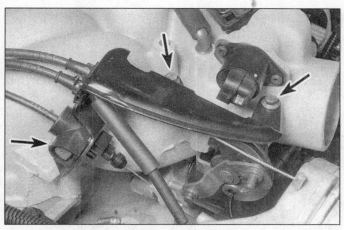

15.12 Remove the three bolts (arrows) from the plenum and lift the bracket off the plenum

15.13a Loosen the clamps and the wing nut (arrows) and . . .

8   When the ECM energizes the injector solenoid, pressurized fuel flows through the fuel tubes to each poppet nozzle. There are six poppet nozzles (one for each cylinder). An increase in fuel pressure will cause the poppet nozzle ball to lift from its seat against spring force and spray fuel at approximately 52 psi. De-energizing the injector solenoid closes the armature and reduces the fuel pressure on the poppet nozzle ball.

CPI unit removal and installation

Refer to illustrations 15.10, 15.11a, 15.11b, 15.11c, 15.12, 15.13a, 15.13b, 15.14, 15.17, 15.19, 15.22, 15.24 and 15.25
Note: *Do not attempt to disassemble the CPI unit. It is a non-serviceable part.*

Removal

9   Read the **Warning** at the beginning of Section 14, then relieve the fuel pressure (see Section 2). Remove the Torx screws and lift off the plastic cover from the air intake plenum.
10   Disconnect the electrical connectors on the TPS, IAC motor, MAP sensor and intake

15.13b . . . disconnect the electrical connector from the air intake sensor - then lift the air intake tube from the engine compartment

manifold tuning valve assembly **(see illustration)**.
11   Disconnect the TV linkage, cruise control cable and accelerator cable **(see illustrations)** from the throttle valve assembly.
12   Remove the bolts **(see illustration)** that

15.14 Remove the nuts (arrows) from the air intake plenum mounting studs (right side shown)

retain the bracket to the air intake plenum.
13   Remove the intake air ducts from the plenum and the fan shroud **(see illustrations)**.
14   Remove the ignition coil **(see illustration)**.
15   Disconnect the PCV hose from the

4

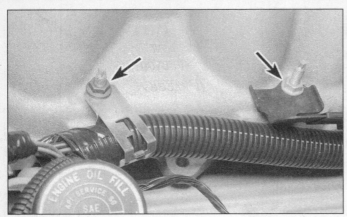

15.17 Remove the nuts (arrows) from the mounting studs located on the air intake plenum and lift the brackets (left side shown)

15.19 Lift the gasket off the intake manifold

15.22 Squeeze the tab (arrow) to disconnect the injector electrical connector

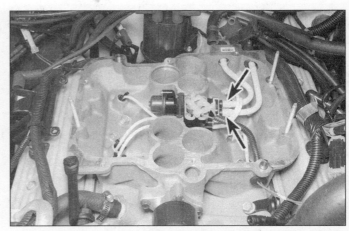

15.24 Carefully remove the inlet and return line from the injector assembly

plenum and the valve cover.

16   Disconnect the vacuum lines from the front and rear of the air in- take plenum.

17   Remove the ignition wire and harness bracket from the plenum. Be sure to mark the position of each stud and nut **(see illustration)**.

18   Remove the bolts and nuts from the air intake plenum. Start on the front bolt and work your way counter-clockwise (standing directly in front of the engine compartment) around the circumference of the plenum.

19   Lift the air intake plenum from the intake manifold. Remove the gasket from the intake manifold **(see illustration)**.

20   Inspect the gasket surface on the plenum and the intake manifold for any chips, burrs or cracks. If the plenum is damaged, replace it with a new unit.

21   Clean the gasket surface on the plenum and the intake manifold with a soft cloth and solvent.

22   Detach the electrical connector from the CPI assembly **(see illustration)**.

23   Disconnect the fuel fitting clip and dispose it.

24   Disconnect the fuel inlet and outlet lines from the CPI assembly **(see illustration)**.

Remove the O-ring seals and dispose them. Use new seals for assembly.

25   Squeeze the poppet nozzle locking tabs **(see illustration)** while lifting the nozzle out of the intake manifold.

26   After disconnecting the six poppet nozzles, lift the CPI assembly out of the intake manifold as a single unit.

Installation

27   Align the CPI assembly grommet with the casting grommet slots and push down until it is seated at the bottom of the guide hole.

28   Push the poppet nozzles into the casting sockets. **Caution:** *Be sure the poppet nozzles are seated and secured in the casting sockets before installing the plenum. Check by pulling each poppet nozzle firmly until it is in its correct place. This will prevent fuel leaks and consequently any fire danger.*

29   Connect the fuel inlet and outlet lines to the CPI assembly. Be sure to install new O-rings. Coat the new O-rings with clean engine oil.

30   Install the new fuel fitting clip.

31   Be sure the fuel pump relay is connected and pressurize the fuel pump by turn-

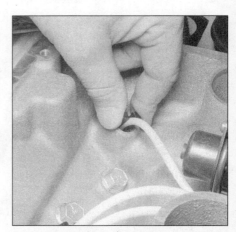

15.25 Squeeze the two tabs and lift the assembly to remove the poppet nozzle from the intake manifold

ing the ignition key "ON". Do not start the engine. Check all the fittings for fuel leaks before installing the air intake plenum.

32   Install the air intake plenum. Be sure to use a new gasket. Tighten the plenum fasteners to the torque listed in this Chapter's

16.2 Remove the exhaust pipe to manifold mounting bolts (arrows)

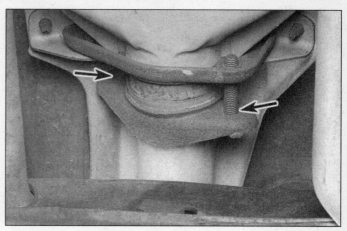

16.3 Remove the clamp (arrow) that secures the exhaust pipe to the catalytic converter

Specifications. **Note:** *Be sure the plenum does not pinch any fuel lines or nozzles.*

16 Exhaust system components - removal and installation

Warning: *The vehicle's exhaust system generates very high temperatures and should be allowed to cool down completely before any of the components are touched. Be especially careful around the catalytic converter, where the highest temperatures are generated.*

Note: *Due to the high temperatures and exposed locations of the exhaust system components, rust and corrosion can "freeze" parts together. Liquid penetrating oils are available to help loosen frozen fasteners. However, in some cases it may be necessary to cut the pieces apart with a hacksaw or cutting torch. The latter method should be employed only by persons experienced in this work.*

1   Raise the vehicle and support it securely on jackstands.

Front exhaust pipe

Refer to illustrations 16.2 and 16.3

2   Remove the bolts securing the exhaust pipe to the exhaust manifold(s) **(see illustration).**

3   Remove the clamp securing the exhaust pipe to the catalytic converter **(see illustration).**

4   Separate the exhaust pipe from the exhaust manifold(s) and the catalytic converter.

5   Installation is the reverse of the removal procedure. Be sure to install new "doughnut" gaskets in the exhaust manifold(s) and new nuts and bolts.

Catalytic converter

Caution: *Make sure the catalytic converter has been allowed sufficient time to cool before attempting removal.*

6   Remove the converter-to-front exhaust pipe clamp **(see illustration 16.3).**

7   Remove the converter-to-crossmember

bracket at the crossmember.

8   Remove the bolts securing the rear of the converter to the converter/intermediate pipe and remove the converter.

9   Installation is the reverse of the removal procedure. Be sure to use new nuts and bolts.

Intermediate exhaust pipe, muffler and tailpipe

10   The intermediate pipe, muffler and tailpipe are all one unit.

11   Remove the intermediate pipe-to-frame bracket.

12   Remove the bolts securing the intermediate pipe to the catalytic converter.

13   Remove the muffler/tailpipe assembly rear hanger bolts at the crossmember just behind the muffler and at the frame near the end of the tailpipe. Separate the muffler/tailpipe/intermediate pipe assembly from the vehicle.

14   Installation is the reverse of removal. Be sure to use new nuts and bolts.

4

Notes

Chapter 5
Engine electrical systems

Contents

	Section
Air gap (1.9L engine) - adjustment	8
Alternator - removal and installation	14
Alternator brushes - replacement	15
Battery - emergency jump starting	3
Battery - removal and installation	2
Battery cables - check and replacement	4
Charging system - check	13
Charging system - general information and precautions	12
"Check engine" light	See Chapter 6
Distributor - removal and installation	6
Hall effect switch - check and replacement	11
Ignition coil - removal, check and installation	10
Ignition key lock cylinder - removal and installation	See Chapter 10
Ignition module - check and replacement	9

	Section
Ignition pick-up coil - check and replacement	7
Ignition switch - replacement	See Chapter 10
Ignition system - check	5
Ignition system - general information and precautions	1
Ignition timing - check and adjustment	See Chapter 1
Spark plug replacement	See Chapter 1
Spark plug wires, distributor cap and rotor - check and replacement	See Chapter 1
Starter motor - removal and installation	18
Starter motor - testing in vehicle	17
Starter motor brushes - replacement	20
Starter solenoid - removal and replacement	19
Starting system - general information	16

Component location

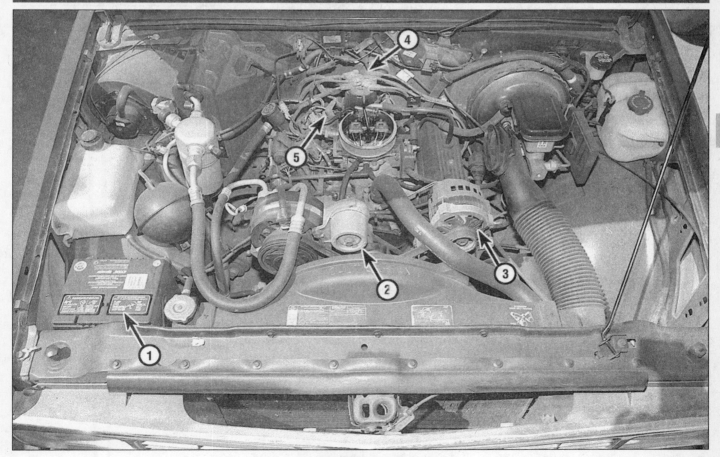

Engine electrical system

1 Battery
2 Serpentine drivebelt tensioner
3 Alternator
4 Distributor (HEI)
5 Ignition coil

Specifications

Ignition pick-up coil resistance (except 1.9L)..	500 to 1500 ohms
Ignition pick-up coil air gap (1.9L only)..	0.12 to 0.20 inch
Starter motor brush length (type two)	
Standard..	0.62 inch
Service limit...	0.47 inch

1   Ignition system - general information and precautions

Warning: *Some parts on later model vehicles have an electrostatic discharge sensitive sticker applied to them. When installing or servicing any parts with this sticker, the following guidelines should be followed:*

Avoid touching the electrical terminals of the part.

Always ground the package to a known good ground on the vehicle before removing the part from the package.

Always touch a known good ground before handling the part.

General information

The ignition system is composed of the battery, distributor, coil, ignition switch, spark plugs and the primary (low tension) and secondary (high tension) wiring circuits.

A high energy ignition (HEI) distributor is used on all vehicles, and all models use a separately mounted coil. Vehicles equipped with the 2.8L or 4.3L engine also incorporate electronic spark timing (EST) and an electronic control module (ECM), which monitors data from various engine sensors, computes the desired spark timing and signals the distributor to change the timing accordingly. Early models are equipped with vacuum and centrifugal advance mechanisms. On all models the distributor uses a magnetic pick-up assembly which contains a permanent magnet, a pole piece with internal teeth and a pick-up coil in place of the traditional ignition point assembly.

The secondary (spark plug) wire used with the HEI system is a carbon impregnated cord conductor encased in an 8 mm (5/16-inch) diameter rubber jacket with an outer silicone jacket. This type of wire will withstand very high temperatures and still provide insulation for the HEI's high voltage. For more information on spark plug wiring refer to Chapter 1. **Warning:** *Because of the very high voltage generated by the HEI system, extreme care should be taken whenever an operation involving ignition components is performed. This not only includes the distributor, coil, control module and spark plug wires, but related items that are connected to the system as well (such as the plug connections, tachometer, and testing equipment). Consequently, before any work is performed, the ignition should be turned off and the negative battery cable disconnected.*

2   Battery - removal and installation

1   The battery is located at the front of the engine compartment. It is held in place by a hold-down clamp near the bottom of the battery case.

2   Hydrogen gas is produced by the battery, so keep open flames and lighted cigarettes away from it at all times.

3   Always keep the battery in an upright position. Spilled electrolyte should be rinsed off immediately with large quantities of water. Always wear eye protection when working around a battery.

4   Always disconnect the negative (-) battery cable first, followed by the positive (+) cable.

5   After the cables are disconnected from the battery, remove the hold-down clamp.

6   Carefully lift the battery out of the engine compartment.

7   Installation is the reverse of removal. The cable clamps should be tight, but do not overtighten them as damage to the battery case could occur. The battery posts and cable ends should be cleaned prior to connection (see Chapter 1).

3   Battery - emergency jump starting

Refer to the *Booster battery (jump) starting* procedure at the front of this manual.

4   Battery cables - check and replacement

1   Periodically inspect the entire length of each battery cable for damage, cracked or burned insulation and corrosion. Poor battery cable connections can cause starting problems and decreased engine performance.

2   Check the cable-to-terminal connections at the ends of the cables for cracks, loose wire strands and corrosion. The presence of white, fluffy deposits under the insulation at the cable terminal connection is a sign the cable is corroded and should be replaced. Check the terminals for distortion, missing mounting bolts or nuts and corrosion.

3   If only the positive cable is to be replaced, be sure to disconnect the negative cable from the battery first.

4   Disconnect and remove the cable(s) from the vehicle. Make sure the replacement cable(s) is the same length and diameter.

5   Clean the threads of the starter or ground connection with a wire brush to remove rust and corrosion. Apply a light coat of petroleum jelly to the threads to ease installation and prevent future corrosion. Inspect the connections frequently to make sure they are clean and tight.

6   Attach the cable(s) to the starter or ground connection and tighten the mounting nut(s) securely.

7   Before connecting the new cable(s) to the battery, make sure they reach the terminals without having to be stretched.

8   Connect the positive cable first, followed by the negative cable. Tighten the nuts and apply a thin coat of petroleum jelly to the terminal and cable connection.

5   Ignition system - check

Refer to illustrations 5.3 and 5.5

Warning: *Because of the very high voltage generated by the ignition system, extreme care should be taken whenever an operation is performed involving ignition components. This not only includes the coils, control module and spark plug wires, but related items connected to the system as well, such as the plug connections, tachometer and any other test equipment. When handling secondary spark plug leads with the engine running, insulated pliers must be used and care exercised to prevent a possible electric shock.*

1   Check all ignition wiring connections for tightness, cuts corrosion or any other signs of a bad connection. A faulty or poor connection at a spark plug could also result in a misfire. Also check for carbon deposits inside the spark plug boots.

2   Remove the distributor cap (if equipped) and check the cap and rotor as described in Chapter 1. Remove the spark plugs, if necessary, and check for fouling.

3   Use a calibrated ignition tester to verify adequate available secondary voltage at the spark plug **(see illustration)**. If there's no spark on one wire, check another wire to insure that an open is not present in a spark plug wire. **Note**: *A few sparks and then nothing is considered no spark.* If spark is found, check for fuel, fuel pressure (see Chapter 4) and the spark plugs, distributor cap and rotor (see Chapter 1). If no spark is found, see the next Step.

4   If no spark was found, unplug the coil-to-cap wire, connect the wire to the spark tester and crank the engine. A spark indi-

5.3 To use a calibrated ignition tester (available at most auto parts stores), simply disconnect a spark plug wire, attach the wire to the tester, clip the tester to a convenient ground and operate the starter - if there's enough power to fire the plug, sparks will be visible between the electrode tip and the tester body

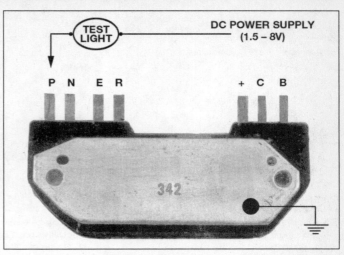

5.5 Typical ignition module terminal identification

cates that the problem must be in the distributor cap or rotor. **Note:** *A few sparks followed by no spark is the same condition as a no spark at all.* Disconnect the 4 terminal distributor connector and check for spark. If spark is now present, replace the pick-up coil. If no spark is found, see the next Step.

5   Normally, there should be battery voltage at the "C" and "+" terminals of the ignition module **(see illustration)**. Low voltage indicates an open or high resistance circuit from the distributor to the coil or ignition switch. If the "C" terminal voltage is low, but the "+" terminal voltage is 10 volts or more, the circuit from "C" terminal to the ignition coil primary winding is open. Disconnect the distributor two-terminal "C/+" connector. Turn the ignition switch to the "on" position, with the engine stopped. Check the volts at "+" and "C" terminals of distributor harness connector. If the reading is under 10 volts at the "C" terminal only, check for an open op poor ground in the circuit from "C" terminal to the ignition coil. If circuit is OK, the fault is either the ignition coil or connection. If both terminals are under 10 volts, repair the wire from module "+" terminal to the "B" terminal of black ignition coil connector or primary circuit to ignition switch. If both terminal are 10 volts or more, see the next Step.

6   Reconnect the two-terminal electrical connector. Check the voltage between the TACH terminal and ground. **Note:** *The terminal may be taped back in harness, making it hard to find.* If the module is turned on, the voltage will be low, but above one volt. This could cause the ignition coil to fail from excessive heat. With an open ignition coil primary winding, a small amount of voltage will leak through the module from the "BAT" to the tach terminal.

7   Applying a voltage (1.5 to 8V) to module terminal "P" should turn the module on and the tach terminal voltage should drop to about 7 to 9 volts. Reconnect the distributor 2 terminal connection and turn the ignition to the "on" position. Check the voltage from the

tach. terminal to ground. If the voltmeter reading is 1 to 10 volts: Replace the module and check for spark from the coil. If spark occurs the system is OK. If no spark occurs replace the ignition coil, it too is faulty and needs to be replaced. If the voltmeter reading is under 1 volt, repair the open tach lead or connection and repeat the voltage check. If the voltmeter reading is over 10 volts, connect a test light from the tach terminal to ground and crank the engine while observing the light. If the light blinks, replace the ignition coil and recheck for spark with a spark tester. If still no spark occurs, re-install the original coil and replace the distributor module. If the light is on steady, see the next Step.

8   This test will determine whether the module or coil is faulty or if the pick-up coil is not generating the proper signal to turn the module on. This test can be performed by using a DC battery with a rating of 1.5 to 8 volts. The use of the test light is to allow the "P" terminal to be probed more easily. Some digital multimeters can also be used to trigger the module by selecting ohms, usually the diode position. In this position, the meter may have a voltage across its terminals which can be used to trigger the module. The voltage in the ohms position can be checked by using a second meter or by checking the manufacturer's specifications for the tool being used. Disconnect the distributor 4 terminal connector, remove the distributor cap and disconnect the pick-up coil connector from module. Connect a voltmeter from the tach terminal to ground and turn the ignition to the "on" position. Insulate a test light probe to 1/4-inch from the tip and note voltage, as test light is momentarily connected from a voltage source (1.5 to 8V) to module term. "P" **(see illustration 5.5)**. If the voltage doesn't drop, check the module ground. If the ground is OK replace the module. If the voltage drops, see the next Step.

9   Connect the coil wire to a spark tester (or hold it about 1/4-inch from a good ground with an insulated tool). Remove the test light -

this should turn off the module and cause a spark. If no spark occurs, the fault is most likely in the ignition coil because most module problems would have been found before this point in the procedure. A GM HEI module tester (available at some auto parts stores or specialty tool dealers) can determine which is at fault. **Note:** *Many auto parts stores are equipped to test the module for you.*

6   Distributor - removal and installation

Four-cylinder engine

Refer to illustrations 6.4 and 6.5

Removal

1   Disconnect the cable from the negative battery terminal.
2   Remove the coil wire from the distributor cap.
3   Remove the distributor cap.
4   Note the position of the rotor and the distributor-to-block alignment. Make alignment marks on the distributor to indicate the

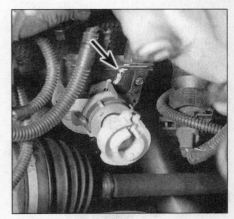

6.4 Mark the position of the rotor to the distributor before removing the rotor

6.5 The distributor hold-down clamp and bolt must be removed before the distributor can be removed from the engine

6.22 Make a mark on the distributor housing base (arrow) to show the direction the rotor is pointing before removing the distributor

6.23 Mark the position of the distributor in relation to the engine (arrow) before loosening the distributor hold-down clamp

position of the rotor and the distributor housing (see illustration).

5   Remove the distributor hold-down clamp bolt and clamp (see illustration). Remove the distributor from the engine. **Caution:** *Do not turn the crankshaft while the distributor is removed from the engine. If the crankshaft is turned, the position of the rotor will be altered and the engine will have to be re-timed.*

Installation (crankshaft not turned after distributor removal)

6   Insert the distributor into the engine in exactly the same relation to the block in which it was removed. To mesh the gears, it may be necessary to turn the rotor slightly. At this point the distributor may not seat down against the block completely. This is due to the lower end of the distributor shaft not mating properly with the oil pump shaft. If this is the case, check again to make sure the distributor is aligned with the block in the same position it was in before removal and that the rotor is correctly aligned with the distributor body. The gear on the distributor shaft is engaged with the gear on the camshaft, and this relationship cannot change as long as the distributor is not lifted from the engine. Use a socket and breaker bar on the crankshaft bolt to turn the engine over in the normal direction of rotation. The rotor will turn, but the oil pump shaft will not because the two shafts are not engaged. When the proper alignment is reached the distributor will drop down over the oil pump shaft, and the distributor body will seat properly against the block.

7   Install the hold-down clamp and tighten the bolt securely.

8   Install the distributor cap and coil wire.

9   Connect the cable to the negative terminal of the battery.

Installation (crankshaft turned after distributor removal)

10   Remove the number one spark plug.

11   Place your finger over the spark plug

hole while turning the crankshaft in the normal direction of rotation with a wrench on the pulley bolt at the front of the engine.

12   When you feel compression, continue turning the crankshaft slowly until the timing mark on the crankshaft pulley is aligned with the "0" on the engine timing indicator.

13   Position the rotor to point to between the number one and number three distributor terminals.

14   Insert the distributor into the engine in exactly the same relation to the block in which it was removed. To mesh the gears, it may be necessary to turn the rotor slightly. If the distributor does not seat fully against the block it is because the oil pump shaft has not seated in the distributor shaft. Make sure the distributor drive gear is fully engaged with the camshaft gear, then use a socket on the crankshaft bolt to turn the engine over in the normal direction of rotation until the two shafts engage and the distributor seats against the block.

15   Install the hold-down clamp and tighten the bolt securely.

16   Install the distributor cap and coil wire.

17   Connect the cable to the negative terminal of the battery.

V6 engine

Refer to illustrations 6.22 and 6.23

Removal

18   Detach the cable from the negative terminal of the battery.

19   Remove the air cleaner housing assembly, adapter and gaskets.

20   Unplug the wiring harness connectors from the side of the distributor base.

21   Remove the distributor cap (see Chapter 1) and move it out of the way.

22   Scribe a mark on the distributor housing base to show the direction the rotor is pointing (see illustration).

23   Mark the position of the distributor housing in relation to the engine (see illustration).

7.3 Before removing the pick-up coil, unplug the lead from the ignition module

24   Remove the distributor hold-down bolt and clamp.

25   Remove the distributor. **Caution:** *Avoid turning the crankshaft while the distributor is removed. Turning the crankshaft while the distributor is removed will change the timing position of the rotor and require re-timing the engine.*

Installation (crankshaft not turned after distributor removal)

26   Position the rotor in the exact location it was in when the distributor was removed.

27   Lower the distributor into the engine. To mesh the gears at the bottom of the distributor it may be necessary to turn the rotor slightly. It is possible that the distributor may not seat down fully against the block because the lower part of the distributor shaft has not properly engaged the oil pump shaft. Make sure the distributor and rotor are properly aligned with the marks made earlier, then use a large socket and breaker bar on the crankshaft bolt to turn the engine in the normal direction of rotation until the two shafts engage and the distributor drops down against the block.

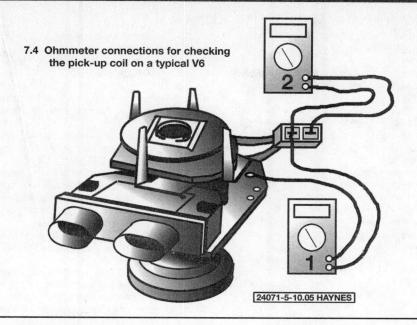

7.4 Ohmmeter connections for checking the pick-up coil on a typical V6

24071-5-10.05 HAYNES

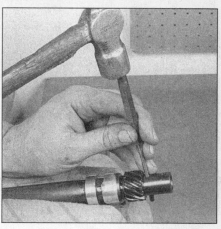

7.11a Mount the distributor shaft in a soft-jawed vise and, using a drift punch and hammer, knock out the roll pin

28 With the base of the distributor seated against the engine block turn the distributor housing to align the marks made on the distributor base and the engine block.
29 Place the hold-down clamp in position and loosely install the hold-down bolt.
30 Reconnect the ignition wiring harness.
31 Install the distributor cap.
32 Reconnect the coil connector.
33 With the distributor in its original position, tighten the hold-down bolt.
34 Check the ignition timing (see Chapter 1).

Installation (crankshaft turned after distributor removal)

35 Remove the number one spark plug.
36 Place your finger over the spark plug hole while turning the crankshaft with a wrench on the pulley bolt at the front of the engine.
37 When you feel compression, continue turning the crankshaft slowly until the timing mark on the vibration damper is aligned with the "0" on the engine timing indicator.
38 Position the rotor between the number one and six spark plug terminals on the cap.
39 Lower the distributor into the engine. To mesh the gears at the bottom of the distributor, it may be necessary to turn the rotor slightly. If the distributor does not drop down flush against the block it is because the distributor shaft has not mated to the oil pump shaft. Place a large socket and breaker bar on the crankshaft bolt and turn the engine over in the normal direction of rotation until the two shafts engage properly, allowing the distributor to seat flush against the block.
40 With the base of the distributor properly seated against the engine block, turn the distributor housing to align the marks made on the distributor base and the engine block.
41 Place the hold-down clamp in position and loosely install the hold-down bolt.

42 Reconnect the ignition wiring harness.
43 Install the distributor cap. If the secondary wiring harness was removed from the cap, reinstall it.
44 Reconnect the coil connector.
45 With the distributor in its original position, tighten the hold-down bolt and check the ignition timing.

7 Ignition pick-up coil - check and replacement

Refer to illustrations 7.3, 7.4, 7.11a, 7.11b, 7.11c, 7.14a and 7.14b

Check

Note: *This procedure does not apply to the magnetic-type pick-up assembly used on the 1.9L four-cylinder engine.*

1 Detach the cable from the negative terminal of the battery.
2 Remove the distributor cap and rotor (see Chapter 1).
3 Detach the pick-up coil leads from the module **(see illustration)**.
4 Connect one lead of an ohmmeter to the terminal of the pick-up coil lead and the other

to ground as shown **(see illustration)**. Flex the leads by hand to check for intermittent opens. The ohmmeter should indicate infinite resistance at all times. If it doesn't, the pick-up coil is defective and must be replaced.
5 Connect the ohmmeter leads to both terminals of the pick-up coil. Flex the leads by hand to check for intermittent opens. The ohmmeter should read one steady value between 500 and 1500 ohms as the leads are flexed by hand. If it doesn't, the pick-up coil is defective and must be replaced.

Replacement

V6, 2.0L and 2.5L four-cylinder engines

6 Remove the distributor from the engine as previously described.
7 Remove the two rotor mounting screws and remove the rotor.
8 Disconnect the pick-up coil leads from the module.
9 On models with a Hall-effect switch remove the switch retaining screws and the switch.
10 Mark the distributor gear and shaft so they can be reassembled in the same position.
11 Carefully mount the distributor in a soft-jawed vice and, using a hammer and punch, remove the roll pin from the distributor shaft and gear **(see illustrations)**.

5

7.11b Remove the driven gear and spacer washers from the end of the shaft, making sure to note the order in which you removed any spacers

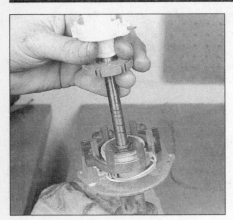

7.11c Remove the shaft from the distributor

12   Remove the gear and washers from the shaft.
13   Carefully pull the shaft out through the top of the distributor.
14   Remove the "C" washer retaining ring at the center of the distributor **(see illustration)** and remove the pick-up coil **(see illustration).**
15   Installation is the reverse of the removal procedure.

7.14a To remove the pick-up coil from a V6 engine distributor, remove the retaining clip

1.9L four-cylinder engine

16   Remove the distributor from the engine as described in Section 6.
17   Remove the rotor.
18   Remove the mounting screws from the vacuum controller and remove the vacuum controller.
19   Disconnect the wires from the pick-up coil. Remove the screw retaining the wiring harness and remove the harness from the distributor housing.
20   Using two screwdrivers, carefully pry the reluctor from the rotor shaft.
21   Remove the mounting screws from the breaker plate assembly and remove the assembly from the distributor housing.
22   Remove the pick-up coil mounting screws and separate the pick-up coil from the breaker plate.
23   Installation is the reverse of the removal procedure.
24   Adjust the air gap after replacing the pick-up coil (see Section 8).

8   Air gap (1.9 liter engine) - adjustment

1   Before measuring the air gap, the engine must be rotated until one of the four reluctor teeth line up with the stator (an assistant or remote starter switch is helpful here). Crank the starter motor intermittently until the reluctor and stator line up.
2   Using a feeler gauge, measure the air gap between the reluctor and the stator and compare it to the Specifications.
3   If necessary, adjust the air gap by loosening the two stainless steel screws and moving the pole piece.
4   Recheck the air gap and tighten the screws.

9   Ignition module - check and replacement

Refer to illustrations 9.11 and 9.15
Note: *It is not necessary to remove the distributor to check or replace the module.*

Check

1   Disconnect the tachometer lead (if so equipped) at the distributor.
2   Check for a spark at the coil and spark plug wires (see Section 5).
3   If there is no spark, remove the distributor cap. Remove the ignition module from the distributor but leave the connector plugged in.
4   With the ignition switch turned On, check for voltage at the module positive terminal **(see illustration 5.5)**.
5   If the reading is less than ten volts, there is a fault in the wire between the module positive (+) terminal and the ignition coil positive connector or the ignition coil and primary circuit-to-ignition switch.
6   If the reading is ten volts or more, check the "C" terminal on the module **(see illustration 5.5)**.
7   If the reading is less than one volt, there is an open or grounded lead in the distributor-to-coil "C" terminal connection or ignition coil or an open primary circuit in the coil itself.
8   If the reading is one to ten volts, replace the module with a new one and check for a spark (see Section 5). If there is a spark the module was faulty and the system is now operating properly. If there is no spark, there is a fault in the ignition coil.
9   If the reading in Step 4 is 10 volts or more, unplug the pick-up coil connector from the module. Check the "C" terminal voltage with the ignition switch On and watch the voltage reading as a test light is momentarily (five seconds or less) connected between the battery positive (+) terminal and the module "P" terminal **(see illustration 5.5)**.
10   If there is no drop in voltage, check the module ground and, if it is good, replace the module with a new one.
11   If the voltage drops, check for spark at the coil wire as the test light is removed from the module terminal. If there is no spark, the module is faulty and should be replaced with a new one. If there is a spark, the pick-up coil or connections are faulty or not grounded **(see illustration)**.

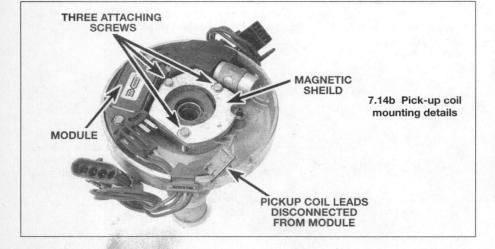

THREE ATTACHING SCREWS

MODULE

MAGNETIC SHEILD

7.14b Pick-up coil mounting details

PICKUP COIL LEADS DISCONNECTED FROM MODULE

9.11 As the test light is removed, check for a spark at the coil wire (arrow)

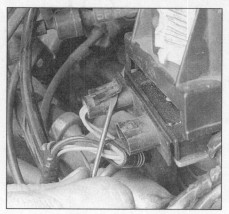

9.15 Unplug both electrical connectors from the module

Replacement

12   Detach the cable from the negative terminal of the battery.
13   Remove the distributor cap and rotor (see Chapter 1).
14   Remove both module attaching screws and lift the module up and away from the distributor.
15   Disconnect both electrical leads from the module **(see illustration)**. Note that the leads cannot be interchanged.
16   Do not wipe the grease from the module or the distributor base if the same module is to be reinstalled. If a new module is to be installed, a package of silicone grease will be included with it. Wipe the distributor base and the new module clean, then apply the silicone grease on the face of the module and on the distributor base where the module seats. This grease is necessary for heat dissipation.
17   Install the module and attach both electrical leads.
18   Install the distributor rotor and cap (see Chapter 1).
19   Attach the cable to the negative terminal of the battery.

---

10   Ignition coil - removal, check and installation

Refer to illustration 10.7
1   Disconnect the cable from the negative terminal of the battery.

Removal

2   Unplug the coil high tension wire.
3   Unplug both electrical leads from the coil.
4   Remove both mounting nuts and remove the coil from the engine.
5   On models with the later style coil, drill out the rivets holding the coil bracket to the engine bracket and separate the coil from the bracket.
6   Lift the coil from the engine compartment. **Note:** *When installing it, use bolts and nuts with lock washers as a substitute.*

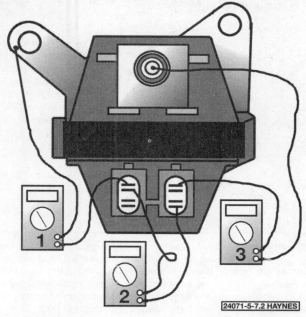

10.7 To check the ignition coil, use an ohmmeter to perform the following three checks (if the coil fails any of these tests, replace it)

1   *On high scale, the ohmmeter should read infinity*
2   *On low scale, the ohmmeter should read very low or zero*
3   *On high scale, the ohmmeter should read high, but not infinity*

24071-5-7.2 HAYNES

Check

7   Check the coil for opens and grounds by performing the following three tests with an ohmmeter **(see illustration)**.
8   Using the ohmmeter's high scale, hook up the ohmmeter leads as illustrated **(see test #1 in illustration 10.7)**. The ohmmeter should indicate a very high, or infinite, resistance value. If it doesn't, replace the coil.
9   Using the low scale, hook up the leads as illustrated **(see test #2 in illustration 10.7)**. The ohmmeter should indicate a very low, or zero, resistance value. If it doesn't, replace the coil.
10   Using the high scale, hook up the leads as illustrated **(see test #3 in illustration 10.7)**. The ohmmeter should not indicate an infinite resistance. If it does, replace the coil.

Installation

11   Installation of the coil is the reverse of the removal procedure.

11   Hall effect switch - check and replacement

Refer to illustration 11.2
1   Some HEI distributors are equipped with a Hall effect switch which is located above the pick-up coil assembly. The Hall effect switch is used in place of the R terminal of the HEI distributor to send engine RPM information to the ECM.
2   Test the switch by connecting a 12-volt power supply and voltmeter as shown **(see illustration)**. Check the polarity markings carefully before making any connections.
3   When the knife blade is not inserted as shown, the voltmeter should read less than 0.5-volts. If the reading is more, the Hall effect switch is faulty and must be replaced by a new one.
4   With the feeler gauge inserted, the voltmeter should read within 0.5-volts of battery

5

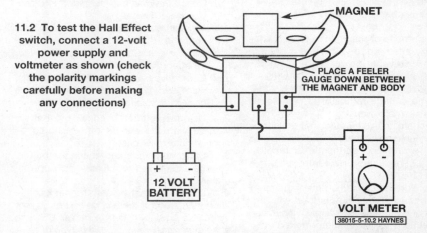

11.2 To test the Hall Effect switch, connect a 12-volt power supply and voltmeter as shown (check the polarity markings carefully before making any connections)

MAGNET

PLACE A FEELER GAUGE DOWN BETWEEN THE MAGNET AND BODY

12 VOLT BATTERY

VOLT METER

38015-5-10.2 HAYNES

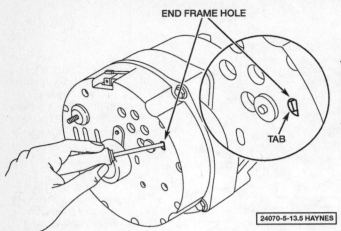

END FRAME HOLE

TAB

13.5 To full field an SI-type alternator, ground the tab located inside the hole by inserting a screwdriver blade into the hole and touching the tab and case at the same time

24070-5-13.5 HAYNES

14.2 Disconnect the BAT terminal wire and electrical connector from the alternator

voltage. Replace the switch with a new one if the reading is more.

5   Remove the Hall effect switch by unplugging the connector and removing the retaining screws.

6   Installation is the reverse of removal.

12 Charging system - general information and precautions

The charging system consists of a belt-driven alternator with an integral voltage regulator and the battery. These components work together to supply electrical power for the ignition system, the lights and all accessories.

There are two types of alternators used. Earlier vehicles use the SI type and later models are equipped with the CS type. There are two types of CS alternators in use, the CS-130 and the CS-144. All types use a conventional pulley and fan.

To determine which type of alternator is installed on your vehicle, look at the fasteners employed to attach the two halves of the alternator housing. All CS models use rivets instead of screws. CS alternators are rebuildable once the rivets are drilled out. However, we don't recommend this practice. For all intents and purposes, CS types should be considered non-serviceable and, if defective, should be exchanged as cores for new or rebuilt units.

The purpose of the voltage regulator is to limit the alternator's voltage to a preset value. This prevents power surges, circuit overloads, etc., during peak voltage output. On all models with which this manual is concerned, the voltage regulator is contained within the alternator housing.

The charging system does not ordinarily require periodic maintenance. The drivebelts, electrical wiring and connections should, however, be inspected at the intervals suggested in Chapter 1.

Take extreme care when making circuit connections to a vehicle equipped with an alternator and note the following. When making connections to the alternator from a bat-tery, always match correct polarity. Before using arc welding equipment to repair any part of the vehicle, disconnect the wires from the alternator and the battery terminal. Never start the engine with a battery charger connected. Always disconnect both battery cables before using a battery charger.

The charging indicator lamp on the dash lights when the ignition switch is turned on and goes out when the engine starts. If the lamp stays on or comes on once the engine is running, a charging system problem has occurred.

13 Charging system - check

Refer to illustration 13.5

1   If a malfunction occurs in the charging circuit, do not immediately assume that the alternator is causing the problem. First check the following items:

a) *The battery cables where they connect to the battery. Make sure the connections are clean and tight.*

b) *The battery electrolyte specific gravity. If it is low, charge the battery.*

c) *Check the external alternator wiring and connections. They must be in good condition.*

d) *Check the drivebelt condition and tension (see Chapter 1).*

e) *Make sure the alternator mounting bolts are tight.*

f) *Run the engine and check the alternator for abnormal noise (may be caused by a loose drive pulley, loose mounting bolts, worn or dirty bearings, defective diode or defective stator).*

2   Using a voltmeter, check the battery voltage with the engine off. It should be approximately 12-volts.

3   Start the engine and check the battery voltage again. It should now be approximately 14 to 15-volts.

4   Locate the test hole in the back of the alternator. **Note:** *If there is no test hole, your vehicle is equipped with a newer CS type alternator. Further testing of this type of alter-nator must be done by a dealer or automotive electrical shop.*

5   Ground the tab that is located inside the hole by inserting a screwdriver blade into the hole and touching the tab and the case at the same time **(see illustration)**. **Caution:** *Do not run the engine with the tab grounded any longer than necessary to obtain a voltmeter reading. If the alternator is charging, it is running unregulated during the test. This condition may overload the electrical system and cause damage to the components.*

6   The reading on the voltmeter should be 15-volts or higher with the tab grounded in the test hole.

7   If the voltmeter indicates low battery voltage, the alternator is faulty and should be replaced with a new one (see Section 14).

8   If the voltage reading is 15-volts or higher and a no charge condition is present, the regulator or field circuit is the problem. Remove the alternator (see Section 14) and have it checked further by an auto electric shop.

14 Alternator - removal and installation

Refer to illustrations 14.2 and 14.3

1   Disconnect the cable from the negative battery terminal.

2   Disconnect the two electrical connectors from the rear of the alternator **(see illustration)**.

3   Remove the bolt retaining the alternator to the adjusting bracket **(see illustration)**.

4   Remove the alternator pivot bolt and remove the alternator from the vehicle.

5   Installation is the reverse of removal.

6   Adjust the alternator drivebelt (see Chapter 1).

15 Alternator brushes - replacement

Refer to illustrations 15.2, 15.3a, 15.3b, 15.4, 15.5, 15.6, 15.7 and 15.10

Note: *The following procedure applies only to*

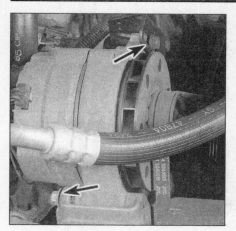

14.3 Alternator mounting details (typical)

15.2 Mark the drive end frame and rectifier end frame assemblies with a scribe or paint before separating the two halves

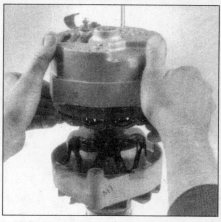

15.3a Carefully separate the drive end frame and the rectifier end frame assemblies

SI type alternators. CS types have riveted housings and shouldn't be disassembled.

1   Remove the alternator from the vehicle (see Section 15).

2   Scribe or paint marks on the front and rear end frame housings of the alternator to facilitate reassembly **(see illustration)**.

3   Remove the four through-bolts holding

the front and rear end frames together, then separate the drive end frame from the rectifier end frame **(see illustrations)**.

4   Remove the bolts holding the stator to the rear end frame and separate the stator from the end frame **(see illustration)**.

5   Remove the nuts attaching the diode

trio to the rectifier bridge and remove the trio **(see illustration)**.

6   Remove the screws attaching the resistor (not used on all models) and brush holder to the end frame and remove the brush holder **(see illustration)**.

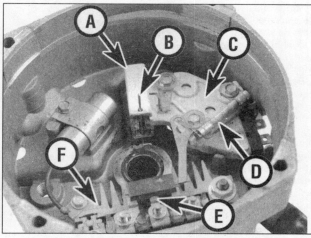

15.3b Inside the SI-type alternator

A   Brush holder
B   Paper clip retaining brushes
C   Regulator (beneath brush holder
D   Resistor (not all models)
E   Diode trio
F   Rectifier bridge

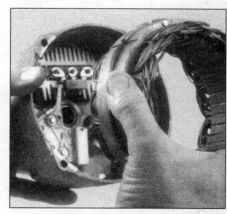

15.4 After removing the bolts holding the stator assembly to the end frame, remove the stator

5

15.5 Remove the nuts attaching the diode trio to the rectifier bridge and remove the trio

15.6 After removing the screws that attach the brush holder and the resistor (if equipped) to the end frame, remove the brush holder

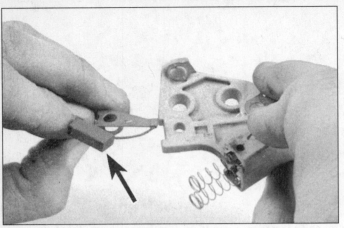

15.7 Remove the brushes from the brush holder

15.10 To hold the brushes in place during reassembly, insert a paper clip like this though the hole in the end frame nearest the rotor shaft

7   Remove the brushes from the brush holder **(see illustration)**.

8   Remove the springs from the brush holder.

9   Installation is the reverse of the removal procedure, noting the following:

10   When installing the brushes in the brush holder, install the brush closest to the end frame first. Slip a straightened paper clip through the rear of the end frame to hold the brush, then insert the second brush and push the paper clip in to hold both brushes while reassembly is completed **(see illustration)**. The paper clip should not be removed until the front and rear end frames have been bolted together.

16   Starting system - general information

The starting system is composed of a starter motor, solenoid and battery. The battery supplies the electrical energy to the solenoid, which then completes the circuit to the starter motor which does the actual work of cranking the engine.

The solenoid and starter motor are mounted together at the lower right side of the engine. No periodic lubrication or maintenance is required.

The electrical circuits of the vehicle are arranged so the starter motor can only be operated when the clutch pedal is depressed (manual transmission) or the transmission selector lever is in Park or Neutral (automatic transmission).

Never operate the starter motor for more than 15 seconds at a time without pausing to allow it to cool for at least two minutes. Excessive cranking can cause overheating, which can seriously damage the starter.

17   Starter motor - testing in vehicle

Refer to illustration 17.6

1   If the starter motor does not turn at all

when the switch is operated, make sure that the shift lever is in Neutral or Park (automatic transmission) or that the clutch pedal is depressed (manual transmission).

2   Make sure that the battery is charged and that all cables, both at the battery and starter solenoid terminals, are secure.

3   If the starter motor spins but the engine is not cranking, the overrunning clutch in the starter motor is slipping and the motor must be removed from the engine for replacement.

4   If, when the switch is actuated, the starter motor does not operate at all but the solenoid clicks, then the problem lies with either the battery, the main solenoid contacts or the starter motor itself. **Note:** *Before diagnosing starter problems, make sure that the battery is fully charged.*

5   If the solenoid plunger cannot be heard when the switch is actuated, the solenoid itself is defective or the solenoid circuit is open.

6   To check the solenoid, connect a jumper lead between the battery (+) and the "S" terminal on the solenoid **(see illustration)**. If the starter motor now operates, the solenoid is OK and the problem is in the ignition switch, neutral start switch or in the wiring.

7   If the starter motor still does not operate, remove the starter/solenoid assembly for disassembly, testing and repair.

8   If the starter motor cranks the engine at an abnormally slow speed, first make sure that the battery is charged and that all terminal connections are tight. If the engine is partially seized, or has the wrong viscosity oil in it, it will crank slowly.

9   Run the engine until normal operating temperature is reached, then disconnect the coil wire from the distributor cap and ground it on the engine.

10   Connect a voltmeter positive lead to the starter motor terminal of the solenoid and then connect the negative lead to ground.

11   Crank the engine and take the voltmeter readings as soon as a steady figure is indicated. Do not allow the starter motor to turn for more than 15 seconds at a time. A reading of 9-volts or more, with the starter motor turning at normal cranking speed, is normal.

17.6 Typical starter solenoid "S" terminal location (arrow)

If the reading is 9-volts or more but the cranking speed is slow, the motor is faulty. If the reading is less than 9-volts and the cranking speed is slow, the solenoid contacts are probably burned.

18   Starter motor - removal and installation

Refer to illustration 18.3

1   Disconnect the cable from the negative battery terminal.

2   On four-wheel drive models remove the skid plate (if equipped) and the cross member. Remove the starter brace and shield, if so equipped.

3   From beneath the vehicle, remove the two starter motor-to-engine bolts **(see illustration)**. **Note:** *On 1.9L four-cylinder engines there is a bolt under the starter and a nut on a stud at the top. Let the starter drop down far enough to allow removal of the nuts attaching the wires to the starter solenoid and battery cable. Support the starter while the wires are removed.*

4   Remove the starter.

18.3 To remove the starter from the engine, detach the wires from the solenoid terminals, then remove both mounting bolts (arrows)

19.3 Withdraw the solenoid assembly from the starter housing

5   Installation is the reverse of removal. Make sure that the shims, if so equipped, are properly reinstalled.

19   Starter solenoid - removal and installation

V6, 2.0L and 2.5L four-cylinder engines

Refer to illustration 19.3

1   After removing the starter as described in Section 18, disconnect the field strap from the solenoid.

2   Remove the two screws which secure the solenoid housing to the starter end frame.

3   Twist the solenoid in a clockwise direction to disengage the flange from the starter body **(see illustration)**.

4   To install, first make sure the return spring is in position on the plunger, then insert the solenoid body into the starter housing and turn the solenoid counterclockwise to engage the flange.

5   Install the two solenoid screws and connect the field strap.

1.9L four-cylinder engine

6   After removing the starter as described in Section 18, disconnect the strap from the "M" terminal on the solenoid.

7   Remove the two bolts which secure the solenoid to the starter and remove the solenoid.

8   Installation is the reverse of the removal procedure.

20   Starter motor brushes - replacement

V6, 2.0L and 2.5L four-cylinder engines

Refer to illustrations 20.3, 20.4, 20.6 and 20.8

1   Remove the starter and solenoid assembly from the vehicle (see Section 18).

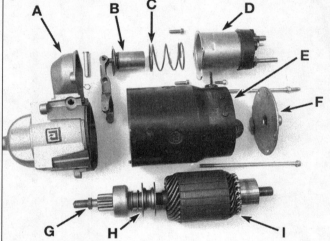

20.3 Exploded view of the starter motor (V6, 2.0L and 2.5L engines)

A   *Drive end housing*
B   *Plunger and shift lever*
C   *Plunger return spring*
D   *Solenoid (switch)*
E   *Frame and field assembly*
F   *Commutator end cap/frame*
G   *Piston stop collar*
H   *Drive assembly*
I   *Armature*

5

20.4 Removing the end frame from the field frame housing

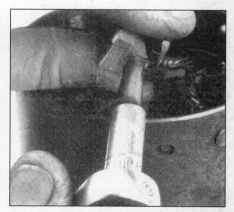

20.6 Unbolting a brush and brush support from the brush holder

2   Remove the solenoid from the starter housing (see Section 19).

3   Remove the starter motor through-bolts after marking the relationship of the commutator end frame to the field frame housing to simplify reassembly **(see illustration)**.

4   Remove the end frame from the field frame housing **(see illustration)**.

5   Mark the relationship of the field frame housing to the drive end housing and pull the field frame housing away from the drive end housing and over the armature.

6   Unbolt the brushes and brush supports from the brush holders in the field frame housing **(see illustration)**.

7   To install new brushes, attach the brushes to the brush supports, making sure they are flush with the bottom of the supports, and bolt the brushes/supports to the brush holders.

8   Install the field frame over the armature, with the brushes resting on the first step of the armature collar at this point **(see illustration)**.

9   Make sure the field frame is properly aligned with the drive end housing, then push the brushes off the collar and into place on the armature.

10   The remaining installation steps are the reverse of those for removal.

1.9L four-cylinder engine

11   Remove the starter and solenoid assembly from the vehicle (see Section 18).

12   Remove the solenoid from the starter housing (see Section 19).

13   Remove the dust cover, ring and thrust washer.

14   Remove the two screws and the through-bolts.

15   Remove the rear cover from the starter housing.

16   Raise the brush spring and remove the brush. Remove the brush holder assembly.

17   The brush and brush lead can now be removed from the starter housing.

18   Installation is the reverse of removal.

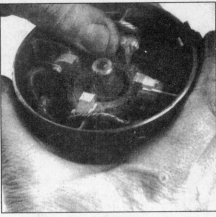

20.8 Installing the field frame over the armature (note the position of the brushes on the armature collar)

Chapter 6
Emissions control systems

Contents

	Section		Section
Air management system	9	Exhaust Gas Recirculation (EGR) system	10
Catalytic converter	15	Feedback carburetor system	2
Computer Command Control (CCC) system and trouble codes	3	General information	1
Early Fuel Evaporation (EFE) system	8	Information sensors	5
Electronic Control Module (ECM)/Programmable Read		Positive Crankcase Ventilation (PCV) system	12
Only Memory (PROM)/CALPAK/MEM-CAL	4	Thermostatic air cleaner (THERMAC) (carbureted and	
Electronic Spark Control (ESC) system	7	TBI models only)	13
Electronic Spark Timing (EST)	6	Transmission Converter Clutch (TCC)	14
Evaporative Emission Control System (EECS)	11		

Component location

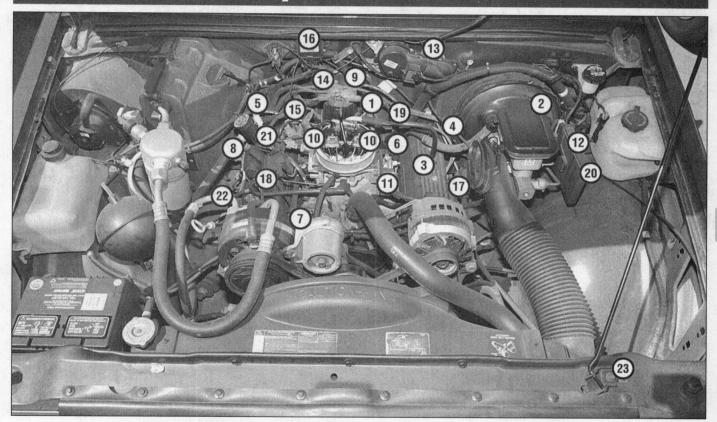

Emission control system and related component locations - 4.3L V6 engine (Throttle Body Injection)

1	ECM harness ground	10	Fuel injector	17	Oil pressure switch
2	Fuel pump test connector	11	Idle Air Control (IAC) motor	18	Electric Air Control (EAC) solenoid
3	Crankcase breather hose	12	Fuel pump relay	19	Exhaust Gas Recirculation vacuum
4	Oxygen sensor (Federal)	13	Transmission Converter Clutch		solenoid
5	Oxygen sensor (California)		connector	20	A/C Relay
6	Throttle Position Sensor (TPS)	14	Electronic Spark Timing (EST)	21	Positive Crankcase Ventilation (PCV)
7	Coolant temperature sensor		distributor		valve
8	Electronic Spark Control (ESC) sensor	15	Remote ignition coil	22	Air pump
9	EGR vacuum diagnostic switch	16	Electronic Spark Control (ESC) module	23	Fuel Vapor Canister

Component location

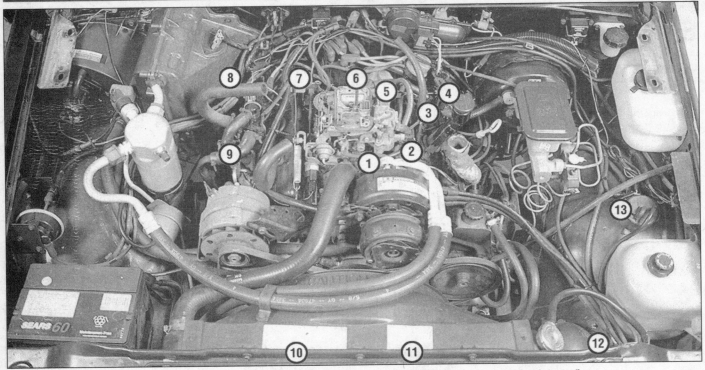

Locations of the emission system components on a California 2.8L V6 model (carbureted)

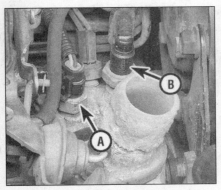

1 Coolant temperature sensor (A),
   Thermal vacuum switch (B)

2 Throttle Position Sensor

3 Heated EFE grid connector (arrow)

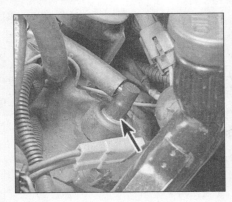

4 PCV valve
   (arrow)

5 Mixture
   control solenoid
   (arrow)

Component location

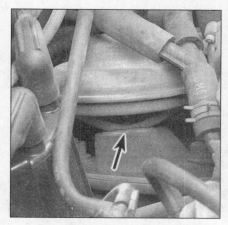

6 Exhaust Gas Recirculation (EGR)
   valve (arrow)

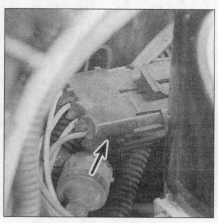

7 Electronic Spark Timing (EST)
   connector (arrow)

8 Oxygen sensor (arrow)

9 Air diverter valve (arrow)

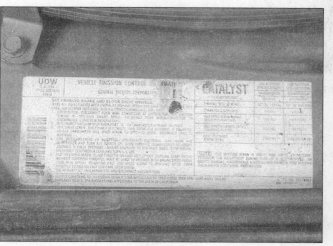

10 VECI label

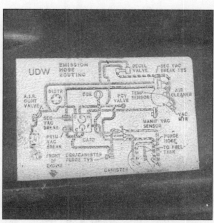

11 Vacuum hose routing diagram

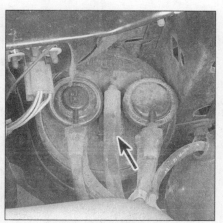

12 Vapor canister (arrow)

13 Manifold Absolute Pressure (MAP)
    sensor (arrow)

6

Component location

Emissions and fuel injection components on a 4.3L V6 engine (Central Port Injection)

1	Fuel pump relay	5	MAP sensor	8	IAC valve
2	Distributor	6	Air cleaner	9	PCV valve
3	Intake manifold tuning assembly	7	Throttle Position Sensor (TPS)	10	Coil
4	Air intake plenum				

1   General information

Refer to illustration 1.7

To prevent pollution of the atmosphere from incompletely burned and evaporating gases, and to maintain good driveability and fuel economy, a number of emission control devices are incorporated.

They include the:

Closed Loop Emissions Control system
Air management system
Feedback carburetor system
Electronic Spark Timing (EST)
Electronic Spark Control (ESC) system
Exhaust Gas Recirculation (EGR) system
Evaporative Emission Control System (EECS)
Positive Crankcase Ventilation (PCV) system
Transmission Converter Clutch (TCC)

Catalytic converter
Thermostatic air cleaner (THERMAC)
Air conditioning control

All of these systems are linked, directly or indirectly, to the Computer Command Control (CCC or C3) system.

The Sections in this Chapter include general descriptions, checking procedures within the scope of the home mechanic and component replacement procedures (when possible) for each of the systems listed above.

Before assuming that an emissions control system is malfunctioning, check the fuel and ignition systems carefully. The diagnosis of some emission control devices requires specialized tools, equipment and training. If checking and servicing become too difficult or if a procedure is beyond the scope of your skills, consult your dealer service department.

This doesn't mean, however, that emis-sion control systems are particularly difficult to maintain and repair. You can quickly and easily perform many checks and do most (if not all) of the regular maintenance at home with common tune-up and hand tools. **Note:** *The most frequent cause of emissions problems is simply a loose or broken vacuum hose or wiring connection, so always check the hose and wiring connections first.*

Pay close attention to any special precautions outlined in this Chapter. It should be noted that the illustrations of the various systems may not exactly match the system installed on your vehicle because of changes made by the manufacturer during production or from year-to-year.

A Vehicle Emissions Control Information (VECI) label is located in the engine compartment **(see illustration)**. This label contains important emissions specifications and ignition timing procedures, as well as a vacuum

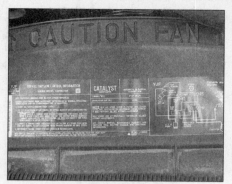

1.7 The Vehicle Emission Control Information (VECI) label is located on the fan shroud and contains information on idle speed adjustment, ignition, timing, location of emission devices on your vehicle, vacuum line routing, etc.

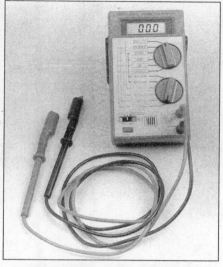

3.1 Digital multimeters can be used for testing all types of circuits; because of their high impedance, they are much more accurate than analog meters for measuring millivolts in low-voltage computer circuits

3.2 Scanners like the Actron Scantool and the AutoXray XP240 are powerful diagnostic aids - programmed with comprehensive diagnostic information, they can tell you just about anything you want to know about your engine management system, but they are expensive

hose schematic and emissions components identification guide. When servicing the engine or emissions systems, the VECI label in your particular vehicle should always be checked for up-to-date information.

2   Feedback carburetor system

General description

1   The function of this system is to control the flow of fuel through the carburetor main metering circuits. The major components of the system are the mixture control (M/C) solenoid and the oxygen sensor.

2   The M/C solenoid changes the fuel/air mixture by allowing more or less fuel to flow through the carburetor. The M/C solenoid, located in the carburetor air horn, is in turn controlled by the ECM, which provides a ground for the solenoid. When the solenoid is energized the fuel flow through the carburetor is reduced, providing a leaner mixture, and when the ECM removes the ground path the solenoid de-energizes and allows more fuel flow.

3   The ECM determines the proper fuel mixture required by monitoring a signal sent by the oxygen sensor located in the exhaust stream. When the mixture is lean, the oxygen sensor voltage is low and the ECM commands a richer mixture. Conversely, when the mixture is rich, the oxygen sensor voltage is higher and the ECM commands a leaner mixture.

Check

Oxygen sensor

4   If the vehicle is equipped with a 1.9 liter engine, make sure that the oxygen sensor is replaced every 30,000 miles.

5   The proper operation of the sensor depends on the four conditions which follow:

6   Electrical conditions: The low voltages and low currents generated by the sensor depend upon good, clean connections which

should be checked whenever a malfunction of the sensor is suspected or indicated.

7   Outside air supply: The sensor is designed to allow air circulation to the internal portion of the sensor. Whenever the sensor is removed and installed or replaced, make sure the air passages are not restricted.

8   Proper operating temperature: The ECM will not react to the sensor signal until the sensor reaches approximately 600-degrees F (360-degrees C). This factor must be taken into consideration when evaluating the performance of the sensor.

9   Non-leaded fuel: The use of non-leaded fuel is essential for proper operation of the sensor. Make sure the fuel you are using is of this type.

10   In addition to observing the above conditions, special care must be taken whenever the sensor is handled. Violation of any of these cautionary procedures may lead to sensor failure. **Note:** *Do not attempt to measure the voltage output of the oxygen sensor with an analog voltmeter, because the current drain from an analog voltmeter would be enough to permanently damage the sensor.*

Mixture control solenoid

11   Check the electrical connectors and wires leading to the mixture control solenoid for looseness, fraying and other damage. Repair or replace any damaged wiring as necessary.

12   Check the mixture control solenoid for apparent physical damage. Replace it if damage is found.

Component replacement

Oxygen sensor

13   To replace the sensor, refer to Section 5.

Mixture control solenoid

14   See Chapter 4 for the M/C solenoid replacement procedure..

3   Computer Command Control (CCC) system and trouble codes

Diagnostic tool information

Refer to illustrations 3.1, 3.2 and 3.3

1   A digital multimeter is necessary for checking fuel injection and emission related components **(see illustration)**. A digital volt-ohmmeter is preferred over the older style analog multimeter for several reasons. The analog multimeter cannot display the volts, ohms or amps measurement in hundredths and thousands increments. When working with electronic circuits which are often very low voltage, this accurate reading is most important. Another good reason for the digital multimeter is the high impedance circuit. The digital multimeter is equipped with a high-resistance internal circuitry (10 million ohms). Because a voltmeter is hooked up in parallel with the circuit when testing, it is vital that none of the voltage being measured should be allowed to travel the parallel path set up by the meter itself. This dilemma does not show itself when measuring larger amounts of voltage (9 to 12 volt circuits) but if you are measuring a low voltage circuit such as the oxygen sensor signal voltage, a fraction of a volt may be a significant amount when diagnosing a problem.

2   Hand-held scanners are the most powerful and versatile tools for analyzing engine management systems used on later model vehicles **(see illustration)**. Each brand scan tool must be examined carefully to match the year, make and model of the vehicle you are working on. Often interchangeable cartridges

6

3.3 Trouble code tools simplify the task of extracting the trouble codes

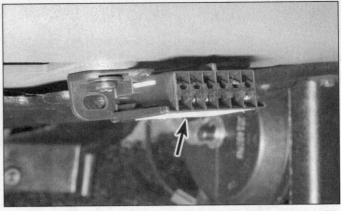

3.8a The assembly Line Data Link (ALDL) (arrow) is located under the dash near the fuse panel

are available to access the particular manufacturer (Ford, GM, Chrysler, etc.). Some manufacturers will specify by continent (Asia, Europe, USA, etc.).

3   Another type of code reader and less expensive is available at auto parts stores **(see illustration)**. These tools simplify the procedure for extracting codes from the engine management computer by simply "plugging in" to the diagnostic connector on the vehicle wiring harness.

General description

4   The Computer Command Control (CCC) system consists of an Electronic Control Module (ECM) and information sensors which monitor various functions of the engine and send data back to the ECM.

5   There are two types of ECMs used. Vehicles equipped with a four-cylinder engine have an ECM with a MEM-CAL (Memory and Calibration) unit. Vehicles equipped with a V6 engine have an ECM with a PROM and a CALPAK. **Note:** *1992 models equipped with a 2.5L or 4.3L (CPI) engine have an ECM referred to as the GMP4 with two serviceable parts; a controller without MEM-CAL and a MEM-CAL unit. 1992 models with a V6 engine without a 4L80-E transmission have an ECM referred to as a GMCM with three parts for service; a controller, a PROM and CAL-PAK. 1992 models with the Hydramatic 4L80-E transmission have a PCM referred to as GMP6 with two parts for service; a controller and a MEM-CAL.* The ECM controls the following systems:

   Feedback carburetor (see Section 2)
   Electronic Spark Timing (EST)
   Electronic Spark Control (ESC)
   Air management (TBI only)
   Exhaust Gas Recirculation (EGR)
   Transmission Converter Clutch (TCC)
   Manual transmission shift light
   Air conditioning clutch control

The CCC system is analogous to the central nervous system in the human body. The sensors (nerve endings) constantly relay information to the ECM (brain), which pro-

cesses the data and, if necessary, sends out a command to change the operating parameters of the engine (body).

6   Here's a specific example of how one portion of this system operates: An oxygen sensor, located in the exhaust manifold, constantly monitors the oxygen content of the exhaust gas. If the percentage of oxygen in the exhaust gas is incorrect, an electrical signal is sent to the ECM. The ECM takes this information, processes it and then sends a command to the fuel injection system, telling it to change the air/fuel mixture. This happens in a fraction of a second and it goes on continuously when the engine is running. The end result is an air/fuel mixture ratio which is constantly maintained at a predetermined ratio, regardless of driving conditions.

7   One might think that a system which uses an on-board computer and electrical sensors would be difficult to diagnose. This is not necessarily the case. The CCC system has a built-in diagnostic feature which indicates a problem by flashing a "Service Engine Soon" light on the instrument panel. When this light comes on during normal vehicle operation, a fault in one of the information sensor circuits or the ECM itself has been detected. More importantly, the source of the malfunction is stored in the ECM's memory.

Testing

Refer to illustrations 3.8a and 3.8b

8   To retrieve this information from the ECM memory, you must use a scan tool, code reader or a short jumper wire to ground a diagnostic terminal. This terminal is part of an electrical connector known as the Assembly Line Data Link (ALDL) **(see illustrations)**. The ALDL is located underneath the dashboard, just below the instrument panel and to the left of the center console. To use the ALDL, remove the plastic cover by sliding it toward you. With the electrical connector exposed to view, push one end of the jumper wire into the diagnostic terminal (B) and the other end into the ground terminal (A).

9   When the diagnostic terminal is

grounded with the ignition on and the engine stopped, the system will enter the Diagnostic Mode. In this mode the ECM will display a "Code 12" by flashing the "Service Engine Soon" light, indicating that the system is operating. A code 12 is simply one flash, followed by a brief pause, then two flashes in quick succession. This code will be flashed three times. If no other codes are stored, Code 12 will continue to flash until the diagnostic terminal ground is removed. After flashing Code 12 three times, the ECM will display any stored trouble codes. Each code will be flashed three times, then Code 12 will be flashed again, indicating that the display of any stored trouble codes has been completed.

10   When the ECM sets a trouble code, the

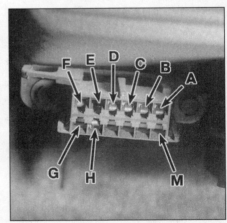

3.8b The Assembly Line Data Link (ALDL) terminal identification

A   *Ground*
B   *Diagnostic terminal*
C   *AIR (if used)*
D   *Check Engine light (if used)*
E   *Serial data (special tool required - do not use)*
F   *TCC (if used)*
G   *Fuel pump (if used)*
H   *Brake sense speed input*
M   *Serial data (four-cylinder engine only, special tool required - do not use)*

Service Engine Soon light will come on and a trouble code will be stored in memory. If the problem is intermittent, the light will go out after 10 seconds, when the fault goes away. However, the trouble code will stay in the ECM memory until the battery voltage to the ECM is interrupted. Removing battery voltage for 10 seconds will clear all stored trouble codes. Trouble codes should always be cleared after repairs have been completed. **Caution:** *To prevent damage to the ECM, the ignition switch must be Off when disconnecting or connecting power to the ECM.*

11   Following is a list of the typical trouble codes which may be encountered while diagnosing the Computer Command Control System. Also included are simplified troubleshooting procedures. If the problem persists after these checks have been made, more detailed service procedures will have to be done by a dealer service department.

Trouble codes	Circuit or system	Probable cause
Code 12 (1 flash, pause, 2 flashes)	No distributor reference pulses to ECM	This code will flash whenever the diagnostic terminal is grounded with the ignition turned On and the engine not running. If additional trouble codes are stored in the ECM they will appear after this code has flashed three times. If this code appears while the engine is running, no reference pulses from the distributor are reaching the ECM.
Code 13 (1 flash, pause, 3 flashes)	Oxygen sensor circuit	Check for a sticking or misadjusted throttle position sensor. Check the wiring and connectors from the oxygen sensor. Replace the oxygen sensor.
Code 14 (1 flash, pause, 4 flashes)	Coolant sensor/high temp	If the engine is experiencing overheating problems the problem must be rectified before continuing. Check all wiring and connectors associated with the coolant temperature sensor. Replace the coolant temperature sensor.*
Code 15 (1 flash, pause, 5 flashes)	Coolant sensor/low temp	See above, then check the wiring connections at the ECM.
Code 21 (2 flashes, pause, 1 flash)	Throttle position sensor/voltage high	Check for a sticking or misadjusted TPS plunger. Check all wiring and connections between the TPS and the ECM. Adjust or replace the TPS (see Chapter 4).*
Code 22 (2 flashes, pause, 2 flashes)	Throttle position sensor/voltage low	Check the TPS adjustment (Chapter 4). Check the ECM connector. Replace the TPS (Chapter 4).*
Code 23 (carbureted) (2 flashes, pause, 3 flashes)	Mixture control solenoid	The mixture control solenoid is open or grounded.
Code 23 (fuel-injected) (2 flashes, pause, 3 flashes)	MAT low temp indication	Sets if the manifold air temperature sensor, connections or wires are open for 3 seconds.
Code 23 (1992 CPI only) (2 flashes, pause, 3 flashes)	IAT low temp indication	Sets if the manifold air temperature sensor, connections or wires are open for 3 seconds.
Code 24 (2 flashes, pause, 4 flashes)	Vehicle speed sensor	A fault in this circuit should be indicated only when the vehicle is in motion. Disregard Code 24 if it is set when the drive wheels are not turning. Check the connections at the ECM. Check the TPS setting.
Code 25 (2 flashes, pause, 5 flashes)	ATI sensor/high air	High temperature indication. Sets if the sensor or signal line becomes grounded for 3 seconds.
Code 32 (carbureted) (3 flashes, pause, 2 flashes)	BARO circuit low	Barometric pressure sensor circuit low.
Code 32 (fuel-injected) (3 flashes, pause, 2 flashes)	EGR	Vacuum switch shorted to ground on start-up, switch not closed after the ECM has commanded the EGR for a specified period of time or the EGR solenoid circuit is open for specified period of time. Replace the EGR valve.*
Code 33 (3 flashes, pause, 3 flashes)	MAP sensor	Check the vacuum hoses from the MAP sensor. Check the electrical connections at the ECM. Replace the MAP sensor.*
Code 34 (3 flashes, pause, 4 flashes)	Vacuum sensor or MAP sensor	Code 34 will set when the signal voltage from the MAP sensor is too low. Instead the ECM will substitute a fixed MAP value and use the TPS to control fuel delivery. Replace the MAP sensor.*
Code 35 (carbureted) (3 flashes, pause, 5 flashes)	ISC valve	Idle Speed Control error. Replace the ISC.*
Code 35 (fuel-injected) (3 flashes, pause, 5 flashes)	IAC valve	Idle Air Control error. Code will set when closed throttle speed is 50 rpm above or below the correct idle speed for 30 seconds. Replace the IAC.*

6

Trouble codes	Circuit or system	Probable cause
Code 42 (4 flashes, pause, 2 flashes)	Electronic Spark Timing (EST)	Electronic Spark Timing bypass circuit or EST circuit is grounded or open. A malfunctioning HEI module can cause this code.
Code 43 (4 flashes, pause, 3 flashes)	Electronic Spark Control	The ESC retard signal has been on for too long or the system has (ESC) unit failed a functional check.
Code 44 (4 flashes, pause, 4 flashes)	O2 sensor indicates lean	Check the ECM wiring connections, particularly terminals 15 and 8. exhaust Check for vacuum leakage at the TBI base gasket, vacuum hoses or the intake manifold gasket. Replace the oxygen sensor.*
Code 45 (4 flashes, pause, 5 flashes)	O2 sensor indicates rich	Check the evaporative charcoal canister and its components for the exhaust presence of fuel. Replace the oxygen sensor.
Code 51 (5 flashes, pause, 1 flash)	PROM or MEM-CAL	Make sure that the PROM or MEM-CAL is properly installed in the ECM. Replace the PROM or MEM-CAL.*
Code 52 (5 flashes, pause, 2 flashes)	CALPAK	Check the CALPAK to insure proper installation. Replace the CALPAK.*
Code 53 (5 flashes, pause, 3 flashes)	System over-voltage (indicates a basic alternator problem)	Check charging system.
Code 54 (fuel injected) (5 flashes, pause, 4 flashes)	Fuel pump	Low fuel pump voltage. Sets when the fuel pump voltage is less than 2 volts when reference pulses are being received.
Code 54 (carbureted) (5 flashes, pause, 4 flashes)	M/C solenoid	Check all M/C solenoid and ECM wires and connections. *Replace if necessary with a new unit.
Code 55 (5 flashes, pause, 5 flashes)	ECM	Be sure that the ECM ground connections are tight. If they are, replace the ECM.*

* Component replacement may not cure the problem in all cases. For this reason, you may want to seek professional advice before purchasing replacement parts.
Note: *There are additional codes that relate only to models equipped with the 4L60-E electronic controlled transmission. These codes represent internal transmission problems that should be left to a dealer service department or transmission repair shop. These codes are as follows: 37, 38, 39 and 58 through 82.*

4 Electronic Control Module (ECM)/Programmable Read Only Memory (PROM)/CALPAK/MEM-CAL

Refer to illustrations 4.8a, 4.8b, 4.13, 4.14 and 4.17

Note: *1992 models equipped with a 2.5L or 4.3L (CPI) engine have an ECM referred to as the GMP4 with two serviceable parts; a controller without MEM-CAL and a MEM-CAL unit. 1992 models with a V6 engine without a 4L80-E transmission have an ECM referred to as a GMCM with three parts for service; a controller, a PROM and CAL-PAK. 1992 models with the Hydramatic 4L80-E transmission have a PCM referred to as GMP6 with two parts for service; a controller and a MEM-CAL.*

1 The Electronic Control Module (ECM) is located inside the body under the dash. Different models may vary in the exact location.
2 Disconnect the negative battery cable from the battery.

3 Remove the screws from the trim panel under the dashboard.
4 Remove the mounting bolts from the bracket.
5 Carefully push any wire harness or cable to the side.
6 Remove the retaining bolts and carefully slide the ECM out far enough to unplug the electrical connector.
7 Unplug both electrical connectors from the ECM. **Caution:** *The ignition switch must be turned off when pulling out or plugging in the electrical connectors to prevent damage to the ECM.*

PROM

8 To allow one model of ECM to be used for many different vehicles **(see illustration)**, a device called a PROM (Programmable Read Only Memory) is used. To access the PROM remove the cover. The PROM **(see illustration)** is located inside the ECM and contains information on the vehicle's weight, engine, transmission, axle ratio, etc. One ECM part number can be used by many GM vehicles but the PROM is very specific and

must be used only in the vehicle for which it was designed. For this reason, it is essential to check the latest parts book and Service Bulletin information for the correct part number when replacing a PROM. An ECM purchased at the dealer is purchased without a PROM. The PROM from the old ECM must be carefully removed and installed in the new ECM.

CALPAK

9 A device known as a CALPAK **(see illustration 4.8b)** is used to allow fuel delivery if other parts of the ECM are damaged. The CALPAK has an access door in the ECM and replacement is the same as that described for the PROM.

MEM-CAL

10 The MEM-CAL contains the functions of the PROM, CALPAK and ESC module used on other GM applications. Like the PROM, it contains the calibrations needed for a specific vehicle as well as the back-up fuel control circuitry required if the rest of the ECM becomes damaged or faulty.

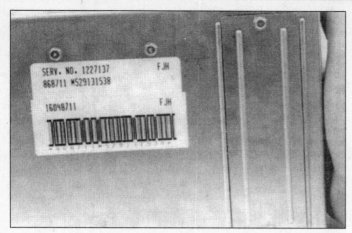

4.8a If you are replacing the ECM, compare the service numbers on the label on the old unit to the numbers on the new one

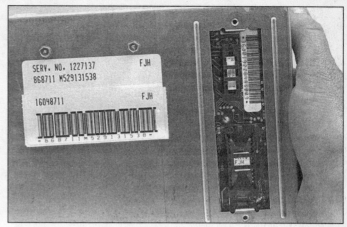

4.8b The CALPAK (top) and PROM (bottom) inside an ECM for a V6 (ECMs for the four-cylinder are similar but have a MEM-CAL instead of a PROM and CALPAK

ECM/PROM/CALPAK replacement

11   Turn the ECM so that the bottom cover is facing up and place it on a clean work surface.

12   Remove the PROM/CALPAK access cover.

13   Grasp the PROM carrier at the narrow ends **(see illustration)**. Gently rock the carrier from end to end while applying firm upward force. The PROM carrier and PROM should lift off the PROM socket easily.

14   Note the reference end of the PROM carrier **(see illustration)** before setting it aside.

15   If you are replacing the ECM, remove the new ECM from its container and check the service number to make sure that it is the same as the number on the old ECM.

16   If you are replacing the PROM, remove the new PROM from its container and check the service number to make sure that it is the same as the number of the old PROM.

17   Position the PROM and carrier assembly squarely over the PROM socket with the small notched end of the carrier aligned with the small notch in the socket at the pin 1 end. Press on the PROM carrier until it seats firmly in the socket **(see illustration)**.

18   If the PROM is new, make sure that the notch in the PROM is matched to the small notch in the carrier. **Caution:** *If the PROM is installed backwards and the ignition switch is turned on, the PROM will be destroyed.*

19   Using the tool, install the new PROM carrier in the PROM socket of the ECM. The small notch of the carrier should be aligned with the small notch in the socket. Press on the PROM carrier until it is firmly seated in the socket. **Caution:** *Do not press on the PROM - press only on the carrier.*

20   Attach the access cover to the ECM and tighten the two screws.

21   Install the ECM in the support bracket, plug in the electrical connectors to the ECM and install the hush panel.

22   Start the engine.

23   Enter the diagnostic mode by grounding the diagnostic terminal of the ALDL (see Section 3). If no trouble codes occur, the PROM

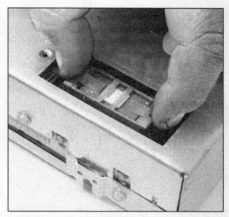

4.13 Grasp the PROM carrier at the ends and gently rock it until the PROM is unplugged from the socket

6

is correctly installed.

24   If Trouble Code 51 occurs, or if the Service Engine Soon light comes on and remains

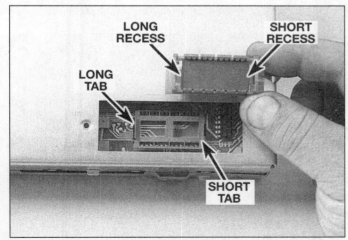

4.14 Note how the notch in the PROM carrier is matched up with the smaller notch in the socket

LONG RECESS
SHORT RECESS
LONG TAB
SHORT TAB

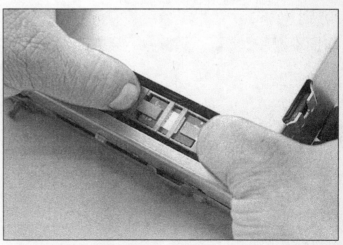

4.17 Press only on the ends of the PROM carrier - pressure on the area in between could result in bent or broken pins or damage to the PROM

5.1 The coolant temperature sensor (arrow) is located near the thermostat housing (V6 engine)

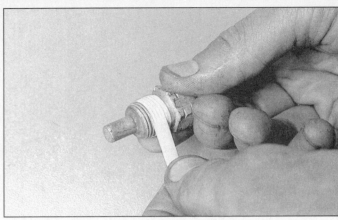

5.3 To prevent leakage, wrap the threads of the coolant temperature sensor with Teflon tape before installing it

lit, the PROM is not fully seated, is installed backwards, has bent pins or is defective.

25   If the PROM is not fully seated, pressing firmly on both ends of the carrier should correct the problem.

26   If the pins have been bent, remove the PROM, straighten the pins and reinstall the PROM. If the bent pins break or crack when you attempt to straighten them, discard the PROM and replace it with a new one.

27   If careful inspection indicates that the PROM is fully seated, has not been installed backwards and has no bent pins, but the Service Engine Soon light remains lit, the PROM is probably faulty and must be replaced.

MEM-CAL replacement

28   Remove the MEM-CAL access cover.

29   Using two fingers, push both retaining clips back away from the MEM-CAL. At the same time, grasp the MEM-CAL at both ends and lift it up out of its socket. Do not remove the MEM-CAL cover itself. **Caution:** *Use of unapproved removal or installation methods may damage the MEM-CAL or socket.*

30   Verify the numbers on the old ECM and new ECM match up (or that the numbers of the old and new MEM-CALs match up,

depending on which component(s) you're replacing) as described in the procedure for removing and installing the PROM and CAL-PAK.

31   To install the MEM-CAL in the MEM-CAL socket, press only on the ends of the MEM-CAL.

32   The small notches in the MEM-CAL must be aligned with the small notches in the MEM-CAL socket. Press on the ends of the MEM-CAL until the retaining clips snap into the ends of the MEM-CAL. Do not press on the middle of the MEM-CAL - press only on the ends.

33   The remainder of the installation is similar to that for the PROM/CALPAK.

34   Once the new MEM-CAL is installed in the old ECM (or the old MEM-CAL is installed in the new ECM), check your installation to verify that it has been installed properly by doing the following test:

a) *Turn the ignition switch on.*
b) *Enter the diagnostics mode at the ALDL (see Section 3).*
c) *Allow Code 12 to flash four times to verify that no other codes are present. This indicates that the MEM-CAL is installed properly and the ECM is functioning properly.*

35   If trouble codes 41, 42, 43, 51 or 55 occur, or if the Service Engine Soon light is on constantly but is flashing no codes, the MEM-CAL is either not fully seated or is defective. If it's not fully seated, press firmly on the ends of the MEM-CAL. If it is necessary to remove the MEM-CAL, follow the above Steps again.

---

5   Information sensors

Refer to illustrations 5.1, 5.3, 5.5a, 5.5b, 5.13a, 5.13b, 5.35, 5.47a and 5.47b

Engine coolant temperature sensor

1   The coolant sensor **(see illustration)** is a thermistor (a resistor which varies the value of its voltage output in accordance with temperature changes). A failure in the coolant sensor circuit should set either a Code 14 or a Code 15. These codes indicate a failure in the coolant temperature circuit, so the appropriate solution to the problem will be either repair of a wire or replacement of the sensor.

2   To remove the sensor, release the locking tab, unplug the electrical connector, then

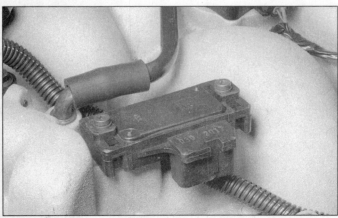

5.5a Location of the Manifold Absolute Pressure (MAP) sensor assembly on a 4.3L V6 engine

5.5b Location of the MAP sensor (arrow) on a four-cylinder engine

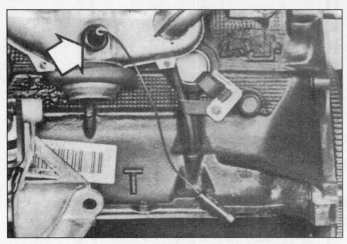

5.13a The oxygen sensor for the four-cylinder engine is located in the exhaust manifold (engine removed from vehicle for clarity)

5.13b The oxygen sensor on the V6 engine is located in the left exhaust manifold

carefully unscrew the sensor. **Caution:** *Handle the cool- ant sensor with care. Damage to this sensor will affect the operation of the entire fuel injection system.*

3   Before installing the new sensor, wrap the threads with Teflon sealing tape to prevent leakage and thread corrosion **(see illustration)**.

4   Installation is the reverse of removal.

Manifold Absolute Pressure (MAP) sensor

5   The Manifold Absolute Pressure (MAP) sensor **(see illustrations)** monitors the intake manifold pressure changes resulting from changes in engine load and speed and converts the information into a voltage output.

6   The ECM uses the MAP sensor to control fuel delivery and ignition timing.

7   A failure in the MAP sensor circuit should set a Code 33 or a Code 34.

Power steering pressure switch

8   Turning the steering wheel increases power steering fluid pressure and engine load. The pressure switch will close before the load can cause an idle problem.

9   The power steering switch is normally open to ground and the voltage supply circuit will be near battery voltage. Closing the switch causes the supply circuit to read less than 1-volt.

10   A pressure switch that will not open or an open circuit will cause timing to retard at idle and may affect idle quality.

11   A pressure switch that will not close may cause the engine to die when power steering loads are high.

12   The pressure switch can be checked with an ohmmeter.

Oxygen sensor

General description

13   The oxygen sensor, which is located in the exhaust manifold **(see illustrations)**, monitors the oxygen content of the exhaust gas stream. The oxygen content in the exhaust reacts with the oxygen sensor to produce a voltage output which varies from 0.1-volt (high oxygen, lean mixture) to 0.9-volt (low oxygen, rich mixture). The ECM constantly monitors this variable voltage output to determine the ratio of oxygen to fuel in the mixture. The ECM alters the air/fuel mixture ratio by controlling the pulse width (open time) of the fuel injectors. A mixture ratio of 14.7 parts air to 1 part fuel is the ideal mixture ratio for minimizing exhaust emissions, thus allowing the catalytic converter to operate at maximum efficiency. It is this ratio of 14.7 to 1 which the ECM and the oxygen sensor attempt to maintain at all times.

14   The oxygen sensor produces no voltage when it is below its normal operating temperature of about 600-degrees F (360-degrees C). During this initial period before warm-up, the ECM operates in open loop mode.

15   If the engine reaches normal operating temperature and/or has been running for two or more minutes, and if the oxygen sensor is producing a steady signal voltage between 0.35 and 0.55-volts, even though the TPS indicates that the engine is not at idle, the ECM will set a Code 13.

16   A delay of two minutes or more between engine start-up and normal operation of the sensor, followed by a low voltage signal or a short in the sensor circuit, will cause the ECM to set a Code 44. If a high voltage signal occurs, the ECM will set a Code 45.

17   When any of the above codes occur, the ECM operates in the open loop mode - that is it controls fuel delivery in accordance with a programmed default value instead of feedback information from the oxygen sensor.

18   The proper operation of the oxygen sensor depends on four conditions:

a) *Electrical - The low voltages generated by the sensor depend upon good, clean connections which should be checked whenever a malfunction of the sensor is suspected or indicated.*

b) *Outside air supply - The sensor is designed to allow air circulation to the internal portion of the sensor. Whenever the sensor is removed and installed or replaced, make sure the air passages are not restricted.*

c) *Proper operating temperature - The ECM will not react to the sensor signal until the sensor reaches approximately 600-degrees F (315-degrees C). This factor must be taken into consideration when evaluating the performance of the sensor.*

d) *Unleaded fuel - The use of unleaded fuel is essential for proper operation of the sensor. Make sure the fuel you are using is of this type.*

19   In addition to observing the above conditions, special care must be taken whenever the sensor is serviced.

a) *The oxygen sensor has a permanently attached pigtail and connector which should not be removed from the sensor. Damage or removal of the pigtail or connector can adversely affect operation of the sensor.*

b) *Grease, dirt and other contaminants should be kept away from the electrical connector and the louvered end of the sensor.*

c) *Do not use cleaning solvents of any kind on the oxygen sensor.*

d) *Do not drop or roughly handle the sensor.*

e) *The silicone boot must be installed in the correct position to prevent the boot from being melted and to allow the sensor to operate properly.*

Replacement

Note: *Because it is installed in the exhaust manifold or pipe, which contracts when cool, the oxygen sensor may be very difficult to loosen when the engine is cold. Rather than risk damage to the sensor (assuming you are planning to reuse it in another manifold or pipe), start and run the engine for a minute or*

6

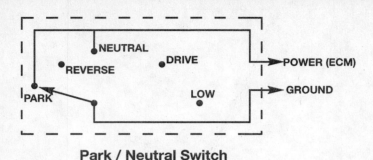

Park / Neutral Switch

24070-6-5.34b HAYNES

5.35 Electrical schematic for the Park/Neutral switch on 2.5L engines

two, then shut it off. Be careful not to burn yourself during the following procedure.

20   Disconnect the cable from the negative terminal of the battery.

21   Raise the vehicle and place it securely on jackstands.

22   Carefully unsnap the electrical connector from the sensor.

23   Carefully unscrew the sensor from the exhaust manifold. **Caution:** *Excessive force may damage the threads.*

24   Anti-seize compound must be used on the threads of the sensor to facilitate future removal. The threads of new sensors will already be coated with this compound, but if an old sensor is removed and reinstalled, recoat the threads.

25   Install the sensor and tighten it securely.

26   Reconnect the electrical connector of the pigtail lead to the main engine wiring harness.

27   Lower the vehicle and reconnect the cable to the negative terminal of the battery.

Throttle Position Sensor (TPS)

28   The Throttle Position Sensor (TPS) is located on the end of the throttle shaft on the TBI unit.

29   By monitoring the output voltage from the TPS, the ECM can determine fuel delivery based on throttle valve angle (driver demand). A broken or loose TPS can cause intermittent bursts of fuel from the injector and an unstable idle because the ECM thinks the throttle is moving.

30   A problem in any of the TPS circuits will set a Code 21 or 22.

31   Once a trouble code is set, the ECM will use an artificial default value for TPS and some vehicle performance will return.

32   Should the TPS require replacement, the complete procedure is contained in Chapter 4.

Park/Neutral switch (automatic transmission equipped models only)

General description

33   The Park/Neutral (P/N) switch, located on the steering column indicates to the ECM when the transmission is in Park or Neutral. This information is used for Transmission Converter Clutch (TCC), Exhaust Gas Recirculation (EGR) and Idle Air Control (IAC) valve operation.

34   **Caution:** *The vehicle should not be driven with the Park/Neutral switch disconnected because idle quality will be adversely affected and a false Code 24 (failure in the Vehicle Speed Sensor circuit) may be set.*

35   The switch is closed to ground in Park or Neutral and open in Drive ranges **(see illustration)**.

Adjustment

36   To adjust the Park/Neutral switch, move the switch housing all the way toward the low gear position.

37   Move the gear selector to the Park position. The main housing and the housing back should ratchet, providing proper switch adjustment.

Replacement

38   To replace the switch, place the gear selector in Neutral.

39   Unplug the electrical connectors.

40   Spread the tangs on the housing and pull the switch out.

41   To install a new switch, align the actuator on the switch with the hole in the shift tube.

42   Position the rearmost portion of the switch (the connector side) to fit into the cutout in the lower jacket.

43   Push down on the front of the switch to engage the two tangs.

44   Move the gear selector to Park and the switch is adjusted.

45   Plug in the electrical connectors.

Vehicle Speed Sensor (VSS)

46   The Vehicle Speed Sensor (VSS) is located next to the speedometer cable fitting on the back of the instrument cluster on early models and mounted in the transmission on later models. It sends a pulsing voltage signal to the ECM, which the ECM converts to miles per hour. The VSS is part of the Transmission Converter Clutch (TCC) system.

47   To replace the VSS, remove the instrument cluster (see Chapter 12). Detach the sensor retaining screw **(see illustration)** and unplug the sensor **(see illustration)**. Trace the pigtail of the VSS to its connector with the main wiring harness and unplug it.

48   Installation is the reverse of removal.

5.47a To replace the Vehicle Speed Sensor, remove the sensor mounting screw . . .

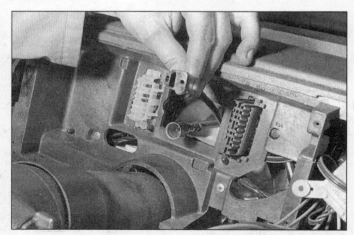

5.47b . . . then trace the sensor pigtail lead to the electrical connector and unplug it from the wire harness

Distributor reference signal

49   The distributor sends a signal to the ECM to tell it both engine rpm and crankshaft position. See Section 6 for further information.

6   Electronic Spark Timing (EST)

General description

Note: *Always consult the VECI label for the exact timing procedure for your vehicle.*

1   To provide improved engine performance, fuel economy and control of exhaust emissions, the Electronic Control Module (ECM) controls distributor spark advance (ignition timing) with the Electronic Spark Timing (EST) system.

2   The EST system consists of the distributor HEI module, an ECM and the connecting wires. The four terminals for the EST are lettered on the module. The distributor four-terminal connector is lettered left-to-right, A-B-C-D. These circuits perform the following functions:

a) *Terminal A - Reference Ground Low. This wire is grounded in the distributor and insures that the ground circuit has no voltage drop which could affect performance. If it is open, it may cause poor performance.*

b) *Terminal B - Bypass. At about 400 rpm the ECM applies 5-volts to this circuit to switch spark timing control from the HEI module to the ECM. An open or grounded bypass circuit will set a Code 42 and the engine will run at base timing, plus a small amount of advance built into the HEI module.*

c) *Terminal C - Distributor Reference High. This provides the ECM with rpm and crankshaft position information.*

d) *Terminal D - EST. This circuit triggers the HEI module. The ECM doesn't know what the actual timing is, but it does know when it gets the reference signal. It advances or retards the spark from that point. If the base timing is set incorrectly, the entire spark curve will be incorrect.*

3   The ECM receives a reference pulse from the distributor, which indicates both engine rpm and crankshaft position. The ECM then determines the proper spark advance for the engine operating conditions and sends an EST pulse to the distributor.

Check

4   The ECM will set spark timing at a specified value when the diagnostic "Test" terminal in the ALCL connector is grounded. To check for EST operation, the timing should be checked at 2000 rpm with the terminal ungrounded. Then ground the test terminal. If the timing changes at 2000 rpm, the EST is operating. A fault in the EST system will usually set Trouble Code 42.

7.3 The Electronic Spark Control (ESC) knock sensor on some V6 engines is located on the right side of the block, near the oil filter (other V6 engines use an additional knock sensor, located on the opposite bank of cylinders)

Setting base timing

5   To set the initial base timing, locate, then disconnect the timing connector (the location and wire color of the timing connector is on the VECI label).

6   Set the timing as specified on the VECI label. This will cause a Code 42 to be stored in the ECM memory. Be sure to clear the memory after setting the timing (see Section 3).

7   For further information regarding testing and component replacement procedures for either the HEI/EST distributor or the distributorless (DIS or C3I) ignition systems, refer to Chapter 5.

7   Electronic Spark Control (ESC) system

Refer to illustration 7.3

General description

1   Irregular octane levels in modern gasoline can cause detonation in an engine. Detonation is sometimes referred to as "spark knock."

2   The Electronic Spark Control (ESC) system is designed to retard spark timing up to 20-degrees to reduce spark knock in the engine. This allows the engine to use maximum spark advance to improve driveability and fuel economy.

3   The ESC knock sensor **(see illustration)** sends a voltage signal of 8 to 10-volts to the ECM when no spark knock is occurring and the ECM provides normal advance. When the knock sensor detects abnormal vibration (spark knock), the ESC module turns off the circuit to the ECM and the voltage at ECM terminal B7 drops to zero volts. The ECM then retards the EST distributor until spark knock is eliminated.

4   Failure of the ESC knock sensor signal or loss of ground at the ESC module will cause the signal to the ECM to remain high. This condition will result in the ECM controlling the EST as if no spark knock is occurring. Therefore, no retard will occur and spark knock may become severe under heavy engine load conditions. At this point, the

ECM will set a Code 43.

5   Loss of the ESC signal to the ECM will cause the ECM to constantly retard EST. This will result in sluggish performance and cause the ECM to set a Code 43.

Check

6   To check the ESC system, connect a timing light in accordance with the tool manufacturer's instructions. Start the engine and point the timing light at the timing scale on the front of the engine. Have an assistant strike the right side exhaust manifold while watching the timing marks - the timing should retard noticeably each time the block is struck. If the timing does not retard, either the knock sensor, the ESC module or the ECM (or any related wiring) is defective.

Component replacement

ESC sensor

7   Detach the cable from the negative terminal of the battery.

8   Disconnect the electrical connector from the ESC sensor.

9   Remove the ESC sensor from the block.

10   Installation is the reverse of the removal procedure.

ESC module

11   Detach the cable from the negative terminal of the battery.

12   Remove the engine cover.

13   Locate the module at the rear of the engine compartment.

14   Detach the wiring harness connector from the module.

15   Remove the module mounting bolts and remove the module.

16   Installation is the reverse of removal.

8   Early Fuel Evaporation (EFE) system

Refer to illustration 8.7

General description

1   This unit provides rapid heat to the

**8.7 Typical thermal vacuum switch (arrow) -
2.8L V6 engine shown**

9.5 AIR system deceleration valve (2.8L V6 engine)

intake air supply by means of a ceramic heater grid which is integral with the carburetor base gasket and located under the primary bore.

2   The components involved in the EFE's operation include the heater grid, a relay, electrical wires and connectors and the ECM.

3   The EFE heater unit is controlled by the Electronic Control Module (ECM) through a relay. The ECM senses the coolant temperature and applies voltage to the heater unit only when the engine temperature is below a predetermined level. At normal operating temperatures the heater unit is off.

4   If the EFE heater is not coming on, poor cold engine performance will be experienced. If the heater unit is not shutting off when the engine is warmed up, the engine will run as if it is out of tune (due to the constant flow of hot air through the carburetor).

Check

ECM-equipped models

5   If the EFE system is suspected of malfunctioning while the engine is cold, first check all electrical wires and connectors to be sure they are clean, tight and in good condition.

6   With the ignition switch in the ON position, use a circuit tester or voltmeter to check that current is reaching the relay. If not, there is a problem in the wiring leading to the relay, in the ECM's thermo switch or the ECM itself.

7   Next, with the engine cold but the ignition switch On, disconnect the heater unit electrical connector and use a circuit tester or voltmeter to see if current is reaching the heater unit **(see illustration)**. If so, use a continuity tester to check for continuity in the connector attached to the heater unit. If continuity exists, the system is operating correctly in the cold engine mode.

8   If current is not reaching the heater unit, but is reaching the relay, replace the relay.

9   To check that the system turns off at normal engine operating temperature, first allow the engine to warm up thoroughly. With

the engine idling, disconnect the heater unit electrical connector and use a circuit tester or voltmeter to check for current at the heater unit.

10   If current is reaching the heater unit a faulty ECM or relay is indicated.

11   For confirmation of the ECM's condition, refer to Section 3 or have the system checked by a dealer or automotive repair shop.

Non-ECM equipped models

12   If the EFE system is suspected of malfunctioning while the engine is cold, first check all wires and connectors to be sure they are clean, tight and in good condition.

13   With the ignition ON and the engine cold, connect a test light lead to a good ground and probe, alternately, the two terminal leads at the coolant sensor/heater switch.

14   If the light glows at both terminals probe the pink wire at the heater unit connector to be sure current is reaching the heater unit. If the light glows again the EFE system should be functioning properly.

15   If the test light only glows at one of the terminals, the heater switch is defective and must be replaced.

16   If the test light does not glow at all and the lead is definitely connected to a good ground, the wiring between the heater switch and ignition switch is faulty. Locate the short circuit and repair as necessary.

9   Air management system

Refer to illustrations 9.5, 9.11, 9.27, 9.31, 9.43, 9.44 and 9.49

General description

1   The air management system is used to reduce carbon monoxide and hydrocarbon emissions. The system used on these vehicles, the Air Injection Reaction (AIR) system, adds air to the exhaust manifold to continue combustion after the exhaust gases leave the combustion chamber.

2   The AIR system consists of an air pump, a diverter valve (Federal/carbureted models) or an Electric Air Control (EAC) valve (California/carbureted and all fuel-injected models), a pair of check valves and the plumbing between these components.

3   A belt-driven air pump supplies air through a centrifugal filter fan to the EAC valve.

4   A check valve on either side of the engine prevents the back flow of exhaust into the air pump if there is an exhaust backfire or pump drivebelt failure.

5   To help prevent backfiring during high vacuum conditions, Federal/carbureted engines utilize a deceleration (gulp) valve to allow air to flow into the intake manifold **(see illustration)**. This air enters the air/fuel mixture to lean the rich condition created by high vacuum when the throttle valve closes on deceleration.

Check

Electric air control (EAC) valve

6   During cold starting, the ECM completes the ground circuit, the EAC solenoid is energized and air is directed to the exhaust ports.

7   As the coolant temperature increases the ECM opens the ground circuit, the EAC solenoid is de-energized and air goes to the air cleaner.

8   The AIR system is not completely noiseless. Under normal conditions, noise rises in pitch as engine speed increases. To determine if the excessive noise is the fault of the AIR system pump, operate the engine with the pump drivebelt removed.

9   If the noise is caused by the AIR system pump, check for a seized air pump, proper mounting and bolt torque of the pump and the proper routing and connections of the hoses.

Air pump

10   The air pump is a permanently lubricated positive displacement vane type

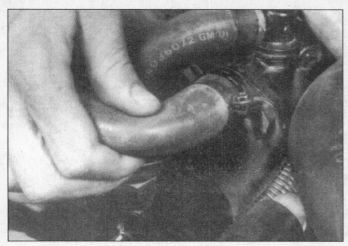

9.11 The air pump hose can be squeezed to check pump output

9.27 To remove the drivebelt, loosen the adjusting bolt and mounting brace bolt (arrows)

design which requires no periodic maintenance. If it is making noise, replace it. Do not attempt to lubricate it.

11   To check air flow from the hoses, accelerate the engine to about 1500 rpm, squeeze the air hose and feel for the pulsations **(see illustration)**. If air flow increases as the engine is accelerated, the pump is operating satisfactorily. If air flow does not increase or is not present, proceed as follows:

12   Check the drivebelt for proper tension (see Chapter 1).

13   Inspect the pressure relief valve for air leaks. If the valve is leaking, you can hear it leak when the pump is running.

Check valve

14   Inspect the check valve(s) whenever the corresponding hose is disconnected or whenever check valve failure is suspected. A pump that has become inoperative and shows indications of having exhaust gases in the pump indicates check valve failure.

15   Blow through the check valve (toward the cylinder head), then attempt to blow through the valve in the other direction. Flow should only be in one direction (toward the exhaust manifold). Replace the valve if it does not operate properly.

Deceleration valve

16   Remove the air cleaner housing assembly and adapter (see Chapter 4), plug the air cleaner vacuum source and connect a tachometer.

17   With the engine running at the specified idle speed, remove the small deceleration valve signal hose from the manifold vacuum source.

18   Reconnect the signal hose and listen for air flow through the ventilation pipe and into the deceleration valve. There should also be a noticeable speed drop when the signal hose is reconnected.

19   If the air flow does not continue for at least one second, or the engine speed does not drop noticeably, check the deceleration

valve hoses for restrictions or leaks.

20   If no restrictions or leaks are found, replace the deceleration valve.

Hoses and pipes

21   Inspect the hoses and pipes for deterioration and holes.

22   Inspect all hose and pipe clamps for tightness.

23   Check the routing of all hoses and pipes. Interference can cause wear.

24   If a leak is suspected on the pressure side of the system, or if a hose or pipe has been disconnected on the pressure side, the connections should be checked for leaks with a soapy water solution. With the pump running, bubbles will form if a leak exists.

Drivebelt

25   Inspect the drivebelt for wear, cracks or deterioration (see Chapter 1) and replace as necessary. When installing a new belt, make sure that it is fully seated in the V-belt grooves of the air conditioning compressor, air pump, alternator and crankshaft pulleys.

Component replacement

Air pump and centrifugal filter fan

26   Detach the cable from the negative terminal of the battery.

27   Immobilize the pump pulley by compressing the drivebelt and loosen the pump pulley bolts. Loosen the drivebelt tension adjusting bolt and, if necessary, the mounting brace bolts **(see illustration)**. Pivot the air pump toward the block to remove belt tension and remove the drivebelt.

28   Clearly label, then detach, the pump hoses, vacuum lines and electrical connectors.

29   Remove the belt tension adjusting bolt and the mounting brace bolt and remove the air pump.

30   Remove the pulley bolts, the pulley and the pulley spacer.

31   Use needle-nose pliers to pull the filter fan from the pump hub **(see illustration)**.

Caution: *Do not allow any filter fragments to enter the air pump intake hole during removal. Do not remove the filter fan by inserting a screwdriver between the pump and the filter fan. You will damage the pump sealing lip. Do not attempt to clean the centrifugal filter fan with either compressed air or solvents. If it is dirty, it must be replaced.*

32   Install the new filter fan on the pump hub.

33   Install the spacer and pump pulley against the centrifugal fan.

34   Install the pump pulley bolts and snug them finger tight.

35   Install the air pump and snug the bolts finger tight.

36   Install the drivebelt and adjust the belt tension (see Chapter 1).

37   Tighten the air pump mounting brace bolt and belt tension adjusting bolt securely.

38   Tighten the pulley bolts securely. This compresses the centrifugal filter fan onto the pump hole. Do not attempt to drive the filter fan on with a hammer. **Note:** *A slight amount*

6

9.31 Removing the air pump filter fan (remove as shown - do not insert any tool behind the fan as damage to the pump may result)

9.43 A typical EAC valve

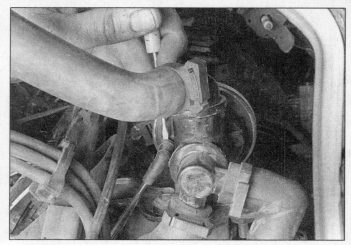

9.44 To detach the manifold vacuum signal tube from the EAC valve, pry it off with a small screwdriver

of interference with the housing bore is normal.
39   Attach the cable to the negative terminal of the battery.
40   Check the air management system for proper operation. **Note:** *After a new filter fan has been installed, it may squeal upon initial operation until the sealing lip has worn in.*

EAC valve
41   Detach the cable from the negative terminal of the battery.
42   Locate the EAC valve **(see illustration)** on the right side of the engine compartment.
43   Detach the electrical connector from the terminal on the lower front of the valve.
44   Detach the manifold vacuum signal hose **(see illustration)**.
45   Detach the air inlet and outlet hoses from the valve.
46   Remove the EAC valve.
47   Installation is the reverse of removal.

Check valve
48   Detach the cable from the negative terminal of the battery.
49   Locate the check valve you wish to replace **(see illustration)**.
50   Release the clamp and detach the hose

from the valve.
51   Using a backup wrench, unscrew the valve from the threaded fitting on the air injection pipe.
52   Installation is the reverse of removal.

Air injection pipe assembly
53   Detach the cable from the negative terminal of the battery.
54   Locate the pipe assembly you wish to replace.
55   Unscrew the check valve.
56   Unscrew the pipe assembly threaded fitting from the manifold.
57   Remove the pipe assembly mounting bracket bolts.
58   Remove the pipe assembly.
59   Installation is the reverse of removal.

Deceleration valve
60   Detach the cable from the negative terminal of the battery.
61   Detach the vacuum hoses from the valve.
62   Remove the screws securing the valve to the engine bracket.
63   Remove the deceleration valve.
64   Installation is the reverse of removal.

10   Exhaust Gas Recirculation (EGR) system

Refer to illustrations 10.12 and 10.20

General description
1   The EGR system is used to lower NOx (oxides of nitrogen) emission levels caused by high combustion temperatures. It does this by decreasing combustion temperatures.
2   The EGR system consists of a negative backpressure EGR valve, a ported manifold vacuum source tube and, on the V6, a solenoid which controls this vacuum source.

Check
3   Too much EGR flow tends to weaken combustion, causing the engine to run rough or stop. When EGR flow is excessive, the engine can stop after a cold start or at idle after deceleration, the vehicle can surge at cruising speeds or the idle may be rough. If the EGR valve remains constantly open, the engine may not idle at all.
4   Too little or no EGR flow allows combustion temperatures to get too high during acceleration and load conditions. This can cause spark knock (detonation), engine overheating or emission test failure.
5   A procedure for performing a check of the EGR is contained in Chapter 1.

Component replacement
EGR valve
6   When buying a new EGR valve, make sure you get the correct replacement part.
7   Detach the cable from the negative terminal of the battery.
8   Remove the fresh air tube from the air cleaner housing.
9   Remove the air cleaner housing assembly and adapter (see Chapter 4). If you're working on a 4.3L V6 equipped with CPI fuel injection, remove the air intake plenum.

9.49 Typical air management system check valve (2.8L V6 engine shown)

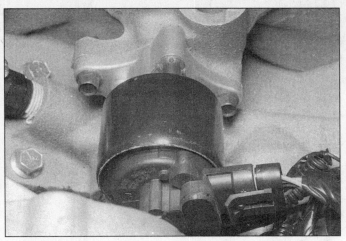

10.12 On 4.3L V6 engines with CPI, first remove the air intake plenum to gain access to the EGR valve solenoid

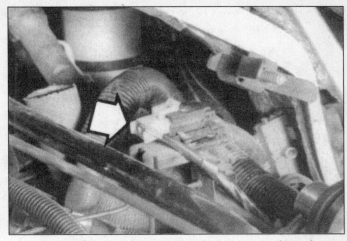

10.20 EGR valve solenoid electrical connector (arrow)

10   Detach the vacuum line from the EGR valve vacuum tube.

11   If you are replacing the EGR valve itself, trace the temperature switch pigtail lead to the main engine wire harness and unplug the electrical connector, then remove the switch from the valve. If you are replacing the EGR valve gasket, unplug the lead but do not remove the switch from the valve.

12   Remove the EGR valve mounting bolts **(see illustration)**.

13   Remove the EGR valve and gasket from the manifold. Discard the gasket.

14   With a wire wheel, buff the exhaust deposits from the EGR valve mounting surface on the manifold and, if you plan to reuse the same valve, the mounting surface of the valve itself. Look for exhaust deposits in the valve outlet. Remove deposit build-up with a screwdriver. **Caution:** *Never wash the valve in solvents or degreaser - both agents will permanently damage the diaphragm. Sand blasting is also not recommended because it will affect the operation of the valve.*

15   If the EGR passage evinces an excessive build-up of deposits, clean it out with a wire wheel. Make sure that all loose particles are completely removed to prevent them from clogging the EGR valve or from being ingested into the engine.

16   Installation is the reverse of removal.

Hoses

17   When replacing hoses, use hose identified with the word *"Fluorelastomer."* Use the VECI label (on the fan shroud) as a hose routing guide. For further information regarding hose inspection and service, see Chapter 1.

EGR vacuum solenoid

18   Detach the cable from the negative terminal of the battery.

19   Remove the air cleaner housing assembly and adapter (see Chapter 4).

20   Unplug the electrical connector from the solenoid **(see illustration)**.

21   Clearly label, then detach, both vacuum hoses.

22   Remove the solenoid mounting screw and remove the solenoid.

23   Installation is the reverse of removal.

EGR temperature switch

24   Detach the cable from the negative terminal of the battery.

25   Trace the pigtail lead to the main engine wire harness and unplug the electrical connector.

26   Remove the switch.

27   Installation is the reverse of removal. Be sure to use anti-seize compound on the switch threads.

11   Evaporative Emission Control System (EECS)

Refer to illustrations 11.2 and 11.16

General description

1   This system is designed to trap and store fuel vapors that evaporate from the fuel tank, throttle body and intake manifold.

2   The Evaporative Emission Control System (EECS) consists of a charcoal-filled canister and the lines connecting the canister to the fuel tank, ported vacuum and intake manifold vacuum **(see illustration)**.

3   Fuel vapors are transferred from the fuel tank, throttle body and intake manifold to a canister where they are stored when the engine is not operating. When the engine is running, the fuel vapors are purged from the canister by intake air flow and consumed in the normal combustion process.

Check

4   Poor idle, stalling and poor driveability can be caused by an inoperative purge valve, a damaged canister, split or cracked hoses or hoses connected to the wrong tubes.

5   Evidence of fuel loss or fuel odor can be caused by liquid fuel leaking from fuel line, a cracked or damaged canister, an inoperative bowl vent valve, an inoperative purge valve,

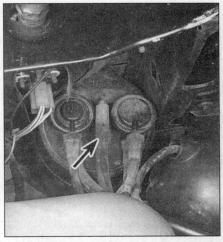

11.2 Typical charcoal canister (arrow)

disconnected, misrouted, kinked, deteriorated or damaged vapor or control hoses or an improperly seated air cleaner or air cleaner gasket.

6   Inspect each hose attached to the canister for kinks, leaks and breaks along its entire length. Repair or replace as necessary.

7   Inspect the canister. It is cracked or damaged, replace it.

8   Look for fuel leaking from the bottom of the canister. If fuel is leaking, replace the canister and check the hoses and hose routing.

9   Check the filter at the bottom of the canister. If it's dirty, plugged or damaged, replace the filter.

10   Apply a short length of hose to the lower tube of the purge valve assembly and attempt to blow through it. Little or no air should pass into the canister (a small amount of air will pass because the canister has a constant purge hole).

11   With a hand vacuum pump, apply vacuum through the control vacuum signal tube to the purge valve diaphragm.

6

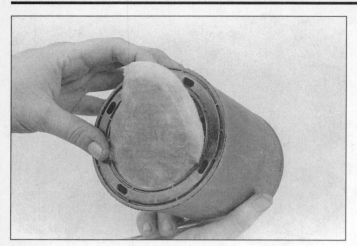

11.16 To replace the canister filter, peel it out and install a new one

12.1a The PCV valve (arrow) on most models fits into a grommet in the valve cover

12   If the diaphragm does not hold vacuum for at least 20 seconds, the diaphragm is leaking and the canister must be replaced.

13   If the diaphragm holds vacuum, again try to blow through the hose while vacuum is still being applied. An increased flow of air should be noted. If it isn't, replace the canister.

Component replacement

14   Clearly label, then detach, all vacuum lines from the canister.

15   Loosen the canister mounting clamp bolt and pull the canister out.

16   Check the filter and replace it if it is dirty **(see illustration)**.

17   Installation is the reverse of removal.

12   Positive Crankcase Ventilation (PCV) system

Refer to illustrations 12.1a and 12.1b

1   The Positive Crankcase Ventilation (PCV) system reduces hydrocarbon emissions by scavenging crankcase vapors. It does this by circulating fresh air from the air cleaner through the crankcase, where it mixes with blow-by gases and is then rerouted through a PCV valve to the intake manifold **(see illustrations)**.

2   The main components of the PCV system are the PCV valve, a fresh air filtered inlet and the vacuum hoses connecting these two components with the engine and the EECS system.

3   To maintain idle quality, the PCV valve restricts the flow when the intake manifold vacuum is high. If abnormal operating conditions arise, the system is designed to allow excessive amounts of blow-by gases to flow back through the crankcase vent tube into the air cleaner to be consumed by normal combustion.

4   Checking and replacement of the PCV valve and filter is covered in Chapter 1.

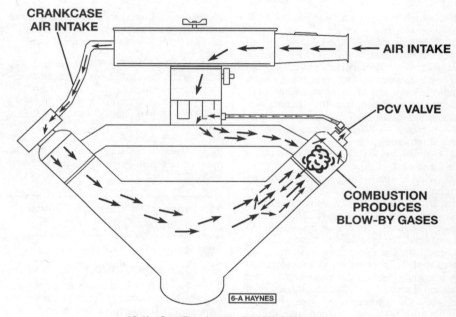

12.1b Gas flow in a typical V6 PCV system

13   Thermostatic air cleaner (THERMAC) (carbureted and TBI models only)

Refer to illustrations 13.2, 13.18, 13.27 and 13.28

General description

1   A heated air intake system is used to provide good driveability under varying climatic conditions. By having a uniform inlet air temperature, the fuel system can be calibrated to reduce exhaust emissions and to eliminate throttle valve icing.

2   The THERMAC air cleaner used on some models **(see illustration)** is operated by heated air and manifold vacuum. Air can enter the air cleaner from outside the engine compartment or from a heat stove built around the exhaust manifold. A temperature sensor located inside the air cleaner housing determines the operational mode of the THERMAC.

Check

3   If the engine hesitates during warm-up:

a) *The heat stove tube could be disconnected.*

b) *The vacuum diaphragm motor could be inoperative, leaving the snorkel (mouth) of the air cleaner housing open to outside air.*

c) *There may be no manifold vacuum.*

d) *The damper door does not move.*

e) *The air cleaner housing assembly-to-TBI adapter seal may be missing.*

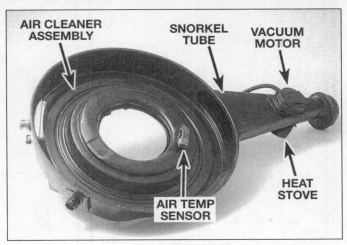

13.2 Typical THERMAC air cleaner

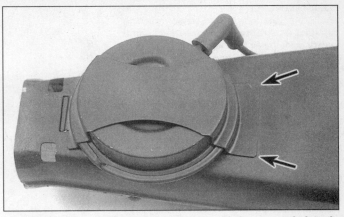

13.18 Once the air cleaner housing assembly is removed, detach the vacuum line from the temperature sensor, drill out the spot welds (arrows) with a 1/16-inch drill, then enlarge as necessary to remove the retaining strap

f) *The air cleaner housing assembly cover seal may be missing.*

g) *The air cleaner housing assembly cover may be loose.*

h) *The air cleaner housing assembly may be loose.*

4 Lack of power and/or sluggish or spongy throttle response can be caused by:

a) *A stuck damper door that does not open to outside air.*

b) *A temperature sensor that does not bleed off vacuum.*

5 Inspect the system to be sure that all hoses and the heat stove tube are connected. Check for kinked, plugged or deteriorated hoses.

6 Check for the presence and condition of air cleaner to carburetor gasket seal.

7 With the air cleaner assembly installed, the damper door should be open to outside air.

8 Start the engine. Watch the damper door in the air cleaner snorkel. When the engine is first started, the damper door should move and close off outside air. As the air cleaner warms up, the damper door should open slowly to the outside air.

9 If the air cleaner fails to operate as described above, the door may not be moving at the right temperature. If the driveability problem is during warm-up, make the temperature sensor check below.

10 With the engine off, disconnect the vacuum hose at the vacuum diaphragm motor.

11 Apply at least 7 inches of vacuum to the vacuum diaphragm motor. The damper door should completely block off outside air when vacuum is applied. If it doesn't, check to see if the linkage is hooked up correctly.

12 With vacuum still applied, trap vacuum in the vacuum diaphragm motor by bending the hose. The damper door should remain closed. If it doesn't, replace the vacuum diaphragm motor assembly. Failure of the vacuum diaphragm motor is more likely to be caused from binding linkage or a corroded snorkel than from a failed diaphragm. Check

13.27 Note the position of the sensor in the air cleaner housing

this first before replacing the diaphragm.

13 If the vacuum motor checks out okay, check the vacuum hoses and connections. If they're okay, replace the temperature sensor.

14 Start the test with the air cleaner temperature below 86-degrees F. If the engine has been run recently, remove the air cleaner cover and place the thermometer as close as possible to the sensor. Let the air cleaner cool until the thermometer reads below 86-degrees F for about 5 to 10 minutes. Reinstall the air cleaner.

15 Start and idle the engine. The damper door should move to close off outside air immediately if the engine is cool enough. When the damper door starts to open the snorkel passage (in a few minutes), remove the air cleaner and read the thermometer. It must read about 131-degrees F.

16 If the damper door is not open to outside air at the indicated temperature, the temperature sensor is malfunctioning and must be replaced.

Component replacement
Vacuum diaphragm motor

17 Remove the air cleaner (see Chapter 4).

18 Detach the vacuum tube from the motor

(see illustration).

19 Drill out the two spot welds with a 1/16-inch drill, then enlarge as required to remove the retaining strap. Do not damage the snorkel tube.

20 Bend the strap up and out of the way.

21 Lift up the motor, cocking it to one side to unhook the motor linkage at the control damper assembly.

22 To install a new motor, drill out the spot welds at the end of the vacuum motor retaining strap.

23 Install the vacuum motor linkage into the control damper assembly.

24 Use the motor retaining strap and sheet metal screw provided in the motor service package to secure the motor to the snorkel tube. Make sure that the screw does not interfere with the operation of the damper assembly. Shorten the screw if necessary.

25 Install the air cleaner housing assembly (see Chapter 4). Be sure to attach the vacuum hose to the motor.

Sensor

26 Remove the air cleaner housing assembly (see Chapter 4).

27 Note the position (see illustration) of the sensor in the air cleaner housing to facili-

6

tate reinstallation.

28 Pry up the tabs on the sensor retaining clip **(see illustration)**. Remove the clip and sensor from the air cleaner.

29 Installation is the reverse of removal. Be sure to attach the two vacuum lines to the sensor pipes.

14 Transmission Converter Clutch (TCC)

General description

1 The Transmission Converter Clutch (TCC) uses a solenoid-operated valve in the automatic transmission to mechanically lock up the torque converter. This reduces the slippage losses in the converter, reducing emissions because engine rpm at any given speed is reduced. It also increases fuel economy.

2 For the converter clutch to operate properly, two conditions must be met:

   a) *The engine must be warmed up before the clutch can apply. The engine coolant temperature sensor (see Section 4) tells the ECM when the engine is at operating temperature.*

   b) *The vehicle must be traveling at the necessary minimum speed to raise the pressure to the level necessary to apply the valve. If the hydraulic pressure is correct, the ECM signals the solenoid to apply the converter clutch.*

3 After the converter clutch applies, the ECM uses the information from the TPS to release the clutch when the car is accelerating or decelerating at a certain rate.

4 Another switch used in the TCC circuit is a brake switch which opens the power supply to the TCC solenoid when the brake is applied.

5 The transmission on the V6 engine uses a 4th gear switch to send a signal to the ECM telling it what gear the transmission is in. The ECM uses this information to vary the conditions under which the clutch applies or releases. However, the transmission does not have to be in high gear in order for the ECM to turn on the clutch. Transmissions using gear select switches can be identified by three wires coming out of the TCC connector.

6 The transmission also uses a 4-3 pulse

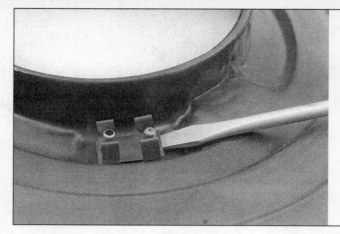

13.28 Pry off the sensor retaining clips with a small screwdriver

switch to open the TCC solenoid circuit momentarily during a downshift.

7 A third gear switch is placed in series on the battery side of the TCC solenoid to prevent TCC application until the transmission is in third gear.

Check

8 If the converter clutch is applied at all times, the engine will stall immediately, just like a manual transmission with the clutch applied.

9 If the converter clutch does not apply, fuel economy may be lower than expected. If the Vehicle Speed Sensor (VSS) (see Section 5) fails, the TCC will not apply.

10 A TCC-equipped transmission has different operating characteristics than an automatic transmission without TCC. If you detect a "chuggle" or "surge" condition, perform the following check.

11 Install a tachometer.

12 Drive the vehicle until normal operating temperature is reached, then maintain a 50 to 55 mph speed.

13 Lightly touch the brake pedal and feel for a slight bumpy sensation, indicating that the TCC is releasing. A slight increase in rpm should also be noted.

14 Release the brake and check for reapplication of the converter clutch and a slight decrease in engine rpm.

15 If the TCC fails to perform satisfactorily during this test, take your vehicle to a dealer to have the TCC serviced.

15 Catalytic converter

General description

1 The catalytic converter is an emission control device added to the exhaust system to reduce pollutants from the exhaust gas stream. A single-bed converter design is used in combination with a three-way (reduction) catalyst. The catalytic coating on the three-way catalyst contains platinum and rhodium, which lowers the levels of oxides of nitrogen (NOx) as well as hydrocarbons (HC) and carbon monoxide (CO).

Checking

2 The test equipment for a catalytic converter is expensive and highly sophisticated. If you suspect that the converter on your vehicle is malfunctioning, take it to a dealer or authorized emissions inspection facility for diagnosis and repair.

3 Whenever the vehicle is raised for servicing of underbody components, check the converter for leaks, corrosion and other damage. If damage is discovered, the converter should be replaced.

4 Because the converter is part of the exhaust system, converter replacement requires removal of the exhaust pipe assembly (see Chapter 4). Take the vehicle, or the exhaust pipe system, to a dealer or a muffler shop.

Chapter 7 Part A
Manual transmission

Contents

	Section		Section
Clutch start switch - check, replacement and adjustment	8	Manual transmission overhaul - general information	5
Extension housing oil seal - replacement	6	Manual transmission - removal and installation	4
General information	1	Shift lever - removal and installation	3
Lubricant change	See Chapter 1	Speedometer driven gear oil seal - replacement	7
Lubricant level check	See Chapter 1	Transmission mount - check and replacement	2

Specifications

Torque specifications

	Ft-lbs
Transmission-to-clutch housing bolts (77mm four-speed and all five-speed transmissions)	55
Transmission-to-engine bolts (77.5mm four-speed transmission)	
Four-cylinder engine	25
V6 engine	55
Crossmember-to-frame bolts	25
Mount-to-crossmember bolts	25
Mount-to-transmission bolts	35
Shift lever nut	28

7A

1 General information

These models are equipped with a standard four-speed or optional five-speed manual transmission. Two different four-speed transmissions are used; a 77mm and a 77.5mm (the figure represents the distance between the mainshaft and countershaft centerlines). The easiest way to tell the difference between the 77mm and 77.5mm four-speed transmissions is that, on the 77.5mm transmission, the gearbox and clutch housing are one piece. On the 77mm transmission, the gearbox bolts to the clutch housing. All manual transmissions are operated through a floor-mounted gearshift lever assembly attached to the top of the transmission extension housing.

2 Transmission mount - check and replacement

Check
Refer to illustration 2.7

1   Raise the vehicle and support it securely with jackstands. Make sure the vehicle is stable as you may jostle it somewhat in the course of checking the mount.
2   Push up on the transmission extension housing and note the amount the housing moves.
3   Pull down on the extension housing and note the amount of movement available.
4   If the extension housing can be pushed up a greater distance than it can be pulled down it is an indication that the rubber is worn and the mount has bottomed out.
5   If the rubber portion of the mount separates from the metal plate when you push up the mount should be replaced.

Replacement

6   Support the transmission with a floor jack and a block of wood.
7   Remove the nuts and bolts, raise the transmission and slide the mount out **(see illustration)**.
8   Installation is the reverse of removal.

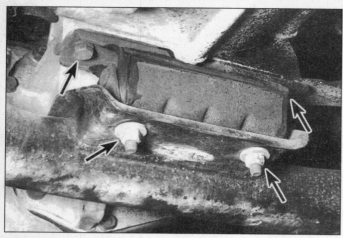

2.7 With the transmission supported with a jack, remove the nuts and bolts (arrows), then remove the transmission mount

3.2 Remove the four bolts (arrows) and lift the shift lever out

3   Shift lever - removal and installation

Refer to illustration 3.2

1   With the transmission in Neutral, remove the screws from the shift lever boot retainer and slide the boot up the lever.

2   Remove the shift lever retaining bolts at the transmission **(see illustration)** and remove the lever assembly by pulling it straight up and out of the extension housing.

3   Installation is the reverse of the removal procedure.

4   Manual transmission - removal and installation

Refer to illustrations 4.16 and 4.18

Removal

1   Disconnect the negative battery cable from the battery.

2   On models equipped with a 77.5mm

transmission only, remove the starter motor upper mounting bolt.

3   Remove the shift lever assembly from the transmission (refer to Section 3).

4   Raise the vehicle and support it securely on jackstands.

5   Remove the driveshaft, referring to Chapter 8 if necessary.

6   Remove the transfer case on four-wheel drive vehicles (refer to Chapter 7C).

7   Disconnect the speedometer cable from the transmission.

8   Label and detach the wire connectors at the transmission.

9   On 1982 and 1983 models, disconnect the clutch cable at the transmission (see Chapter 8). On 1984 and later models, disconnect the clutch slave cylinder from the transmission without disconnecting the hydraulic line (see Chapter 8).

10   On 77.5mm transmissions only, disconnect the exhaust pipe(s) at the manifold. Remove the appropriate body mounting bolts and raise the body as described in Chapter 2F, Section 7. This will provide the clearance needed to remove the upper bellhousing

bolts.

11   Support the engine/transmission by placing a jack and a block of wood under the engine oil pan.

12   Remove the transmission mount bolts.

13   Remove the hanger supporting the catalytic converter. Take care not to damage the converter.

14   Place a jack under the transmission and secure the transmission to the jack with safety chains. Raise the transmission slightly with the jack. Remove the crossmember bolts, then remove the crossmember and transmission mount.

15   If the clutch housing is being removed, remove the dust cover bolts.

16   On models equipped with the 77.5mm transmission, remove the transmission-to-engine bolts. On 77mm transmissions, remove the transmission-to-clutch housing upper bolts **(see illustration)**, install guide pins in the holes then remove the lower bolts. The guide pins can be made by cutting the heads off of appropriate size bolts.

17   Lower both jacks until the transmission can be withdrawn to the rear and removed.

4.16 Remove the upper transmission bolts (the upper left bolt is indicated by the arrow) first, then install guide pins (77mm transmission)

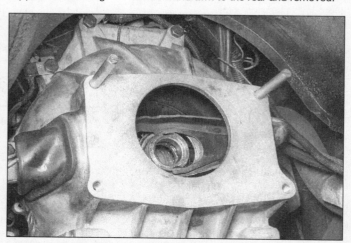

4.18 With the guide pins installed, the transmission and the input shaft are easily aligned with the bellhousing and pilot bearing (77mm transmission)

Installation

18 Installation is the reverse of removal. On 77mm transmissions, use the guide pins **(see illustration)** as an installation aid. Apply a light coat of high-temperature grease to the input shaft bearing retainer and to the splined portion of the shaft to ensure free movement of the clutch and transmission components during installation. If the transmission input shaft splines won't align with the clutch hub splines, place the transmission in high gear and rotate the output shaft while pressing the transmission against the engine. Be sure to tighten all nuts and bolts to the specified torque.

19 Refill the transmission with the recommended lubricant (see Chapter 1).

5 Manual transmission overhaul - general information

Overhauling a manual transmission is a difficult job for the do-it-yourselfer. It involves the disassembly and reassembly of many small parts. Numerous clearances must be precisely measured and, if necessary, changed with select fit spacers and snap-rings. As a result, if transmission problems arise, it can be removed and installed by a competent do-it-yourselfer, but overhaul should be left to a transmission repair shop. Rebuilt transmissions may be available - check with your dealer parts department and auto parts stores. At any rate, the time and money involved in an overhaul is almost sure to exceed the cost of a rebuilt unit.

Nevertheless, it's not impossible for an inexperienced mechanic to rebuild a transmission if the special tools are available and the job is done in a deliberate step-by-step manner so nothing is overlooked.

The tools necessary for an overhaul include internal and external snap-ring pliers, a bearing puller, a slide hammer, a set of pin punches, a dial indicator and possibly a hydraulic press. In addition, a large, sturdy workbench and a vise or transmission stand will be required.

During disassembly of the transmission, make careful notes of how each piece comes off, where it fits in relation to other pieces and what holds it in place.

Before taking the transmission apart for repair, it will help if you have some idea what area of the transmission is malfunctioning.

Certain problems can be closely tied to specific areas in the transmission, which can make component examination and replacement easier. Refer to the Troubleshooting section at the front of this manual for information regarding possible sources of trouble.

6 Extension housing oil seal - replacement

Refer to illustration 6.7

1 The extension housing oil seal can be replaced without removing the transmission from the vehicle.

2 Raise the vehicle and support it securely on jackstands.

3 Remove the driveshaft as described in Chapter 8.

4 Carefully pry out the old seal. Do not nick or scratch the output shaft.

5 Clean the counterbore and examine it for damage.

6 Lubricate the area between the lips of the new seal with transmission lubricant and coat the outer diameter with sealant.

7 Carefully install the seal, with the lip in, until the flange seats. A proper seal driver is the preferred tool for installing the seal, but a piece of pipe of the proper diameter used with a hammer may be substituted **(see illustration)**.

8 Reinstall the driveshaft (refer to Chapter 8).

9 Check the transmission lubricant level and refill as needed with the recommended lubricant (see Chapter 1).

7 Speedometer driven gear oil seal - replacement

1 The speedometer driven gear seal can be replaced without removing the transmission from the vehicle.

2 Raise the vehicle and support it securely on jackstands.

3 Disconnect the speedometer cable, remove the lock plate to extension housing bolt and lock washer, then remove the lock plate.

4 Insert a screwdriver in the lock plate fitting and pry the fitting, gear and shaft from the extension housing.

5 Pry out the O-ring and seal.

6 Installation is the reverse of removal, but

6.7 An appropriate diameter piece of pipe, a socket, or a special seal installer tool housing is needed to install the extension oil seal evenly so it won't leak

lubricate the new O-ring and seal with transmission lubricant and hold the assembly so that the slot in the fitting is toward the lock plate boss on the extension.

8 Clutch start switch - check, replacement and adjustment

Check

1 This switch is a safety device intended to prevent the engine from being started with the clutch pedal released. It is attached to the clutch pedal mounting bracket and is activated by a plunger-type shaft. To check the switch, disconnect its electrical connector and place a jumper wire between the two terminals of the connector. If you can now start the vehicle, but you could not with the connector hooked up to the switch, the switch is faulty. Replace it.

Replacement and adjustment

7A

2 Remove the screws retaining the hush panel and remove the panel.

3 Disconnect the wiring harness connector at the switch.

4 Remove the switch mounting screw from the clutch pedal bracket and disengage the shaft from the clutch pedal.

5 Installation is the reverse of removal.

6 To adjust the switch simply move the slider towards the switch and depress the clutch pedal as far as possible.

Notes

Chapter 7 Part B
Automatic transmission

Contents

	Section
Automatic transmission fluid change	See Chapter 1
Automatic transmission - removal and installation	6
Diagnosis - general	2
Extension housing oil seal - replacement	See Chapter 7A
Fluid level check	See Chapter 1
General information	1
Neutral safety and back-up light switch - replacement and adjustment	5

	Section
Shift linkage - check and adjustment	3
Speedometer gear seal - replacement	See Chapter 7A
Throttle valve (TV) cable assembly - description and adjustment	4
Transmission mount - check and replacement	See Chapter 7A

Specifications

Transmission type
Three-speed 180C/200C
Four-speed 700-R4/4L60/4L60-E

Torque Specifications
Ft-lbs
Driveplate-to-torque converter bolts 35
Transmission-to-engine bolts
Four-cylinder engines 25
V6 engines 55

1 General information

All vehicles covered in this manual come equipped with either a four- or five-speed manual transmission or a three- or four-speed automatic transmission. All information on the automatic transmission is included in this Part of Chapter 7. Information on the manual transmission can be found in Part A of this Chapter.

Due to the complexity of the automatic transmissions covered in this manual and the need for specialized equipment to perform most service operations, this Chapter contains only general diagnosis, routine maintenance, adjustment and removal and installation procedures.

If the transmission requires major repair work, it should be left to a dealer service department or an automotive or transmission repair shop. You can, however, remove and

install the transmission yourself and save the expense, even if the repair work is done by a transmission shop.

The 4L60-E electronic controlled transmission is not equipped with the Throttle valve (TV) cable assembly. The transmission functions controlled by the TV cable on other models are controlled electronically in this transmission.

2 Diagnosis - general

Note: *Automatic transmission malfunctions may be caused by five general conditions: poor engine performance, improper adjustments, hydraulic malfunctions, mechanical malfunctions or malfunctions in the computer or its signal network. Diagnosis of these problems should always begin with a check of the easily repaired items: fluid level and condition (see Chapter 1), shift linkage adjustment and*

throttle linkage adjustment. Next, perform a road test to determine if the problem has been corrected or if more diagnosis is necessary. If the problem persists after the preliminary tests and corrections are completed, additional diagnosis should be done by a dealer service department or transmission repair shop. Refer to the Troubleshooting Section at the front of this manual for information on symptoms of transmission problems.

Preliminary checks
1 Drive the vehicle to warm the transmission to normal operating temperature.
2 Check the fluid level as described in Chapter 1:
   a) *If the fluid level is unusually low, add enough fluid to bring the level within the designated area of the dipstick, then check for external leaks (see below).*

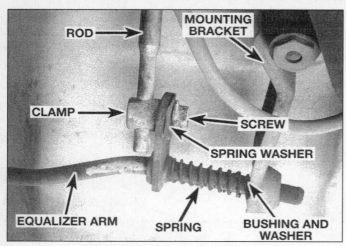

3.2 Shift linkage adjustment details

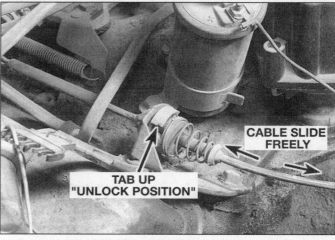

4.9 After releasing the readjust tab on the TV cable, rotate the throttle to the fully open position to automatically readjust the cable

b) *If the fluid level is abnormally high, drain off the excess, then check the drained fluid for contamination by coolant. The presence of engine coolant in the automatic transmission fluid indicates that a failure has occurred in the internal radiator walls that separate the coolant from the transmission fluid (see Chapter 3).*

c) *If the fluid is foaming, drain it and refill the transmission, then check for coolant in the fluid or a high fluid level.*

3   Check the engine idle speed. **Note:** *If the engine is malfunctioning, do not proceed with the preliminary checks until it has been repaired and runs normally.*

4   Check the throttle valve cable for freedom of movement. Adjust it if necessary (see Section 4). **Note:** *The throttle cable may function properly when the engine is shut off and cold, but it may malfunction once the engine is hot. Check it cold and at normal engine operating temperature.*

5   Inspect the shift control linkage. Make sure that it's properly adjusted and that the linkage operates smoothly.

Fluid leak diagnosis

6   Most fluid leaks are easy to locate visually. Repair usually consists of replacing a seal or gasket. If a leak is difficult to find, the following procedure may help.

7   Identify the fluid. Make sure it's transmission fluid and not engine oil or brake fluid (automatic transmission fluid is a deep red color).

8   Try to pinpoint the source of the leak. Drive the vehicle several miles, then park it over a large sheet of cardboard. After a minute or two, you should be able to locate the leak by determining the source of the fluid dripping onto the cardboard.

9   Make a careful visual inspection of the suspected component and the area immediately around it. Pay particular attention to gasket mating surfaces. A mirror is often helpful for finding leaks in areas that are hard

to see.

10   If the leak still cannot be found, clean the suspected area thoroughly with a degreaser or solvent, then dry it.

11   Drive the vehicle for several miles at normal operating temperature and varying speeds. After driving the vehicle, visually inspect the suspected component again.

12   Once the leak has been located, the cause must be determined before it can be properly repaired. If a gasket is replaced but the sealing flange is bent, the new gasket will not stop the leak. The bent flange must be straightened.

13   Before attempting to repair a leak, check to make sure that the following conditions are corrected or they may cause another leak. **Note:** *Some of the following conditions cannot be fixed without highly specialized tools and expertise. Such problems must be referred to a transmission repair shop or a dealer service department.*

Gasket leaks

14   Check the pan periodically. Make sure the bolts are tight, no bolts are missing, the gasket is in good condition and the pan is flat (dents in the pan may indicate damage to the valve body inside).

15   If the pan gasket is leaking, the fluid level or the fluid pressure may be too high, the vent may be plugged, the pan bolts may be too tight, the pan sealing flange may be warped, the sealing surface of the transmission housing may be damaged, the gasket may be damaged or the transmission casting may be cracked or porous. If sealant instead of gasket material has been used to form a seal between the pan and the transmission housing, it may be the wrong sealant.

Seal leaks

16   If a transmission seal is leaking, the fluid level or pressure may be too high, the vent may be plugged, the seal bore may be damaged, the seal itself may be damaged or improperly installed, the surface of the shaft

protruding through the seal may be damaged or a loose bearing may be causing excessive shaft movement.

17   Make sure the dipstick tube seal is in good condition and the tube is properly seated. Periodically check the area around the speedometer gear or sensor for leakage. If transmission fluid is evident, check the O-ring for damage.

Case leaks

18   If the case itself appears to be leaking, the casting is porous and will have to be repaired or replaced.

19   Make sure the oil cooler hose fittings are tight and in good condition.

Fluid comes out vent pipe or fill tube

20   If this condition occurs, the transmission is overfilled, there is coolant in the fluid, the case is porous, the dipstick is incorrect, the vent is plugged or the drain back holes are plugged.

3   Shift linkage - check and adjustment

Refer to illustration 3.2
Note: *Apply the parking brake and block the wheels to prevent the vehicle from rolling.*

1   Position the shift lever in the Neutral position.

2   Working under the vehicle, loosen the clamp screw attaching the shift rod to the transmission control lever (B) **(see illustration)**.

3   Make sure that the transmission lever (A) is in the neutral detent.

4   Hold the clamp flush against the control lever while tightening the clamp screw finger-tight.

5   Tighten the clamp screw while making sure no force is exerted in either direction against the shift rod.

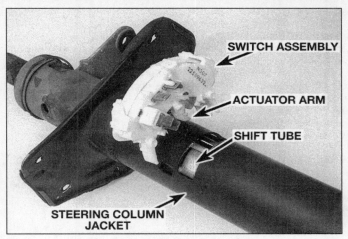

5.4 Neutral safety switch details

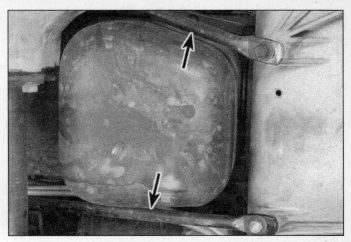

6.12 Transmission support brackets (arrows)

4   Throttle valve (TV) cable assembly - description and adjustment

Refer to illustration 4.9

1   The throttle cable should not be thought of as just an automatic downshift cable, but rather as a cable that controls the line pressure, shift feel and shift timing, as well as part throttle and detent downshifts. The function of the cable combines the functions of the vacuum modulator and downshift (detent) cable found on other model transmissions.

2   The TV cable is attached to the link at the throttle lever and bracket assembly at the transmission and to the throttle lever at the carburetor or fuel injection throttle body.

3   Whenever the TV cable has been disconnected from the carburetor or fuel injection throttle body it must be adjusted after reconnection.

4   The engine should be Off.

5   If not previously done, remove the air cleaner, labeling all hoses as they are removed to simplify installation.

6   Depress and hold down the metal readjust tab at the engine end of the TV cable.

7   While holding the tab down move the slider until it stops against the fitting.

8   Release the readjust tab.

9   Manually open the carburetor or fuel injection throttle lever to the full throttle stop position. The cable will ratchet through the slider and automatically re-adjust itself **(see illustration)**.

10   Release the carburetor or fuel injection throttle lever.

11   Road test the vehicle. If delayed or only full-throttle shifts occur, have the vehicle checked by a transmission specialist.

5   Neutral safety and back-up light switch - replacement and adjustment

Refer to illustration 5.4

1   When the switch is operating properly,

the back-up lights should come on only when the transmission is in Reverse and the engine should start only with the transmission lever in Park or Neutral.

Replacement (and initial adjustment)

2   The neutral safety and back-up light switch is mounted on the lower part of the steering column. To replace the switch, simply remove the two mounting bolts and separate the switch from the column.

3   Move the shift lever to the Neutral position.

4   Insert a 5/64-inch diameter gauge pin 3/8-inch into the gauge hole on the new switch **(see illustration)**.

5   Insert the carrier tang on the switch into the shift tube slot in the steering column and install and tighten the switch mounting bolts.

6   Remove the gauge pin.

7   Move the shift lever into the Park position.

8   Return the shift lever to the Neutral position. The gauge pin should now fit into the switch gauge hole without any binding. If the pin does not fit readjust the switch as described in the following steps:

Adjustment

9   To reset the adjustment on the original switch, move the shift lever to the Neutral position and loosen the switch mounting bolts.

10   Insert the gauge pin as described in Step 4.

11   Tighten the mounting bolts and remove the gauge pin.

12   Check the operation of the switch.

6   Automatic transmission - removal and installation

Refer to illustration 6.12

Note: *Before removing the transmission from four-wheel drive vehicles the transfer case*

must be removed as described in Chapter 7C.

1   Disconnect the cable from the negative battery terminal.

2   Remove the air cleaner, labeling all hoses as they are disconnected to simplify installation.

3   Disconnect the TV cable at the carburetor or fuel injection throttle body.

4   Remove the transmission fluid dipstick from the tube.

5   Remove the upper bolt retaining the dipstick tube and separate the tube from the transmission.

6   Raise the vehicle and support is securely on jackstands.

7   Remove the driveshaft (refer to Chapter 8).

8   Disconnect the speedometer cable at the transmission.

9   Disconnect the TCC wire connector at the transmission if so equipped.

10   Separate the brake line from the crossmember.

11   If necessary for clearance, remove the mounting bolts from the exhaust crossover pipe and catalytic converter and remove the crossover pipe and converter as an assembly (see Chapter 4).

12   Remove the support bracket bolts at the inspection cover, if so equipped **(see illustration)**.

13   Remove the bolts retaining the inspection cover and detach the cover.

14   Remove the now-exposed torque converter-to-driveplate bolts. It will be necessary to turn the crankshaft to bring each of the bolts into view (use a wrench on the large bolt at the front of the crankshaft). Mark the relative position of the converter and driveplate with a scribe so they can be reinstalled in the same position. Engage a large screwdriver in the teeth of the driveplate to prevent movement as the bolts are loosened.

15   Disconnect the catalytic converter support bracket, if not done previously.

16   Disconnect the exhaust pipe(s) at the manifold.

17   Remove the appropriate body mounting

7B

bolts and raise the body of the vehicle as described in Chapter 2F, Section 7. This will provide the clearance needed to remove the upper bellhousing bolts.

18   Using a transmission jack, preferably one with safety chains, support the transmission and remove the rear mount bolts. Remove the crossmember mounting bolts and detach the crossmember by sliding it toward the rear.

19   Lower the transmission as far as possible without causing the engine or transmission to contact the firewall, then disconnect the TV cable assembly and the oil cooler lines at the transmission.

20   Support the engine at the oil pan rail with a jack and remove the transmission-to-engine bolts. The upper bolts should be removed first.

21   Move the transmission to the rear and down. If necessary, carefully pry it free from the driveplate. Keep the rear of the transmission down at all times to keep the converter from falling out. The converter can be held in place with a strap.

22   Installation is the reverse of the removal procedure, with the following additional instructions.

23   Before installing the driveplate-to-converter bolts make sure that the weld nuts on the converter are flush with the driveplate and that the converter can be turned freely by hand in this position. Start the mounting bolts and tighten them finger-tight, then tighten them securely. This will insure proper alignment of the converter.

24   Adjust the shift linkage (refer to Section 3).

25   Adjust the TV cable (refer to Section 4).

Chapter 7 Part C
Transfer case

Contents

	Section			Section
Lubricant level - checking	See Chapter 1		Transfer case - disassembly, inspection and reassembly	4
Shifter - removal and installation	1		Transfer case - lubricant change	See Chapter 1
Shift linkage - adjustment	2		Transfer case - removal and installation	3

Specifications

Torque specifications

	Ft-lbs
Front output yoke nut	90 to 100
Vacuum switch	20
Shift lever nut	15
Transfer case half attaching bolts	20 to 25
Rear retainer bolts	15 to 20
Extension housing bolts	20 to 25
Drain/fill plug	35
Transfer case adapter bolts (automatic only)	25
Shift bracket bolt	55
Shift pivot bolt	85 to 100
Shifter adjusting bolt	30

1.4 Loosen the jam nut (arrow) from the bottom of the shifter

1.8 Transfer case shift pivot bolt location (arrow)

1   Shifter - removal and installation

Refer to illustrations 1.4 and 1.8

1   Disconnect the negative cable from the battery.
2   From inside the vehicle, remove the shifter console mounting screws and lift out the console.

3   Remove the shifter boot.
4   Loosen the jam nut from the bottom of the shifter and unscrew the shifter from its base **(see illustration)**.
5   Detach the electrical connectors and remove the mounting bolt from the selector switch. Remove the selector switch.
6   Raise the vehicle and support it securely on jackstands.

7   Disconnect the shift rod from the shifter by prying it out with a screwdriver.
8   Remove the pivot and adjusting bolts **(see illustration)**.
9   Installation is the reverse of removal. Adjust the shifter mechanism as described in Section 2.

2.1 Loosen the shift lever bracket bolt (arrow)

2.5 A 5/16-inch drill bit works fine as a gauge pin
when adjusting the shift linkage

2   Shift linkage - adjustment

Refer to illustrations 2.1 and 2.5

1   Loosen the small bolt on the shift lever bracket attached to the transmission extension housing **(see illustration)**.
2   Loosen the shifter pivot **(see illustration 1.8)**.
3   Move the transfer case shifter (inside the vehicle) to the 4 HI position.
4   Remove the shifter console and boot. Slide the boot up the shifter.
5   Insert an 8mm gauge pin (a 5/16-inch drill bit works fine) through the shifter and shifter bracket **(see illustration)**.
6   Insert a locking bolt or screw through the transfer case shift lever.
7   Tighten the small bolt to the torque listed in this Chapter's Specifications.
8   Tighten the shifter pivot bolt to the torque listed in this Chapter's Specifications.
9   Remove the gauge pin and lock bolt or screw.
10   Install the shifter boot and console.

3   Transfer case - removal and installation

Refer to illustrations 3.6, 3.10 and 3.14

1   Move the transfer case shifter to the 4 HI position.
2   Disconnect the negative battery cable.
3   Raise the vehicle and support it securely on jackstands.
4   Remove the skid plate mounting bolts and detach the skid plate, if equipped.
5   Drain the lubricant from the transfer case.
6   Mark the transfer case front output shaft yoke and driveshaft so they can be reassembled in the same relative position **(see illustration)**. Disconnect the front driveshaft from the transfer case.
7   Mark the rear axle yoke and driveshaft to simplify reassembly, then remove the rear driveshaft.
8   Disconnect the speedometer cable (or electrical connector) and vacuum harness at the transfer case.

9   Remove the shifter lever as described in Section 1. Disconnect the shift rod from the transfer case.
10   Remove the catalytic converter hanger bolts at the converter **(see illustration)**.
11   Place a floor jack under the transmission oil pan and raise the transmission slightly. Position a block of wood between the jack head and the oil pan to prevent damage to the pan.
12   Remove the transmission mount bolts. Remove the mount and catalytic converter hanger.
13   Lower the transmission and transfer case.
14   While supporting the weight of the transfer case with the floor jack **(see illustration)**, remove the transfer case mounting bolts. On automatic transmission equipped vehicles the shifter bracket must be removed from the transfer case adapter before the upper mounting bolt can be removed.
15   Separate the transfer case from the extension housing and remove it from the vehicle.

3.6 Mark the front driveshaft yoke so it can be reinstalled
in the same position

3.10 Remove the catalytic converter hanger bolts prior to
removing the transfer case/transmission mount

3.14 Use a floor jack to support the transfer case weight during the removal procedure

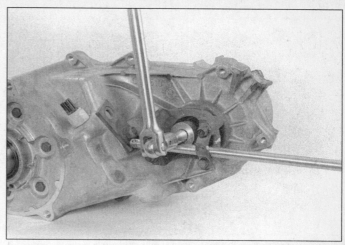

4.2 A breaker bar can be inserted through the front yoke to facilitate removal of the yoke nut

16   Before installation position a new gasket on the transfer case.

17   Install the transfer case, aligning the splines of the input shaft while sliding the transfer case forward until seated against the transmission.

18   Install the transfer case mounting bolts and tighten them to the torque listed in this Chapter's Specifications. Be sure to install the shift lever bracket on vehicles equipped with an automatic transmission.

19   Raise the transfer case and install the mount and hanger bracket. Install the retaining bolts and tighten them to the torque listed in this Chapter's Specifications.

20   Install the catalytic converter hanger bolts at the converter and tighten them securely.

21   Attach the shift linkage to the transfer case and install the shift lever.

22   Connect the speedometer cable and vacuum hose.

23   Install the front and rear driveshafts, using the alignment marks for reference.

24   Fill the transfer case with the specified lubricant.

25   Install the skid plate (if equipped) and lower the vehicle.

26   Connect the negative battery cable.

4   Transfer case - disassembly, inspection and reassembly

Disassembly

Refer to illustrations 4.2, 4.5, 4.13 and 4.14

1   Remove the fill and drain plugs.

2   Remove the front yoke **(see illustration)**.

3   Remove the yoke seal washer. Discard the seal washer and yoke nut.

4   Set the transfer case on its side, positioning the front case on wood blocks.

5   Shift the transfer case to the 4 LO position **(see illustration)**. The top of the transfer case lever should be in the far left detent.

6   Remove the extension housing mounting bolts and detach the extension housing. Tap the shoulder of the extension housing with a soft-faced hammer to break the seal.

7   Remove and discard the snap-ring from the mainshaft rear bearing.

8   Remove the rear retainer mounting bolts and tap the shoulder of the retainer to break the seal.

9   Remove the rear retainer and pump housing from the transfer case.

10   Remove the pump seal from the pump housing.

11   Remove the speedometer driven gear from the mainshaft.

12   Remove the pump gear from the mainshaft.

13   Remove the rear case attaching bolts from the front case. Separate the cases by prying only at the slots cast into the ends of the transfer case **(see illustration)**.

14   Remove the front output shaft and drive

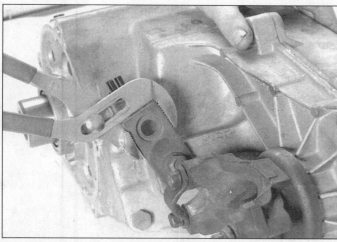

4.5 Before beginning disassembly, the top of the shifter must be in the far left (4 LO) detent position

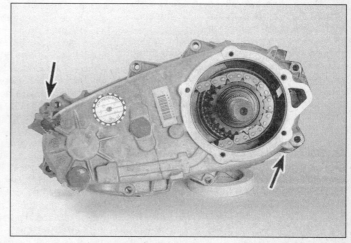

4.13 The case must be pried apart only at the pry slots cast into the case

7C

4.14 Raising the mainshaft slightly will allow the output shaft and drive chain to be removed as an assembly

4.68 Install the planetary assembly in the transfer case as shown

chain as an assembly. The mainshaft can be raised slightly to allow the front output shaft to clear the case **(see illustration)**.

15   Pull up on the mode fork rail until it clears the range fork. Rotate the mode fork and rail and remove them from the transfer case.

16   Pull up on the mainshaft, separating it from the planetary assembly and remove the mainshaft from the transfer case.

17   Remove the planetary assembly and range fork from the transfer case.

18   Remove the planetary thrust washer and input gear from the transfer case.

19   Remove the input gear thrust bearing and front thrust washer from the transfer case.

20   Remove the shift sector detent spring and retaining bolt.

21   Remove the shift sector, shaft and spacer from the transfer case.

22   Remove the retaining bolts from the lock plate and separate the lock plate from the transfer case.

23   Using an expansion tool and a slide hammer, remove the input gear pilot bearing.

24   Using a screwdriver or a brass drift, remove the front output shaft seal, the input shaft seal and the rear extension seal.

25   Press the two input gear roller bearings from the transfer case, using a press with the proper adapters. **Note:** *Before removing the bearings, measure their installed depth.*

26   Using an expansion tool and slide hammer, remove the output shaft rear bearing. **Note:** *Before removing the bearing, measure its installed depth.*

27   Using a hammer and drift, remove the rear mainshaft bearing from the rear retainer.

28   Using a screwdriver, pry out the snap-ring retaining the front output shaft bearing.

29   Remove the front output shaft bearing from the case using a hammer and punch. **Note:** *Before removing the bearing, measure its installed depth.*

30   Press the extension housing bushing from the housing using the proper adapters.

31   To disassemble the mainshaft, first remove the synchronizer hub snap-ring.

32   Tap the synchronizer hub from the mainshaft, using a soft-faced hammer.

33   Remove the drive sprocket and thrust washer.

34   Using an appropriately sized collar, press the two roller bearings from the drive sprocket.

35   Remove the synchronizer keys and retaining rings.

36   To disassemble the planetary gear, first remove the snap-ring that retains the planetary gear to the annulus gear.

37   Remove and discard the outer thrust ring.

38   Remove the planetary assembly from the annulus gear.

39   Remove the inner thrust ring from the planetary assembly and discard it.

Inspection

40   Wash all parts thoroughly in solvent. Make sure that all old lubricant, dirt and metal particles are removed. Clean out each oil feed port and channel in each case half with compressed air. After cleaning, the parts should be laid out for inspection.

41   Inspect all gear teeth for evidence of excessive wear or damage. Check all gear splines for burrs, nicks, wear or damage. Minor nicks or scratches can be removed with an oil stone, but replace any part showing significant wear or damage.

42   Inspect all snap-rings and thrust washers and replace any that show signs of wear, distortion or damage.

43   Inspect the two case halves for cracks, damaged mating surfaces, stripped bolt threads or distortion. Replace as necessary.

44   Inspect the low range lockplate in the front case. If the lock plate teeth or the plate hub are cracked, chipped or excessively worn, replace the lock plate and the lock plate attaching bolts.

45   Inspect all needle, roller and thrust bearings. Check the condition of the bearing

bores in both cases. Also check the bearing bores in the input gear, rear output shaft and rear retainer. Replace any part that shows signs of excessive wear or damage.

Reassembly

Refer to illustrations 4.68, 4.70 and 4.75

46   To assemble the planetary gear, begin by installing the inner thrust ring.

47   Install the planetary assembly in the annulus gear.

48   Install the outer thrust ring. Install the retaining snap-ring.

49   Begin assembling the mainshaft by using an appropriately sized collar to press the front drive sprocket bearing into place.

50   Press the rear bearing into the front drive sprocket with an appropriately sized collar.

51   Install the drive sprocket thrust washer on the mainshaft.

52   Install the drive sprocket on the mainshaft.

53   Install the blocker ring and synchronizer assembly on the mainshaft. Install a new snap-ring.

54   Install the pump gear on the mainshaft, tapping it with a soft-faced hammer until it is seated.

55   Install the speedometer gear on the mainshaft.

56   Begin transfer case reassembly by installing the lock plate. Coat the case and lock plate surfaces around the bolt holes with a non-hardening thread locking compound.

57   Position the lock plate on the case, aligning the bolt holes. Install the mounting bolts and tighten them to the torque listed in this Chapter's Specifications.

58   Install the two input shaft roller bearings in the transfer case. Press the bearing in until they are installed to the depth measured in Step 25. **Note:** *All of the bearings used in the transfer case must be correctly aligned with the bearing oil feed holes. After installing each bearing, check the bearing position to be sure the oil feed hole is not in any way*

4.70 Install the mode fork rail and bracket as shown here

4.75 The pump gear and speedometer drive gear are installed on the mainshaft as shown

obstructed by the bearing.

59   Install the front output shaft rear bearing to the depth measured in Step 26.

60   Install the front output shaft front bearing to the depth measured in Step 29.

61   Install the front output shaft bearing snap-ring.

62   Install the front output shaft seal using a length of pipe of the appropriate diameter.

63   Install the spacer on the shift sector shaft and install the sector in the transfer case.

64   Install the shift lever and retaining nut and tighten the nut to the specified torque.

65   Install the shift sector detent spring and retaining bolt.

66   Press the input gear pilot bearing into place.

67   Install the input gear front thrust bearing and input gear in the transfer case.

68   Install the planetary gear thrust washer on the input gear. Install the range fork on the planetary assembly and install the planetary assembly in the transfer case **(see illustration)**.

69   Install the mainshaft in the transfer case, making sure the thrust washer is aligned with the input gear and planetary assembly.

70   Install the mode fork on the synchronizer sleeve and rotate it so that it lines up with the range fork. Slide the mode fork rail down through the range fork until the rail bottoms out in the case bore **(see illustration)**.

71   Position the drive chain on the front output shaft and on the mainshaft drive sprocket. Install the front output shaft in the transfer case. The mainshaft can be raised slightly to allow the output shaft to seat completely.

72   Install the magnet in the pocket in the transfer case.

73   Apply a 1/8-inch bead of anaerobic sealant to the mating surface of the front case half.

74   Install the rear case on the front case, aligning the dowel pins. Install the attaching bolts and tighten them to the specified torque. Install the two bolts and washers used in the dowel pin holes.

75   Install the pump gear and speedometer drive gear on the mainshaft **(see illustration)**.

76   Install the output bearing in the rear retainer. Press the bearing in until it is completely seated in the bore.

77   Install the pump seal in the pump housing using a seal driver or a pipe of the appro-

priate diameter. Apply some petroleum jelly to the pump housing tabs and install the pump housing in the rear retainer.

78   Apply a 1/8-inch bead of anaerobic sealant to the mating surface of the rear retainer. Attach the rear retainer to the transfer case. Tighten the bolts to the specified torque.

79   Install a new snap-ring on the mainshaft. Pull up on the mainshaft to seat the snap-ring.

80   Install the extension housing bushing using an installation tool. Press the bushing in until it bottoms in the bore.

81   Install the new extension housing seal. Seat the seal completely in the bore.

82   Apply a 1/8-inch bead of anaerobic sealant to the mating surface of the extension housing. Install the extension housing. Tighten the attaching bolts to the specified torque.

83   Install the front yoke on the output shaft, using a new seal washer and nut. Tighten the nut to the torque listed in this Chapter's Specifications).

84   Install the drain and filler plugs and tighten them to the specified torque.

Notes

Chapter 8
Clutch and drivetrain

Contents

	Section
Axleshaft - removal and installation	13
Axleshaft bearing - replacement	15
Axleshaft oil seal - replacement	14
Clutch - general information	1
Clutch cable and adjuster - replacement	26
Clutch components - removal, inspection and installation	3
Clutch hydraulic system - bleeding	7
Clutch master cylinder - removal, overhaul and installation	6
Clutch pedal freeplay check and adjustment (1982 and 1983 models only)	See Chapter 1
Clutch pedal - removal and installation	2
Clutch pilot bearing - removal and installation	4
Clutch release cylinder - removal, overhaul and installation	5
CV joint boot - replacement (split-type boot)	20
Driveshaft - general information	8
Driveshaft - removal and installation	11
Driveshaft - out-of-balance correction	10
Front differential carrier bushing - replacement	25
Front driveaxles - general information	19
Front differential carrier - removal and installation	24
Front differential output shaft pilot bearing - replacement	23
Front driveaxle - removal, boot replacement and installation	21
Front output shaft tube and tube seal - removal and installation	22
Rear axle assembly - removal and installation	16
Rear differential - oil change	See Chapter 1
Rear differential - oil level check	See Chapter 1
Rear differential pinion flange - replacement	18
Rear differential pinion seal - replacement	17
Universal joints - disassembly, inspection and reassembly	12
Universal joints - wear check	9

Specifications

General
Clutch fluid type	See Chapter 1
Clutch pedal freeplay (1982 and 1983 models)	See Chapter 1

Torque specifications
	Ft-lbs (unless otherwise indicated)
Clutch pedal-to-mounting bracket	25
Clutch master cylinder-to-cowl	120 in-lbs
Clutch pressure plate-to-flywheel	20
Release cylinder-to-bellhousing	15
Universal joint retainer strap bolts	15
Brake assembly-to-rear axle housing	35
Rear differential pinion shaft lock screw	20
Rear differential carrier cover bolts	20
Filler plug	20
Shift cable housing attaching bolts	35
Driveaxle-to-output shaft flange bolts	60
Output shaft tube bracket-to-frame bolts	55
Output shaft tube-to-differential carrier bolts	36
Driveaxle/hub retaining nut	174
Wheel lug nuts	See Chapter 1

8

1 Clutch - general information

Refer to illustration 1.1

All manual transmission-equipped vehicles utilize a single dry plate, diaphragm spring-type clutch **(see illustration)**. Operation is through a foot pedal and cable or hydraulic system. The unit consists of a pressure plate assembly which contains the pressure plate, diaphragm spring and fulcrum rings. The assembly is bolted to the rear face of the flywheel.

The driven plate (friction or clutch plate) is free to slide along the transmission input shaft and is held in place between the flywheel and pressure plate by the pressure exerted by the diaphragm spring. The friction lining material is riveted to the clutch plate, which incorporates a spring-cushioned hub designed to absorb driveline shocks and to assist in ensuring smooth starts.

Depressing the clutch pedal pushes the throwout bearing forward to bear against the fingers of the diaphragm spring. This action causes the diaphragm spring outer edge to deflect and move the pressure plate to the rear to disengage the pressure plate from the clutch plate.

When the clutch pedal is released, the diaphragm spring forces the pressure plate into contact with the friction linings of the clutch plate and at the same time pushes the clutch plate forward on its splines to ensure full engagement with the flywheel. The clutch plate is now firmly sandwiched between the pressure plate and the flywheel and the drive is taken up.

A hydraulic clutch assembly is employed on all 1984 and later models. The assembly consists of a remote reservoir, a clutch master cylinder and a release cylinder.

The clutch master cylinder is mounted on the cowl panel in the engine compartment and the release cylinder is mounted on the transmission bellhousing. The master cylinder operates directly off the clutch pedal.

When the clutch pedal is pushed in, hydraulic fluid (under pressure from the clutch master cylinder) flows into the release cylinder. Because the release cylinder is also connected to the clutch fork, the fork moves the throwout bearing into contact with the pressure plate release fingers, disengaging the clutch plate.

The hydraulic clutch system locates the clutch pedal and provides clutch adjustment automatically, so no adjustment of the clutch linkage or pedal position is required. **Caution:** *Prior to servicing the clutch or vehicle components that require the removal of the release cylinder (i.e. transmission and bellhousing removal), the master cylinder pushrod must be disconnected from the clutch pedal. If this is not done, permanent damage to the release cylinder will occur if the clutch pedal is depressed while the release cylinder is disconnected.*

If a malfunction of the hydraulic clutch assembly is suspected, verify it by removing

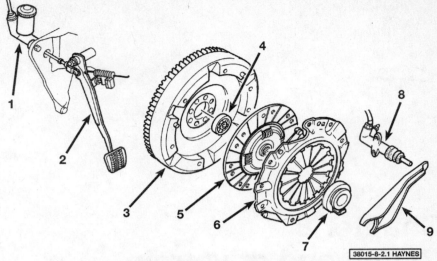

1.1 Exploded view of the clutch components

1	Clutch master cylinder	6	Clutch cover
2	Clutch pedal	7	Clutch release bearing
3	Flywheel	8	Clutch slave cylinder
4	Pilot bearing	9	Clutch release lever
5	Clutch disc		

the clutch housing dust shield and measuring the clutch release cylinder pushrod travel as follows.

Raise the vehicle and place it securely on jackstands. Remove the bolts retaining the clutch housing dust shield to the clutch housing and remove the shield. Note the position of the release cylinder pushrod. Have an assistant push the clutch pedal all the way to the floor. Measure the distance the pushrod travels while engaging the clutch fork. If it extends substantially (approximately 1/2-inch or more), the clutch hydraulic system is operating correctly. Do not remove it. If the release cylinder pushrod does not travel at least the specified distance check the reservoir fluid level (the release cylinder must be in place when the fluid level is checked).

2.6 To disconnect the clutch master cylinder pushrod from the clutch pedal, remove the retainer clip (arrow) and push out the clevis pin

Note: *Carefully clean the top of the reservoir before removing it to prevent contamination of the system. Fill the reservoir to the proper level, indicated by a step in the reservoir. Do not overfill the reservoir, as the upper portion must accept fluid that is displaced from the release cylinder as the clutch wears.*

If the reservoir required fluid, examine the hydraulic system components for leakage by removing the rubber boots from the master and release cylinders and checking for leakage past the pistons. A slight wetting of the surfaces is acceptable, but if excessive leakage is evident, the clutch hydraulic system must be replaced, as a whole, with a new one.

2 Clutch pedal - removal and installation

Refer to illustration 2.6

1 Disconnect the cable from the negative battery terminal.
2 Disconnect the clutch pedal return spring.
3 Remove the screws retaining the under-dash hush panel, then remove the hush panel.
4 Disconnect and remove the neutral start switch from the clutch pedal (see Chapter 7A).
5 Remove the turn signal and hazard warning flasher mounting bracket screws.
6 Disconnect the clutch cable (see Section 26) or the clutch master cylinder pushrod from the clutch pedal **(see illustration)**.
7 Remove the nut from the clutch pedal pivot bolt.

NORMAL FINGER WEAR   **EXCESSIVE FINGER WEAR**   **BROKEN OR BENT FINGERS**

3.1a Replace the pressure plate if excessive wear is noted

3.1b Check the clutch plate lining, spring and splines (arrows) for wear

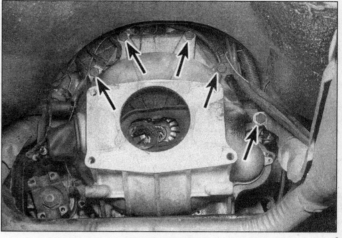

3.2 Locations of the bellhousing mounting bolts (not all are visible)

8   Pull the bolt out only far enough to allow removal of the clutch pedal, leaving it engaged through the brake pedal pivot and bracket.

9   Before installing the clutch pedal assembly, inspect and clean all components. Replace all components showing wear with new ones. **Note:** *Do not clean the bushings with solvent; simply wipe them off with a clean rag.*

10   Installation is the reverse of the removal procedure. After installation is complete, adjust the clutch pedal freeplay (1982 and 1983 models only) (see Chapter 1).

3   Clutch components - removal, inspection and installation

Refer to illustrations 3.1a, 3.1b, 3.2, 3.9, 3.19 and 3.23

Warning: *Dust produced by clutch wear and deposited on clutch components may contain asbestos, which is hazardous to your health. DO NOT blow it out with compressed air and DO NOT inhale it. DO NOT use gasoline or petroleum-based solvents to remove the dust. Brake system cleaners should be used to flush the dust into a drain pan. After the clutch components are wiped clean with*

a rag, dispose of the contaminated rags and cleaner in a covered, marked container.

1   Access to the clutch is normally accomplished by removing the transmission, leaving the engine in the vehicle. If, of course, the engine is being removed for major overhaul, then the opportunity should always be taken to check the clutch assembly for wear at the same time **(see illustrations).**

2   Disconnect the clutch cable and spring, then remove the transmission (see Chapter 7A) and bellhousing from the engine block (on models where the bellhousing is not an integral part of the transmission case) **(see illustration).** On models equipped with a hydraulic clutch assembly, remove the release cylinder heat shield and release cylinder from the bellhousing before removing the bellhousing.

3   Slide the clutch fork from the ball stud and remove the fork from the dust boot.

4   If necessary, the ball stud can be removed from the bellhousing by unscrewing it.

5   If there are no alignment marks on the pressure plate (an X-mark or white, painted letter) scribe or center-punch marks for indexing purposes during installation.

6   Unscrew the bolts securing the pressure plate and cover assembly one turn at a time in a diagonal sequence to prevent distortion

3.9 The throwout bearing must be lubricated at these points before installation

of the clutch cover.

7   With all the bolts and lock washers removed, carefully lift the pressure plate away from the flywheel. Be careful not to drop the clutch plate.

8   It is not practical to dismantle the pressure plate assembly.

9   If a new clutch plate is being installed, replace the throwout bearing at the same time **(see illustration).** This will preclude hav-

8

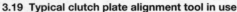

3.19 Typical clutch plate alignment tool in use

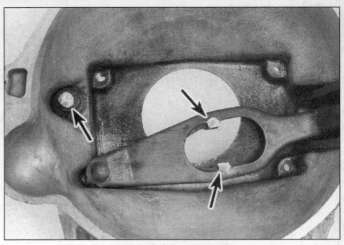

3.23 Clutch fork lubrication points

ing to replace it at a later date when wear on the clutch plate is still very little.

10   If the pressure plate assembly must be replaced, a rebuilt unit may be available.

11   Examine the clutch plate friction lining for wear and loose rivets, and the disc for rim distortion, cracks, broken hub springs and worn splines. The surface of the friction linings may be highly glazed, but as long as the clutch material pattern can be seen clearly, this is satisfactory. Compare the amount of lining remaining with a new clutch plate, if possible. If in doubt, replace the clutch plate with a new one.

12   Check the machined faces of the flywheel and the pressure plate. If either are grooved, they should be machined until smooth or replaced.

13   If the pressure plate is cracked or split, replace it with a new one; also, if the condition of the diaphragm spring is suspect, the spring should be checked and replaced if necessary.

14   Check the throwout bearing for smoothness of operation. There should be no harsh or loose spots in it. It should spin reasonably freely, bearing in mind that it has been prepacked with grease. If in doubt, replace the bearing with a new one.

15   It is important that no oil or grease gets on the clutch plate friction linings or the pressure plate and flywheel faces. Always handle the clutch with clean hands and wipe down the pressure plate and flywheel faces with a clean, dry rag before assembly begins.

16   Place the clutch plate against the flywheel, making sure that the longer splined boss faces toward the flywheel (thicker torsional spring assembly projection toward the transmission).

17   Install the pressure plate and clutch cover assembly so that the marks are in alignment. Tighten the bolts only finger tight so that the driven plate is gripped, but can still be moved sideways.

18   The clutch plate must now be aligned so that when the engine and transmission are mated, the input shaft splines will pass

through the splines in the center of the clutch hub plate.

19   Alignment can usually be carried out by inserting a round bar or long screwdriver through the hole in the center of the clutch so that the end of the bar rests in the small hole in the end of the crankshaft containing the input shaft pilot bearing **(see illustration)**. Ideally, an old transmission input shaft or alignment tool should be used. These alignment tools are inexpensive and available at your local auto parts retailer.

20   Using the bearing as a fulcrum, move the bar sideways or up and down to move the clutch plate in whichever direction is necessary to align (center) it.

21   Alignment can be verified by removing the bar and viewing the clutch plate hub in relation to the hole in the center of the clutch cover plate diaphragm spring. When the hub appears exactly in the center of the hole, all is correct. On pressure plates that have cutaway edges, the clutch plate can be centered by using the fingers to line up its edges with the edge of the flywheel.

22   Tighten the pressure plate bolts a little at a time to the torque listed in this Chapter's Specifications. Tighten them in a diagonal sequence to ensure that the cover plate is pulled down evenly and without distortion of the flange.

23   Lubricate the clutch fork fingers at the throwout bearing end, and the ball and socket, with a high melting point grease **(see illustration)**. Also lubricate the throwout bearing collar and groove.

24   Install the clutch fork and dust boot in the clutch housing and attach the throwout bearing to the fork.

25   Install the bellhousing (if separated from the transmission).

26   Install the transmission (see Chapter 7A).

27   Connect the fork pushrod and spring, lubricating the spring and pushrod ends. On models with hydraulic clutch assemblies, attach the release cylinder and release cylinder heat shield to the bellhousing.

28   Adjust the clutch pedal freeplay (see Chapter 1) on models not equipped with a hydraulic clutch release assembly.

4   Clutch pilot bearing - removal and installation

Refer to illustrations 4.5a, 4.5b, 4.5c and 4.6
Note: *If the engine has been removed from the vehicle, disregard the following steps that do not apply.*

1   Remove the transmission (see Chapter 7A).

2   Remove the bellhousing and clutch (see Section 3).

3   The clutch pilot bearing (or bushing), which is pressed into the end of the crankshaft, supports the forward end of the transmission input shaft. It requires attention whenever the clutch is removed from the vehicle.

4   Clean the bearing thoroughly and inspect it for excessive wear or damage. If wear is noted, the bearing must be replaced with a new one.

5   Removal can be accomplished with a special puller, but an alternative method, and one that works very well, is to remove the bearing hydraulically. First, locate a solid steel bar with a diameter that is slightly less than the inside diameter of the bearing (19/32-inch should be very close). The bar should just slip into the bearing with very little clearance. Next, pack the bearing and the area behind it (in the crankshaft recess) with heavy grease **(see illustrations)**. Try to eliminate as much air as possible from the recess behind the bearing. Insert the bar into the bearing bore and rap the end of the bar with a hammer **(see illustration)**. The pressure exerted on the grease will be transferred to the back side of the bearing, forcing it out of the recess. Be sure to clean the grease out of the crankshaft after the bearing has been removed.

6   To install the new bearing, lubricate its

4.5a A grease gun works very well for filling the area behind the pilot bearing with heavy grease

4.5b After packing the area behind and in the bearing with grease . . .

4.5c . . . insert a close fitting steel bar and strike it with a hammer

4.6 A socket or a steel bar can be used to install the new pilot bearing

outside surface with oil, then drive it into the recess with a socket and a soft-faced hammer **(see illustration)**. The radius in the bore of the bearing must face out. Select a socket that is slightly smaller than the outside diameter of the bearing.

7   Reinstall the clutch and transmission.

5   Clutch release cylinder - removal, overhaul and installation

Refer to illustrations 5.2 and 5.5

1   Raise the vehicle and support it securely on jackstands.
2   Disconnect the hydraulic line at the release cylinder **(see illustration)**.
3   Remove the release cylinder retaining fasteners and detach the cylinder.
4   Remove the pushrod and dust cover from the release cylinder.
5   Using snap-ring pliers, remove the snap-ring from the release cylinder **(see illustration)**.
6   Shake out the plunger and spring assembly.

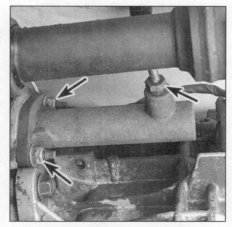

5.2 To remove the release cylinder, unscrew the hydraulic line fitting (right arrow), then remove the mounting fasteners (left arrows)

7   Carefully remove the seal from the plunger.
8   Replace the seal and clean all other

5.5 Remove the snap-ring from the release cylinder

parts in clean brake fluid. Do not use solvent!
9   Inspect the cylinder bore for scoring and scratches. The bore should be smooth to the touch. Replace the release cylinder if the

8

bore is not smooth.
10   Carefully install the seal in the groove on the plunger.
11   Install the spring on the plunger.
12   Lubricate the seal and cylinder bore with clean brake fluid.
13   Install the plunger and spring assembly in the cylinder bore.
14   Press in on the plunger and install the snap-ring.
15   Apply some grease to the inside of the rubber dust cover (there should be some included with the rebuild kit). Install the dust cover on the release cylinder.
16   Install the pushrod through the dust cover.
17   Attach the cylinder to the vehicle by first installing the hydraulic line.
18   Fill the clutch master cylinder reservoir with clean brake fluid of the specified type and bleed the clutch hydraulic system (see Section 7).
19   Attach the release cylinder to the bell-housing and install the retaining fasteners, tightening them to the specified torque.

6   Clutch master cylinder - removal, overhaul and installation

Refer to illustration 6.9
1   Remove the under-dash panel.
2   Disconnect the master cylinder pushrod from the clutch pedal.
3   Remove the master cylinder mounting bolts.
4   Disconnect and plug the reservoir hose at the master cylinder.
5   Disconnect and plug the hydraulic line for the release cylinder at the master cylinder.
6   Remove the master cylinder.
7   Be sure to disassemble the master cylinder on a clean working surface.
8   Slide the dust cover back.
9   Use snap-ring pliers to remove the pushrod circlip and detach the pushrod **(see illustration)**.

6.9 Push in on the pushrod and remove the snap-ring with snap-ring pliers

10   Shake out the plunger and spring assembly.
11   Remove the reservoir adapter from the top of the master cylinder by twisting and pulling out.
12   Remove the spring, seal support, recuperation seal and shim from the front of the plunger. Be careful not to damage the plunger surface.
13   Remove the back seal from the rear of the plunger.
14   Replace all seals and clean the remaining parts with clean brake fluid. Inspect the cylinder bore for scoring and scratches. The bore should be smooth to the touch. Replace the master cylinder if any roughness is noted.
15   Reassemble the master cylinder using new seals.
16   Install the back seal in the groove in the plunger.
17   Install the shim and recuperation seal on the plunger, with the flat of the seal against the shim.
18   Install the seal support in the recuperation seal and snap the ring over the plunger nose.
19   Lubricate the seals and cylinder bore with clean brake fluid.
20   Carefully install the plunger assembly into the master cylinder bore.
21   Install the plunger and circlip in the master cylinder.
22   Install the new reservoir adapter seal and press in the adapter.
23   Attach the master cylinder to the vehicle and tighten the retaining bolts to the specified torque.
24   Connect the pushrod to the clutch pedal and install the retaining clip.
25   Install the under-dash panel.
26   Connect the reservoir hose and hydraulic line to the master cylinder.
27   Fill the reservoir with the recommended brake fluid and bleed the clutch system (see Section 7).

7   Clutch hydraulic system - bleeding

1   The clutch hydraulic system should be bled whenever any part of the system is disconnected or when a low fluid level has allowed air to be drawn into the master cylinder.
2   Fill the master cylinder with the specified grade of clean brake fluid (see Chapter 1).
3   Raise the vehicle and support it securely on jackstands.
4   Have an assistant depress the clutch pedal all the way while you loosen the bleed screw.
5   Tighten the bleed screw and release the clutch pedal.
6   Repeat Steps 5 and 6 until all air is evacuated from the system.
7   Check the fluid level in the master cylinder reservoir and refill if necessary.

8   Driveshaft - general information

The driveshaft is of tubular construction and may be a one or two-section type depending upon the wheelbase of the vehicle.

On four-wheel drive vehicles the rear wheel driveline is very similar to that described above, but in order to drive the front wheels a driveshaft is incorporated between the transfer case and the front axle. This shaft is basically similar to the shafts used to drive the rear axle.

All driveshafts used to drive the rear wheels have needle bearing type universal joints. Single-section shafts have a splined sliding sleeve at the front end connecting to the output shaft of the transmission, while the two-section shafts have a central slip joint. The purpose of these devices is to accommodate, by retraction or extension, the varying shaft length caused by the movement of the rear axle as the rear suspension deflects. On some four-wheel drive models, due to the extent of the front driveshaft angle, a constant velocity joint is used at the transfer case end of the driveshaft.

The universal joints are lubricated for life and are not serviceable on the vehicle. If a universal joint becomes worn or noisy, a service kit containing cross and bearing assemblies is available. The kit also contains snap-rings which must be installed to substitute for the nylon injection rings installed at the factory during shaft assembly. The entire driveshaft must be removed from the vehicle whenever servicing is necessary and care must be taken when handling it to preserve the balance produced at the factory. Care should also be taken if the vehicle is undercoated. Never allow undercoating or any other foreign material to adhere to the driveshaft as it will disturb the factory balance.

9   Universal joints - wear check

1   Universal joint problems are usually caused by worn or damaged needle bearings. These problems are revealed as vibration in the driveline or clunking noises when the transmission is put in Drive or the clutch is released. In extreme cases they are caused by lack of lubrication. If this happens, you will hear metallic squeaks and ultimately, grinding and shrieking sounds as the bearings are destroyed.
2   It is easy to check the needle bearings for wear and damage with the driveshaft in place on the vehicle. To check the rear universal joint, turn the driveshaft with one hand and hold the differential yoke with the other. Any movement between the two is an indication of wear. The front universal joint can be checked by holding the driveshaft with one hand and the sleeve yoke in the transmission with the other. Any movement here indicates the need for universal joint repair.

11.2a Mark the driveshaft and pinion flange relationship with paint

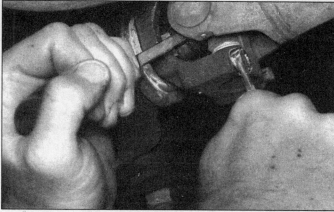

11.2b Insert a screwdriver through the U-joint to keep the driveshaft from turning and remove the retaining bolts with a wrench

3   If they are worn or damaged, the universal joints will have to be replaced with new ones. Read over the procedure carefully before beginning.

10 Driveshaft out-of-balance correction

1   Vibration of the driveshaft at certain speeds may be caused by any of the following:

*Undercoating or mud on the shaft
Loose rear strap mounting bolts
Worn universal joints
Bent or dented driveshaft*

2   Vibration which is thought to be coming from the driveshaft is sometimes caused by improper tire balance. This should be one of your first checks.

3   If the shaft is in a good, clean, undamaged condition, it is worth disconnecting the rear end mounting bolts and turning the shaft 180-degrees to see if an improvement is noticed. Be sure to mark the original position of each component before disassembly so the shaft can be returned to the same location.

4   If the vibration persists after checking for obvious causes and changing the position of the shaft, the entire assembly should be checked out by a repair shop or replaced.

11 Driveshaft - removal and installation

One-piece driveshaft

Refer to illustrations 11.2a and 11.2b

1   Raise the vehicle and place it securely on jackstands.

2   Refer to the illustrations for the driveshaft removal procedure **(see illustrations)**.

3   Make sure that the driveshaft is handled carefully during the removal and installation procedures, as it must maintain the factory balance to operate smoothly and quietly.

4   Make sure that the outer diameter of the transmission sleeve yoke is not burred, as it could damage the transmission seal when the driveshaft is installed.

5   Lubricate the sleeve yoke splines with engine oil, then slide the yoke onto the transmission output shaft. Do not force it or use a hammer. If resistance is met, check the splines for burrs.

6   Attach the shaft to the pinion flange. Be sure to align the marks on the shaft and pinion flange that were made before removal.

7   Install the rear bolts and tighten them to the specified torque.

8   Remove the jackstands and lower the vehicle.

Two-piece rear driveshaft

Refer to illustration 11.9

9   The procedure is the same as the one described above with the exception of the need to remove the two bolts which support the center bearing assembly **(see illustration)**. Be sure to mark the relationship of the front half to rear half of the driveshaft at the center joint.

10   Install the front half first. Attach the center bearing support loosely to the crossmember.

11   Slide the front yoke into the transmission until it bottoms and tighten the center bearing support bolts to the torque listed in this Chapter's Specifications.

12   Slide the rear half into position and tighten the U-joint retaining bolts to the torque listed in this Chapter's Specifications.

Front driveshaft (four-wheel drive models only)

13   Raise the vehicle and support it securely on jackstands. Remove the two transmission mount-to-crossmember retaining nuts.

14   Using a hydraulic jack, raise the transfer case about 1/2-inch.

15   Remove the two bolts and nuts from each end of the crossmember (four total), working through the frame access holes as necessary.

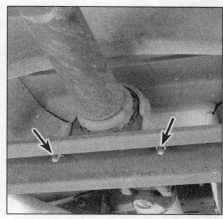

11.9 Two-piece driveshaft center support mounting bolts

16   Centerpunch or mark the relationship of the driveshaft to the pinion flanges at the transfer case and front differential.

17   Remove the U-joint retaining bolts and detach the driveshaft.

18   Be sure to align the marks during installation.

19   Tighten the U-joint retaining bolts to the specified torque.

20   Install the crossmember and tighten the attaching bolts and nuts securely.

21   Lower the jack supporting the transfer case.

22   Install the transmission mount-to-crossmember retaining nuts and tighten them securely.

23   Remove the jackstands and lower the vehicle.

12 Universal joints - disassembly, inspection and reassembly

Refer to illustrations 12.2, 12.3a, 12.3b, 12.4, 12.11, 12.13, 12.14 and 12.15

Note: *Always purchase a universal joint service kit(s) for your model vehicle before start-*

8

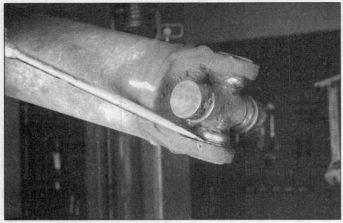

12.2 Remove the snap-rings from the U-joint by tapping them off with a screwdriver and hammer

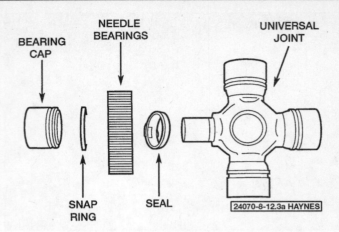

12.3a Exploded view of a typical universal joint

12.3b To remove the U-joint from the driveshaft, use a vise as a press - the small socket will push the cross and bearing cup into the large socket

12.4 Removing a bearing cup from the yoke ear after it has been pressed out

ing the procedure which follows. Also, read through the entire procedure before beginning work.

1   Remove the driveshaft (see Section 11).

2   Place the shaft on a workbench equipped with a vise. **Note:** *Production universal joints cannot be reassembled because there are no bearing retaining grooves in the production bearing cups. All U-joint service kits contain snap-rings, which will be used when the replacement U-joints are assembled. If your driveshaft has previously had the original U-joints replaced with snap-ring types, remove the snap-rings before pressing the bearing cups out* **(see illustration)**.

3   Place the universal joint in the vise with a 1-1/8 inch socket against one ear of the shaft yoke and a 5/8-inch socket placed on the opposite bearing cup **(see illustrations)**. **Note:** *Never clamp the driveshaft tubing itself in a vise, as the tube may be bent.*

4   Press the bearing cup out of the yoke ear, shearing the plastic retaining ring on the bearing. **Note:** *If the cup does not come all the way out of the yoke, it may be pulled free with pliers, then removed* **(see illustration)**.

5   Turn the driveshaft 180-degrees and

press the opposing bearing cup out of the yoke, again shearing the plastic retainer.

6   Disengage the cross from the yoke and remove the cross.

7   If the remaining universal joint is being replaced, press the bearing cups from the slip yoke as detailed in Steps 3 through 6.

8   When reassembling the driveshaft, always install all parts included in the U-joint service kit.

9   Remove all remnants of the plastic bearing retainers from the grooves in the yokes. Failure to do so may keep the bearing cups from being pressed into place and prevent the bearing retainers from seating properly.

10   Using multi-purpose grease to retain the needle bearings, assemble the bearings, cups and washers. Make sure the bearings do not become dislodged during the assembly and installation procedures.

11   In the vise, assemble the cross and cups in the yoke, installing the cups as far as possible by hand **(see illustration)**.

12   Move the cross back and forth horizontally to assure alignment, then press the cups into place a little at a time, continuing to center the cross to keep the proper alignment.

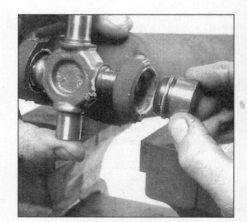

12.11 Assembling a new cross and bearing cup in the driveshaft

13   As soon as one snap-ring groove clears the inside of the yoke, stop pressing and install the snap-ring **(see illustration)**.

14   Continue to press on the bearing cup until the opposite snap-ring can be installed. If difficulty is encountered, strike the yoke

12.13 Installing a snap-ring in the groove

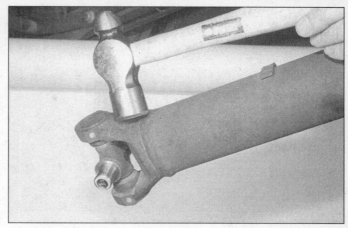

12.14 Strike the tube yoke ear firmly but not on the cup area

12.15 Installing a grease fitting in the U-joint

13.3 Remove the lock screw and pull the pinion shaft out of the differential far enough to clear the inner end of the axleshaft

13.4 Push the axleshaft in and remove the C-lock

sharply with a hammer. This will spring the yoke ears slightly and allow the snap-ring groove to move into position **(see illustration)**.

15   Install the grease fitting **(see illustration)** and lubricate the U-joint.

16   Install the driveshaft (see Section 11).

13 Axleshaft - removal and installation

Refer to illustrations 13.3 and 13.4

1   Raise the rear of the vehicle, support it securely and remove the wheel and brake drum (see Chapter 9).

2   Unscrew and remove the pressed steel cover from the differential carrier and allow the lubricant to drain into a container.

3   Remove the lock bolt from the differential pinion shaft **(see illustration)**. Remove the pinion shaft.

4   Push the outer (flanged) end of the axleshaft in and remove the C-lock from the inner end of the shaft.

5   Withdraw the axleshaft, taking care not

to damage the oil seal in the end of the axle housing as the splined end of the axleshaft passes through it.

6   Installation is the reverse of removal. Tighten the lock bolt to the torque listed in this Chapter's Specifications.

7   Always use a new cover gasket and tighten the cover bolts to the torque listed in this Chapter's Specifications.

8   Refill the differential with the correct quantity and grade of lubricant (see Chapter 1).

14 Axleshaft oil seal - replacement

Refer to illustration 14.3

1   Remove the axleshaft (see Section 13).

8

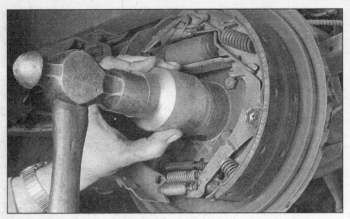

14.3 Installing a rear axleshaft oil seal with a large socket

15.2 Bearing puller and slide hammer being used to remove a rear axleshaft bearing

2   Pry out the old oil seal from the end of the axle housing, using a large screwdriver or the inner end of the axleshaft itself as a lever.

3   Apply high melting point grease to the oil seal recess and tap the seal into position **(see illustration)** so that the lips are facing in and the metal face is visible from the end of the axle housing. When correctly installed, the face of the oil seal should be flush with the end of the axle housing.

4   Install the axleshaft (see Section 13).

15   Axleshaft bearing - replacement

Refer to illustration 15.2

1   Remove the axleshaft (see Section 13) and the oil seal (see Section 14).

2   A bearing puller will be required or a tool which will engage behind the bearing will have to be fabricated **(see illustration)**.

3   Attach a slide hammer and pull the bearing from the axle housing.

4   Clean out the bearing recess and drive in the new bearing using a piece of pipe applied against the outer bearing race. Lubricate the new bearing with gear lubricant. Make sure that the bearing is tapped into the full depth of its recess and that the numbers on the bearing are visible from the outer end of the housing.

5   Discard the old oil seal and install a new one, then install the axleshaft.

16   Rear axle assembly - removal and installation

1   Raise the rear of the vehicle and support it securely on jackstands placed under the frame rails.

2   Position a floor jack under the differential housing. Raise the jack just enough to take up the weight of the rear axle assembly, but not far enough to take the weight of the vehicle off the jackstands.

3   Disconnect the shock absorbers.

4   Remove the brake line junction block bolt at the axle housing, then disconnect the brake lines at the junction block.

5   Lower the jack under the differential housing enough to remove the springs.

6   Remove the rear wheels and brake drums (see Chapter 9).

7   Remove the cover from the rear axle assembly and drain the lubricant into a container.

8   Remove the axleshafts (see Section 13).

9   Disconnect the brake lines from the axle housing clips.

10   Remove the backing plates.

11   Mark the driveshaft and companion flange, unbolt the driveshaft and support it out of the way on a wire hanger.

12   Remove the rear axle assembly from under the vehicle.

13   Installation is the reverse of the removal procedure. When installation is complete fill the differential with the recommended lubricant (see Chapter 1) and bleed the brake system (see Chapter 9).

17   Rear differential pinion seal - replacement

Refer to illustrations 17.5, 17.7, 17.9, 17.10, 17.11 and 17.15

1   Raise the vehicle and support it securely on jackstands.

2   Mark the rear of the driveshaft and the pinion flange so they can be reassembled in the same position.

3   Disconnect the driveshaft from the pinion flange and secure it out of the way by wiring it to the exhaust pipe.

17.5 The rear pinion flange, shaft and nut must be marked before disassembly

17.7 Checking the pinion bearing preload

17.9 Using a puller to remove the pinion flange

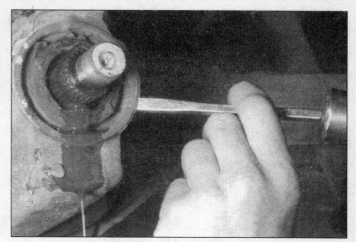

17.10 Use a blunt chisel to remove the old seal, being careful not
to damage the differential carrier

4   If the U-joint bearings are not equipped with a retainer strap, tape the bearings to their journals.

5   Mark the position of the pinion flange, pinion shaft and nut so the proper bearing preload can be set during reassembly **(see illustration)**.

6   It is a good idea to check the bearing preload before disassembly. This measurement will be needed if a replacement pinion flange has to be installed.

7   To check the pinion bearing preload, remove both rear wheels and brake drums. Using an inch-pound torque wrench, check the pinion bearing preload and record it for future reference **(see illustration)**. The preload is the torque required to just begin turning the pinion shaft.

8   Using a socket and a flange holding tool or a breaker bar inserted through the flange yoke, remove the pinion flange nut and washer.

9   Position a drain pan under the differential and remove the pinion flange with a puller **(see illustration)**.

10   Drive the oil seal out with a blunt chisel,

being careful not to damage the differential carrier **(see illustration)**.

11   Examine the seal surface of the pinion flange for tool marks, nicks or wear marks **(see illustration)**. If any damage is found, replace the pinion flange (see Section 18).

12   Lubricate the lips of the new seal with multi-purpose grease.

13   Install the replacement seal with a large section of pipe and a hammer.

14   Install the pinion flange and tighten the nut to the position it was marked at before disassembly.

15   Install the flange holder or breaker bar and tighten the flange nut to 1/16-inch (1.59 mm) beyond the alignment marks **(see illustration)**.

18 Rear differential pinion flange - replacement

1   Raise the vehicle and support it securely on jackstands.

2   Remove both rear wheels and brake drums.

3   Mark the driveshaft and pinion flange and then disconnect the driveshaft at the rear U-joint. Secure the driveshaft out of the way by wiring it to the exhaust pipe. Tape the joint bearings in place if they are not held by a retainer strap.

4   Check the preload with an inch-pound torque wrench (a dial-type is best) and record it for future use.

5   Remove the pinion flange nut and washer (see Section 18 if necessary).

6   Apply multi-purpose grease to the outside diameter of the replacement pinion flange.

7   Install the pinion flange, washer and pinion flange nut finger tight.

8   While holding the pinion flange as shown in the accompanying illustration, tighten the nut a little at a time, turning the drive pinion several revolutions each time to set the rollers. Check the preload of the bearing each time. Continue until the preload is 3 to 5 inch-pounds more than the measurement obtained before disassembly.

9   Install the brake drums and wheels, then lower the vehicle.

19 Front driveaxles - general information

The front driveaxle utilizes a right side output shaft tube which can be removed independently to service the tube bearing, seal and output shaft pilot bearing. CV joints are used on each driveaxle, with inner and outer sealing boots.

Note: *Some auto parts stores carry "split" type replacement boots, which can be installed without removing the driveaxle from the vehicle (see Section 20). This is a convenient alternative; however, it is recommended that the driveaxle be removed and the CV joint disassembled and cleaned to ensure that the joint is free from contaminants such as moisture and dirt, which will accelerate CV joint wear (see Section 21).*

8

17.11 The sealing surface of the pinion flange should be free of nicks and gouges

17.15 On pinion seal replacement only, tighten the flange nut to 1/16-inch beyond the alignment marks

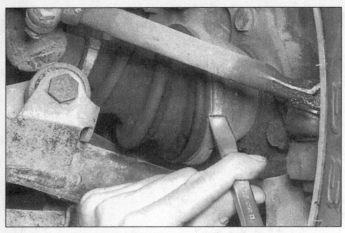

20.2 Removing the boot retaining bands

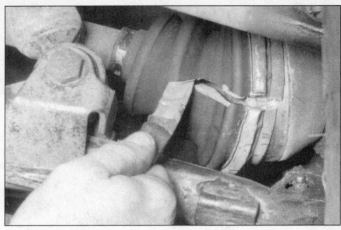

20.3 After removing the inner and outer retaining bands, the old boot can be cut off and removed

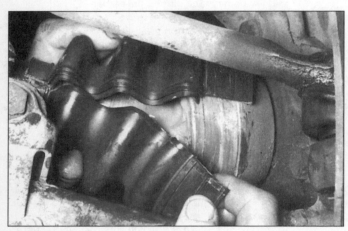

20.5 The replacement CV boot can be slipped into place and secured with the adhesive and retaining bands

21.4 To remove the driveaxle hub nut, hold the driveaxle by inserting a large screwdriver or prybar between the wheel studs as shown and use a large breaker bar to loosen the nut

20   CV joint boot - replacement (split-type boot)

Refer to illustrations 20.2, 20.3 and 20.5

1   The inner and outer CV joints (axleshaft U-joints) on the four-wheel drive models must be kept dirt free. It is a very good idea to check the CV joint dust boots regularly for splits and tears. The CV joint boots can be replaced by the home mechanic without disassembling the front axle by using one of the "wraparound" aftermarket boots available from your local auto parts retailer.
2   Using a chisel and hammer, remove the retaining bands from the affected boot **(see illustration)**.
3   Cut the old boot off and remove it from the axle **(see illustration)**.
4   If any sign of dirt is evident inside the boot, remove the grease and thoroughly clean the CV joint, then repack it with the grease supplied with the boot kit.
5   Install the replacement boot following the directions included with the kit **(see illustration)**. **Note:** *Be sure not to get any grease on the adhesive area at the seams.*

6   Install the replacement retaining bands and let the adhesive set (according to manufacturer's instructions) before driving the vehicle.

21   Front driveaxle - removal, boot replacement and installation

Note: *If the CV joints exhibit signs of wear indicating need for an overhaul (usually due to torn boots), explore all options before beginning the job. Complete driveaxles are available on an exchange basis, which eliminates much time and work. Whichever route you choose to take, check on the availability of parts before disassembling the vehicle.*

Removal

Refer to illustrations 21.4 and 21.7

1   Loosen the lug nuts on the wheel(s) to be removed.
2   Raise the vehicle and support it securely on jackstands.
3   Remove the wheel(s).
4   Using a deep socket (1-3/8 inch) and breaker bar, remove the axle nut. Wedge a

long prybar or screwdriver between two of the wheel studs to prevent the hub from turning **(see illustration)**.
5   Unbolt the lower end of the shock absorber (see Chapter 10) and move it out of the way.
6   Disconnect the tie-rod end from the steering knuckle (see Chapter 10).
7   Remove the six bolts attaching the tri-pot housing to the drive flange **(see illustration)**. Angle the inner end of the driveaxle forward.
8   Remove the driveaxle. If the splines of the stub shaft stick in the hub, press the shaft through the hub with a two-jaw puller (this will require removal of the brake caliper and disc - see Chapter 9).

Boot replacement

9   Place the driveaxle in a vise lined with rags to avoid damage to the shaft.

Inner CV joint

Refer to illustrations 21.13, 21.19 and 21.20

10   Cut off the boot retaining clamps and slide the boot towards the center of the driveaxle.
11   Mark the tri-pot housing and driveaxle

21.7 Remove the six tri-pot housing-to-drive flange
attaching bolts

21.13 Use snap-ring pliers to remove both the inner and outer
retaining rings

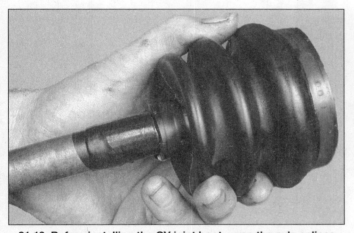

21.19 Before installing the CV joint boot, wrap the axle splines
with tape to prevent damage to the boot

21.20 When installing the spider assembly on the driveaxle, make
sure the recess in the counterbore (arrow) is facing the
end of the driveaxle

so they can be reinstalled in the same relative positions.

12   Slide the housing off the spider assembly.

13   Remove the spider assembly from the axle by first removing the inner retaining ring and sliding the spider assembly back to expose the outer retaining ring. Remove the outer retaining ring and slide the joint off the driveaxle **(see illustration).**

14   Use tape or a cloth wrapped around the spider bearing assembly to retain the bearings during removal and installation.

15   Remove the spider assembly from the axle.

16   Slide the boot off the axle.

17   Clean all of the old grease out of the housing and spider assembly. Carefully disassemble each section of the spider assembly, one at a time, and clean the needle bearings with solvent. Inspect the rollers, spider, bearings and housing for scoring, pitting and other signs of abnormal wear. Apply a coat of CV joint grease to the inner bearing surfaces to hold the needle bearings in place when reassembling the spider assembly.

18   Pack the housing with half of the grease

furnished with the new boot and place the remainder in the boot.

19   Wrap the driveaxle splines with tape to avoid damaging the boot, then slide the boot onto the axle **(see illustration).**

20   Install the spider assembly with the recess in the counterbore facing the end of the driveaxle **(see illustration).**

21   Install the tri-pot housing.

22   Seat the boot in the housing and axle seal grooves, then install the retaining clamps.

Outer CV joint

Refer to Illustrations 21.23, 21.25, 21.28, 21.29, 21.30, 21.31, 21.32a, 21.32b, 21.35 and 21.36

23   Tap lightly around the outer circumfer-

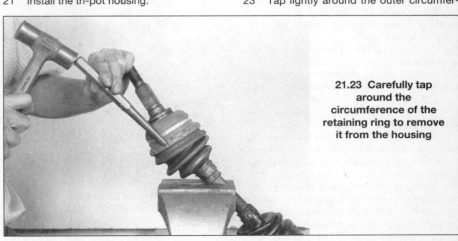

21.23 Carefully tap
around the
circumference of the
retaining ring to remove
it from the housing

8

21.25 Use snap-ring pliers to expand the inner retaining ring, then slide the joint off the shaft

21.28 Gently tap the inner race with a brass punch to tilt is enough to allow the ball bearings to be removed

21.29 Using a dull screwdriver, carefully pry the balls out of the cage

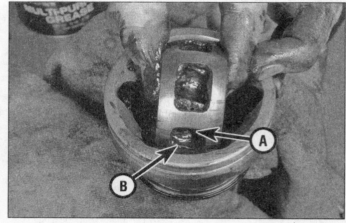

21.30 Tilt the inner race and cage 90-degrees, then align the windows in the cage (A) with the lands (B) and rotate the inner race up and out of the outer race

ence of the seal retaining ring with a hammer and punch to dislodge and remove it. Be very careful not to deform the ring or it won't seal properly **(see illustration)**.

24   Cut off the clamp retaining the boot to the shaft.

25   Expand the snap-ring and slide the joint assembly off **(see illustration)**.

26   Slide the old boot off the driveaxle.

27   Place marks on the inner race and cage so they both can be installed facing out when reassembling the joint.

28   Press down on the inner race far enough to allow a ball bearing to be removed. If it's difficult to tilt, tap the inner race with a brass punch and hammer **(see illustration)**.

29   Pry the balls out of the cage, one at a time, with a dull screwdriver or wooden tool **(see illustration)**.

30   With all of the balls removed from the cage and the cage/inner race assembly tilted 90-degrees, align the cage windows with the outer race lands and remove the assembly from the outer race **(see illustration)**.

31   Remove the inner race from the cage by turning the inner race 90-degrees in the cage, aligning the inner lands with the cage win-

dows and rotating the inner race out of the cage **(see illustration)**.

32   Clean the components with solvent to remove all traces of grease. Inspect the cage and races for pitting, score marks, cracks and other signs of wear and damage. Shiny,

polished spots are normal and won't adversely affect CV joint operation **(see illustrations)**.

33   Install the inner race in the cage by reversing the technique described in Step 31.

34   Install the inner race and cage assembly

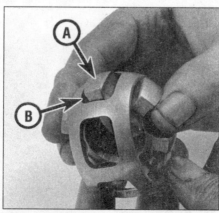

21.31 Align the inner race lands (A) with the cage windows (B) and rotate the inner out of the cage

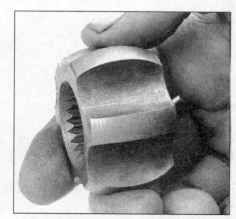

21.32a Check the inner race lands and grooves for pitting and score marks

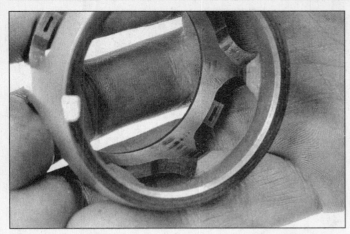

21.32b Check the cage for cracks, pitting and score marks -
shiny spots are normal and don't affect operation

21.35 Align the cage windows and the inner and outer race
grooves, then tilt the cage and inner race to insert the balls

21.36 Apply grease through the splined hole, then insert a
wooden dowel through the splined hole and push down - the
dowel will force the grease into the joint (do this until the joint is
completely full of grease)

22.2a To remove the shift cable from the vacuum actuator,
disengage the locking spring and press in on the
vacuum actuator . . .

in the outer race by reversing the procedure in Step 30. The marks that were previously applied to the inner race and cage must both be visible after the assembly is installed in the outer race.

35   Press the balls into the cage windows **(see illustration)**.

36   Pack the CV joint assembly with grease through the inner splined hole. Force the grease into the bearing by inserting a wooden dowel through the splined hole and pushing it to the bottom of the joint. Repeat this procedure until the bearing is completely packed **(see illustration)**.

37   Install the boot on the driveaxle as described in Step 19. Apply a liberal amount of grease to the inside of the axle boot.

38   Position the CV joint assembly on the driveaxle, aligning the splines. Using a soft-face hammer, drive the CV joint onto the driveaxle until the retaining ring is seated in the groove.

39   Seat the inner end of the boot in the seal groove and install the retaining clamp.

40   Install the seal retainer securely by tapping evenly around the outer circumference with a hammer and punch.

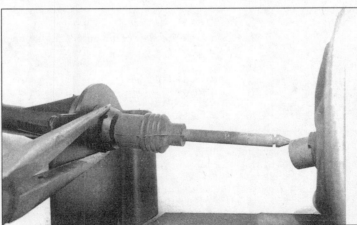

22.2b . . . then squeeze the cable locking fingers and remove the cable from the bracket

Installation

41   Installation is the reverse of the removal procedure. Be sure to tighten all fasteners to the torque values listed in this Chapter's Specifications (and the Chapter 9 and 10 Specifications for brake, suspension and suspension components).

22   Front output shaft, tube and tube seal - removal and installation

Refer to illustrations 22.2a, 22.2b, 22.13, 22.14 and 22.16

1   Disconnect the negative cable from the battery.

8

22.13 The shift cable can be removed after pulling the cable housing away from the output shaft tube flange

22.14 To detach the output shaft tube from its support bracket, remove these two nuts (arrows)

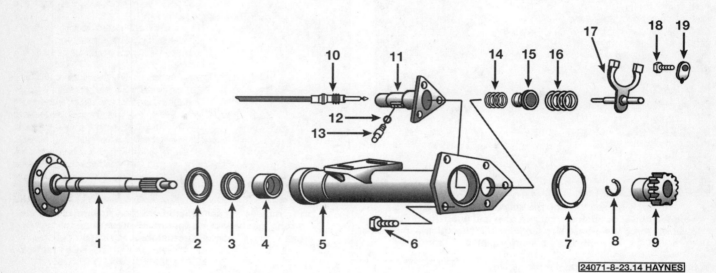

22.16 An exploded view of the output shaft tube assembly

1	Output shaft	6	Bolt	11	Shift cable housing	16	Spring
2	Deflector	7	Thrust washer	12	Gasket	17	Shift shaft and fork
3	Seal	8	Snap-ring	13	Indicator switch	18	Bolt
4	Bearing	9	Carrier connector	14	Spring	19	Locking tab
5	Output shaft tube	10	Shift cable	15	Seal		

2   Remove the shift cable from the vacuum actuator on top of the right fenderwell by first disengaging the locking spring (see illustrations). Push in on the vacuum actuator diaphragm to release the grooved cable end.
3   Squeeze the two locking fingers of the cable with pliers and pull the cable out of the bracket.
4   Unlock the steering wheel at the steering column.
5   Loosen the front wheel lug nuts.
6   Raise the vehicle and support it securely on jackstands.
7   Remove the front wheels.
8   Remove the engine drivebelt shield.
9   Remove the skid plate (if equipped).

10   Support the lower control arm with a floorjack. **Warning:** *The jack must remain in this position throughout the entire procedure.* Disconnect the right side upper balljoint (see Chapter 10).
11   Remove the driveaxle-to-output shaft attaching bolts (see illustration 21.7). Insert a drift through the opening in the top of the brake caliper and into a brake disc vane to keep the axle from turning.
12   Disconnect the four-wheel drive indicator light electrical connection from the switch.
13   Remove the switch/cable housing mounting bolts from the inner flange on the output shaft tube. Pull the housing away enough to gain access to the cable locking

spring and disengage the spring (see illustration). Remove the cable assembly. Do not unscrew the cable coupling nut unless the cable is being replaced.
14   Remove the two tube assembly mounting nuts/bolts from the frame (see illustration).
15   Remove the two remaining tube assembly bolts from the differential housing.
16   Carefully remove the tube assembly from the vehicle (see illustration).
17   Remove the output shaft from the tube by striking the inside of the flange with a soft-faced hammer while holding the tube.
18   Using a large screwdriver, pry the output shaft tube seal from the tube.

19   Remove the tube bearing using a bearing removal tool. **Note:** *Before removing the bearing, measure its installed depth.*

20   Drive the shift cable housing seal out of the tube flange with a drift punch or socket.

21   Install the new shift cable housing seal using an appropriate size socket.

22   Install the tube bearing to the depth measured in Step 19.

23   Install the output shaft tube seal using a socket equivalent to the diameter of the seal outer flange. The flange of the seal must be flush with the tube outer surface when installed.

24   Before installing the tube assembly, make sure that the sleeve, thrust washers and connectors are in place in the differential.

25   Apply RTV sealant to the tube-to-differential carrier mating surface.

26   Apply some grease to the thrust washer and install the washer.

27   Carefully install the tube assembly and install the first mounting bolt at the one o'clock position (but don't tighten it yet).

28   Pull the assembly down and install the cable and switch housing, and remaining four attaching bolts. Tighten the bolts to the specified torque.

29   Install the two tube assembly mounting bolts in the frame and tighten the nuts to the torque listed in this Chapter's Specifications.

30   Install the shift cable by pushing it into the shift fork hole (the cable will automatically snap into place).

31   Connect the wire for the four-wheel drive indicator light to the indicator switch.

32   Connect the upper balljoint (see Chapter 11).

33   Connect the driveaxle to the output shaft flange (see Section 21).

34   Install the skid plate (if equipped) and drivebelt shield.

35   Install the wheel and lower the vehicle.

36   Push the shift cable into place in the

vacuum actuator and attach the negative battery cable.

23   Front differential output shaft pilot bearing - replacement

1   Remove the tube and output shaft assembly (see Section 22).

2   Remove the pilot bearing from the output shaft.

3   Install the replacement bearing.

24   Front differential carrier - removal and installation

1   Remove the output shaft (see Section 22). Both sets of front wheel lug nuts should be loosened before raising the vehicle.

2   Remove the bolt securing the steering stabilizer to the frame.

3   Scribe the location of the steering idler arm and remove the idler arm mounting bolts from the frame member.

4   Move the steering linkage towards the front of the vehicle.

5   Remove the axle vent hose from the fitting on the carrier.

6   Remove the left driveaxle from the output shaft by removing the six bolts. Insert a drift punch through the top of the caliper and into a brake disc vane to keep the axle from turning.

7   Disconnect the front driveshaft (see Section 11).

8   Remove the two carrier-to-frame mounting bolts. An 18mm combination wrench inserted through the frame will be needed to hold the upper nut from turning.

9   Lift up and rotate the carrier until the necessary clearance is gained for removal.

10   Installation is the reverse of removal.

25   Front differential carrier bushing - replacement

1   Remove the tube and shaft assembly (see Section 22).

2   Remove the differential carrier (see Section 24).

3   Press the bushing out of the carrier ear.

4   Press the replacement bushing into the carrier ear using a press tool. Use a spacer to prevent the bushing from being installed too deeply.

26   Clutch cable and adjuster - replacement

Note: *This procedure applies to 1982 and 1983 models only.*

1   Pull the clutch pedal back all the way and support it in this position. Remove the under-dash panel.

2   Disconnect the clutch cable from the release lever at the transmission.

3   Unbolt the clutch pedal stop from the pedal bracket.

4   Remove the clutch pedal pivot bolt and separate the pedal from the bracket.

5   Detach the end of the clutch cable from the detent. Raise the locking pawl away from the detent, then pass the cable forward between the detent and the pawl.

6   Working in the engine compartment, remove the bolts that attach the cable casing to the firewall. Remove the cable assembly from the vehicle.

7   If the teeth on the detent or locking pawl (the components that make up the self-adjuster mechanism) are worn, separate them from the pedal and install new ones.

8   Installation is the reverse of removal. Adjust the pedal freeplay (see Chapter 1).

8

Notes

Chapter 9   Brakes

Contents

	Section
ABS system trouble codes - general information and retrieval	17
Anti-lock Brake System (ABS) - general information	16
Brake check	See Chapter 1
Brake pedal - removal and installation	14
Brake rotor (disc) - inspection, removal and installation	5
Combination valve (non-ABS models) - check and replacement	10
Fluid level check	See Chapter 1
Front disc brake caliper - overhaul	4
Front disc brake caliper - removal and installation	3
Front disc brake pads - replacement	2

	Section
General information	1
Hydraulic brake hoses and lines - inspection and replacement	9
Hydraulic system - bleeding	13
Master cylinder - removal, overhaul and installation	8
Parking brake - adjustment	11
Power brake booster - check, removal and installation	12
Rear drum brake shoes - replacement	6
Stop light switch - removal, installation and adjustment	15
Wheel cylinder (drum brakes) - removal, overhaul and installation	7

Specifications

Brake fluid type .... See Chapter 1

Disc brakes

Minimum brake pad thickness	See Chapter 1
Disc thickness after resurfacing	0.980 inch minimum
Disc discard thickness	0.965 inch*
Lateral runout	0.004 inch maximum
Disc thickness variation (parallelism)	0.0005 inch

*Refer to the marks cast into the disc. They supersede information printed here.

Drum brakes

Minimum brake lining thickness	See Chapter 1
Drum diameter after resurfacing	9.56 inch maximum
Drum discard thickness	9.59 inch*
Out-of-round	0.006 inch maximum
Taper	0.003 inch maximum

*Refer to the marks cast into the drum. They supersede information printed here.

Parking brake travel .... 9 to 13 clicks

Torque specifications

Ft-lbs (unless otherwise specified)

Master cylinder mounting nuts	21
Power booster mounting nuts	21
Caliper mounting bolts	37
Wheel cylinder mounting bolts	156 in-lbs
Brake hose-to-caliper banjo bolt	32
Wheel lug nuts	See Chapter 1
Brake pedal shaft nut	28

9

Component location

Typical front brake assembly

1   Brake disc
2   Wheel bearing grease cap
3   Outer brake pad
4   Caliper
5   Brake line (metal)
6   Flexible brake line

1   General information

The vehicles covered by this manual are equipped with hydraulically operated front and rear brake systems. The front brakes are disc type and the rear brakes are drum type. Both the front and rear brakes are self adjusting. The front disc brakes automatically compensate for pad wear, while the rear drum brakes incorporate an adjustment mechanism which is activated as the brakes are applied when the vehicle is driven in reverse.

Later models are equipped with an Antilock Braking System (ABS). ABS is designed to maintain vehicle steerability, directional stability and optimum braking under most conditions. It does so by monitoring the speed of each wheel and controlling the brake pressure to each wheel during braking. All parts and procedures listed in this Chapter also apply to models with ABS. More information on the ABS, and the components which are unique to it, can be found in Section 16.

Hydraulic system

The hydraulic system consists of two separate circuits. The master cylinder has separate reservoirs for the two circuits and in the event of a leak or failure in one hydraulic circuit, the other circuit will remain operative. A visual warning of circuit failure or air in the system is given by a warning light activated by displacement of the piston in the pressure differential switch portion of the combination valve from its normal "in balance" position.

Combination valve

A combination valve, located in the engine compartment below the master cylinder, consists of three sections providing the following functions. The metering section limits pressure to the front brakes until a predetermined front input pressure is reached and until the rear brakes are activated. There is no restriction at inlet pressures below 3 psi, allowing pressure equalization during non-braking periods. The proportioning section proportions outlet pressure to the rear brakes after a predetermined rear input pressure has been reached, preventing early rear wheel lock-up under heavy brake loads. The valve is also designed to assure full pressure to one brake system should the other system fail. The pressure differential warning switch incorporated into the combination valve is designed to continuously compare the front and rear brake pressure from the master cylinder and energize the dash warning light in the event of either a front or rear brake system failure. The design of the switch and valve are such that the switch will stay in the "warning" position once a failure has occurred. The only way to turn the light off is to repair the cause of the failure and apply the brake pedal firmly.

Power brake booster

The power brake booster, utilizing engine manifold vacuum and atmospheric pressure to provide assistance to the hydraulically operated brakes, is mounted on the firewall in the engine compartment.

Component location

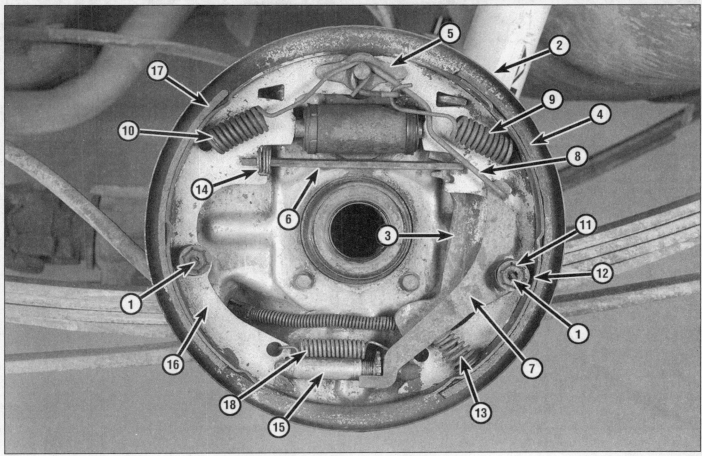

Exploded view of the drum brake components

1	Hold-down pins	7	Actuator lever	13	Lever return spring
2	Backing plate	8	Actuator link	14	Strut spring (rear only)
3	Parking brake	9	Return spring	15	Adjusting screw assembly
4	Secondary shoe	10	Return spring	16	Adjusting screw spring
5	Shoe guide	11	Hold-down spring	17	Primary shoe
6	Parking brake strut	12	Lever pivot		

Parking brake

The parking brake operates the rear brakes only, through cable actuation. It's activated by a pedal mounted on the left side kick panel.

Service

After completing any operation involving disassembly of any part of the brake system, always test drive the vehicle to check for proper braking performance before resuming normal driving. When testing the brakes, per-

form the tests on a clean, dry flat surface. Conditions other than these can lead to inaccurate test results.

Test the brakes at various speeds with both light and heavy pedal pressure. The vehicle should stop evenly without pulling to one side or the other. Avoid locking the brakes because this slides the tires and diminishes braking efficiency and control of the vehicle.

Tires, vehicle load and front-end alignment are factors which also affect braking performance.

2   Front disc brake pads - replacement

Refer to illustrations 2.6a thru 2.6k

1   **Warning:** *Disc brake pads must be replaced on both wheels at the same time. Whenever you are working on the brake system be aware that asbestos dust may be present and be careful not to inhale any of it, because it has been proven to be harmful to your health. Never blow the dust out with com-*

9

2.6a Use an Allen wrench to remove the two caliper mounting bolts. Check the bolt threads for damage

2.6b Remove the brake line retaining clip (mounted to the frame rail at the upper left) and separate the brake line from the retainer. Pull off the caliper and remove the inside pad from the caliper

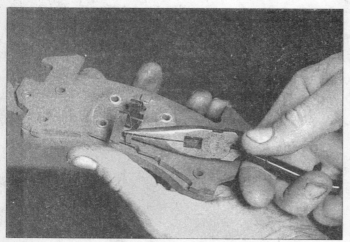

2.6c Remove the anti-rattle clip with pliers

2.6d Use a screwdriver to detach the outer pad from the caliper

pressed air, and wear an approved filtering mask when working on the brakes. *Do not, under any circumstances, use petroleum-based solvents to clean brake parts. Use brake system cleaner only!*

2   Remove the cover from the brake fluid reservoir and siphon off about two ounces of the fluid into a container and discard it.

3   Raise the front of the vehicle and place it securely on jackstands.

4   Remove the front wheel, then, on 4WD models, reinstall two wheel lugs (flat side toward the rotor) to hold the rotor in place. Work on one brake assembly at a time, using the assembled brake for reference if necessary.

5   Push the piston back into its bore. If necessary, a C-clamp can be used, but a flat bar will usually do the job. As the piston is depressed to the bottom of the caliper bore, the fluid in the master cylinder will rise. Make sure that it does not overflow. If necessary, siphon off more of the fluid as directed in

2.6e Separate the outer pad from the caliper

Step 2.

6   Now see the illustrations and perform the procedure described. Start with **illustration 2.6a**.

2.6f After cleaning the caliper, install the anti-rattle clip to the new pad and install the inner pad

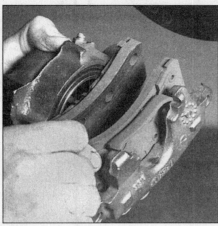

2.6g Attach the outer pad to the caliper

2.6h Apply multi-purpose grease to the ends of the caliper mounting bracket surfaces

2.6i Install the caliper over the disc onto the mounting bracket. Do not get any grease on the pad lining

2.6j Install the mounting bolts and tighten them securely, then reattach the brake hose to the retaining clip on the frame

2.6k After refilling the master cylinder and pumping the brake pedal to seat the pads, use pliers to bend the upper ears of the outer pad until the ears are flush with the caliper housing, with no radial clearance

3 Front disc brake caliper - removal and installation

Refer to illustrations 3.6a and 3.6b

1   Whenever you are working on the brake system be aware that asbestos dust is present and be careful not to inhale any of it, because it has been proven to be harmful to your health (see the **Warning** in Section 2).

2   Remove the cover from the brake fluid reservoir and siphon off about two ounces of the fluid into a container and discard it.

3   Raise the front of the vehicle and place it securely on jackstands.

4   Remove the front wheel. Remove the caliper from one brake assembly at a time, using the assembled brake for reference if necessary.

5   Push the piston back into its bore. If necessary, a C-clamp can be used, but a flat bar will usually do the job. As the piston is depressed to the bottom of the caliper bore, the fluid in the master cylinder will rise. Make sure that it does not overflow. If necessary,

3.6a Remove the brake fluid hose banjo bolt (arrow)

siphon off more of the fluid as directed in Step 2.

6   Remove the banjo fitting bolt holding the brake hose **(see illustration)**, then remove

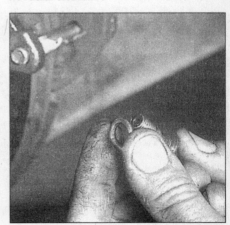

3.6b Always install new copper seal rings when installing the brake hose

and discard the copper seal rings found on either side of the banjo fitting. **Note:** *Always use new copper seals when reinstalling the brake hose* **(see illustration)**.

9

4.4 Compressed air is used to move the piston out of the caliper bore (use a wooden block as a cushion)

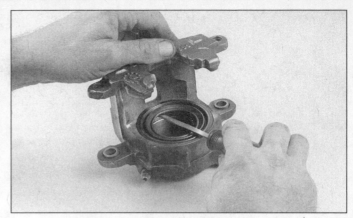

4.5 Pry the dust boot out of the caliper bore

4.6 Remove the piston seal from the caliper groove

4.10 Position the seal in the caliper bore groove

4.11 Install a new dust boot in the piston groove with the folds toward the open end of the piston

7   Remove the Allen head bolts holding the caliper to the mounting bracket and separate the caliper from the rotor.

8   Installation is the reverse of removal. Lubricate the ends of the caliper mounting bracket surfaces before attaching the caliper to the bracket. Tighten all bolts securely.

4   Front disc brake caliper - overhaul

Refer to illustrations 4.4, 4.5, 4.6, 4.10, 4.11, 4.12 and 4.13

Note: *Purchase a brake caliper overhaul kit for your particular vehicle before beginning this procedure. Complete overhauled calipers are available at many auto parts stores. These may be more cost effective, particularly if the piston or piston bore in the caliper is damaged.*

1   Remove the caliper (see Section 3).

2   Remove the brake pad assemblies (see Section 2).

3   Clean the exterior of the brake caliper with brake fluid (never use gasoline, kerosene or cleaning solvents), then place the caliper on a clean workbench.

4   Place a wooden block or shop rag in the caliper as a cushion, then use compressed

air to remove the piston from the caliper **(see illustration)**. Use only enough air pressure to ease the piston out of the bore. If the piston is blown out, even with the cushion in place, it may be damaged. **Caution:** *Never place your fingers in front of the piston in an attempt to catch or protect it when applying compressed air - serious injury could occur.*

5   Carefully pry the dust boot out of the caliper bore **(see illustration)**.

6   Using a wood or plastic tool, remove the piston seal from the groove in the caliper bore. Metal tools may cause bore damage **(see illustration)**.

7   Remove the caliper bleeder valve, then remove and discard the sleeves and bushings from the caliper ears. Also discard all rubber parts.

8   Clean the remaining parts with brake fluid. Allow them to drain and then shake them vigorously to remove as much fluid as possible.

9   Carefully examine the piston for nicks and burrs and loss of plating. If surface defects are present parts must be replaced. Check the caliper bore in a similar way, but polishing with crocus cloth is permissible to remove light corrosion and stains. Discard the mounting bolts if they are corroded or damaged.

10   When assembling, lubricate the piston bores and seal with clean brake fluid. Position the seal in the caliper bore groove **(see illustration)**.

11   Lubricate the piston with clean brake fluid, then install a new boot in the piston groove with the fold toward the open end of the piston **(see illustration)**.

12   Insert the piston squarely into the caliper

4.12 Square the piston in the bore

4.13 Use a hammer and driver to seat the boot in the caliper housing counterbore

bore, then apply force to bottom the piston in the bore **(see illustration)**.

13 Position the dust boot in the caliper counterbore, then use a drift to drive it into position **(see illustration)**. Make sure that the boot is evenly installed below the caliper face.

14 Install the bleeder valve.

15 The remainder of the installation procedure is the reverse of the removal procedure. Always use new copper gaskets when connecting the brake hose and bleed the system (see Section 13).

5 Brake rotor (disc) - inspection, removal and installation

Refer to illustrations 5.5 and 5.6

Inspection

1 Raise the vehicle and place it securely on jackstands.

2 Remove the appropriate wheel.

3 Remove the brake caliper assembly (see Section 3 or 5). **Note:** *It is not necessary to disconnect the brake hose. After removing the caliper mounting bolts, hang the caliper out of the way on a piece of wire. Never hang the caliper by the brake hose because damage to the hose will occur.*

4 Inspect the brake disc surfaces. Light scoring or grooving is normal, but deep grooves or severe erosion is not. If pulsating has been noticed during application of the brakes, suspect disc runout. On 4WD models, reinstall the lug nuts with the beveled sides facing out. This secures the disc for the following check.

5 Attach a dial indicator to the caliper mounting bracket, turn the brake disc and note the amount of runout. Check both inner and outer surfaces **(see illustration)**. If the runout is more than the maximum allowable, the disc must be removed from the vehicle and taken to an automotive machine shop for resurfacing. **Note:** *Professionals recommend resurfacing of disc brakes regardless of the dial indicator reading (to produce a smooth, flat surface that will eliminate brake pedal pulsations and other undesirable symptoms related to questionable discs). At the very least, if you elect not to have the discs resurfaced, deglaze them with sandpaper or emery cloth (using a swirling motion to ensure a nondirectional finish).*

6 Using a micrometer, measure the thickness of the disc **(see illustration)**. If it is less than the minimum specified, replace the disc with a new one. Also measure the disc thickness at several points to determine variations in the surface. Any variation over 0.0005 inch may cause pedal pulsations during brake application. If this condition exists and the disc thickness is not below the minimum, the disc can be removed and taken to an automotive machine shop for resurfacing.

Removal and installation

7 To remove and install the disc on 2WD models, refer to Chapter 1, *Wheel bearing check and repack*. On 4WD models, the disc should pull off the studs after the caliper has been removed. There may be a pressed-metal nut over one of the studs that secures the disc. This does not need to be replaced when installing the disc.

6 Rear drum brake shoes - replacement

Refer to illustrations 6.3 and 6.4a through 6.4v

Warning: *Drum brake shoes must be replaced on both wheels at the same time - never replace the shoes on only one wheel. Also, the dust created by the brake system may contain asbestos, which is harmful to your health. Never blow it out with compressed air and don't inhale any of it. An approved filtering mask should be worn when working on the brakes. Do not, under any circumstances, use petroleum-based solvents to clean brake parts. Use brake system cleaner only!*

Caution: *Whenever the brake shoes are replaced, the retractor and hold-down springs should also be replaced. Due to the continuous heating/cooling cycle that the springs are subjected to, they lose their tension over a period of time and may allow the shoes to drag on the drum and wear at a much faster rate than normal.*

Note: *All four rear brake shoes must be replaced at the same time, but to avoid mixing up parts, work on only one brake assembly at a time.*

1 Loosen the wheel lug nuts, raise the rear of the vehicle and support it securely on jackstands. Block the front wheels to keep the vehicle from rolling.

2 Release the parking brake and remove the wheel.

3 Remove the brake drum. **Note:** *If the brake drum cannot be easily pulled off the*

5.5 Check the brake disc runout with a dial indicator

5.6 Check the disc thickness with a micrometer

9

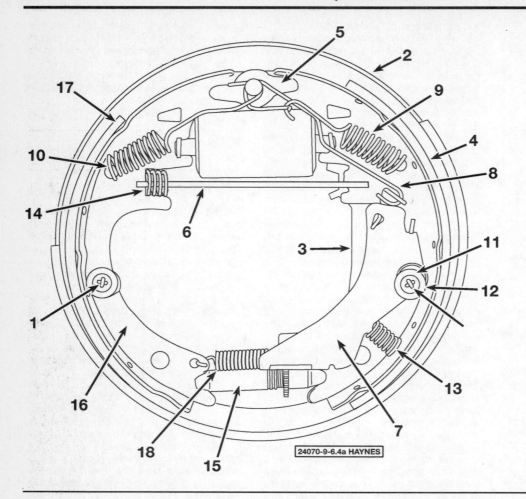

**6.4a Exploded view of the drum
brake components**

1   *Hold-down pins*
2   *Backing plate*
3   *Parking brake lever*
4   *Secondary shoe*
5   *Shoe guide*
6   *Parking brake strut*
7   *Actuator lever*
8   *Actuator link*
9   *Return spring*
10 *Return spring*
11 *Hold-down spring*
12 *Lever pivot*
13 *Lever return spring*
14 *Strut spring*
15 *Adjusting screw assembly*
16 *Adjusting screw spring*
17 *Primary shoe*

24070-9-6.4a HAYNES

*axle and shoe assembly, make sure that the
parking brake is completely released, then
squirt some penetrating oil around the center
hub area. Allow the oil to soak in and try to
pull the drum off. If the drum still cannot be
pulled off, the brake shoes will have to be
retracted. This is accomplished by first
removing the plug from the backing plate with
a hammer and chisel. With the plug removed,
push the lever off the adjusting screw wheel
with one small screwdriver while turning the
adjusting wheel with another small screwdriver, moving the shoes away from the drum
(see illustration). The drum should now
come off. Replace the plug with a press-in
rubber plug (available at auto parts stores).*

4   Follow the accompanying illustrations
(see illustrations 6.4a through 6.4v) for the
inspection and replacement of the brake
shoes. Be sure to stay in order and read the
caption under each illustration.

**6.4b Remove the shoe return springs - the spring tool shown
here is available at most auto parts stores and makes this job
much easier and safer**

**6.4c Pull the bottom of the actuator lever toward the secondary
brake shoe, compressing the lever return spring - the actuator
link can now be removed from the top of the lever**

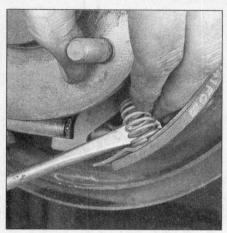

6.4d Pry the actuator lever spring out with a large screwdriver

6.4e Slide the parking brake strut out from between the axle flange and primary shoe

6.4f Remove the hold-down springs and pins - the hold-down spring tool shown here is available at most auto parts stores

6.4g Remove the actuator lever and pivot - be careful not to let the pivot fall out of the lever

6.4h Spread the top of the shoes apart and slide the assembly around the axle

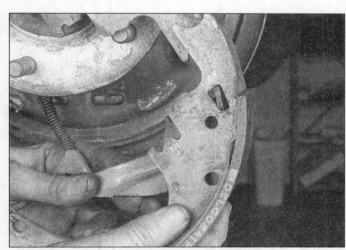

6.4i Unhook the parking brake from the secondary shoe - on some models you'll have to pry off an E-clip with a small screwdriver before the shoe pin will slide out of the lever - you may have to drive the pin out of the old shoe with a hammer and punch and transfer it to the new shoe

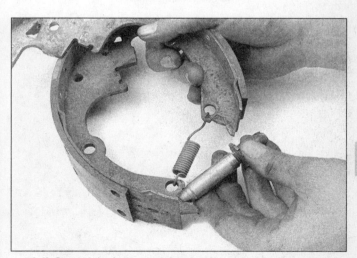

6.4j Spread the bottom of the shoes apart and remove the adjusting screw assembly

9

6.4k Clean the adjusting screw with
solvent, dry it off and lubricate the threads
and end with multi-purpose grease, then
reinstall the adjusting screw assembly
between the new brake shoes

6.4l Lubricate the shoe contact points on
the backing plate with high-temperature
brake grease

6.4m Insert the parking brake lever into
the opening in the secondary brake shoe
or insert the pin in the shoe through the
lever and install a new E-clip

6.4n Spread the shoes apart and slide them into position
on the backing plate

6.4o Install the hold-down pin and spring through the backing
plate and primary shoe

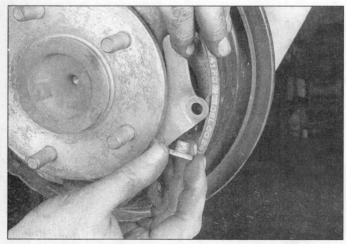

6.4p Insert the lever pivot into the actuator lever, place the lever
over the secondary shoe hold-down pin and install the
hold-down spring

6.4q Guide the parking brake strut behind the axle flange and
engage the rear end of it in the slot on the parking brake lever -
spread the shoes enough to allow the other end to seat against
the primary shoe

6.4r Place the shoe guide over the anchor pin

6.4s Hook the lower end of the actuator link to the actuator lever, then loop the top end over the anchor pin

6.4t Install the lever return spring over the tab on the actuator lever, then push the spring up onto the brake shoe

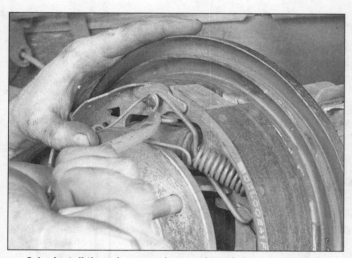
6.4u Install the primary and secondary shoe return springs

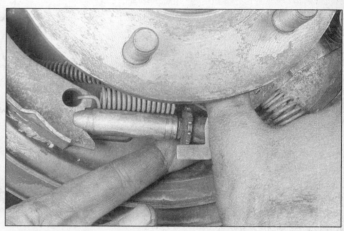
6.4v Pull out on the actuator lever to disengage it from the adjusting screw wheel, turn the wheel to adjust the shoes in or out as necessary - the brake drum should slide over the shoes and turn with a very slight amount of drag (then turn the adjuster until they don't drag)

5   Before reinstalling the drum it should be checked for cracks, score marks, deep scratches and hard spots, which will appear as small discolored areas. If the hard spots cannot be removed with fine emery cloth or if any of the other conditions listed above exist, the drum must be taken to an automotive machine shop to have it resurfaced. **Note:** *Professionals recommend resurfacing the drums whenever a brake job is done. Resurfacing will eliminate the possibility of out-of-round drums. If the drums are worn so much that they can't be resurfaced without exceeding the maximum allowable diameter (stamped into the drum), then new ones will be required. At the very least, if your elect not to have the drums resurfaced, remove the glazing from the surface with medium-grit emery cloth using a swirling motion.*
6   Install the brake drum on the axle flange.
7   Mount the wheel, install the lug nuts, then lower the vehicle.
8   Make a number of forward and reverse

stops to adjust the brakes until satisfactory pedal action is obtained.

7   Wheel cylinder (drum brakes) - removal, overhaul and installation

Refer to illustrations 7.2, 7.3a, 7.3b, 7.3c and 7.12
Note: *Obtain the wheel cylinder rebuild kits before beginning this procedure. Complete rebuilt or new wheel cylinders are available at many auto parts stores. These may be more cost-effective than overhauling the cylinders yourself, particularly if the pistons or wheel cylinder bore is damaged.*

Removal

1   Remove the brake shoes (see Section 6).
2   Remove the brake line fitting from the rear of the wheel cylinder **(see illustration)**. Cap the brake line to prevent contamination.

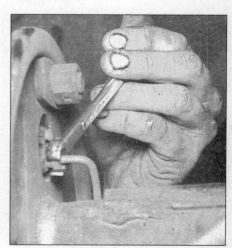
7.2 Unscrew the brake line fitting from the rear of the wheel cylinder

9

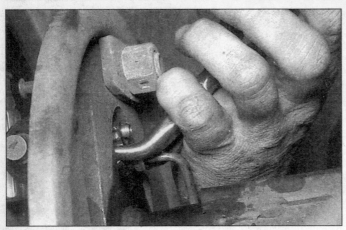

7.3a Remove the wheel cylinder retaining clip, using needle-nose pliers . . .

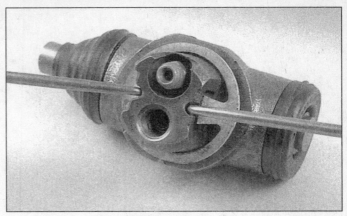

7.3b . . . or use two awls or similar tools to remove the retaining clip as shown here (cylinder removed from backing plate for clarity)

3   On 1991 and earlier models, use curved needle-nose pliers to remove the wheel cylinder retaining clip **(see illustration)** from the rear of the wheel cylinder. Alternatively, insert two awls into the access slots between the cylinder pilot and the retainer locking tabs and bend both tabs away at the same time **(see illustration)**. On 1992 and later models, the wheel cylinder can be simply unbolted from the backing plate **(see illustration)**.

Overhaul

4   Remove the cylinder and place it on a clean workbench.
5   Remove the bleeder valve, seals, pistons, boots and spring assembly from the cylinder body.
6   Clean the wheel cylinder with brake fluid, denatured alcohol or brake system cleaner. Do not, under any circumstances, use petroleum-based solvents to clean brake parts.
7   Use compressed air to remove excess fluid from the wheel cylinder and to blow out the passages.
8   Check the cylinder bore for corrosion and scoring. Crocus cloth may be used to remove light corrosion and stains, but the cylinder must be replaced with a new one if the defects cannot be removed easily, or if the bore is scored.
9   Lubricate the new seals with clean brake fluid.
10   Assemble the brake cylinder, making sure the boots are properly seated.

Installation

11   Place the wheel cylinder in position in the backing plate.
12   Secure the cylinder in place with a new retaining clip or bolts by first starting the brake line fitting into the threads of the wheel cylinder, and installing and tightening bolts (later models) or placing a screwdriver handle between the wheel cylinder and the axle flange to hold the cylinder in place while the retaining clip is pushed into place with curved needle-nose pliers **(see illustration)**. Make

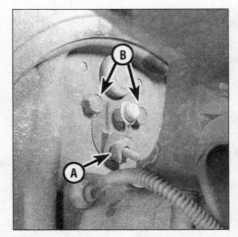

7.3c On later model cylinders, completely loosen the brake line fitting (A), then remove the two mounting bolts (B)

sure the clip and cylinder are securely in place, then remove the screwdriver. On all models, tighten the brake line fitting.
13   Bleed the brake system (see Section 13).

---

8   Master cylinder - removal, overhaul and installation

Removal

1   A master cylinder overhaul kit should be purchased before beginning this procedure. The kit will include all the replacement parts necessary for the overhaul procedure. The rubber replacement parts, particularly the seals, are the key to fluid control within the master cylinder. As such, it's very important that they be installed securely and facing in the proper direction. Be careful during the rebuild procedure that no grease or mineral-based solvents come in contact with the rubber parts.
2   Completely cover the front fender and

7.12 Place a screwdriver handle between the wheel cylinder and axle flange to hold the cylinder in place while installing the retaining clip or bolts

cowling area of the vehicle, as brake fluid can ruin painted surfaces if it is spilled.
3   Disconnect the brake line connections. Rags or newspapers should be placed under the master cylinder to soak up the spilled fluid.
4   Remove the two master cylinder mounting nuts, move the bracket retaining the combination valve forward slightly, taking care not to bend the hydraulic lines running to the combination valve, and remove the master cylinder from the vehicle.

Overhaul

Refer to illustrations 8.6, 8.9, 8.14, 8.15 and 8.18
Note: *Complete rebuilt master cylinders are available at many auto parts stores. These may be a more cost-effective alternative than overhaul, particularly if the cylinder bore is corroded or damaged.*
5   Remove the reservoir cover and reservoir diaphragm, then discard any remaining fluid in the reservoir.

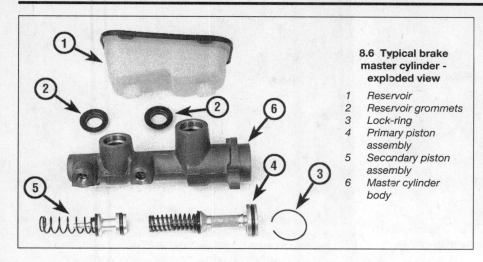

8.6 Typical brake master cylinder - exploded view

1 Reservoir
2 Reservoir grommets
3 Lock-ring
4 Primary piston assembly
5 Secondary piston assembly
6 Master cylinder body

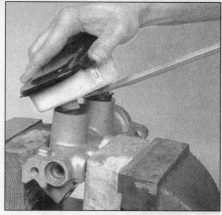

8.9 Pry the plastic reservoir from the master cylinder body

6   Remove the primary piston lock-ring by depressing the piston and prying the ring out with a screwdriver **(see illustration)**.
7   Remove the primary piston assembly with a wire hook, being careful not to scratch the bore surface.
8   Remove the secondary piston assembly in the same manner.
9   Place the master cylinder in a vise and pry the reservoir from the cylinder body with a pry bar **(see illustration)**.
10   Do not attempt to remove the quick take-up valve from the cylinder body, as this valve is not serviceable.
11   Remove the reservoir grommets.
12   Inspect the cylinder bore for corrosion and damage. If any corrosion or damage is found, replace the master cylinder body with a new one, as abrasives cannot be used on the bore.
13   Lubricate the new reservoir grommets with silicone brake lube and press the grommets into the master cylinder body, making sure they are properly seated.
14   Lay the reservoir on a hard surface and press the master cylinder body onto the reservoir, using a rocking motion **(see illustration)**.

15   Remove the old seals from the secondary piston assembly and install the new seals so that the cups face out **(see illustration)**.
16   Attach the spring retainer to the secondary piston assembly.
17   Lubricate the cylinder bore with clean brake fluid and install the spring and secondary piston assembly in the cylinder.
18   Disassemble the primary piston assembly, noting the position of the parts, then lubricate the new seals with clean brake fluid and install them on the piston **(see illustration)**.
19   Install the primary piston assembly in the cylinder bore, depress it and install the lock-ring.
20   Inspect the reservoir cover and diaphragm for cracks and deformation. Replace any damaged parts with new ones and attach the diaphragm to the cover.
21   **Note:** *Whenever the master cylinder is removed, the complete hydraulic system must be bled. The time required to bleed the system can be reduced if the master cylinder is filled with fluid and "bench bled' (refer to Steps 22 through 25) before the master cylinder is installed on the vehicle.*

22   Insert threaded plugs of the correct size into the cylinder outlet holes and fill the reservoirs with brake fluid (the master cylinder should be supported in such a manner that brake fluid will not spill out of it during the bench bleeding procedure).
23   Loosen one plug at a time and push the piston assembly into the bore to force air from the master cylinder. To prevent air from being drawn back into the cylinder, the appropriate plug must be tightened before allowing the piston to return to its original position.
24   Stroke the piston three or four times for each outlet to assure that all air has been expelled.
25   Refill the master cylinder reservoirs and install the diaphragm and cover assembly. **Note:** *The reservoirs should only be filled to the top of the reservoir divider to prevent overflowing when the cover is installed.*

Installation

26   Carefully install the master cylinder by reversing the removal steps, then bleed the brakes at the wheel bleed valves (see Section 13).

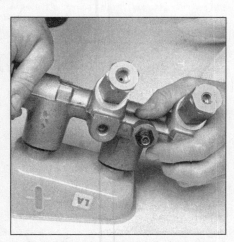

8.14 Press the master cylinder body onto the reservoir

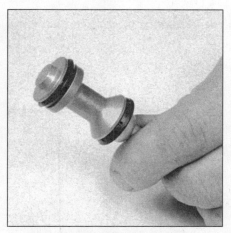

8.15 The secondary seals must be installed with the lips facing out

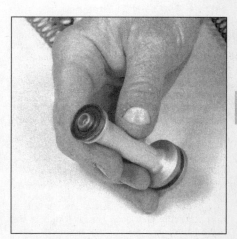

8.18 The primary seal must be installed with the lip facing away from the piston

9

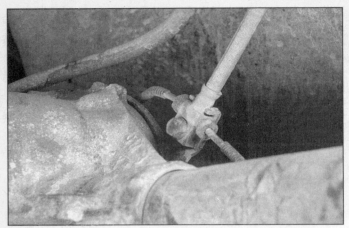

9.11 Typical rear brake hose routing and mounting details

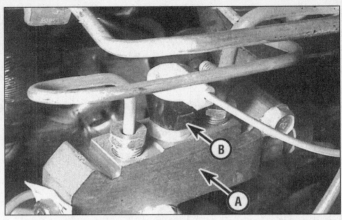

10.1 On most models, the combination valve (A) is located just under the master cylinder, and the pressure differential switch (B) is in the center of the valve

9 Hydraulic brake hoses and lines - inspection and replacement

1   About every six months, with the vehicle raised and placed securely on jackstands, the flexible hoses which connect the steel brake lines with the front and rear brake assemblies should be inspected for cracks, chafing of the outer cover, leaks, blisters and other damage. These are important and vulnerable parts of the brake system and inspection should be complete. A light and mirror will prove helpful for a thorough check. If a hose exhibits any of the above conditions, replace it with a new one as follows:

Front brake hose

2   Using a back-up wrench, disconnect the brake line from the hose fitting, being careful not to bend the frame bracket or brake line.
3   Use pliers to remove the U-clip from the female fitting at the bracket, then remove the hose from the bracket.
4   At the caliper end of the hose, remove the bolt from the banjo fitting then remove the hose and the copper gaskets on either side of the banjo fitting.
5   When installing the hose, always use new copper gaskets on either side of the banjo fitting and lubricate all bolt threads with clean brake fluid before installing them.
6   With the fitting flange engaged with the caliper locating ledge, attach the hose to the caliper and tighten it securely.
7   Without twisting the hose, install the female fitting in the hose bracket (it will fit the bracket in only one position).
8   Install the U-clip retaining the female fitting to the frame bracket.
9   Using a back-up wrench, attach the brake line to the hose fitting and tighten it securely.
10   When the brake hose installation is complete there should be no kinks in the hose. Also, make sure the hose does not contact any part of the suspension. Check this by turning the wheels to the extreme left

and right positions. If the hose makes contact, remove the hose and correct the installation as necessary.

Rear brake hose

Refer to illustration 9.11
11   Locate the junction block at the rear axle and disconnect the two steel brake lines from the block **(see illustration)**.
12   Using a back-up wrench, remove the hose at the female fitting, being careful not to bend the bracket or steel lines.
13   Remove the U-clip with pliers and separate the female fitting from the bracket.
14   Note the position of the junction block carefully so that it may be reinstalled in precisely the same position.
15   Remove the bolt attaching the junction block to the axle and remove the hose from the block.
16   When installing, thread both steel line fittings into the junction block at the rear axle.
17   Bolt the junction block to the axle, then tighten the block bolt and steel lines securely.
18   Without twisting the hose, install the female end of the hose in the frame bracket (it will fit the bracket in only one position).
19   Install the U-clip retaining the female end to the bracket.
20   Using a back-up wrench, attach the steel line fitting to the female fitting, tightening it securely. Again, be careful not to bend the bracket or steel line.
21   Check that the hose installation did not loosen the frame bracket. Retorque the bracket if necessary.
22   Fill the master cylinder reservoirs and bleed the system (see Section 13).

Steel brake lines

23   When it becomes necessary to replace steel lines, use only double-walled steel tubing. Never substitute copper tubing because copper is subject to fatigue cracking and corrosion. The outside diameter of the tubing is used for sizing.
24   Auto parts stores and brake supply houses carry various lengths of prefabricated

brake line. These sections can be bent in a tubing bender.
25   When installing the brake line, leave at least 3/4-inch clearance between the line and any moving parts.

10 Combination valve (non-ABS models) - check and replacement

Check

Refer to illustration 10.1
1   Disconnect the electrical connector from the pressure differential switch **(see illustration)**. **Note:** *When disconnecting the connector, squeeze the connector side lock releases, moving the inside tabs away from the switch, then pull up. Pliers may be used as an aid if necessary.*
2   Using a jumper wire, connect the switch wire to a good ground, such as the engine block.
3   Turn the ignition key to the On position. The warning light in the instrument panel should light up.
4   If the warning light does not light, either the bulb is burned out or the electrical circuit is defective. Replace the bulb (see Chapter 12) or repair the electrical circuit as necessary.
5   When the warning light functions correctly, turn the ignition switch off, disconnect the jumper wire and reconnect the wire to the switch terminal.
6   Make sure the master cylinder reservoirs are full, then attach a bleeder hose to one of the rear wheel bleeder valves and immerse the other end of the hose in a container partially filled with clean brake fluid.
7   Turn the ignition switch on.
8   Open the bleeder valve while a helper applies moderate pressure to the brake pedal. The brake warning light on the instrument panel should light.
9   Close the bleeder valve before the helper releases the brake pedal.
10   Reapply the brake pedal with moderate to heavy pressure. The brake warning light

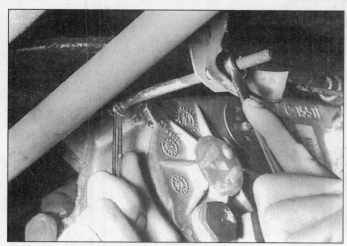

11.4 Use one wrench to hold the brake cable stud from turning while turning the adjusting nut with another wrench

12.9 Remove the four booster mounting nuts (arrows)

should go out.

11   Attach the bleeder hose to one of the front brake bleeder valves and repeat Steps 8 through 10. The warning light should react in the same manner as in Steps 8 and 10.

12   Turn the ignition switch off.

13   If the warning light did not come on in Steps 8 and 11, but does light when a jumper is connected to ground, the warning light switch portion of the combination valve is defective and the combination valve must be replaced with a new one since the components of the combination valve are not individually serviceable.

Replacement

14   Place a container under the combination valve and protect all painted surfaces with newspapers or rags.

15   Disconnect the hydraulic lines at the combination valve, then plug the lines to prevent further loss of fluid and to protect the lines from contamination.

16   Disconnect the electrical connector from the pressure differential switch (refer to Step 1 if necessary).

17   Remove the bolts holding the valve to the mounting bracket and remove the valve from the vehicle.

18   Installation is the reverse of the removal procedure.

19   Bleed the entire brake system (see Section 13). Do not move the vehicle until a firm brake pedal is attained.

11 Parking brake - adjustment

Refer to illustration 11.4

1   The parking brake cables may stretch over a period of time, necessitating adjustment. Also, the parking brake should be checked for proper adjustment whenever the rear brake cables have been disconnected. If the parking brake handle travel is less or more clicks than those listed in the Specifica-

tions Section at the beginning of this Chapter, the parking brake needs adjustment.

2   Apply the parking brake pedal exactly two (2WD) or three (4WD) ratchet clicks.

3   Raise the vehicle and support it securely on jackstands.

4   Locate the adjusting nut on the rear side of the equalizer bracket. To keep the brake cable stud from turning, hold it with one wrench and turn the adjusting nut with another wrench until the left rear wheel can just be turned in reverse (using two hands) but is locked when you attempt to turn it forward **(see illustration)**.

5   Release the parking brake and make sure that both rear wheels turn freely and that there is no brake drag in either direction, then remove the jackstands and lower the vehicle.

12 Power brake booster - check, removal and installation

1   The power brake unit requires no special maintenance apart from periodic inspection of the hoses and inspection of the air filter beneath the boot at the pedal pushrod end.

Operating check

2   Depress the pedal and start the engine. If the pedal goes down slightly, operation is normal.

3   Depress the brake pedal several times with the engine running and make sure that there is no change in the pedal reserve distance.

Airtightness check

4   Start the engine and turn it off after one or two minutes. Depress the brake pedal several times slowly. If the pedal goes down farther the first time but gradually rises after the second or third depression, the booster is airtight.

5   Depress the brake pedal while the engine is running, then stop the engine with

the pedal depressed. If there is no change in the pedal reserve travel after holding the pedal for 30 seconds, the booster is airtight.

Removal and installation

Refer to illustration 12.9

6   Dismantling of the power brake unit requires special tools. If a problem develops, it is recommended that a new or factory-exchange unit be installed rather than trying to overhaul the original booster.

7   Remove the mounting nuts which hold the master cylinder to the power brake unit. Position the master cylinder out of the way, being careful not to strain the lines leading to the master cylinder. If there is any doubt as to the flexibility of the lines, disconnect them at the cylinder and plug the ends.

8   Disconnect the vacuum hose leading to the front of the power brake booster. Cover the end of the hose.

9   Inside the vehicle, loosen the four nuts that secure the booster to the firewall **(see illustration)**. Do not remove these nuts at this time.

10   Disconnect the power brake pushrod from the brake pedal. Do not force the pushrod to the side when disconnecting it.

11   Now remove the four booster mounting nuts and carefully lift the unit out of the engine compartment.

12   When installing, loosely install the four mounting nuts and then connect the pushrod to the brake pedal. Tighten the nuts securely and reconnect the vacuum hose and master cylinder. If the hydraulic brake lines were disconnected, the entire brake system should be bled to eliminate any air which has entered the system (see Section 13).

13 Hydraulic system - bleeding

Refer to illustration 13.8

Warning: *Wear eye protection when bleeding the brake system. If the fluid comes in con-*

9

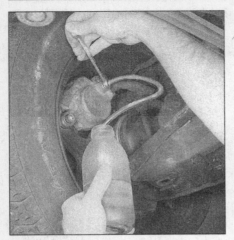

13.8 When bleeding the brakes, a hose is connected to the bleeder valve and then submerged in brake fluid - air will be seen as bubbles in the container and the hose

tact with your eyes, immediately rinse them with water and seek medical attention.

Note 1: *Bleeding the hydraulic system is necessary to remove any air that manages to find its way into the system when it's been opened during removal and installation of a hose, line, caliper or master cylinder.*

Note 2: *If the EHCU valve in the Four-Wheel Anti-lock (4WAL) brake system is suspected of having air in it, it must be separately bled by a dealer service department.*

1   It will probably be necessary to bleed the system at all four brakes if air has entered the system due to low fluid level, or if the brake lines have been disconnected at the master cylinder.

2   If a brake line was disconnected only at a wheel, then only that caliper or wheel cylinder must be bled.

3   If a brake line is disconnected at a fitting located between the master cylinder and any of the brakes, that part of the system served by the disconnected line must be bled.

4   Remove any residual vacuum from the brake power booster by applying the brake several times with the engine off.

5   Remove the master cylinder reservoir cover and fill the reservoir with brake fluid. Reinstall the cover. **Note:** *Check the fluid level often during the bleeding operation and add fluid as necessary to prevent the fluid level from falling low enough to allow air bubbles into the master cylinder.*

6   Have an assistant on hand, as well as a supply of new brake fluid, a clear container partially filled with clean brake fluid, a length of plastic, rubber or vinyl tubing to fit over the bleeder valve and a wrench to open and close the bleeder valve.

7   Beginning at the right rear wheel, loosen the bleeder valve slightly, then tighten it to a point where it is snug but can still be loosened quickly and easily.

8   Place one end of the tubing over the bleeder valve and submerge the other end in brake fluid in the container **(see illustration)**.

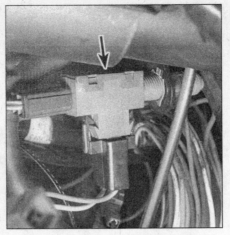

15.4 Stop light installation details

9   Have the assistant push the brake pedal down, then hold the pedal firmly depressed.

10   While the pedal is held depressed, open the bleeder valve just enough to allow a flow of fluid to leave the valve. Watch for air bubbles to exit the submerged end of the tube. When the fluid flow slows after a couple of seconds, close the valve and have your assistant release the pedal slowly.

11   Repeat Steps 9 and 10 until no more air is seen leaving the tube, then tighten the bleeder valve and proceed to the left rear wheel, the right front wheel and the left front wheel, in that order, and perform the same procedure. Be sure to check the fluid in the master cylinder reservoir frequently.

12   Never use old brake fluid. It contains moisture which can boil, rendering the brakes useless.

13   Refill the master cylinder with fluid at the end of the operation.

14   Check the operation of the brakes. The pedal should feel solid when depressed, with no sponginess. If necessary, repeat the entire process. **Warning:** *Do not operate the vehicle if you are in doubt about the effectiveness of the brake system.*

14 Brake pedal - removal and installation

1   Disconnect the cable from the negative battery terminal.

2   Disconnect the clutch pedal return spring (if equipped with a manual transmission).

3   Remove the clip retainer from the pushrod pin which travels through the pedal arm.

4   Remove the nut from the pedal shaft bolt. Slide the shaft out far enough to clear the brake pedal arm.

5   The brake pedal can now be removed, along with the spacer and bushing. The clutch pedal (if equipped) will remain in place.

6   When installing, lubricate the spacer and bushings with multi-purpose grease and

tighten the pivot nut to the torque listed in the Specifications Section.

15 Stop light switch - removal, installation and adjustment

Refer to illustration 15.4

1   The switch is located on a flange or bracket protruding from the brake pedal support.

2   With the brake pedal in the fully released position, the plunger on the body of the switch should be completely pressed in. When the pedal is pushed in, the plunger releases and sends electrical current to the stop lights at the rear of the vehicle.

3   If the stop lights are inoperative and it has been determined that the bulbs are not burned out, push the stop light switch into the tubular clip, noting that audible clicks can be heard as the threaded portion of the switch is pushed through the clip toward the brake pedal.

4   Pull the brake pedal all the way to the rear against the pedal stop until no further clicks can be heard **(see illustration)**. This will seat the switch in the tubular clip and provide the correct adjustment.

5   Release the brake pedal and repeat Step 4 to ensure that no further clicks can be heard.

6   Make sure that the stop lights are working.

7   If the lights are not working, disconnect the electrical connectors at the stop light switch and remove the switch from the clip.

8   Install a new switch and adjust it by performing Steps 3 through 6, making sure the electrical connectors are hooked up.

16 Anti-lock Brake System (ABS) - general information

Description

The Anti-lock Brake System is designed to maintain vehicle maneuverability, directional stability and optimum deceleration under severe braking conditions on most road surfaces. It does so by monitoring the rotational speed of the wheels and controlling the brake pressure during braking. This prevents the wheels from locking up prematurely.

Two types of systems are used: Rear Wheel Anti-Lock (RWAL) and Four Wheel Anti-Lock (4WAL). RWAL only controls lockup on the rear wheels, whereas 4WAL prevents lockup on all four wheels.

Components
Actuator assembly

The actuator assembly includes the master cylinder and control valve which consists of a dump valve and an isolation valve. The valve operates by changing the brake fluid pressure in response to signals from the control unit.

Component location

Assembly Line Data Link (ALDL)

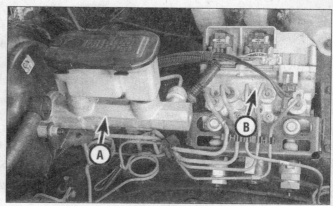

Master cylinder (A); 4WAL EHCU valve (B)

Combination valve

Brake pedal switch

Parking brake switch

Wheel speed sensor

Warning lights

16.4 Four-Wheel Anti-lock (4WAL) brake system components

Control unit

Refer to illustration 16.4

The control unit for the anti-lock brakes is called the Control Module on RWAL and Electro-Hydraulic Control Unit (EHCU) on 4WAL systems. The unit is mounted in the engine compartment below the master cylinder and is the "brain" for the system **(see illustration)**. The function of the control unit is to accept and process information received from the speed sensor(s) and brake light switch to control the hydraulic line pressure, avoiding wheel lockup. The control unit also constantly monitors the system, even under normal driving conditions, to find faults within the system.

If a problem develops within the system the BRAKE (RWAL system) or ANTI-LOCK (4WAL system) warning light on the dashboard will glow. A diagnostic code will also

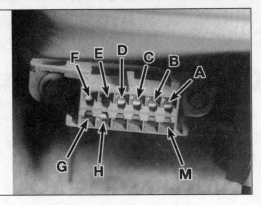

17.2 ALDL terminal details - connect a jumper between the A and H terminals to access the ABS codes

be stored, which, when retrieved by a technician, will indicate the problem area or component.

Speed sensor

On RWAL systems, a rear wheel speed sensor is located in the transmission extension housing on 2WD models or in the transfer case on 4WD models. On 4WAL systems, a speed sensor is located at each wheel. These sensors send a signal to the control unit, indicating wheel speed.

Brake light switch

The brake light switch signals the control unit when the driver steps on the brake pedal. Without this signal the anti-lock system won't activate.

Diagnosis and repair

If the dashboard BRAKE or ANTI-LOCK warning light comes on and stays on, make sure the there's no problem with the brake hydraulic system. If that's not the cause, the anti-lock system is probably malfunctioning. Although special test procedures are necessary to properly diagnose the system, the home mechanic can perform a few preliminary checks before taking the vehicle to a

dealer service department.

a) *Make sure the brakes, calipers and wheel cylinders are in good condition.*
b) *Check the electrical connectors at the control unit.*
c) *Check the fuses.*
d) *Follow the wiring harness to the speed sensor(s) and brake light switch and make sure all connections are secure and the wiring isn't damaged.*

If the above preliminary checks don't rectify the problem, first try to identify the area of trouble using the trouble codes in the next section, then take the vehicle to a dealer service department.

---

17   ABS system trouble codes - general information and retrieval

Refer to illustration 17.2

The on-board computer that operates the RWAL or 4WAL system also has a built-in diagnostic feature. This feature allows you to pinpoint a problem because the computer detects faults and stores them as trouble codes, which can then be easily retrieved. While it may not be possible for the home

mechanic to repair all of these faults, the codes can allow you to be better informed when explaining a problem to the mechanic.

Every time the vehicle is started, the system checks itself and the BRAKE/ANTI-LOCK light on the dash comes on, then goes off when the check is completed. When a code is stored, the light on the dash will light and stay on. The codes can then be retrieved and displayed. These codes are represented as flashes, indicating the problem area or component in the system.

Retrieving codes

1   Locate the ALDL connector under the dash **(see illustration 16.4)**.
2   Connect a jumper wire between the H and A terminals **(see illustration)**. After about 20 seconds the codes will flash on the BRAKE/ANTILOCK light. Write down the codes as they are displayed. Once the codes are retrieved, check them against the chart for your vehicle. Two-digit codes will consist of a long and short flash. Begin counting each code with the long flash (include the long flash in the count). If there is more than one ABS system failure, only the first code recognized will be stored.

Clearing codes

3   After codes have been retrieved and repairs made, they should be cleared from the ECU memory.

RWAL system

4   With the ignition Off, remove the "Brake" fuse from the fuse block for at least five seconds, then reinstall it.

4WAL system

5   Turn the ignition switch On, install the jumper wire between the H and A terminal for two seconds, remove it for one second, then install it for two seconds. The ANTI-LOCK/BRAKE light should light, then go off.

RWAL system

Trouble codes	Circuit or system	Probable cause
Code 1 (1 flash)	ECU	Faulty Electronic Control Unit (ECU).
Code 2 (2 flashes)	Isolation valve, ECU	The isolation valve is stuck or the ECU is faulty.
Code 3 (3 flashes)	Pressure dump valve or ECU	The dump valve is stuck open or the ECU is faulty.
Code 4 (2 flashes)	Anti-lock valve switch	The anti-lock valve is stuck open.
Code 5 (5 flashes)	Pressure dump valve	If the rear brake anti-lock action is excessive during hard braking, the pressure dump valve could be faulty.
Code 6 (6 flashes)	Speed sensor	Erratic brake action at low speeds and pedal pressure is a sign of a fault in the speed sensor or speedometer circuit.
Code 7 (7 flashes)	Isolation valve, ECU	Isolation valve short circuited or ECU faulty.
Code 8 (8 flashes)	Dump valve, ECU	Dump valve short circuit or ECU faulty.
Code 9 (9 flashes)	Speed sensor circuit	Open in the speed sensor circuit or a faulty speedometer.

RWAL system (continued)

Trouble codes	Circuit or system	Probable cause
Code 10 (10 flashes)	Brake light switch circuit	The brake light switch is faulty or needs adjustment.
Code 11 (1 flash, pause, 1 flash)	ECU	Faulty Electronic Control Unit (ECU).
Code 12 (1 flash, pause, 2 flashes)	ECU	Faulty Electronic Control Unit (ECU).
Code 13 (1 flash, pause, 3 flashes	ECU	Faulty Electronic Control Unit (ECU).
Code 15 (1 flash, pause, 5 flashes)	ECU	Faulty Electronic Control Unit (ECU).

4WAL system

Trouble codes	Circuit or system	Probable cause
Code 21 (2 flashes, pause, 1 flash)	Right front wheel circuit	Faulty wheel sensor or open circuit.
Code 22 (2 flashes, pause, 2 flashes)	Right front wheel circuit	No signal. Remove the wheel. Check for a damaged sensor or loose electrical connectors.
Code 23 (2 flashes, pause 3 flashes)	Right front wheel circuit	Intermittent signal, indicating a loose electrical connector.
Code 25 (2 flashes, pause, 5 flashes)	Left front wheel circuit	No signal. Remove the wheel. Check for a damaged sensor or a loose electrical connector.
Code 26 (2 flashes, pause, 6 flashes)	Left front wheel circuit	Intermittent signal, indicating a loose electrical connector.
Code 27 (2 flashes, pause, 7 flashes)	Left front speed sensor circuit	Faulty sensor or loose electrical connector.
Code 28 (2 flashes, pause, 8 flashes)	Speed sensor signal	Erratic brake action at low speeds and pedal pressures indicates a fault in the speed sensor circuit or speedometer.
Code 29 (2 flashes, pause, 9 flashes)	EHCU circuit	A loss of signal from all four sensors indicates a loose EHCU connector.
Code 31 (3 flashes, pause, 1 flash)	Right rear speed sensor circuit	An intermittent code indicates a loose electrical connector.
Code 32 (3 flashes, pause, 2 flashes)	Right rear wheel circuit	No signal. Remove the wheel and check for a damaged sensor and loose connectors.
Code 33 (3 flashes, pause, 3 flashes)	Right rear wheel circuit	The signal is intermittent, indicating a loose electrical connector.
Code 35 (3 flashes, pause, 5 flashes)	Left rear wheel circuit	The signal is intermittent. Check for a loose connection or faulty sensor unit.
Code 36 (3 flashes, pause, 6 flashes)	Left rear speed sensor circuit	No signal. Remove the wheel and check the sensor wheel for damage and the sensor for a loose or damaged connection.
Code 37 (3 flashes, pause, 7 flashes)	Left rear speed sensor circuit	An inconsistent anti-lock action at low speeds and pedal pressure is a sign of a fault in the speed sensor unit or connectors.
Code 38 (3 flashes, pause, 8 flashes)	EHCU valve circuit	A pulsing pedal indicates a defective wheel sensor or faulty EHCU valve.
Codes 41 through 66	4WAL control unit	Check for a loose ground connection at the motor circuit. Clear the code and drive the vehicle. If any of these codes return, the EHCU valve may be faulty.
Codes 71 through 74	4WAL control unit	Clear the code and drive the vehicle. If any of these codes return, the EHCU valve may be faulty.

9

4WAL system (continued)

Trouble codes	Circuit or system	Probable cause
Code 67 (6 flashes, pause, 7 flashes)	Motor circuit	Check the motor for loose electrical connections.
Code 68 (6 flashes, pause, 8 flashes)	Motor circuit	A locked motor or an open circuit. Check the motor for loose electrical connections.
Code 81 (8 flashes, pause, 1 flash)	Brake switch circuit	Make sure the driver hasn't been riding the brake. Check the brake switch adjustment and electrical connections.
Code 86 (8 flashes, pause, 6 flashes)	Anti-lock warning light	Check the light and wiring for a short circuit.
Code 88 (8 flashes, pause, 8 flashes)	Brake warning light	Check the light and wiring for a short circuit.

Chapter 10
Suspension and steering systems

Contents

	Section
Chassis lubrication	See Chapter 1
Front coil springs (2WD models) - removal and installation	9
Front shock absorber - removal and installation	2
Front suspension - general information	1
Lower control arms - removal and installation	8
Power steering gear - removal and installation	16
Power steering pump - removal and installation	17
Power steering system - bleeding	15
Power steering system - general information	14
Rear leaf spring - removal and installation	11
Rear shock absorber - removal and installation	3
Stabilizer bar - removal and installation	4
Steering column switches - removal and installation	19

	Section
Steering knuckle and balljoints (2WD models) - removal and installation	5
Steering knuckle, balljoints and front wheel bearing (hub) assembly (4WD models) - removal and installation	6
Steering linkage - inspection, removal and installation	13
Steering system - general information	12
Steering wheel - removal and installation	18
Suspension and steering check	See Chapter 1
Tire and tire pressure checks	See Chapter 1
Tire rotation	See Chapter 1
Tors on bar (4WD models) - removal and installation	10
Upper control arms - removal and installation	7

Specifications

Torque specifications

	Ft-lbs (unless otherwise indicated)
Steering linkage	
Steering knuckle-to-tie-rod end nut	40
Tie-rod clamp nuts	14
Tie-rod-to-relay rod nut	40
Pitman arm-to-relay rod nut	40
Pitman arm-to-steering gear nut	185
Idler arm-to-relay rod nut	40
Idler arm-to-frame nut	50
Steering column support bracket	
Nuts	20
Bolts	22
Power steering pump	
Reservoir bolt	35
Flow control fitting	35
Pressure hose fitting	20
Power steering gear	
Gear-to-frame bolts	80
High pressure line fitting at gear	20
Oil return line fitting at gear	20
Coupling flange bolt	30
Coupling flange nut	20
Steering wheel and column	
Steering wheel-to-shaft nut	30
Bracket-to-steering column support nuts	25
Toe-pan-to-dash screws	45 in-lbs
Toe-pan clamp screws	60 in-lbs
Bracket-to-steering column bolt	30
Cover-to-housing screws	100 in-lbs
Clamp-to-steering shaft nut	55
Support-to-lock plate screws	60 in-lbs

10

Front suspension (2WD models)

Shock absorber upper nut	96 in-lbs
Shock absorber-to-control arm bolts	20
Upper control arm-to-frame nuts	45
Lower control arm-to-frame nuts (weight on wheels)	65
Upper control arm pivot shaft nuts	85
Stabilizer bar link nuts	156 in-lbs
Stabilizer bar bracket-to-frame bolts	24
Lower balljoint	90
Upper balljoint	65

Front suspension (4WD models)

Shock absorber nuts	55
Lower control arm-to-frame nuts	92
Upper control arm-to-frame nuts	70

Component location

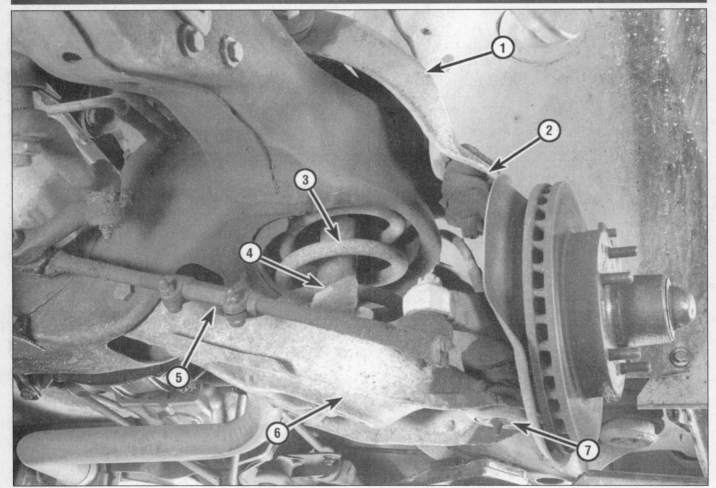

Front suspension components (2WD models)

1	Upper control arm	3	Coil spring	5	Tie-rod adjustment sleeve	7	Lower balljoint
2	Upper balljoint	4	Rubber bump stop	6	Lower control arm		

Lower balljoint 83
Upper balljoint 50
Driveaxle hub/retaining nut.. See Chapter 8
Front wheel bearing (hub) assembly-to-steering knuckle bolts
    1985 and earlier models... 78
    1986 and later models.. 86
Torsion bar crossmember retainer bolts 25

Rear suspension
Shock absorber upper bolts.. 15
Shock absorber lower nut 50
Leaf spring U-bolts (final torque) 85
Leaf spring eye bolts 88
Leaf spring rear shackle-to-frame bolt 88

Component location

Suspension and steering components (4WD models)

1	Tie-rod	3	Relay rod	5	Stabilizer bar
2	Lower control arm	4	Steering stabilizer	6	Torsion bar

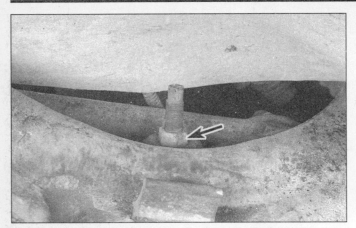

2.2 Remove upper stem nut (arrow) (2WD models)

2.6 Location of the front shock absorber
upper mount (4WD models)

1   Front suspension - general information

The front suspension on both 2WD and 4WD models is fully independent, allowing each wheel to compensate for road surface changes without appreciably affecting the opposite wheel.

Each wheel is connected independently to the frame by a steering knuckle, upper and lower balljoints and upper and lower control arms. The front wheels are held in proper relationship to each other by tie-rods, which are connected to the steering knuckles and to a relay rod assembly.

2WD models

Chassis suspension is handled by coil springs mounted between the lower control arms and the frame. Shock absorbers are mounted inside each coil spring, bolted to the lower control arm and passing through the upper control arm to bolt to the upper control arm frame bracket.

Side roll is controlled by a stabilizer bar mounted to the frame in rubber bushings. Rubber grommeted link bolts attach the ends of the stabilizer bar to the lower control arms.

4WD models

The basic layout of the front suspension on 4WD models is the same as that of 2WD models, with the exception of the replacement of the coil springs with torsion bars. These allow the front driveaxles access to the drive hubs.

The torsion bars are mounted to the lower control arms and are anchored in a frame crossmember with an adjustable arm to control the trim height of the vehicle.

2   Front shock absorber - removal and installation

2WD models

Refer to illustration 2.2

1   Raise the vehicle and support it securely on jackstands.
2   Remove the upper shock absorber stem nut **(see illustration)**. Use an open end wrench to keep the upper stem from turning.
3   Remove the two bolts at the lower shock mount and pull the shock absorber out through the bottom of the lower control arm.
4   Installation is the reverse of removal. Be

sure to tighten the nuts/bolts to the torque listed in this Chapter's Specifications.

4WD models

Refer to illustration 2.6

5   Raise the vehicle and support it securely on jackstands.
6   Remove the nut and bolt from the upper shock absorber mount **(see illustration)**.
7   Remove the nut and bolt from the lower mount on the control arm.
8   Compress the shock absorber enough to slide it off the mounts and remove it from the vehicle.
9   Installation is the reverse of removal. Be sure to tighten the nuts/bolts to the torque listed in this Chapter's Specifications.

3   Rear shock absorber - removal and installation

Refer to illustrations 3.2 and 3.3

1   Raise the vehicle and support it securely on jackstands.
2   Remove the two bolts and nuts at the upper shock absorber mount **(see illustration)**.

3.2 Location of the rear shock absorber upper mount

3.3 Rear shock absorber lower mount (arrow)

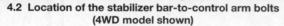

**4.2 Location of the stabilizer bar-to-control arm bolts
(4WD model shown)**

**4.3 Location of the stabilizer bar-to-frame bolts
(4WD model shown)**

3   Remove the nut and washer at the lower mount **(see illustration)**.
4   Slide the shock absorber off the lower mount and detach it from the vehicle.
5   Installation is the reverse of removal. Be sure to tighten the nuts/bolts to the torque listed in this Chapter's Specifications.

4   Stabilizer bar - removal and installation

Refer to illustrations 4.2 and 4.3
1   Raise the vehicle and support it securely on jackstands.
2   On 2WD models, remove the bolts from each end of the stabilizer bar at the lower control arms. Note the positions of the grommets and spacers. On 4WD models, remove the stabilizer bar mounting cups from the lower control arms **(see illustration)**.
3   Remove the mounting bolts from the

frame and detach the stabilizer bar, bushings and brackets **(see illustration)**
4   Installation is the reverse of removal. Install the control arm nuts first, then the frame bolts. **Note:** *On 4WD models you may have to loosen the torsion bar adjustment bolts or raise the outer ends of the control arms in order to install the mounting cups. Tighten all fasteners to the torque listed in this Chapter's Specifications.*

5   Steering knuckle and balljoints (2WD models) - removal and installation

Refer to illustrations 5.5, 5.6, 5.10, 5.11 and 5.12
1   Raise the vehicle and support it securely on jackstands.
2   Remove the wheel and tire.
3   Place a floor jack under the lower con-

trol arm spring seat, raising it just enough to take all spring pressure off the upper control arm.
4   Remove the tie-rod from the steering knuckle (see Section 13).
5   Remove the cotter pin and nut from the lower balljoint stud **(see illustration)**.
6   Separate the balljoints from the steering knuckle using a balljoint separator to press the balljoints out of the knuckle **(see illustration)**.
7   Remove the cotter pin and nut from the upper balljoint stud.
8   Separate the balljoint from the knuckle **(see illustration 5.6)**.
9   Remove the lower balljoint from the control arm by pressing it out with a special balljoint press (available at some auto parts stores, equipment rental yards and specialty tool dealers). If this tool is not available, remove the lower control arm (see Section 8) and take it to an automotive machine shop to have the balljoint replaced.

10

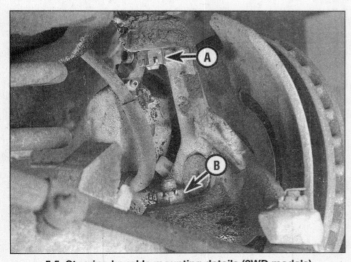

5.5 Steering knuckle mounting details (2WD models)

A   Upper balljoint nut   B   Lower balljoint nut

**5.6 A special tool for pushing the balljoint studs out of the
steering knuckle can be fabricated from a large bolt, nut, washer
and socket**

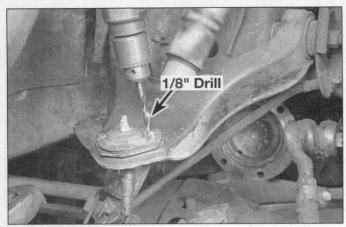

5.10 Drill through the rivets with a 1/8-inch drill bit . . .

5.11 . . . then drill the heads off with a 1/2-inch drill bit

5.12 The balljoint rivets must be driven out with a punch

6.6 Remove the cotter pin and driveaxle/hub nut

10   The upper balljoint is removed by using a 1/8-inch diameter bit to drill 1/4-inch deep into the four mounting rivets **(see illustration)**.

11   Drill off the rivet heads using a 1/2-inch bit **(see illustration)**.

12   Remove the rivets with a small punch **(see illustration)** and slide the balljoint out of the control arm.

13   To install the lower balljoint position the new unit in the lower control arm and press it in until it bottoms. The grease purge opening on the seal must be facing in, towards the engine.

14   Place the balljoint stud in the steering knuckle, thread on the nut and tighten it to the torque listed in this Chapter's Specifications. Tighten additionally as necessary to line up the slot in the nut with the hole in the stud and install the cotter pin.

15   Lubricate the balljoint with chassis grease.

16   Install the new balljoint in the upper control arm, using the four attaching bolts which came with the balljoint, and tighten the nuts to 96 in-lbs. **Note:** *The bolts should be inserted from the underside of the control arm.*

17   Place the balljoint stud in the steering knuckle, thread on the nut and tighten it to the torque listed in this Chapter's Specifica-

tions. Install the cotter pin.

18   Lubricate the balljoint with chassis grease.

19   Install the wheel and lower the vehicle.

---

6   **Steering knuckle, balljoints and front wheel bearing (hub) assembly (4WD models) - removal and installation**

Steering knuckle and balljoints

Refer to illustration 6.6

1   Loosen the lug nuts of the wheel to be removed.

2   Raise the vehicle and support it securely on jackstands.

3   Remove the wheel.

4   Position a hydraulic jack under the lower control arm to support the control arm.

5   Remove the tie-rod from the steering knuckle (see Section 13).

6   Remove the driveaxle/hub nut cotter pin, nut cover, nut and washer **(see illustration)**.

7   If the steering knuckle seal is to be changed remove the three bolts holding the hub and bearing assembly to the steering

knuckle and slide the hub out of the knuckle.

8   Remove the cotter pins and nuts from the upper and lower balljoint studs.

9   Using a balljoint separator, remove the balljoint studs from the steering knuckle. **Note:** *Do not use a "pickle fork" type of balljoint tool unless the balljoints are to be replaced, as this can damage the balljoint seals.*

10   Use a 1/8-inch diameter drill bit to drill 1/4-inch deep into the balljoint mounting rivets (four rivets on the upper control arm and four on the lower).

11   Drill off the rivet heads using a 1/2-inch drill bit.

12   Use a small punch to remove the rivet shafts and the balljoints will fall out of the control arms.

13   Install the new balljoints using the attaching nuts and bolts which came with the new balljoints. Tighten the nuts to 96 in-lbs.

14   Place the balljoint studs in the steering knuckle and thread on the nuts. Tighten the balljoint nuts to the torque listed in this Chapter's Specifications. Tighten the nuts further as necessary to install the cotter pins.

15   Connect the tie-rod end and tighten it.

16   Grease the new balljoints.

17   The remainder of the installation is the reverse of the removal procedure.

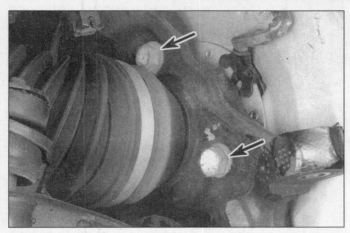

6.21a To detach the hub and bearing assembly from the steering knuckle, remove these bolts (arrows) . . .

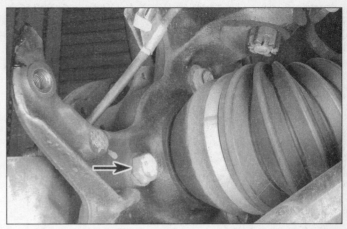

6.21b . . . and this bolt (arrow) (upper bolt is the same upper bolt shown in the previous photo)

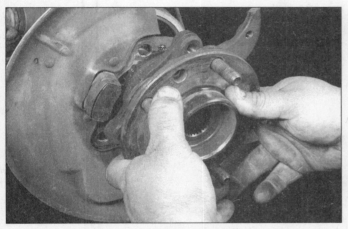

6.22 Remove the hub and bearing assembly from the steering knuckle, then remove the brake disc shield and set it aside

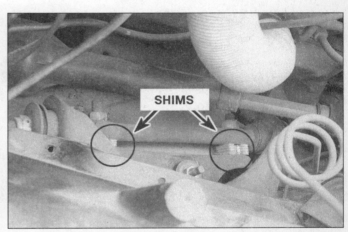

7.5a On 2WD models, note the location of the alignment shims and return them to their original positions

Front wheel bearing (hub) assembly)

Refer to illustrations 6.21a, 6.21b and 6.22

18   Loosen the wheel lug nuts, raise the vehicle and support it securely on jackstands.
19   Remove the driveaxle/hub nut **(see illustration 6.6)**.
20   Remove the brake caliper and brake disc (see Chapter 9).
21   Remove the hub assembly-to-steering knuckle bolts **(see illustrations)**.
22   Tap the hub assembly from side-to-side to free it from the steering knuckle. Pull the hub assembly off the driveaxle **(see illustration)**. If the hub is stuck on the driveaxle splines, push the end of the driveaxle out of the hub with a two-jaw puller. **Caution:** *Be careful not to overextend the inner CV joint of the driveaxle.* Remove the brake disc splash shield.
23   Installation is the reverse of removal. Be sure to lubricate the splines of the driveaxle with multi-purpose grease, and tighten the hub-to-knuckle bolts to the torque listed in this Chapter's Specifications. Tighten the driveaxle/hub nut to the torque listed in the

Chapter 8 Specifications. Tighten the brake caliper mounting bolts to the torque listed in the Chapter 9 Specifications.

7   Upper control arms – removal and installation

Refer to illustrations 7.5a and 7.5b

1   Raise the vehicle and support it securely on jackstands.
2   Support the lower control arm with a hydraulic jack. The support point must be as close to the balljoint as possible to give the maximum leverage on the coil spring or torsion bar.
3   Remove the wheel.
4   Disconnect the upper balljoint from the steering knuckle (see Section 5 or 6).
5   On 2WD models, remove the upper control arm bolts and detach the upper control arm. Note the position of the alignment shims which are installed between the pivot shaft and frame **(see illustration)**. They will have to be reinstalled in the same position when replacing the control arm. On 4WD models,

7.5b When removing the upper control arm on a 4WD model, make sure you mark the relationship of the eccentric cams to the frame bracket before removing the front and rear pivot nuts and bolts

10

mark the positions of the camber adjusting cups then remove the pivot bolts **(see illustration)**.

8.12a The nut for the 4WD lower control arm's front pivot bolt is located inside this hole in the lower crossmember

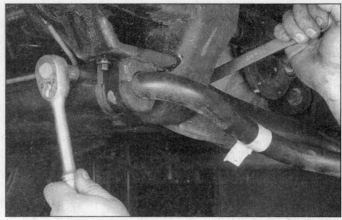

8.12b Using a backup wrench on the front pivot bolt, break the nut loose with a deep socket

6   Replace the bushings in the control arm, if necessary. A threaded puller and receiver cup works well to remove the bushings.

7   Installation is the reverse of removal. Tighten all bolts to the torque listed in this Chapter's Specifications.

---

8   Lower control arms - removal and installation

2WD models

1   Remove the coil spring (see Section 9).

2   Disconnect the lower balljoint stud from the steering knuckle (see Section 5).

3   Remove the lower control arm, guiding it out through the opening in the splash shield.

4   Using a blunt chisel, drive the bushing flare down flush with the rubber bushing.

5   Remove the bushings and install new ones, if necessary.

6   Use a flaring tool to flare the replacement bushing.

7   Installation is the reverse of the removal procedure.

4WD models

Refer to illustrations 8.12a, 8.12b and 8.12c

8   Raise the vehicle and support it on jackstands.

9   Unload the torsion bar (see Section 10, Steps 2 and 3).

10   Unbolt the stabilizer bar mounting cups on both sides and pivot the stabilizer bar down to clear the control arm (see Section 4).

11   Remove the lower shock absorber mounting bolt.

12   Remove the inner control arm pivot bolts **(see illustrations)**.

13   Detach the lower balljoint stud from the steering knuckle (see Section 6).

14   Remove the old control arm bushings and install new ones, if necessary.

15   Installation is the reverse of the removal procedure.

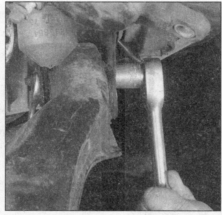

8.12c Using a backup socket on the rear pivot bolt, break the nut loose with a wrench

---

9   Front coil springs (2WD models) - removal and installation

Refer to illustration 9.5

1   Raise the vehicle and support it on jackstands placed under the outside frame rails. The lower control arms must be free to move.

2   Remove the wheel.

3   Remove the shock absorber (see Section 3).

4   Disconnect the stabilizer bar at the lower control arm.

5   Install a spring compressor tool up through the center of the spring **(see illustration)**. Tighten the compressor until all spring force is relieved from the control arm.

6   Remove the control arm rear pivot bolt, then the front bolt.

7   Lower the control arm and spring. Remove the compressed spring out of the control arm pocket. Do not apply force to the control arm-to-steering knuckle balljoint to remove the spring. **Warning:** *Handle the spring carefully and set it aside in a safe area.*

8   Installation is the reverse of the removal procedure. Be sure the spring is positioned correctly.

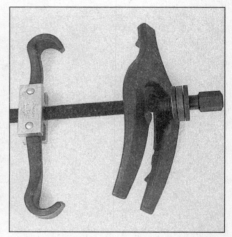

9.5 A typical aftermarket internal spring compressor tool: The hooked arms grip the upper coils of the spring, the plate is inserted below the lower coils, and when the nut on the threaded rod is turned, the spring is compressed

---

10   Torsion bar (4WD models) - removal and installation

Refer to illustrations 10.2a, 10.2b, 10.4, 10.5a, 10.5b, 10.5c and 10.9

1   Raise the vehicle and support it securely on jackstands.

2   Mark the relationship of the torsion bar adjusting bolt to the adjuster nut **(see illustration)**. Install a two-jaw puller over the torsion bar support as shown **(see illustration)**.

3   Remove the torsion bar adjusting bolt.

4   Remove the adjuster nut **(see illustration)**.

5   Mark the relationship of the torsion bar to the lower control arm **(see illustration)**. Slide the torsion bar forward in the lower control arm until it clears the torsion bar support **(see illustration)**. Remove the adjusting arm from the torsion bar support **(see illustration)**.

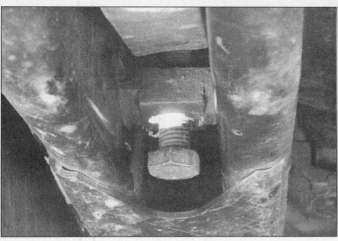

10.2a To ensure proper adjustment of the torsion bar upon reassembly, count the number of threads showing on the torsion bar adjuster bolt and mark the relationship of the bolt to the torsion bar adjuster nut as insurance

10.2b Install a two-jaw puller as shown, with the fingers hooked around the flange running along each side of the crossmember; make sure the puller bolt is centered on the dimple in the torsion bar adjuster arm, then tighten the puller bolt until all tension is removed from the adjuster nut

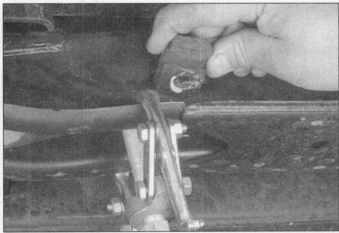

10.4 With tension removed from the adjuster nut, remove the adjuster nut

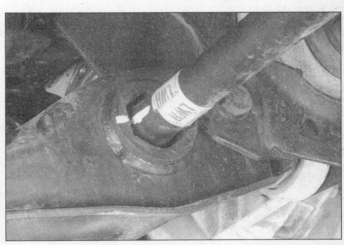

10.5a Mark the relationship of the torsion bar to the lower control arm

10.5b Slide the torsion bar forward through the lower control arm far enough to pull the rear end of the bar out of the crossmember . . .

10.5c . . . and remove the torsion bar adjuster arm. Hold your hand under the arm as you slide out the torsion bar to prevent the arm from falling

10

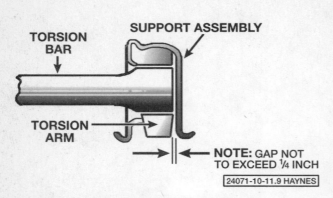

10.9 The clearance measurement indicated here should be checked after torsion bar installation

11.3 The rear leaf spring must be free to pivot down, so loosen the spring-to-shackle nut

11.4 Side view of the rear leaf spring assembly (all models)

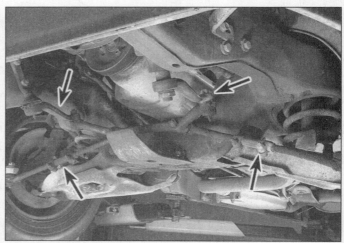

12.1 Steering linkage assembly

6   Pull down on the torsion bar and detach it from the control arm.

7   Before installing the torsion bar apply some grease to the top of the adjusting arm and to the end of the adjusting bolt. Also, apply some grease to the hex-shaped surface of the torsion bar.

8   Install the torsion bar by reversing the removal procedure.

9   Finally, check the torsion arm-to-support assembly clearance after installation **(see illustration)**.

10   Install the wheel and lug nuts and lower the vehicle. Tighten the wheel lug nuts to the torque listed in the Chapter 1 Specifications.

11   Measure the vehicle ride height on each side, from equal points on the frame to the ground. If the side that has been worked on is higher or lower than the other side, turn the torsion bar adjusting screw accordingly until the vehicle sits level. This may take a few tries, and it's important to roll the vehicle back-and-forth and jounce the front end between adjustments, to settle the suspension and get an accurate reading.

11   Rear leaf spring - removal and installation

Refer to illustrations 11.3 and 11.4

1   Loosen the wheel lug nuts, raise the vehicle and support it securely on jackstands placed under the frame. Remove the wheel.

2   Support the rear axle with a floor jack positioned under the axle tube on the side being worked on.

3   Loosen, but do not remove, the spring-to-shackle retaining nut **(see illustration)**.

4   Remove the U-bolt retaining nuts **(see illustration)** and detach the U-bolts.

5   Rotate the spring anchor plate on the shock absorber until the plate clears the spring.

6   Remove the nut and bolt securing the spring shackle to the frame.

7   Remove the nut and bolt from the front hanger and detach the spring.

8   If the spring eye bushings are worn or damaged they must be replaced by an automotive repair shop with the necessary hydraulic press and associated tools.

9   Clean the axle spring pad before installing the spring.

10   Attach the spring at the front hanger but do not tighten the bolt to the final torque.

11   Attach the spring shackle to the frame (be sure the open end of the shackle faces forward, but do not tighten the bolt to the final torque.

12   Make sure that the shackle bolt in the rear spring eye is loose.

13   Position the axle spring pad on the spring so that the center bolt head seats into the hole in the spring pad seat.

14   Rotate the anchor plate into position and install the U-bolts fingertight.

15   Tighten the U-bolt nuts, in a criss-cross pattern, to 20 ft-lbs.

16   Lower the vehicle completely and tighten the U-bolt nuts to the torque listed in this Chapter's Specifications.

17   Check to be sure that the leaves are properly seated by comparing the overhang dimensions on each side.

18   Install the wheel and lug nuts and lower the vehicle. Tighten the lug nuts to the torque listed in the Chapter 1 Specifications.

13.8 Remove the cotter pin, then loosen - but don't yet remove - the castle nut on the tie-rod end ballstud

13.9 Install a two-jaw puller on the tie-rod end ballstud and separate the ballstud from the steering knuckle - leaving the nut in place will prevent the parts from separating violently

19   Tighten the front and rear spring eye bolts and the shackle-to-frame bolts to the torque listed in this Chapter's Specifications.

12 Steering system - general information

Refer to illustration 12.1

The steering linkage **(see illustration)** connects both front wheels to the steering gear through the Pitman arm. The right and left tie-rods are attached to the steering knuckles and to the relay rod by balljoints. The left end of the relay rod is supported by the Pitman arm, which is driven by the steering gear. The right end of the relay rod is supported by the idler arm, which pivots on a support bolted to the frame rail. The Pitman arm and idler arm move in symmetrical arcs and remain parallel to each other.

13 Steering linkage - inspection, removal and installation

Inspection

1   The steering linkage connects the steering gear to the front wheels and keeps the wheels in proper relation to each other. The linkage consists of the Pitman arm, the idler arm, the relay rod, two adjustable tie-rods and a steering damper. The Pitman arm, which is fastened to the steering gear shaft, moves the relay rod back-and-forth. The relay rod is supported on the other end by a frame-mounted idler arm. The back-and-forth motion of the relay rod is transmitted to the steering knuckles through a pair of tie-rod assemblies. Each tie-rod is made up of an inner and outer tie-rod end, a threaded adjuster tube and two clamps.
2   Set the wheels in the straight-ahead position and lock the steering wheel.
3   Raise one side of the vehicle until the tire is approximately 1-inch off the ground.

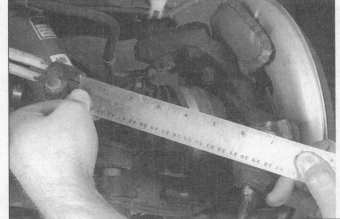

13.11 Measure the distance from the end of the adjuster tube to the center of the ballstud and record your measurement before loosening the adjuster tube clamp and unscrewing the tie-rod end

4   Mount a dial indicator with the needle resting on the outside edge of the wheel. Grasp the front and rear of the tire and, using light pressure, wiggle the wheel back-and-forth and note the dial indicator reading. The gauge reading should be less than 0.108-inch. If the play in the steering system is more than specified, inspect each steering linkage pivot point and ball stud for looseness and replace parts, if necessary.
5   Raise the vehicle and support it on jackstands. Push up, then pull down on the relay rod end of the idler arm, exerting a force of approximately 25 pounds each way. Measure the total distance the end of the arm travels. If the play is greater than 1/4-inch, replace the idler arm.
6   Check for torn ball stud boots, frozen joints and bent or damaged linkage components.

Removal and installation

Tie-rod

Refer to illustrations 13.8, 13.9, 13.11 and 13.15
Note: *This procedure covers replacing the tie-rod ends as well as the entire tie-rod. If you'll only be replacing a tie-rod end, ignore the Steps that don't apply.*

7   Loosen the wheel lug nuts, raise the vehicle and support it securely on jackstands. Apply the parking brake. Remove the wheel.
8   Remove the cotter pin and loosen, but do not remove, the castellated nut(s) from the ball stud(s) **(see illustration)**. If only the outer tie-rod end will be replaced, only loosen the outer nut. If only the inner tie-rod end will be replaced, only loosen the inner nut. If the entire tie-rod will be replaced, loosen both nuts.
9   If the outer tie-rod end or the entire tie-rod will be replaced, use a two-jaw puller to separate the tie-rod end from the steering knuckle **(see illustration)**. Remove the castellated nut and pull the tie-rod end from the knuckle.
10   If the inner tie-rod end or the entire tie-rod will be replaced, separate the inner tie-rod end from the relay rod (see Steps 8 and 9).
11   If the inner or outer tie-rod end must be replaced, measure the distance from the end of the adjuster tube to the center of the ball stud and record it **(see illustration)**. Loosen the adjuster tube clamp bolts and unscrew the tie-rod end.
12   Lubricate the threaded portion of the tie-rod end with chassis grease. Screw the new

10

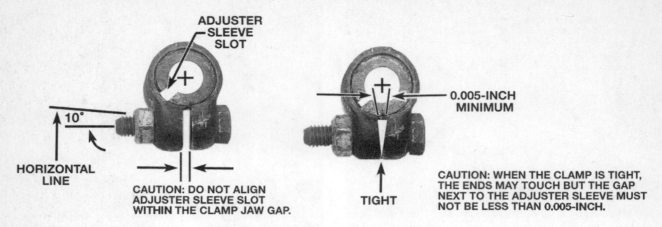

13.15 Relationship of the tie-rod clamp and sleeve

tie-rod end into the adjuster tube and adjust the distance from the tube to the ball stud to the previously measured dimension. The number of threads showing on the inner and outer tie-rod ends should be equal within three threads. Don't tighten the clamp yet.

13   Connect the disconnected ball stud nut(s). Tighten the nut(s) to the torque listed in this Chapter's Specifications and install a new cotter pin. If the ball stud spins when attempting to tighten the nut, force it into the tapered hole with a large pair of pliers. If necessary, tighten the nut slightly to align a slot in the nut with the hole in the ball stud.

14   Insert the inner tie-rod end ball stud into the relay rod until it's seated. Install the nut and tighten it to the torque listed in this Chapter's Specifications.

15   Tighten the clamp nuts. The center of the bolt should be nearly horizontal and the adjuster tube slot must not line up with the gap in the clamps **(see illustration)**.

16   Install the wheel and lug nuts, lower the vehicle and tighten the lug nuts to the torque listed in the Chapter 1 Specifications. Drive the vehicle to an alignment shop to have the front end alignment checked and, if necessary, adjusted.

Idler arm

17   Raise the vehicle and support it securely on jackstands. Apply the parking brake.

18   Loosen but do not remove the idler arm-to-relay rod nut.

19   Separate the idler arm from the relay rod with a two jaw puller **(see illustration 17.9)**. Remove the nut.

20   Remove the idler arm-to-frame bolts.

21   To install the idler arm, position it on the frame and install the bolts, tightening them to the torque listed in this Chapter's Specifications.

22   Insert the idler arm ball stud into the relay rod and install the nut. Tighten the nut to the specified torque. If the ball stud spins when attempting to tighten the nut, force it into the tapered hole with a large pair of pliers.

Relay rod

23   Raise the vehicle and support it securely on jackstands. Apply the parking brake.

24   Separate the two inner tie-rod ends from the relay rod (see Step 10).

25   Separate the relay rod from the Pitman arm.

26   Separate the relay rod from the idler arm.

27   Installation is the reverse of the removal procedure. If the ball studs spin when attempting to tighten the nuts, force them into the tapered holes with a large pair of pliers. Be sure to tighten all of the nuts to the torque listed in this Chapter's Specifications.

Pitman arm

Refer to illustration 13.32

28   Raise the vehicle and support it securely on jackstands.

29   Remove the relay rod nut from the Pitman arm ball stud. Discard the nut - don't reuse it.

30   Using a puller, separate the relay rod

13.32 Remove the Pitman arm with a Pitman arm puller, available at most auto parts stores

from the Pitman arm ball stud.

31   Remove the Pitman arm nut and washer. Mark the Pitman arm and the steering gear shaft to ensure proper alignment at reassembly time.

32   Remove the Pitman arm with a Pitman arm puller or a two-jaw puller **(see illustration)**.

33   Inspect the ball stud threads for damage. Inspect the ball stud seals for excessive wear. Clean the threads on the ball stud.

34   Installation is the reverse of removal. Make sure the marks you made on the Pitman arm and Pitman shaft are aligned. **Note:** *If a clamp type Pitman arm is used, spread the arm just enough, with a wedge, to slip the arm onto the Pitman shaft. Don't spread the arm more than necessary to slip it over the shaft with hand pressure. Do not hammer the arm onto the shaft or you may damage the steering gear.*

Steering damper

35   Inspect the steering damper for fluid leakage. A slight film of fluid near the shaft seal is normal, but if there's excessive fluid present and it's obviously coming from the steering damper, replace the damper.

36   Inspect the steering damper bushing for excessive wear. If it's in bad shape, replace the damper.

37   To test the damper itself, disconnect it from the frame or axle end (see next step). Using as much travel as possible, extend and compress the damper. The resistance should be smooth and constant for each stroke. If any binding or unusual noises are present, replace the damper.

38   Remove the damper ballstud-to-relay rod cotter pin, then remove the nut. Separate the damper from the relay rod, using the technique shown in **illustration 17.9**.

39   Remove the steering damper mounting bolt and nut, then remove the damper.

40   Installation is the reverse of removal. Tighten all the fasteners securely.

16.7 To remove the steering gear, remove these three bolts

17.3 You'll need a special puller to remove the power steering pump pulley

14 Power steering system - general information

With the optional power steering gear, hydraulic pressure is generated in an engine-driven pump and supplied through hoses to the steering box spool valve. When the steering wheel is turned and force is applied to the steering shaft, hydraulic pressure is added and power assistance is given to the turning effort.

15 Power steering system - bleeding

1   This is not a routine operation and normally will only be required when the system has been dismantled and reassembled.
2   Fill the reservoir to the correct level with the recommended fluid and allow it to remain undisturbed for at least two minutes.
3   Start the engine and run it for two or three seconds only. Check the reservoir and add more fluid as necessary.
4   Repeat the operations described in the preceding paragraph until the fluid level remains constant.
5   Raise the front of the vehicle until the wheels are clear of the ground.
6   Start the engine and run it at about 1500 rpm. Turn the steering from stop to stop. Check the reservoir fluid level.
7   Lower the vehicle to the ground and, with the engine still running, move the vehicle forward sufficiently to obtain full right lock, followed by full left lock. Recheck the fluid level. If the fluid in the reservoir is getting foamy allow the vehicle to stand for a few minutes with the engine off, then repeat the previous operations. At the same time check the belt tightness. Check to make sure the power steering hoses are not touching any part of the vehicle such as sheet metal or the exhaust manifold.
8   The procedures above will normally

remedy an extreme foam condition and/or a noisy pump. If, however, either or both conditions persist after a few trials, the power steering system will have to be checked by a dealer. Do not drive the vehicle until the conditions have been remedied.

16 Power steering gear - removal and installation

Refer to illustration 16.7
1   Disconnect the cable from the negative battery terminal.
2   Remove the coupling shield.
3   Disconnect the pressure and return hoses attached to the power steering gear assembly.
4   Plug or tape the ends of the disconnected hoses and the holes in the power steering housing to prevent contamination.
5   Remove the nuts, lockwashers and bolts at the steering coupling-to-steering shaft flange.
6   Remove the Pitman arm locknut and washer. Mark the position of the Pitman arm in relation to the shaft and disconnect the Pitman arm with a puller **(see illustration 13.32)**.
7   Remove the bolts securing the steering gear to the frame and separate it from the vehicle **(see illustration)**.
8   When installing the gear place it in position so that the coupling mounts properly to the flanged end of the steering shaft. Secure the gear to the frame, install the washers and bolts, then tighten down the bolts to the torque listed in this Chapter's Specifications.
9   Secure the steering coupling to the flanged end of the column with the lock washers and nuts. Tighten the nuts.
10   Install the Pitman arm, lining up the marks made during disassembly, and tighten the nut.
11   Connect the coupling shield and negative battery cable.

17 Power steering pump - removal and installation

Refer to illustrations 17.3 and 17.4
1   Disconnect the hydraulic hoses from the pump and keep them in the raised position to prevent the fluid from leaking out until they can be plugged.
2   Remove the pump drivebelt by loosening the pump mounts and pushing it in toward the engine.
3   Unscrew and remove the pump mounting bolts and braces and remove the pump. **Note**: *On some models, it may be necessary to remove the power steering pump pulley to access the mounting bolts. A power steering pump pulley remover/installer (available at automotive parts stores) will be required to complete the procedure* **(see illustration)**.
4   Installation is the reverse of removal. If you removed the pulley, install it using a pulley installation tool or equivalent **(see illustration)**.

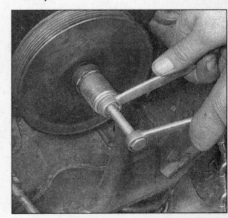

17.4 To install the pulley on the shaft, use a long bolt with the same thread pitch as the internal threads of the power steering pump shaft, a nut, washer and socket that's the same diameter as the pulley hub

10

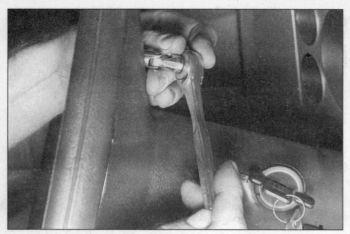

18.2 Removing the steering wheel horn pad screws

18.3 Unplugging the horn wire and spring

18.5 The steering wheel and shaft should be marked before removing the steering wheel

18.6 Using a steering wheel puller to remove the steering wheel

5   Prime the pump by turning the pulley in the reverse direction to that of normal rotation (counterclockwise as viewed from the front) until air bubbles cease to emerge from the fluid when observed through the reservoir filler cap.

6   Install the drivebelt and adjust it (see Chapter 1).

7   Bleed the system (see Section 15).

18   Steering wheel - removal and installation

Refer to illustrations 18.2, 18.3, 18.5 and 18.6

1   Disconnect the negative battery cable from the battery.

2   Use a 7mm socket to remove the horn pad screws on the underside of the steering wheel **(see illustration)**. Detach the horn pad.

3   Unplug the horn wire **(see illustration)**.

4   Remove the retainer clip and steering wheel retaining nut. A socket and breaker bar will be needed to remove the retaining nut.

5   Mark the steering wheel and steering

shaft so the wheel can be reinstalled in the same position **(see illustration)**.

6   Use a steering wheel puller to remove the steering wheel from the column **(see illustration)**.

7   Installation is the reverse of removal. Tighten the nut to the torque listed in this Chapter's Specifications.

19   Steering column switches - removal and installation

Refer to illustrations 19.2, 19.3, 19.8, 19.9, 19.11, 19.13 and 19.15

1   Remove the steering wheel (see Section 18).

19.2 Removing the steering column shaft lock cover

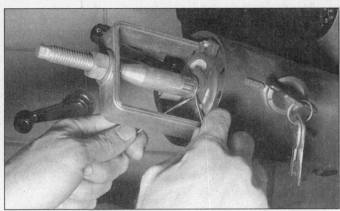

19.3 Depress the lockplate and pry out the retaining ring (the special tool shown here greatly simplifies this step and is available at most auto parts stores)

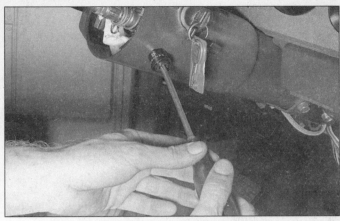

19.8 Removing the hazard signal knob

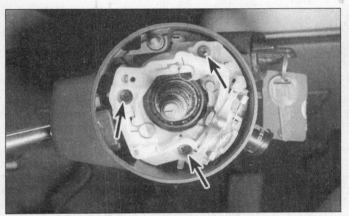

19.9 Location of the turn signal switch mounting screws

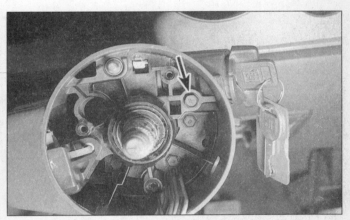

19.11 Location of the ignition lock cylinder retaining screw

2   Pry the shaft lock cover off the steering column **(see illustration).**

3   Depress the lockplate and remove the lockplate retaining ring **(see illustration).**

4   Remove the lockplate.

5   Remove the cancelling cam.

6   Remove the upper bearing spring and washer.

7   Remove the mounting screw from the base of the turn signal lever and detach the turn signal lever.

8   Remove the hazard signal knob screw on the outside of the steering column and detach the hazard signal knob **(see illustration).**

9   Remove the three mounting screws **(see illustration)** from the signal switch assembly and pull the switch out of the column shroud.

10   If the switch assembly is not being replaced, it can be left hanging from the steering column.

11   To remove the ignition lock cylinder, first remove the lock cylinder retaining screw from inside the column **(see illustration).**

12   Turn the ignition lock cylinder to the Run position and pull the lock cylinder out.

13   To replace the signal switch assembly, first remove the steering column trim cover **(see illustration).**

14   Remove the four bolts and two nuts

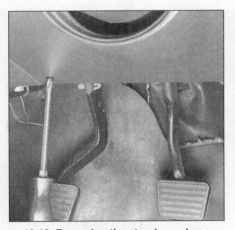

19.13 Removing the steering column trim cover

19.15 The turn signal switch wiring harness is disconnected at the bottom of the steering column

from the steering column-to-dashboard brace to free the wiring harness.

15   Disconnect the switch wiring harness at the bottom of the column **(see illustration)** and attach a routing wire to the end of the switch harness.

16   Remove the switch and wiring harness from the steering column.

17   Attach the replacement switch wiring

harness to the routing wire and install the harness in the column.

18   Connect the wiring harness. Install the two bracket nuts and the four bolts, tightening them to the torque listed in this Chapter's Specifications.

19   The rest of installation is the reverse of removal.

10

Notes

Chapter 11 Body

Contents

	Section		Section
Body - maintenance	2	Grille - removal and installation	17
Body repair - major damage	7	Hinges and locks - maintenance	5
Body repair - minor damage	6	Hood - removal, installation and adjustment	12
Bumpers - removal and installation	16	Liftgate - removal, installation and adjustment	15
Door exterior handle and lock cylinder - removal and installation	10	Rear cab window - removal and installation	18
		Tailgate latch and handle - removal and installation	14
Door glass and window regulator - removal and installation	11	Tailgate - removal and installation	13
Door trim panel - removal and installation	9	Upholstery and carpets - maintenance	3
General information	1	Vinyl trim - maintenance	4
		Windshield and fixed glass - replacement	8

1 General information

These models feature separate body and frame construction. The frame is ladder-type, consisting of two C-section steel side rails joined by crossmembers.

Certain components are particularly vulnerable to accident damage and can be unbolted and repaired or replaced. Among these parts are the body moldings, bumpers, the hood and trunk lids and all glass.

Only general body maintenance practices and body panel repair procedures within the scope of the do-it-yourselfer are included in this Chapter.

2 Body - maintenance

1   The condition of your vehicle's body is very important, because it is on this that the second-hand value will mainly depend. It is much more difficult to repair a neglected or damaged body than it is to repair mechanical components. The hidden areas of the body, such as the fenderwells, the frame, and the engine compartment, are equally important, although obviously do not require as frequent attention as the rest of the body.

2   Once a year, or every 12 000 miles, it is a good idea to have the underside of the body and the frame steam cleaned. All traces of dirt and oil will be removed and the underside can then be inspected carefully for rust, damaged brake lines, frayed electrical wiring, damaged cables, and other problems. The front suspension components should be greased after completion of this job.

3   At the same time, clean the engine and the engine compartment using either a steam cleaner or a water soluble degreaser.

4   The fenderwells should be given particular attention, as undercoating can peel away and stones and dirt thrown up by the tires can cause the paint to chip and flake, allowing rust to set in. If rust is found, clean down to the bare metal and apply an anti-rust paint.

5   The body should be washed once a week (or when dirty). Wet the vehicle thoroughly to soften the dirt, then wash it down with a soft sponge and plenty of clean soapy water. If the surplus dirt is not washed off very carefully, it will in time wear down the paint.

6   Spots of tar or asphalt coating thrown up from the road should be removed with a cloth soaked in solvent.

7   Once every six months, give the body and chrome trim a thorough wax job. If a chrome cleaner is used to remove rust from any of the vehicle's plated parts, remember that the cleaner also removes part of the chrome, so use it sparingly.

3 Upholstery and carpets - maintenance

1   Every three months, remove the carpets or mats and clean the interior of the vehicle (more frequently if necessary). Vacuum the upholstery and carpets to remove loose dirt and dust.

2   If the upholstery is soiled, apply upholstery cleaner with a damp sponge and wipe it off with a clean, dry cloth.

4 Vinyl trim - maintenance

Vinyl trim should not be cleaned with detergents, caustic soaps or petroleum-based cleaners. Plain soap and water or a mild vinyl cleaner is best for stains. Test a small area for color fastness. Bubbles under the vinyl can be corrected by piercing them with a pin and then working the air out.

11

5   Hinges and locks - maintenance

Every 3000 miles or three months, the door, hood and tailgate hinges and locks should be lubricated with a few drops of oil. The striker plates should also be given a thin coat of grease to reduce wear and ensure free movement.

6   Body repair - minor damage

See photo sequence

Repair of minor scratches

If the scratch is very superficial and does not penetrate to the metal of the body, repair is very simple. Lightly rub the scratched area with a fine rubbing compound to remove loose paint and built-up wax. Rinse the area with clean water.

Apply touch-up paint to the scratch, using a small brush. Continue to apply thin layers of paint until the surface of the paint in the scratch is level with the surrounding paint. Allow the new paint at least two weeks to harden, then blend it into the surrounding paint by rubbing with a very fine rubbing compound. Finally, apply a coat of wax to the scratch area.

If the scratch has penetrated the paint and exposed the metal of the body, causing the metal to rust, a different repair technique is required. Remove all loose rust from the bottom of the scratch with a pocket knife, then apply rust-inhibiting paint to prevent the formation of rust in the future. Using a rubber or nylon applicator, coat the scratched area with glaze-type filler. If required, the filler can be mixed with thinner to provide a very thin paste, which is ideal for filling narrow scratches. Before the glaze filler in the scratch hardens, wrap a piece of smooth cotton cloth around the tip of a finger. Dip the cloth in thinner and then quickly wipe it along the surface of the scratch. This will ensure that the surface of the filler is slightly hollow. The scratch can now be painted over as described earlier in this section.

Repair of dents

When repairing dents, the first job is to pull the dent out until the affected area is as close as possible to its original shape. There is no point in trying to restore the original shape completely as the metal in the damaged area will have stretched on impact and cannot be restored to its original contours. It is better to bring the level of the dent up to a point which is about 1/8-inch below the level of the surrounding metal. In cases where the dent is very shallow, it is not worth trying to pull it out at all.

If the back side of the dent is accessible, it can be hammered out gently from behind using a soft-faced hammer. While doing this, hold a block of wood firmly against the opposite side of the metal to absorb the hammer blows and prevent the metal from being stretched out.

If the dent is in a section of the body which has double layers, or some other factor that makes it inaccessible from behind, a different technique is required. Drill several small holes through the metal inside the damaged area, particularly in the deeper sections. Screw long, self-tapping screws into the holes just enough for them to get a good grip in the metal. Now the dent can be pulled out by pulling on the protruding heads of the screws with locking pliers.

The next stage of repair is the removal of paint from the damaged area and from an inch or so of the surrounding metal. This is easily done with a wire brush or sanding disk in a drill motor, although it can be done just as effectively by hand with sandpaper. To complete the preparation for filling, score the surface of the bare metal with a screwdriver or the tang of a file (or drill small holes in the affected area). This will provide a very good grip for the filler material. To complete the repair, see the Section on filling and painting.

Repair of rust holes or gashes

Remove all paint from the affected area and from an inch or so of the surrounding metal using a sanding disk or wire brush mounted in a drill motor. If these are not available, a few sheets of sandpaper will do the job just as effectively. With the paint removed, you will be able to determine the severity of the corrosion and decide whether to replace the whole panel, if possible, or repair the affected area. New body panels are not as expensive as most people think and it is often quicker to install a new panel than to repair large areas of rust.

Remove all trim pieces from the affected area (except those which will act as a guide to the original shape of the damaged body, i.e. headlight shells, etc.). Then, using metal snips or a hacksaw blade, remove all loose metal and any other metal that is badly affected by rust. Hammer the edges of the hole in to create a slight depression for the filler material.

Wire brush the affected area to remove the powdery rust from the surface of the metal. If the back of the rusted area is accessible, treat it with rust-inhibiting paint.

Before filling is done, block the hole in some way. This can be done with sheet metal riveted or screwed into place, or by stuffing the hole with wire mesh.

Once the hole is blocked off, the affected area can be filled and painted (see the following sub-section on filling and painting).

Filling and painting

Many types of body fillers are available, but generally speaking, body repair kits which contain filler paste and a tube of resin hardener are best for this type of repair work. A wide, flexible plastic or nylon applicator will be necessary for imparting a smooth and contoured finish to the surface of the filler material.

Mix up a small amount of filler on a clean piece of wood or cardboard (use the hardener sparingly). Follow the manufacturer's instructions on the package, otherwise the filler will set incorrectly.

Using the applicator, apply the filler paste to the prepared area. Draw the applicator across the surface of the filler to achieve the desired contour and to level the filler surface. As soon as a contour that approximates the original one is achieved, stop working the paste. If you continue, the paste will begin to stick to the applicator. Continue to add thin layers of filler paste at 20-minute intervals until the level of the filler is just above the surrounding metal.

Once the filler has hardened, the excess can be removed with a body file. From then on, progressively finer grades of sandpaper should be used, starting with a 180-grit paper and finishing with 600-grit wet-or-dry paper. Always wrap the sandpaper around a flat rubber or wooden block, otherwise the surface of the filler will not be completely flat. During the sanding of the filler surface, the wet-or-dry paper should be periodically rinsed in water. This will ensure that a very smooth finish is produced in the final stage.

At this point, the repair area should be surrounded by a ring of bare metal, which in turn should be encircled by the finely feathered edge of good paint. Rinse the repair area with clean water until all of the dust produced by the sanding operation is gone.

Spray the entire area with a light coat of primer. This will reveal any imperfections in the surface of the filler. Repair the imperfections with fresh filler paste or glaze filler and once more smooth the surface with sandpaper. Repeat this spray-and-repair procedure until you are satisfied that the surface of the filler and the feathered edge of the paint are perfect. Rinse the area with clean water and allow it to dry completely.

The repair area is now ready for painting. Spray painting must be carried out in a warm, dry, windless and dust-free atmosphere. These conditions can be created if you have access to a large indoor work area, but if you are forced to work in the open, you will have to pick the day very carefully. If you are working indoors, dousing the floor in the work area with water will help settle the dust which would otherwise be in the air. If the repair area is confined to one body panel, mask off the surrounding panels. This will help minimize the effects of a slight mismatch in paint color. Trim pieces such as chrome strips, door handles, etc., will also need to be masked off or removed. Use masking tape and several thicknesses of newspaper for the masking operations.

Before spraying, shake the paint can thoroughly, then spray a test area until the spray painting technique is mastered. Cover the repair area with a thick coat of primer. The thickness should be built up using several thin layers of primer rather than one thick one. Using 600-grit wet-or-dry sandpaper, rub down the surface of the primer until it is

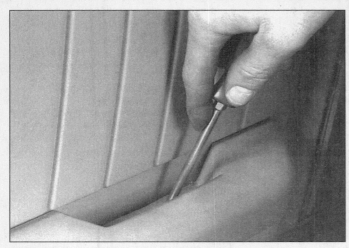

9.2 On most models, the armrest can be removed by removing the screws and sliding it to the rear

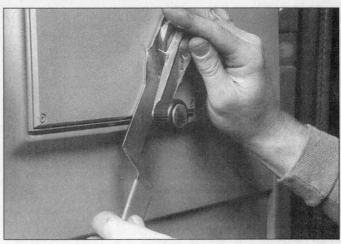

9.3a Use a screwdriver or the inexpensive tool shown here to remove the window regulator handle retaining clip

very smooth. While doing this, the work area should be thoroughly rinsed with water and the wet-or-dry sandpaper periodically rinsed as well. Allow the primer to dry before spraying additional coats.

Spray on the top coat, again building up the thickness by using several thin layers of paint. Begin spraying in the center of the repair area and then, using a circular motion, work out until the whole repair area and about two inches of the surrounding original paint is covered. Remove all masking material 10 to 15 minutes after spraying on the final coat of paint. Allow the new paint at least two weeks to harden, then use a very fine rubbing compound to blend the edges of the new paint into the existing paint. Finally, apply a coat of wax.

7 Body repair - major damage

1   Major damage must be repaired by an auto body shop specifically equipped to perform body repairs. These shops have available the specialized equipment required to

do the job properly.
2   If the damage is extensive, the frame must be checked for proper alignment or the vehicle's handling characteristics may be adversely affected and other components may wear at an accelerated rate.
3   Due to the fact that all of the major body components (hood, fenders, etc.) are separate and replaceable units, any seriously damaged components should be replaced rather than repaired. Sometimes these components can be found in a wrecking yard that specializes in used vehicle components (often at considerable savings over the cost of new parts).

8 Windshield and fixed glass - replacement

Replacement of the windshield and fixed glass requires the use of special fast-setting adhesive/caulk materials and some specialized tools and techniques. These operations should be left to a dealer service department or a shop specializing in glass work.

9 Door trim panel - removal and installation

Refer to illustrations 9.2, 9.3a, 9.3b and 9.4
1   Remove the door handle trim frame.
2   Remove the armrest mounting screws and slide the armrest to the rear **(see illustration)**. Remove the armrest.
3   Using a special tool available at your local auto parts retailer **(see illustrations)** or a small screwdriver, remove the window handle retaining spring clip.
4   Carefully remove the clips retaining the trim panel to the door, using a screwdriver **(see illustration)**, or special tool (available at your local auto parts retailer).
5   Release the two latches at the top of the trim panel and detach the panel.
6   Installation is the reverse of removal. If any trim panel retaining clips were broken during removal, they can be inexpensively replaced (available at your local auto parts retailer).

9.3b Window handle retaining clip

9.4 Detach the clips by prying the door trim panel

11

These photos illustrate a method of repairing simple dents. They are intended to supplement *Body repair - minor damage* in this Chapter and should not be used as the sole instructions for body repair on these vehicles.

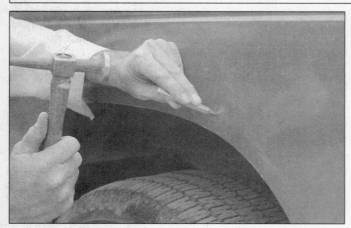

1   If you can't access the backside of the body panel to hammer out the dent, pull it out with a slide-hammer-type dent puller. In the deepest portion of the dent or along the crease line, drill or punch hole(s) at least one inch apart . . .

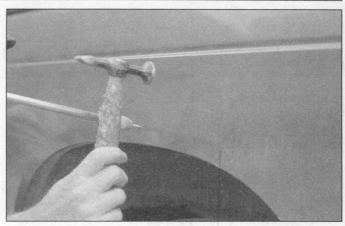

2   . . . then screw the slide-hammer into the hole and operate it. Tap with a hammer near the edge of the dent to help 'pop' the metal back to its original shape. When you're finished, the dent area should be close to its original contour and about 1/8-inch below the surface of the surrounding metal

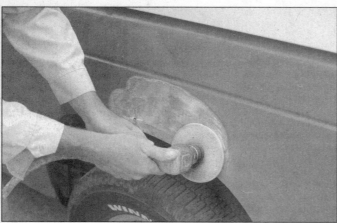

3   Using coarse-grit sandpaper, remove the paint down to the bare metal. Hand sanding works fine, but the disc sander shown here makes the job faster. Use finer (about 320-grit) sandpaper to feather-edge the paint at least one inch around the dent area

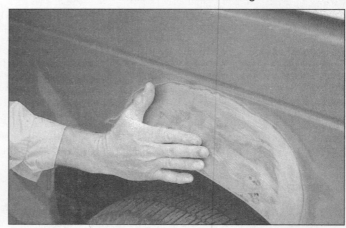

4   When the paint is removed, touch will probably be more helpful than sight for telling if the metal is straight. Hammer down the high spots or raise the low spots as necessary. Clean the repair area with wax/silicone remover

5   Following label instructions, mix up a batch of plastic filler and hardener. The ratio of filler to hardener is critical, and, if you mix it incorrectly, it will either not cure properly or cure too quickly (you won't have time to file and sand it into shape)

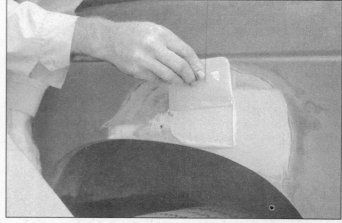

6   Working quickly so the filler doesn't harden, use a plastic applicator to press the body filler firmly into the metal, assuring it bonds completely. Work the filler until it matches the original contour and is slightly above the surrounding metal

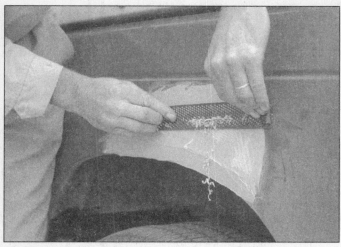

7   Let the filler harden until you can just dent it with your fingernail. Use a body file or Surform tool (shown here) to rough-shape the filler

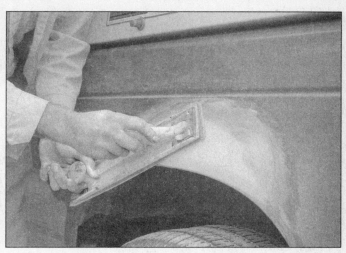

8   Use coarse-grit sandpaper and a sanding board or block to work the filler down until it's smooth and even. Work down to finer grits of sandpaper - always using a board or block - ending up with 360 or 400 grit

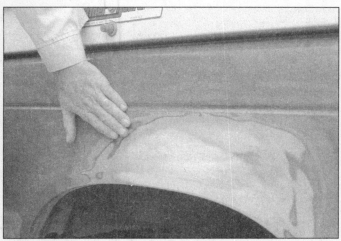

9   You shouldn't be able to feel any ridge at the transition from the filler to the bare metal or from the bare metal to the old paint. As soon as the repair is flat and uniform, remove the dust and mask off the adjacent panels or trim pieces

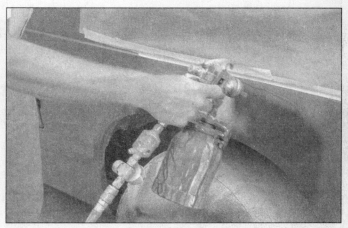

10   Apply several layers of primer to the area. Don't spray the primer on too heavy, so it sags or runs, and make sure each coat is dry before you spray on the next one. A professional-type spray gun is being used here, but aerosol spray primer is available inexpensively from auto parts stores

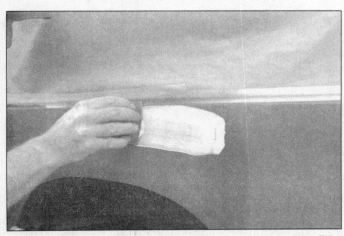

11   The primer will help reveal imperfections or scratches. Fill these with glazing compound. Follow the label instructions and sand it with 360 or 400-grit sandpaper until it's smooth. Repeat the glazing, sanding and respraying until the primer reveals a perfectly smooth surface

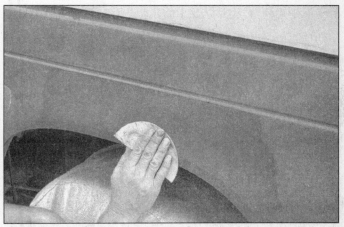

12   Finish sand the primer with very fine sandpaper (400 or 600-grit) to remove the primer overspray. Clean the area with water and allow it to dry. Use a tack rag to remove any dust, then apply the finish coat. Don't attempt to rub out or wax the repair area until the paint has dried completely (at least two weeks)

10.4 Remove the exterior handle retaining nuts (arrows) and pry the linkage rod (arrow) out of the handle

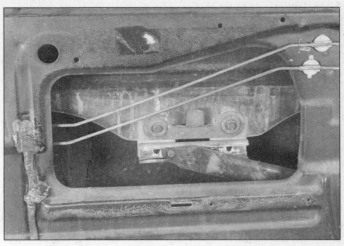

11.4 Lower the glass and remove regulator mounting bolts

10 Door exterior handle and lock cylinder - removal and installation

Refer to illustration 10.4

1   Raise the window completely.

2   Remove the door trim panel as described in Section 9.

3   Pry back the water deflector enough to gain access to the exterior handle mounting hardware.

4   Pry the linkage rod out of the door handle lever with a screwdriver **(see illustration)**.

5   Remove the two nuts retaining the handle to the door sheet metal and detach the handle.

6   Installation is the reverse of removal.

7   To remove the lock cylinder detach the linkage rod from the lock lever and slide the retainer forward with pliers to disengage it from the lock unit. The lock can be removed from the outside.

8   Installation is the reverse of removal.

11 Door glass and window regulator - removal and installation

Refer to illustrations 11.4 and 11.7

1   Remove the trim panel as described in Section 9.

2   On models equipped with power windows, disconnect the negative battery cable from the battery.

3   Use a putty knife to completely remove the water deflector.

4   Replace the window glass by first lowering the glass until the window regulator roller is visible through the door access hole **(see illustration)**.

5   Remove the window glass retaining bolts and disengage the window regulator roller from the sash channel. Lower the glass into the door and rotate it up to remove it.

6   To replace the window regulator raise the window completely and tape both sides of the glass to the top of the door with a single piece of cloth-backed tape.

7   Remove the window regulator mounting bolts **(see illustration)**.

8   On power windows maneuver the regulator as necessary and disconnect the motor wiring harness.

9   Disengage the roller or regulator lift arm from the glass run channel.

10   Remove the regulator through the door panel access hole.

11   Installation is the reverse of removal.

12 Hood - removal, installation and adjustment

Note: *The hood is heavy and somewhat awkward to remove and install - at least two people should perform this procedure.*

Removal and installation

Refer to illustration 12.2

1   Use blankets or pads to cover the cowl area of the body and the fenders. This will protect the body and paint as the hood is lifted off.

2   Apply marks around the bolt heads to

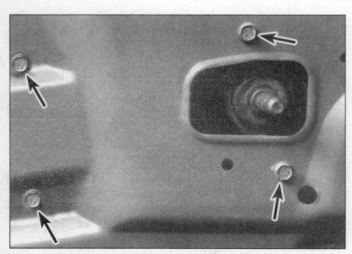

11.7 Door glass regulator bolt locations (arrows)

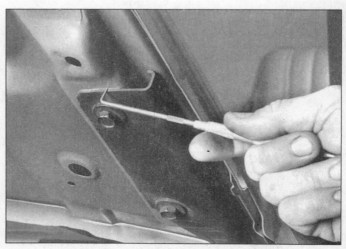

12.2 Use a scribe or marking pen to mark the location of the hood mounting plate

12.11 The hood bumpers can be screwed in or out to adjust the front edge of the hood in relation to the fenders

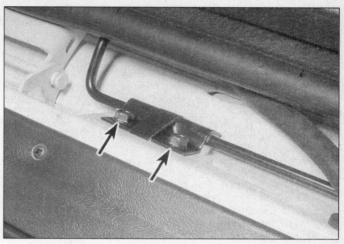

13.3 The torque rod is held in place by bolts (arrows)

insure proper alignment during installation **(see illustration).**

3   Disconnect any cables or wire harnesses which will interfere with removal.

4   Have an assistant support the weight of the hood. Remove the hinge-to-hood nuts or bolts.

5   Lift off the hood.

6   Installation is the reverse of removal.

Adjustment

Refer to illustration 12.11

7   Fore-and-aft and side-to-side adjustment of the hood is done by moving the hood in relation to the hinge plate after loosening the bolts or nuts.

8   Scribe a line around the entire hinge plate so you can judge the amount of movement **(see illustration 12.2).**

9   Loosen the bolts or nuts and move the hood into correct alignment. Move it only a little at a time. Tighten the hinge bolts or nuts and carefully lower the hood to check the alignment.

10   If necessary after installation, the entire

hood latch assembly can be adjusted up-and-down as well as from side-to-side on the radiator support so the hood closes securely and is flush with the fenders. To do this, scribe a line around the hood latch mounting bolts to provide a reference point. Then loosen the bolts and reposit on the latch assembly as necessary. Following adjustment, tighten the mounting bolts securely.

11   Finally, adjust the hood bumpers on the radiator support so the hood, when closed, is flush with the fenders **(see illustration).**

12   The hood latch assembly, as well as the hinges, should be periodically lubricated with white lithium-base grease to prevent sticking and wear.

13   Tailgate - removal and installation

Refer to illustrations 13.3 and 13.4

1   Support the tailgate in the open position.

2   Disconnect all cables and wire harness

connectors that would interfere with removal of the tailgate.

3   Detach the support cables. On later models, remove rod bolts and detach the torque rod **(see illustration).**

4   While an assistant supports the tailgate, remove the hinge pins **(see illustration).**

5   Detach the tailgate from the vehicle.

6   Installation is the reverse of removal.

14   Tailgate latch and handle - removal and installation

Refer to illustration 14.1

1   Remove the handle mounting screws from the inside **(see illustration).**

2   Detach the linkages from the retaining clips at the handle.

3   Remove the latch mounting bolts at each side.

4   Remove the latches and linkages through each side of the tailgate and liftgate.

5   Installation is the reverse of removal.

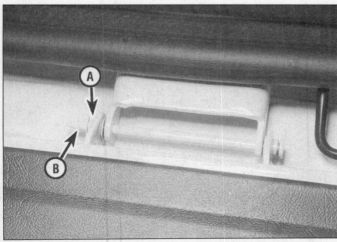

13.4 Detach the clips (A), drive the hinge pins out (B), then remove the tailgate

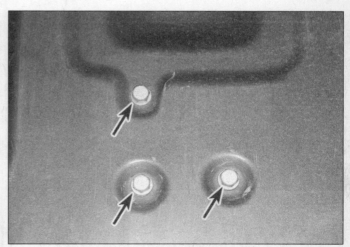

14.1 Remove the handle mounting screws (arrows)

11

15 Liftgate - removal, installation and adjustment

Refer to illustrations 15.4, 15.5 and 15.7

1   Open the liftgate and cover the upper body area around the opening with pads or cloths to protect the painted surfaces when the liftgate is removed.

2   Disconnect all cables and wire harness connectors that would interfere with removal of the liftgate.

3   Paint or scribe around the hinge flanges.

4   While an assistant supports the liftgate, detach the support struts **(see illustration)**.

5   Remove the hinge bolts and detach the liftgate from the vehicle **(see illustration)**.

6   Installation is the reverse of removal.

7   After installation, close the liftgate and make sure it's in proper alignment with the surrounding body panels. Adjustments are made by moving the position of the hinge bolts in the slots **(see illustration)**. To adjust it, loosen the hinge bolts and reposition the hinges either side-to-side or fore-and-aft the desired amount and retighten the bolts.

8   The engagement of the liftgate can be adjusted by loosening the lock striker bolts, repositioning the striker and retightening the bolts.

16 Bumpers - removal and installation

Front

Refer to illustration 16.3

1   Remove the right and left side parking lights from the housings in the bumper.

2   If equipped, remove the air deflector mounting bolts at the right and left side lower fender flanges.

3   Remove the bumper-to-frame bolts, the bumper brace-to-frame bolts and detach the bumper **(see illustration)**.

4   Installation is the reverse of removal.

Rear

5   Remove the license plate light housing(s) from the bumper and disconnect

15.4 Detach the strut clips by inserting a small screwdriver or punch here (arrow)

the lamp lead(s).

6   Remove the bumper brace-to-bumper bolts and detach the bumper.

7   Installation is the reverse of removal.

17 Grille - removal and installation

1   Remove the headlight trim frames.

2   Remove the grille mounting screws from the front of the grille.

3   Remove the grille.

4   Installation is the reverse of removal.

18 Rear cab window - removal and installation

1   Using a screwdriver from the inside of the cab, pry carefully around the weatherstrip lip, forcing the weatherstripping out. Have an assistant pull on the window assembly to remove it with the weatherstripping attached.

2   On sliding type rear windows, using a screwdriver and pliers, remove the sliding glass stopper from the channel.

3   From the channel track, remove the four screws holding the two fixed frames.

4   With the window assembly standing vertically on its lower edge, place a folded rag near the center of the window frame to

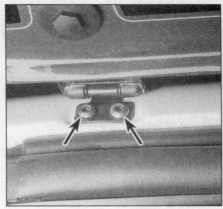

15.5 After marking the position of the hinge, remove the bolts (arrows)

protect the channel.

5   Stand on the rag with one foot and gently lift the top edge of the frame and remove the sliding windows and fixed frames.

6   Move the rag toward either end of the channel frame and remove the two non-sliding windows in the same manner.

7   To install the rear window, first transfer the weatherstripping from the non-sliding window(s) being replaced to the new window(s).

8   Apply soapy water to the contact face of the weatherstripping surrounding the glass channel and to the glass channel flange.

9   The remaining assembly steps are the reverse of those for disassembly. It is probable that the old weatherstripping has become weather-hardened and may develop water leaks. Replace the weatherstripping with new material if any such deterioration is indicated.

10   Once the rear window is assembled, apply a working cord along the weatherstripping groove.

11   Begin the installation in the center of the lower part of the glass.

12   Attach the window assembly to the body by pulling on the cord from the inside while an assistant pushes along the weatherstripping from the outside.

13   Seat the window assembly by tapping around the circumference of the glass with your open hand.

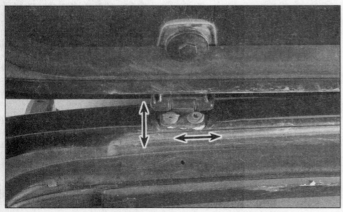

15.7 Adjust the liftgate by moving the hinge side-to-side or fore-to-aft

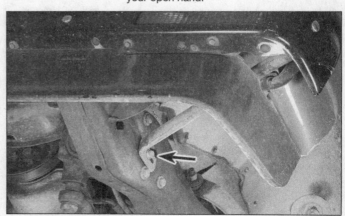

16.3 Remove the bumper brace to frame bolts (arrow) (left side shown)

Chapter 12
Chassis electrical system

Contents

	Section			Section
Bulbs - replacement	9		Instrument cluster - removal and installation	11
CHECK ENGINE light	See Chapter 6		Neutral safety and backup light switch	See Chapter 7B
Circuit breakers - general information	5		Neutral start switch	See Chapter 7A
Electrical troubleshooting - general information	2		Radio - removal and installation	10
Fuses - general information	3		Speedometer cable - replacement	12
Fusible links - general information	4		Steering column switches - removal and installation	14
General information	1		Stoplight switch - adjustment and replacement	See Chapter 9
Headlights - adjustment	8		Turn signal and hazard flashers - check and replacement	6
Headlights - removal and installation	7		Wiring diagrams - general information	15
Headlight switch - removal and installation	13			

1 General information

The electrical system is a 12-volt, negative ground type. Power for the lights and all electrical accessories is supplied by a lead/acid-type battery which is charged by the alternator.

This chapter covers repair and service procedures for the various electrical components not associated with the engine. Information on the battery, alternator, distributor and starter motor can be found in Chapter 5.

It should be noted that whenever portions of the electrical system are worked on, the negative battery cable should be disconnected to prevent electrical shorts and/or fires.

2 Electrical troubleshooting - general information

A typical electrical circuit consists of an electrical component, any switches, relays, motors, fuses, fusible links or circuit breakers related to that component and the wiring and connectors that link the component to both the battery and the chassis. To help you pinpoint an electrical circuit problem, wiring diagrams are included at the end of this book.

Before tackling any troublesome electrical circuit, first study the appropriate wiring diagrams to get a complete understanding of what makes up that individual circuit. Trouble spots, for instance, can often be narrowed down by noting if other components related to the circuit are operating properly. If several components or circuits fail at one time, chances are the problem is in a fuse or ground connection, because several circuits are often routed through the same fuse and ground connections.

Electrical problems usually stem from simple causes, such as loose or corroded connections, a blown fuse, a melted fusible link or a bad relay. Visually inspect the condition of all fuses, wires and connections in a problem circuit before troubleshooting it.

If testing instruments are going to be utilized, use the diagrams to plan ahead of time where you will make the necessary connections in order to accurately pinpoint the trouble spot.

The basic tools needed for electrical troubleshooting include a circuit tester or voltmeter (a 12-volt bulb with a set of test leads can also be used), a continuity tester, which includes a bulb, battery and set of test leads, and a jumper wire, preferably with a circuit breaker incorporated, which can be used to bypass electrical components. Before attempting to locate a problem with test instruments, use the wiring diagram(s) to decide where to make the connections.

Voltage checks

Voltage checks should be performed if a circuit is not functioning properly. Connect one lead of a circuit tester to either the negative battery terminal or a known good ground. Connect the other lead to a connector in the circuit being tested, preferably nearest to the battery or fuse. If the bulb of the tester lights, voltage is present, which means that the part of the circuit between the connector and the battery is problem free. Continue checking the rest of the circuit in the same fashion. When you reach a point at which no voltage is present, the problem lies between that point and the last test point with voltage. Most of the time the problem can be traced to a loose connection. **Note:** *Keep in mind that some circuits receive voltage only when the ignition key is in the Accessory or Run position.*

12

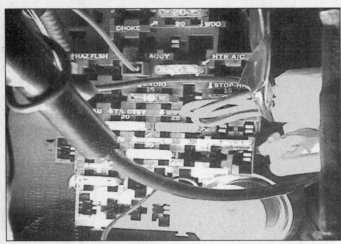

3.1 The fuse block is located under the instrument panel
to the left of the steering column

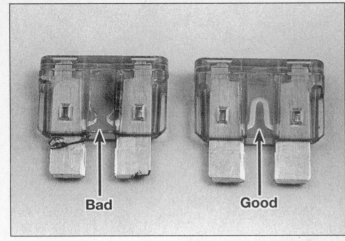

3.3 When a fuse blows, the element between the terminals melts
- the fuse on the left is blown, the fuse on the right is good

Finding a short

One method of finding shorts in a circuit is to remove the fuse and connect a test light or voltmeter in its place to the fuse terminals. There should be no voltage present in the circuit. Move the electrical harness from side-to-side while watching the test light. If the bulb goes on, there is a short to ground somewhere in that area, probably where the insulation has rubbed through. The same test can be performed on each component in the circuit, even a switch.

Ground check

Perform a ground test to check whether a component is properly grounded. Disconnect the battery and connect one lead of a self powered test light, known as a continuity tester, to a known good ground. Connect the other lead to the wire or ground connection being tested. If the bulb goes on, the ground is good. If the bulb does not go on, the ground is not good.

Continuity check

A continuity check is done to determine if there are any breaks in a circuit - if it is passing electricity properly. With the circuit off (no power in the circuit), a self-powered continuity tester can be used to check the circuit. Connect the test leads to both ends of the circuit (or to the "power" end and a good ground), and if the test light comes on the circuit is passing current properly. If the light doesn't come on, there is a break somewhere in the circuit. The same procedure can be used to test a switch, by connecting the continuity tester to the switch terminals. With the switch turned On, the test light should come on.

Finding an open circuit

When diagnosing for possible open circuits, it is often difficult to locate them by sight because oxidation or terminal misalignment are hidden by the connectors. Merely wiggling a connector on a sensor or in the electrical harness may correct the open circuit condition. Remember this when an open circuit is indicated when troubleshooting a circuit. Intermittent problems may also be caused by oxidized or loose connections.

Electrical troubleshooting is simple if you keep in mind that all electrical circuits are basically electricity running from the battery, through the wires, switches, relays, fuses and fusible links to each electrical component (light bulb, motor, etc.) and to ground, from which it is passed back to the battery. Any electrical problem is an interruption in the flow of electricity to and from the battery.

3   Fuses - general information

Refer to illustrations 3.1 and 3.3

The electrical circuits of the vehicle are protected by a combination of fuses, circuit breakers and fusible links. The fuse block is located under the instrument panel on the left side of the dashboard in the electrical harness **(see illustration)**. Later models also have a convenience center, located under the dash near the fuse block which contains certain components such as the horn relay and hazard flasher.

Each of the fuses is designed to protect a specific circuit, and the various circuits are identified on the fuse panel itself.

Miniaturized fuses are employed in the fuse block. These compact fuses, with blade terminal design, allow fingertip removal and replacement. If an electrical component fails, always check the fuse first. The best way to check the fuses is with a test light. Check for power at the exposed terminal tips of each fuse. If power is present on one side of the fuse but not the other, the fuse is blown. A blown fuse can also be confirmed by visually inspecting it **(see illustration)**.

Be sure to replace blown fuses with the correct type. Fuses of different ratings are physically interchangeable, but only fuses of the proper rating should be used. Replacing a fuse with one of a higher or lower value than specified is not recommended. Each electrical circuit needs a specific amount of protection. The amperage value of each fuse is molded into the fuse body.

If the replacement fuse immediately fails, don't replace it again until the cause of the problem is isolated and corrected. In most cases, the cause will be a short circuit in the wiring caused by a broken or deteriorated wire.

4   Fusible links - general information

On some models the circuit breaker resets itself automatically, so an electrical overload in a circuit breaker protected system will cause the circuit to fail momentarily, then come back on. If the circuit does not come back on, check it immediately. Once the condition is corrected, the circuit breaker will resume its normal function. Some circuit breakers must be reset manually.

Some circuits are protected by fusible links. The links are used in circuits which are not ordinarily fused, such as the ignition circuit.

Although the fusible links appear to be a heavier gauge than the wire they are protecting, the appearance is due to the thick insulation. All fusible links are four wire gauges smaller than the wire they are designed to protect.

Fusible links cannot be repaired, but a new link of the same size wire can be put in its place. The procedure is as follows:

a) *Disconnect the negative cable from the battery.*
b) *Disconnect the fusible link from the electrical harness.*
c) *Cut the damaged fusible link out of the wiring just behind the connector.*

7.3 Remove only the retainer screws (arrows) - do not disturb the headlight aim adjusting screws unless you're adjusting the headlights

8.1a The adjustment screw on the side of the headlight moves it left-or-right

d) Strip the insulation back approximately 1/2-inch.
e) Position the connector on the new fusible link and crimp it into place.
f) Use rosin core solder at each end of the new link to obtain a good solder joint.
g) Use plenty of electrical tape around the soldered joint. No wires should be exposed.
h) Connect the battery ground cable. Test the circuit for proper operation.

5 Circuit breakers - general information

Circuit breakers protect components such as power windows, power door locks and headlights. Some circuit breakers are located in the fuse box.

On some models the circuit breaker resets itself automatically, so an electrical overload in a circuit breaker protected system will cause the circuit to fail momentarily, then come back on. If the circuit does not come back on, check it immediately. Once the condition is corrected, the circuit breaker will resume its normal function. Some circuit breakers must be reset manually.

6 Turn signal and hazard flashers - check and replacement

Turn signal flasher

1   The turn signal flasher, a small canister-shaped unit located in the fuse block, flashes the turn signals.
2   When the flasher unit is functioning properly, an audible click can be heard during its operation. If the turn signals fail on one side or the other and the flasher unit does not make its characteristic clicking sound, a faulty turn signal bulb is indicated.
3   If both turn signals fail to blink, the prob-lem may be due to a blown fuse, a faulty flasher unit, a broken switch or a loose or open connection. If a quick check of the fuse box indicates that the turn signal fuse has blown, check the wiring for a short before installing a new fuse.
4   To replace the flasher, simply pull it out of the fuse block.
5   Make sure the replacement unit is identical to the original. Compare the old one to the new one before installing it.
6   Installation is the reverse of removal.

Hazard flasher

7   The hazard flasher, a small canister-shaped unit located in the fuse block or convenience center, flashes all four turn signals simultaneously when activated.
8   The hazard flasher is checked in a fashion similar to the turn signal flasher (see Steps 2 and 3).
9   To replace the hazard flasher, pull it from the fuse block or convenience center.
10   Make sure the replacement unit is identical to the one it replaces. Compare the old one to the new one before installing it.
11   Installation is the reverse of removal.

7 Headlights - removal and installation

Refer to illustration 7.3
1   Disconnect the negative cable from the battery.
2   Remove the retaining screws and detach the headlight bezel.
3   Remove the headlight retainer screws, taking care not to disturb the adjustment screws (see illustration).
4   Remove the retainer and pull the headlight out enough to allow the connector to be unplugged.
5   Remove the headlight.
6   To install the headlight, plug the connector in, place the headlight in position and install the retainer and screws. Tighten the screws securely.
7   Place the headlight bezel in position and install the retaining screws. Connect the negative battery cable.

8 Headlights - adjustment

Refer to illustrations 8.1a, 8.1b and 8.2
Note: The headlights must be aimed correctly. If adjusted incorrectly they could blind the driver of an oncoming vehicle and cause a serious accident or seriously reduce your ability to see the road. The headlights should be checked for proper aim every 12 months and any time a new headlight is installed or front end body work is performed. It should be emphasized that the following procedure is only an interim step which will provide temporary adjustment until the headlights can be adjusted by a properly equipped shop.
1   Headlights have two spring loaded adjusting screws, one on the top controlling up-and-down movement and one on the side controlling left-and-right movement (see illustrations).

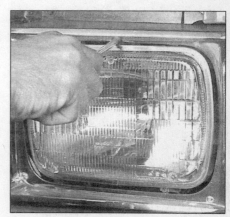

8.1b The screw at the top of the headlight adjusts it up-and-down

12

2   There are several methods of adjusting the headlights. The simplest method requires a blank wall 25 feet in front of the vehicle and a level floor **(see illustration)**.

3   Position masking tape vertically on the wall in reference to the vehicle centerline and the centerlines of both headlights.

4   Position a horizontal tape line in reference to the centerline of all the headlights. **Note:** *It may be easier to position the tape on the wall with the vehicle parked only a few inches away.*

5   Adjustment should be made with the vehicle sitting level, the gas tank half-full and no unusually heavy load in the vehicle.

6   Starting with the low beam adjustment, position the high intensity zone so it is two inches below the horizontal line and two inches to the right of the headlight vertical line. Adjustment is made by turning the top adjusting screw clockwise to raise the beam and counterclockwise to lower the beam. The adjusting screw on the side should be used in the same manner to move the beam left or right.

7   With the high beams on, the high intensity zone should be vertically centered with the exact center just below the horizontal line. **Note:** *It may not be possible to position the headlight aim exactly for both high and low beams. If a compromise must be made, keep in mind that the low beams are the most used and have the greatest effect on driver safety.*

8   Have the headlights adjusted by a dealer service department or service station at the earliest opportunity.

9   Bulbs - replacement

Refer to illustrations 9.3, 9.8 and 9.9

Front

1   The bulbs for the parking and turn signal lights are accessible from the rear of each unit.

2   Reach behind the front bumper and twist the socket out of the housing.

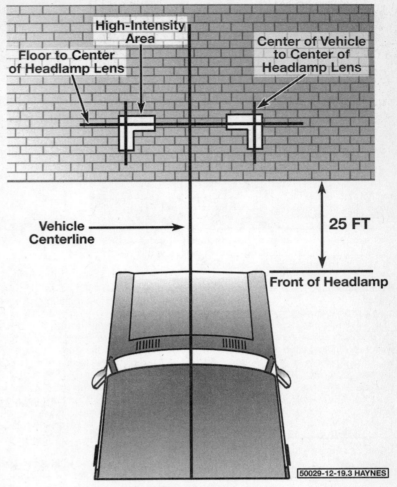

8.2 Headlight adjustment details

3   Pull the bulb out of the socket and install the replacement **(see illustration)**.

Side marker

4   The front side marker lights are accessible from under the front wheel well.

5   Turn the bulb socket counterclockwise 90-degrees to detach it.

6   Pull the bulb out of the socket and install the replacement.

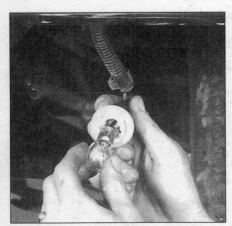

9.3 The parking/turn signal bulbs can be replaced without removing the lens assembly

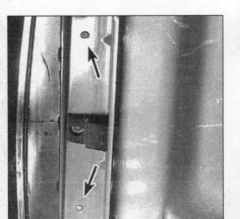

9.8 These two mounting screws for the tail light lens assembly are accessible after lowering the tailgate

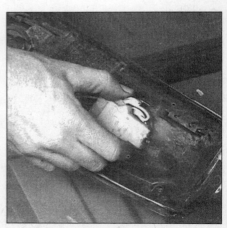

9.9 All rear light bulbs are accessible from the rear of the tail light lens assembly

10.3 Radio retaining screw locations (arrows)

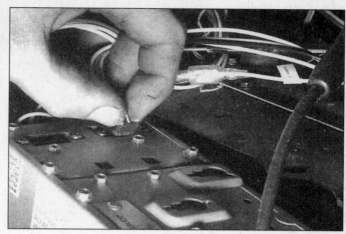

10.5 Pull the radio out and unplug the electrical connectors

11.2 Typical instrument cluster bezel mounting screws
(two are out of view on the right side)

11.3 Instrument cluster screw locations (arrows)

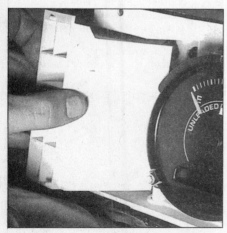

11.4 Grasp the instrument light grid
securely and detach it

Rear

7   The bulbs for the tail lights, brake lights, turn signal lights and backup lights are all accessible after removing the lens assembly.

8   Using a Torx bit screwdriver, remove the four lens assembly mounting screws. The inner two screws can be removed after lowering the tailgate **(see illustration)**.

9   Remove the appropriate bulb socket by squeezing the lock on the assembly and turning it counterclockwise, or by simply turning the socket out of the panel **(see illustration)**.

10   Pull the bulb out of the socket and install the replacement.

License plate bulb

11   Remove the screw retaining the lens/socket assembly and pull the assembly out of the bumper.

12   Twist the socket out of the lens and replace the bulb.

10   Radio - removal and installation

Refer to illustrations 10.3 and 10.5

1   Disconnect the negative cable from the battery.

2   Remove the center instrument panel bezel (a number 15 Torx bit driver may be needed on some models).

3   Remove the four mounting screws from the radio bracket and pull the radio forward **(see illustration)**.

4   Disconnect the antenna lead from the rear of the radio.

5   Disconnect the speaker and electrical connectors from the rear of the radio **(see illustration)**.

6   Installation is the reverse of removal.

11   Instrument cluster - removal and installation

Refer to illustrations 11.2, 11.3, 11.4, 11.5a, 11.5b and 11.6

1   Disconnect the negative battery cable.

2   Remove the five mounting screws from the instrument cluster trim plate and detach the trim plate **(see illustration)**.

3   Remove the four mounting screws from the instrument panel face plate and detach the face plate **(see illustration)**.

4   Remove the instrument light grid from the center of the cluster **(see illustration)**.

5   From behind the instrument cluster, reach behind the speedometer and discon-

12

11.5a Pull the speedometer out, reach behind it, then . . .

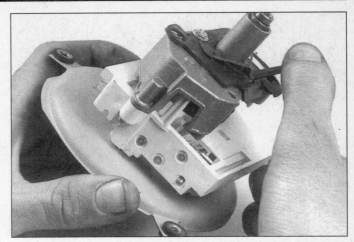

11.5b . . . press the retaining tab to disengage the cable

nect the speedometer cable by releasing the tab **(see illustrations)**.

6   Pull the instrument cluster away from the dashboard just enough to detach the "Check Engine" light bulb from the center of the instrument cluster **(see illustration)**.

7   Remove the instrument cluster from the dashboard.

8   The fuel gauge and speedometer can now be detached by removing the three mounting bolts on either component.

9   Installation is the reverse of removal.

12   Speedometer cable - replacement

1   Disconnect the cable from the negative battery terminal.

2   Disconnect the speedometer cable from the transmission or transfer case, as applicable.

3   Remove the instrument cluster as described in Section 11.

4   Slide the old cable out of the upper end of the casing, or, if broken, from both ends of the casing.

5   If speedometer operation has been noisy, but the speedometer cable appears to be in good condition, take a short piece of speedometer cable with a tip that fits the speedometer and insert it in the speedometer socket. Spin the piece of cable between your fingers. If binding is noted, the speedometer is faulty and should be replaced.

6   Inspect the speedometer cable casing for sharp bends and cracks, especially at the transmission end. If cracks are noted replace the casing with a new one.

7   When installing the cable perform the following operations to ensure quiet operation:

8   Wipe the cable clean with a lint-free cloth.

9   Flush the bore of the casing with solvent and blow it dry with compressed air.

10   Place some speedometer cable lubricant in the palm of one hand.

11   Feed the cable through the lubricant and into the casing until the lubricant has been applied to the lower two-thirds of the cable. Do not over-lubricate.

12   Seat the upper cable tip in the speedometer and snap the retainer onto the casing.

13   The remaining installation steps are the reverse of those for removal.

13   Headlight switch - removal and installation

Refer to illustrations 13.3, 13.5, 13.6 and 13.7

1   Disconnect the negative cable from the battery.

2   Disconnect the parking brake release cable from the ratchet mechanism.

3   Press in on the retaining fingers of the release cable handle and remove the handle **(see illustration)**.

4   Pull the dashboard panel insert down to gain access to the switch assembly.

5   Pull the headlight switch knob out and press in on the release button **(see illustration)**. Remove the switch knob.

6   Using needle-nose pliers, remove the switch retaining nut **(see illustration)**.

7   Disconnect the headlight switch from the electrical connector and remove the switch **(see illustration)**.

8   Installation is the reverse of removal.

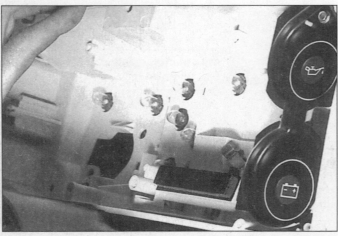

11.6 Pull the instrument cluster away just enough to detach the CHECK ENGINE light bulb

13.3 Press on the retaining fingers (arrows) to release the brake release handle cable

13.5 Headlight switch release button location (arrow)

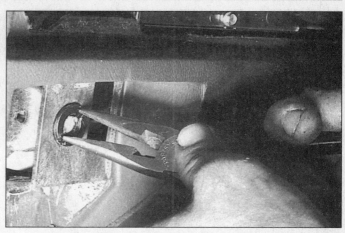

13.6 Use needle-nose pliers to unscrew the headlight switch retaining nut

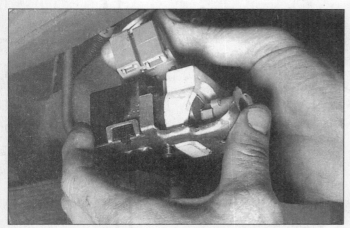

13.7 Unplug the electrical connectors from headlight switch

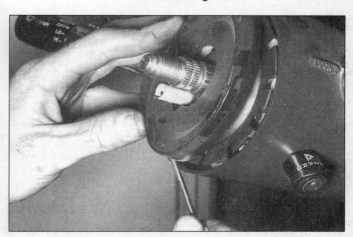

14.2 Pry the steering column lock cover off with a small screwdriver

14 Steering column switches - removal and installation

Refer to illustrations 14.2, 14.3, 14.8, 14.9, 14.11, 14.13 and 14.15

1   Disconnect the negative battery cable.

Remove the steering wheel (see Chapter 10).
2   Pry off the column lock plate cover **(see illustration)**.
3   Depress the shaft lock plate and remove the retaining clip **(see illustration)**.
4   Remove the shaft lock plate.
5   Remove the cancelling cam and spring

6   Remove the upper bearing spring and washer.
7   Remove the mounting screw from the base of the turn signal lever and detach the turn signal lever
8   Remove the hazard flasher knob **(see illustration)**.

14.3 Use a depressor tool to depress the lockplate, then pry the retaining ring out

14.8 Unscrew the hazard warning knob with a Phillips head screwdriver

14.9 Turn signal switch mounting screw locations (arrows)

14.11 Ignition lock cylinder screw location (arrow)

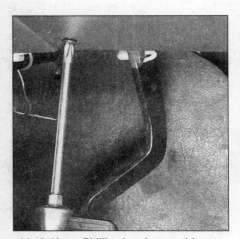

14.13 Use a Phillips head screwdriver to remove the steering column trim cover

14.15 Unplug the turn signal switch harness at the base of the steering column

9   Remove the three screws and detach the turn signal switch assembly **(see illustration)**.
10   If the switch is not being replaced, it can be left hanging from the steering column.
11   To remove the ignition lock cylinder, first remove the switch retaining screw **(see illustration)**.
12   Turn the ignition switch to the Run position and pull the lock cylinder out. Installation is the reverse of removal.

13   To replace the turn signal switch assembly, remove the column trim cover **(see illustration)**.
14   Remove the four bolts and two nuts from the steering column-to-dashboard bracket, to release the electrical harness.
15   Disconnect the switch electrical harness at the lower end of the column and attach a length of wire to the pigtail to pull the pigtail back through during installation **(see illustration)**.

16   Remove the switch and electrical harness from the steering column.
17   Install the new switch, attach the wire to the new pigtail and pull it into position. Remove the wire and plug in the electrical connector.
18   Install the bracket nuts and the four bolts.
19   The remainder of installation is the reverse of removal. Tighten the steering column nuts/bolts to the torque values listed in the Chapter 10 Specifications.

15   Wiring diagrams - general information

Since it isn't possible to include all wiring diagrams for every year covered by this manual, the following diagrams are those that are typical and most commonly needed.

Prior to troubleshooting any circuits, check the fuse and circuit breakers (if equipped) to make sure they're in good condition. Make sure the battery is properly charged and check the cable connections (see Chapter 1).

When checking a circuit, make sure that all connectors are clean, with no broken or loose terminals. When unplugging a connector, do not pull on the wires. Pull only on the connector housings themselves.

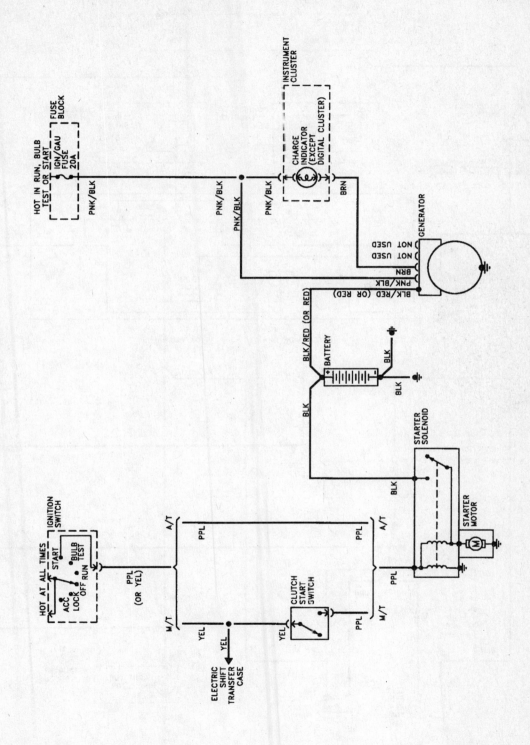

Starting and charging system

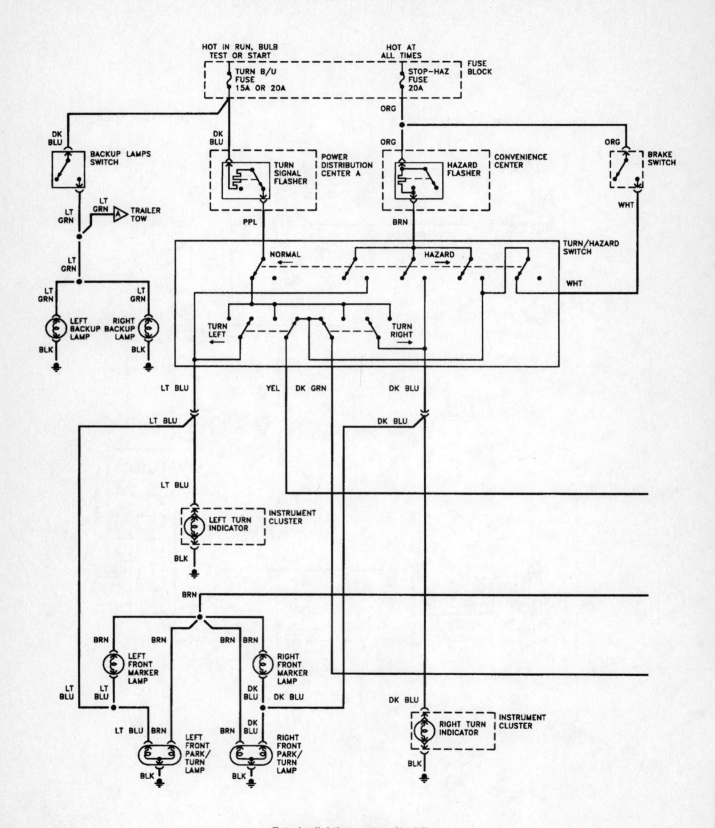

Exterior lighting system (1 of 2)

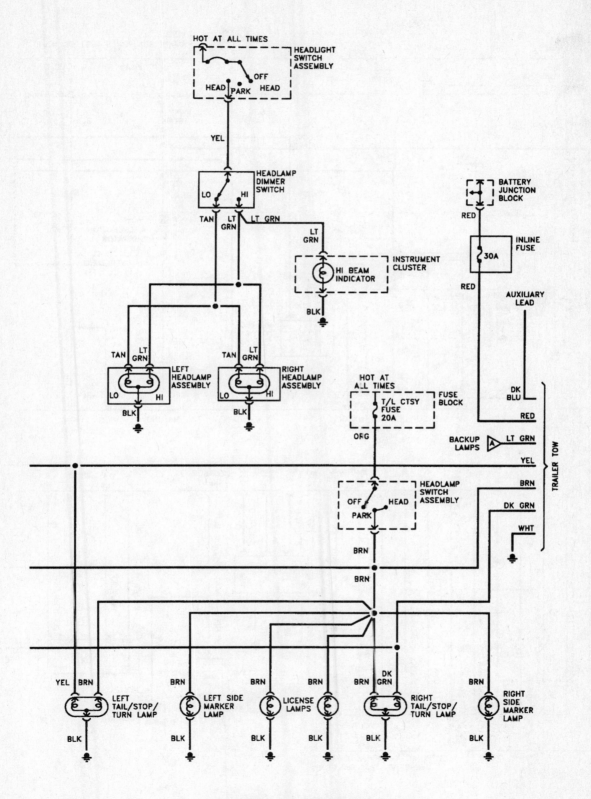

Exterior lighting system (2 of 2)

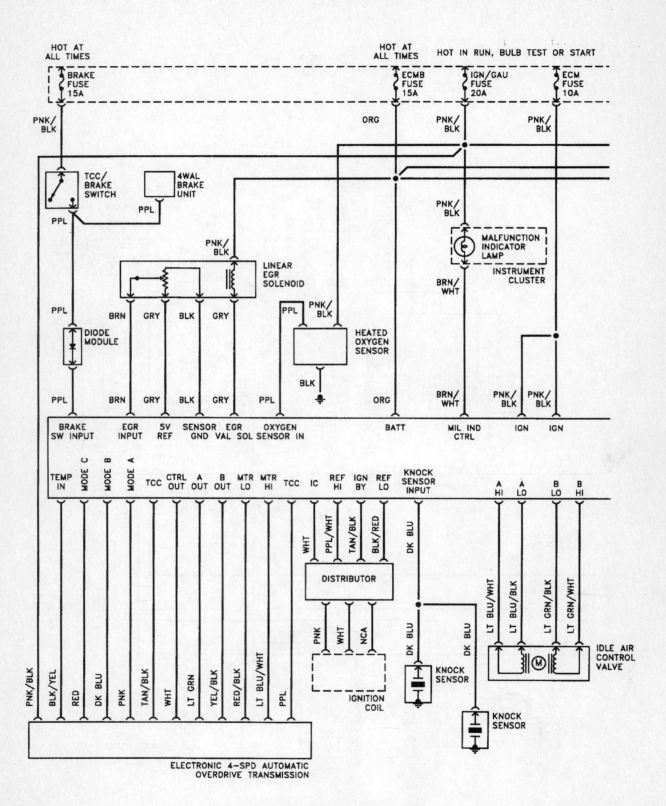

1992 and later engine controls (1 of 2)

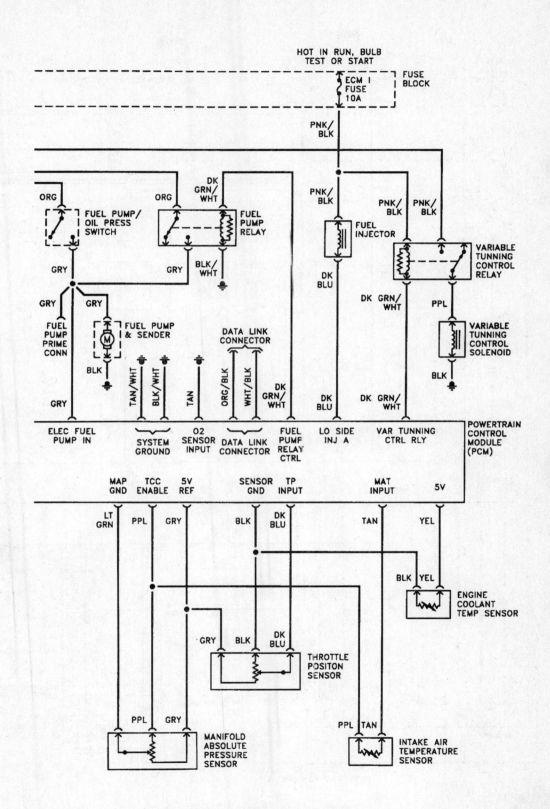

1992 and later engine controls (2 of 2)

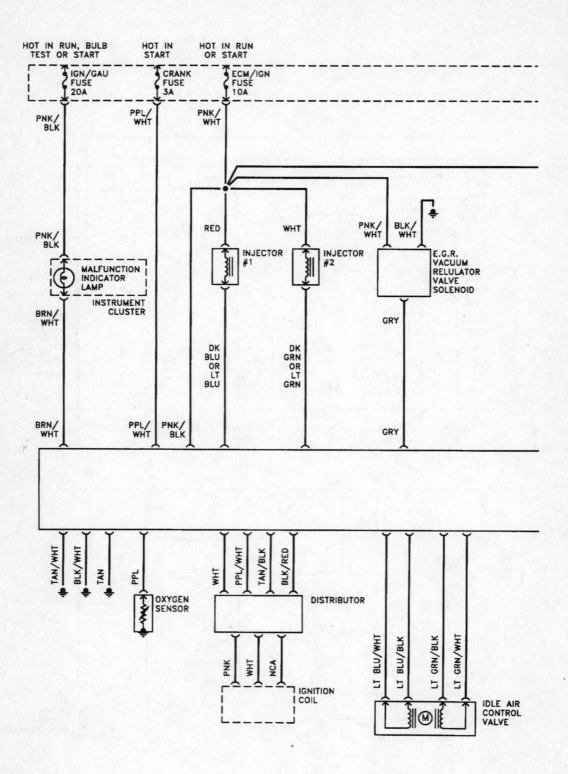

1991 and earlier engine controls (1 of 2)

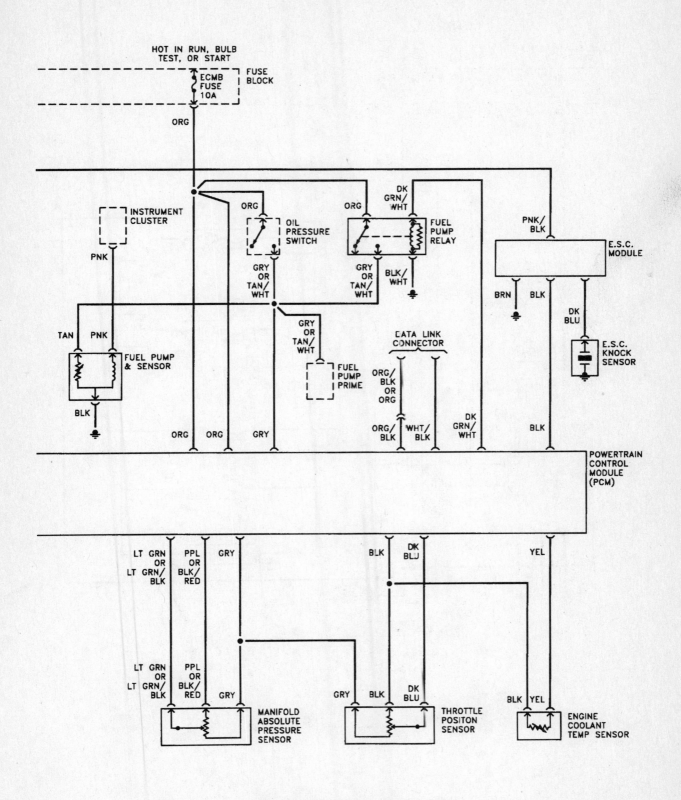

1991 and earlier engine controls (2 of 2)

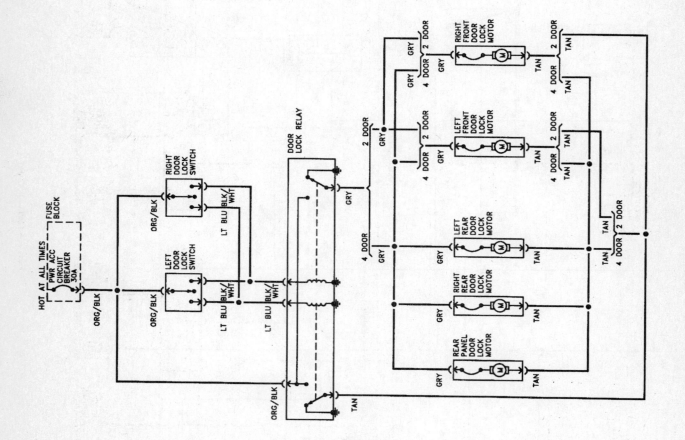

Power door lock system

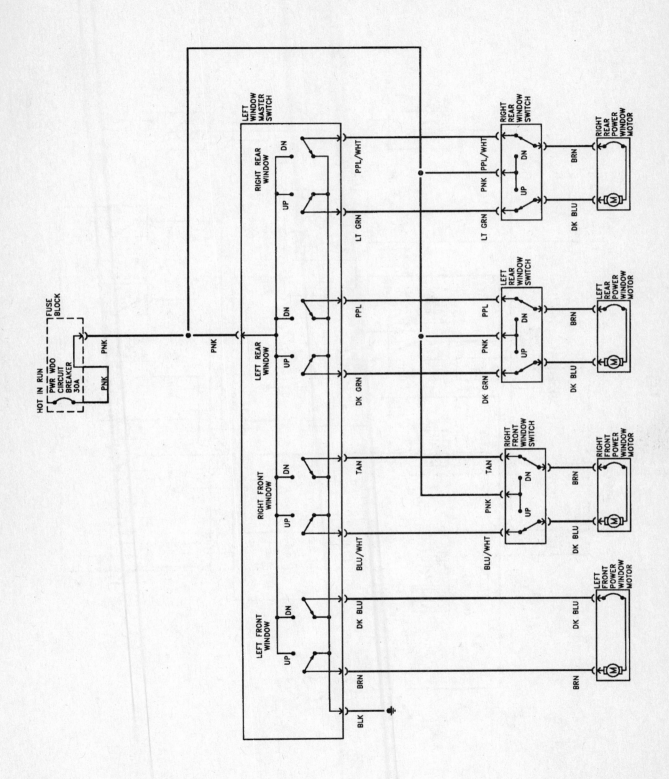

Power window system

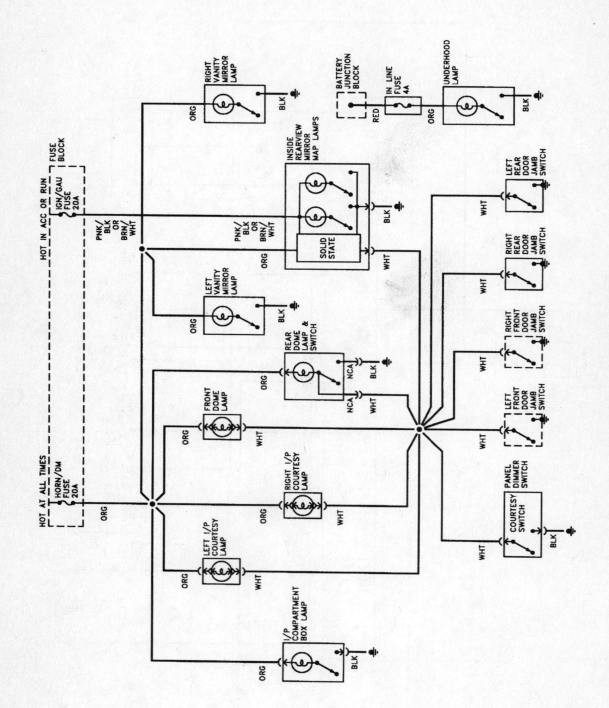

1992 and later interior lighting system

Shifter, removal and installation, 7C-1
Shock absorber, removal and installation
    front, 10-4
    rear, 10-4
Spark plug
    replacement, 1-31
    wires, distributor cap and rotor check and
        replacement, 1-32
Speed sensor, 9-18
Speedometer
    cable, replacement, 12-6
    driven gear oil seal, replacement, manual
        transmission, 7A-3
Stabilizer bar, removal and installation, 10-5
Starter
    motor
        brushes, replacement, 5-11
        removal and installation, 5-10
        testing in vehicle, 5-10
    solenoid, removal and installation, 5-11
Starting system, general information, 5-10
**Steering column switches, removal
and installation, 12-7**
Steering damper, 10-12
Steering system
    column switches, removal and installation, 10-14
    general information, 10-11
    power steering
        gear, removal and installation, 10-13
        pump, removal and installation, 10-13
        system
            bleeding, 10-13
            general information, 10-13
    steering linkage, inspection, removal and
        installation, 10-11
        idler arm, 10-12
        Pitman arm, 10-12
        relay rod, 10-12
        steering damper, 10-12
        tie-rod, 10-11
    wheel, removal and installation, 10-14
**Stop light switch, removal, installation and
adjustment, 9-16**
Suspension and steering check, 1-17
Suspension and steering systems, 10-1 through 10-16
Suspension system
    coil springs, front (2WD models), removal and
        installation, 10-8
    control arms
        lower, removal and installation
            2WD models, 10-8
            4WD models, 10-8
        upper, removal and installation, 10-7
    front suspension, general information, 10-4
        2WD models, 10-4
        4WD models, 10-4
    leaf spring, rear, removal and installation, 10-10
    shock absorber
        front, removal and installation, 10-4
        rear, removal and installation, 10-4
    stabilizer bar, removal and installation, 10-5
    steering knuckle and balljoints (2WD models),
        removal and installation, 10-5
    steering knuckle, balljoints and front wheel bearing
        (hub) assembly (4WD models), removal and
        installation, 10-6
    torsion bar (4WD models), removal
        and installation, 10-8

T

Tailgate
    latch and handle, removal and installation, 11-7
    removal and installation, 11-7
**Thermo-controlled Air Cleaner (TAC) check
(carbureted and TBI models only), 1-21**
Thermostat
    bench-testing the thermostat, 3-4
    check and replacement
        1.9L four-cylinder engine, 3-2
        2.0L and 2.5L four-cylinder engines, 3-3
        V6 engines, 3-4
    on-vehicle check, 3-2
**Thermostatic Air Cleaner (THERMAC) (Carbureted
and TBI only), 6-18**
Throttle linkage check, 1-21
Throttle Position Sensor (TPS), 6-12
**Throttle valve (TV) cable assembly, description
and adjustment, 7B-3**
Tie-rod, removal and installation, 10-11
Timing chain
    and sprockets, inspection, removal and installation
        1.9L four-cylinder engine, 2A-4
        2.0L four-cylinder engine, 2B-6
        2.8L V6 engine, 2D-10
        4.3L V6 engine, 2E-12
Timing cover seal, replacement
    1.9L four-cylinder engine, 2A-4
    2.0L four-cylinder engine, 2B-5
    2.5L four-cylinder engine, 2C-10
    2.8L V6 engine, 2D-10
    4.3L V6 engine, 2E-16
Tire and tire pressure checks, 1-8
Tire rotation, 1-23
Tools, 0-11
Top Dead Center (TDC) for number 1 piston, locating
    four-cylinder engines, 2C-11
    V6 engines, 2E-11
**Torsion bar (4WD models), removal
and installation, 10-8**

Transfer case, 7C-1 through 7C-6
    disassembly, inspection and reassembly, 7C-3
    identification number, 0-7
    lubricant change, 1-24
    removal and installation, 7C-2
    shift linkage, adjustment, 7C-2
    shifter, removal and installation, 7C-1
Transmission
    automatic, 7B-1 through 7B-4
        diagnosis, general, 7B-1
        fluid and filter change, 1-23
        fluid leak diagnosis, 7B-2
        general information, 7B-1
        neutral safety and back-up light switch,
            replacement and adjustment, 7B-3
        removal and installation, 7B-3
        shift linkage, check and adjustment, 7B-2
        Throttle valve (TV) cable assembly, description
            and adjustment, 7B-3
    manual, 7A-1 through 7A-4
        clutch start switch, check, replacement and
            adjustment, 7A-3
        extension housing oil seal, replacement, 7A-3
        general information, 7A-1
        lubricant change, 1-24
        mount, check and replacement, 7A-1
        overhaul, general information, 7A-3
        removal and installation, 7A-2
        shift lever, removal and installation, 7A-2
        speedometer driven gear oil seal, replacement, 7A-3
Transmission Converter Clutch (TCC), 6-20
Trouble codes, 6-7
Troubleshooting, 0-21
Tune-up and routine maintenance, 1-1 through 1-34
Tune-up general information, 1-8
    major tune-up, 1-8
    minor tune-up, 1-8
Turn signal and hazard flashers, check and
    replacement, 12-3

U

Underbody flushing, 1-34
Underhood hose check and replacement, 1-15
Universal joints
    disassembly, inspection and reassembly, 8-7
    wear check, 8-6
Upholstery and carpets, maintenance, 11-1

V

Valve clearance adjustment (1.9 liter engine only), 1-33
Valve cover, removal and installation
    1.9L four-cylinder engine, 2A-3
    2.0L four-cylinder engine, 2B-3
    2.5L four-cylinder engine, 2C-3
    2.8L V6 engine, 2D-2
    4.3L V6 engine, 2E-2
Valve lash, adjustment
    1.9L four-cylinder engine, 1-33
    2.0L four-cylinder engine, 2B-4
    2.8L V6 engine, 2D-5
Valve springs, retainers and seals, replacement
    1.9L four-cylinder engine, 2A-3
    2.0L four-cylinder engine, 2B-3
    2.5L four-cylinder engine, 2C-3
    2.8L V6 engine, 2D-3
    4.3L V6 engine, 2E-4
Valves, servicing, 2F-13
Vehicle identification numbers, 0-6
    axle/differential numbers, 0-7
    certification label, 0-6
    engine identification number, 0-6
    service parts identification label, 0-6
    transfer case identification number, 0-7
    transmission identification number, 0-7
    Vehicle Emissions Control Information (VECI) label, 0-7
Vehicle Speed Sensor (VSS), 6-12
Vibration damper, removal and installation,
    2.8L V6 engine, 2D-9
Vinyl trim, maintenance, 11-1

W

Water pump
    check, 3-5
    removal and installation, 3-6
Wheel
    bearing check and repack (2WD models only), 1-25
    cylinder (drum brakes), removal, overhaul and
        installation, 9-11
    steering, removal and installation, 10-14
Windshield
    and fixed glass, replacement, 11-3
    wiper blade inspection and replacement, 1-15
Wiring diagrams, general information, 12-8
Working facilities, 0-15

Haynes Automotive Manuals

ACURA
*12020 Integra '86 thru '89 & Legend '86 thru '90

AMC
Jeep CJ - see JEEP (50020)
14020 Mid-size models, Concord, Hornet, Gremlin & Spirit '70 thru '83
14025 (Renault) Alliance & Encore '83 thru '87

AUDI
15020 4000 all models '80 thru '87
15025 5000 all models '77 thru '83
15026 5000 all models '84 thru '88

AUSTIN-HEALEY
Sprite - see MG Midget (66015)

BMW
*18020 3/5 Series not including diesel or all-wheel drive models '82 thru '92
*18021 3 Series except 325iX models '92 thru '97
18025 320i all 4 cyl models '75 thru '83
18035 528i & 530i all models '75 thru '80
18050 1500 thru 2002 except Turbo '59 thru '77

BUICK
Century (front wheel drive) - see GM (829)
*19020 Buick, Oldsmobile & Pontiac Full-size (Front wheel drive) all models '85 thru '98
Buick Electra, LeSabre and Park Avenue;
Oldsmobile Delta 88 Royale, Ninety Eight and Regency; Pontiac Bonneville
19025 Buick Oldsmobile & Pontiac Full-size (Rear wheel drive)
Buick Estate '70 thru '90, Electra'70 thru '84, LeSabre '70 thru '85, Limited '74 thru '79
Oldsmobile Custom Cruiser '70 thru '90, Delta 88 '70 thru '85,Ninety-eight '70 thru '84
Pontiac Bonneville '70 thru '81, Catalina '70 thru '81, Grandville '70 thru '75, Parisienne '83 thru '86
19030 Mid-size Regal & Century all rear-drive models with V6, V8 and Turbo '74 thru '87
Regal - see GENERAL MOTORS (38010)
Riviera - see GENERAL MOTORS (38030)
Roadmaster - see CHEVROLET (24046)
Skyhawk - see GENERAL MOTORS (38015)
Skylark '80 thru '85 - see GM (38020)
Skylark '86 on - see GM (38025)
Somerset - see GENERAL MOTORS (38025)

CADILLAC
*21030 Cadillac Rear Wheel Drive all gasoline models '70 thru '93
Cimarron - see GENERAL MOTORS (38015)
Eldorado - see GENERAL MOTORS (38030)
Seville '80 thru '85 - see GM (38030)

CHEVROLET
*24010 Astro & GMC Safari Mini-vans '85 thru '93
24015 Camaro V8 all models '70 thru '81
24016 Camaro all models '82 thru '92
Cavalier - see GENERAL MOTORS (38015)
Celebrity - see GENERAL MOTORS (38005)
24017 Camaro & Firebird '93 thru '97
24020 Chevelle, Malibu & El Camino '69 thru '87
24024 Chevette & Pontiac T1000 '76 thru '87
Citation - see GENERAL MOTORS (38020)
*24032 Corsica/Beretta all models '87 thru '96
24040 Corvette all V8 models '68 thru '82
*24041 Corvette all models '84 thru '96
10305 Chevrolet Engine Overhaul Manual
24045 Full-size Sedans Caprice, Impala, Biscayne, Bel Air & Wagons '69 thru '90
24046 Impala SS & Caprice and Buick Roadmaster '91 thru '96
Lumina - see GENERAL MOTORS (38010)

24048 Lumina & Monte Carlo '95 thru '98
Lumina APV - see GM (38035)
24050 Luv Pick-up all 2WD & 4WD '72 thru '82
*24055 Monte Carlo all models '70 thru '88
Monte Carlo '95 thru '98 - see LUMINA (24048)
24059 Nova all V8 models '69 thru '79
*24060 Nova and Geo Prizm '85 thru '92
24064 Pick-ups '67 thru '87 - Chevrolet & GMC, all V8 & in-line 6 cyl, 2WD & 4WD '67 thru '87; Suburbans, Blazers & Jimmys '67 thru '91
*24065 Pick-ups '88 thru '98 - Chevrolet & GMC, all full-size pick-ups, '88 thru '98; Blazer & Jimmy '92 thru '94; Suburban '92 thru '98; Tahoe & Yukon '98
24070 S-10 & S-15 Pick-ups '82 thru '93, Blazer & Jimmy '83 thru '94,
*24071 S-10 & S-15 Pick-ups '94 thru '96 Blazer & Jimmy '95 thru '96
*24075 Sprint & Geo Metro '85 thru '94
*24080 Vans - Chevrolet & GMC, V8 & in-line 6 cylinder models '68 thru '96

CHRYSLER
25015 Chrysler Cirrus, Dodge Stratus, Plymouth Breeze '95 thru '98
25025 Chrysler Concorde, New Yorker & LHS, Dodge Intrepid, Eagle Vision, '93 thru '97
10310 Chrysler Engine Overhaul Manual
*25020 Full-size Front-Wheel Drive '88 thru '93
K-Cars - see DODGE Aries (30008)
Laser - see DODGE Daytona (30030)
*25030 Chrysler & Plymouth Mid-size front wheel drive '82 thru '95
Rear-wheel Drive - see Dodge (30050)

DATSUN
28005 200SX all models '80 thru '83
28007 B-210 all models '73 thru '78
28009 210 all models '79 thru '82
28012 240Z, 260Z & 280Z Coupe '70 thru '78
28014 280ZX Coupe & 2+2 '79 thru '83
300ZX - see NISSAN (72010)
28016 310 all models '78 thru '82
28018 510 & PL521 Pick-up '68 thru '73
28020 510 all models '78 thru '81
28022 620 Series Pick-up all models '73 thru '79
720 Series Pick-up - see NISSAN (72030)
28025 810/Maxima all gasoline models, '77 thru '84

DODGE
400 & 600 - see CHRYSLER (25030)
*30008 Aries & Plymouth Reliant '81 thru '89
30010 Caravan & Plymouth Voyager Mini-Vans all models '84 thru '95
*30011 Caravan & Plymouth Voyager Mini-Vans all models '96 thru '98
30012 Challenger/Plymouth Saporro '78 thru '83
30016 Colt & Plymouth Champ (front wheel drive) all models '78 thru '87
*30020 Dakota Pick-ups all models '87 thru '96
30025 Dart, Demon, Plymouth Barracuda, Duster & Valiant 6 cyl models '67 thru '76
*30030 Daytona & Chrysler Laser '84 thru '89
Intrepid - see CHRYSLER (25025)
*30034 Neon all models '95 thru '97
*30035 Omni & Plymouth Horizon '78 thru '90
*30040 Pick-ups all full-size models '74 thru '93
*30041 Pick-ups all full-size models '94 thru '96
*30045 Ram 50/D50 Pick-ups & Raider and Plymouth Arrow Pick-ups '79 thru '93
30050 Dodge/Plymouth/Chrysler rear wheel drive '71 thru '89
*30055 Shadow & Plymouth Sundance '87 thru '94
*30060 Spirit & Plymouth Acclaim '89 thru '95
*30065 Vans - Dodge & Plymouth '71 thru '96

EAGLE
Talon - see Mitsubishi Eclipse (68030)
Vision - see CHRYSLER (25025)

FIAT
34010 124 Sport Coupe & Spider '68 thru '78
34025 X1/9 all models '74 thru '80

FORD
10355 Ford Automatic Transmission Overhaul
*36004 Aerostar Mini-vans all models '86 thru '96
*36006 Contour & Mercury Mystique '95 thru '98
36008 Courier Pick-up all models '72 thru '82
36012 Crown Victoria & Mercury Grand Marquis '88 thru '96
10320 Ford Engine Overhaul Manual
36016 Escort/Mercury Lynx all models '81 thru '90
*36020 Escort/Mercury Tracer '91 thru '96
*36024 Explorer & Mazda Navajo '91 thru '95
36028 Fairmont & Mercury Zephyr '78 thru '83
36030 Festiva & Aspire '88 thru '97
36032 Fiesta all models '77 thru '80
36036 Ford & Mercury Full-size, Ford LTD & Mercury Marquis ('75 thru '82); Ford Custom 500,Country Squire, Crown Victoria & Mercury Colony Park ('75 thru '87); Ford LTD Crown Victoria & Mercury Gran Marquis ('83 thru '87)
36040 Granada & Mercury Monarch '75 thru '80
36044 Ford & Mercury Mid-size, Ford Thunderbird & Mercury Cougar ('75 thru '82); Ford LTD & Mercury Marquis ('83 thru '86); Ford Torino,Gran Torino, Elite, Ranchero pick-up, LTD II, Mercury Montego, Comet, XR-7 & Lincoln Versailles ('75 thru '86)
36048 Mustang V8 all models '64-1/2 thru '73
36049 Mustang II 4 cyl, V6 & V8 models '74 thru '78
36050 Mustang & Mercury Capri all models Mustang, '79 thru '93; Capri, '79 thru '86
*36051 Mustang all models '94 thru '97
36054 Pick-ups & Bronco '73 thru '79
36058 Pick-ups & Bronco '80 thru '96
36059 Pick-ups, Expedition & Mercury Navigator '97 thru '98
36062 Pinto & Mercury Bobcat '75 thru '80
36066 Probe all models '89 thru '92
36070 Ranger/Bronco II gasoline models '83 thru '92
*36071 Ranger '93 thru '97 & Mazda Pick-ups '94 thru '97
36074 Taurus & Mercury Sable '86 thru '95
*36075 Taurus & Mercury Sable '96 thru '98
*36078 Tempo & Mercury Topaz '84 thru '94
36082 Thunderbird/Mercury Cougar '83 thru '88
*36086 Thunderbird/Mercury Cougar '89 and '97
36090 Vans all V8 Econoline models '69 thru '91
*36094 Vans full size '92-'95
*36097 Windstar Mini-van '95-'98

GENERAL MOTORS
*10360 GM Automatic Transmission Overhaul
*38005 Buick Century, Chevrolet Celebrity, Oldsmobile Cutlass Ciera & Pontiac 6000 all models '82 thru '96
*38010 Buick Regal, Chevrolet Lumina, Oldsmobile Cutlass Supreme & Pontiac Grand Prix front-wheel drive models '88 thru '95
*38015 Buick Skyhawk, Cadillac Cimarron, Chevrolet Cavalier, Oldsmobile Firenza & Pontiac J-2000 & Sunbird '82 thru '94
*38016 Chevrolet Cavalier & Pontiac Sunfire '95 thru '98
38020 Buick Skylark, Chevrolet Citation, Olds Omega, Pontiac Phoenix '80 thru '85
38025 Buick Skylark & Somerset, Oldsmobile Achieva & Calais and Pontiac Grand Am all models '85 thru '95
38030 Cadillac Eldorado '71 thru '85, Seville '80 thru '85, Oldsmobile Toronado '71 thru '85 & Buick Riviera '79 thru '85
*38035 Chevrolet Lumina APV, Olds Silhouette & Pontiac Trans Sport all models '90 thru '95
General Motors Full-size Rear-wheel Drive - see BUICK (19025)

(Continued on other side)

Haynes North America, Inc., 861 Lawrence Drive, Newbury Park, CA 91320-1514 • (805) 498-6703

Haynes Automotive Manuals (continued)

NOTE: New manuals are added to this list on a periodic basis. If you do not see a listing for your vehicle, consult your local Haynes dealer for the latest product information.

GEO

Metro - *see CHEVROLET Sprint (24075)*
Prizm - *'85 thru '92 see CHEVY (24060), '93 thru '96 see TOYOTA Corolla (92036)*
*40030 **Storm** all models '90 thru '93
Tracker - *see SUZUKI Samurai (90010)*

GMC

Safari - *see CHEVROLET ASTRO (24010)*
Vans & Pick-ups - *see CHEVROLET*

HONDA

42010 **Accord CVCC** all models '76 thru '83
42011 **Accord** all models '84 thru '89
42012 **Accord** all models '90 thru '93
42013 **Accord** all models '94 thru '95
42020 **Civic 1200** all models '73 thru '79
42021 **Civic 1300 & 1500 CVCC** '80 thru '83
42022 **Civic 1500 CVCC** all models '75 thru '79
42023 **Civic** all models '84 thru '91
*42024 **Civic & del Sol** '92 thru '95
*42040 **Prelude CVCC** all models '79 thru '89

HYUNDAI

*43015 **Excel** all models '86 thru '94

ISUZU

Hombre - *see CHEVROLET S-10 (24071)*
*47017 **Rodeo** '91 thru '97; **Amigo** '89 thru '94; **Honda Passport** '95 thru '97
*47020 **Trooper & Pick-up**, all gasoline models Pick-up, '81 thru '93; Trooper, '84 thru '91

JAGUAR

*49010 **XJ6** all 6 cyl models '68 thru '86
*49011 **XJ6** all models '88 thru '94
*49015 **XJ12 & XJS** all 12 cyl models '72 thru '85

JEEP

*50010 **Cherokee, Comanche & Wagoneer Limited** all models '84 thru '96
50020 **CJ** all models '49 thru '86
*50025 **Grand Cherokee** all models '93 thru '98
50029 **Grand Wagoneer & Pick-up** '72 thru '91 Grand Wagoneer '84 thru '91, Cherokee & Wagoneer '72 thru '83, Pick-up '72 thru '88
*50030 **Wrangler** all models '87 thru '95

LINCOLN

Navigator - *see FORD Pick-up (36059)*
59010 **Rear Wheel Drive** all models '70 thru '96

MAZDA

61010 **GLC Hatchback (rear wheel drive)** '77 thru '83
61011 **GLC (front wheel drive)** '81 thru '85
*61015 **323 & Protegé** '90 thru '97
*61016 **MX-5 Miata** '90 thru '97
*61020 **MPV** all models '89 thru '94
Navajo - *see Ford Explorer (36024)*
61030 **Pick-ups** '72 thru '93
Pick-ups '94 thru '96 - *see Ford Ranger (36071)*
61035 **RX-7** all models '79 thru '85
*61036 **RX-7** all models '86 thru '91
61040 **626 (rear wheel drive)** all models '79 thru '82
*61041 **626/MX-6 (front wheel drive)** '83 thru '91

MERCEDES-BENZ

63012 **123 Series Diesel** '76 thru '85
*63015 **190 Series** four-cyl gas models, '84 thru '88
63020 **230/250/280** 6 cyl sohc models '68 thru '72
63025 **280 123 Series** gasoline models '77 thru '81
63030 **350 & 450** all models '71 thru '80

MERCURY

See FORD Listing.

MG

66010 **MGB** Roadster & GT Coupe '62 thru '80
66015 **MG Midget, Austin Healey Sprite** '58 thru '80

MITSUBISHI

*68020 **Cordia, Tredia, Galant, Precis & Mirage** '83 thru '93
*68030 **Eclipse, Eagle Talon & Ply. Laser** '90 thru '94
*68040 **Pick-up** '83 thru '96 & **Montero** '83 thru '93

NISSAN

72010 **300ZX** all models including Turbo '84 thru '89
*72015 **Altima** all models '93 thru '97
*72020 **Maxima** all models '85 thru '91
*72030 **Pick-ups** '80 thru '96 **Pathfinder** '87 thru '95
72040 **Pulsar** all models '83 thru '86
*72050 **Sentra** all models '82 thru '94
*72051 **Sentra & 200SX** all models '95 thru '98
*72060 **Stanza** all models '82 thru '90

OLDSMOBILE

*73015 **Cutlass** V6 & V8 gas models '74 thru '88
For other OLDSMOBILE titles, see BUICK, CHEVROLET or GENERAL MOTORS listing.

PLYMOUTH

For PLYMOUTH titles, see DODGE listing.

PONTIAC

79008 **Fiero** all models '84 thru '88
79018 **Firebird** V8 models except Turbo '70 thru '81
79019 **Firebird** all models '82 thru '92
For other PONTIAC titles, see BUICK, CHEVROLET or GENERAL MOTORS listing.

PORSCHE

*80020 **911** except Turbo & Carrera 4 '65 thru '89
80025 **914** all 4 cyl models '69 thru '76
80030 **924** all models including Turbo '76 thru '82
*80035 **944** all models including Turbo '83 thru '89

RENAULT

Alliance & Encore - *see AMC (14020)*

SAAB

*84010 **900** all models including Turbo '79 thru '88

SATURN

87010 **Saturn** all models '91 thru '96

SUBARU

89002 **1100, 1300, 1400 & 1600** '71 thru '79
*89003 **1600 & 1800** 2WD & 4WD '80 thru '94

SUZUKI

*90010 **Samurai/Sidekick & Geo Tracker** '86 thru '96

TOYOTA

92005 **Camry** all models '83 thru '91
92006 **Camry** all models '92 thru '96
92015 **Celica Rear Wheel Drive** '71 thru '85
*92020 **Celica Front Wheel Drive** '86 thru '93
92025 **Celica Supra** all models '79 thru '92
92030 **Corolla** all models '75 thru '79
92032 **Corolla** all rear wheel drive models '80 thru '87
92035 **Corolla** all front wheel drive models '84 thru '92
*92036 **Corolla & Geo Prizm** '93 thru '97
92040 **Corolla Tercel** all models '80 thru '82
92045 **Corona** all models '74 thru '82
92050 **Cressida** all models '78 thru '82
92055 **Land Cruiser** FJ40, 43, 45, 55 '68 thru '82
92056 **Land Cruiser** FJ60, 62, 80, FZJ80 '80 thru '96
*92065 **MR2** all models '85 thru '87
92070 **Pick-up** all models '69 thru '78
*92075 **Pick-up** all models '79 thru '95
*92076 **Tacoma** '95 thru '98, **4Runner** '96 thru '98, & **T100** '93 thru '98
*92080 **Previa** all models '91 thru '95
92085 **Tercel** all models '87 thru '94

TRIUMPH

94007 **Spitfire** all models '62 thru '81
94010 **TR7** all models '75 thru '81

VW

96008 **Beetle & Karmann Ghia** '54 thru '79
96012 **Dasher** all gasoline models '74 thru '81
*96016 **Rabbit, Jetta, Scirocco, & Pick-up** gas models '74 thru '91 & Convertible '80 thru '92
96017 **Golf & Jetta** all models '93 thru '97
96020 **Rabbit, Jetta & Pick-up** diesel '77 thru '84
96030 **Transporter 1600** all models '68 thru '79
96035 **Transporter 1700, 1800 & 2000** '72 thru '79
96040 **Type 3 1500 & 1600** all models '63 thru '73
96045 **Vanagon** all air-cooled models '80 thru '83

VOLVO

97010 **120, 130 Series & 1800 Sports** '61 thru '73
97015 **140 Series** all models '66 thru '74
*97020 **240 Series** all models '76 thru '93
97025 **260 Series** all models '75 thru '82
*97040 **740 & 760 Series** all models '82 thru '88

TECHBOOK MANUALS

10205 **Automotive Computer Codes**
10210 **Automotive Emissions Control Manual**
10215 **Fuel Injection Manual, 1978 thru 1985**
10220 **Fuel Injection Manual, 1986 thru 1996**
10225 **Holley Carburetor Manual**
10230 **Rochester Carburetor Manual**
10240 **Weber/Zenith/Stromberg/SU Carburetors**
10305 **Chevrolet Engine Overhaul Manual**
10310 **Chrysler Engine Overhaul Manual**
10320 **Ford Engine Overhaul Manual**
10330 **GM and Ford Diesel Engine Repair Manual**
10340 **Small Engine Repair Manual**
10345 **Suspension, Steering & Driveline Manual**
10355 **Ford Automatic Transmission Overhaul**
10360 **GM Automatic Transmission Overhaul**
10405 **Automotive Body Repair & Painting**
10410 **Automotive Brake Manual**
10415 **Automotive Detailing Manual**
10420 **Automotive Eelectrical Manual**
10425 **Automotive Heating & Air Conditioning**
10430 **Automotive Reference Manual & Dictionary**
10435 **Automotive Tools Manual**
10440 **Used Car Buying Guide**
10445 **Welding Manual**
10450 **ATV Basics**

SPANISH MANUALS

98903 **Reparación de Carrocería & Pintura**
98905 **Códigos Automotrices de la Computadora**
98910 **Frenos Automotriz**
98915 **Inyección de Combustible 1986 al 1994**
99040 **Chevrolet & GMC Camionetas** '67 al '87 Incluye Suburban, Blazer & Jimmy '67 al '91
99041 **Chevrolet & GMC Camionetas** '88 al '95 Incluye Suburban '92 al '95, Blazer & Jimmy '92 al '94, Tahoe y Yukon '95
99042 **Chevrolet & GMC Camionetas Cerradas** '68 al '95
99055 **Dodge Caravan & Plymouth Voyager** '84 al '95
99075 **Ford Camionetas y Bronco** '80 al '94
99077 **Ford Camionetas Cerradas** '69 al '91
99083 **Ford Modelos de Tamaño Grande** '75 al '87
99088 **Ford Modelos de Tamaño Mediano** '75 al '86
99091 **Ford Taurus & Mercury Sable** '86 al '95
99095 **GM Modelos de Tamaño Grande** '70 al '90
99100 **GM Modelos de Tamaño Mediano** '70 al '88
99110 **Nissan Camionetas** '80 al '96, Pathfinder '87 al '95
99118 **Nissan Sentra** '82 al '94
99125 **Toyota Camionetas y 4Runner** '79 al '95

---

* Listings shown with an asterisk (*) indicate model coverage as of this printing. These titles will be periodically updated to include later model years - consult your Haynes dealer for more information.

Over 100 Haynes motorcycle manuals also available

5-98

Haynes North America, Inc., 861 Lawrence Drive, Newbury Park, CA 91320-1514 • (805) 498-6703